The John Hotson Memorial Series

MELTDOWN

MONEY, DEBT AND THE WEALTH OF NATIONS

How
ZERO INFLATION POLICY AND DEREGULATION
have turned the world economy into a
GLOBAL CASINO

as documented in the first decade of
Economic Reform

WILLIAM KREHM, EDITOR

Other titles:

All You Must Know About Economics
William Henry Pope

It's Your Money
William F. Hixson

COMER Publications
Toronto

THE FUNDAMENTALS ARE SOUND!
WE'RE STILL GOING UP!
TITANIC

Canadian Cataloguing in Publication Data

Main entry under title:

Meltdown : money, debt and the wealth of nations : how zero inflation policy and deregulation have turned the world economy into a global casino : as documented in the first decade of *Economic Reform*

(The John Hotson memorial series)
Includes bibliographical references and index.
ISBN 0-9680681-2-X

1. Inflation (Finance). 2. Economic policy. 3. Banks and banking, Central. I. Krehm, William, 1913- II. Series.

HG229.M45 1999 332.4'1 C99-900072-1

Printed and bound in Canada.

COMER Publications
Suite 107
245 Carlaw Street
Toronto, ON M4M 2S6

Telephone 416-466-2642
Fax 416-466-5827

Look for COMER Online on the World Wide Web at www.comer.org.

Typesetting & Design: Larry Farquharson, Larkson Communications
Cartoonist: Allen Good
Printing: The Aylmer Express Limited

"Among the costs
of 'zero inflation' push
is the demolition of economics
as a discipline that might tell us
something useful about
the economy."
— p. 121

Contents

Article Titles

Preface

Economic Reform was launched as *COMER Comments* in the summer of 1988. COMER, acronym for Committee on Monetary and Economic Reform, had been organized at a conference of the Eastern Economic Association in Washington DC in the mid-1980s. Its purpose was to study the strange turn that monetary policy was taking under the aggressive leadership of the world's central banks. COMER's founding group had been brought together by the late John Hotson of the University of Waterloo. When the newly appointed governor of the Bank of Canada, John Crow, proclaimed "zero inflation" the one concern of the central bank, we launched our newsletter to meet the challenge. In the early nineties, on the suggestion of one of our subscribers, Mel Hurtig, the name was changed to *Economic Reform*.

In preparing this anthology, I have been struck by the relative accessibility of governments and the media in our early years for much of what we had to say. A meeting of the provincial premiers in the fall of 1988 contacted us for information. That was apparent in their releases. Their request for an interview with the Governor of the Bank of Canada, however, was rebuffed, and a torrent of ridicule poured on their heads by the press. In our issue of June 1989, we were able to report extensive newspaper coverage of the highly critical report of the Commons Finance Committee on the central bank's policy. But within a year or two, such things became unthinkable. Thus the same committee's rejection of the Government's attempt to put "zero inflation" into the *Bank of Canada Act* in February 1992 did not rate a mention in the same papers. A bill was slipped through Parliament in 1991 phasing out the statutory reserves that banks had to put up with the central bank.

From its earliest issues some COMER members felt that we should write only on subjects that would not tax the understanding of the broadest public. However, the view prevailed that our limited resources be concentrated on vital matters that were being neglected — above all the covert campaign to roll back economic theory and policies to the orthodoxy of the early thirties.

The task we set ourselves involved more than resurrecting the ideas of John Maynard Keynes. Only since World War II had a mixed peacetime economy arisen, and the immense implications of that on statistics, accountancy, and economic theory had been disregarded. In the course of our first ten years *ER* has published original work of significance.

The first few issues were edited by John Hotson and printed at the University of Waterloo. Soon, however, that became impossible, and the active editing and publication passed to Toronto where it has been handled by William Krehm. John Hotson's activities as an organizer not only of COMER but of a variety of other activities — Results, TOES, Sovereignty — demanded more and more of his time and extended not only to the United States but involved two speaking tours of Australia, New Zealand, and trips to Europe. His untimely death took place in January 1996.

Because an important purpose of this book is to establish a record, I have attempted to reproduce faithfully the essence of what was said when it was said. However, to cut down the repetitions, the occasional updating of information is provided, but these are set off in rectangular parentheses. Space-saving considerations have prompted condensations and rewriting the odd sentence. Care has been taken throughout to avoid stretching what claims we may have to foresight. That explains why minor discrepancies may appear in statistical data between two treatments of the same subject at different dates.

William Krehm
January 1999

C.O.M.E.R COMMENTS

The Newsletter of the Committee On Monetary and Economic Reform (C.O.M.E.R.)

Vol 1 No 1 Summer, 1988

Here We Go Again!!

Real GNP Creeps Up • Money GNP Crawls Up • Wages and Profits Struggle Up • Taxes Surge Up • Interest Explodes Up

The Bank of Canada's Phony War on Inflation

Economic Reform

(formerly COMER Comment)

NEWSLETTER OF THE COMMITTEE ON MONETARY AND ECONOMIC REFORM

June, 1991 Volume 3, Number 6

CRACK IN CERTAINTY?

Economic Reform

NEWSLETTER OF THE COMMITTEE ON MONETARY AND ECONOMIC REFORM

December, 1994 Volume 6, Number 12

THREE STRIKES AND OUT!

TEN YEARS

ER

ECONOMIC REFORM

THE COMMITTEE ON MONETARY AND ECONOMIC Reform

Volume 8, Number 5

May 1996

Bank for International Settlements

In the shade of a *tottering* tower?

As much humanity as computers mated with suction pumps

ER ECONOMIC REFORM

Volume 9, Number 9 • SEPTEMBER 1997

OTTAWA WHISPERS CONFESSION TO PRIVATIZATION SCAM

the newsletter of the COMMITTEE ON MONETARY AND ECONOMIC REFORM

ER ECONOMIC REFORM

Volume 10, Number 12 ¥ DECEMBER 1998

LOCKED IN DEREGULATION'S VICIOUS CIRCLE

the newsletter of the COMMITTEE ON MONETARY AND ECONOMIC REFORM

The Articles

Vol. 1, No. 1 — Summer 1988

It is irrational to seek to lower prices by policies which raise costs. It is inefficient to use blunt instruments such as high interest rates, when selective credit and income controls are so much more cost-effective.

Now, just as it is possible to get from Chicago to New York by travelling west, north, or south instead of east, since the earth is a ball, so is it possible to reduce inflation with high interest rates. It is just an extraordinarily inefficient and expensive way to "get there."

John Hotson

The one statistic by which the state of the economy is judged is the price index. Any increase in the price level is taken as a sign of an overheated economy which must be cooled with higher interest rates.

Prices, however, may very well have moved up for reasons quite other than an overheated economy. It might be that more essential public services are being provided and that the taxation to pay for these finds its way substantially into the price level.

Particularly in the sixties, Canada made huge public investments in education, health and social welfare for an expanding population. This initiated a break-away upward movement of Canadian prices. Mistaking the price effects of the changing structures of our society for an overheated economy, our Central Bank attempted to suppress it with ever higher interest rates, thus adding an unnecessary layer of "policy push" inflation.

By the early eighties those rates had been driven into the mid-twenties and we were faced with economic breakdown. Only then did the price rise slow down. That has been hailed as a victory over inflation, but the costs of that spurious victory are still coming in. High rates in the United States, strengthened the dollar and priced American exports out of the world markets. The strong dollar multiplied the Third World debt; most of which had been contracted in American currency. Instead of using their liquid resources to modernize their plant, American industrial firms hoarded their cash reserves. That in turn made them tempting prey for take-over raiders. While the real economy languished, the fictitious economy, engaged in reshuffling claims on the real product, grew rank. Ultimately the cost of this must contribute to the cost and prices of real production.

William Krehm

Vol. 1, No. 2 — Fall 1988

Ten Premiers Go A-calling

In mid-August Canada's ten [provincial] premiers unanimously demanded of the Bank of Canada a reduction in interest rates. Premier Devine of Saskatchewan was delegated to deliver the message to Governor Crow. The Governor declined to receive him. Instead, as though someone had thrown a switch, the section of the media that toes the Bank's line started pouring abuse on the premiers. The Governor does not take kindly to those who question what he is up to.

In an editorial captioned 'Look Who's Giving Advice' *The Financial Post* delivered itself of the following: "This year's provincial budgets show a total deficit of $5.7 billion. That's about $2 billion lower than in fiscal 1987-8. But after five years of strong overall economic growth it's appalling that the provinces remain so heavily in the red and depend upon borrowing."

But the provinces' debt, like Ottawa's, was run up in large part to pay the crushing interest charges imposed by our central bank. When rates started their wild climb almost a decade ago, the federal debt was about 26% of the GDP. Today it is more than twice that. If the Bank of Canada reverts to its insane policy of the early eighties, the consequences will be even more shattering.

Whenever we are confronted with problems of survival, the central bank's obsession with driving up interest rates dictates nonsense responses. There are areas of our West where the drought reduced crops by as much as 80%. The Worldwatch Institute of Washington warns that the world's grain reserves are half what they were a year ago — enough for 54 days' consumption. One more year like this and there could be widespread famine on several continents.

Inescapably this will show up in higher food prices. And when our central bank picks up the blip in the index, it will screw rates up even further. Such policy has already driven tens of thousands of farmers off their land. Surely with the prospects ahead for this planet, we should be encouraging farmers to go on farming.

Many scientists relate the drought to the destruction of our ozone layer. That, along with such things as the recent PCB fire at St. Basile in Quebec, has added to the mounting alarm over our ravished environment. The provincial premiers must deal with problems such as these. Fighting pollution calls for costly measures — scrubbers to keep down the harmful emissions, safe disposal of noxious waste. Whether these are paid for by governments or private firms, their costs will show up in the price level. But the Bank of Canada has resisted all suggestions that it analyse price rises for their very different causes. Instead, it seizes upon any upward movement of the very inaccurate index as a pretext for promoting its "zero inflation" goal.

As a result we will have to pay our money-lenders an added ransom before we can undertake critical conservation schemes.

Peter Cook filled his *Globe and Mail* column with gems such as the following: "After a three-hour breakfast, the premiers showed that they cannot tell a financial market from a fruit loop, by announcing that they favour a low interest rate policy for Canada. ...Why should Canada be part of [the world monetary system] when Czechoslovakia isn't?"

That international system, however is run by the Bank for International Settlements — a sort of central bankers' club that operates out of low-profile Basel headquarters that *Forbes* once likened to a speakeasy of Prohibition days.

At the moment these gentlemen are having a bit of falling out. Washington has been pressuring Western Germany to stimulate its economy to help improve the American trade balance. But even though unemployment in West Germany has reached a record level for recent years, its central bank is as hooked on high rates as is ours. It countered by proposing that the Fed drop its rate instead. Rather than that the Fed chose to raise its rate. So to maintain the previous differential West Germany and Britain have pushed theirs up as well. The prospect is for a competitive screwing up of bank rates that bodes no good.

The only major holdout in this mad race is Japan. "The Bank of Japan takes the view is that its priority is to keep borrowing costs in Japan low to maintain the rapid pace of economic expansion, which benefits other countries by sucking in imports. Moreover, the bank fears that a rise in Japanese rates could easily spark a round of worldwide rate increases." (*Financial Times*, London 9/2/88)

Better Ways of Fighting Inflation

Mainstream economists, however, have been drilled to see price as determined by the balancing of supply and demand on the market and nothing else. All factors that do not fit into this model are dismissed as 'cognitive dissonance.' Let me quote a specialist in system analysis, Anatol Rapoport of the University of Toronto: "Cognitive dissonance — the tendency of not admitting certain kinds of information that threatens to clash with previously formed ideas — involves a censor or gatekeeper who sees to it that certain information does not penetrate into the system in question."

How overworked that gatekeeper is these days was shown by the experience of our Finance Minister, Michael Wilson. More than a year ago he extended the sales tax to cover services as well as goods. Inevitably that tax was reflected in a higher price index. And the Governor of the BoC John Crow, disregarded a memo from his own staff to make allowance for Mr. Wilson's new tax before deciding how 'overheated' the market really was. Instead Governor Crow raised the bank rate repeatedly to make the price effect of the sales tax disappear, until he finally helped bring on the stock market collapse of October 1987. Still more amazing, Mr. Wilson, in the last analysis responsible both for the Bank's policy and the offending tax, voiced his approval of what Mr. Crow had done.

The dogma that higher prices necessarily mean that 'too many dollars chasing too few goods' has closed the minds of our policymakers to the basic lemma of a mixed economy: the cost of public services is not only the additional taxes we pay, but also the higher prices that must result from these added taxes.

The mere recognition of this lemma would have powerful anti-inflationary effects:

1) So long as the belief persists that added taxation is the total cost of new public services, hope springs eternal that the other guy will be stuck with the taxes, while we will enjoy the public services gratis.

2) A better perception of the full cost of public services would enjoin greater responsibility on our politicians. It should be made mandatory for any parliamentarian proposing new public services to include an estimate of their influence on the price level.

3) Today not only our trade unions but our governments equate our living standard with the purchasing power of our take-home pay. The fallacy of this emerges if we consider the case of a new public dental scheme. We would no longer have to cover our dentist's bills out of our take-home pay. Most of the costs would be borne by our employers and the government, and these would turn up in higher prices. If we went on measuring our living standard by our real take-home pay, we would be ignoring the portion of our dental bills that were being paid for us. This would introduce a vicious inflationary spiral into the economy; as does the indexing of civil servants' salaries — and those of the private sector — to the price level. Such arrangements ignore the greater basket of public services that all of us are getting.

Alternate Policies Do Exist for Managing Our Price Mobility Without Wrecking the Economy

The common feature of these policy options consists of seeking ways of easing the burden of taxation on price. Reducing interest rates is closely related to this. If we take as our point of departure the basic lemma of a mixed economy — the relationship between taxation and price — we would find other ways of funding essential government services.

But first we need a rational system of accountancy for the public sector. Today the federal government has no capital budget. It writes off purchases of land, buildings, and equipment in a single year.

Were private firms allowed such write-offs, they would have to hoist their prices drastically. There is no reason to believe that such flawed accountancy has a different effect in the public sector.

No inventory of our government's non-financial assets exists to set off against its debt. It should be compiled — not only for physical assets that remain within the jurisdiction of the federal government, but for a reasonable portion of such assets created through grants to other levels of government and to the private sector. The sole criterion for regarding an expenditure as an investment is whether it contributes to an expanded tax-base.

Recently our Prime Minister announced a $110 million program to combat illiteracy. He cited estimates that placed the annual costs to us of the 20 percent functional illiteracy amongst our population at $14 billion each year. Obviously spending to curtail that loss is an enduring investment. Such public investment should be amortized over its useful life, as is done in the market economy.

Vol. 1, No. 3 — Winter 1989

Correspondence — to John Hotson / from Finance Minister Michael Wilson

Ottawa, 22/12/88

Professor John H. Hotson
University of Waterloo

The Prime Minister has forwarded for my consideration a copy of your June 15 /88 letter concerning monetary policy and your proposal for the establishment of a Royal Commission. I am pleased to offer some comments.

Let me first mention that the high interest rates of the early 1980s were largely a reflection of sustained inflationary pressures which had developed over the previous decade when economic policies were generally less attentive to the risks posed by inflation. The sharp economic correction which followed was a direct result of the build-up and persistence of inflationary pressures. Our policies have sought to avoid a repeat of this performance and the economy has responded well; Canada has been a world leader in economic growth and job creation in recent years, and there have been sustained improvements in terms of reduced inflation, interest rates and unemployment since the early 1980s.

However, despite the decline in inflation and our success in keeping it under control, the current strength of our economy has pushed many Canadian industries to near capacity and threatened a renewal of inflationary pressures. In these circumstances monetary policy has been aimed at discouraging inflationary impulses that would bring an early end to our economic expansion. You are correct, of course, that not all price level increases are inflationary. There is a clear distinction between a one-time jump in the price index because of special factors and a general rise in costs and prices throughout the economy. I can assure you that these developments are monitored closely in formulating policy.

While interest rates have no doubt played a role in the recent strengthening of the Canadian dollar vis-a-vis the US dollar, favourable market reactions to our improved economic performance and to higher commodity prices have also been important. We do not consider short-run fluctuations of interest rates and the exchange rate as detracting from the substantial opportunities which the Free Trade Agreement will open up to Canadians. Monetary policy can best enhance our long-term prospects through resisting inflationary pressures and facilitating a return to reasonable price stability.

Regarding your proposal for setting up a Royal Commission on the theory of monetary policy, may I refer you to the background documents produced in 1985 by the MacDonald Royal Commission on the Economic Union and Development Prospects for Canada. You will find a review in those documents of theoretical issues related to the formation of monetary policy.

In closing, let me thank you for your comments and interest in these important economic issues.

Michael H. Wilson
Minister of Finance

8/2/89

Michael Wilson
Minister of Finance
Ottawa

Dear Mr. Minister:

Thank you for your letter of 22/12/88 in response to mine of 15/6/88 to the Prime Minister. My letter urged the establishment of a Royal Commission on the Theory of Monetary Policy to consist of experts on scientific method, control theory, and general systems analysis, rather than economists or bankers. COMER offers to pay $250,000 of the prospective $1 million cost of such a Commission out of a realization that present-day monetary policies are not scientifically well-based.

The many months which elapsed between the dispatch of my letter and the receipt of yours led me to believe that you and your staff were giving our proposal the thoughtful, careful consideration which it deserves. However, your letter makes it clear that this was not the case. Your letter merely restates the conventional wisdom concerning monetary policy. It is the purpose of the proposed Commission to subject this wisdom to scientific examination.

As you suggest, I have reviewed the background materials prepared for the 1985 MacDonald Royal Commission on the Economic Union and Development Prospects for Canada. As you know, these materials do not constitute a scientific analysis of the premises of the Theory of Monetary Policy and therefore are not germane to the present issue.

As we see it, Canada faces a number of major problems which will involve us in major expenditures over the near term. These problems can only be compounded if the Bank of Canada puts "ending inflation" above all else, and attempts this with counterproductive cost and deficit-increasing interest rate hikes.

I am disturbed that you seem to believe that essential long-term projects will involve only a one-time step-up in our price indices.

Our population is rapidly aging and will certainly require a sustained increase in medical and social services.

During the election campaign the Prime Minister spoke eloquently about the widespread illiteracy in the country, and as I remember, placed the economic loss resulting from that at $10 billion a year. Our airports are getting so dangerously congested that near misses have become frequent. Is there a one-shot solution to this as well?

The government is committed to spend major sums on a "war" on pollution. This is a necessity, not a luxury. Will you insist on financing this war at low interest rates, as we financed World War II, or will you continue to allow the Bank of Canada to hobble with high interest rates any effort to save our environment?

Mr. Wilson, economists, unlike scientists, have shown themselves to be unable, or unwilling to establish criteria for recognizing, correcting and avoiding error. By forcing economists to submit to the discipline natural scientists take for granted, the proposed Royal Commission can perform a great service for Canada and the world.

Please direct your staff to set up an early day-long session at which economists from COMER can share insights on the reform of monetary policy with your advisers from the Finance Department and the Bank of Canada. We do not claim to have all the answers, but we do know that the current "answers" are part of the problem.

John Hotson

Executive Director, COMER

Bulgarian Tenors and Central Bankers

I recall a lecture some years ago by the great accompanist Gerald Moore.

He told of his experience with a famous Bulgarian tenor. Having some discomfort with the high notes of a song they were performing, he turned to Moore and asked, "Could you transpose it down a half tone?"

Moore obliged. But then the tenor was in trouble with the low notes. After a moment in deep thought, he surfaced with a solution,"Don't you have anything in between?"

As I follow the efforts of our central bank, I am tempted to believe that our tenor abandoned singing to become a central banker.

For the Bank of Canada, too, has been trying to find something "in between." Last February Governor John Crow proclaimed that "any degree of inflation is unacceptable." That is a pretty tight groove, when you consider that not once in the past 35 years, i.e. since our mixed economy came into existence, have we experienced a year when our prices have not moved forward — slowly or fast. The Governor then has little to base himself on in his search of those green pastures between C and B.

This process of "fine tuning" with a complete disregard of scales must lead to ever more bizarre results.

This was evident from the stock market crash of October, 1987. Repeatedly before it happened, the Bank upped the bank rate — because Ottawa and some of the provinces had raised some of their taxes. And when the Governor increased the rates once too much, the market not only fell — but collapsed. Immediately the Bank of Canada — along with the US Fed — pulled back a full point and a half.

Although the Bank has subsequently dictated reams of self-congratulation about its vigilance in "heading off inflation," a few cynics ask why it had to bring the roof down on our heads, before pulling rates back a percent and a half. Couldn't it have left them where they were in the first place?

Worse yet: Why is it shoving them up again?

wk

Vol. 1, No. 4 — May 1989

Is There a Virus in Michael Wilson's Software?

Readers will remember the prank of a Cornell student who hid a "virus" in his software that upset the functioning of computers across the country. That bright lad has been brought to trial. Yet the "worm" in our Finance Minister's software, though more damaging, goes unchallenged.

The Globe and Mail (23/03) summed up the situation: "(Wilson) stands completely behind ... John Crow in his belief that inflation must be fought through raising interest rates to slow down the economy. In doing that, Mr. Wilson digs the federal treasury into a deeper hole. Each time interest rates go up, it costs Ottawa more interest payments on the country's debt."

Because he has identified high rates with "fighting inflation" Wilson has done just about everything wrong in managing the public debt. For years COMER tried explaining that prices would edge up for "non-inflationary" reasons — i.e. reasons having nothing to do with demand outstripping productive capacity. Had he listened to us, he would have tried locking in government borrowings on a long-term, fixed-rate basis. Private corporations have done that to survive.

Instead Wilson did just the opposite. He relied heavily on Canada Saving Bonds that allow redemption at par. Repeatedly the Finance Ministry upped the coupon on the CSBs, but found that the central bank had beat it to the draw, and pushed up short term rates even higher. "Canadians cashed in $5.4 billion of CSBs between Feb. 1 and March 15....The money coming out of the CSBs seems to be headed directly into treasury bills. So much for the BoC's claim that higher rates are needed to attract savings. The same savings are being recycled at ever steeper rates. The taxpayers have been set up for ransom by our Finance Minister. For ultimately he is responsibly for the central bank's policy.

The Case for Regionally Sensitive Interest Rates

The current high interest rate policy of the Bank of Canada is causing serious problems in many parts of the country where unemployment — as opposed to inflation — is still the principal problem. As Table 1 clearly shows, this policy has the perverse impact of imposing the highest real rates of interest in regions with the highest unemployment and the lowest rate of inflation. Toronto, the target of the anti-inflation policy, has the lowest real rate of interest in the country. It is also clear that inflation — and unemployment for that matter — is a regionally disaggregated phenomenon.

It is argued that there are no alternatives to this policy of undifferentiated high interest rates. I believe, however, that alternatives are possible. My alternative of developing a system of variable loan costs by regions relies upon a system of compensating balances and quantitative credit controls that are regionally sensitive. As well, simple regulation will be necessary to ensure that most borrowers do not borrow out of region without paying the equivalent cost. I have developed this model with Bernard Bouska of Concordia University after having studied the Japanese system of credit control.

The Japanese central bank has relied upon the policy of direct quantitative credit controls known as "window guidance" to control credit conditions in the country. Window guidance has had the effect of tightening credit conditions so that the commercial banks themselves ration out their loans to customers in hotter markets by using what are called "compensating balances" on loans. These compensating balances increase the effective interest rate on a loan. Less heated markets are offered loans without these balances, hence ensuring cheaper loans in slower growth regions.†

In addition, Section 18 of the *Bank Act* permits the central bank to purchase securities issued or guaranteed by the provinces. These purchases could be used to help develop greater regional sensitivity to both monetary and fiscal policy. For example, by varying its purchasing policy in provincial markets, the central bank could restrain or stimulate credit conditions where appropriate.

I think we should not hesitate to develop a system of our own which uses the techniques of compensating balances and quantity credit controls to ensure that regions suffering high unemployment are not forced to pay the price for inflation in Toronto.

Unemployment, inflation and interest rates by region

Region	Unemployment	Inflation	Real rate of interest
Montreal, PQ	10.8	4.1	9.4
Calgary, AB	8.0	2.2	11.3
Edmonton, AB	9.2	3.0	11.0
Saskatoon, SK	10.9	3.0	10.5
Saint John, NF	12.8	3.6	9.9
Saint John's, NB	11.5	3.6	10.8
Vancouver, BC	8.0	4.3	9.2
Toronto, ON	4.6	6.5	7.0

Inflation and real interest rates are for February 1989; unemployment rates are for March 1989.

Harold Chorney
Professor of Economics and Public Policy
Concordia University

† "Compensatory balances" are frequently imposed by banks for their own purposes — the client is required leave part of the money he borrows from the bank in his account for a zero or token rate of interest. By this device the banks with a minimum of publicity increase the effective interest rate on what borrowings the client is free to use. [Editor]

Vol. 1, No. 5 — June 1989

Can We Afford to Survive?

Are we finally going to roll up our sleeves and clean up the environment? President Bush, Prime Minister Mulroney, and the Iron Lady beyond the great waters have raised that cause to a position alongside motherhood.

Yet "balancing" government budgets and "licking inflation" have become causes above even motherhood. Budgets cannot possibly be balanced so long as we unbalance them with ever higher interest rates; and what we must do to save the environment will raise the price index. Thus we are driven to the conclusion: before we can hope to clean up the environment, we must first clean up what passes for accountancy in the government sector.

Forbes (15/5/89) estimates the cost of cleaning up the 10,000 waste dumps in the US as $500 billion (about Canada's GDP in 1989) over the coming fifty years — and that, with ever higher interest rates to finance the economy, threatens to be pushed beyond our means. With such monetary policy we simply cannot afford to survive. Such nonsense end-results don't just occur. They are brought about by viruses in the software of our thinking.

One of the major flaws is in the price index (GDP deflator or the CPI) by which central banks try running the economy. These indexes will register the cost of the clean-up job, but will ignore the benefits of the improved environment. That is because these benefits will be unpriced, unmarketed, and available to everybody, a common good. Our price index is the weighted average of a representative basket of goods and services. Into that master ratio the benefits of a cleaner environment can be introduced in a simple way. Its price would be entered as zero, since the cleaner environment would not be sold or priced. Its costs would already have turned up in the increased prices of the other items in the basket resulting from higher [direct] costs to firms of the cleanup, and the taxation to pay for the government's part in such costs. The weighting given the clean-up item is arrived at by dividing its total costs — both to industry and government — by the Gross Domestic Product. Since we are adding to the price index an item priced at zero and properly weighted, that index will be reduced [corresponding to the greater benefits now recognised as arising from the costs previously recognised]. Similar rectifications would have to be applied to many other items — the improved quality of medical services, education and so forth.

The recognised budgetary deficit is also not a reliable guide to policy. This misleading statistic comes from the public accounts, a cash-flow exercise that makes no distinction between current spending like pencils and capital spending of government that will benefit the economy for years to come.

What in the current jargon passes for a "balanced budget" would pay for total current and capital expenditure out of current taxation. Such a concept is wholly foreign to business accountancy. A corporation that sought to be so "conservative" as to finance its capital investment entirely out of current receipts would set itself up for a takeover by more skilful managers — if it did not succumb to the competition of its more intelligent rivals.

Consider the case of a sewage treatment facility created by a private firm and the same plant built by the federal government. In the first case it would be amortised over its useful life — say 30 years. Each year one thirtieth of its cost would be written off as current spending plus the costs of financing the unamortised portion of that cost. In the second it would be written off entirely in a single year. Clearly this discrepancy puffs up the advantages of the current rage for the privatisation of public services. There may be advantages in many proposed privatisations, but how are we to know if we do not use the same accountancy in making comparisons between public and private ownership?

Three years ago a joint report of the Office of the Auditor-General of Canada and the United States General Accounting Office entitled *Federal Government Reporting Study* recommended that "the cost of long-lived physical assets ... be allocated (as depreciation) over the period in which the produce benefits."

A Neglected Aspect of the Buyout Mania

There has been much commentary on the leveraged buyout wave, but a crucial aspect has been overlooked. Without the high-interest policy of our central bank, this bizarre development could not have happened.

The present value of any investment is calculated by discounting its future income flow at the current interest rate. If an investment is projected to yield one dollar each year and the rate of interest is 10%, its present value will be the sum of a series beginning with 9/10ths of $1 plus $1x(.9)^2$ plus $1x(.9)^3$ ... and so on to infinity. High-school algebra will show that the sum of such a series is about $9. Raise the interest rate to 20% and the value of the series will drop to about $4. [With a higher interest rate the present value of the annual return discounts to near zero far sooner.]

Moreover, the 20% interest rate, by depressing the economy, may reduce that one dollar or even possibly bankrupt the enterprise so that the income disappears entirely. When the present value of an investment becomes less than the cost of the project, the investment no longer makes sense. If it has already been made, its value may drop to the point where its value is only what its sale as scrap will bring in. Driven high enough, interest rates can thus destroy capital values. And capital values, after all, are what capitalism is about.

That does not help our banks. Under the fractional reserve system, banks are among the highest leveraged operators outside casinos. They are able to lend 20 times and more than their liquid reserves. And when the high rates set by the central bank finally destroy the value of the security that backs their loans, it is not only others' money that they lose, but their own capital. Thus, unless the central bank comes to their aid, the banks must call in 20 or more times of their losses in loans. It isn't just a churlish disposition that impels your friendly banker, once it starts raining, to take back the umbrella that he lent you when the sun was out.

These mysteries of money creation are prudishly hidden from the layman, but they do determine how our world spins. When rates are high, the floor is littered with bargains. Firms that no longer make sense as functioning units may be sold off at a fraction of their replacement cost. Those who pick up their pieces are able to put together new empires for a song.

When rates are finally allowed to subside, fortunes are made.[Then the process described above goes into reverse.] On every such occasion armies of accountants, lawyers, underwriters, tax-shelter promoters, and purveyors of inside information are given employment. Kohlberg, Kravis, Roberts & Co. Inc, the most spectacular firm in the field, has earned its investors as much as 40% annually. The fees of Drexel Burnham Lambert Inc.'s Michael R. Milken, wizard of junk bondery at present under a bit of cloud, amounted to a half a billion dollars in a single year.

Eventually all this must show up in the costs of the real economy. The symbolic economy, engaged in reshuffling claims on the real economy, enjoys fabulous capital gains while the real economy lies in the gutter. From a society of producers, we revert to the more primitive patterns of hunters and collectors The hero of our times is the man who tracks his corporate quarry and scores a kill.

Originally KKR specialised in friendly takeovers with the management of the captured firms serving as partners, who provided access to company records. But competition has become so furious that KKR began turning up more frequently in the role of unfriendly aggressors. A management manning the battlements is hardly likely to be forthcoming with facts and figures to an enemy encamped on the other side of the moat.

Corporate managers who survived the credit crunch of the early eighties determined never again to expose themselves to such an experience. So they backed off investing heavily in new plant or technology. Instead they hoarded their profits and put them out on the money market. Some of the larger ones even set up financial subsidiaries and themselves become quasi bankers. No human arrangement, however, is perfect, and the very cash they accumulated made them tempting prey for a new breed of *condottieri*. Buying up the shares of such companies on a stock market that high interest-rates depressed, the aggressors financed their raids by issuing high-coupon "junk bonds," stripping the acquired companies of their cash, and selling off some of their parts.

Sometimes the besieged management, to ward off the raiders, scrambles to get rid of the cash hoards that make them attractive prey. They can achieve this by declaring large one-time dividends, or by acquiring other firms, thus adding to the froth of the take-over game. A whole technology of "poison pills" and "golden parachutes" has arisen to the same end.

At times the predator does not even have to have real claws and teeth. Paul Bilzerian, one of the most notorious raiders, has been convicted of fraud. Though lacking enough resources of his own to represent a serious threat to the firms he targets, he operates with borrowed funds to relieve his victims in "greenmail" before surrendering to them his accumulation of their shares.

Natural predators are believed to contribute to the well-being of the herds they prey upon, by culling their weaker members. In the strange universe created by high-interest policy, this is hardly the case. Successful or not, a raid is likely to leave the targeted corporation stripped of the cash reserves needed to meet the next credit crunch. If taken over, it is weighed down under a load of high-interest bonds.

Such firms, too, are likely to be headed for labour strife. With their liquidity seriously curtailed, one of the few ways left to them of cutting costs is at the expense of labour.

William Krehm

Vol. 1, No. 6 — September 1989

Crow's House of Distorting Mirrors

If you start with a dogma that stands the real world on its head, and proclaim it an absolute truth, you are committing yourself to nonsensical results. That is why the Bank of Canada is coming to resemble a fun-house of distorting mirrors.

The Globe and Mail (19/5/89) carries the following pearl: "Mr. Gordon Thiessen, the bank's second-in-command also points to car sales which slumped earlier in the year, but rebounded in April. He said cheap financing offered by auto dealers had exacerbated inflation."

Now anybody who has bought a car will realize that the financing charges are part of its cost, and when financing is provided by the manufacturer or dealer at a below-market rate, he is in fact reducing his price. At least one American manufacturer is giving its buyers the choice between loss-leader financing and a price rebate. Such below-cost financing would thus rank as an anti-inflationary measure, especially since auto plants are being shut down because of excess inventories. Certainly no bottlenecks there.

But anyone who dares reduce any interest rate is desecrating the most hallowed of the BoC's altars.

The Financial Post (21/6/89) informs us that Ottawa is "counting on an alternative form of consumer price index to help moderate wage pressures in the wake of the introduction of a goods and services tax. Statscan is working on a version of the CPI that excludes price changes caused by commodity taxes, including the GST. The new index will support the government's claim that although the GST will cause a price blip in 1991, the underlying rate of inflation will not be affected. Finance officials say they hope wage negotiators will consult this underlying index when they embark on wage bargaining over the next two years."

In short there will be two measures of inflation. The higher one by which the central bank will screw up interest rates. And the lower one for use in resisting higher wage demands because of the same inflation.

When COMER and others proposed differential monetary and fiscal policies to deal with the overheated Southern Ontario economy without penalizing depressed regions, we were stonewalled by the central bank. We were told by the BoC that it was absolutely essential to have the one punitive high-rate policy from sea to sea. But having two price indices to choose from, as it may be to suit the purpose of the BoC and the Finance Ministry is okay. Just like a card sharper who keeps a reserve card up his sleeve for special occasions.

William Krehm

Vol. 1, No. 7 — November 1989

Correspondence — to Don Blenkarn, MP / from William Krehm

The Hon. Don Blenkarn, MP
Chairman, Standing Committee on Finance and Economic Affairs
House of Commons, Ottawa

I am writing to request an opportunity to present my views on the proposed GST before your Committee.

There is a distinct linkage between the effects of the GST and the high-interest rate fanaticism of the Bank of Canada.

The Finance Minister has admitted that the GST will produce a 2.25 percent increase in the price level. But he has evaded the implications of this by declaring that this will be a one-time rise. That is wishful thinking. Nowhere in the utterances of the Governor of the Bank of Canada has there been the slightest recognition of any difference between one-time increases in the price level and sustained increases. He watches every wiggle of our highly imperfect price statistic like a hawk and responds to any rise by restricting the money supply.

It is therefore entirely predictable that the price effects of the GST will bring on a sharp rise in the bank rate, and that in turn will result in a jump in the budgetary deficit, which will necessitate a further rise in the GST, which will lead to a further supposedly "one-time" jump in the price level that will provoke still higher interest rates...and so forth. What we have is a vicious spiral that can only lead to long-term pain for no gain.

There is a further point. Mr. Wilson has not revealed the basis for his claim that the jump in the price level brought on by the GST will be a "one-time" affair. The only way in which one could form a serious opinion on that would be to examine what the increase in government revenue produced by the GST would be spent on. The answer is — absent a drastic change in the mind-set of the Governor of the Bank of Canada — that it would go to increase still further the transfer payment to our money lenders engineered to "lick inflation."

The present distortion [in the measure of "inflation"] is a double one. During the years when the ravaging of our environment was going on, the cost and prices of our production were understated. And the need not only to prevent further spoliation of the environment, but to make good the damage already sustained, will further distort the picture. The repair of the damage must therefore be treated as an investment to be amortized over a long period. Rectifying the CPI in this way would take a dangerous toy out of the hands of our Central Bank.

William Krehm
Board Chairman of COMER

Correspondence — to Prime Minister Brian Mulroney / from John Hotson and William Krehm

Dear Mr. Prime Minister:

Canadian Press (14/10) carries a report of a speech by Governor Crow of the Bank of Canada in Tokyo which in part reads as follows: "Some Canadian monetary specialists have suggested that the Bank of Canada could make interest rates reflect regional economic disparities in Canada 'as the Japanese do.'"

A year ago at Saskatoon the provincial premiers protested against the high interest rate policy of the BoC that was penalising the depressed regions of the country to fight inflation in Southern Ontario. At the request of one of the premiers, the Committee on Monetary and Economic Reform (COMER) outlined a policy by which our central bank, while keeping interest rates relatively low, might apportion credit differentially amongst the various regions and industries of the country according to the real productive bottlenecks.

We were told not only that this was impossible, but that it had in fact never happened in Japan as COMER claimed. In your own public utterances you seemed to identify high interest rates with "fighting inflation." More effective techniques for managing market inflation outlined by COMER and others have been systematically ignored.

We are comforted then to learn that Governor Crow has not tried telling the Japanese that monetary policy differentiating between industries and regions has been unknown in Japan. Much of the Japanese performance in fact can be traced to the inexpensive credit made available to strategic industries.

We would also draw to your attention that in its preamble the *Bank of Canada Act* provides that our central bank shall "regulate credit and currency...to mitigate...fluctuations in the general level of production, trade, prices and employment." It does not authorize the Governor to plot violent fluctuations in the general level of production, trade and employment in pursuit of "zero inflation." That could be obtained only by achieving a "zero economy." For that the BoC studiously avoids analysing price movement into its very different components, some of which have nothing to do with an overheated market.

With Friday's stock market crash, you must certainly understand the urgency of such a measure. It is common knowledge amongst economists that it takes about 18 months for a central bank to create a depression — twice the time that it takes a woman to produce a child. That in itself underlines the irresponsible brinkmanship of our central bank in throttling the economy until the Governor's pipe-dream of "zero inflation" has shown up in our highly defective statistics.

Depressions, Mr. Prime Minister, are easier to bring on than to undo. The one that threatens the country today is imposing severe strains on the very fabric of Confederation, and is visiting hardship on millions of Canadians. The realities of a depression would leave in tatters these buzzwords of over-orchestrated PR — "short-term pain for long-term gain" and "soft landing." The electorate is likely to prove unforgetting and unforgiving.

Yours respectfully,
John H. Hotson, Executive Director
William Krehm, Board Chairman
Committee for Monetary and Economic Reform

A Lexicon of Central Bank Newspeak

In his *1984* George Orwell wrote of a totalitarian state twisting words like pretzels until they took on the exact opposite of their original meaning. Abused in this way, language can imprison minds as dungeons do bodies.

The practice is not confined to totalitarian regimes. Conventional economic theory is based on the notion of a "pure and perfect market" that acts much like the thermostat of your heating system. Without anybody's intervention it is supposed to keep prices at a steady level. If prices do go up for a while, that will choke off demand and encourage greater supply, so that they will tend to return to their original level.

This notion of a self-balancing market is imbedded in the very language in which economists are drilled to communicate. Higher prices are *defined* to mean "too much demand and/or not enough supply." The trouble is that when policy-makers start plotting recessions to enforce "zero inflation," they destroy their credentials. Where a functioning thermostat really exists, there is no need for the householder to apply a crowbar to it.

There was plenty wrong with this theory — marginal value theory — when it was introduced over a century ago. Its great attraction, at a time of rising labour unrest, was that it attributed the maldistribution of wealth to impersonal market forces. "In the long run" things were supposed to work out to everybody's satisfaction. The theory hardly lived up to its promises: the Great Depression of the thirties showed that.

Since then it has become patently irrelevant. Our economy has become a mixed economy, with the public sector in the advanced countries accounting for anywhere from 30 to over 50% of the national output. Trying to explain what might be going on in such economies entirely by the balancing of market supply and demand means relegating the public sector to outer space.

Thus until very recently it was taught in our universities that an increase in taxation had an anti-inflation effect — it "syphoned off excess purchasing power." Over 20 years ago John Hotson and I, quite independently, reached the conclusion that this was nonsense, and that the growth of the public sector within the economy was giving rise to an ever broader layer of taxation to price.

This meant that increases in the price level were not necessarily "inflationary," i.e. due to an "overheated market." They could be due wholly or in part to the changing structures of our society. The growth of public services, essential for our urbanized high-tech world, was only one of these. In the US you cannot reverse the price effects of abolishing Jim Crow by raising the bank rate. For that Congress would have to pass a bill reinstating Jim Crow.

The very term "inflation" sends our minds racing down the wrong track. It comes from the Latin "to blow up," and implies that whatever you stick that label onto can be deflated. Any serious understanding of a particular price surge, however, must begin by asking whether it might be due to too much demand or merely reflects higher costs created by legislative or other non-market events.

The data for such analysis are readily available. But we got nowhere in trying to alert mainstream economists to so obvious a relationship.

Since their survival depends on such distinctions, the Inuit are said to have dozens of words for different types of snow. We, however, are still using a single expression for the many different causes of upward price movement.

When Ottawa first proposed a version of the Value Added Tax, I thought that might at least awaken it to the fact that higher taxes must give rise to higher prices having nothing to do with an overheated market. Vain hope. In the past few months our Finance Minister and media have come to talk of the General Sales Tax adding two to three percent to "inflation." Everything is in place for the BoC to respond with higher interest rates that will take care of the extra revenue that the Finance Ministry will collect. It has been earmarked in advance to increase the transfer payments to the moneylenders.

These days the BoC is increasingly making use of the "Non-accelerating inflation rate of unemployment" (NAIRU). This is defined as the rate of unemployment that would allow a non-accelerating rate of inflation. It is assumed that such a rate exists, i.e. that inflation is caused by an "overheated labour market." Here again we are being dealt marked cards.

wk

What Advice to the Soviets?

There is a danger of our trivializing the lessons to be learned from the crumbling of the Soviet empire. What the Soviets, Poles and Hungarians can hope to move into is not capitalism but a mixed economy. Even in the West it is some decades since anything resembling a pure capitalist economy has existed. There is no way of running a modern country without a substantial and growing public sector.

Boxed in by their respective ideologies, both the West and the Communist world have disregarded the circuits that splice together the public and private sectors. In the West we go on trying to interpret the behaviour of a mixed economy in terms of a pure and perfect market model. We treat any upward price movement as an aberration to be righted by "wrestling inflation to the ground."

Yet in our day climbing prices may have nothing to do with overheated markets: they could just mirror the changing structures of our economy. To run our society, for example, we have need of ever more public services.

The Soviets, too, have tried running a mixed economy by an ideological model based on a single sector — in their case the public sector. And yet a mixed economy of sorts was established under Lenin. To be sure, he did foresee an eventual stage when even a formal market and money would disappear to give way to an all-embracing public sector with the lemma: "from each according to his means, to each according to his needs." But to pave the way to this heavenly realm, the Soviets adopted a money economy. More than theory, economic breakdown led them to tolerate private businesses under the New Economic Policy of 1921.

Though lip-service was paid to the concept of a mixed economy, the show was run with little regard for market logic. Prices of the nationalized sector of the economy were set by fiat. As a result abysmal quality and chronic shortages of goods became the norm.

How great the gap that opened between theory and reality can be judged from the current state of affairs.

For decades even possessing foreign money could land a Soviet citizen in a Siberian prison camp.

Today the currency black market operates quite in the open. On occasion the tourist guides themselves take a hand in its activities and help the tourists under their charge participate in the great game. While the official rate is $1.65 US dollars to the rouble, the going black rate is 10 roubles to the dollar or better — a differential of some 1500 percent.

The basic law of price in a mixed economy is that the costs of the unpriced output of the public sector must show up as a layer in the prices of the marketed output of the economy. That this law has been ignored on either side of the Iron Curtain in no way makes it less valid.

In the United States the public sector accounts for about 30 percent of the economy. That means that some 3/7's of the American price index will merely reflect the layer of taxation in price that goes to pay for the unpriced output of state services.

Let us examine the corresponding situation in the Soviet Union. A Moscow subway ticket costs 5 kopeks. At the official rate this is about 8 US cents. At the black-market rate it is less than a penny. Rent for a modest apartment in Moscow is 20 roubles — if you are lucky enough to get one after waiting for ten years or more. That translates into some $35 at the official rate and about $2.50 at the black market rate. The military establishment is not incommensurate with the American, but the economy that supports it is frail and even fictitious. If the proportion of the unpriced to the priced economy in the US is of the order of 3:7, it is a fair guess that the corresponding proportion in the USSR is likely to be something like 5:1. That explains much of the gap between the official and black-market rates for the rouble, the empty store shelves and the ever longer queues.

We share a basic weakness with the Communist economies. Like theirs, our particular dogma has prevented us, too, from working out the basic relationships between the two sectors of our economy. With a theological faith in the ability of the free market to take care of all problems, we have been drilled to mistake all price rises as a sign of an 'overheated economy' that must be cooled with higher interest rates. Our eyes have been sealed to the non-cyclical price gradient that has arisen over the past four decades to reflect the changing structures of our society.

That blind spot severely limits the assistance we can offer the peoples of the Soviet bloc in their present crisis. They do have need of a free market, but as a tool rather than a religion. In our own house the reigning free-market code has left us with some ugly social problems. Transferred blindly to the Eastern block countries it would almost certainly produce violent dislocations, and heighten the danger of civil war.

Imagine for a moment what a sweeping program of privatisation, financed with leveraged buyouts and junk bonds would do for the sorely tried citizens of the Soviet empire. Or a central bank that would try to lick inflation according to the high-interest-rate prescriptions of the Federal Reserve.

To date Gorbachev's victories have been largely confined to international politics. On the domestic front time is running out on him. Unless it is carefully planned, the very transition to market freedom can lead to unbridled speculation, increased hardship, and disturbances.

Free markets will have to be introduced with careful forethought focussing to begin with on those areas that would have the greatest effect in boosting public morale.

Anybody who has visited Russia would have no difficulty in identifying some of these areas.

In the free market at Kishenev in Moldava last summer I was astonished to see melons being sold by a Mongolian woman. Behind her was a small passenger car loaded with the melons that had obviously been brought from Central Asia perhaps two thousand kilometers away. On a previous trip at an airport in the Urals I was astounded to see potatoes roll out onto the floor when the suitcase of an elegantly dressed man had inadvertently come open. It is by such primitive means that much of the provisioning of Russia's great cities takes place.

A bold program to introduce a modern food distribution system, would give Gorbachev what he needs most — credibility in coping with the country's economic mess. That requires outside financial help and expertise. The United States and Canada must provide it — *with strings attached*. Drastic cuts in the Soviet armament program — to be matched by that of the NATO countries — would make available the funds to finance shipments of refrigerated railway cars and trucks, the building of food terminals, and foodstuffs.

By now we should have learned that the burden of taxation to support a growing public sector is sapping the efficiency of the private economy. Clearly the state must find other sources of funding than taxation. Surely it would be a serious mistake for the Soviets to privatise their ownership of land and buildings in a wholesale way. It would make more sense to lease out urban lots on a long-term basis. That would reserve to the state the prospect of capital gains, without interfering with the establishment of robust markets.

Nor would it help much for the Communist countries to copy our present bank system too closely. Under this our governments assign their money-creating powers to the private banks and then proceed to borrow back their needs at usurious rates set by the central banks. Fractional reserve banking as it exists in the West allows private banks to lend up to twenty times or more their cash reserves. In hot pursuit of profit that highly leveraged system has already gotten our banks into trouble. As great as the Soviet need is of private banks, there is little in our recent banking practice that merits imitation.

Transferred to the Soviet Union, the programmed high unemployment quotas that make up a key portion of our central bank's agenda could well be the final tinder to ignite civil war.

To help the Soviet Union make its difficult transition, we must help ourselves by rethinking our programmed unemployment and high-interest policy. That has been going on now for some 35 years — just about half the time that it took Soviet Communism to reduce their empire to a basket-case. It is a sobering thought what the state of the West might be after another thirty-five years of central bank folly.

wk

Vol. 1, No. 8 — December 1989

If It Is Not Broken, Break It!

At times one cannot help admiring the inventiveness of the Bank of Canada in hoodwinking its boss, the Government, the media and the public.

Prices have been moving upwards relentlessly every year since the Second World War with the exception of a slight downward blip in 1953. Our country has changed beyond recognition. We have thrown up schools, university campuses, air fields, expressways to provide the public infrastructures needed for a high-tech world. Inevitably the taxes to pay for all this cannot but show up as a growing layer of taxation in price. Our central bank, however, insists on confusing the price effects of this transformation with the inflation due to an overheated economy. But the transformation — and its cost and price effects — will not go away.

How are higher interest rates supposed to get around this little difficulty? The BoC arranges things so that such troublesome questions cannot be asked. From a problem to be analysed, "inflation" is cast as a dragon, the Governor of the Bank of Canada as St. George, and the rest of us as innocent if dumb damsels to be rescued. We must stand aside and ask no distracting questions.

As every playwright knows, the language spoken by his characters must fit their roles. A dragon must snort fire and not hold forth like an economist. All St. George has to do is brandish his gleaming sword. Strictly speaking, he doesn't have to talk at all.

A modern St. George, however, is unthinkable without press agents, and they are all over the place merchandising. Instead of answering questions, they are busy doctoring the language so that they cannot be asked.

But a time comes when all such successes must crumble. Events in the Soviet Empire should remind us that the greatest of all subversives is reality itself.

Two years ago the central bank responded to the October stock market crash by dropping the bank rate in panic by almost a percent and a half. That helped prevent things from falling apart. But in October of this year, our central bank decided that was no proper way to play Russian roulette. After all there had been no recession two years ago, and the stock market had gone into a feverish speculative fever based largely on leveraged buyouts made possible in large part by the mad lurchings of interest rates.

All this is being hailed as success by our central bank. When it runs into a brick wall with its foot on the accelerator, it explains that the bump on its forehead is where the halo sat too tight.

Let us take a leaf from Albert Einstein. He specialised in what he called "thought experiments" that required only a pencil and a sheet of paper. Plus an open mind that checked out alternative explanations. His special theory of relativity resulted from his reexamining the electro-magnetic equations that had been around for some decades and contradicted the orthodox laws of physics. Without that discovery, the modern world in all its miseries and glories would not have come into being.

Let us then attempt a little thought experiment of our own. Assume that St. George has slain the dragon and "zero inflation" has been achieved. Prices are lying flat on their backs as is the economy. The only industries working extra shifts are the bankruptcy courts. Governor Crow blows the whistle to allow rates to come down. The surviving entrepreneurs crawl out of their mouse holes and set up shop again. But they will do so only if they have the prospect of earning some profit. That means that prices will have to start moving up from the liquidation levels that constituted the "final victory over inflation."

Then won't the whole murderous experiment have to start all over again? Little will be left to which the central bank can apply its unspoken lemma "If it isn't broken, break it!"

The Missing Foundation for Public Policy Formulation

The national product estimates serve as a framework for many different aspects of economic analysis. In the December,1988 *Journal of Economic Literature*, Robert Eisner published a scholarly review of the literature on this subject. His list of weaknesses in the national product estimates includes the following:

1. Neglect of Concept of Total National Product

The total national product obviously includes both that portion that is produced and marketed commercially, and that portion that is produced and consumed within each family unit. The long-term trend has been away from non-commercial and towards an increasing proportion of commercial output. Therefore the long-term increase in real per-capita *commercial* output overstates the increase in real per-capita *total* output.

For example, in recent years the increasing proportion of women in the workforce, many with young children, has increased the demand for commercial services in education, child care, food preparation, etc.,services that were supplied previously in the non-commercial home economy. That shift increased the reported real commercial output, but may well have reduced the quantity and quality of those services.

The shift in services provided by women may be the single most important reason for the increase in the share of services in the commercial national output. Currently, the national output aggregates such as GNP are not specifically identified with commercial output only. That should be corrected. Failure to recognize household output obscures the role of family life both in the nurture and education of children and in producing the satisfactions of adult life.

2. Need for a Value-Added Concept

If environmental considerations are to be fully recognized, both the consumption of natural resources and the degradation of the environment must be considered. The introduction of a rigorous concept of value added in the estimates of total national product would achieve that goal. Total national value added would have to be net of natural resources consumed, of previously produced physical capital consumed, and of the environmental degradation.

The net value added by the household economy could also be estimated to obtain a total net value added figure.

3. Eliminating the Double Accounting of Output in Joint Purchase Situations

Merchants frequently offer some additional products "free of charge" as a bonus to stimulate sales. For example, a free $100 bicycle might be offered as a bonus with each purchase of a $400 television. How should such a transaction be measured for national output purposes? Did a $400 joint purchase take place, or did the buyer receive a free bicycle worth $100 plus a $400 TV?

Most observers would agree that a joint purchase took place at a total price of $400, and that the amount should be allocated appropriately to each item.

Now, instead of a free bicycle, think of free government services. Using a joint purchase example again, assume that the government levies taxes that can only be recovered from increased prices of goods sold over what the prices could otherwise be. Funds from the taxes then permit the government to pay for goods and services that are given away, yet their costs are also included in GNP. This illustrates how the cost of government services are included once in GNP through the higher prices necessary to recover tax costs, and a second time by including a cost-based value of "free" government output. *That double counting overstates the nominal value added and distorts measures of inflation.* Inflation should measure increases in factor costs, not increases in joint purchase costs. The elimination of the double counting of output in joint purchase situations would reduce the size of reported national output, and show a more realistic ratio of taxes to national output.

4. Need for Use of Full Accrual-Basis Accounting.

Current macroeconomic statistics reflect the continued partial usage of outdated cash-basis accounting. In defining GNP the current rhetorical device of assuming an identity between production, spending, and income makes each into a term of art that violates both common sense and established usage in other areas. Production cannot be equal to value added if capital consumption in the productive process is ignored. Nor can income be equal to both production as defined and value added. Expenditure is a flow-of-funds concept that cannot be meaningfully related to production, value added or income.

Harvey Wilmeth

Comment on Wilmeth

It is by the monthly trends of the GNP that our central bank ladles out to us a further dose of deflationary purgative. From Eisner's work, elaborated by Harvey Wilmeth, it becomes clear that a statistic could hardly be more misleading.

• Whenever any one leaves the household sector for the commercial sector, the GDP goes up. Hence the classic joke in freshmen economics courses: the GDP drops whenever a man marries his housekeeper. The discrepancy is less amusing today when millions of women are going out to work. That means greater dependence on market services such as fast foods, child-care.

• Perceiving the resulting rise in the GNP, our central bank may decide the economy is overheated and push up interest rates. But this may really mean that because of previous increases in the bank rate, too many wives have had to take jobs to help with mortgage payments.

• The GDP in effect counts the output of the public sector doubly. Because the taxation to pay for marketed government services turns up substantially as a layer of price, the cost of government is already included in the dollar amount of the private sector. But then its costs are added once again in the cost of public services to arrive at the GDP.

Harvey Wilmeth's ingenious analogy of the "free" bike offered with the TV set should do much to popularize the basic algorithm of a mixed economy: Aggregate price in a mixed economy includes *grosso modo* the cost of the unpriced public sector. Unless we assimilate this into our thinking, our policies will be an ongoing web of disaster.

This growing layer of taxation in our price structure I have termed the *social lien*. The value of the output of the public sector must be seen as transferred to the output of the private sector through the social lien. Aggregate price would thus include the value produced by both sectors, though it is attached to the output of the private sector alone.

"The external diseconomies of the private sector would come into better focus. We would be less likely to find our government promising to clean up the environment, and in the next breath threatening to inflict deflation on their economies if prices go on rising. Prices can do nothing but climb if such external diseconomies are integrated into the costs of private firms through taxation." (W. Krehm, *Price in a mixed economy — our record of disaster*, 1975, p. 131)

Wilmeth's remark about the output of the public sector being counted twice in the GNP says something very similar. If the Output of the Public Sector (P) is subtracted from the GNP (G) to correct this, the average price of the GDP will be shown to have grown by the factor G/(G-P). This is equivalent to the infinite series

$1 + P/G - (P/G)^2 + (P/G)^3 - ...$

This is a remarkable result achieved with some tuppenny mathematics. It shows that the effect on the price level of unpriced government services is in fact more complex than just simple addition. That is because the cost of state [services] must be borne by a real GDP that is in fact smaller than would first appear — in its pricing the cost of the public services turns up twice.

But a smaller private product as a proportion of GDP means that the output of the public sector is relatively greater. And since it is counted twice this means a further shrunken real GDP to support [this correction], and so forth. The double counting echoes back and forth between the P and G and gives rise to a converging infinite series to show the ultimate effect on price of unpriced public services.

Getting back to Wilmeth's analogy: if you were to ignore the value of the bike you get free with the TV, and attributed the $400 to the cost of a TV set you previously had been able to buy alone [say] for $300, you would conclude that there had been a 33% inflation. That, indeed, is what we have been doing by ignoring the value of public services.

There is no need to *assume* that taxes can only be recovered from increased prices of goods sold. The case of excise, sales, and value-added taxes should be evident even to the blind. Yet not only trade unions but governments too often identify the real standard of living of workers with the purchasing power of their take-home pay (thus ignoring the increased basket of unpriced public services we receive). On purely doctrinal grounds, it has been assumed by the orthodox that corporation income tax could not shift into price. (Since by marginalist theory price is determined on the margin where profits are zero, a tax on profit [according to the prevailing dogma] could not possibly affect price.)

Some of these extended conceptual frameworks catalogued by Eisner can be applied without further ado. Others are not so readily incorporated into workaday statistics. That is the case with the work performed in the non-commercial household sector. But even here recognizing that they exist can serve as an important *caveat*.

In his catalogue Eisner omits the social lien effect. That is like inspecting power consumption without checking the wiring at the meter. Nevertheless, Eisner has once again made a monumental contribution to clearing up some of the fog that envelops economic thought.

William Krehm

Correspondence — to Don Blenkarn / from John Hotson

10/11/89

Don Blenkarn
Chairman of the Standing Committee on Finance
House of Commons
Ottawa

Dear Mr. Blenkarn:

Thank you for your letter of 30/10 in which you comment on ours of 16/10 addressed to the Prime Minister. It was encouraging to read in it: "I think you are on the right track...In my view our Governor does not listen and has now institutionalized 5% inflation. As you rightly point out once interest rates stay high enough for a long enough period, the interest rates themselves get built into the cost of doing business and people pay them because they seem inevitable like death and taxes."

As gratifying as it was to learn that there was some substantial agreement between us, your letter left COMER all the more perplexed why we should have been denied our request to testify before recent hearings on the GST held by the Standing Committee on Finance.

COMER is a non-profit organization with a membership of some 200 including many academic and business economists. It is particularly interested in seeking out neglected options for managing inflation without wrecking the economy. From the press we gather that most of the depositions before your committee had to do with exemptions from the GST and the rate at which that tax should be set. The brief we had prepared, on the other hand, emphasized the linkage between the deficit and the policy of the Bank of Canada. The latter guarantees that any additional revenue raised through the GST will be assigned in advance to the money-lenders in an attempt to suppress the inevitable price effects of that very GST.

In *The Globe and Mail* of 8/11 you are quoted: "If people know that they are being gouged and screwed...perhaps they will make less demands on government." Though as ever we admire your colourful forthrightness, we cannot dismiss the real need for essential public services as simply the screwing and gouging of the tax-payer.

In actual fact our society is being starved of adequate public services. In the coming years we shall be experiencing the graying of our population, and a growing concern with our ravaged environment. Rather than planning greater unemployment to achieve the unattainable goal of "zero inflation," we should be upgrading our infrastructures against the day when fewer Canadians of working age will be called upon to support a growing population of retirees.

But we can hardly prepare for that day so long as we are obsessed with a government deficit that reflects mostly the wretched state of Ottawa's accountancy. Since the latter forties several Royal commissions on tax reform have recommended establishing a capital budget. I note your remark that the GST would bring into the open the effect on the price level of increased public spending. That, however, should remind us that trying to write off Ottawa's purchases of land, buildings and equipment in a single year must add needlessly to the layer of taxation in price. And this in turn triggers higher bank rates that further dislocate the budget.

Members of our board had already written to the Standing Committee on Finance over two years ago requesting a hearing on such matters. In reply to William Krehm, our chairman, you wrote at the time that the off-budget deficits of Crown Corporations make up for the disregard of the federal government's tangible capital assets.

You might as well argue that it is unnecessary for private firms to keep track of their capital assets because they may have subsidiaries running at a loss.

On that earlier occasion, too, we were not given an opportunity to present our views to your committee. Parliamentary committees and their hearings, must be considered no man's private fief. What is at stake is the livelihood of 26 million Canadians, and possibly the survival of Canadian confederation.

Alternate options to the GST-Zero Inflation combination do exist. As you point out in your letter, Governor Crow's mistake is that he won't listen. By his refusal to do so, he is incurring an awesome responsibility. I am sure you would not wish to be perceived in a similar position.

John H. Hotson,
Executive Director, COMER

We Salute

The Financial Post has published about a half dozen columns by Diane Francis on aspects of the recent COMER Conference, and an article by Andrew Cohen on our view of inflation. It also ran the following reply by William Krehm to a column by William Watson:

"*The Financial Post* carried a remarkable column by William Watson (13/10). In it he took Diane Francis to task for "[failing] to tell her readers that the Committee on Monetary and Economic Reform is widely regarded in mainstream economics as a committee of cranks."

"He is gracious enough to go on to say that 'cranks are occasionally right.'

When they are, he might have added, they are often so in a big way — a bit like oil explorers drilling in elephant country. That is because they question assumptions that may have boxed in the wits of the orthodox.

"To establish what is crankery and what is re-examination of a failed paradigm, one should begin by listening to what the 'crank' is saying. This Mr. Watson fails to do.

"A quarter of a century ago, I reached the conclusion that market imbalances of supply and demand could not alone account for the rise of prices that had begun taking over. A growing public sector was providing more and more of the infrastructures needed for our urbanizing, high-tech society. Inevitably this was feeding a broadening stratum of taxation into price. Declaring "inflation" the "main enemy" without taking the trouble to analyse it into its very different components, is a sure formula for trouble.

"I also identified other structural factors in our secular, non-cyclical upward creep of prices — legislation for fairer treatment of women and minorities, the depletion of our resources. Higher interest rates could not possibly reverse the effects of such non-market factors in our price movement.

"We can talk about only one thing at a time. At the Environment Conference at Waterloo that Ms. Francis covered, we were concerned that the funding of environmental programs would trigger further increases in the bank rate. For Mr. Watson to tell us that "inflation is due to more than high interest rates and taxes" is unnecessary.

"Mr. Watson writes: 'It would be hard to attribute our current inflations — which had its origins in the 1970s — to the post-1984 hike in the tax burden.

"In fact you would not have to. The ratio of consolidated government revenue to gross national product, which stood at 28.5% in 1965, had risen to 34.9% by 1969 and 41% by 1980. Like Rossini's *Calumny* aria, what started as a mere whisper gradually built up to the present roar, amplified by the mindless policy of the Bank of Canada. So, too, did the perceived 'inflation,' that the central bank was allegedly wrestling to the ground: 2.48%, 4.5% and 10.2% were the increases of the CPI for the same three years.

"Now here we have an acid test not only for COMER's crankery, but for Mr. Watson's credentials as journalist and economist. In my *Price in a Mixed Economy*, published in 1975, I not only detected the initial whisper of this process, but foretold its present roar. Since Mr. Watson is a writing gent, he should be able to produce his own forecasts at that time. Or establish when he stopped teaching — along with the rest of the 'mainstreamers' — that higher taxation was deflationary, since it 'siphoned off excess purchasing power' — presumably into the outer spaces of their flat world."

Vol. 2, No. 1— January 1990

Correspondence — to John Hotson and William Krehm / from Michael Wilson

20/11/89

Mr. John H. Hotson & Mr. William Krehm
The Committee on Monetary and Economic Reform
University of Waterloo

Dear Sirs:

The Prime Minister has forwarded to me a copy of your letter dated 16/10/89 recommending the use of credit controls as a means to moderate demand in our economy.

You suggest that a federal policy of directing credit regionally or industrially would be more effective in containing inflationary pressures than a policy relying on market forces and interest rates. The international record on credit controls, however, has been far less successful than you suggest, and I have serious reservations about applying them in Canada.

You refer to the use of "window guidance" in Japan, an informal approach used by the Bank of Japan in the past to limit the extension of credit by banks, to support your views that controls can work. Even in Japan, however, which has a more regulated financial system than many other industrial countries, this form of control has been used less frequently in recent years. Similar trends have developed in other industrial countries as well, as financial markets worldwide have become more deregulated. Adoption of credit controls in Canada would clearly be a step backward at a time when other countries around the world are moving towards more market based policies.

As for regional controls in Canada, you will note that there is no feasible way of operating these in our country. Our financial markets are too fully-integrated and competitive for that. Credit restrictions in one area of the country could be easily avoided by borrowers with access to other markets.

Nation-wide controls applied to lending in particular sectors would entail similar problems of avoidance, and would likely lead to the uneven and inefficient treatment of borrowers. By limiting credit supplied by institutional lenders we would hasten the expansion of markets for direct lending and borrowing outside of financial institutions, and drive an increasing number of borrowers, particularly the large borrowers into offshore markets. To the extent that sectoral controls did limit credit, they would fall most heavily on the small businesses, farmers and households who have less access than large corporate borrowers to alternatives sources of funds.

In these circumstances, how would lenders decide among qualified borrowers who should receive loans and who should be refused loans? There would be no assurance that funds would go to those who could make the most efficient use of them.

Disciplined policies which act to moderate demand and ease inflationary pressures offer the most reliable long-term answers to the strains and problems that currently affect our economy. Our monetary and fiscal policies are working together to promote an environment in which durably lower interest rates and sustainable economic growth are possible, and the structural policies and reforms we are implementing are laying the foundation for a stronger, more competitive economy for Canadians now and in the future.

Yours sincerely,
Michael Wilson
Minister of Finance

The Honourable Michael H. Wilson
Minister of Finance
Ottawa

Thank you for your letter of 20/11 in reply to ours to the Prime Minister of 16/10.

The views you express to support the Bank of Canada's high-rate policy suffer from two fundamental defects.

We are puzzled that you should identify the BoC's "zero inflation" goal with a reliance on "market forces and interest rates." Not in a single year since 1953 has our price index lain flat. Nor is it likely to in the future. What Governor Crow chooses to call "inflation" includes increases that have nothing to do with an overheated market, but merely reflect the ever-broader layer of taxation entering our price index. Substantially that increased taxation in recent years has gone to pay for the burden of interest imposed on the budget by our central bank's own perverse policy.

Imagine, Mr. Minister, what would happen if firefighters made no distinction between smoke caused by an electrical short-circuit, and smoke caused by a smouldering fire, and insisted on dousing any source of smoke with their water-hoses as the sole means of combatting "smoke." Clearly we would all long since have gone up in flames.

In any branch of engineering the identification of such a vicious circuit, where the problem fattens on the alleged solution, would send the designers back to square one. It is disturbing that your Ministry should shut its eyes to so basic a flaw. This guarantees not only that perfectly foreseeable disasters will be acted out, but will be endlessly repeated.

Nor do the facts support your presentation of Governor Crow's high rate policy as being in agreement with "other countries around the world....moving towards more market-based policies." Because of the gathering recession in the US the Federal Reserve has slashed its discount rate twice in two weeks. Governor Crow's stubborn refusal to follow suit has increased the spread between Canadian and American short-term rates to 451 basis points — almost double what it was last January. That has driven the Canadian dollar to new highs and put Canadian industry at a crippling disadvantage at the very time that the Free Trade Treaty is removing barriers between the two economies.

You need only consult the widening gap between the short-term and long-term rates to appreciate how unfounded is your attempt to pass our central bank's policy off as market-based. The short-term rates, of course, reflect the manipulation of the central bank, the longer-term ones economic reality. The differential is the measure of central bank intervention to control the money market.

You write that "credit restrictions in one area of the country could easily be avoided by borrowers with access to other markets." That problem is readily handled by requiring an affidavit from the borrower attesting that the loan would be used for the declared purpose. Any borrower violating that undertaking would be liable to prosecution for tax-evasion.

Many of the other objections you raise have equally simple answers. Can you, for example, really believe that the present brutal curtailment of credit does *not* fall most heavily on "the small businesses, farmers and households who have less access to alternative sources of funds"? Or that our banks under the current arrangement do not decide "who should receive and who should be refused loans?"

Yours truly,
William Krehm
John Hotson

Vol. 2, No. 2 — February 1990

Correspondence — to John Hotson / from Don Blenkarn

20/12/89

Mr. John H. Hotson
Executive Director, COMER

Thank you for the copies of your correspondence with the Honourable Michael Wilson. I very much agree with the thrust of your letter and I very much believe that the current policy of the government with respect to the current monetary policy is absolutely dead wrong.

Last spring I advocated credit controls to the government in lieu of the broad axe of the monetary policy. Unfortunately I received essentially the same answer you have received from Mr. Wilson.

It strikes me though that in a country where we have six large banks and no more than a half dozen other major financial institutions that it is very easy for the finance officials to exercise control over the system in order to effect a system of credit controls.

Congratulations on the work you are doing. Please keep it up.

Don Blenkarn, MP Mississauga South
cc. Rt. Hon Brian Mulroney
Hon. Michael Wilson

Hokum in the Black Box

The soft landing promised by John Crow is turning out a head-on crash. When a plane falls out of the sky, the authorities go to great lengths to reconstruct what brought on the tragedy. They comb the debris for miles around seeking the blackbox to obtain clues. Enquiries are held, witnesses cross-examined. No effort is spared to salvage from the catastrophe the lessons that may prevent its recurrence.

In our economic policy failures, we pursue quite the opposite course. Here the goal is coverup. Were a blackbox to turn up, it would yield little more than buzzwords. Our very language has been rigged to assure that we will have the same mishaps in ever grander format.

As the coverup grows bolder and more embracing, we are becoming a nation of economic illiterates, unable even to communicate meaningfully on economic matters.

The time has come when we must recapture the ability to deal with our problems.

There are some very simple, straight-forward rules for achieving this. First we must identify the real problems on which our future hangs. And having done so, we must judge proposed policies by whether they expedite or hinder our dealing with those real problems.

Real problems require real solutions: there must be at hand enough resources — trained labour, material, equipment. If that is so, it should always be possible to design financial arrangements for such real solutions. But if we postpone dealing with real problems until we have resolved some issue in our symbolic economy — balancing the budget, "licking inflation," we may be chasing a phantom. We can no longer afford the luxury of dogma-driven policies that are not open to verification.

And if we can show that a proposed solution in fact adds to the problem it is supposed to solve, we must scratch it at the starting gate. For what we are confronted with is what systems analysts call a "positive feed-back." If we allow them to, such positive feedbacks always lead to the breakdown of the system.

Unless they start grouping our problems according to their effective causes, our policy-makers are in the position of medical men who would apply radiation and chemotherapy to all "swellings," including those resulting from bumps, bee-bites and pregnancies.

There is too much murk in our blackbox.

wk

The Bundesbank up to Bat

With their economies crumbling into a recession of their own making, the American Fed and the BoC would like to climb down from their high-interest perches. But that is not going to be easy. Suddenly our all-powerful central banks have awakened to the realisation that they have put themselves in a position where they must dance to somebody else's tune. The chief piper at the moment seems to be West Germany where the Bundesbank is striking out on a high-interest kick of its own.

For years West Germany has enjoyed a great prosperity not only due to its own efficiency, but to the artificially high US dollar. And now European economic unification and the collapse of the Soviet Empire have opened up vast prospects for its economy. Investment flooding into the country and has pushed up its currency. In the past year the mark has risen by 14% against the yen. West Germany's trade balance has surpassed that of Japan for the first time in a decade.

Undoubtedly this creates inflationary dangers. To deal with them a whole menu of measures other than high interest rates could be designed. Unfortunately, the Bundesbank President, Karl Otto Poehl, is the dominant spirit at the Bank for International Settlements at Basel, the central bankers' private club that has imposed its high-rate doctrine on the western world. So instead of serving as the locomotive to pull the real economy of the world out of its predicament, the Bundesbank is tugging it into a higher-interest-rate zone.

The Japanese, whose economic miracle has depended on cheap financing, are being pressured into the stampede towards higher rates. Since the US Fed is unwilling to resort to lower rates and a weaker dollar to recoup American competitive fortunes, it is badgering the Japanese into raising their rates. And in this it is being seconded by Herr Poehl.

The Wall Street Journal (8/2) quotes him, "We thought the yen would move in parallel with the European currencies, but it didn't happen. The main reason is that Japan didn't raise its interest rates." While the Bank of Japan has since raised its rates, Mr. Poehl is still unhappy that it did so "hesitantly and not to the same extent" as Germany.

As a result Western German government bonds have a 1.62% higher yield than those in Japan.

If the Bundesbank persists in this course, it is not hard to foresee grief. For years the performance of the Tokyo market has been a miracle of levitation with averages 70 and more time earnings. Those has made it possible for Japanese industries to raise money at low rates. Putting the arm on the Japanese to drive up their rates will not just blunt Japan's export advantages. It could trigger a stock market crash to make anything that happened in Wall St. since 1929 look like child's play. And then Tokyo's funds will be pulled back from abroad in panic.

For all its economic power, West Germany has enough problems of its own, ranging from its dying lakes and forests to the growing unemployment in a country with an aging population. Mass unemployment — eight percent at the beginning of Poehl's high-rate binge — can only make an explosive mixture with Europe's increasingly liquid frontiers. Nor can East Germans flocking into the country be treated like disposable Turkish *Gastarbeiter* and sent back where they came from.

K.

Vol. 2, No. 3 — March 1990

Thermostat or Empty Tank?

Anything that might lead to a price increase prompts Governor Crow of the Bank of Canada to up interest rates — whether it is expenditure to clean up the environment, to educate our people or look after their health. By this definition such things are deemed bad. Unemployment, closed factory gates, and increased bankruptcies — since they "cool the economy" — are good. In this way we are torn between two contradictory value systems. We are faced not only with an economic crisis, but with a moral one.

The only intellectual footings to which the central bank's "zero inflation" policy can lay claim is the model of a self-equilibrating economy developed in the 19th century. That theory argued that if too much were produced, the price would go down and production would drop, and that in time would lead to higher prices and more production. And in this way prices, production and everything else in the economy, it is argued, tends to oscillate around equilibrium points. The economy supposedly works very much like the thermostat in your home. When the house gets cold, the furnace is switched on until the temperature at which it was set is reached and then it is automatically cut off.

That is a cozy paradigm. But it suffers from grave defects.

To begin with, when the thermostat on your furnace stops performing, the first thing to do, would be to go down into the basement and look at the oil gauge to make sure the tank isn't empty. Fuel deliveries are another subsystem that the temperature of your home depends upon.

And fuel deliveries will take place only if your payments for the fuel have been made. Together these three subsystems — and several more — add up to a system. Going at your thermostat with a crowbar would not make much sense, no matter how much resolve you brought to the act. In fact it would demolish your premise of a self-balancing system. Yet that is what Governor Crow has been doing.

We call our economy a mixed economy, because it consists not only of the market, but of a public sector. The two work by distinct codes. The public sector is responsible for many of our infrastructures and our common goods and services, even though it may contract with private firms to deliver these. What is important is that the cost of such services are paid for mostly through taxation. For the most part these services are not even priced. But the taxes that pay for them do turn up substantially in the prices of goods that are marketed. When you buy an automobile, you are really paying as well for a basket of public services that permit our society to go on functioning.

There are still other subsystems in our economy. There is the ecology that runs by laws of its own. The laws of supply and demand hardly hold in the upper atmosphere, and the most ardent entrepreneurial types need a minimum of oxygen to go on entrepreneuring. It is therefore wrong to treat the costs of conserving the environment when they turn up in the price level as just "inflation." Before we go at our thermostat with a crowbar, we should make sure that it is calibrated properly. The same holds for the price index.

In any of the natural sciences a model pretending to take more energy out of a system than is there, is at once dismissed as charlatanry (perpetual motion). Not so in the economic theory in style today. There, if you manage to hammer prices down to where they used to be, that is taken as a sign that supply and demand are in balance and that God is in His heaven. That is why Governor Crow is prepared to go on raising interest rates until he achieves "zero inflation" without asking where those usurious rates are to come from.

Dressing up this thermostat model of the economy in fancy mathematics in no way helps. It merely intimidates the illiterate into taking this bizarre theory for science. The professors who propound it in our universities, when hard pressed, argue that economics is a "non-normative science." Translated into the language of five-year-olds that means that it is a "pretending" science having nothing to do with the real world.

That places a heavy responsibility on our academics, Their intellectual parlour-game has made possible policies that have blighted untold lives. They are in fact faced with a dilemma parallel to that of true believers in the former Communist world. Some of these started expressing doubts about the Communist blueprint as early as the Moscow trials of the thirties. The faith of others went on burning bright right until Khruschev's revelations about Stalin in the mid-fifties. Still others hung on into the age of Gorbachev in the latter eighties. For good enough reason we grade ex-Communists according to the date of their exit from that Nirvana, Eventually the same is bound to be the case with our economists.

Saving the Savings Concept

Avuncular sermons on how little we save are not in short supply. They all press the conclusion that our Finance Minister should wield an axe on all government spending. In that way, it is argued, we shall be able to reduce our deficits, and even pay off our debts. And at the end of this virtuous path will lie our reward.

There are many things wrong with this hard sell. Much of our society's savings in a modern mixed economy takes place in the public sector — its vast investment in physical infrastructures — highways, airfields, and so forth — and in human capital such as health and education. Little of this is kept track of: Ottawa has no capital budget. Its deficit is arrived at by expensing its acquisitions even of land, building and equipment in a single year.

We hear a great deal of the high rate of saving in Japan. However, Japanese investment in such essential physical infrastructures is lamentably wanting. It is enough to wander off the main streets in Tokyo to come across unpaved roads without sewage service.

From the eloquent lips of our Prime Minister we have had shocking figures on the functional illiteracy of Canadians, and its economic costs. Consistency would require Mr. Mulroney to be equally eloquent in emphasizing that expenditures on education are a vital investment. There the Japanese are far ahead of us. Instead Ottawa has been cutting grants to the provinces for education and other human capital. At the same time the provinces are under pressure to step up their own budget-balancing.

It is commonly acknowledged that a good education is likely to increase a person's earning powers over his lifetime. However, the debts incurred by both governments and individuals for such purposes are taken as a sign of national decadence. How deeply this schizophrenia is rooted in established economic theory can be seen from a recent paper of Thomas J. Courchene of Queen's, 'Rethinking the Macro Mix: The Case for Provincial Stabilization Policy.'

"The national-income-accounting identity can be re-arranged in the 'twin deficits' form: (G-T) = (M-X) + (S-I) where the fiscal deficit (G-T) is identically equal to the current account deficit (M-X) plus the private sector net savings (S-I)." (M is imports, X is exports, S is Savings; I investment of the private sector.)

Into this "identity" you could not squeeze public sector investment with a shoehorn. And deductions from it are bound to be little more than ideological exercises.

Savings are made not from corporative losses or relief payments, but out of profits and wages earned. So long as real factors of production — qualified labour and talent, equipment and plant — are available, money can be created to put these to work. That was the lesson of the grimmest stretch of human history to date — the thirties and forties. During the Great Depression the emphasis — as today — was on balancing budgets, and savings hit an all-time low.

Only with the outbreak of World War II were people put to work on borrowed money — in the US at interest rates kept between .5 and 2%. Then savings scored a dramatic comeback. Though much of the national production was blown up on the battlefields, savings grew at such a pace that they prevented the post-war depression that most people expected. With low-interest rates, they made possible the financing of European reconstruction. After a quarter of a century of "encouraging savings with high interest rates," however, today we are unable to reduplicate the Marshall Plan in Eastern Europe.

Vol. 2, No. 4 — May 1990

Putting Humpty Dumpty Together Again

Until recently everything was headed upward — not only the bank rate, but the self-orchestrated acclaim Governor Crow was getting in the media for bestowing on us "short-term pain for long-term gain." Now the act of levitation has come to a sudden halt. Interest rates and the Canadian dollar may still be headed upward, but all else is in nose-dive. Once a believer, *The Financial Post* (9/04) now informs us: "[Finance Minister] Wilson is the second federal official in less than a week to admit the battle against inflation is failing. On Monday, BoC Governor John Crow said the central bank's high interest policy has not been as successful as expected."

In the circumstance, the Governor could use some consolation. It has come in the form of salary increases over the past three years in the 12% to 21% annual range. All that remains is for him to cite these figures as a reason for a further hike in the bank rate to enforce better anti-inflationary discipline.

Greg Ip in *The Financial Post* (30/03) writes: "Interest rates resumed their upward march yesterday raising concerns among some economists that the price of the BoC's battle against inflation may be too great." The point is not that the product is overpriced, but that it is fraudulent, adding to the very problem it is advertised to solve.

Until a couple of years ago, the orthodox view was that higher taxes kept inflation down. One could have hoped that the Goods and Services Tax, appearing on the final consumer's invoice, would make it clear that some of our price rise merely reflects the cost of more public services; and that higher interest rates, driving those taxes higher, can only add to inflation. Vain hope. To get around that little embarrassment the term "tax inflation" has been introduced.

And economists react to the word "inflation" as unthinkingly as a slot-machine to an inserted coin.

We are witnessing the breakdown of professional self-respect amongst mainline economists as they close in to defend a discredited dogma. Thus David Laidler of the C.D. Howe Institute is quoted (*FP* 9/04): "To compare what's happening to monetary policy and the outcome in the same year is not legitimate — there's a couple of years' lag in there." That's fine. Repeatedly we have pointed out that it takes twice as long for the central bank to engineer a depression as for a woman to produce a child. But we do not recall Dr. Laidler protesting when John Crow jacked up rates because the week's statistics did not show the economy in total collapse in response to the rate boost a couple of weeks earlier.

Antecedents — John Maynard Keynes

Like Joseph's coat of many colours, Keynes's dazzling gifts were bound to get him into trouble. It was risky enough questioning the inherited wisdom of the counting houses. But while doing so, in true Bloomsbury fashion Keynes could not resist scandalising the Philistines. Thus to illustrate the need for the state making up shortfalls in aggregate demand, he delivered himself of the following:

"Ancient Egypt was doubly fortunate, and doubtless owed to this its fabled wealth, in that it possessed *two* activities, namely pyramid-building as well as the search for the precious metals, the fruits of which because they could not serve the needs of man by being consumed, did not stale with abundance. The Middle Ages built cathedrals and sang dirges. Two pyramids, two masses for the dead, are twice as good as one: but not so two railways from London to York. Thus we are so sensible, having schooled ourselves to so close a semblance to prudent financiers, taking careful thought before we add to the "financial" burdens of posterity by building them houses to live in, that we have no such easy escape from the sufferings of unemployment."

Inevitably the burghers took their sweet revenge. For decades Keynes has been treated as a non-person, exhumed from time to time only to be hung in irons.

After the October 1987 market debacle, a scholar of Ronald Regan's standing mocked Keynes for not having a degree in economics — his speech-writers were apparently unaware the same could be said of Adam Smith, David Ricardo, and John Stuart Mill, to say nothing of Karl Marx.

If mentioned at all, Keynes is presented as the patron saint of inflation. Yet whenever he dealt with that problem, he looked beyond the symptoms to deeper causes. As a young Treasury official at the Peace Conference, he cautioned against the inflationary effects of trying to squeeze out of Germany reparations that wildly exceeded her power to pay in foreign currency.

For its deafness to these warnings, the world was to pay a heavy price — not only in the collapse of the German currency in 1923, but eventually of its own social structures.

Keynes had been brought up to do his thinking within the framework of the *laissez faire* model: the economy was viewed as a self-equilibrating machine that ground out prosperity and social justice. But no sooner did the Depression strike, than he turned his back on his own writings to wrestle with the spirit again. In *The General Theory*, we are given a glimpse of the anguish involved: "The great puzzle of Effective Demand vanished from economic literature. ... It could only live on furtively below the surface in the underworlds of Karl Marx, Silvio Gesell or Major Douglas."

He wrote of his "long struggle of escape ... from habitual modes of thought and expression ... which ramify for those brought up in them, as most have been, into every corner of our minds."

To come to grips with the problem of effective demand, Keynes had to reject the quaint article of orthodoxy known as Say's Law. This held that by the very act of its production every commodity created its own demand, and that a general state of overproduction was thus impossible. That hardly equipped economists to deal with the Great Depression. Their prescription — cutting wages and government spending — served only to shrink effective demand further.

With the help of his brightest students, he analysed this vicious spiral, long familiar to socialists. But whereas Marx had celebrated it as a terminal disorder, Keynes devised techniques for turning it around. Increased state expenditures would reverse the fall of prices, encourage investment, expand the tax-base, and, feeding upon itself, the spiral, turned benign, would get the economy moving upward once again.

He had but partial success in convincing his government to pull its economy out of the depression in this way. That was left to World War II.

And here Keynes scored his greatest practical triumph. In his pamphlet *How to Pay for the War* he proposed freezing a portion of the wages and salaries to be released only at the end of hostilities. These accumulated savings helped prevent the postwar depression that almost everybody expected. Along with low interest rates maintained throughout and after the war, this made possible the rapid reconstruction of non-Communist Europe.

Unfortunately, pressure by his academic peers led Keynes to do his most basic thinking in a very private manner, much as a gentleman performs his ablutions. In the words of G.L.S. Shackle: "Keynes spares his readers, even in the deliberately provocative *General Theory* of 1936 the ultimate force of his conclusion uttered in speech: "Equilibrium is blither."

On reading the proofs of *The General Theory*, Roy Harrod, his future biographer, offered this advice: "(Your) effectiveness is diminished if you try to eradicate every deep-rooted habit of thought *unnecessarily*. I am not merely thinking of the aged and fossilized, but of the younger generation. ... It is doing a great violence to their fundamental groundwork of thought if you tell them that two independent demand and supply functions won't jointly determine price and quantity. Tell them that we don't know the supply functions. Tell them that the *ceteris paribus* clause is inadmissible and that we can discover more important relationships governing price and quantity in this case that render the supply and demand analysis nugatory. But don't impugn the analysis itself."

Keynes, so adept in dealing with opponents, was less so in standing up to friends. Rather than overturned, the apparatus of marginalism was merely by-passed. Everything remained in place for the grand counter-revolution that was to engulf the Western economy and bring it to its present plight.

When Keynes did his mature work, rising prices were hardly the problem. The public sector still made up a quite negligible portion of the economy.

With the peace, however, a mixed economy came into existence. The new social pluralism, urbanization, the population explosion, mass migrations, new technologies all called for costly infrastructures that only the state could provide. The patterns of price changed radically to reflect this.

William Krehm

Moving the Clock Back to "Lick Inflation?"

As a working journalist in the forties, I got to know Guatemala under its perennial dictator, Jorge Ubico. Indians worked on the coffee plantations for ten and twenty cents a day, and put in two weeks of unpaid labour on the direct roads. Rural teachers were paid seven dollars a month to teach classes of fifty or sixty. This happy state of affairs was maintained by a murderous reign of terror that created the impression that an epidemic of laryngitis had descended on the land.

Four months before Ubico was swept away by a popular revolution in 1944, *The Reader's Digest* praised him as a hero in the battle against inflation. He had persuaded Washington to lower the wages paid for the building of its Guatemalan air base from a dollar to fifty cents a day. Similarly, he had forced the United Fruit Company to reduce the pay of the workers laying out its new plantations on the Pacific coast. With such wages, of course, the bulk of the population could afford no imports, and the local currency, the *quetzal*, even fetched a penny premium over the US dollar.

Came the democratic revolution, and all this began to change. An educator, Juan Jose Arevalo, was elected president in a democratic vote. Trade unions came into existence for the first time in years. Wages inched up. Schools and hospitals were built. And inevitably, prices also started rising.

That left me with a gnawing question: could you classify such price increases as "inflation"? Were these really attributable to a pathological condition of the market that called for correction? Clearly you could not bring back the wages so admired by *The Reader's Digest* without the repressive system that had enforced it. And further down the line should we then see the death squads that assassinated tens of thousands of Guatemalans and Salvadorans in recent decades as "fighters against inflation?"

The case of Ubico's Guatemala was an extreme one. But the same questions beg replies before we can claim to know what we are doing closer home in our attempts to manage price movement. In the past quarter of a century the advanced countries of the world have undergone profound structural changes. A new social pluralism has come into being. Legislation has been put on the books limiting discrimination on the basis of race, nationality or sex. Such transformations must have a powerful effect on the price level. And yet in our discussions of inflation this is completely ignored.

We are free, of course, to attach any name to anything we may wish. But to a considerable degree our language programs our thinking. To know what we are doing, we must classify effects according to their causes. For only by addressing the cause can we control the effect.

Were we to use the same word to designate an electrical short circuit and a flame ignited by a match, we would be led to douse a short-circuit with water.

A clear distinction must be made between price movements that are market-determined — i.e. too much or too little demand in relation to the available supply — and price movements originating outside the market. The former could be called "market-inflationary" or "truly inflationary." The latter could be termed "structural price movements."

In turn, such "structural price movements" having their origins in legislation rather than the market, fall into two categories. The government itself pays for additional public services that are neither priced nor marketed, and all taxation, directly or indirectly, must substantially find its way into the costs of the private sector and hence into prices. Accordingly it is impossible to reverse such price increases by depressing the economy with higher interest rates.

There is another type of "structural price increase." In this case the state itself does not spend more money for unpriced public services, but orders the private sector to do things that add to its costs. Thus it may set new standards to limit pollution of the environment. Or it may impose an obligatory schedule of wages on employers, wiping out the traditional differentials between the pay of men and women, or between white and black workers. The latter we could call *social revalorisation.*

It is this last sort of structural price increase that we are concerned with in this article.

The most obvious thing in managing our price movement would be the need to break down each given movement of price into its very distinct components. If a higher minimum wage or equal pay legislation has been brought in, it is possible to estimate the contribution that such laws would make to a higher price level. Likewise, if higher taxes are going to be collected, it is easy enough to estimate the likely increase in the layer of taxation in price.

And the residue that cannot be accounted for by price increases traceable to such non-market factors could be attributed to true market inflation.

But you are barking up the wrong tree if you apply higher interest rates to reverse a price jump that merely reflects the higher costs imposed on producers by legislation making more equal the pay of men and women, whites and blacks. To reverse these price increases, you would have to repeal the laws in question, or reintroduce Jim Crow.

wk

Vol. 2, No. 5 — June 1990

Ken Bohnsack's Sovereignty Petition

COMER member Ken Bohnsack has put his energy and enthusiasm behind his Sovereignty Petition to the US Congress. The proposal is that, as a modest step away from the public debt mess and the starvation of public services, Congress make interest free loans of government-created money to state and local tax authorities for voter-approved capital projects. Many thousand voters in 41 states have signed the petition and it has been endorsed by twenty tax-supported bodies including four county governments, six city councils, and a number of school districts and townships. These range in size from Cuyahoga County's 1.5 million down.

In all probability the program would start off fairly small — say $1 billion for the first year. That amount of new money — created, one supposes, by the issue of cheques which will be deposited in banks and added to their reserves — will be but a small addition to the annual increase of the money supply (M3) of some $125 billion. If, however, it is considered undesirable to make this net addition to the money supply, the Fed can easily offset this by reducing its open market bond purchases

Indeed, an excellent way to start the whole Sovereignty plan would be to require the Treasury to deposit to the credit of the first public bodies endorsing Sovereignty loans the $322,539,016 in President Lincoln's Treasury money "Greenbacks" which in recent years the Treasury has kept under lock and key. These US Notes played a vital role in financing Lincoln's war to save the union.

The useful $1, $2, $5 US Notes which my older US readers will remember have all been withdrawn and destroyed, large denomination US notes have been printed to replace them *and then locked in a vault* where they sit to this day! Why? During the over 100 years these "greenbacks" circulated interest free, they saved the US public more than $1 billion in interest they would have had to pay to keep an equal amount of private bank money circulating!

So the bankers don't want the US Notes to circulate? Fine. Deposit them to the credit of Cuyahoga Country and Elyria, Ohio and Freeport, Illinois, and use them to build some fine schools and water treatment plants — schools and plants which the taxpayers of Ohio and Illinois will only pay for *once*, instead of several times over when they float a bond issue to pay with bank money.

Since the loans will be financing essential capital projects, they will add not only to society's well-being, but to its productivity and hence to the federal government's tax base.

John H. Hotson

We Risk a Sorry Epitaph

There are those who explain BoC policy by a secret clause in the Free Trade Agreement pledging Canada to keep its dollar at 85 cents or better. That theory has been mentioned in Parliament, but confirmation may not be available until the archives are opened some decades ahead.

Far more menacing than possible plots are the carefully nurtured outbreaks of ideological distemper. Not only is the effect of the latter more sweeping, but they do leave behind a "paper trail." Ensnaring the public mind with ideological birdlime carries with it a legitimization that a second-storey job could never provide.

In Britain the reigning dogma was a belief in balancing budgets at all costs and keeping the currency strong to satisfy national pride and as a buffer against inflation. And if that meant high interest rates, deflation, unemployment, the decay of exports, so be it: it would not only work for those who had money to breed interest, but keep the great unwashed in their place.

This helped bring on the British General Strike of 1926, and eventually the Great Depression and World War II. These were hardly the goals that central banks had in mind, but then to foresee what lies ahead you must exercise your brain rather than your prejudices.

Our readers will have no difficulty recognizing in the Treasury View of the twenties the wisdom that shapes our monetary policy today.

The Bank for International Settlements (BIS), like the Communist International in its day, holds that people are not to be trusted in deciding what is good for them. That is why the BIS, established in 1930 to help manage the international balance of payments, became a central bankers' club operating in the shadows.

The policy of "zero inflation" was cooked up at the BIS. Our central bank head, John Crow, is unique only in the ingenuous way in which he has trumpeted his goal. For mindless fervour, Crow occupies a position in the central banking community similar to that of Albania in the Communist constellation.

In the thirties the wisdom of the world's central bankers led to the near collapse of Western social structures. Eventually, however, popular pressures forced an opening for new ideas; and an age of public programs financed at low interest rates was ushered in. That not only saved capitalism, but made possible the financing of World War II, and two decades of growth after its end.

The war ushered in a period of profound transformation throughout the non-Communist world. Mass migrations, rapid urbanization, technological revolutions, the pluralistic society, new expensive military hardware called for massive infrastructures. With broadening layers of taxation in price, price patterns were no longer determined wholly by the market.

During the thirties, governments, grappling for shares of a shrinking world market, devalued their currencies — a strategy that came to be known as "beggaring your neighbour." Today our governments are following a contrary course. By pushing up their bank rates, they have strengthened their currencies as well as their dependence on short-term financing for their deficits. Up to now lower rates not only gave Germany and Japan a competitive edge, but permitted these countries to provide the markets to prevent the collapse of the world economy. Now Washington has begun leaning on them to raise their interest rates. What threatens is a competitive tug-of-war for short-term funds to fill the holes eaten in balance sheets by high rates. And as the game goes on, it is bound to trigger some bad surprises. A major sell-off on the Tokyo stock and bond market could reproduce the trauma of the Austrian Kreditanstalt collapse of 1931. At that time the recall of US short-term money in the New York stock market's hour of need precipitated an international financial crisis.

The new surge of high-interest rates on world money markets could spell the collapse of social structures in the Third World. The deep wounds of the early eighties are being torn open again when they have hardly begun to scar. Worse still, thinking on the whole question of inflation has become so muddled as to verge on the grotesque. Thus to stifle inflation, the new Brazilian regime has frozen all bank accounts, including the operating capital of producing firms. This has obliged them to borrow the money from the same banks at fancy interest rates to keep going.

By mirror-image deduction, the peoples of Eastern Europe are crediting the Western system with virtues as absolute as the defects of their own Communism. This great illusion is unlikely to last. Our high-interest cult makes our governments more prolific in bad advice than in effective aid. Mass unemployment and soaring prices will go ill with ancestral hatreds and quizzical frontiers. In the wings, champing at the bit, are the steeds of the apocalypse, freshly shod and snorting brimstone.

We risk a sorry epitaph: *Here lies a civilization whose prowess in the natural sciences impelled it to poke around in the very genitals of Creation. But in the conduct of its own affairs it failed the most rudimentary test of logic.*

wk

Lower Interest Rates to Save Meech Lake

Just when the true believers were awaiting that velvety landing promised by our central bank, everything sacred seems to be breaking up — Canadian Confederation itself. In its warped perspective these unpleasant surprises are only arguments for the BoC driving interest rates still higher. Like a fly on the ceiling, it sees everything standing on its head.

Throughout the world today, in the Soviet Union, Yugoslavia, India, economic stress is imparting a jagged edge to nationalist conflicts. Canada is no exception.

Of the three provinces that withdrew their support from the Meech Lake Agreement, two are the most depressed — Newfoundland with its 16% unemployment and New Brunswick not too far behind. The farm economy of Manitoba has been particularly vulnerable to high interest rates.

Last summer a US State Department alumnus, Francis Fukuyama, announced the end of history — because of the collapse of the Soviet Empire. The quaint notion of history coming to an end with the arrival of the millennium was first developed by the German philosopher Hegel and borrowed by Marx. The trouble with such fanatics is that they are not only prepared to abolish future history; they are also prone to bury or reinvent the past.

Canadian Confederation was negotiated in the teeth of the continent's geography. Essentially it was an act of faith — a rosary with more string than beads. Rightly or wrongly, the Fathers of Confederation were agreed that independence from the United States was worth the high-cost economy it entailed. To bring in the scattered colonies separated by many hundreds of miles of rock, they negotiated tough compromises — expensive infrastructures such as railways and financial compensation for the outlying provinces. Such an economy is exceptionally capital-intensive. Hence it is particularly vulnerable to high interest rates.

Were John Crow and his "zero inflation" in place in 1867, the Fathers would have headed for Washington not Charlottetown.

Vol. 2, No. 6 — July 1990

Making Our Statistics More Liar-proof

Only belatedly is the hoax of salvation through usury being uncovered. That task seems already underway at Statistics Canada. Thus it reports that the Consumer Price Index posted a 4.5% increase in the 12 months ending in May, down from 5.0% in April. That was the biggest monthly drop in nearly six years. The most important reason for the drop was the removal of the federal excise increases on tobacco and gasoline.

Douglas Peters, chief economist of the Toronto-Dominion Bank, summed up the disclosure: "The inflation numbers tell us what we've known for a long time — inflation has stayed at 4% for the last six years except for the idiot taxes that keep getting added in." The "core rate of inflation," that excludes volatile factors of food and energy, fell to 4.4% in April from 4.9% a year earlier. The concept of a "core inflation" was introduced by the late Otto Eckstein in 1981 — a mincing step in the right direction.

Far more important than the volatility of certain market factors is the part played in price movement by factors not originating in the market at all. Rather than just segregating increases in the tobacco and gasoline taxes, or in food and energy prices, it is essential that Statscan unbundle our statistical indices according to their causes.

A significant move already made in this sense is a new multi-factor measure of productivity. Up to now the labour productivity index had measured the value produced only against labour inputs. Between 1961 and 1986, for example, the labour productivity index increased by an average of 2.1% annually — almost twice as much as the new multiple-factor measure of productivity. When productivity lagged, this was commonly misinterpreted to place the blame entirely on labour's performance. Several of the inputs that now enter the denominator — new equipment, technology — are obviously influenced by the level of interest rates.

Infrastructure Deficit

Like antibodies developed by an infected organism, significant questionings are starting to appear even among conservatives.

The latest blockbuster has come from David A. Anschauer, Senior Economist of the Chicago Federal Reserve. (*The Wall Street Journal* 30/07): "The Fed economist attributes as much as 60% of the productivity slump [in the US] to neglect of our core infrastructures, by which he means streets and highways, mass transit, airports, water and sewer systems and electrical and gas facilities." If Mr. Anschauer had included human infrastructures — education, health and social services — in his definition, he would have come up with an even more shocking figure.

The article goes on to quote Peggy L. Cuciti of the University of Colorado: "She notes that the budget includes $43.8 billion for nonmilitary physical capital, or about the same amount, adjusted for inflation, that was spent in 1979, even though the economy has grown some 40% since then. The 1991 infrastructure outlay comes to 3.6% of all proposed spending, sharply below the 1979 rate of 5.3%. The Federal Highway Administration has estimated that 23% of the nation's 575,000 bridges are structurally deficient and more than 25% of interstate roadway has deteriorated. If poor roads cause traffic jams, it's likely that more gasoline will be consumed and more overtime paid. This will tend, at least in the short run, to increase the gross national product. But it hardly represents a desired economic trend."

wk

Shades of Mussolini

Governor Crow has run into a further difficulty in delivering his promised "soft landing." In our central bank's scheme of saving us from "inflation," there are two statistics that it watches.

One is the price index. The other is the unemployment rate, which Crow insists must rise to 8%, before rates come down. Both these figures must be in favourable constellation, plus an endless number of other improvised conditions: the Meech Lake Accord was supposed to sail through uneventfully, the federal debt must be down, and there must be no drought on the Prairies. The beauty of this arrangement is that the resolute governor can dream up new reasons for not relaxing the bank rate faster than the old ones are satisfied.

Now he has really run into a bonanza: though the economy has been slowing down for eighteen months, the unemployment rate actually dropped from 7.5 to 7.4% between May and June, and from 8% since August, 1988. So a warning is being sounded of a continued inflationary menace. The tocsin for the purpose, of course, is the money-lenders' cash register ringing up higher receipts.

There is, however, a clear reason for the static unemployment figures, but clear reasons are not the BoC's specialty.

In the 1970s the Canadian labour force grew on the average by 3.2 % a year. Now that rate is down to about one percent. That is because those entering the labour force for the first time in the seventies were born in the high-birth years of the late 50s and early sixties, when there were 480,000 births a year. Those entering the labour force today were born in the following years when the birth rate touched a low of 340,000 in 1973. The entry of women into the labour force which contributed powerfully to the unemployment statistic a few years back is now tending to stabilize.

In the US, Fed Chairman Alan Greenspan has also remarked how puzzled he is on how little impact the slower growth of the economy has had on employment. One of the remarkable things about central bank heads is that quite obvious things leave them puzzled, while they have such absolute certainty about the most arrant nonsense.

For example, with the prospect of fewer active workers and more long-lived retirees in the decades ahead, you might conclude that every willing worker should be employed putting our infrastructures in order, introducing labour-saving technologies, and contributing to retirement funds. But in the cuckoo-land of central bankers, the right answer is: fewer available workers means that interest rates must continue in the clouds, making it impossible to finance labour-saving technologies, our infrastructures must be allowed to crumble, and we must create more unemployment amongst our dwindling work force.

But not to despair. The late Fascist Dictator had the formula that might still enable us to look forward to a relaxing of the bank rate, if only a generation hence. To ensure himself enough cannon-fodder for his imperial ambitions, the Duce awarded medals and prizes to mothers who had birthed at least twelve children. Perhaps we should adopt a similar scheme for breeding unemployed for Crow.

Vol. 2, No. 7 — August 1990

After the Party Comes the Clean-up

The party is over, and the table is littered with the debris of yesterday's wisdom. Headlines tell us that the bankruptcy rate is worse than in the 1982 recession. Just yesterday the analysts of investment houses were rooting for higher interest charges. As stocks plummeted, their commissions from bond-trading on BoC account gained in persuasiveness even as the Great White Father's logic dwindled. Now more and more of these houses are shutting their doors, while others are writing almost as many pink-slips as orders.

Canada was unsuccessful in persuading the G7 summit to "highlight the continued danger of inflation at Houston." (*Financial Post* 9/7) "'The Big Three — the US, Germany and Japan — just don't want to think about inflation,' a frustrated Canadian official says. 'The US administration,' he explains, 'is feuding with the Federal Reserve to ease monetary policy. The West Germans want to de-emphasize inflation in light of unification.'" The one thick-tongued guest still refilling his glass to toast gods of crumbling clay is Governor John Crow. And yet of all G7 countries Canada is by far the most vulnerable to high interest rates — both because of its resource economy, and its unusually high overhead.

The *FP* quotes the same Canadian official: "capital utilisation rates are too high in most industrial countries." The same paper (29/6) wrote of the drop in the utilisation rate in Canadian manufacturing as peaking at 86.2% of capacity in 1987, and falling for the seventh consecutive quarter to a mere 80.4% during the first three months of 1989. Such is reality dimly perceived through the bottom of an ideological wine-glass.

For some years we have been subjected to a powerfully orchestrated campaign on how the saving habits of the Japanese contrasted with our own profligacy. Now Martin Mittelstaedt in *The Globe and Mail* (23/7) quotes the research firm Nuala Beck & Associates: "By this measure, Canada had total debts of all levels of government, businesses and consumers of 208% (of the GNP) at the end of 1988. The United States was slightly worse, at 234%. The real shocker is Japan which is in hock up to 317% of the total domestic product. Most shocking of all is the difference in the debt burden of the various economic players. In Japan it is the corporate sector that is wallowing in debt — 125%. Borrowing by Canadian companies is 47%, and by US companies it is 67%.

Book Review — *Enough Is Enough! Dear Mr. Camdessus : an Open Letter of Resignation to the Managing Director of the International Monetary Fund*

[Budhoo, Davison L. *Enough is enough! Dear Mr. Camdessus: an open letter of resignation to the Managing Director of the International Monetary Fund.* New York : New Horizons Press, 1990]

In May 1988, Davison Budhoo, for 23 years a middle-echelon IMF economist from Grenada, handed in his resignation in the form of a 113-page bombshell.

That letter, now available in book form, created a stir in the Third World, but — significantly — hardly a ripple in the developed countries.

Mr. Budhoo's disillusionment began with his experience in Trinidad and Tobago where the government refused to swallow the IMF medicine. The retribution of the IMF was quick and thorough. In its Briefing Paper for its 1987 consulting mission to Trinidad and Tobago, the IMF stated that "unit labour costs in manufacturing relative to (its) main trading partners had increased at an average rate of 20% (per year)" and concluded that "a further devaluation of the TT dollar is needed...The mission will propose a significant initial devaluation (e.g. from TT $3.6 to TT $5.0 per US dollar) perhaps to be followed by other small step adjustments."

Budhoo goes on to say: "But there is a catch in all this — viz the index for T&T was never what we were proclaiming it to be. What we had done over those years was to "manufacture" statistical indices — the RULC (Relative Unit Labour Cost) and several others — that would allow us to prove our point and push a particular policy line, irrespective of economic realities."

"On the basis of calculations made by our divisional statistician last year after the

Fund mission returned from the field, the RULC in T&T increased by 69% only instead of the 145.8% as stated in our 1985 report. Over 1983-5 relative unit labour costs moved up only 14.9%, not by the 36.9% that was mooted in the world community in 1986." Budhoo tabulates no less than eight instances where figures were contrived to justify the harshest policy prescriptions, only to be debunked in later internal reports of the IMF itself.

"Our previous 'mistakes' were never mentioned to the authorities. We went glibly on to ask for more devaluation, great public sector lay-offs, further real wage cuts and the whole gamut of demand management measures, as if the Briefing Paper's evaluation was still absolutely valid."

"What exactly did we do when we found that the T&T authorities had already achieved the adjustment in the fiscal accounts that we were going to get them to achieve in our own particular way?

"Well, we stiffened the targets that you had approved in the Briefing Paper. We went to them and said something like this:"our detailed research tells us now that the 3% GDP deficit that we had mentioned before for 1988-92 is no longer acceptable. You must reduce it further. And have no fancy idea of reducing it further on your own. No, no, you have to let us dictate to you what to do. You have to leave room for us to use the Steamroller (Heaviest)."

Among the measures dictated in this way was "Accumulating international reserves equivalent to five months of imports (Aide Memoire of 21/7/87) or six months of imports (Staff Report of 25/9/87).

"What developing country on earth starting from a stock of almost zero reserves would want to subject its people to more and more unemployment, hardship and deprivation for the sake of holding surplus and redundant funds on deposit in US and European banks, and in doing its bit(in Fund parlance) to finance the US deficit?"

"I want to remind you that T&T is only one country from the host of Third World nations where we are perpetrating the same economic nonsense, with the same catastrophic consequences for 'screaming-in-pain' governments and people forced to bend on their knees before us, and begging for a sliver of reasonableness and decency on our part? What are we doing to the world?"

The bitter medicine of the IMF usually consists of devaluation of the local currency, removal of price controls even on the most basic essentials, accelerated reduction of real wages, removal of exchange controls on external capital and current transactions, spectacular cuts in the public sector wage bills, deep reduction in transfers to persons, cuts in social services, including health and education, systematic increases in interest rates, restructuring of the taxation system to increase its regressiveness, indiscriminate divestment of public enterprises.

"Quite frankly, our 'program' is nothing but a hotchpotch of irreconcilable and conflicting elements and objectives; it reduces economics to a farce. It is the recipe for comprehensive disorder and all-enfolding disintegration of the fabric of national life. The staff through time has twisted and changed whatever may have been the original epistemology of the Fund into a dogma to emasculate the Third World and to wield unholy power there, and to line their pockets with the good things of life for doing so. The conceptual backdrop sprang overwhelmingly from the 19th century vision of Pax Britannica, now writ large as Pax Atlantica — i.e. 'perfect competition' and 'world allocation of resources' and 'international division of labour' and 'general equilibrium in the (Western) world economy.'

There is one expenditure in the Third World that the IMF has never challenged. "In 1980 Third World countries utilized about $60 billion as military expenditure; by 1983 this had risen by about 50%; by 1986 it had doubled. In many instances Fund programs have collapsed because it proved impossible to get the government concerned to reduce the public sector by another ½ or 1% of GDP through 'demand management.' In the developing world as a whole, military expenditures in recent years averaged over 10% of GDP. If 1/5 of this could have been diverted to 'adjustment' certainly a lot of Fund programs that went astray could have been saved. "The IMF, however, argues that recommending a reduction in arms spending would be an invasion of national sovereignty. To which Budhoo replies, "When you control nations (as you do), governments are nothing but puppets in your hands. It is an accepted norm that the Fund may withdraw, at its beck and call, fundamental constitutional rights of a

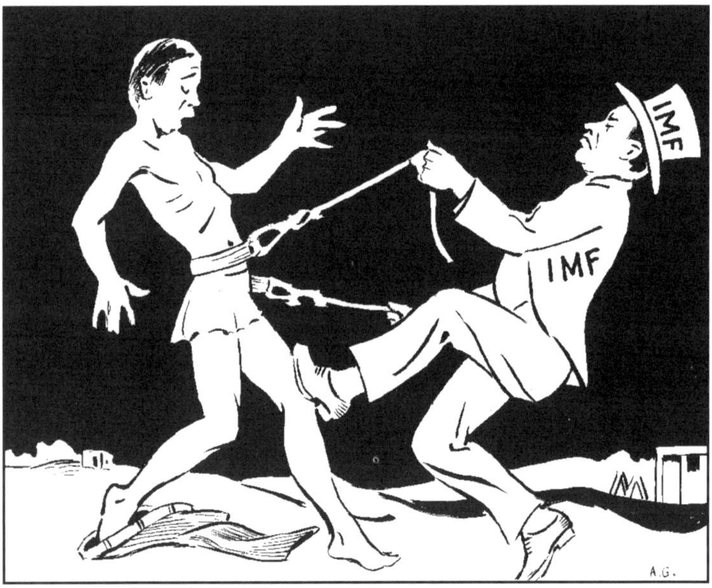

people, forcing the government concerned to sentence masses of its poor to even greater hardship. How can the argument be sustained that on the peripheral issue of surplus arms purchases from developed countries 'national sovereignty' must be meticulously respected?"

On the rewards of playing God to the Third World: "I want to get on with the juicy details of the Honeypot. And in doing so I will refer to my own situation. Admittedly, that is not a very good example, for my Fund career has been punctuated with rebelliousness and non-conformity. "My total salary/benefits package (is)US $143,000. My allowances are relatively modest because my family group is small. Assume, for instance, that I had my grandmother residing with me in Washington, and I had chosen to have five children attend school/college in say Geneva. In such circumstances my gross package would shoot up towards the US $200,000 mark. If, in addition, I was in field assignment in say, Guyana, as Fund Resident (I was, you know, some years back) I would have earned close to US$300,000 per year.

"The Big Family Man with my identical basic pay but on assignment in the Third World even as his five kids learn Social Graces in Geneva, compliments of our Honeypot, would receive more than the basic pay of every head of state in the world, including the President of the US. In relation to the developing world, his gross earnings would probably be about ten to fifteen times more than the budgeted salary of a typical African or Latin American or Asian Head of State."

How could such rewards no exercise a corrupting power on many local politicians? "In scores of Ministries of Finance and Central Banks around the world, the hearts of aspiring "technocrats flutter when a Fund mission is announced, for hope springs eternal in the human breast — hope to gain access to the Honeypot's Lusciousness by picking up 'big work' in Washington. The means to achieve this dream is by being 'nice' to and by 'cooperating' with Fund missions, by doing all the things our Visiting Priests would have them do."

V

Vol. 2, No. 8 — October 1990

From Santa's Bag to Pandora's Box

By now it must be clear that those who promised us "long-term gain" for the "short-term pain" of high interest rates had got things badly mixed up. For Santa's Bag has suddenly turned into Pandora's Box. Growing unemployment and bankruptcies stretch before us as far as the eye can see. Social dissent, military confrontations, bizarre political upheavals are taking over at home and abroad.

Before the immensity of the disaster, we must step back and make a serious effort to understand how this could have happened. Several decades ago, the late French economist, François Perroux, developed the concept of a *dominant revenue* that can help us into the light. It is the revenue of a particular class the volume which is taken as the index of well-being of society as a whole. Were we by some magic to attain a stable price level, even while more non-marketed public benefits were provided, it would mean that money-lenders would be uniquely rewarded. Producers of goods and services would be left with the burden of paying for those benefits. But the money-lenders, producing nothing directly and hence not hit by regulations for environmental conservation, would come out unscathed. To them the advantages of an improved environment would come as a freebie,

Indeed, their bonanza would be even greater. Obviously those new costs would have to show up in prices, or in the long run the producers could not go on producing. And as prices bulged, the central bank would show no curiosity about what might be behind the phenomenon — an overheated market, or just non-discretionary costs imposed by the new regulations. Instead, it would merely push up the bank rate in order "not to accommodate" the higher prices. Though the entrepreneur is currently celebrated in verse and song, our central banks have packaged him as pet food for our rentiers.

There is one catch to all this. In a market economy it is the entrepreneur — not the rentier — who keeps accounts and underwrites other people's claims. What our central bank has done is separate the dominant revenue from the ultimate financial responsibility for keeping the economy functioning.

That bodes no good even for the rentiers. Prices can be kept flat only to the point at which entrepreneurs are driven into bankruptcy and their wares are put on the block. But that destroys the collateral for the rentiers' loans, and indeed rattles the banking system and the entire economy.

k

The Swoosh of Upward Mobility

Since John Crow has scratched his mark on an epoch of Canadian history, it is fitting that he should rate a biography. *The Globe and Mail* fills the bill with a two-page spread by Edward Greenspon and Harvey Enchin out of England. Like all good biographers they sought out the seeds of future greatness in the early years. And they turned up humble beginnings indeed in East-end London. But from the start there was a Thatcher-like determination to put all that behind. Scholarships to fashionable schools and Oxford, supplemented with good performance at soccer and cricket, sped our hero on his upward clamber.

Up to this point I read the tale with admiration and even a faint glimmer of hope. There is a great literature enjoying a good market during the Christmas season devoted to powerful men, who amidst the swoosh of their upward mobility, suddenly remember their harsh childhood and consider what they might do for those in such a plight.

But then I came upon a section that caused me to lay aside all hope. It turns out that Mr. Crow's entire career before coming to the Bank of Canada was with the International Monetary Fund specializing in Latin America. Insofar as the Spanish Inquisition and Teddy Roosevelt's Big Stick diplomacy have a successor, it is the IMF. It dictates devaluations and belt-tightenings to hungry nations, and mixes the arrogance and life styles of Eastern potentates with the power-gluttony of Russian *apparatchiki*.

That provides the key to much of Mr. Crow's policy since he took over the governance of the BoC — in particular his inability to distinguish between an upward inching of the price level due to non-market factors and the runaway inflation of countries like Brazil, the Argentine, and Peru that has its roots in social breakdown. Indeed, Canada, with the fatuous connivance of its government, has been treated by the Governor as just another of the IMF's wretched clients.

And here again he has shown himself an over-achiever. To such an extent that the IMF in its annual report warns that the Bank of Canada's "heavy reliance on high interest rates could have adverse consequences for the exchange rate and international competitiveness, as well as domestic investment."

It is revealing that the day after the publication of the IMF report Governor Crow should have beat a retreat from his mindless course. Some months ago when he chose to ignore the softening of the US Fed's stance and drove the differential between Canadian and short term rates up to a ruinous 5% points, his claque hailed it as a "Made in Canada" policy. Now it should be clear to the most trusting where BoC policy is really begotten.

Vol. 2, No. 9 — November 1990

Our Foundling Recession — Is it a Boy or a Girl?

In some areas we have made spectacular progress. The expectant mother is no longer left in doubt whether to do her knitting in pink or blue. But when it comes to economic forecasting, our learned doctors argue even into the ninth month whether or not the lady is in an interesting condition. Now that all but the odd central banker have agreed that we are in recession, the debate has shifted to another question: "Is it going to be a long bad recession or just a short, benign one?"

There is also a reluctance on the part of the father in taking credit for the brat he had worked so enthusiastically to beget. Finance Minister Wilson tries to pass it off as just one of those cyclical things that are inevitable after seven years of a booming economy. The fact is that cyclical recessions no longer just happen of themselves as they used to before World War II. The public sector has grown to such proportions to meet the needs of our urbanized, high-tech world, that there is ever a backlog of demand for physical and social infrastructures.

The Wall Street Journal (10/10) quotes Paul J. Markowski of Buckingham Research in New York: "We've grown accustomed to equating the advent of a recession with physical problems in the economy. But financial problems can be equally important."

The deregulation of the banking system in the seventies freed interest rates to soar like a lark ascending. The take-over orgy that followed has left both the industries and the banking system of the US under a crushing burden of junk bonds. We enter the adventure of recession with the Third World still a basket case from the high interest binge of the early eighties.

Let us review some of the key lessons of the past that have been buried. We might call these the Theorems of Disinformation, drummed into our skulls with a thoroughness that the Communist propagandists of yesteryear might envy.

1. The "Nobody here but us chickens" theorem. After being fed for years with PR about our central bankers' resolve in "wrestling inflation to the ground" we are now assured that the market alone is responsible for high rates. The fact is that short-term rates are basically set by the weekly intervention of the central bank buying or selling treasury bills.

2. The "Herbert Hoover theorem": we have to cut government expenditure until we balance the budget. Actually, poor Hoover has been maligned, because privately his Quaker conscience was bothered about not putting the unemployed to work when there were too many things that needed doing.

3. The "Mixed Metaphor" Theorem. Instead of analysing the very different factors that tend to push up the price level, the government picks a muscular, emotion-laden metaphor without the slightest relevance to the problems at hand. This it plays to the hilt, making up with decibels for the lack of logic. "Wrestling inflation to the ground," "Wringing inflation out of the economy," "Short-term pain for long-term gain" are samples.

The trouble is that when in the wrestling ring you force your opponent's shoulders to the ground, you are proclaimed winner and the match is over. Were John Crow to attain zero inflation and the economy started recovery, the game would immediately start again.

Correspondence — to Hon. Bob Rae, Premier of Ontario / from John Hotson and William Krehm

9/10/90

The Honourable Bob Rae
Premier of Ontario
Toronto, On. M7A1A2

Dear Mr. Rae:

The Committee on Monetary and Economic Reform (COMER) is a non-partisan think-tank devoted to exploring new bases for the symbiosis between our public and private sectors. In particular we see an urgent need to seek out new ways of funding government while lightening the burden of taxation. The present effort to balance the federal budget through tax hikes and expenditure cuts hides an unacknowledged agenda: to return to the good old Canada of the 1920s. Instead, the attempt appears to be setting the clock back not to the 1920s, but to the 1930s.

In the recession which the Bank has created it will be difficult for you to finance the forward-looking programs you envision: to de-pollute the environment, to improve our schools, and to care for our people better. That is why we write to ask you to consider alternative ways to finance needed public infrastructures.

Perhaps the most promising of these for a provincial government is what we call "tax-bonds." We enclose an article on tax-bonds which will be appearing in the next issue of our newsletter.

We would welcome the opportunity to meet with you or members of your staff to discuss the plan.

John H. Hotson, Executive Director
William Krehm, Board Chairman
COMER

[The material on "tax bonds" can be found on page 163.]

Vol. 2, No. 10 — December 1990

Discord on Olympus

Discord has broken out on Olympus, where the fate of lesser mortals is decided. After almost three years of harmony in ruining the economy with high interest rates, Finance Minister Michael Wilson and the Governor of the BoC no longer see eye to eye.

In *The Globe and Mail* (23/10) we read: "After six years of insisting that zero is the only acceptable target for inflation, the federal government appears to be undergoing a change of heart.

"Finance Minister Wilson told reporters that there were discussions going on between his department and the BoC over whether targets higher than zero should be made public.

"This may be a way of allowing us to set a course that the country can understand

and learn to live with." This can only mean that what he has been serving us as policy defies understanding and is not to be lived with.

"(Wilson) indicated that zero would still be the long-term goal of monetary policy but that something short of that would be acceptable in the short term."

No sooner had Mr. Wilson made this announcement, than BoC Governor Crow "in a speech yesterday in Moncton said even a low rate of inflation is not acceptable because it leads to social and economic losses that accumulate over time. People who advise the BoC that it should fight inflation only when it is accelerating are in effect suggesting that at all other times monetary policy should ignore inflation, addressing itself, say, to printing money to finance deficits or to drive down the exchange rate." (*G&M* 26/10)

This was a most unusual way for Governor Crow to be talking about his boss, the Finance Minister.

Who Said Nothing Is Sacred Any More?

"Spending cuts are a must," everyone in and out of Congress agreed. "Everything is on the table, no spending program is sacred," said some. "A 5 percent cut or more across-the-board is the best way to go. What they all believed, and what a few sheepishly admitted to believing, is that "there is nothing you can do about interest on the government debt. That has to be paid."

There is, it turns out, nothing sacred about the government's obligations to the aged, the infirm, the unemployed. There is nothing sacred about spending on environmental protection or deteriorating infrastructures. There is nothing sacred about AIDS research, or free lunches for kiddies in school, or, indeed, about education in general and at any level. What is sacred is the income of the money-lenders.

And yet the government's interest burden could be abated without reneging on any promise. All that is needed is to refinance the debt at lower — much lower — interest rates. The government knows how to finance its debt at much lower rates, because it has done so in the past.

In 1942-3-4-5, with a debt that on average amounted to 93% of GNP, and with annual deficits that averaged over 25% of GNP, the government borrowed all the money it wanted at an average rate of about 2%. Forty years later, for 1982-3-4-5, with a debt that on average amounted to only 49% of GNP, the government paid a rate that averaged four times as much. Why? Because, unlike the 1940s when the Federal Reserve "pegged" interest rates on 3-month T-bills, for example, at 3/8ths of 1%, for 1982-3-4-5 the Fed connived with rentiers and the T-bill rate was driven to over 9% — 24 times as high.

What is required to bring down interest rates is for the Fed to create more interest-free money for the government and make the government less dependent on interest-bearing money created by the private banking system.

The ratio of money created by the Fed to the USA M2 money supply was about 42% in 1940. By 1960 that ratio had dropped by half. By 1980 it had dropped to less than half of the 1960 level and less than a fourth of the 1940 level. Why? Because it was Fed policy, Administration policy, Congressional policy, to make it drop. "Free market forces" in "the money market" had little to do with the change in the ratio, but government policy, cravenly responsive to the lobbies of the bankers and other money-lenders, had almost everything to do with it.

William Hixson

Empty Pew

There is a revealing oddity in the monthly *Bank of Canada Review*. In its B211 series the *Review* reports the Bank's Advances to the Government of Canada. But month after month that column is blank. Alongside it are busy advances to the Members of the Canadian Payments Association, "amounts held under purchase and resale agreements" of government paper. But direct advances to the government are nil.

The mere existence of that column is like an empty church pew. It tells of the abandonment of an earlier faith. Clearly it harks back to a bygone age when it was accepted as one of the functions of the BoC to create money directly for the government. The interest charged for such loans would revert to the Government since it owns the central bank. However, direct money creation for the government has fallen into disrepute. You might ask why the column — if only to cut printing costs — is not eliminated, since nothing rides in it. I suspect it is retained as a badge of respectability — to emphasize to fellow central bankers that the BoC does not directly create money for use by the Government of Canada.

But the BoC does a brisk business trading Government of Canada paper of every possible maturity from short-term treasury bills to bonds over 10 years. In August 1990 it held some $22,290 million of such paper. It is in fact the agent of the Government in marketing its securities. It is by buying and selling government securities, particularly short-term treasury bills that make up most of its holdings, that injects or drains liquidity from the banking system. But most of its interventions in recent years have been to drive up interest rates on treasury bills to raise the interest rate that Ottawa pays its private lenders — "to lick inflation." Such payments do *not* come back to the government. On the contrary, they account for most of the federal government's cash flow deficit. Jack Biddell in his recent book has remarked on the conflict of interest involved in the financial agent of the Government entrusted with marketing its bonds exerting itself to keep the yield as high as possible.

To satisfy a gnawing curiosity, I betook myself to the library and worked my way through the 50 years of the *Bank of Canada Review* and its predecessor, the *Bank of Canada Statistical Summary*, to see when that column Advances to the Government started being empty. The answer would seem to be November 1961. During the war and postwar years the central bank had been used not only to finance the greatest conflict in our history and to help reconstruct Europe and Asia, but to reduce the debt incurred to proportions entirely manageable by a flourishing economy. Subsequently, by an adroit counter-revolution, the powers of the central banks came to be redirected towards making the world safe for our money-lenders. Ever higher interest rates, the rescinding of usury laws, the deregulation of financial institutions were steps in that direction.

k

Canada's [Misguided] Economic Plan and How it Affects You

Ottawa has spent a reported $1.3 million supplying Canadians with the 8-page flyer, 'Important Information About Canada's Economic Plan and How it Affects You.' That is a sinful waste of trees as the flyer contains sinful untruths.

The first untruth occurs in the definition of the word "deficit."

Deficit: The amount by which government spending exceeds revenues. Governments then have to borrow this amount, which gets added to the "public debt."

It is not true that "Governments have to borrow" when they run a deficit. Any sovereign government can create money rather than borrow at interest from private banks the money they produce. Even before the Bank of Canada was created in 1935, half the currency and all the coins were supplied by the Dominion Government.

The flyer points out that the government is currently running an operating surplus — meaning that its revenues exceed the amount it spends on programs and services. Thus it could even reduce its debt if it created Canada's money.

The BoC produced only 2% of the money added last year. What would be wrong with going back to earlier policies when the Bank and the chartered banks shared the privilege of creating money more evenly? When the BoC was new it sparked a partial recovery from the Depression by producing almost half (46%) of the increased money supply from 1935 to 1939. During the much greater expansion in World War II is provided 47% of the new money. These policies, together with sensible wage and credit controls, gave Canada the fullest employment ever, very low interest rates and no inflation during the last two years of the greatest war in history.

To restrict the chartered banks to creating half the money, the BoC must raise their reserve requirements and restrict their ability to add to their high interest accounts. Instead, our government intends to allow them to operate with zero reserves.

A second untruth reads:

"There are two ways to slow the growth of the debt and reduce the amount of borrowed money needed to meet interest payments. One is to increase government revenues through higher taxation. The other is to restrain government spending."

There is a third way to reduce interest payments — reduce the rate of interest. The BoC can make the rate of interest at which it lends to the chartered banks any number it chooses, and can peg the rate on government bonds there also. In WWII it pegged the rate on T-bills as low as 0.36% and on longer-term bonds at 2.5% when government deficits were as much as 27% of Canada's GNP and the money supply was increasing at a 20% clip. Now the deficit is less than 4% and would not even exist if the BoC had not raised interest rates beyond all reason.

J.H.H.

Vol. 3, No. 2 — February 1991

Sending John Crow off to the Wars

The war to which we propose sending Governor Crow is not the Gulf War. Into that conflict he has already waded with what threatens to be devastating results. In mid-January he told the Canadian Manufacturers' Association that the slow economy may not prevent inflation from being pushed up during a war in the Gulf. "And that's not the kind of process that monetary policy should finance, of course." Accordingly Canada will finance her war effort at current or even higher interest rates.

No matter what the TV coverage might suggest, our "#1 enemy" is thus still inflation. And we can judge how formidable an enemy it is by the depth of its camouflage: the price index that the Governor follows in his bunker is only vaguely related to an excess of market demand. A rise in that index may merely be reflecting the effects of legislation or government regulation, or the high financing costs the BoC has imposed on our production.

That is why we decided to conscript John Crow to run the BoC in a replay of World War II. During the first 22 months of the war 25% of the $1.9 billion raised at home resulted from the BoC's acquisition of Government securities. Since profits of the central bank revert to the government, the "net effect of this, therefore, was to provide a sort of interest-fee loan to the Government" (A.F.W. Plumptre, *Mobilising Canada's Resources for War*, Toronto, 1941, p. 155).

As the unemployed were taken out of the bread-lines and put to work in war industries, the tax-base expanded explosively, and Canada was able to resort to more conventional financing. After all, the first governor of the BoC, Graham Towers, was anything but a radical — he had been recruited to head the new central bank in 1935 from his post as assistant general manager of the Royal Bank. But he did have a keen sense of reality. By 1946 the holdings of government securities by the central bank had fallen to 22.8% of domestic borrowings — partly because the expanded war-economy provided other sources of financing, and partly because the vast pool of idle productive capacity at the beginning of the war was no longer there.

In the post-war, to meet the needs of an expanding economy, direct money-creation by the BoC for the government started climbing again to attain a peak of some 26% in the latter seventies.

What money the Government did borrow from the public during the war was at very modest rates. when the central bank opened for business in 1935, it continued the 2 1/2% discount rate that had been in force under the preceding Finance Act. In February, 1944 it was dropped to 1 ½%, because 2 1/2% was "out of line with the current market." In October 1950 it was increased to 2%, and no further change was made until it was cut to 1 1/2% in 1955. Financing at such rates made possible the transformation of Canada beyond recognition in the post-war years — a vast immigration was assimilated, the baby-boom housed, new technologies brought in, costly infrastructures built.

In the 1943 Bank of Canada Report, Governor Towers proclaimed his easy money program. "The rate of interest is only one of many factors...and it is probably not as important an instrument of control as was once supposed. The prospect of unstable interest rates could make it exceedingly difficult for business to formulate long-term plans. Moreover, high borrowing costs would hamper new investment in plant, equipment and housing, restrict the expansion of employment, and would seriously complicate the task of government financing."

Towers had headed the marketing of the last five issues of Victory bonds, and "he believed that to drive bond prices down by following a tight money policy could easily produce panic selling of bonds, and would have brought renewed inflationary pressures."

But many will argue that such lack of monetary restraint would be inflationary. In actual fact the cost of living between 1939 and 1945 rose some 19.5% — little more than 3% a year. By 1944 and 1945 this had been brought down to .5% yearly by a combination of price controls and forced savings. When released at the end of the war, those savings eased the transition to a peacetime economy.

But were 2% and even 1 3/4% coupons on two-year Victory bonds and 3 1/4% and 3% interest rates on longer-term bonds not unfair to lenders? During the thirties lenders had enjoyed bountiful innings at the expense of society. The cost of living index had fallen from 121.7 in 1929 to 101.2 in 1937. Only by 1946 did it recover to 123.6. The war was a time of sacrifice, and lenders not unjustly bore their share.

The federal debt that had amounted to 135% of GNP in 1946, was shrunk to a mere 44% by 1958. And these figures do not even take note of the vast public investment that had been financed by this retreating proportion of borrowing to GNP: raising and educating the postwar baby-boomers, putting in the services for mushrooming suburbs, new transportation systems.

Now let us replace Graham Towers with John Crow, the knight-errant ever ready to break not only a lance but the entire economy in pursuit of "zero inflation."

Nine Victory Bond campaigns had yielded the government some $12.5 billion at a real interest rate of zero percent or less. Until the present collapse of our economy, the BoC had exerted itself to keep the real yield on government paper in the 7% range. Had Governor Crow headed the BoC in WWII, he would have run the show in the conviction that "enemy #1" was "inflation." Financing $12.5 billions of Victory bonds at 7% real interest would have increased the federal debt by $3 billion.

At present the BoC holds about 10% of the federal debt — mostly short-term paper used to manipulate the short-term market. During the war the corresponding figures for BoC holdings were 25% during the first 22 months and gradually dropping to 12.8%. Reducing that to 10% would have made a difference in interest charges up to the end of the war of some $100 million. That would have raised the resulting federal debt from $16 billion in 1946 to around $19 billion.

That is not the whole story. The government's suppliers also had their financing costs set by the bank rate. To cover these another $1 billion would have been needed. That would have brought the total debt by 1946 to $20 billion with annual additional interest charges of $280 million.

What would have happened with John Crow as head of the Bank of Canada in WWII is just a bad dream. But John Crow's current effort to combine the blessings of a war and a depression is a living nightmare.

wk

Vol. 3, No. 3 — March 1991

Heading off a Bigger and Better Depression for 1997

There is a striking parallel between the struggle against Saddam Hussein and the economic war raging at home. To some it might seem that with Saddam Hussein out of Kuwait, the war is over. However, allowing Saddam the time to perfect his non-conventional arsenal might leave the door open for unpleasant surprises in the years ahead.

Something similar is happening with the high-interest policy that plunged us into the present recession. In January the unemployment rate in Canada jumped from 9.3% to 9.7%. 1,300,000 Canadians are now out of work. But because of the quaint way in which Canadian unemployment figures are put together, this is gentlemanly understatement. Anyone who has worked for one hour in the previous week is considered "employed," and those too discouraged to seek work during the past month are not seen as "unemployed." 85,000 of the 90,000 jobs that disappeared in January were in the services sector. Relatively untouched until now, the services sector has begun looking like the Tigris bridges.

"This is really bad," remarked Philip Cross, chief of current analysis for Statistics Canada. "For those people who have set up a recovery watch, it's going to be a lonely vigil."

Reluctantly, the BoC has begun pulling out of its particular Kuwait. But in its retreat it is fighting every inch of the way. While one-year treasury bill yield dropped to a 2 3/4 year low from 9.89% to 9.22%, in the third week of February, the BoC intervened to keep the bank rate at 10.49%. Last spring the rate peaked at 14.05%.

But to believe that the damage done by two years of brutally high interest rates can be remedied by lowering interest rates alone would be naive. So long as the public ignores the effect of taxation on the price level, it will go on demanding more public services, not all of them strictly necessary. For hope springs eternal that the new taxes will hit the other guy and not us. But nobody can escape a higher price level.

"Zero inflation" which encourages such pipe-dreams could in fact be called "other guyism." It is a grand exercise in getting "the other guy" to swallow costs without asking whether it is possible for him to do so. Today government offices routinely identify real living standards with the purchasing power of employees' take-home pay. Yet if public dental insurance were introduced to-morrow and part of its costs deducted from pay envelopes, it would turn up as a decline in "real living standards" although government and the employers might be covering most of your dental fees.

What we lack in fact is a serious social accountancy that will stop sweeping other people's costs under the table.

k

Turning Out the Lights

The following letter was carried by *The Financial Post* and *The Globe and Mail*:

Canada's record with respect to research and development is nothing short of wretched. While Japan devotes 2.9% of its GNP to such purposes, and West Germany 2.6%, Canada trails the US figure of 2.0% with a mere 1.33%. Moreover, despite much vocal concern about productivity, the axe is being applied to this modest budget.

Our scientific community is being reduced to panhandling for financing vital work.

Yet our government has a ready solution for such things. When it has a problem, it simply turns out the lights. Its brand of rhetoric fares better in the dark.

Statscan reports that it must stop compiling research and development figures because its budget has been slashed $4.5 million to help pay for the military deployment in the Persian Gulf.

In this same spirit, we can expect our government to solve our growing unemployment by discontinuing unemployment statistics. Those figures have certainly given our Finance Minister a hard time. Projecting this program, Statscan's output could be reduced to a single misleading statistic, the Consumer Price Index, which is about the only figure Governor John Crow of the BoC misreads to justify keeping our interest rates and our dollar at artificial heights. High enough, in fact, to reduce our government to the idiocy of abolishing statistics vital for running a country to help finance a war.

William Krehm
Chairman of COMER

Ten days after the letter was published, Statscan announced that the government had restored the R&D budget and instead was eliminating — among much else — the midyear survey of capital spending intentions.

Vol. 3, No. 4 — April 1991

The Iceman Cometh

Two recent volumes published by AISMEA (*Archives de Sciences et Mathematiques et Economiques Appliquees* of France) present the deflationary obsession of our central banks under a revealing light. Alain Parguez and the group around him see the banks caught up in a creed that attributes our woes to a perpetual lack of savings. And that in turn serves as an argument for ever greater exactions on behalf of the rentier. The so-called "circuit economists"" take their departure from the circuit of production that reaches back to the 18th century French Physiocrats through Marx. Augusto Graziani and others analyse its modern version — the financial circuit that underlies every investment They show that where the real factors of production are at hand, it is credit created by the banking system rather than preexistent savings in money form that sets the circuit in motion.

These days our money supply has the highly evanescent form of debt. Society's significant savings are to be found in the real factors of production. Where these are available and the project to be financed promises to be profitable, financing is essentially an institutional arrangement. When the circuit is completed, the debt is repaid, and the debt-money vanishes,

In the thirties Keynes "already had been worried by the propensity of the so-called Practical Men in Business and Government to blindly believe in some conventional view of economics contradicting the whole structure of the real world" (Parguez). He confronted this with a vision of his own — a world of full employment that would bring on increasing plenty and make full use of credit within the constraints of the real resources present. In this way it would create an abundance of capital — the fruit of previous labours. Where the social structures within capitalism failed to produce the necessary purchasing power and recession ensued, the state would step in with massive investments to start things rolling again.

Though Keynes has been pilloried as a champion of inflation, he in fact formulated the anti-inflationary policy that served the Anglo-Saxon countries so well in World War II. Once the market was working at near capacity, the government would rein in activity by achieving fiscal surpluses and other such devices. The policy worked during the war, and gave the world an unprecedented two decades of prosperity after its end. But in the late sixties this goal of full employment, low interest rates, and a sustained rise in living standards, came to be replaced by the vision of Austerity.

Alain Parguez sees the Keynesian model as relating financial gains to real growth: increased investment leads to an increase in real wealth, a greater abundance of capital, lower interest rates, and hence higher prices for both stocks and bonds. "The enrichment is real." The growth of society's real wealth goes hand in hand with the increased value of financial assets.

The austerity vision on the other hand seeks a cure for higher prices by bringing on unemployment, squeezing out commodity inflation, while swelling the revenue of lenders. Underlying this is the long discredited Say's Law by which every product by the mere act of its production brings sufficient buyers to the market. There is no question in the minds of the austerity apostles that unemployment brought on to "purge the economy of inflation" might shrink the market and empty the government coffers.

The outcome is an enrichment of the "financial economy" combined with a deflation of labour income and profits. The increase in financial wealth is fictitious, even parasitic, unsupported as it is by an expansion of the real economy. This can only lead to breakdown.

Hanging on a tooth of faith, it is a vision that blocks out sight. It leaves no room for doubt or verification.

"This society where fiction is reality is the Pure Rentier Economy. Its 'Law of the Prophets' is the expansion of 'pure wealth,' relieved of all exposure to dynamic risks. Enjoy, enjoy, o ye Rentiers, who grow ever richer only by acquiring debts and collecting interest and capital gains...."

"The longer it goes on, the greater the gulf it opens between paper profits and real profit. Moreover, it is necessary to intensify the austerity to prevent the drop in security prices. But the more austerity deepens, the more real profit goes down...

"There are those who have convinced themselves that there is liberalism involved in the Rentier Economy. But the Welfare state does not disappear under the Rentier Economy: its benefits are simply directed to the Rentiers!"

Though impressive, the picture is done in too broad strokes. The contributors attribute inflation to the increased "financial mark-up" exacted by the central bank (the "Rentier-in-Chief"). But the analysis ignores a more basic factor in our price rise — the "tax mark-up" that reflects the inevitable growth of the public sector in a mixed economy. In France, the land of Value Added Tax triumphant, this should be easy to discern.

Throughout the Second World War and well into the mid-fifties interest rates were kept low and many rentiers were receiving negative real rates on their loans. Keynes's "euthanasia of the rentier" was well on the way to being realised. That helps explain the blind ferocity of the counter-revolution staged by the international central bank fraternity in the mid-sixties, when prices started moving up rapidly as a result of the changing structures of the economy.

Government regulation, necessary and unnecessary, has added another component of price rise having nothing to do with the market supply-and-demand balancing act.

As prices started soaring in the mid-sixties to reflect the huge public spending to set up new university campuses, health and welfare systems, and general infrastructures, it was treated as excess market demand run wild that had to be suppressed by higher interest rates.

Those high rates compounded the trouble to a far greater extent than appears even in the circuit models of Parguez and his group.

What is closing in on us is a new Ice Age. Ice-fields spreading out from our central banks threaten to make Iceberg Alleys even of the remotest tropical seas.

Vol. 3, No. 6 — June 1991

Correspondence — to *Economic Reform* / from *Journal of Business Ethics*

24/11/91

Journal of Business Ethics
University of Guelph

Economic Reform is by far the best buy of over 70 journals and newsletters to which I subscribe. You are performing a real public service in the best sense of that phrase.

Alex Michalos
Editor-in-Chief

Vol. 3, No. 7 — July 1991

Correspondence — to John Hotson / from M.A. Baltzan

Saskatoon
22/5/91

Dear Professor Hotson:

This morning while shaving, I was listening to Canada AM and I was startled by an economist speaking logically, sensibly, and reasonably.

Since this event is rare in my experience, without cutting my face any further, I ran into the bedroom and discovered it was you on television.

My faith in the fundamental fallacy of economists was further shattered by the most recent [*Economic*] *Reform* publication which finally suggests that Bob Rae may not be crazy in the head running a deficit at this time.

These shocks are taking a terrible toll on me.

M.A. Baltzan, MD, FRCPC, FACP

Vol. 3, No. 8 — August 1991

Dunking Doughnut Holes in Creamless Coffee

President Bush and our own P.M. are spending an increasing amount of their time abroad telling ex-Communists how simple it is running a capitalist economy. You merely let the reins drop to the buggy floor and shout an encouraging giddy-yap from time to time. However, while they revel on photo opportunities in exotic settings, embarrassments are mounting at home. In the US the S&L and banking crises continue to flower like carnivorous jungle blooms. The estimate of what the first item will cost the taxpayer has in a matter of months risen from $50 to $500 billion and is still going strong. Commercial banks are crumbling. And now some major insurance companies have begun folding.

The two largest to date are Executive Life of California and Mutual Benefit of New Jersey. The trouble? Very much the same as with the S&Ls and the banks. A murderously competitive market led underwriters to shave their premiums below their costs (an "anti-inflationary" move if ever there was one). But to make up the difference they invested increasingly in junk-bonds and real estate mortgages. Of course, there was nothing to support those high returns in an economy that the Fed was doing its utmost to deflate.

Public indignation has moved from the CEOs of the failed institutions to the accountancy profession. Why did the accountants not knock down the alleged assets of the banks and insurance companies to their true market value? But that was easier said than done in the near-panic provoked by the central bank. Subsequently, the central bank itself, aghast at what it had done, was recommending "forbearance" to its inspectors.

In their zeal our central banks forgot to ask a simple question: where was the money to pay all that interest coming from? Debt that cannot be serviced because its payments cannot fit within the net operating income (NOI) of the investment for which it was borrowed is no longer an asset but a fiction. The effective money supply supposed to determine the price level thus shrivelled. For money these days *is* debt. We are on a debt-standard.

All this brings to mind the novel *Dead Souls* of the 19th century Russian writer Nikolai Gogol. In those days Russian estates were appraised by the number of "souls," i.e. serfs, that went with the land. That determined the amount of the mortgage that could be put on a property. To maximise these loan values Gogol's heroes did their research in the local graveyards, resurrecting hard-working peasants long gone to their rest. Our central bank tends to plow under their peasants; Gogol's appraisers raised them from the dead.

Our central banks have mistaken the hole for the doughnut. And until we clear up this little misunderstanding we shall go on trying to subsist on dunking doughnut holes in very creamless coffee.

k.

The Scud as Star of Bethlehem

These must be stressful times for John Crow, Governor of the BoC. From absolute if uncrowned king, his image is hastily being retailored to that of constitutional monarch. Only yesterday a hundred editors cheered him on to save us by making sure that not we but our money-lenders lived beyond our means. And now, as at the press of a button, they are suggesting that his decisions be subordinated to a council of regional representatives.

At first glance this is the stuff of Shakespearean drama — of crowns surrendered, dungeons dank, impalement on irons red-hot, and bloody blocks. True enough, we have already taken our readers backstage and shown that the play is but a windy thing of paintpots and manipulated perception. Into the new constitution the stage director is sneaking a provision that will engrave the will of the reduced monarch as the basic law of the land. That is why I seized an invitation for a luncheon in the Ajax Community Centre at which John Crow was the guest speaker. I was curious to see how the great man was handling so delicate a transition.

The answer is in a thoroughly professional manner. No matinee idol could do better — especially considering that the new piece was opening — of all places — in Ajax. Ajax, some miles to the east of Toronto, is a new town, with a large cluster of young industries. All of them are smarting under the high-interest-rate policy.

The Governor struck a human note many miss in his policies. He spoke of his young sons wanting him to help them over some money embarrassments by signing some more of those banknotes. Was this a subtle prod at his critics? If so, the rapier was turned when the chairman — the local MP — observed that Mr. Crow's two young sons are probably the last supporters of his policies in the land. But it was all clean fun as it should be among folks with municipal chicken to digest

Before an audience more familiar with baseball than cricket, Mr. Crow shared a memory of having played cricket on an Ajax green long since built over. However, a few more years of his policies and it should be possible to play cricket in downtown Ajax once more.

Mr. Crow's evasion of the questions from the floor blended sheer cheek with virtuosity. To a complaint about the homicidal effect of the high Canadian dollar, his reply was: the bank is not interested in targeting exchange values for the dollar, only in defending its purchasing power at home.

To a question whether the Consumer Price Index ought not to be disaggregated to disclose the different factors involved in price movement, he replied that he was not running Statistics Canada and everybody was free to do his own disaggregation of the CPI. He did make placating references to "phoney inflation" factors and "one-time price increases," Trouble is that when the cows come home, Governor Crow forgets about the CPI's "phoney inflationary" components and "one-time inflationary factors," and uses the statistic to clobber the economy.

P.S. The trouble with history at its most final is that there is always a footnote. And the footnote to the delightful Ajax luncheon came a few weeks later. Our Prime Minister was in London using the other six heads of the G7 powers as photo props, when the news broke that a justice of the peace back home had ordered an enquiry into the bribery and fraud charges raised by a Quebec businessman against some 14 persons at the highest level of the cabinet and the civil service. At once the Canadian dollar dropped 75 basis points in a single day. Might this not have been providence, disguised as human frailty in high places, stepping in with a bit of mercy? Hadn't we heard from Governor Crow's own lips that the BoC had no target for the exchange value of the dollar? Wasn't a lower Canadian dollar what the country was begging for?

But at once the central bank started unloading treasury bills to drain cash from the market and buying Canadian dollars to support them at their oppressive heights.

wk

Peter Cook Wins COMER Award

Peter Cook, Economics Editor of *The Globe and Mail*, has been announced as winner of the $500 COMER Award for Business Journalists.

Economic Reform last April explained the basis for the award: "The prize is to go to the business journalist outstanding for rethinking his views on monetary policy. The prize is not for 20-20 vision. Prophets too far-sighted tend to get relegated to the desert and a diet of locusts. We are talking about journalists who in better times may have been given to a breezy acceptance of whatever came from on high — much like the rules of baseball. But then as they saw what was being inflicted on the country, more and more of these have been driven to question buzzwords once taken for gospel. That is a courageous and painful step.

The *G&M* is itself to be congratulated for carrying Mr. Cook's brilliant critique of BoC policy.

Since Peter Cook requested that his prize money go to a good cause of our choosing, it has been sent to the Daily Bread Food Bank.

From Cook's Recent Writings

"When the Bank of Canada set targets for reducing inflation, it was a case of following Napoleon's dictum about taking Vienna. If you want to take Vienna, do it.

"But, increasingly, financial markets appear to interpret the bank's action as an advance on Moscow in the middle of winter. As things are now, we have a perverse relationship between the bank's probability of success in meeting its inflation targets and the level of the dollar. The less likely the attainment of the target, the more currency markets assume the bank has a vested interest in maintaining, even strengthening, the dollar." (27/6)

"But few business people are prepared to say that the choice is between Mr. Crow and chaos. Instead, the consensus is that when Mr. Crow drives unemployment up and drives away profits to get marginally lower inflation, he is acting the fanatic." (29/7)

Vol. 3, No. 9 — September 1991

Once Again — Lights Out

Once again our Finance Department is unhappy with Statistics Canada. It has a way of switching out the lights when the Mulroney team needs shadows for what it is up to.

In its June issue a Statscan publication *Economic Observer* carried a feature article 'The Growth of the Federal Debt' by H. Mimoto and P. Cross that was taken for high heresy.

"Broadly speaking, government program spending as a share of the GDP did not rise significantly over the whole period from 1975. ... This moderation would have been more evident but for a sharp increase in interest payments on the public debt. Deficits also became steadily larger initially more from a shortfall of revenues than higher spending."

This debunked the campaign of misinformation on which the Government has been piddling away so much money. Between 1965 and 1975, when key components of Canada's social security and much more generous funding of post-secondary education were being put in place, spending on such social programs rose from 6% of the GDP to 9%. Over the last 16 years, however, spending on such programs has not increased as a percentage of the GDP. If the debt between 74-5 and 89-90 has shot up from $56 to $400 billion, and from 37 to 60% of the GDP, it was primarily because the average interest rate had almost doubled, and through the marvels of compound interest, debt service charges had exploded from $3.3 billion to $39.2 — by almost a multiple of 12.

"From 1965 to 1975 revenues generally kept pace with rapidly-growing federal spending. Since 1975-5, however, the ratio of program spending to GDP grew slowly, while revenues have gone down relative to GDP...Meanwhile, spending was raised by the 1981-2 recession, and has remained at these higher levels due to the growth of rising interest payments to service the debt."

"The sluggish performance of the economy since the mid-1970s, at least compared to the previous two decades, undoubtedly served to depress revenues and raise expenditures. ... In fact the OECD estimates that the cyclically-adjusted budget balance would been in surplus until 1982 if not for the slower growth and higher levels of unemployment." That is hardly the picture the Government had been painting. According to them, program spending had gone crazy, making it necessary for the government regretfully to raise taxes."

Inevitably Opposition MPs seized on the article to embarrass a government that already had its fill of embarrassments.

What went on behind the scenes we can only surmise. The August issue of *The Observer* published a note: "This position was not argued in the body of the article and should not have appeared in the conclusion." It added that the "slow growth in tax revenues was 'overdrawn.' Statistics Canada regrets any inconvenience that may have been caused by these aspects of the article." Stewart Wells, assistant chief statistician at the federal agency said yesterday that Finance Department officials had pointed out problems in the article, but he said other economists had done the same. The Finance Department has never lacked for economists to shove out front to present its views as the fruit of independent thinkers.

And yet more than half the conclusion of *The Observer* study had been devoted to emphasizing the scope for debate left by the study. "The choice of an appropriate base year, or what revenues and expenditures would have been under different economic scenarios and policies, or even what is an appropriate level of debt, are inherently contentious issues. It is hoped this paper has contributed to the public debate on the federal debt and deficits by sketching the broad trends in higher spending and lower revenues since 1975, relative to overall growth of the economy, and the sources of these trends."

But it is exactly such debates that the Mulroney government has been shunning as the devil does holy water.

Morality Play

Some forgotten sage formulated a helpful axiom: a man bound for salvation should find himself morally strengthened as he moves toward his goal. The early Christian martyrs thrown into the lion's den certainly passed that test. Their pain was short-lived enough, and their uplift as they faced it showed they at least believed in the prospect of long-term gain.

The opposite was the case with the Communist empire. Lenin had promised that the state would wither and every cook become a statesman. Instead the state, like an athlete on steroids, never stopped putting on muscle. And it was the statesmen who cornered the groceries and ended up doing most of the cooking.

So we need only check the moral progress of our society as we draw closer to this "long-term gain." Even if we must pull in our belts a notch, are we faring better spiritually?

Our TV recently showed us an Austrian and a Hungarian border guard jointly patrolling their border to make sure that no Rumanian refugee slipped through. And with unfailing national wit, the Hungarian remarked to his colleague: "We shouldn't have torn down that barbed wire fence. Instead we should just have leased it to you Austrians."

Perhaps the same could be said of the Berlin Wall. Instead of tearing it down, perhaps the West Germans should simply have leased it from their Eastern co-nationals to stem the unwelcome westward flood of Germans, Poles, Russians.

The same program brought us scenes of Rumanians bedded down in Budapest's Keleti railway station. Come to think of it, a picture not unlike the shots of homeless in North American cities. Except that you can send Rumanians and Albanians back to where they came from, but what do you do with your own homeless?

And that dilemma has ethical dimensions. How much love of your neighbour can you afford with real interest rates in the midst of a self-inflicted recession at 6% or better? Come to think of it, how many *neighbours* can you afford when you are running the New Testament tape in reverse, converting wine to water, and diminishing the loaves and the fishes?

Was Jesus fiscally responsible in driving the money changers from the temple?

k

Vol. 3, No. 10 — October 1991

Like Thieves in the Night

When Finance Minister Mazankowski ran his used car lot in Edmonton, he had to observe legal constraints in pushing his wares. He would not have dared foist on an unsuspecting client an old jalopy burning oil, with a rigged odometer, that would hurtle brakeless downhill leaving a trail of hit-and-run victims. Why should he and colleagues assume that as the government they have the right to do just that?

Why would they choose this particular time to smuggle into our Constitution a policy that has failed in every key and colour and contributed to our present constitutional crisis?

For years the BoC has shamelessly contravened the first paragraph of the *Bank of Canada Act* that enjoins it "to mitigate fluctuations in the general level of production, trade, prices and employment." Expecting quick results from its high-rate policy, it manipulated the media so that we would not notice this passing irregularity. Once Governor Crow had rushed us from our "short-term pain" through the pearly gates into "long-term gain," nobody would quibble about his having used the BoC as doggies do the nearest lamppost.

That game has failed miserably. And foolishly Governor Crow and the PM set themselves a schedule of targets for bringing inflation down. To meet these, Crow finds himself maneuvered into doing what he had for years avoided: distinguishing between one sort of "inflation" and another. The grounds on which he does this are of course the wrong ones: instead of disaggregating price movements according to their causes, he does so according to whether the inflation is "one-time" or not. The truth is that there is nothing one-time in a throttled economy in which all deficits fatten on one another. So the Governor finds himself with scorecard in hand watching a race to see whether "inflation" or the economy hits zero bottom first.

With this prospect of a long haul to nowhere, the BoC has suddenly come to feel the need for legitimization. That is why, like thieves in the night, it is smuggling the failed "zero inflation" policy into the *Bank of Canada Act*.

Such a goal formally set would reduce the provision for "regional directors" to window-dressing. Bruce Little in *The Globe and Mail* (25/9) describes it as a feel-good lollipop in the form of consultations. The proposed new directive would put the bank on one track. Regionally sensitive directors might advise the governor on how fast the train should be going, but if the law of the land directs him to reduce inflation, he would be in a stronger position to fend off easy-money critics."

Less happily, Little demonstrates how unschooled the media have become about the economy. "The current *Bank of Canada Act* directs the governor and his staff to fret about a mish-mash of economic goals — production, trade, prices, employment, the exchange rate and generally the economic and financial welfare of Canada."

That "mish-mash" in fact reflects the basic interrelationships of our mixed economy. Ignoring these is a sure formula for disaster. The high interest rates shrink the tax-base while increasing the carrying charges of the debt. They drive up our dollar and undermine our competitiveness. Then as we try balancing an unbalanceable budget, taxes push up prices still more and we are readied for another turn of the interest-rate screw.

The government must keep its sticky thumbs off the *Bank of Canada Act*!

Vol. 3, No. 11 — November 1991

The Ghost of Our Economy Walks the Battlements

While the press is full of the tidings of lay-offs, shut-downs and bankruptcies, Governor Crow bestrides the carnage like Napoleon at Austerlitz. "The Canadian economy already has paid most of the price of achieving the BoC's inflation targets. The paper by Bank of Canada economists Barry Cozier and Gordon Wilkinson examines data from 1964 to 1988 to find out how much gross domestic product has to fall to get inflation down, the so-called 'sacrifice ratio.' They conclude it costs 2% of a year's GDP to achieve each percentage point of permanent reduction in inflation." (*The Financial Post* 15/10)

We have rigorous laws that prosecute peddlers of snake oil claiming their wares to be "permanent" cures for cancer. It is not clear why we should not impose similar standards on our central bank.

When the BoC talks about decreased production, it is a goal it achieves through high interest rates. But that is therapy that does not stop on a dime. Raise interest rates and you destroy capital values throughout the economy. Perfectly viable factories become scrap. Productive humans are made derelict. You devastate the financial system by savaging the collateral for its loans and inundating it with bad debts. Even a casual reading of the business press should alert one to the fact that we are still haunted by the ravages of the high-rate orgy of 1981.

High interest rates drive up the exchange rate of our currency and put our products at a disadvantage both abroad and on the home market. The gap in our international balance of payments is filled by expensive foreign borrowings. That dependence is like an addiction — the longer it goes on the harder it is to break.

While the BoC reports that "the war against inflation is won" the budget deficit that was in the $30 billion rate last year is currently heading for $40 billion. That will cause both the BoC and foreign lenders to keep interest rates high or drive them still higher.

Still more disturbing, the BoC and its faithful camp-followers are intent on cutting off our retreat from the edge of the chasm. As usual it is The C.D. Howe Institute in its fervour that has let the cat out of the bag. Recently Thomas Courchene of Queen's, attacking central bank policy, called for a lower Canadian dollar. The Institute's reply, written by David Laidler, has the revealing passage: "It is hard to imagine US legislators failing to react if Canada were to attempt to gain competitive advantage through an active policy of devaluation and wage-and-price controls."

So all the while that Governor Crow has been keeping our dollar high with higher interest rates he was leading us into a trap — easier to get into than to get out of. No American protectionist legislator could possibly object to our shooting ourselves in the foot with interest rates so much higher than theirs. If the Lord made us that stupid it must simply be the will of Heaven. But once we try bringing that dollar down again, it becomes an unfair trade practice. Or at least the C.D. Howe Institute wants us to believe that.

Vol. 3, No. 12 — December 1991

Gastric Juices

I recall reading of the imperfect healing of a stomach wound of a Civil War veteran. Through the remaining opening, doctors were for the first time able to study the flow of gastric juices.

Likewise, in its far from perfect healing, our financial system recently granted us an unusual glimpse of its inner mysteries.

It all began when President Bush "urged banks to lower credit-card interest rates as a way to spur community purchases. Capitalising on the president's remarks, Sen. Alphonse d'Amato (R.-N.Y.) who has tried unsuccessfully for years to cap credit-card rates, introduced his proposal, and it passed overwhelmingly.

"The Senate measure would set credit card rates at four percentage points over the rate the Internal Revenue Service charges on the underpayment of taxes, requiring an immediate reduction to 14% from the current 18.94% average.

"Yesterday, the administration tried to derail the cap movement by arguing it will hurt the economy. 'The administration strongly supports lower credit-card rates,' Treasury Secretary Nicholas Brady said. 'But we should let the market-place determine the rates, not inflexible legislation that could reduce credit to Americans by $100 billions and impede the economic recovery.'" (*Wall Street Journal*, 15/11).

In response to the d'Amato bill the N.Y. Stock Exchange dropped 120 points. "Stocks of the largest card-issuing banking companies fell as much as 26% yesterday. Banks such as Citicorp and First Chicago earn more than 50% of earnings from credit-card operations."

"'It would blow away the profitability of the banking system,' said James McDermott, president of Keefe, Bruyette and Woods Inc. Adds Richard Pike, a vice-president of Chancellor Capital Management, 'It's one of the few things banks had going for them.'"

"A ceiling on credit card interest rates could force the banks to add capital to support billions of dollars of credit-card receivables that may have to be brought back onto their balance sheets. Those receivables had been packaged and sold as securities. Banks must set aside 4% in equity capital and 8% of total capital for most assets. If interest rates are capped, these securities would no longer earn sufficient returns for bondholders, and would therefore be called."

In short not only our recovery, but the solvency of the banking system hangs on banks charging their credit card clients 19% or so when the rate charged on 3-month treasury bills at the end of October was fully 14.51 percentage points lower. (In Canada the spread between these two items is 11.66 points, and in Britain 17.46.)

"Bankers, retailers, oil companies and other credit-card issuers claim that high interest rates on the $230 billion of debt outstanding are necessary to cover the cost of delinquencies on card operations." But is it not one of the functions of banks to screen borrowers for creditworthiness?

"The typical American family has 4.6 credit cards, and many credit-card rates have remained near 20% while most other interest rates have fallen sharply in the period of economic weakness."

The string upon which the solvency of our banking system hangs would seem pretty tenuous.

In Canada "today's typical bankrupt consumer has 7.62 credit cards, all of them fully extended." (*Financial Post* 26/11) And how did they get their mitts on so much dangerous plastic? The answer : lenders have been pushing credit cards like dope peddlers do their wares.

And why has the Bush Administration been pressuring its bank inspectors to lay off too rigorous inspections of the affairs of the banks when their most lucrative business — credit cards — is clearly usury-driven? To the point where interest charges are likely to get even creditworthy clients into trouble. The mere fact that a person will pay such rates is enough to make him suspect in the eyes of the lenders.

The outcry of the banks was so great that the House banking subcommittee put the whole issue on indefinite hold.

W

Vol. 4, No. 1 — January 1992

Correspondence — to COMER / from Lynn Turgeon

24/11/91

In William Krehm's comments on 'Right-thinking Illiteracy' he mentioned that "there has been a preference for central bankers with deep voices who stand well over six feet in their socks, and move in a cloud of PR that emphasizes their unbendable resolve to 'lick inflation.'" This may have applied to Paul Volcker, but Alan Greenspan is quite short and hunched.

Lynn Turgeon
Professor Emeritus of Economics
Hofstra University

Editorial reply: My reference to the preference for central bankers who stand over six feet in their socks was not only to Volcker but to our own John Crow who meets these specs. Note well that our Crow raised our bank rate at the very time that your Greenspan chickened out just because the economy was crumbling and dropped his a full percent. Which suggests that central bankers on nomination should be weighed in and measured like boxers.

wk

Vol. 4, No. 2 — February 1992

Introducing the Entropy Concept to Economics

('An Intercom for the Tower of Babel,' February 1992; 'Entropy II', March 1992)

In the seventies I applied the entropy concept to the systems within our mixed economy.[†] But at the time there were few takers for such subtleties. Why so complicated a model for something so simple as our economy?

So in the first 31 issues of *Economic Reform* we have not so much as mentioned the word "entropy." But we have come to a period of cracking timbers. It is going to take more than piety to keep the temple from collapsing on our heads. We must work out the ground rules for the symbiosis of the different subsystems in our economy. There is no way of doing this without borrowing the entropy concept from physics.

Some ecologists in the past twenty years have made use of the notion of entropy. It remains only to extend it from the environment to society itself.

Early in the 19th century a French engineer pondered something familiar to every housewife: heat will flow only from a hotter to a colder body. In time this led to the science of thermodynamics. Its second law — the entropy law — tells us that energy can be put to work only if a difference in energy levels (potential) exists. As energy flows from a higher to a lower level, that potential difference is dissipated. When the potential difference is used up, the energy remaining becomes unavailable — i.e. entropy builds up.

That stood physics on its ear. Up to then its equations had been taken to be as valid read backward as forward. But with the concept of potential differences running out, time became as unidirectional as the rest of us.

The notion of entropy — the running out of "negentropy" (potential difference) — has become the dominant symbolism of our day. It is coming to pervade every area of social thinking with but a single exception — economic theory. There the equations are timeless and self-balancing. There is nothing to run out — unless it is our credulity.

In the physical world as one system builds up entropy, it can tap the negentropy in another to keep going. Energy in those various systems may be in different forms — gravitational, electro-magnetic, nuclear, thermal.

That suggests a pattern for managing our economy. There the entropy pattern is rarely a purely physical one. In the economy what may be involved are both the means and the motivations that drive the various subsystems. But as different as these may be, one subsystem can be cannibalised to keep another going. Negentropy can be transferred from one system and another to recharge its batteries.

There is, however, a condition that must be respected: if the system tapped is vital for the economy as a whole — and if it were not it would not by definition be a subsystem — it must not be stripped of the means to continue functioning. As its negentropy is run down, it must be replenished.

In this the entrepreneur appears as a negentropy scout with a flair for seeking out other entropy systems to be drained to keep his own going. But he cannot, without urging from without, be too concerned about the fate of the systems that he is tapping.

In every instance a ratio can be found to meter the negentropy of a system. In the case of carbon-dioxide pollution it will be the maximum component of CO_2 tolerable in the atmosphere less the amount actually present. If the automobile industry prospers by polluting the atmosphere with carbon dioxide beyond the tolerable level, it has drained off a vital reserve of the environmental system, and thus threatens the future of society as a whole.

We can set up similar negentropy meters within the economy itself.

In the private sector the Net Operating Income (NOI) is the entropy gauge. This is the balance of revenue after operating costs have been paid. From it the firm must pay its financing costs and its corporation tax. What remains is its profit. If the financing costs gobble up the entire NOI, the economy is in trouble.

In the short run the financial subsystem — the one dealing with claims on wealth instead of producing it — might seem to be doing fine bagging most of the NOI. Central bankers might even call this "stabilization," but our negentropy meter would warn us that we are approaching a massive collapse.

The public sector must be seen as another entropy subsystem within our mixed economy. Technological revolutions have made necessary ever more costly infrastructures that only our government can provide. For the most part these can be delivered only as common services with costs covered by taxation. Inevitably that taxation turns up in producers' costs. What results is a growing layer of taxation in price that reflects the rising proportion of public to private sector in the economy. When prices go up, that can no longer be taken as a sign that demand has outstripped supply. It might merely register the growth of the public sector within the economy. Or that environmental standards have been stepped up.

This in itself constitutes an entropy build-up for the private sector. When more of the costs of producers come to be determined by taxation and regulation and fewer by market forces, the very price signals no longer mean quite what they used to. That is confusing, especially when the monetary authorities insist on misreading all price increases as a sign of an excess of demand, and proceed to deflate the economy with higher interest rates. In that way they respond to an entropy build-up in one subsystem (the invasion of the price system by non-market determinants of price) by cannibalizing another entropy subsystem (assigning more of the NOI to lenders).

An entropy model codifies the interdependence of the various subsystems of the economy. Any policy that focuses entirely on stabilizing a single statistic can be dismissed as mischievous nonsense.

Significantly, the proportion of total costs of the private sector that originate outside the market has now begun turning up in discussions of the economy. But almost invariably that is taken as an argument for slashing public services across the board.

However, depriving society of essential public services originating outside the market would undermine essential subsystems of the economy. The need is rather to detax the economy as much as possible by finding complementary sources to taxation for funding the state. The entropy approach discloses ways of doing this.

The problem has become so serious that we must go back to simple observations. Let us therefore rejoin Isaac Newton under his apple tree. He has already learned and taught us why ripened apples fall to the ground. So we can turn our gaze to the dusty road skirting the orchard. We may note that over stretches it climbs rather as our prices do. By his discovery of gravity Newton taught us that when that road climbs it gives rise to potential energy. That we can take advantage of when we coast downhill.

Let us transfer this knowledge to our price problem. It is easy enough to identify that part of our price rise that is due not to an overheated market, but to what might be called our "structural price gradient." This can be traced to the increase of public services within the economy and to higher regulatory standards.

Once we are aware of the structural price gradient we are no longer in the position of the foolish architect who plans a building without first surveying the slope of the lot. It won't do assuming that the lot is level because we believe that God made the world flat.

The government in fact has valuable inside information regarding the future pitch of that structural price gradient. It need only look at what legislation is in the works. Any entrepreneur would put such information to timely use to obtain capital gains.

When a highway or subway is built, capital gains are created for landowners along its route. There is no reason why the government should not position itself for a share in such capital gains resulting from its own investment. They could help stabilize the price level to a degree by detaxing the economy.

Since the government has advance knowledge of its own investment plans, this is easily arranged. If it is about to finance a subway, it need only option some strategic sites along its course. Then at the proper time it can lease such sites long-term to developers in return for a share of the profits. When the project becomes profitable, the government would be free to sell part or all of its interest.

There are other advantages in such an arrangement. At present the private capital gains based on the future appreciation of the site are capitalised, borrowed against or sold, and the proceeds reinvested in further projects of this kind. The driving force is the allure of speculative gains. This has contributed to a wild over-development of commercial and office space. Under this proposal both the risks and the speculative attraction of such investments would be trimmed. Far more modest land acquisition costs would find their way into the rent of the finished project.

William Krehm

† 'The Entropy Concept as a Tool of Economic Analysis,' in *Economie Appliquee*, Paris, 1977-1. See also *Babel's Tower — the Dynamics of Economic Breakdown*, Toronto, 1977.

We Are the Victims of Bum Metaphors

Irrelevant metaphors shape our destinies. BoC Governor Crow fancies himself a gladiator wrestling "inflation to the ground." Or a hero in a hand laundry "wringing inflation out of the economy."Unfortunately by now John Crow should realize that what he is wringing is the neck of that economy.

Most significantly he has cast himself as a white-robed surgeon tracking down the last cancer cell with a sharp scalpel. You need only assume that inflation behaves like cancer and it follows like night does day that he is saving the economy from a fate worse then death.

However, if you stick to the historical record rather than to irrelevant metaphors, you might come to another conclusion. Runaway inflation occurs not from the neglect of "creeping inflation," but from social breakdown — from defeat in a war, or from a civil war, or for that matter from steering the economy long enough by the wrong metaphors.

More recently Governor Crow has bombed disastrously in his key role — that of cancer surgeon. For key role it was, most faithfully mirroring his economic model. Despite much groaning and grunting, it isn't unusual for both contenders in a wrestling match to come out of the ring undamaged. In laundering, failure to wring the last drop of water out of the long johns will not bring back the biblical flood. But in oncology the result can be grim if even a few malignant cells remain.

The politicians who had handed over the economy to Dr. Crow's mercies, seem to have gotten cold feet as the polls showed that they were sliding into zero popularity.

The Globe and Mail (23/10) reported: "After six years of insisting that zero is the only acceptable target for inflation, the federal government appears to be having a change of heart.

And at the recent Repap Conference in Montreal Mr. Crow's deputy, Charles Freedman, explained that "what we really meant by 'zero inflation' was one or 1.5% inflation."

But allow for a moment that the patient can live with two ounces of inflation, or that their removal could be postponed until after the next general election. Where would that leave Dr. Crow? The next thing folks would be insisting that you have a serious diagnosis before you embarked on the surgeon act. And then you would find that the Consumer Price Index registers the costs but not the benefits of a lot of essential public services that are not priced or marketed. For example, new laws for cleaning up the environment must show up in the prices of the output of our smelters and paper mills. That is really not more "inflation" but — something that should be of interest to our oncologist — less cancer.

But where does that leave the dazed patient? He is still on the operating table with a couple of pounds already cut out from him, while the surgeon and his director argue whether what was excised was cancer or just some vital organ.

And while the debate goes on, steps are underway to write Dr. Crow's surgical innovations into the Hippocratic Oath, pardon me, the *Bank of Canada Act* and the Constitution.

wk

Correspondence — to Murray Dorin / from William Krehm

20/1/92

Mr. Murray Dorin, MP
Chairman of the Standing Committee on Finance of the House of Commons

Dear Mr. Dorin:

Under date of August 1st last you wrote me in reply to a letter of mine: "I have taken the liberty of forwarding a copy of your letter to the Clerk of the Finance Committee in order that you be contacted to appear as a witness before the Committee when we deal with the Bank of Canada."

Under date of October 9th Mr. Don Blenkarn, MP the former chairman of the Standing Committee on Finance sent me a copy of his letter to you which read in part: "William Krehm is a good friend of mine who knows what he is talking about. I think you might be interested in having him make a presentation."

Mr. Blenkarn was good enough to write that letter entirely on his own initiative. I had contacted him on quite another matter, and had mentioned in passing that I had heard from about my appearance before the standing committee.

Early in December the clerk of the standing committee, Susan Baldwin, tried contacting me by phone and left her number, but no further message.

I replied at once and gave my home number. She left her name with my answering service, but with no further message. In subsequent days I made several attempts to reach her, invariably leaving my name. On the last occasion I was informed she had begun her holidays. I left my fax number with the request that she inform me of a couple of available dates for an appearance, and I would confirm one at once.

I was still awaiting a reply to that message when I was surprised to read in *The Globe and Mail* (17/1) "Mr. Crow's appearance wrapped up the finance committee's study of proposed changes to the Bank of Canada's mandate and method of operation, included in the government's constitutional proposals."

I would be unhappy to have to conclude that I have been denied a hearing before your committee. *Economic Reform*, the newsletter of the Committee for Monetary and Economic Reform, has over the past four years devoted much of its attention to the manner in which the Bank of Canada was violating the very clause that the Government now proposes to replace — mandating the central bank "to mitigate by its influence fluctuations in the general level of production, trade, prices and employment."

The February issue of *Economic Reform* goes to press on January 30th. We should like to be able to report that your committee has rectified what we trust was an unfortunate bureaucratic blunder.

William Krehm
Publisher, *Economic Reform*

Correspondence — from Gerald Bouey / from Peter Cook

2/1/92

Your December 1991 issue includes on page 5 a letter from Peter Cook which contains the following statement: "In 1973, the then-Governor Bouey was so incensed by a piece I wrote in Ottawa that he phoned up my publisher and tried to get me fired."

This statement is untrue.

Yours sincerely,

Gerald K. Bouey

24/1/92

The only reply I would make is:

"If Mr. Bouey says the incident did not happen, then I accept that — contrary to what I was told at the time."

Best wishes,

Peter Cook

Vol. 4, No. 3 — March 1992

Writing on a Crumbling Wall

Of a sudden we find ourselves as guests at Belshazzar's feast. Celebrating the collapse of the Evil Empire, we had drunk the wine, praised the gods of gold, silver, brass and stone. Some of us went so far as to toast "the end of history," and looked forward to a "peace dividend" and a "new world order." But then out of nowhere came forth the fingers of a man's hand and wrote over against the candlestick upon the plaster of the wall: MENE, MENE TEKE, UPHARSIN. But we had long since forgotten how to read the clearest messages. Nor were we given to calling in oddball prophets to translate for us.

We assumed the inscription was but another arcane equation proving the market endlessly wise that had netted some pious academic the Nobel prize for economics. What changed our countenance, troubled our thoughts and caused our knees to smite one against the other was that we beheld the wine in our cups turning to vinegar, and the victuals vanishing from our gold plates before we could set tooth to them.

The ceilings and walls crumbled and a surfeit of history came tumbling down on us, all of it of the wrong sort. In a trice the Good Empire seemed headed the way of the wicked one. Taught to worship the god Maximisation, we found ourselves sorely minimised.

Whether they know it or not, all Canadians are indebted to the Commons Finance Subcommittee on the *Bank of Canada Act* for having taken a hard look at the scrawl on our crumbling walls. Though still far from having fully deciphered it, the minutes of their hearings show that they have started asking the right questions.

That is why we are devoting a major portion of this issue of *ER* to the subcommittee's hearings.

The Arrogance of Infallibility

We had been left with few enough illusions on that score, but still the degree of Governor Crow's arrogance before the Subcommittee shocked us.

Herbert Gray (Liberal, Windsor W.): Mr. Crow, if the government's proposals were in fact law, what, if anything, would you do differently? For example, last Thursday the bank rate went up. It was also reported a few days ago that the BoC intervened to prevent the Canadian dollar from falling...

Mr. Crow: I don't accept your characterisation of what happened last week. Not everything we see in the newspaper is correct.

Mr. Gray: Didn't the bank last Thursday announce a rate slightly higher than the preceding week?

Mr. Crow: The bank rate was higher than the week before, yes.

Mr. Gray: And you announced it?

Mr. Crow: We could announce that tomorrow is going to be a sunny day, for that matter. I am not sure what the point is you're making, Mr. Gray.

Mr. Gray: Well, did you make an announcement or not last Thursday?

Mr. Crow: We made an announcement. What the bank rate was, yes.

Mr. Gray: Also, a few days ago, didn't the BoC intervene in international exchange markets to prevent the Canadian dollar from falling?

Mr. Crow: I think I have to start at a place that is more consistent with the facts. .... The bank, when it undertakes an intervention operation in foreign exchange markets, is acting as the agent [of the Government of Canada], not as the principal.

Mr. Blenkarn (Mississauga S., P.C.): Could you explain that further? Do you get direction from [Finance Minister] Mazankowski to enter into a trading activity with the Canadian dollar?

Mr. Crow: We give advice, of course, on these matters, and on many matters, to the government. In the end what we do — and there's no doubt about it, Mr. Blenkarn — is follow the instructions of the government. In that situation I feel somewhat reluctant to confirm or deny what the bank did last week, but I will say that as a general rule, exchange market interventions are taken to steady the market as it moves up or moves down. ... Whatever happened, or whatever you read about what happened in the market last week, Mr. Gray, took place in that context.

Mr. Gray: Quite apart from whose instructions are acted on, did the BoC intervene in the exchange markets in a way that prevented the Canadian dollar from falling?

Mr. Crow: This is a little difficult, Mr. Chairman. This gets us into the question of under what rules we were operating from the Minister of Finance...

Mr. Gray: Why are you denying what everybody in the financial community seems to know and which is reported — that is, the Bank from time to time intervenes in the exchange markets. Why are you being so coy with this committee?

Mr. Crow: I think there are some laws, Mr. Gray, that preclude me also from speaking about this. In fact I think there are some fairly heavy [fines] for giving away information. My colleague says six months in jail, but...

Mr. Gray: Well, I am not asking you...

Mr. Crow: I am not sure what you are asking me, Mr. Gray.

Mr. Gray: I want to know what the BoC did last week with respect to the exchange markets. Did it buy or sell Canadian currency? I am not asking for the amounts.

Mr. Crow: This is not an inspiring beginning, Mr. Chairman. We're not going to tell you, Mr. Gray.

Mr. Langdon (Essex-Windsor, NDP): I wonder if it might be possible to ask the witness to lower his level of animosity and simply answer the questions that are put by members of the committee?

Crow's Dance of Seven Veils

Prime Minister Mulroney recently promised greater "transparency" in the government's monetary policy. But though the glass tower of the Bank of Canada's headquarters is burnished to a shine, it was less than transparent when the Common Subcommittee tried peeking in.

Mr. Blenkarn: Can you explain money to us?

Mr. Crow: I'm using "money" in the broad sense. Money is what monetary policy deals with, which, of course, is circular. There are various kinds of money. This is the awkwardness, and I guess it is a point that should be borne in mind. There is central bank money. What we manage and in a real sense control are the liabilities of the Bank of Canada.

Mr. Blenkarn: What does it look like?

Mr. Crow: It looks like bank notes. It looks like bank deposits. ... That's what it is.

Then you have all kinds of other definitions of money: M1, M2, M3, M2 plus, which all have various properties we certainly aim to examine and put out many learned papers on the properties of. Their interest and importance to us is that they do convey, in a sense that is linked to spending in the economy and interest rates, something about the dimensions of monetary policy.

That monetary policy in the end is about monetary expansion, however you measure it whether you look at it in terms of our instrument, let's say our balance sheet, or its relationship to these broader definitions of money, which in the end is not something we supply to the market. We don't go around with helicopters dropping money. What happens is there is a demand for money related to income, related to interest Z=s, but if it's at all reasonably behaved, it gives you a kind of path to which you can relate and which is in the same dimension as your instrument...

Mr. Blenkarn: Is this money? It says Murray Dorin, the Royal Bank of Canada 451505288?

Mr. Dorin: If I go to a restaurant or a store in most places in Canada, I can have your currency notes or I can have this. Both will be accepted equally.

Mr. Crow: Yes, I think this is a case of what I would call misplaced concreteness, in a broad sense capacity to acquire goods and services. It can be through borrowing — the use of a credit card is a form of borrowing, which is credit, or it can be balances that one holds, which can be used to finance transactions. When we look at money in this broad sense — I must say this is getting a bit technical, but I believe it is the right way to look at it — we look at it in terms of the stability, this relationship of, say, transaction balances, as best we can measure them, or personal balances with broad numbers such as money, GDP, with short-term interest rates, in order to see whether we can work out some reasonably stable relationships between money and spending, which we can use as a guide to our policy.

... For example, to give you an idea of what I am thinking about here or trying to convey, when you get, say, double-digit pace, especially if you see credit as well, you kind of begin to wonder whether you are not storing up trouble from, let us say, an inflation point of view. Credit Card balances are neither M1 nor M2 because they are not a balance. That is a form of credit. They are in consumer credit, which is the other side of the balance sheet. I am right there?....

Mr. Blenkarn: ... as far as the ordinary guy is concerned, he spends that money as if he had cash in his pocket.

Mr. Crow: I will put it this way. If you look at a balance sheet...

Mr. Blenkarn: Mr. Crow, you don't even print it.

Mr. Crow: ... at a balance sheet of a bank, it'll have various assets, of course, and various liabilities. One can say that the counterpart to your consumer if you look at credit — I am sorry if I get personal — which is an asset of the bank, has a liability on the other side of some kind, which ...will pay off your personal credit. What we think is that we can get a better eye on what is happening to spending through the prism, let us say, of money and credit through the money side, generally speaking, than through the credit side.

Mr. Crow can be most articulate when he chooses to be. It is just that if you make a career of hiding things from the peasants for their own good, you develop a pea-soup style.

The sub-committee's questions could have been answered briefly as follows:

Ours is a debt-money system. That immediately links the soundness of our money to the health of the real economy. You cannot sacrifice the health of the real economy to protect the money supply as our central bank has been trying to do. If you depress the real economy with high interest rates, you convert good debts into bad debts.

That was the point that Mr. Crow skirted. Like a coy shepherdess eluding the goat-god, he tripped nimbly over mount and dale. But with so much cavorting a tatter of truth will eventually drop by the wayside. This happened when Mr. Crow remarked: "We can get a better eye on what is happening ... through the money side, generally speaking, than through the credit side."

When you concentrate on money rather than "the credit side," you are in fact turning your back on the real economy that determines whether debts are fact or fiction. The central bank is kidding itself when it believes that deflating the economy with high interest rates can preserve the circulating medium.

The deregulation of the banking system wiped out the distinction between checking accounts and interest-bearing accounts. It was no longer possible to distinguish between transaction money (that could contribute to inflation) and savings (which in the monetarist creed is the supreme engine of virtue). In the US, Fed Chairman Paul Volcker's blindness to the point brought on the devastating recession of the early eighties.

From the Other Side of the Mirror

The testimony of David Slater was of special interest. A retired academic, Dr. Slater served both in the Department of Finance and as Director of the Bank of Canada a couple of decades ago. He comes then from the other side of the mirror, from a world the very traces of which have been erased by the militant new orthodoxy.

"I am sure you are familiar with the fact that almost any central bank in the world now refers to M-1, M-1A, M-2, M-4, M-5 etc. The degree of moneyness about many of them has come about in spite of central banks rather than because of them. Indeed one of the principal errors, I would now call it, of both the federal reserve system and the BoC in the 1970s and early 1980s was the failure to recognize how the institutions, beliefs and practices of the public were changing the amount of work that a given supply of narrow money could do, how effectively it could do it, and enormously increasing the moneyness characteristics of things that were previously not included in money..."

And then Blenkarn put the mother of questions: "We were in a depression in the 1930s. The Nazis took over Germany and managed to put their people back to work without massive inflation, using their Deutschmark (sic). How did they do that?"

Slater: "If you have a sufficiently depressed economy and one which has gone through the ravages of a hyper-inflation you can pursue an expansionary policy, both fiscally and monetarily, and they did."

Surely we are rapidly qualifying as a "sufficiently depressed economy" And does the fact that much of the German production was going into armaments not put us at an advantage over the Nazis?

Then Blenkarn pressed on to his next question: "Did they not create enough new work and new physical assets to cover the money they created?"

That drove Slater into still more delicate areas, where even a tale half told can be subversive. "We started into the war, with a still very depressed economy. We had an expansion of the real national product of this country by 50% within about a four-year period. We had, in the earliest part of the war, some reliance on new money creation to finance the government, but it was the policy to have that on a strictly limited basis and to build up the tax and borrowing system that would permit the war to be financed during the war."

"The heart of the war finance was not price controls, but taxation and borrowing operations and the public's participation in savings programs. Canadian households saved and made available to the government 25% of their disposable income in war bond purchases for several years in a row during the war."

While describing the workings of the US Fed, Slater stated: "If you have banks in North Dakota and find you have farm credit problems and those banks have to get their reserves to some extent by going to the discount window of the regional central bank, the attitudes of that regional central bank to providing reserves and liquidity base to their regional banks can be different from what it is in California. That is a very good thing."

It is something, too, that is provided for in the present *Bank of Canada Act* (articles 18 and 19) for differential treatment of various regions in the re-discounting of certain bank loans. Little if any use has been made of that in recent years. On the contrary Governor Crow has headed off questions on the matter by highjacking the language. Repeatedly he has stated that only a single monetary policy was possible for the entire country, identifying "monetary policy" with the rate of interest. However, the availability of credit, too, is an important aspect of monetary policy.

Likewise he has identified "fighting inflation" with pushing up interest rates. And at the hearing academic after academic made thoughtless use of the Queen's English as amended by Crow.

Vol. 4, No. 4 — April 1992

Just Working on the Railroad

The character-twisting effects of political power have come in for much comment. Not so the case of the central banker. At home he is given to fancying himself an absolute monarch — what other meaning could we attribute to the recently defeated move to proclaim the independence of the Bank of Canada?

On the other hand your central banker's policies fit into an international ideological hierarchy. His strategies are laid out by the Bank for International Settlements at Basel, Switzerland. It is there, for example, that the objectives of both "zero inflation" and the independence of the central bank from the local government were launched.

Toward the international power centre an ambitious central banker in a lesser land can prove himself only by over-achievement. The analogy with the late Communist International is inescapable: the last outpost of Stalinism significantly was Albania.

In line with this New Zealand has actually put "zero inflation" into its constitution. And it was by the grace of God rather than of Brian Mulroney that Canadians at the last moment managed to keep it out of theirs.

The parallel between the international central bankers' club and the Communist International does not stop there. Both have fancied themselves agents of a super-social force — the historical process in the case of the Communists, the free market in the case of central bankerdom. Yet theirs is an intrusive, hands-on style. Critics might see a logical contradiction in this. But for practitioners of the art, the ambiguity is instead a tactical resource.

Very much a child of the great railway-building age, Marx saw history as a super-railroad with the steel laid out to socialism as final stop. That allowed his Communist heirs to duck responsibility for the victims strewn along the right-of-way. But for others it left a nagging question: with the destination already assured, courtesy of the historical process, why did you have to work so hard getting there.

You might ask the same question of John Crow. But you will note that now that the good train "zero inflation" lies overturned in the ditch, the good Governor is posing as a humble conductor who simply worked on the railroad.

"The recession wasn't the made-in-Canada malaise that many economist have said," according to Mr. Crow. "Instead it can be blamed on economic problems common to industrialized countries in the past few years," Crow wrote in the central bank's 1992 annual report.

The most basic of the economic problems common to the industrialized countries has in fact been the high interest rates imposed by their central banks to achieve zero inflation.

In the past, countries experienced the credit cycle in random sequence, and those on the upward leg took turns pulling the depressed economies out of the trough. But the credit cycle has become heavily ideologized. The very shakiness of their dogma stoked the proselytising fervour of the believers. Over the past couple of years we have witnessed the incredible situation where the Federal Reserve of the US, a country heavily dependent on Japanese funds to finance the deficits created by its own high-rate policy, has pressured the Japanese central bank to raise its discount rate so that the Fed could postpone dropping its own. And not so many months ago when American interest rates did come down substantially, the BoC expressed unhappiness at the Fed's failure to "stay the course."

Governor Crow apparently feels that his princely status bestows on him the right of the first night with the facts.

Let us consult these to see how much of this recession was in fact homemade. That can be gauged from the spread between Canadian real short-term rates and those elsewhere.

Real short-term rates			
	1988	1989	1990
Canada	5.0	8.3	10.9
United States	4.8	5.5	4.7
Germany	2.7	4.6	5.1
Japan	3.6	2.9	5.1

And yet if ever there was a land vulnerable to high rates, it is Canada. The vast gaps of wilderness separating its pockets of population, its climate, its bilingualism, mark it out as a high-overhead economy with a high break-even point. Deflate the economy and deficits must spread through such a land like a bad case of measles. The cost of government per unit of production as a result weighs all the more heavily — and contributes needlessly to higher prices.

The Next Bigger and Better Bust

If there is one subject taboo among conventional economists it is money creation. For good enough reason. On the one hand, the monetarists have chosen high interest rates, supposedly a neutral means of preserving the value of the currency that favours no one, and ("in the long run") is for the benefit of all. But it assigns an unsustainable cut of the national income to money-lenders. So huge, in fact that the economy cannot survive the drain, and eventually collapses.

An article by Martin Feldstein, former chairman of the US Council of Economic Advisers, in *The Wall Street Journal* (6/03), provides a virtual catscan of the monetarist brain.

"After a series of meetings in the Swiss city of Basel in the late 1980s, the bank regulators of the major industrial countries agreed on a new common standard of capital requirements for commercial banks. These rules became officially effective in the US at the beginning of this year and will be fully phased in by year-end."

"Before this standard became effective, domestic regulators imposed the leverage capital requirements on American banks. The leverage standard varies from bank to bank based on the judgment of each bank's own supervisors. Every bank is required to have at least $3 of equity capital for every $100 of loans. In practice, the supervisors generally require banks to have between $4.50 and $5.50 of equity capital per $100 of assets (i.e. loans) with the amount depending on the supervisors' judgment about the quality of the bank's assets and earnings."

"The Basel standard requires banks to have $4 of equity for every $100 of 'risk-weighted' assets. In calculating its risk-weighted assets, a bank gives full weight to business loans but only a 50% weight to home mortgages and no weight at all to Treasury bonds. Thus a bank with $800 million of business loans, $400 million of mortgages, and $200 million of government bonds would have $1.4 billion of total assets but only $1 billion of risk-weighted assets'; the Basel rules would require it to have at least $40 million of equity capital. It is often easier for a bank to meet the Basel standard than the leverage capital standard. If the bank actually had the $50 million of equity capital, it could do an additional $250 million of lending before it was limited by the Basel standard, but it would be prevented from doing any additional lending because of the leverage standard. Indeed, it would have to shrink in size by some $400 million to comply with its leverage capital requirement. Current bank capital requirements limit the ability of healthy banks to expand their lending to businesses and households. Without additional bank lending, the recovery as a whole will be weakened."

What is left unmentioned is the killer at the centre of this gossamer web. The same Bank for International Settlements in Basel where these new banking standards were designed is also the place where the "zero inflation" drive was hatched. By raising interest rates to whatever level is needed to knock prices flat, the scheme destroys the solvency of borrowers and the banks' collateral. While claiming to stabilise the price level by controlling the money supply, it in fact annihilates the money supply which in our world consists not of gold, but of debt.

Take the case of home mortgages, only 50% of the value of which is reckoned as "risk-weighted assets." Raise interest rates to "lick inflation," and many of your homeowners will lose their jobs. The value of the house mortgages will drop and may leave little if any of the owners' equity. Good loans become bad loans. It is anybody's guess what the state of a bank's solvency and indeed the money supply might be. It is like planning a trip to Mars fuelled by burning the spaceship to get you there. Bon voyage!

Correspondence — to William Krehm / from Murray Dorin

27/2/1992

William Krehm
Publisher, *Economic Reform*
Toronto

I sincerely regret that an apparent communications mix-up between yourself and the Clerk of the Finance Committee may have denied you the opportunity to appear before the Sub-Committee on the Bank of Canada.

I do wish to point out, however, that the Committee issued a press release on November 11th stating that the Committee's intention to undertake an examination of the Bank of Canada and inviting submissions to, and expressions of interest to appear before the Committee.

The Committee would have welcomed any submission by you on the subject of the enquiry if scheduling difficulties made a personal appearance by yourself impossible. Be that as it may, I hope that you will be gratified by the results of the enquiry which led the Committee in an unanimous report released Monday to reject the government's proposal to narrow the mandate of the Bank of Canada. I am enclosing a copy.

Murray Dorin, MP
Chairman, Standing Committee on Finance

In reply the following letter was sent to Mr. Dorin on 15/3:

Thank you for yours of February 27. I note your reference to the "press release on November 11th inviting submissions and expressions of interest to appear before the

Committee." However, since under date of August 1st you informed me that you had forwarded my letter to the Clerk in order that I could be contacted to appear as a witness, there was no reason for my responding to subsequent press releases.

William Krehm

Vol. 4, No. 5 — May 1992

All the News Fit to Print

For months the government and the BoC had prepared their daring coup. With the economy already reduced to tatters to the beat of the "zero inflation" drum, the plan was to elevate the policy to a state religion unexposed to worldly testing. First came the scholarly papers churned out by friendly think-tanks proving the scientific necessity of putting "zero inflation" into the *Bank of Canada Act*, and to establish the sovereignty, pardon, the independence of the central bank from the elected government. Like Strasbourg geese, the media was force-fed with disinformation describing the Bank's present mandate to mitigate fluctuations in trade, employment as well as in price as a "mishmash" of goals.

All the more remarkable then was the fact that when the parliamentary subcommittee studying the government's initiatives finished its hearings, its three party caucuses of the committee joined in recommending that the proposed amendments be turned down.

Not a word of this appeared in the two leading business papers of the land, *The Globe and Mail* and *The Financial Post*.

We had been led to believe that dog bites man is no news, but that man bites dog is. But here this proved not so. It depends very much on what man and whose dog.

The Tool Becomes the Program

Marshall McLuhan's keen summary of our world: "the medium is the message" is proving a harbinger of worse variants still to come. The tool becomes the program, and we become the environment, abused as environments tend to be.

The current efforts to entrust our environmental concern to the market illustrates the point. *The Wall Street Journal* (14/04) quotes Richard L. Sandor, a director of the Chicago Board of Trade: "Commodities exchanges such as the Board of Trade are competing to run legally sanctioned markets that would trade rights to emit sulfur dioxide, nitrogen oxide, and reactive vapors. Utilities, refineries and manufacturers would buy and sell pollution rights, which are supposed to ease the transition to increasingly stringent emission limits."

The *WSJ* informs us that in Torrance, California, Mobil Oil Corp. has just bought the right "to spew an additional 900 lbs. of noxious gas per day. For about $3 million, Mobile acquired pollution "credits' from the nearby city of South Gate. South Gate had acquired the credits from General Motors Corp, which closed a plant there in 1985 and sold the city the property. Mobil bought the rights under a rudimentary version of market-based environmental regulation. The program has been around since the 1970s, but its rules are so cumbersome that pollution "trades" are rare. For every 1.2 lbs. of pollution eliminated in a shutdown, the program allows creation of only one lb. of new credits."

The US Environmental Protection Agency "hopes to do better with its new sulfur-dioxide program. Companies will only get enough credits for 30% to 50% of what they used to pollute."

If you are a true believer in the higher morality of the market, this may arouse your enthusiasm. It could be that we will finally get a handle on homicide in our cities by introducing murder rights (30% to 50% of previous killings). The plan capitalises pollution that took place in the past — converts it into a property right. The pollution of an obsolescent rust-belt industry, about to be shut down in any case, is made a capital asset.

Contrast this with the treatment of efforts to clean up the environment. If the government itself does the job, the costs show up in higher taxation that must affect the price level. This is seen not as an investment in a better environment, but as "inflation." That in turn is taken by the central bank as a pollution of the price system, and causes it to screw up interest rates. If industries are required to clean up their act, their cost of doing so, recaptured in price, gets the same treatment.

Pollution thus becomes the capital investment, and eliminating it an inflationary evil. Just how insane can a value system get?

Vol. 4, No. 6 — June 1992

Extra! Extra! The Millennium Arrived Last Year!

In understatement, let us say that the reality of zero inflation has fallen short of the promised long-term gain. What had been offered was a final segregation of good from evil: a sort of celestial bliss where halos would replace sphincters, and there would be little need for landfills or plumbing — indeed for earthly infrastructures of any sort. These do have a way of involving us in public spending that does rough up prices. A buck would always be worth a good old buck, and those who lived on interest would get their share of costly public services thrown in free.

However, since that alluring prospect has failed, we are reduced to picking up the pieces and figuring out things all over again.

We are told that we have "licked inflation." In Canada it is down to an official 1.6%. But what passes for "inflation" is a cluster of different things — part might really be due to too much market demand and too little supply. But prices might move up just to reflect our getting more for our money than the goods crossing the counter in earlier years. Higher standards may have been set by law, and producers have no choice but to meet them. When we buy a car today, seat-belts are no longer an option, but mandatory and are thus included in the list price. To treat that part of the higher price that pays for the seat-belts as "inflation" is madness. Essential public services can often not be delivered on a market basis. To do that you would have to carry around your clean atmosphere in cylinders.

In reorganizing society's affairs we must sort out those different factors at work in price movement. And we will have to label each carefully to distinguish it — just as we do the specimens in a medical laboratory. That would permit us to monitor the full costs of public services. It would enable us to segregate that portion of any price increase that was really due to an overheated market. That we could call "Market

Inflation" That due to higher legislated standards could be labelled "mandated standards costs" Any increase in the layer of taxation in price could be named "increased public services costs" or "social lien."

Let us make a stab at quantifying some of the different factors in our perceived "inflation."

The Wall Street Journal (15/4) quotes a study of the German Economic Institute on the percentage of the Gross National Product spent to protect the air, water, and land in 1991: Germany 1.7%, Austria 1.9%, the Netherlands 1.5%, the US 1.4%, Japan 1.02%, and France 0.9%.

No figure is given for Canada, but we can take it to be somewhat higher than the US, say 1.6%.

Nearly two-thirds of German spending on environmental cleanup was borne by industry as compared with 62% in France, 78% in Holland and 88% in Japan. Environmental concerns in Canada have come to the fore as never previously: You need only consider the recycling of our trash, the clean-up of emissions and effluents imposed on our industries, the growing number of environmental enquiries under way affecting housing, airports, aboriginal peoples, mega-projects like James Bay. At the same time the denominator of this crucial proportion — our GNP — is shrinking due to the prolonged recession. A plausible guesstimate is that over the past year environmental spending as a proportion of the GNP has jumped by a third or .5%.

Between 1960-1982 health spending by all levels of government rose from 5.3% to 8.5% of Canada's GNP (Canada Year Book 1988). Given the advance of medical technology and our aging population, a ballpark guess of the increase over the past year would lie in the .5% range.

Between 1980 and 1984 spending on social welfare rose from 9.0% of GNP to about 10.9%. In these troubled times the increase over the past year is likely to be in the .5% range.

The three above items alone would account for almost the entire perceived "inflation" over the past year. Given the many other non-market factors driving up prices, it is likely that a zero rate of "market inflation" was achieved a year ago or even earlier. But at that time short-term interest rates had been pushed up into the 12% range "to lick inflation." The truth is that non-market factors pushing up prices were actually eclipsing the brutal deflation of the economy even in the early stages of our "zero inflation" saga.

Lands of Fiction

At no time in its history has Latin America been unacquainted with fiction as a mode of life. It learned early to discount the rhetoric of kings, popes, statesmen, and international bankers. It improvised underground arrangements of survival while its masters went through their charades.

Under Spanish rule the Madrid Court went on churning out instructions for the Christian treatment of the natives. To these the Viceroys on the scene merely added the marginal notation: "To be obeyed, but not carried out." That in fact could serve as the heraldic device for the region.

In the Wars of Independence romantic young generals (with due quota of Irishmen) crisscrossed the snow-covered Andes with ragged armies and issued proclamations echoing the ideals of the American and French revolutions. To all of this, reality added its sordid counterpoint. The great Liberator Simon Bolivar, departing into exile, summed it up in wormwood: "Like plowing the sea."

Tough, illiterate caudillos took over and ran the countries like their private ranches. In lands with 90% illiteracy, they might erect Temples to Minerva to the acclaim of foreign journalists. The inflation of words matched that of the currencies.

What met the eye was not the effective social structure. In the Peruvian village of Moche an American anthropologist identified more than a dozen types of "godfather" relationships beyond the baptismal tie: the midwife who delivered a child, the woman who first cut its nails or hair, first hung a scapular around its neck, presided over engagements or marriages, house-warmings, the opening of a festive keg of maize beer. There was an avid need to reach out and touch fellow-humans.

Illegitimate progeny in all classes served a similar purpose. Even in modern times a dictator like Anastasio Somoza of Nicaragua might assign rawer chores to a natural son, while the more elegant official offspring graced diplomatic posts. The compadre or illegitimacy tie could even cross class lines and afford either party the advantage of a toe in the other camp.

There is no way of appraising the news coming out of Latin America without keeping these deeper realities in mind. Thus the drug economies that have taken over in Bolivia, Peru and Colombia persist because they fill an economic vacuum. They can only be supplanted by introducing substitute cash crops.

Into this dangerously mined area the IMF has brought an obsession with a few abstract dogmas. Free trade, a panacea the G7 countries are readier to export than practice at home, has a checkered background in Latin America. It calls to mind Guatemalan Indians in the thirties carrying their masters' imported Cadillacs on their backs to highland coffee fincas because, though an item of prestige, there were no roads for them to run on.

The slashing of public services and subsidies ordained by the IMF will undoubtedly strengthen the local currencies and lure back some of the capital that has fled the country. Today, along with lucrative privatisations, this is fuelling a new speculative boom in several of the republics, based on a massive shift of income from the lower middle class. But in the fullness of time the social unrest provoked will join with the world recession in pricking the bubble of lopsided prosperity. At that point the capital accumulated during the boom will once again flee the country, and leave it in a deeper mess than before. This is so recurrent a pattern in Latin America, that only the IMF can overlook it. The strains imposed upon the world economy by the high-interest-rate policies of our central banks are bound to show up first in the snapping of its weakest links — the Third World.

wk

Vol. 4, No. 7 — July 1992

Whirling Dervishes

Mirages are not confined to desert travel. Under the banner caption 'Recovery signs start to show,' *The Financial Post* (6/6) exults, "The recovery is beginning to take hold as positive signs accumulate" and then, before you can rush your parched camel to the shimmering spring, it goes on: "including even a rise in the number of jobless."

The Canadian unemployment rate increased from 11% in April to 11.2% in May. But the hook on which the optimism is hung is this: though the number of people looking for work jumped by 25,000, the number of those working was also up — by 31,000.

The Globe and Mail of the same date sounds the same bright note: "'I think it's a relatively good sign that people were back in the labour market looking for jobs even if a lot them didn't find them,' said Philip Cross, of Statistics Canada. Mr. Cross said the growth in jobs was welcome even if the positions created were mostly part time rather than full time."

That opens the door to more mournful interpretations. Your executive may have lost his job, so his wife takes a part-time appointment checking out groceries at the supermarket, while he looks for another position. That would add a body to the labour force.

There is, too, the possibility that the Finance Minister has hired an additional spin-master to manage the press. For not even the Whirling Dervishes of Konya spin in such superb coordination as our media in prettying up the news out of our moribund economy.

Vol. 4, No. 9 — September 1992

Restructuring

"Neither (Carla) Hills nor Michael Wilson could explain the 'structural changes' that Prime Minister Brian Mulroney claimed President George Bush told him would occur in the way Washington deals with bilateral trade following Mulroney's two-day visit in May." (*The Financial Post*, 10/6)

Whenever we find ourselves knotted in problems a new word is thrown in to decoy our wits. *Restructuring* is the latest such. If unemployment continues to push up, not to worry — it merely reflects the "restructuring" of the economy. The word commits to nothing, but coins advantage from the widespread feeling that our society is rotting-ripe for change.

Let us examine some of these basic restructurings with which we have failed to come to terms.

Technology Transfer

Just enough technology has been transferred to the underdeveloped countries to unleash a population explosion, but not enough to manage it. In 1930 the population of the world was about 2 billion; today is 5.4 billion. The discouragement of family planning and abortion by both the Vatican and Washington has been a major factor in this.

Urbanization

In 1900 there were sixteen cities in the world with a population of a million or more. Today there are 276 in that category and 27 with populations of 10 million and more. Grinding rural poverty has fuelled the trend. Cities are the nodal points of society's ills.

Education

Equipping a migrant from a primitive rural area for survival in a modern city calls for an immense capital investment in education, housing, social welfare. It is certainly no good just "throwing money" at such problems, but how about investing it carefully?

Environmental Damage

The onrush of technology, the population blast, and urbanization have our environment under siege. Not only births, but death and destruction move on an exponential curve. The restructuring of our economy must take place around these core issues.

There are two things that threaten the environmentalist movement.

The first is that it keel over to become just another ideology, extrapolating well-based concerns into certainties even in areas still inadequately researched. We would do well to heed the Heidelberg Appeal, signed last April by 217 prominent scientists including Hans Bethe, Jonas Salk, and Linus Pauling. (see box)

An even greater menace is the monetarist dogma entrenched in our central banks. Assigning top priority to a stable price level, it in effect vetoes any programs to deal with the above core problems as "inflationary." In reality the inevitable effects of such programs on price levels would be for good value received.

The Heidelberg Appeal reads in part: "We are worried, at the dawn of the twenty-first century, at the emergence of an irrational ideology which is opposed to scientific and industrial progress and impedes economic and social development.

"We contend that a Natural State, sometimes idealized by movements with a tendency to look towards the past, does not exist and has probably never existed, insofar as humanity has always progressed by increasingly harnessing Nature to its needs and not the reverse.

"We intend to assess science's responsibilities and duties towards society as a whole.

"We do, however, forewarn the authorities in charge of our planet's destiny against decisions which are supported by pseudo-scientific arguments or false or irrelevant data.

"We draw everybody's attention to the absolute necessity of helping poor countries attain a level of sustainable development which matches that of the rest of the planet, protecting them from troubles and dangers stemming from developed nations...The greatest evils which stalk our Earth are ignorance and oppression, and not Science. Technology and Industry whose instruments, when adequately managed, are indispensable tools of a future shaped by Humanity overcoming overpopulations, starvation and worldwide diseases."

Vol. 4, No. 10 — October 1992

Catalysts

A catalyst is a substance that speeds up a chemical reaction without itself being consumed in the process. It emerges intact, ready to perform the same function over again. Life as we know it depends on biological catalysts known as "enzymes."

First conceived by the Swedish chemist Berzelius in 1835, this model suggests the role of money in our economy. We hear a great deal about the shortage of money due to our failure to save enough. Our economy indeed has been battered into a recession with high interest rates "to encourage savings." Instead what we got are more breadlines and bankruptcies.

The catalyst model suggests why. The catalyst is recovered only if the chemical reaction proceeds to completion. Similarly, the renewal of our money supply takes place only if the real economy completes its producing and marketing cycle and goes on to the next one.

In our day money consists mostly of debt. Undermine the production and marketing processes with high interest rates and good debt will become bad debt. Money is unable to complete its catalyst function. .

But where do we get the money to kick off this ongoing process? Doesn't that require savings? It does indeed, and the crucial part of such savings takes the form of the skills and education of the population, in the physical plant and infrastructures that make production possible. If these are at hand, credit can be created by banks against such security properly positioned for production.

Though the subject is taboo, banks do create money many times their capital or their cash reserves. And if they paint themselves into a corner where they cannot do the job, the government must do it. Whether it is prudent or imprudent will depend entirely on the real activity financed in this way. The amount of coin or bills accumulated in mattresses or tills has little to do with the matter.

William Krehm

On Mortgages and Futures

Should we mortgage our children's future? is one of the most overworked phrases of our day. It throws up a structure jerry-built with different buzzwords. For example, it is a bit cheeky for our government to bring up the word "mortgage" in connection with the federal debt. For "mortgage" means a loan secured by a capital asset, and the budgets both of Washington and Ottawa recognize no non-financial capital assets in the public sector. There is no way of fitting the mortgage concept to such a muddle.

The term "future" invites similar reflections.

The current article of faith is that everything in the economy should be left to the wisdom of the market. Market logic, but not market accountancy, is to be introduced into the public sector. This implies that society must dole out the amount of future it can afford. For the present value of a capital asset is appraised by discounting the expected income flow from it by the going rate of interest. The higher that rate, the sooner the future income discounts to practically zero.

Now the hitch here is that the rate of interest has become the militant arm of the central bank to enforce "zero inflation." Given the growing non-market components buried in our price index and mistaken for "inflation," that translates into a deflated economy.

And the deflated income flows from it are discounted at inflated interest rates to arrive at the present value of investments. Under these circumstances, we cannot undertake projects with long-term paybacks, public or private, because we will never get our investment back. No matter how much politicians may talk in favour of education, environmental cleanup and other motherhood issues, the projects are ruled out in advance. In a nutshell, we simply cannot afford survival.

Under the feudal system the church promised bliss in the after-life in return for submission to injustices in this fleeting existence. With the Communists a classless society stretched endlessly into the sunset. Central banks these days work to a similar blue-print. But since ours is not a theological age, they found it necessary to shrink the pain-period rather than stretch the reward to infinity. That, however, exposes the schedule to verification. It has not stood up well.

You can open up any paper these days and find dramatic debunking of our government's claim to be protecting our children's future.

The Globe and Mail (4/7) carries an article by Salom Alaton: 'The children are back and they are middle-aged.' "Recession and work restructuring have returned some of their grown children to their doorstep, just when the older people had reasonably felt their duties of parenting were completed. Alaton quotes Tom Camarella of the International Senior Citizens Association in Los Angeles: "The old days of raising children, having them go out and raise their children on their own, are gone. I've seen almost an explosion of older people having to take care, on a daily basis of young kids, and not just baby-sitting."

"There is another group that can claim an even tougher spot than the retirees helping out their children, and that's people in their fifties and sixties fighting to reach retirement while taking care of their children and their parents."

You can hardly put a price tag on the psychological damage to three generations. This then is the reality behind President Bush's code-word "family values."

The *G&M* (13/7) writes: "All over Toronto, younger and younger people are committing violent crimes." Then it goes on to report the hold-up of a pizza parlour by four kids aged nine to 15.

Shortly before the Democratic convention, we caught a TV interview with Mario Cuomo, governor of New York state. He cited the costs of keeping one person in prison: to build the cell $160,000; to keep a prisoner in it $30,000 per year. "For that we could send them to Harvard," was the way he summed up the situation.

Who then is mortgaging what future?

Vol. 4, No. 11 — November 1992

Confessional

Unburdening one's soul is a therapy practised by most faiths. In the Catholic Church the confession is received by a priest in the shades of a booth. Amongst evangelicals it may be proclaimed on the market square. With orthodox Jews the casting-off of sin is symbolized by pockets turned inside-out over flowing water.

But in all religions nothing less than full disclosure will do — that is the sense of "coming clean."

Such were the thoughts that raced through our minds as we read in *The Globe and Mail* (3/10) that "The BoC stunned the markets yesterday with a novel move designed to limit the rise in short-term interest rates. Just before 10 a.m., the BoC called a number of key money trading desks at banks and investment dealers offering to lend cash for one day at 7.62 — the same as Thursday's bank rate. Normally dealers would have to pay the rate for the central bank's overnight loans, which was then about 9%.

"By offering the dealers cheaper money, the Bank was effectively helping them buy bills and pushing up their price, which automatically reduces the yield on the bills."

Our first impulse was to welcome this undercutting of the bank's own official rate with tears of reconciliation. But suppose the repentance of the alcoholic were just a plot to finance his next binge? After all it was only a few months ago that Governor

Crow had involved our trusting Government in a carefully planned campaign to revise the *Bank of Canada Act* and our very Constitution to make price stability the only goal of our central bank. To their eternal credit the members of all three parties on the Banking Subcommittee of the Finance Committee joined to turn down the proposal.

But Crow has refused to take "no" for an answer. Having lost his costly gamble with the economy, Crow went so far as to propose a "compromise: he would forget about [his demand for] the independence of the BoC from the government in return for putting "zero inflation" into the Act.

That hardly suggests that the sinner has really given up the juice.

In *The Financial Post* (6/10) Greg Ip cites anonymous financial sources that see this "Psst, I can get it for you wholesale" innovation as the improvisation of a central bank surprised by "a combination of the C$'s collapse, teething troubles with the central bank's new chartered bank reserve management system and a chaotic treasury bill auction."

"Until last year, banks were required to keep a legislated percentage of their deposits at the BoC as reserves. Starting last fall, those required reserves are being phased out and the major lenders are being penalized instead for any (negative) "settlement balance" [in their daily cheque clearance].

To break the speculative freefall of the C$, the BoC intervened to force up the call rate charged by major financial institutions for one-day loans in the market. Its main way of doing this is by shifting federal government cash between its own books and those of the chartered banks. To ease rates it will shift cash from its books to the banks' accounts at the central bank, or effect a "redeposit." To raise rates, it will shift cash back to its own books from the banks," i.e. do a "drawdown."

"On Wednesday, call money had risen far more than the BoC expected. It made a massive redeposit to the banking system. Exactly how much is not clear but central bank figures show that while excess settlement balances had averaged $13 million to $53 million from August 20 to Sept. 30, on Sept. 30 along they stood at a colossal $881 million.

"But instead of dropping, the call loan rate remained between 8% and 10%. Why didn't call money fall? The direct clearers had almost $1 billion in cash sitting at the BoC earning no interest that they were not lending out, contrary to the system's objective. Observers suggest that either those with cash were holding out for better rates; or, the prospect of rates rising left some wanting a cushion against drawdowns that could leave them open to penalties from the BoC."

"That prompted the unprecedented phone call from the BoC to money market dealers offering call money at less than the prevailing overnight rate.

"But rates are now 200 basis points above their pre-crisis level and markets are extremely jittery."

Lucrative gambles in foreign exchange have become a major interest of our financial institutions. And, of course, so high-risk a game calls for substantial reserves. Our banks can't be bothered with prosaic loans to the producing economy.

Vol. 4, No. 12 — December 1992

Lame Duck

For the past five years we have been as an audience in the theatre of the absurd. For the one play in town, the cast wrote its own billing and doubled as claque and critic. Finally it climaxed with our modern Nero torching the theatre and taking a bloody toll of his public. And now, amidst the debris, he has donned a fireman's helmet and is taking his bow.

We refer, of course, to the Governor of the BoC, John Crow.

Some recognition of the extent of the centrally programmed disaster is creeping into the press. But our hero goes right on playing with matches, and indeed conspires to inscribe arson into the basic law of the land.

The moment business really starts recovering, Crow's militant buzzwords of 1988 will resound again throughout the land: "Shall we give up the fight against inflation just because the economy is depressed?" The world of finance has been severed from the real economy. There is a refusal even to consider how the rigged interest rates can fit into the Net Operating Income of firms or the economy as a whole. From the NOI, financing charges, corporation taxes and profits must be covered. If that can't be done, bankruptcy spreads like wildfire. The low prices rapped out by the liquidator's hammer have nothing to do with a victory over inflation. The victory is over the economy.

Meanwhile those interest rates have pushed up the exchange value of our dollar and made it impossible for our producers to meet competition at home or abroad. Yet our PM goes on talking about fundamentals being sound. All we lack is an economy.

That much is becoming apparent to the money traders who up to now have applauded Governor Crow for having delivered the country's wealth to their mercies. But when they sense that the real economy simply cannot come up with the exactions that our central bank has decreed on their behalf, they put sentiment aside and rush in to short our dollar.

These speculative games have bled the country white. John Crow has called all the turns and called them wrong. All the remains to him is a dwindling section of the media. *The Financial Post* (26/11) that walked the narrow path of piety for the past year has finally broken ranks once more. Editor Diane Francis wrote: "Crow's monetary policy is a dismal failure. For years now, Crow has tried to cure Canadians by force-feeding us with Bundesbank medicine. Nobody swallowed and now we are in a mess. Besides, who is Crow to defy the duly elected (if misguided) leaders of this country even if they mortgage away our future?"

There is no provision in our constitution for civil servants, especially eminently failed ones, to conduct international campaigns for their reappointment. It would be prudent for Crow to complete his contract with whatever grace a lame-duck incumbent can muster.

Who Is Crowding Out Whom?

Remember the refrain about government borrowing crowding out private firms on the money markets and driving up interest rates? Well, *The Wall Street Journal* (11/4) carried an article by Richard C. Breeden, chairman of the SEC and William M. Isaac, a former chairman of the FDIC, showing that it simply ain't so.

"In the 1970s the bank regulators from the industrialized nations formed a group — the Basel Committee — under the auspices of the Bank for International Settlements. The Basel Committee laboured during the 1970s and 1980s to produce a uniform standard for credit risk. The new rules required banks to maintain capital equal to 7.25% of business and most consumer loans, with the requirement increasing to 8% at the end of 1992.

"Other bank assets, such as single-family mortgage loans, were assigned lower capital requirements on the theory that they involved less risk. Government bonds were assigned a risk weighting of zero and therefore required no capital. Previous US capital rules required a fixed percentage of capital against all assets on their balance sheets, including government bonds."

Naturally this led bankers to load their portfolios with government bonds.

Though our bankers talk a great deal about the need to balance the budget and reduce the debt, they in fact are bedding down on the avails of the very situation they have been deploring.

Since the new rules went into effect in March 1989,US bank portfolios of government bonds have jumped 68% and their real estate loans by 27%. Their commercial loans, on the other hand, have fallen. Moreover, the gap between the banks' prime rate and their rate on commercial loans has widened.

Large industrial firms can cope with this bank bias by marketing corporate bonds and commercial paper. Smaller firms do not have this recourse.

But surely, you may object, banks *should* play it safe and put their clients' deposits in the most risk-free securities. There, in fact, is the rub. The orthodoxy beamed out of the Bank for International Settlements is that when prices start moving up again (and who can imagine a recovery where this does not happen?) the way to deal with it is to nip it in the bud with higher interest rates. That will find our cautious banks sitting on mountains of long-term bonds with modest coupons . They are in fact exposing themselves to an "interest risk" perhaps more devastating than the "credit risk" they hope to avoid by lightening up their business loans.

The Breeden-Isaac article, which a *WSJ* editorial commends to the new President, concludes with the following paragraph: "The risk-based capital rules were a mistake, and they should not have been adopted. Since the US regulators played a major role in leading other industrialized nations down this path, they should now take the lead in reversing this misguided policy."

wk

Vol. 5, No. 1 — January 1993

Hammerlock

The central fortress has fallen, and with it the port from which Governor Crow of the BoC launched a thousand leaky ships.

On October 26th, a *Globe and Mail* editorial in a heroic *non sequitur* had run up the Governor's Jolly Roger on its mast: "whether it knows it or not, the federal government has been given a mandate in this referendum. The Conservative Government is obliged, in the time it has left, to fulfill the electorate's preferred prescription of its duties. The Government should make good on its earlier promise, and entrench in law the BoC's one true mandate: to maintain a stable monetary standard." The government had actually received a thorough bashing in the constitutional referendum, and although it had originally proposed putting "zero inflation" in the constitution, the matter had been dropped for good enough cause, and nothing further had been heard about it.

And then on 11/12 there appeared a remarkable article by the *G&M*'s editor-in-chief William Thorsell: "Why have we paid so little attention to deflation, its risks and consequences? Because the intellectual priesthood of price stability has a hammerlock on public discourse. Indeed, the most powerful of the current crop of politically correct nostrums insists on the virtue of absolute price stability. There is 'zero tolerance' for anything but zero inflation in the thin-lipped halls of policy analysts these days. ... Our economy contains a deep structural bias against price decreases best addressed by the lubrication of low, stable inflation."

We congratulate Mr. Thorsell on his article, but it does leave us in suspense. For depending upon the follow-up or lack of it, he has said too much or not enough.

On the strength of that article the *G&M* owes its readers an immense catch-up on the economic information it has withheld from them over the years. Uttered by the editor-in-chief of Canada's National Newspaper, "the hammerlock on public discourse" is a most ticklish phrase. Can it mean the *G&M* and other papers are not edited by their editors-in-chief? And if so, who does apply the hammerlock?

Our minds reel with years of constitutional debate that have led nowhere. We have quite lost track of the number of charters to guarantee rights that have been proposed or actually exist. Despite these we now are informed that a faceless *somebody* put a hammerlock on information that has cost 11.8% of Canadians their livelihood.

Vol. 5, No. 2 — February 1993

Canada's Answer to Munchhausen

The Governor of the Bank of Canada is spending more of his time in foreign capitals taking bows for his having "licked inflation" back home. Is he attempting the ultimate in salesmanship — peddling to unsuspecting foreigners the culls that can no longer be sold at home? Or is he merely repaying an old debt to the land that gave us Munchausen, that delightful teller of tales taller than our bankrupt skyscrapers?

The Baron von Munchausen realised that the gullibility of his audience grew with the square of their distance from the settings of his stories. In keeping with this principle, Governor Crow has decided to work the Germans.

"The German business newspaper *Handelsblatt* reported last week that John Crow, governor of the Bank of Canada, had told it that the growing economic recovery in Canada means that there is no further need for interest rate cuts. Bankers and economists in Canada were scrambling for German-English dictionaries for a retranslation of the unusually blunt comments from Mr. Crow.

Along with New Zealand, Canada is being presented abroad as having put "zero inflation" and the independence of our central bank into the law of the land. The facts are different: last February the government's proposal to amend the *Bank of Canada Act* in this sense was turned down by a Parliamentary subcommittee.

The Globe and Mail (13/1) informs us: "Governor Crow had the satisfaction of advising former mentors yesterday when asked, in front of an audience of German financiers, what inflation-fighting advice he could give the Bundesbank?

"Hang in there," said Mr. Crow, with only a small smile playing at the corners of his mouth. "Be persistent!"

"It wasn't so long ago that Germany was giving lessons to the rest of the world on how to keep inflation in check, and Canada was one of many wayward pupils.."

"Now the roles are reversed. Canadian inflation is close to non-existent while German inflation is near 4%."

We have long known that Governor Crow sees the credibility of the central bank as the polar star around which the heavens turn. The trouble is that in his mind credibility is wholly a matter of what you can get away with.

Vol. 5, No. 3 — March 1993

Exit Danny Boy

It is by symbols that we live and die. In Orson Welles' *Citizen Kane* there was a rosebud. With Brian Mulroney it was an episode of early childhood. In Baie Comeau on the lower St. Lawrence his father worked as an electrician in a paper mill of *The Chicago Tribune*. And whenever Col. Robert McCormick, the *Tribune* owner, came to town, little Brian would be placed on a table to sing *Danny Boy* for him. Reward came in the form of a pat on the head and a dollar bill. In a sense Mulroney has never stopped singing *Danny Boy* in his rich baritone voice.

He has lived in the conviction that somewhere on high was a fount of certainties never to be questioned. As *The Globe and Mail* summed it up: "Scarcely a nickel could be placed between his government and the Business Council on National Issues, the big-business bullhorn."

One of the by-products of the arrangement was an honest ignorance on economic matters. If eternal truths are to be had over a telephone line, there is little need for curiosity.

Where Mulroney came to grief was that he encountered a far stronger personality of not dissimilar background. In 1988 he appointed John Crow as Governor of the Bank of Canada. Crow had put his native East End London behind with the upward mobility of an intercontinental rocket. Before landing in Canada he served his apprenticeship in the International Monetary Fund — with the decay of monarchies certainly the best place for cultivating imperial manners. Once at the head of the central bank, he set about compensating for the modesty of his Canadian base with an excess of zeal.

Though "zero inflation" was beamed out in all directions by the Bank for International Settlements in Basel, the various central banks imposed it with varying degrees of fanaticism. Crow was no man for compromises.

With God in his heaven, Mulroney was free to devote himself to other endeavours. Of Irish-French origins in small-town Quebec, he was drawn to constitutional reform to bridge the gulf between the two founding peoples. What escaped him was that there is little room for comity between various social and cultural groups in a shrinking economy. Instead, "leanness and meanness" became the norm.

His brief corporate experience had been as president of the branch plant of an American mining corporation, and prophetically enough it centred on the shutting down of its Canadian operation including the company town.

He loved being loved, and cut a figure on the international arena. There with fewer constraints than at home, he espoused humanitarian causes with high eloquence.

The media were force-fed by his government with reports of studies by dedicated rightist think-tanks quantifying the bliss that would ensue once the price index had been flattened. Less publicized studies calculated the increased unemployment needed to keep prices on the floor. Economists of investment houses prospering on BoC trading commissions were enlisted to testify that there was no recession and/or that recovery was underway. Meanwhile the economy was falling downstairs, picking up momentum as it hit each tread.

With a general election approaching, the polls showed the popularity of the Mulroney government down to 14%. Under such circumstances it is the practice of governments to lean on their central banks to loosen the credit noose. The procedure for doing that had been set down in the *Bank of Canada Act*. But leaning on John Crow was like leaning on a prickly cactus.

Pitiably, the PM told a journalist that his Finance Minister was spending more time with Crow than with his family. But that former used-car dealer was no match for the Governor. What emerged was a sweeping campaign to revise the *Bank of Canada Act* to establish the independence of the central bank and to declare the one goal of the BoC to be zero inflation. The parliamentary subcommittee that considered the proposals was unanimous in turning them down. The decision was not even mentioned in the press.

We still have not worked our way our way out from the depths of that humiliation. That appeared in the coverage of Mulroney's resignation. His failures and vanities were chewed over with a fulsomeness verging on sadism. The one omission was a mention of John Crow's contribution to the regime's disaster. High interest rates, when referred to, were treated as God-given, the inevitable consequences of foreign bondholders' ire over our deficit.

Vol. 5, No. 4 — April 1993

Time to Clean up the Kitchen

On the testimony of both kettle and pot, it is high time to clean up the kitchen.

With undisguised glee, *The Globe and Mail* (20/3) reported mutiny at *The Financial Post*. The writing staff protested against the free space given the Hees Edper empire to defend its operations. However, while kicking up its heels at the discomfiture of its rival, *G&M* was exposing its own soiled petticoats. The issue of press freedom has landed squarely on the table.

"The *FP* went to a daily format in 1988 with the avowed aim of beating the *G&M*'s 'Report on Business' at its own game. It painted the ROB as an anti-business paper.

"It was the ROB's relations with Edper, as much as anything, that were key to this perception. Senator Trevor Eyton, a key Edper executive, became so incensed about ROB coverage at one point that he reportedly leaned over to senior *Globe* figures at a party and told them to fix the *Globe* or sell it to him so that he could fix it."

The notion of Edper "fixing" a newspaper, except in the sense that stock markets and horse races are "fixed," is titillating.

Parlayed from a moderate fortune of the junior, less brilliant branch of the Bronfman family, the Edper empire has been creatively managed by a group of professionals. Its special culture calls to mind a militant monastic order. Executives' salaries are modest, but the company lent them the money to make obligatory purchases of company stock. For such an arrangement to work, the market for the shares had to do consistently well. Just as the Versailles fountains had need of unfailing water pressure to light up the glory of the Sun Monarch, so the well-being of the Edper empire depended on the constant upward spray of dividends from its resource, manufacturing, real estate and financial subsidiaries.

One might then assume that Edper would be acutely aware of the threat that the BoC's "zero inflation" kick represented both to itself and to the economy. Piety, however, goes with monastic orders and can get in the way of thought.

Edper's Trevor Eyton is top brass at the Business Council on National Issues, of which the *G&M* recently wrote: "Scarcely a nickel could be placed between the (Mulroney) government and the BCNI, the big-business bullhorn."

The *G&M* (29/3) reports $235.5 millions owed by 240 Edper executives, while the stock purchased with the loans may be worth 10% or less of the present loan value. Even if the loans were forgiven by the Edper companies, the amount of the gift would immediately become subject to capital gains tax.

The empire has been selling off its crown jewels, control of John Labatt, Royal Trustco, MacMillan Bloedel.

These are the gentlemen who have been instructing our Prime Minister on how to deal with deficits.

This raises a philosophical question: Is disinformation on the economy really helpful to business? The C.D. Howe Institute, for example, is a think-tank only in the sense that an abattoir could be described as a cattle firm — it slaughters thought and markets the carcass. The Institute has issued countless studies "proving" that once "inflation" is licked. a prosperous inflation-free future will stretch into the sunset.

The Edper companies have been prominent contributors to the C.D. Howe Institute.

Since their necks depend upon a buoyant stock market, the irascibility of its executives towards prying business reporters is understandable. "Ira Gluskin, president of an investment firm and author of a regular column in the *FP*, said that if anything the press has been far too gentle on [the Edper] conglomerate that has systematically mismanaged its empire. All of their annual reports and speeches have turned out not even to be garbage."

Correspondence — to Robert Heilbroner / from William Krehm

Dear Mr. Heilbroner:

I was intrigued that in your *Twenty-First Century Capitalism* you conclude that "from the imbalance" between the economy and the state there "emerges the risk of instability for which no remedy exists."

I have admired your eloquent championing of capital budgeting in the public sector. In fact [the introduction of capital budgeting] would merely be the first step towards setting up a rational framework for dealing with the problems closing in on us. You attribute the resistance to capital budgeting in the US to the difficulty of "a people still captivated by the romantic images of the frontier to exchange the values of cowboy society for those of a social-contract-minded society." But that is hardly the whole tale. Beneath the "bugaboo of the deficit" lurks the more basic bugaboo of "licking inflation" with high interest rates that in fact account for much of the deficit.

The use of the term "inflation" for any upward price movement ("too many dollars chasing too few goods") excludes the productivity of the public sector in an even more basic way than the absence of a public capital budget. For most of the output of the public sector is neither priced nor marketed, but is delivered as common services. Its cost is paid for by taxation that must show up as a layer of price. Market dealings in a mixed economy are in fact combined transactions: when we purchase a marketed good we make a non-discretionary payment for some of the public services that we enjoy.

There is no way of fitting this into the marginal utility model. Economists are not drilled to add up columns to arrive at a notion of what a feasible price-level may be. That is deduced in advance from the vision of a self-equilibrating market.

Thus as the environment is cleaned up the costs of the operation will show up in a higher price level. But that is not more "inflation," but less cancer.

Only one conclusion is possible: our misleading price index must be disaggregated to disclose which of several possible causes are responsible for a given price movement.

Turn this price disaggregation process around and you arrived at a properly structured model of price formation for a mixed economy. The market-driven cost components must be kept separate from those originating with government in other non-market areas. Each of these will behave according to its own code, but they will interact. As a first approximation they must be summed up to arrive at feasible prices. In this way we find ourselves summing up costs — a habit that businessmen have never abandoned. This brings us back to something structured not unlike the cost of production theory of value of John Stuart Mill, and one of the value theories used by Adam Smith.

It would reveal at a glance that using interest rates to fight inflation is profoundly destabilizing. For interest rates must fit within the Net Operating Income of both the firm and on a national scale. Yet the "zero inflation" doctrine in force sets no ceiling on how high interest rates may rise "to do the job." It preempts for lenders what social resources may exist for essential programs.

It is only in a prosperous economy that the ticklish problem of "transnational" relations could stand some chance of being managed. A fully employed economy would help make it possible for living standards in the Third World to move slowly in the direction of those in the First.

These days none of us can be wildly sanguine about humanity's prospects. Yet unless we complete the task of setting up a rational framework for assessing our problems, we have no right to declare them without remedy.

William Krehm

We have received the following reply from Mr. Heilbroner:

"Forgive a brief (because hurried and harried) answer to your nice and extremely interesting letter of March 12th. I am, as you have already anticipated, entirely in accord with you as regards the rationalization of the national income accounts which have become a kind of strait jacket on the formulation of national policy. All C (consumption) is deemed to be the same, although it ranges from education to golf club fees. All I (investment) is considered to be dynamic although it includes misinvestment; all G (government spending) is C; and any negative balance is considered to be a drain (like consumption), although it may include considerable imports of capital goods. Meanwhile, there is a great to-do over the "savings shortage," chargeable in considerable degree to these absurd aggregations. On top of which I find it hard to believe that the elemental lessons of Keynes have been so quickly forgotten.

I must say that economics as a whole takes something of a back seat as the political problems of the "New World Order" come boiling up. In the US edition of my *Twenty-First Century Capitalism* I have added a preface and a final chapter that try to put the economic trends into some perspective against these disconcerting events.

None of this belongs, I think, in *Economic Reform* — it is too hurried — but I'm glad you wrote and I expect that we will stay in touch.

Robert Heilbroner

Correspondence — from Alex Michalos / to *The Globe and Mail*

Alex Michalos sends us the following correspondence of the *Journal of Business Ethics* with *The Globe and Mail* which speaks for itself.

1/12/92

Duncan McMonagle

Globe and Mail, Toronto

Thank you for addressing my complaint about current *Globe* editorialists' practice. My complaint is simply that your writers have asserted in a variety of ways over some time that federal government spending requires government borrowing. Because this is false, I want them to stop making such assertions.

Enclosed are three articles in which the false assertion is made in different ways. The three specific sentences are:

1. "In the case of Canada, spending by government equals borrowing by government." (Cook, Nov. 16, p. B2)

2. "When the Mulroney government or the Clinton administration looks in the cupboard for 'new money' to stimulate the North American economies, they will find only borrowed monies." (Simpson, Nov. 17, p. A16)

3. "And, lest we forget: any money Ottawa lends is money Ottawa borrows." (Unsigned editorial, 23/11, p. A16)

Interested people can have a look at the fifth edition of *Economic Principles, Problems and Policies* (1990) by C. R. McConnell, S. L. Brue and W. H. Pope, chapters 23-30.

If the mistake had been made in a single article, it might have been corrected by publishing a brief correction. However, because the error seems to be a matter of "received doctrine" of several writers, a broader remedy is required. Perhaps a memo from you to your writers would suffice. That would not help all readers who have been misled to far, but it would be a good beginning. My main concern is to prevent your writers from continuing to pound a false idea into the heads of millions of Canadians.

As I indicated on the phone, there is no great rush for compliance with my request. But I do think that the sooner you put an end to the misinformation, the better off we will all be. I gather from my conversation with the secretary of the Ontario Press Council that it is standard practice for the Council to get involved only as an arbitrator in case we fail to reach a satisfactory agreement. That seems reasonable to me.

Alex Michalos

25/1/93
Colin McKenzie,
The Globe and Mail, Toronto

Further to my letter for Mr. McMonagle of Dec. 1, I noticed that the claim about federal government spending requiring government borrowing is still being made by *Globe* writers. For example:

1. "...there are only two ways a country can finance its excess spending. It can either borrow money from abroad or sell off assets to foreigners." (Little, Jan. 9, p. B21)

2. "This money, like all subsequent federal contributions, had to be borrowed." (Unsigned editorial, Jan. 19, p. A18)

3. "Governments, federal and provincial, are so burdened with indebtedness and deficits that they cannot easily find new money to throw at social problems. If they do, it is borrowed money, and must be paid back, increasingly to foreign lenders." (Simpson, 1/22)

These writers still show no appreciation of the possibility of the Bank of Canada's capacity to monetise much more of the government debt than it has been willing to do.

So, I still think it is important to stop this misinformation.

Alex Michalos

Vol. 5, No. 5 — May 1993

The Next Trip to the Vomitorium

Twice in a single decade our central banks have used higher interest rates to stabilize prices. Raise interest rates and you devalue existing assets with fixed returns. As their portfolios dropped in value our financial institutions became victims of a central bank that was supposed to protect them.

It was to help the banks recoup their losses that the Bank for International Settlements in 1988 announced a plan for making it no longer necessary for banks to keep reserves with their central banks. Such moneys, lodged with their central banks and earning them no interest, were released for profitable lending. [Editorial note: Though it seems that this was the original intention when the Risk-Based Capital Requirements guideline was drawn up, Canada was only one of three major countries that actually did away with reserves. Significantly the United States and Germany retained them.]

To replace the reserves, banks must now increase their capital in proportion to their new loans. Those proportions are set on a risk basis. Government bonds, judged risk-free, require no additional capital. Non-real-estate loans call for 8%. real-estate loans occupy the middle ground requiring 4 to 5% of the banks' own capital.

But no matter how sound government credit might be, the moment our central bank embarks on its next holy war to "lick inflation," all existing government bonds will plummet below their cost. Far from being "risk-free," in the world of "zero inflation" any fixed-rate security [considering the leverage with which banks can now acquire it for their portfolio] is a bit of a long shot.

The case of business loans will be even more traumatic. With the banks now enjoying far greater leverage in their acquisitions of government debt, they are less than enthusiastic about lending to business firms. Established clients are now treated like fledgling firms approaching venture capitalists. Not only are the banks demanding much higher rates, but fees and a piece of the action.

We hear a great deal about government borrowing "crowding out" the private sector. The real crowding out, however, stems from BIS regulations and in Canada the complete phasing out of statutory reserves. The picture is drawn in a recent article by John Rutledge in *Forbes* (26/4): "My first experience with the late unlamented credit crunch happened in April 1990 at a meeting between one of my corporate clients and his bankers. 'The Eighties are over,' the banker said 'We don't lend into the future any more.' Translation: The bank has reduced the company's working capital line below the level it needed to run its business. However, the banker had brought along his corporate finance man, who could lend us the same money the banker had just taken away, but as subordinated debt. Of course, he would need a much higher interest rate and an equity interest in the company to do it.

"On the street this is called vigorish. In rent-controlled neighborhoods, key money. Done at the point of a gun to a convenience store, it is called armed robbery."

"Banks are using their improved capital positions and enormous government security portfolios to finance aggressive lending campaigns." We are witnessing a feeding orgy of banks that will tax both their digestions and the ability of the real economy to sustain it.

To forestall the financial disaster ahead three measures are necessary: 1) the central banks must acquire the government securities issued to finance public capital projects; 2) central banks must repudiate manipulating interest rates to stabilize prices; 3) the reserve system must be brought back to control the solvency of commercial banks. With that in place all that would be necessary to curb any real inflationary threat would be to raise reserve requirements. That would rein in the amount of lending rather than raising interest rates.

Barring such measures to handle the bankers' next rush to the vomitorium, it will be prudent to have front-end loaders standing by. Mops alone will not be up to the job.

The Publisher

Casino

Forbes (29/3) carries an article by Robert Lenzner and William Heuslein, 'The Age of Digital Capitalism.' It tells of the revolution wrought by high-powered computers in the financial world. Trading in just stocks, bonds and mortgages is "for the fogies." The young super-achievers, backed by complex computer technologies, deal by preference in "derivatives." This "includes options, futures, synthetic securities and mortgage-backed securities that are entitled only to certain portions of the interest and principal thrown off a mortgage pool."

What the article omits, is that this proliferation of abstract financial instruments would have been unthinkable if monetarist policy had not introduced a shrieking pitch of risk into the economy. In fact the production of risk is coming to be the main output of the economy, with goods and services satisfying human needs reduced to little more than pegs on which to hang the risk on.

Without derivatives George Soros and other currency speculators could not have marshalled the buying power to overwhelm Europe's central banks last fall. Using derivatives, a legion of young money managers are surging to the fore, taking huge risks and earning almost incredible returns. Computers are a necessary but not sufficient condition for the changes in the securities business. The other half of the explanation lies in the increasing volatility in interest and exchange rates.

In that environment, essentially a by-product of monetarist "stabilization" practices, it has become impossible to operate many socially useful businesses without hedging against sudden shifts of interest and exchange rates. Oil refiners, for example, lay off the high risk of holding crude by buying oil futures and selling gasoline and heating oil futures.

These days a fixed-rate mortgage is carved up into its components as thoroughly as hogs in an abattoir. The various risk elements are sold to those seeking to hedge the risks in their conventional operations, or to speculators who live by risk.

But in a demented world such instruments are inevitably put to less commendable uses. "The German tax system rewards (German) investors for holding German stocks, while penalizing foreigners for holding the same shares." And yet there is a demand both within and outside Germany for international (equity) diversification. To circumvent that road bump the DAX 30 Index future has been set up in Frankfurt. German investors will buy German stocks that they may not wish to own apart from the tax advantage and then hedge away their equity position by shorting the Dax30 Index,

wk

Vol. 5, No. 6 — June 1993

Requiem for a Party?

The New Democratic Party has come upon evil days. When in 1991 the federal NDP fleetingly touched 41% in the opinion polls and its provincial organizations came to power in three provinces, it seemed that the millennium had a toe in the door. The very economic crisis that had lifted the NDP off the opposition benches bequeathed it a mountain of debt. The BoC's high-interest rate policy scheduled that debt to grow in hothouse splendour.

But to this the Ontario NDP Government added richly. No party can spend sixty years in opposition without piling up obligations. And mated with self-righteous loyalties, dogmas can be deadly.

Once in power the NDP ran headlong into the most formidable thought-control machine ever mounted in the Western world. Some day libraries will be filled by scholars plumbing the depth of the counter-revolution that began in the sixties. Initially it was plotted as old money's revenge for its humiliation when the government saved its neck at the price of its cherished prejudices.

By the late sixties a counterattack was underway to reclaim the bankers' ancestral fiefs. It embraced the universities and the media; it denatured our very language. Its command bunker was in the club of central bankers in Switzerland, the Bank for International Settlements. The NDP failed to appraise or challenge this grand push. It ended up accepting its buzzwords at face value.

Whatever their politics, Canadians owe the NDP a measure of respect. Its forerunner, the CCF, had challenged the indecency of the Great Depression. Much of what it had to say was later appropriated by the Liberals to give Canada its distinctive character as a caring society.

In the grand Disraeli tradition, the Liberals had stolen the NDP's bathing clothes. And now, as though to even the score, the NDP Ontario Government seems to have pinched the Progressive Conservatives' pin-striped suits.

Premier Bob Rae has simplified the art of governing to slashing government services "to lick the deficit." Yet in a depression there is no surer way of rendering an economy dysfunctional.

In 1933 the NDP's predecessor, the Co-operative Commonwealth Federation, had called for the 'socialization" of banking credit and the 'financial system.' And though that was vague enough, the realization that deflation and high real interest rates were ruining the country was there.

With an insight that politicians have still to pick up, William Greider in his *Secrets of the Temple* has remarked that the geological fault in modern society has come to run between lenders and borrowers. That calls for a revision of the traditional rhetoric of the NDP.

The unhappiness within the NDP came to a head when its financial critic in the federal parliament, Steven Langdon, attacked Ontario NDP premier Bob Rae's "very dangerous" policies of spending cuts in a recession. He branded it a betrayal of the party's tradition. Immediately the federal leader, Audrey McLaughlin, relieved Langdon of his position as financial critic.

In his day J.S. Woodsworth, the founding father of the CCF, had pronounced the party an "educational crusade." Rae's greatest sin has been his abandonment of that vision. Though his practical options were limited, he should have spoken out about the ruinous monetary policies of the central bank. The BoC, which has the money-creating powers in the land, is, of course, a federal institution. But article 18 of the *Bank of Canada Act* gives the provinces a vested interest in that institution. It authorizes the Bank to lend to the provincial governments or even against their guarantees.

That article is a key to lifting the country out of the depression. A bold policy of financing essential public infrastructures by the BoC would in effect be at token rates since the profits of the BoC revert to its owner, the federal government. That could open up a new dimension of understanding between Ottawa and the provinces to obviate the cuts in Canada's grants to the provinces. Ontario and the other provinces should be fighting like tigers against the attempt of the Ottawa to revise that Act to leave no other goal for the BoC than "zero inflation." Premier Rae's silence on the matter can be seen as legitimizing that plan.

Banking on the Brink

Financial deregulation was premised on the assumption that reduced regulation would provide increased market choices for large and small savers alike. Interest rate ceilings were the primary obstacle standing in the way of an unfettered free market.

Competitive forces, once unleashed, would bring higher returns to depositors as commercial banks, savings and loans, and credit unions found themselves in the same environment as previously unregulated money markets, such as Eurodollars and mutual funds. Higher interest rates on deposits would encourage private thrift and savings which, guided by an invisible hand, would flow into investment of new capital plant and equipment.

All this was fantasy. Increased interest rates to depositors meant more burdensome lending rates for public and private borrowers, particularly at a time when the total supply of credit was dogmatically restricted by the Fed.

By the end of his first administration, Ronald Reagan had succeeded in ratifying the most radical transformations of American banking since the New Deal: virtually all restrictions on the price of credit were abolished. By the end of Reagan's second term, the advocates of free market capitalism were relying on massive government interventions and a policy of financial bailout to safeguard the entire monetary payments system.

Once upon a time there was a banking crisis so severe that not a single bank was open for business in the entire country. This was the reality as F.D. Roosevelt took his first oath of office on March 4, 1933. The magnitude of the crisis presented policymakers with the opportunity for a major reform of banking.

Signed into law within days, the Emergency Banking Act of 1933 prohibited the payment of interest on demand deposits (checking accounts) and raised minimum capital requirements for federally-chartered banks. The Act also provided the statutory authority for the Federal Reserve Board to implement Regulation Q setting maximum interest rate ceilings payable on time deposits (such as savings accounts).

Underlying the reform was the perception that unrestrained competition had destroyed confidence in the entire banking industry. Throughout the 1920s, in an effort to attract funds, banks had bid up depository rates to excessive levels; "to cover the cost of these funds, the banks in turn were obliged to invest their resources on terms which sacrificed quality for yield." Note the strong similarity between the 1920s and the 1980s when once again banks "sacrificed asset quality for yield" in the form of junk bonds. A major factor in the 1930-33 wave of business failures, mortgage foreclosures and bank closings was the "competitive escalations of interest rates paid on deposits." which induced lenders to make riskier loans at higher interest rates.

For nearly a half century beginning in 1933, the depository interest rate ceilings under Regulation Q formed the basis of financial stability in the United States, allowing the banking system to expand credit without raising lending rates. Meanwhile, state usury laws limited interest rates on loans while providing banks with a comfortable margin for profit.

Banking became a conservative "3-6-3" business: bankers paid out 3% nominal interest to attract deposits, lent deposits out at 6%, and headed for the golf course at 3 in the afternoon. Prudence was valued more than risk, and competition for deposits was restricted to the provision of branches and other services, and offers of toasters.

From 1930 to 1933 more than 9000 commercial banks had failed, with devastating effect on the public's confidence in the entire system.; from 1934 to 1973 only 641 US banks were closed, an average of less than 17 a year.

Throughout the period, the Fed would make periodic adjustments to Regulation Q to achieve the conflicting policy objectives of "maximum employment, production, and purchasing power" embodied in the Employment Act of 1946. However, the intricate system of regulated depository rates depended upon the maintenance of low market interest rates to prevent depositors from withdrawing funds from banks and thrifts to invest in higher-yielding government securities or money-markets. This was at first achieved by the Fed's policy of "pegging" yields on government securities to levels below Regulation Q ceilings. During World War Two and for several years thereafter, the Federal Reserve supplied funds to anyone presenting government securities at pegged prices, which ranged from 3/8 of 1 percent on 90-day maturities to a top of 2 and ½ percent on 25-year Treasury bonds.

However, the Fed was anxious to end this low interest rate regime, particularly as mild price escalation drove the real interest rate to low and even negative levels. With the Federal Reserve-Treasury Accord of 1951, the Fed was finally freed from its pegging policy.

Over the course of the next three decades, real yields on government securities would rise steadily, and the Fed would face sustained lobbying from the banking industry to raise Regulation Q ceilings accordingly. The secular rise in interest rates would contribute to higher levels of both inflation and unemployment.

Interest rate ceilings were progressively relaxed as large institutional savers sought higher market yields by purchasing government debt or money market funds. The irony was that the Fed itself had brought this on by abdicating its policy of setting market interest rates at levels below the Regulation Q ceilings.

[Part II, from Vol. 5, No. 7, July 1993]

Any analysis of financial deregulation should include the influence of those foreign jurisdictions exempt from US taxation, security laws, reserve requirements and other regulations. Their competition poses myriad opportunities for corporations to engage in "regulatory arbitrage," playing one jurisdiction off against another to minimize the regulatory costs.

The same process developed in banking, where a "dual banking system" allowed private interests to shop around for the jurisdiction with the most relaxed regulatory environment. It was State bank regulation which was first to permit some of the most significant financial innovations of the 1970s, thereby undermining the federal regime of regulated interest rates.

US banks found themselves at a competitive disadvantage to offshore banks and offshore funds both in attracting deposits and booking loans.

Low and stable interest rates and the Bretton Woods system of fixed exchange rates had enabled the national government to regulate interest rate ceilings on existing money markets while impeding the development of high interest-bearing financial instruments. But as market interest rates rose above the level of US interest ceilings, and as cross-border financial flows expanded, large depositors could increasingly shop around for the highest returns. Regulators ratified the innovation "by raising interest rate ceilings on close substitutes offered by banks and thrifts."A Democratic administration and a Democratic Congress bowed to the pressures for financial deregulation. Policymakers were continually reminded that price inflation and market interest rates had both risen well above the ceilings imposed by Regulation Q.

Monetarism provided the theoretical justification for tight money and higher interest. The die was cast with Carter's 1979 appointment of Paul Volcker to head the Fed. For the first time in its history, the Fed would ignore the level of interest rates, opting instead to control the entire supply of credit to keep the volatile monetary aggregates M1 and M2 at doctrinaire levels.

Unfortunately, tight money was particularly inappropriate to deal with cost-push inflationary forces.

Throughout 1979 and 1980 US securities dealers invaded the markets for deposits by introducing the money market mutual fund (MMF) which offered many of the deposit services of banks without the costs of reserve requirements and federal deposit insurance. As market interest rates rose into double digits, deposits in money market mutual funds grew from $5 billion in early 1978 to over $40 billion by the end of 1979. Congress refused to bring the money market mutual fund under the authority of Regulation Q. Within months President Carter signed the Depository Institutions Deregulation and Monetary Control Act of 1980 (DIDMCA) which liberalized depository rate ceilings, preempted state usury ceilings on mortgage loans, and allowed depository institutions to offer negotiable order of withdrawal (NOW) accounts. The law of the jungle would uphold any interest rate agreed upon between borrowers and lender, regardless of their wide disparities in bargaining power.

As Ronald Reagan took office, the table was already set for a decisive assault on the New Deal regulatory framework. The administration's first great legislative success, the huge supply-side tax cut of 1981which disproportionately rewarded the highest income tax brackets, was soon overshadowed by deepening recession. With a prime lending rate over 15%, yields on government securities in the double digits, and inflation around 6%, regulators remained under the same pressures which had existed late in the Carter administration to relax and abolish the depository interest rate ceiling, or to extend Regulation Q to encompass mutual funds and other proliferating money substitutes. Congress chose the former. The *Garn-St. Germain Act* set a time table for all depository interest rates limits to expire in 1986. Wall St. could remain secure with the knowledge that the Fed remained in the hands of the "financial bankers" (as opposed to the "industrial capitalists").

Inflation was in the low single digits. But throughout the rest of the decade the real rate of interest (the nominal rate minus the inflation rate) remained at an all-time high.

In such an environment, money market mutual funds grew tremendously throughout the 1980s; from $40 billion in 1979 to $1.6 trillion by 1992. During these years, millions would lend their savings to the money market brokers at high interest, largely unconcerned that those same funds were often channelled into high risk junk bonds, for use in leveraged buyouts fuelling the stock market's rise, and for other speculative investments. Monetarism's high interest rates served as the reward not of effort or risk, but of wealth itself. Meanwhile the weaker members of society were locked in a stiff struggle for jobs, resources, business ownership, and expensive credit.

To cover the higher costs of funding, US banks began pursuing more aggressive lending policies in search of higher yields. Competition to make loans to gas, oil and coal producers became so intense that credit standards started to slip. The 1982 *Garn-*

St. Germain Act had raised the level of federal deposit insurance from $40,000 to $100,000 per account. To restore confidence in the entire system of monetary payments, the FDIC announced that it would insure even the uninsured (i.e. deposits over the $100,000 limit), while the Fed opened a $7.5 billion line of cheap credit to Continental Illinois. The bank was simply "too large to fail."

From 1942 to 1980, 198 US banks failed, but in 1987 alone, 184 banks failed. In 1989 and 1990, another 362 banks failed. With accrued interest burdens, stemming from high real interest rates, the expected costs of the bailout would exceed $1 trillion.

Timothy A. Canova
Adjunct Professor of International Trade and Finance
New College, Hofstra University, New York

Vol. 5, No. 7 — July 1993

The Magna Carta in the Age of Photo Opportunities

No sooner sworn in as the new Prime Minister, Kim Campbell announced "a new, lean, streamlined government more responsive to the real needs of Canadians."

At once this was expressed symbolically. "New cabinet ministers were advised that it might not look so hot if they pulled up at the front door of Rideau Hall in the traditional dark ministerial limousines. Instead, a line of taxis snaked its way up the long front driveway to the front portico where a pair of red-coated Mounties saluted the ministers-to-be." (*Globe and Mail* 26/6)

But the best symbols sometimes show a frumpy hem. "Some of the ministers gave the game away. They arrived in cabs, but had members of their families chauffeured to the Governor-General's residence in those same official cars that will be used to ferry minister around town when they are out of sight of the TV cameras."

There was a lot more than shiny limousines hidden in the bushes. The same *G&M* wrote that "recent polls have shown that the economic despair is focussed on a 11.4% static unemployment rate." Yet the freshly sworn-in Finance Minister, Gilles Loiselle, announced that "he is four-square behind the tough monetary policy of the BoC Governor John Crow. We have the lowest rate of inflation and the lowest interest rates in 20 years. That is wonderful."

At the outset of the campaign Ms. Campbell declared "for the independence of the Bank of Canada." Only once. In days of yore, knights swore fealty on bended knee to their liege a single time. But their oath was binding to the death.

Ms. Campbell's declaration of allegiance opened the coffers of the financial community and assured her election as PC head.

One of the great unadvertised discoveries of our day is that it is possible to undo the primacy of Parliament without bothering to repeal the Magna Carta. Leave Parliament its monopoly of taxing, but quietly drill holes in the government's strongbox, so that no matter what revenues come in, the coffer will stay empty or worse. Achieve that, and you have acquired sweeping powers for reshaping society.

As a sample take an editorial 'An Independent Fed' in *The Wall Street Journal* (10/6). "It is none too early for other vital institutions to demonstrate that they can continue to function whatever the confusion in the White House. Above all, it's time for the

Federal Reserve to affirm its vaunted independence. The early warning board on inflation has been lighting up, after all. Even as Clinton and Co. hash fiscal policy, the Fed can continue to do its job on monetary policy, provided, of course, that it is not conscripted into trying to cover the administration's fiscal errors."

In Canada, on the contrary, we have witnessed an uncharacteristic softening of utterance on the part of Governor John Crow. He has even agreed to meet with the provincial finance ministers (*Financial Post* 10/6). There has been no such gathering since 1982.

Crow's term as Governor expires next January, and he has been busy campaigning on several continents for another 7-year appointment. A federal election is coming up in the fall, and the unpopularity of the PCs is so great that the leading members of the cabinet almost without exception are not even seeking reelection.

Index-numbers

The Gross National Product came to us out of the loins of the Great Depression. Victory in World War II would have been unlikely had the Allies offered only a return to the pinched world of the thirties. Instead there was hope of a more egalitarian society best articulated by John Maynard Keynes. The Gross National Product statistic calibrated reality to that dream. It cut corners to focus on an overriding concern — enough aggregate demand to avoid depressions.

For there were few who did not fear that with the coming of peace we might reenter the thirties — a period that had acted out Carlyle's description of laissez-faire — anarchy plus a constable. Not many statisticians had been enlisted to keep the cop company on his beat. For lack of adequate statistics, we can assume that before World War II public expenditures nowhere exceeded the range of 10%-15% of total peacetime spending. Today in the advanced countries they make up anywhere from 40% to 60%.

Institutional channels for pumping up "aggregate demand" to deal with the Depression did not exist. To set the eardrums of the stone-deaf tingling, Keynes dreamt up outlandish projects to make the point that almost any alternative would be less costly than the forced idleness of millions. Digging up gold or even trash in one hole and burying it in another was only one example of this.

The most fateful defect of our statistics is their failure to sort out government investment from operational spending. In a sense it is a heritage of the Keynesian concern about aggregate demand. Both public and private spending do contribute to aggregate demand. But they influence the economy in different ways. That difference is becoming more important with each passing year.

After World War II new technologies, shelved during a decade and a half of denial, were incorporated into the civilian economy. The baby boom and mass immigration had to be housed in a new urban setting and educated to unprecedented standards. Much of this investment took place in the public sector where investment was not even acknowledged to exist. That seriously skewed the price index. A one-year write-off of an oil company's wells and refineries would drive the price of gasoline into the skies; treating public investment in this way would could only have a similar effect on prices. Incorrectly diagnosed as an overheated market, the chosen cure — high interest rates — did the rest. The age of double-digit inflation had arrived.

The financial community was uniquely elevated. The inflation of their income was proclaimed the cure, the deflation of the rest of the economy the goal. Few mortals benefiting from so smiling an arrangement could resist viewing it as a revealed religion. Not surprisingly, they dug in to defend their faith.

From a working statistic, the Consumer Price Index became a religious icon.

All that was lacking was a miracle. But miracles have their own drawback: they don't stand up well under rescheduling. Rain-checks, however, have become legal tender for promised blessings that fail to materialise.

Nor does it help much for the miracle-workers to blame 'world conditions' for bliss not crossing our doorstep. The most durable of these 'world conditions' has been the spread of the same bad monetary policy throughout the world.

Up to now this game was played in violation of the laws of the land. But now that the miracle has struck out, there is a scramble to proclaim the "independence" of central banks throughout the world. Mexico did so a month ago.

All this moves public spending for the unemployed into a different light. So long as reasonably full employment was the goal, it was possible to regard unemployment insurance as a current outlay. But with the new faith elevated to the state religion, such spending becomes as much an investment as life-boats on a ship or a fire protection system in a building.

The well-fed minority in the thirties were vocal in rejecting proposals for unemployment insurance. Yet a few years later we lacked men in good enough physical condition to fill the ranks of the army. We are heading today into a period of aging population. That will make us all the more dependent for survival on workers who are jobless today.

Mass unemployment ("the natural rate of unemployment") has become the hallmark of our future planned by our central bank. Rather than an enigma, our "jobless recovery" is in fact a program realised. In this age not even getting rid of trash comes without high costs. It is a dangerous illusion that throwing humans on the scrap heap is an economy.

k.

Vol. 5, No. 8 — August 1993

Goose Egg Gambit

In the little red schoolhouse of my remote childhood, a goose egg was the badge of shame. It could turn up on a test paper for one of two reasons: all the answers were wrong, or the scholar was caught cheating. If the little bounder cheated, however, he usually got some of the answers right.

This restriction no longer holds as the goose egg has become the icon in our public affairs.

That new style of score-keeping owes much to John Crow, Governor of the BoC. In February 1988 he launched "zero inflation" as a revealed religion. The slightest upward move of price was viewed like a touch of pregnancy which, neglected, could grow into a full man, who, moreover, might turn out a parricide.

So credit had to be tightened until eyeballs bulged and bones cracked. Such "short-term pain" was scant price for the "long-term gain" foretold. The trouble is that the promises of an imminent inflation-free prosperity have proved a pipe-dream. And meanwhile not only "zero inflation" but crates of other goose-eggs are being delivered by the truckload.

The Governor had obviously gotten his arithmetic wrong. But he has also cheated. The editorialist of *The Times-Colonist* of Victoria (3/7) cites an internal memo of Darryl Merrett of the BoC assessing a proposal by Doug Peters, formerly chief economist of the Toronto-Dominion Bank and now a federal Liberal candidate. Peters wrote: "Employing a million more Canadians (if the central bank lowered interest rates) would reduce unemployment insurance costs by $15 billion, and would probably generate another $5 to $7 billion in tax revenue."

On these proposals Merrett advised his boss: "Reducing this [1.6 million unemployed] by one million would take us well below the natural rate of unemployment."

The Times-Colonist comments: "These people ignore the personal pain and family dislocation of being unemployed." The pain and gain of which Crow spoke were in fact directed to different parties.

Hixson's Corner — The Fed's Deregulation of the Money Supply

The 1992 *Annual Report* of the Board of Governors of the USA Federal Reserve System reveals large management shortcomings of the control mechanisms.

For the period from the fourth quarter of 1991 to the fourth quarter of 1992 the Fed 'targeted" growth of the M-2 money supply at between 2.5 and 6.5 percent. Although the target in this case was about the size of a hay barn or an airplane hangar, the Fed missed it. Actual M-2 growth, by the Fed's own accounting, amounted to only about 1-3/4%.

For the same period the Fed targeted growth of M-3 of between 1.0 and 5.0%. One might think that a comfortably large target, but one would be wrong. Actual M-3 growth was 1/4 of 1% according to the Fed's *Report* but according to the *Survey of Current Business*, M-3 growth was -0.06%.

If you think these failures to hit oversized targets resulted in mass resignations from the Fed Board of Governors or the Fed Open Market Committee, reduction in salaries, or cancellation of juicy perks, guess again.

Looking backward a little we find that for the five years 1986-1990 inclusive, M-3 increased at an average annual rate of 6.8%. The increase was largely the result of private borrowing of money from "depository institutions" at an average "prime rate" of 9.3%. But after 1989 people and corporations showed increasingly less disposition to engage in borrowing the money newly created by banks that brings about increased M-3. Despite a fed-encouraged drop in the average prime rate from 9.3 to 8.4% in 1991, M-3 increased only 1.9%. Then a further reduction in the prime to a near 6.5% average in 1992 did not prevent more money being repaid than borrowed to present the decrease in M-3 bu 0.06%,1992 was the first year since 1960 and, I believe, even since 1948 that M-3 had a negative growth rate.

To encourage money supply growth the Fed had also stepped up the growth of the "adjusted monetary base" (MB). MB is "seed money" or "high-powered money" that enables banks to increase their reserves and then create "fractional reserve money." For the five years 1986-1990 the Fed increased MB an average of 7.5% annually. For 1991 the rate was jumped to 8.4% and for 1992 to a whopping 10.4%. For the first quarter of 1993 the Fed increased MB at the almost incredible annual rate of 26.9%. These are the amounts reported by the Fed's St. Louis District Bank.

The *Annual Report* has nothing to say about MB that I could find. The Fed has set no target for MB. This is especially interesting inasmuch as the Fed can control MB with pinpoint accuracy. This attractive opportunity was passed by because the Fed does not like to talk about its authority to create money, or why it creates so small a percentage of the total, or why it permits banks to create so large a percentage.

In addition the Fed has reduced the reserve requirements of banks to a new all-time low. Thus during 1991 and 1992 the Fed provided increasing enticements to bring the horse to water and make him drink — but the sluggishness of M-2 and M-3 persisted.

William F. Hixson

Vol. 5, No. 9 — September 1993

Smoking Guns

So pervasive is the unspoken agenda to turn back the world's clock, that its critics have been driven to specialisation. Some have concentrated on economic policy, others on the tax system, [still others on monetary policy]. The task will be made easier when we recognise the striking parallelisms in these areas. There is a smoking gun to be found in each of them — decisive evidence that has been removed from public view.

The *Bank of Canada Act* still preserves intact the powers that enabled Canada to pull herself out of the Great Depression and to finance her part in the Second World War. The Act enjoins the Bank to apply its powers to mitigate oscillations in employment, trade, prices and exchange rates. Disregarding that, Governor Crow has focussed his passion on keeping prices stable, employment and trade low and the exchange rate of our currency high.

There is a similar smoking gun on the tax front. It is the report of the Royal Commission headed by Kenneth Carter that completed its labours in 1967. I am indebted to Linda McQuaig's *Behind Closed Doors* for the following:

An American tax expert, Louis Eisenstein, in his *The Ideologies of Taxation* had penetrated the Olympic mists veiling tax theory: "Those who have less property have more votes. Since heads are to be counted, they must first be persuaded. Of course, if an ideology is to be effective, it must convey a vital sense of some immutable principle that rises majestically above partisan preferences."

From 18th century Britain Canada inherited the view: Property was like a tree and the income or rent or harvest was like its fruit. The tree must not be taxed since it was the source of future income. Only the income. But in the hurly-burly of modern finance, trees and much else can be flipped in a matter of days for fancy profits. Moreover, with capital gains (appreciation of the value of the tree) taxed at a lower rate, there was a great temptation to "strip profits" and escape taxation by disguising fruit as trunk and branches. Corporation dividends were taxed albeit at a lower level than salaries because taxes had already been paid by the corporation — in theory at least.

Proposals poured in from the business community to put an end to the questionable practice — not by taxing capital gains more highly, but by removing the tax from dividends. Since such solutions won't stand public scrutiny, strategists of the business community felt that the matter would better be entrusted to a Royal Commission. As chairman, a well-connected conservative accountant, Kenneth Carter, was chosen and as his deputy J. Harvey Perry, long director of the Tax Foundation and executive director of the Canadian Bankers' Association. As the commission opened its sessions, none of its leading members doubted that the Canadian tax system was basically fair.

But as the Commission delved into the evidence, that conviction crumbled. It concluded that there were no good reasons for exempting capital gains, or for giving preferred treatment to those whose income came from capital over those who laboured for theirs. Income was income, and a buck a buck.

The report shocked the conservative business community out of its socks. Carter was ostracised by his social circle. The government was made to feel the heat even more. So much so that the incoming Liberal Prime Minister, Lester Pearson, refused $50,000 to have the report published. At Harvard and other American universities the report overnight became "an underground classic" with 25 students sharing a single copy. A haunting legend it has remained to this day.

The fury of the counter-offensive by business lobbyists raised the fine act of tax-sheltering to new heights.

By deferring taxation in numerous ways devised by prospering tax-lawyers, billions of dollars of taxation have been kept indefinitely in limbo, often never to be paid. Neil Brooks, an Osgoode Hall tax specialist, has identified $8 billion that the federal government loses annually in tax shelters — over 25% of the perceived federal deficit.

In 1983 under the Scientific Research Tax Credit, a fast-talking artist might get a tax credit for any hare-brained "scientific scheme" amounting to 50% of his supposed project budget. This he might sell for cash forthwith to a corporation with taxes to pay, less a premium which motivated the corporation to choose this perfectly legal route. He distributed fat fees to brokers and lawyers, and then could invest only a small portion of the remainder in mortgaged real estate to house the "research." This could leave Ottawa with a massive loss of revenue and scant likelihood that a single cent would be applied to scientific research. Many of these "scientific entrepreneurs" ended up in prison or in foreign havens having no extradition treaties with Canada.

"Tax credits" lavished irresponsibly are not identified in the public mind with shelling out public monies. The involved vocabulary of tax law warns off lay curiosity as effectively as an appropriate spray does unfriendly dogs. In this there is a perfect parallel to the mysteries of money creation. The two, moreover, interlock to assure the ransacking of the public treasury.

Were these twin raids on the public treasury stopped, [and proper accountancy introduced into government affairs], there would be no deficit problem. But that approach is not even raised in the high-pressured debate on the deficit that dominates our political scene.

wk

Greenspan's Retooling of Monetary Policy

At his appearance before the Senate Banking Committee on July 24, 1993, Alan Greenspan indicated that the Federal Reserve would stop relying on money supply growth (specifically M-2) in policy decisions. His reasoning involved the supposed shift out of savings and checking accounts to mutual funds, which are not included in M-2. If this explained the unreliability of money supply growth in predicting overall growth and/or inflation, one wonders why not just include mutual funds in measuring money supply?

To understand the importance of such questions, we must review what has been happening during the past 15 years. The key event was President Carter's appointment of Paul Volcker as Chairman of the Fed in 1979. From Volcker's recent book (*Changing Fortunes*, 1992), we learn the origins of the recently abandoned reliance on money supply growth, rather than the previous policy of watching nominal interest rates.

After Volcker's appointment, he and his predecessor, William Miller, attended a meeting of the International Monetary Fund in Belgrade. Leaving Miller to give the Plenum speech defending US policy, Volcker rushed back to Washington, stopping in Hamburg en route for talks with Helmut Schmidt and Otmar Emminger, President of the West German Bundesbank.

Schmidt and Emminger evidently gave him courage to "bite the bullet" on fighting inflation, something that Milton Friedman and von Hayek had been advocating for some time. With much fanfare, Volcker declared himself a Friedmanite and announced that he would henceforth concentrate on money supply growth and let interest rates soar, if necessary.

This he did and eventually produced what Schmidt referred to as "the highest interest rates since the birth of Christ."

The soaring nominal interest rates produced the highest real (or inflation-adjusted) interest rates since the early thirties. They account for the large passive deficits — non-inflationary deficits coming from the revenue side of the budget — and unprecedented growth of the national debt under Reagan and Bush.

By 1984 it was apparent that something was wrong with Friedman's paradigm. Earlier in the year he had predicted that there would be double-digit inflation by the end of the year because of the large jump in the money supply in 1983. When in fact, the inflation rate had dropped to under five percent by the year-end, Friedman was forced to "eat crow" on TV in 1985.

Volcker's successor since 1987, Alan Greenspan, was even more of an ideologue when it came to fighting inflation. Like his Canadian counterpart, John Crow, Greenspan is a great believer in the possibility of achieving "zero inflation" and he has constantly lowered the goals for money supply growth.

During recent hearings before the Senate Banking Committee — required every six months by the Humphrey-Hawkins Act of 1978 — Greenspan was subjected to critical grilling both by Chairman Donald Riegle and member Paul Sarbanes, Deputy Chairman of the Joint Economic Committee and its most knowledgeable member. Why has he allowed the money supply growth to fall short of his stated goals, and why have his predictions on the economy had such a positive spin and a poor record?

As the anti-monetarist hounds closed in, Greenspan confounded his critics with the announcement that he would begin to pay attention to real interest rates. Sarbanes in particular had been pressing that on him.

Greenspan now claims that the real interest rate is zero or negative, focussing on the Fed Funds rate, the rate at which bankers lend money to one another overnight. As some of his critics pointed out, the real interest rate on consumer credit is close to 15%. Which rate is it appropriate to concentrate on?

In my view, we should look at the record of real rates summarized by the late Sidney Homer's *A History of Interest Rates*, 3rd edition, 1991, revised by Richard Sylla. This edition, by the way, is the first to even deal with real rates.

Using Moody's AAA bonds as guide and estimating expected inflation on the basis of the seven previous years, Sylla calculated that the average real rate for the eighties was 4.7%. In the 70s it was 2.3% and in the sixties 3.2%. In the forties and fifties, the average real rates were negative.

Since 1989 the average real interest rate has been running around 4% higher than in the seventies, but slightly lower than in the sixties. However, if we assume that the Consumers' Price Index in the nineties has an upward bias due to the continued use of a 1982 basket of goods and services, there is very little differences between today and the 1960s.

The debt overhang from the 80s, when there were those astronomically high real interest rates, increased the cost of servicing this debt and contributes to the continued stagnation in the 1990s.

In the 1992 *Economic Report of the President*, Michael Boskin, CEA Chairman, admitted in a similar vein that "currently, real short-term rates are higher than they have been during many comparable periods in the past."

The 1993 *Economic Report of the President* pointed our that the destruction by Hurricane Andrew put upward pressure on real rates as firms and households sought funding to rebuild the damage. The same might be expected from the recent Midwest floods. How will Greenspan react to any upward tick in the CPI as a result of the destruction?

Alan Greenspan is opening a Pandora's box in shifting emphasis to real interest rates. No longer will it be possible to state that "interest rates have fallen to their lowest level in twenty years." When the history of Reaganomics is finally written, the longest period of high real interest rates will surely be recognised as a key factor. Likewise the continued import surplus can be attributed to the overvalued dollar that arose initially from high real interest rates.

Lynn Turgeon
Professor Emeritus of Economics
Hofstra University

Back at the Starting Gate

For an adequate analogy with the nightmare of our financial system, we must reach to the masterpieces of Russian 19th century literature. At Baden Baden the roulette wheel spins ever more madly in an alcoholic mist. The next morning our hero, without quite understanding how or why, awakes to find that he has gambled away the family estate of thousands of souls.

ER has repeatedly emphasised the seismic effects of using high interest rates to stabilise the economy. Those rates come to lead a magic life of their own., ordaining mass transfers of wealth that exceed what is produced. The widening cleft between the fictitious and real worlds offers climactic gains to the more perceptive buccaneers. They draw courage from the very mind-control that has blinded central bankers and right-thinking investors from grasping the vulnerability of the system. And when the time is ripe, they move in with murderous leverage made possible by computer technology. Instead of operating with real money, they work with its merest fragrance — with derivatives that allow them to outgun the central banks.

When they decide that a currency like a hot-air balloon has lost all contact with the terrestrial economy, they buy options to sell the currency away below its trading price.

Because it is so far below that range ("out of the money") they can buy such options ("puts") for a song. They can afford to leverage them by as much as 1000:1. But to counteract that pressure on its currency, the besieged central bank must put out dollar for dollar in foreign currency to support its own currency at an unsupportable level. When it finally throws in the sponge, it is left with a pile of its own currency that has shed ten or twenty percent of its value.

The Wall Street Journal (22/7) informs us that "international bankers made public their campaign to head off government controls on the arcane but lucrative business of trading derivatives. The bankers acknowledge shortcomings in current methods of managing and disclosing the risk of derivatives, but argue for a set of standard practices that would allow major players in this more than $6 trillion global market to police themselves." The study cites "senior managers' concerns that they don't know enough about derivatives and might be 'over-reliant' on a few specialists."

Remember the S&L scandals and the other fruits of deregulation? We are back at the starting gate. But the stakes are higher, the track more slippery, and the nags are doped.

k

Hixson's Corner — The 1993 Budget Debate

After weeks of posturing by both advocates and opponents, the 1993 Budget Bill passed the USA House of Representatives 218 to 216 and the Senate by 51 to 50. Though the media hoopla was designed to make it appear "the battle of the century," the debate was, in fact, "much to do about nothing."

Budget bills always contain many "iffy" assumptions about the rate of growth of the economy, the level of interest rates, and so on, that getting very excited about them is a sign of mild mental illness. The last big "budget battle" was under Bush in 1990. How significant it actually was is suggested by a quote from *The Washington Post* (7/26/93).

"In the warm afterglow of the 1990 budget summit agreement, the Congressional Budget Office estimated this year's deficit would be $170 billion. This January, however, the CBO revised the estimate to $302 billion."

There is little reason to have much more confidence in the prediction of the 1993 Budget Bill for 1996 and beyond. Budget Bill debates need to be classified under the head "games people play" to keep people's minds off the real issues.

The focus of the 1993 Budget Bill debate was on "the deficit." The hocus-pocus was to make appear all-important the "on-budget deficit"whereas what is really significant is the sum of the "on-budget deficit" and the "off-budget deficit" — the "total deficit."

What's at issue is shown by the following table for the Bush years (in billions):

US budget deficit, Bush years 1989-1992

	On-Budget	Off-Budget	Total
1989	$144.7	152.6	$297.3
1990	238.7	175.9	$414.6
1991	292.0	136.3	$428.3
1992	303.8	167.3	$471.1
TOTAL	$979.2	$632.1	$1611.3

Here we see that the on-budget deficit constitutes only about 3/5ths of "the total deficit problem" and that even if the on-budget deficit had been reduced to zero, the total deficit would have still increased in four years by $632.1 billion.

The largest component of the off-budget deficit is money for the bailout of failed banks and savings and loan associations — the result of de-regulation of financial institutions, larger federal guarantees of deposits, and the Federal Reserve doctrine that dozens of debilitated banks are "too large to fail." Neither Democrats nor Republicans are eager to keep recalling this scandal to the attention of the public. Hence the bailout is placed off-budget.

The unwillingness of all parties to grapple with the real issues is further manifested by the absence of any discussion of the importance of accepting the universal practice of businesses and placing operating expenses in an operating budget and capital expenditures in a capital budget. The warped perspective of all parties is further indicated by their making a deficit of less than 10 percent of GNP sound all-important whereas in the 1940s deficits of near 30 percent of GNP caused no furor at all.

The aura of flim-flam surround the Clinton Administration's acceptance of "the deficit" as the crucial issue of 1993 was heightened by its failure to raise two other important issues to the top of the agenda.

First, the Administration seemingly has no plan to disaggregate the Consumer Price Index and stop the Fed from raising interest rates every time there is an uptick in the CPI.

Floods in the Midwest are likely to raise food prices and the Fed is likely, in consequence, to raise interest rates. How silly it would be to tolerate such a reaction is apparently not yet understood by the Administration. In this context we must also note that in an astounding burst of optimism, the Budget Bill projects $65 billion in savings over previous estimates for 1993-1997 in interest on the federal debt. This involves some unrealistic guesses about the future level of interest rates.

Second, Clinton has made no proposal to slow the growth of the debt by having the government create more money and simultaneously slow the rate at which commercial banks create money that the government borrows from them. Clinton accepts the myth that the only way to slow debt growth is by higher taxes or lowering spending.

There are, however, some positive things to be said about Clinton's proposals and certain features of the 1993 Budget Bill. The thrust of taxation laws under Reagan and Bush was to shift the burden from high earners to low earners. One of Clinton's proposals was to raise the top marginal rate on individual incomes. Another proposal was to increase the rate on coporations by a percent or two. Another was to increase the amount of income subject to the medicare tax — to see that high-income earners paid at the same rate as low-income earners. Still another was to exempt from taxation less of the social security payments received by persons with large incomes from other sources. In addition to these moves taxing higher incomes, Clinton proposed an earned income tax credit (EITC) designed to lift "the working poor" above the poverty level.

Taken together these proposals have two aspects. First and properly, they were designed to reverse the thrust of taxation changes during the previous twelve years. Second and deplorably, they amounted to only a piddling move in the right direction.

Under Reagan the highest marginal income tax rate was reduced from 70 to 30 percent. Clinton proposed to raise this rate to a still modest 40 percent. To get the Budget Bill passed, Clinton had to permit his original modest proposals to be whittled away. Even then the Bill was passed by the narrowest of margins.

Though Eisenhower, Nixon and Ford all submitted budgets calling for the 70 percent marginal rate on high incomes, Republicans pretended to be appalled at Clinton's proposed 40 percent rate. Nearly a fifth of the Democrats in the House and more than a tenth in the Senate deserted Clinton in the vote on the whittled-down bill. The much vaunted "checks and balances" built into the USA's political system make it almost impossible to govern.

William F. Hixson

Vol. 5, No. 10 — October 1993

Government by Panic

If we may borrow from the late Sam Goldwyn, our new PM's "inclusive style of politics" "includes us out."

While vowing to kill the deficit within five years Ms. Campbell declines to say what she will cut because "there is no one consistent set of bookkeeping standards within the government." If she goes into federal bookkeeping a bit further, she may come upon far more astounding discoveries. For example, that Ottawa treats its acquisitions of land, buildings and equipment in exactly the same way as it does the replacement of toilet paper — as an operating expense written off in a single year. Private firms with such accountancy would go belly-up within a year. Accordingly, Ms. Campbell's chatter about the deficit has as much substance as her claim to knowing Russian and Yiddish.

The truth is that we have entered an era of Government by Panic. First it was "Inflation is Our #1 Enemy," and now when that policy has reduced government finances to a shambles, it is the Deficit.

Canadians are just beginning to rediscover the costly lesson of the thirties: cutting government services in a recession can only lead to a further collapse of both the economy and state revenues. *The Financial Post* (11/9) reports that for April-July of the current year the deficit is $2,934 million above $15,996 million for the same period last year. Job creation has been half of what was forecast.

Ms. Campbell declares there will be no improvement of the job situation until the year 2000, but the grim symbolism of that date escapes her. That would bring the duration of our economic slump to a full decade, exactly that of the Depression that led the world into the Second World War.

In *The Financial Post* (18/9) David Gillen writes: "With Britain mired in recession, yet obliged to peg the pound closely to the other European currencies, selling pounds had meant easy money for traders and punishingly high interest rate for British businesses. Finally, on September 16, 1992, a humiliated British government was forced to abandon Europe's Exchange Rate Mechanism.

"The pound promptly tumbled about 20% against other European currencies. A year later, PM John Major's ERM failure looks like his biggest economic success. The devaluation of the pound and the subsequent slide in British interest rates have pulled the economy out of one of its longest slumps since the 1930s. The British Treasury [is] $20 billion poorer because of its earlier efforts to support the pound."

"The Bank's base lending rates [were] sliced to a 15-year low of 6% from 10% last September, industrial production was up 3.2%. Unemployment declined for five straight months. Now manufacturers are using a weaker pound and lower rates to carve a bigger slice of European markets."

You might imagine that Ms. Campbell, so concerned with deficits, would be asking what the attempts of the BoC to maintain our dollar at artificial levels have cost the taxpayer. The figure for September-October 1992 alone must have been in the $4,000 million region. Our dollar had been pushed from below 79 US cents in 1986 to just over 87 cents.

Presenting John Crow's Boss

"Kim Campbell has declined to explain just what she meant when she promised to make the BoC more independent." (*G&M* 8/4)

Let us fill that information gap. One thing that independence of the BoC does not mean is freeing it from the dictates of the Bank for International Settlements. Let us then turn to a scholarly work to learn something of that institution: Henry H. Schloss, *The Bank for International Settlements* (New York University, 1970).

The BIS was set up in 1930 to manage the transfer of Germany's reparation payments to the victors of the First World War. BIS shareholders were to consist entirely of central banks, but because the US Federal Reserve was unwilling to participate, a syndicate of American commercial banks (J. P. Morgan & Company, the First National Bank of New York, and the First National Bank of Chicago) took up the United States subscription.

The shareholders and members of the BIS are *central banks* rather than governments as is the case with the International Monetary Fund and the World Bank founded towards the end of World War II.

The BIS voting rights are permanently reserved to the original members in proportions to the shares *originally* subscribed by them, even though they may have sold some of their shares in the interim. BIS seems allergic to anything remotely smacking of democracy.

"The purpose and functions of the IMF are widely known, while those of the BIS remain somewhat clouded and mysterious. ... To safeguard the 'independence' of BIS, a director of BIS shall not be an official of a government or a member of a legislative body, unless he is governor of the central bank. It is this provision that gives the Bank its characteristic as a central bankers' organisation, and it has jealously guarded itself against the intrustion of government officials."

"One of the major stigmas attached to the reputation of the Bank in the 1940s was a widespread feeling that it had been pro-German during the interwar period and collaborated and appeased Germany in the 1930s and during the war. In fact, the charge of collaboration with the Axis was an important reason why the BIS was not transformed into the preeminent international monetary institution in the early postwar period and a new International Monetary Fund was created instead.

"These charges of collaboration by the Bank have been investigated in considerable detail by the author. The Bank may have been guilty of appeasement *in the late 1930s*. But the charges of pro-German conduct by the Bank *during the war* are essentially unfounded." [More recently the question has been raised about the BIS's role in handling gold extracted from concentration camp inmates during the war.]

At the Bretton Woods Conference a resolution was passed recommending the liquidation of the Bank at the earliest possible moment. But by 1951 the dissolution of BIS was a dead issue.

By then banks were well advanced towards recapturing the positions surrendered during the Depression. "In March 1951 President Truman assented to a negotiated settlement between the Treasury and the central bank agreeing to slightly higher rates and granting minor flexibility to the Fed. Within two years, however, Fed officials claimed a more sweeping interpretation of the Treasury-Fed agreement. It was, they attested, a declaration of full independence for the central bank. By that point, the liberal Democrats were gone from the White House." Central banks on the comeback trail had need for an international bunker. BIS filled the bill.

And it is in that bunker that much of Canada's future has been determined. That appears from the annual report of the BIS General Manager, Alexandre Lamfalussy, delivered in Basel on May 23, 1991:

"It has been argued that a quality bias in price level calculations implies that inflation in the range of 1-2% may be considered price stability for all practical purposes. Nonetheless, the move from an environment of low or moderate inflation to one of no inflation implies an important psychological shift. It has proved very difficult in recent decades to do better than achieve merely low inflation and to move to actual price stability, even in those countries with the best price performance.

"From all this it must be clear why central banks — even if they enjoy full independence from governments — find it difficult to pursue the objective of absolute price stability. An obvious condition is a sufficient degree of social consensus, since in a world in which unavoidable price increases need to be offset by price declines, the consequences will be felt very differently by different social groups."

In short, as we have long maintained, "the short-term pain" and the promised "long-term gain" are directed to different people. "But would such a pessimistic conclusion be justified? Perhaps not; several developments, with converging lessons, provide a ray of hope. As the environmental debate illustrates, it is by no means impossible to convince large segments of the population that the systematic undervaluation of future interests needs to be corrected. Something similar has also happened with the public perception of the need to combat inflation...."

In actual fact, environmental clean-up and "zero inflation" rather than converge are irreconcilable. Clean up the environment and the costs of the operation must show up in a higher price level.

Mr. Lamfalussy concluded: "Even more relevant is the behaviour of bond markets. Operators in this market have worldwide acquired a much longer time-horizon with a strong, well-founded interest in the future course of inflation. They are able to deliver a more convincing message to all policy-makers on the appropriateness of monetary policy than any academic speculation regarding the tolerable level of inflation."

That lets the cat out of the bag. Now you know why our media are more and more given to quoting economists from brokerage houses as the "consensus of science" — and why these economists have already proposed the canonisation of John Crow.

William Krehm

Latest Gift from the Bank for International Settlements

The following extract from Canada's statutes does not make easy reading. Yet you had better get to know it. It could cost you your job a few years down the line.

Subsection (4) of Section 457 of Chapter 46 of the Statutes of Canada 1991 phases out the requirement for our chartered bank to maintain reserves with the Bank of Canada.

"On the first day of the first month following the months this section comes into force, the primary reserve referred to in subsection (2) shall be reduced to 3 percent, and thereafter on the first day of the first month of each of the next three succeeding three-month periods, the primary reserve as modified by this subsection shall be reduced by 3 per cent, and on the first day of the twenty-fifth month following the month in which this section comes into force, the primary reserve referred to in subsection (1) shall be nil."

[That bit of bureaucratic gobbledygook finally snuffed out the statutory reserves that our banks had to put up with the BoC. These earned them no interest and had already been whittled down from 10% in legal tender, plus 8% in government debt to less than 4% in legal tender to help bail our banks during the preceding decades.]

A Comparison

From time to time we are asked why we direct so much attention to John Crow, Governor of the Bank of Canada. Would it not be better to leave personalities out of the discussion, and confine ourselves to issues? Our difficulty, however, is that, largely as a result of Mr. Crow's zeal, we have been allowed little serious discussion of monetary policy. The moment Mr. Crow observes the behaviour proper for a civil servant, we will be happy to adopt a more impersonal tone.

To illustrate the point we need only compare Mr. Crow's style with the forthcoming testimony of Graham Towers, the first Governor of the BoC, before the Subcommittee on Banking and Commerce in 1939.

Q: But there is no question about it that banks do create the medium of exchange?

A: (Mr. Towers) That is right...That is banking business just in the same way that a steel plant makes steel. (p. 287)

Q: 95% of all our volume of business is being done with what we call exchange of bank deposits — that is simply bookkeeping entries in banks against which people write cheques?

A: That is a fair statement. (p. 223)

On essential infrastructural projects to pull the country out of the Depression:

Mr. Towers: "The real cost of government expenditure to the country as a whole is the amount of labour and equipment required to carry out the various projects. When the question is asked if we can finance a certain government expenditure, the fundamental problem is whether we can afford to devote a certain amount of our productive resources to the projects in question.

How the government can obtain the money that will give it title to the use of the labour and equipment may present considerable technical difficulties, but it is not the fundamental problem."

In some respects Graham Towers did hold the views of bankers of his day. Though the *Bank Act* set a 5% minimum reserve of the chartered banks' deposits to be held as reserves with the central bank, in practice 10% was required. This effectively cut the credit which could be created by the banks from $2.9 billion to half that amount.

Q: (McGreer) In the event of our being called upon to defend ourselves in a world war, surely that $2,920 million would be available to Finance defence? (p. 140)

A: I should regret that thought. After all, we will recall that what is wanted in the way of defence are men and materials. In the last war the citizens of the country as a whole, being producers, had the wherewithal to pay the war costs each day. But it was not possible to get from the people in taxation sufficient to cover the war.

[It was a bizarre notion that financing the war entirely by taxation might be possible.]

Q: Today we have under our monetary system the means of increasing our bank deposits from $2.5 to $5.4 billions.

A: Oh, far more than that.

Q: I mean to say on the reserves of cash the banks have.

A: Yes we can add to the excess reserves at any time: the sky is the limit.

Q: In any event, we can double, under our laws, the reserve of cash the banks now hold, our bank deposits which we use as 95% of our medium of exchange money?

A: Providing the banks are willing to do it. Yes.

Q: Parliament has given them the power?

A: Yes...The sequence is better if we said a possible increase of the $10.7 billion. If that is superimposed on existing deposits, the total deposits of the Canadian people would be $13.2 billion.

Q: Will you agree with me that of the great changes in monetary practice over the last 20 years, one of them has been the (creation) of a banking system that can supply an abundance of money.

A: Potentially.

Q: In other words, we have provided the means of supplying considerably more than $10 billion of bank deposit money?

A: Yes.

Q: Now, Mr. Towers, would you tell me why, when parliament has created an abundance of money..

Mr. Towers: the means...

Mr. McGreer: Created the means of supplying such an abundance, why our national government, our provincial governments, and our municipal governments are unable to Finance the progress of the Dominion of Canada without resorting to burdensome and confiscatory taxation?

A: Parliament, as far as I know, has never said that it considered money as wealth, nor that by issuing another $ 10 M (sic) the best interest of the country would be served. Should parliament decide otherwise, parliament would do so, no doubt.

Q: You are conversant with the preamble of this act which declares: it is desirable to establish a central bank in Canada to regulate credit and currency... to control and protect the external value of the monetary unit and to mitigate within the scope of monetary action, and generally the economic and financial welfare of the Dominion.

A: So far as may be possible within the scope of monetary action.

Q: Agreed. We are not dealing with tariffs or a thousand and one non-monetary factors. We are dealing only with the creation, issue and circulation of money?

A: Yes.

What distinguished Mr. Towers from his current successor was his open mind. And when the country was once more plunged into war, he was patriot enough to set aside the prejudices of his profession and release the slumbering potential of the country for its defence.

Marvels of the Free Market

Recently we chanced upon a remarkable discussion on Jesse Jackson's TV program *Both Sides* on aid to the Mississippi flood victims. Taking part were the governor of Iowa, a couple of the victims, and a gentleman from the Cato Institute. The last is a think-tank which must have Attila the Hun as its honorary chairman.

The Iowans described the plight of the flood victims, their houses, crops, barns, livestock destroyed, and the urgent need for federal help. To all this the Cato gentleman, dry and comfortable, had an unchanging answer: the government is not to be trusted with spending the victims' money. Better give them tax credits so that they will be able to spend their own money more wisely. The Iowans tried making the point that the victims' possessions were under ten feet of water, that they had no prospects of taxable income unless Washington came to their rescue. The Cato man remained wrapped in his mantra.

Before long we will undoubtedly be treated to a TV panel on some disastrous fire, where the Cato man will be heard arguing against calling the municipal firefighters with their pumps, hoses, extension ladders, and first-aid equipment. Instead we will be urged to give the victims clinging to the upper window sills tax credits.

And even if they had no chances of survival, couldn't their heirs sell their tax credits to corporations with taxes to pay, and keep brokers, tax lawyers and miscellaneous finaglers in cool clover arranging the scam?

Vol. 5, No. 11 — November 1993

Tunnel Vision With All Lights Out

A couple of years ago when the grand plan to revise the *Bank of Canada Act* was under way, the war cry was that the central bank must not be distracted with the "mishmash" of goals prescribed by the Act, attenuating oscillations in employment, prices, trade, and exchange rates. Instead, it was argued, it should be allowed to concentrate on a single goal: zero inflation.

What this proposal avoided mentioning was that "zero inflation" via high interest rates was in fact the flip side of a very definite agenda of depressing trade and employment to make a pancake of a highly flawed statistic.

Fortunately the attempt to put "zero inflation" into the *Bank of Canada Act* was defeated by a parliamentary subcommittee in February 1992. That event somehow escaped the attention of the media.

That was of considerable embarrassment to the Bank for International Settlements, the central bankers' centre in Basel. The victory of Governor Crow, a super-achiever among central bankers, had been taken for granted. For many months international journals such as *The Wall Street Journal* and *The Economist* went right on reporting the granting of independence to the Bank of Canada as an accomplished fact.

But now another strategy has been put in place. This appears from two articles in *The Economist* of 28/9/ One ('Too many pies for the Old Lady') uses the peculiar problems of the Bank of England as a smoke-screen. It refers to "the growing acceptance among academics and commentators, if not politicians, of the case for giving (the Bank) greater independence in the running of monetary policy." That is "a condition for joining the European monetary union (if it happens)." The banks of the member countries by the Maastricht Treaty will simply have to conform to the Bundesbank pattern.

We are told that "the Bank of England performs a ragbag of more tasks than any of the world's other big central banks. It supervises banks; watches over financial regulation; runs the printing works for England's banknotes; manages government funding; promotes London as a financial centre; intervenes in disputes between companies and creditors; and acts as general guardian of the City of London." It could, however, be relieved of any or all of these secondary duties without giving it independence in setting the general direction of monetary policy. For on monetary policy hangs hangs the livelihood of the nation.

In fact *Economic Reform* has suggested relieving the Bank of Canada of one such secondary activity: by putting the assignment of the Bank of Canada's trading business among the various brokers into the hands of a non-political office independent of the Bank. Too much of the Governor's time and the taxpayers' money appears to be devoted to winning friends among the brokerage community, by the selective distribution of the lucrative trading of securities for the account of the Bank. The same should be done in the distribution of research grants to the academic community.

The State of the Art

On October 15th I attended the second annual conference of the John Deutsch Institute for *The Bell Canada Papers on Economic and Public Policy* at Queen's University.

The rupture between the world of theory and the constraints of the real economy is complete: just about everything is seen to depend on the expectations in the heads of the market players. But expectations may be shaped by thought control. At the day's end the test will be whether these expectations are compatible with the arithmetic tables. The real message of the deficits with which we are assailed on all sides is that they aren't.

Most of the papers read presented dogma with just enough hedging to lubricate the forced-feeding process. Thus the paper of John F. Helliwell of the University of B.C. and Harvard assured us that "model diversity is better thought of as an asset to be encouraged." But when I sought traces of some model other than the zero inflation one, none was to be found. Even the man on the street these days is haunted by parallels between our "jobless recovery" with the Depression of the thirties. Yet the successful blending of fiscal and monetary policy by which Canada financed the war and freed us from a decade of depression received no mention in this paper.

So long as idle resources were at hand, the BoC during WWII built up its portfolio of government bonds to provide the government with considerable near-interest-free financing. No "funny-money" was involved in this — as the sole shareholder of the central bank the Government got back as dividends the bulk of the interest paid on the bonds held by the Bank. Once the economy approached capacity production, the central bank tapered off its acquisitions of government bonds and the government relied more on forced savings and bond sales to the public. That not only helped keep inflation in check, but contributed to avoiding a serious postwar recession.

Everything that made this feasible is still in place in the *Bank of Canada Act*. It could be applied to Finance essential infrastructural projects to end our present recession. When I made that point, Tom Courchene, the director of the Deutsch Institute, advanced quite another explanation of the mid-war shift in emphasis from monetary toward fiscal policy. He attributed to Governor John Crow of the BoC the view that the drop in the portion of the government debt held by the Bank of Canada as the war progressed was in response to intelligence reports that the Nazis were deliberately wrecking the economies of the occupied countries by printing money: Ottawa accordingly decided that it made no sense treating our economy as the Nazis did their victims. However, some obstacles stand in the way of this alluring interpretation. Keynes's famous pamphlet *How to Finance the War* proposing the forced savings strategy had appeared in the early months of the war, and outlined a policy for financing the war that essentially foretold the one followed.

Then again, the BoC throughout the war and long after went on keeping various interest rates in the 3/4 to 3% range. Without that the shrinkage of the federal debt/GNP ratio from 135% in 1946 to 44% by 1958 could never have taken place.

Last spring I had attended a conference of the same Deutsch Institute on capital budgeting in the public sector. That is a subject of immense implications for inflation, price statistics, deficits, productivity and the entire economy. At long last the need for capital budgeting in government accounts was receiving some attention even from the International Monetary Fund. That earlier conference was full of promise, but unfortunately there was not the slightest carryover from it to be detected in the Bell Canada Papers gathering.

Instead the Helliwell paper contained the remarkable passage: "an anti-inflationary policy is best seen as an investment that must be purchased over several years, and for which the benefits largely lie several years in the future." Accordingly, a policy-induced recession is to be treated as an "investment," but federal acquisitions of land, buildings, and equipment are still written off in a single year.

Even more interesting than the papers read, were the glimpses of the sociology of the profession afforded by the conference. Much to the fore was a young generation of academics who express their enthusiasm for the official central bank doctrine with a rich admixture of Greek terminology borrowed — not necessarily with any relevance — from physics.

Many of them spend part of their time working at the BoC or carrying on research with the aid of grants from that institution.

Very much on the sidelines were several eminences of an earlier generation who had helped fashion economic policy in a happier era. They read no papers, and their occasional interventions were given short shrift.

They could be overheard exchanging wormwood impressions about "the cartel." "What do you make out of all this talk of hysteresis and exogeneity?" "My son is working on his PhD in physics, but I nagged him into taking an economics course. After a few classes he told me: 'Dad, this stuff is for the birds. It makes no sense. It is too simplistic.'"

Among the costs of "zero inflation" push is the demolition of economics as a discipline that might tell us something useful about the economy.

William Krehm

Vol. 5, No. 12 — December 1993

Who's Who at Canossa

Some matters of high protocol overhung the first meeting of our new Finance Minister, Paul Martin, and the Governor of the BoC. The *Bank of Canada Act* gives the minister the ultimate power to set the general course pursued by the Bank. Mr. Crow, however, is not paying much heed to that Act. There was something symbolic about our new Finance Minister having to await his turn while John Crow flew off to Basel to chair the monthly meeting of the BIS. Priorities had to be established.

On his return, however, Crow made amends. To meet with the minister he journeyed to Windsor, where Martin was attending his mother's funeral. *The Globe and Mail* (15/11) was quick to interpret this as a sort of replay of Canossa, where a medieval Emperor walked barefoot to bow before the Pope's supremacy.

But there are reasons for discounting that interpretation. The Windsor meeting, according to tradition, took place without supporting staff. And that raises a problem. Mr. Crow is a banking technician with command of the facts and much practice in twisting them. There was an element of farce whenever Mulroney's last Finance minister, an alumnus of the used car business, confronted the highly motivated governor, strictly *tête-à-tête*.

There is a more likely explanation of Crow's trip to Windsor. In his 1991 annual report the General Manager of BIS, Alexandre Lamfalussy, had expressed impatience with even those central bankers who had wrestled inflation down to under 2% and then stopped dead there. However, in two subsequent reports Mr. Lamfalussy adopted a more discreet tone. BIS after all has had considerable experience in lying low in the shadow of the noose. Could his BIS masters on his recent trip to Basel have recommended greater tact to Crow because of the bad press closing in on him?

It would be helpful if the Liberals repudiated reports that they have swerved to the view that "having paid a horrendous cost to get inflation under control, it would be foolish not to enjoy the rewards." At the food banks and in the bankruptcy courts the cost of Crow's "victory over inflation" goes on being paid every day.

Vol. 6, No. 1 — January 1994

Time to Turn the Light on Again

If you engage in enforcing tall tales about yesterday and today, tomorrow will soon be around to unmask your game. That is at the bottom of John Crow's troubles. Listen to Greg Ip in *The Financial Post* (1/12): "When the IMF said a year ago that Canada would lead the world in growth at 4.4% this year, many found it unbelievable. The IMF may have found it unbelievable as well."

Ip quotes Festus Osunsade of the IMF in his recent talk in Toronto: "The problem is we cannot say many things in published form that government authorities don't like. The audience of professional economists was surprised less by the admission than the frankness of it."

Ip cites Ernie Stokes of WEFA Canada, a research firm: "He recalls trying to produce a forecast that took the BoC's zero inflation rhetoric seriously, and being unable to convince clients to accept it. 'They thought it was a junk forecast.'"

"Both Finance and the BoC swing a lot of authority in the forecasting community. They have hundreds of economists and huge research budgets. It's not unusual for them to call up an analyst with whose views they disagree to talk it over, but to some of the analysts it can come across as uncomfortable pressure.

"Paul Darby, an economist with the Conference Board of Canada, told a conference that when the Board sharply marked down its 1992 growth forecast to 1%, we got severely chastised by the Department of Finance for sowing lack of confidence. We got into trouble for that, but stuck to our guns."

The Economic Council of Canada, a governmental body, fared even worse when its studies drew the wrath of the government. After almost 30 years of existence, it was simply abolished. A public enquiry into these matters should be held. But can we afford a Royal Commission in this age of cuttings and slashings? Those costs would be unshelled peanuts compared with what John Crow gambled away in a matter of days in October 1992 supporting our dollar at unsustainable levels. Disinformation never comes cheap.

It is time we turned on the lights again.

Vol. 6, No. 2 — February 1994

Supplementals for the Finance Minister

Mr. Martin's economic conferences show him lending ear only to what he wants to hear.

Four members of the COMER board who requested to be heard at a recent confab of this sort were all turned down. We have long been aware that pardon for too timely warnings of disasters ahead comes in heaven, if at all. But more to the point, Mr. Martin has excluded a crucial stretch of our history along with provisions that are still on our law books. It would take a man foolhardy in a very good cause to defy such a paper trail. Good causes, however, have no need for suppressing key evidence.

Our banks are well on the way to becoming government pensioners. According to

BoC figures bonds issued or guaranteed by the federal government and held by the BoC have dropped by 37% between 1987 and the same month in 1993. But over the same period similar securities in the portfolios of our chartered banks have risen by 768%.

The fly in this balm is that when the economy starts recovering and prices point up, the BoC will raise interest rates "to lick inflation."That will collapse the value of the banks' fully leveraged bond holdings and their capital will go up the chimney. We have tried alerting the government and the media to this. To no avail.

Now *The Wall Street Journal* ('The Fed Can't Control Interest Rates,' by Martin Mayer of the Brookings Institute) offers a very similar warning:

"If (an economic) revival should spark an increase in bank lending to business, the Fed will not have the power to determine whether rates will rise, or even when they will rise, if the banks resume lending. From late 1990 until well into this year, the Fed worked to make interest rates very low for short-term borrowings, and rather high for long-term borrowings. The purpose was to generate profits for the banks, which typically borrow most of the funds they need through very short-term instruments and lend or invest on somewhat longer terms. What the policy means in practice was the banks could make money absolutely safely by investing in Treasury and government-guaranteed paper, and didn't have to make loans at all. By 1992, for the first time since the years right after WWII, the banking system's portfolio of Treasury paper was larger than its portfolio of commercial and industrial loans.

"Regulators don't make banks allocate capital against their holdings of government securities, because these securities are in effect the liquidity reserve of the system. If a bank wants to make a loan, it doesn't have to lure money from depositors; it can and will sell its excess Treasury paper.

"Reaching for better yield than from bank certificates of deposit and money-market funds, people have poured hundreds of billions of dollars into bond funds. Rising rates, however, mean declining bond prices. In the past three months, as the economy has begun to improve, rates have edged up, and the total return from bond funds has declined to something like zero. The mutual fund industry has made it a cinch for customers to switch out of bond funds for the price of a telephone call. When the customers want out, the bond fund must sell bonds. Should bond prices really tank — should the yield rise over, say, 7% — investors in bond funds could flee. In the worst scenario, cascading bond prices could drag down stock prices, creating a panic more dangerous than that of 1987, when bonds rose as stocks fell. Thus the Fed keeps jawboning about the need to fight inflation in a time when there's virtually no inflation.

"The decision (to) make what is still a sick banking system look healthy may or may not have been wise, but in either case it wasn't a free lunch. Part of the price to be paid, whether the president, Congress and the Fed's directors like it or not, is that a reduction in the central banks' dependence on commercial and industrial lending as a source of income may mean that banking has become disconnected from the real economy."

Vol. 6, No. 3 — March 1994

End Our Policy of Double-dipping

Rub history out of memory and you end up having it splashed on your face. That is happening with the Chrétien Government and the Thirties. Throughout the Depression Ottawa governments went about slashing spending "to balance the budget." Yet as a proportion of the Domestic Gross Product the debt rose systematically from 47.5% in 1929 to 98.8% in 1933. Only when the benefits of Roosevelt's spending programs started dribbling across the border was the debt/GDP ratio brought down to 78.5% in 1938. Nor was the rise of the figure due to overspending on social programs — such things were simply non-existent in the thirties.

In 1993, despite all the hysteria about the debt, that crucial ratio was 57.1%. It had risen from 37.1% in 1984 in tandem with the "slash and cut to reduce the debt" show that is still gathering speed on the road.

But more than just bad figures we are getting an overpowering whiff of the morality of the 1930s. As unemployed "rode the rods" from one end of the country to the other in search of jobs or handouts, a cry resounded amongst the well-fed: "the country owes no one a living." A "living" in those days did not mean a pension but the chance to earn food and shelter. We are getting back to the game of turning the victims into villains.

The Globe and Mail (16/2) reports Metro Toronto "exploring the possibility of fingerprinting welfare recipients to clamp down on fraud. The municipal government's social services department has canvassed companies for information about new computerized finger-scanning technology. No provincial or municipal governments has ever identified welfare recipients by their fingerprints."Why not just tattoo numbers on their arms?" asked Lynne Toupin, executive director of the National Anti-Poverty Organization.

Since welfare is one of few growth industries, higher technology should not be ruled out. But it should be extended to areas where fraud and inefficiency are even costlier.

We would, for example, propose the introduction of "finger-imaging" to prevent disastrously failed monetary policies from falsifying the record in a multiple-dipping scam of their own.

What has happened to the promise of "short-term pain for long-term gain" that launched us into the "zero inflation" age? We should not allow the same practitioners to change their finger-prints, sorry, their buzzwords, giving us a replay under the heading of "lick the deficit" of what we have already suffered in the name of "licking inflation."

Shrapnel

In the great war underway to make the war safe for speculation, statistics are the shrapnel. Rather than the quality of the fragments, the deciding factor is the area over which they are scattered. To apply tests of logic or morality is beside the point.

We are, however, perverse enough to do just that. Now that our central bankers have just about "wrestled inflation to the ground," the original schedule called for the short-term pain to give way to long-term gain." Yet unemployment is still near its peak, bankruptcies and plant-closings go on, and we are assured that it is a special "jobless recovery" that has overtaken us. We had been told that those who suffered the pain would be the ones compensated with the gain. A more popular expression for a situation where the pain and the reward are directed to different parties is "rip-off."

But to forestall such awkward discussions, the whole matter is raised to a higher plane of abstraction. And that is where the compliant academics come in. They are directing their "research" to prove that there is a negative correlation between the amount of inflation and the growth rate.

In this spirit *The Economist* (7/11/92 'Zero inflation') wrote: "One study by two economists at the BoC, covering 62 countries over 25 years, concludes that a reduction in the inflation rate by one percentage point increases the annual growth rate by one-tenth of a percentage point. A recent OECD study reaches a similar result. That may seem piffling, but over time it adds up. If a country cuts its inflation rate from 5% to 0, say, then in 20 years its output should be 10% higher than it would otherwise have been."

62 is a most impressive number. I suppose 125 would have been still more impressive — don't the textbooks tell us that the broader your sampling the more reliable the results?

But the number of developed countries in the world by the most generous of counts cannot exceed 25 to 30. And even the quality of the statistics of many of these leaves much to be desired. The *Economist* article itself notes: "The most commonly used measure of inflation, the Consumer Price Index (CPI) fails to adjust fully for improvements in quality.

"Robert Gordon, an economist at North Western University, estimates that America's CPI has overstated the rise in the price of consumer durables by an average of 1.5% a year over the past couple of decades."

The above and other failings of the CPI could be found in standard textbooks over the past half century, but except on occasions when they wish to demonstrate their scientific rigour, central banks shut their eyes to them. But there are even greater inaccuracies of our price statistics that standard textbooks still ignore. Over the past half-century a mixed economy has come into being with the public sector called upon to provide more and more essential investment in physical and human capital. Try suppressing their price effects with higher interest rates instead of revising the index, and you will in fact be deflating the economy. It is like a surgeon cutting into lights and liver, while claiming that he is doing a cosmetic job on fat.

Such are the shortcomings of statistics even in the advanced countries. But to come up with 62 countries the Bank of Canada scholars must have drawn extensively on the Third World. In another connection Reuven Brenner at McGill has written: "I am always reminded of the numbers that came out from an area in China in two enumerations. In one the population was 28 million. Five years later it was 105 million. The reason for the difference: the first census was done for tax and military purposes, the second for famine relief."

Such is the nature of the statistical shrapnel with which — for a purpose — we are everlastingly bombarded.

Plowshares into Guided Missiles

Even though there is a reasonably well-intentioned man in the White House, the United States is increasing its lead as the world's premier arms merchant.

The Clinton team has found itself blocked to deliver the promised "Peace Dividend" through a broad program of infrastructural renovation. War industries, however, are the very heart-throb of American conservatism. In that area, too, American technology has maintained an awesome lead. As a result the Clinton recovery seems doomed to depend on exporting more lethal weapons into a world ripening for major blood-lettings.

The situation is not without precedent. In our last issue Lynn Turgeon told how Leon Keyserling finally managed to pull the US out of the Truman recession of 1949.

"Impressed by the productive potential revealed by World War II, he came to the conclusion that a three-fold increase in government spending would permit rises in personal consumption. At about the same time, the cold warriors, especially Paul Nitze, began to look for a means to bleed the Soviet economy. Together Keyserling and Nitze came up with NSC-68 — a secret memorandum of the National Security Council — in early 1950. Instead of a three-fold increase in general government spending, the Keyserling scheme now called for a three-fold increase in military spending. The stagnation of the postwar years came to an end with the outbreak of the Korean conflict in June, 1950."

There is, however, a difference. In its present reincarnation this strategy tends to place most of the burden of arms spending on Third World countries. The major exporters seem to have stumbled upon a dream-boat of salesmanship: every sale produces a ripple of further orders from neighbours of the original customer who feel threatened.

The Wall Street Journal (28/1) provides chilling details:" For decades the US has been reluctant to spread its best armaments over the globe. But since the end of the Cold War, even as Washington urges others to show restraint in the name of global security, it has become the world's pushiest arms merchant.

"From Southeast Asia to Switzerland and across the Mideast, Americans have unleashed a barrage of weapons exports, largely to prop up the declining domestic defense industry."

This is bringing the US into cut-throat competition with Russia. In December 1992 when the Malaysian Defence Minister informed the US Ambassador that he was ordering $660 million of Russian MIG-29R fighters, he added that the Malaysians went to Russia for their shopping because they figured that the Americans would not sell their high-tech planes. At once Washington and the defence corporations went into a huddle, removed that trifling obstacle to clear the path for a sale to Malaysia of F/A-18 attack jets.

Immediately that brought enquiries and orders from the Philippines and Thailand. It heated up the rivalry not only with Russia but with China. To improve their competitive positions, the exporting powers are committing themselves to technology transfer. That puts the importers in line to become exporters themselves. Near Ankara, Turkey, General Dynamics and the US Government helped organize F-16 co-production in the eighties. Today workers there are assembling forty of these jets for export to Egypt.

Taiwan achieved a $6 billion delivery of 150 F-16 fighter planes from the US by threatening to turn to French suppliers. The following year it obtained $1.1 billion in contracts for the production of parts and the maintenance of the F-16s. That did not go down well with Beijing that had bought a far smaller number of Russian jets. This inspired the mainland Chinese to boycott the negotiations to restrict arms sales after the Gulf War. Instead it has stepped up the sale of long-range missiles to Iran and sensitive technologies to North Korea and Pakistan.

American corporations are estimated to have filed 7,000 applications to license Third World clients to acquire American military technology. Such applications were practically unknown before 1990.

European manufacturers are doing deals with Russia to improve their jets to capture more of this booming market. "In the defense field we cannot cooperate with the

Americans," declares Gerard Renon, chairman of the French Snecma and formerly French Secretary of Defence. "The US doesn't favour the existence of a European defence industry."

In this field the Russians have little to learn about markets. Russia not only discounts its weapons to 40% below Western prices, but in the case of Malaysia has accepted half the payment in palm oil. "Typically, weapons contracts call for counter-trade worth 60% to 100% of the value of the weapons — at least twice the amount of a few years ago. Because offsets aren't monitored, related job losses in the US can't be tallied. They more often affect small suppliers, whose work is easier to duplicate."

While Secretary of State Christopher runs up an impressive mileage as archangel of peace, he is not averse to switching mid-flight into the role of drummer for the armament industry. When Litton Industries were up against British competition to sell Greece electronic systems for new F-16s, Christopher wrote Athens praising their product and netted them a $122 million contract.

Moshe Arens, former Israeli defence minister, has stated that since the Gulf War, "commercial considerations have become more important than the growing destabilisation. The Europeans sell to almost anyone."

Hixson's Corner — Some Revealing Figures

Just as in Canada, the commercial banks in the USA are creating money and using it to buy federal debt at a rapid rate. And just as is the case with the BoC, the USA's central bank, the Fed, is creating money and using it to buy federal debt only at a very slow rate.

Going through back issues of the *Survey of Current Business* one may find the relevant statistics. In December 1981, for example, the commercial banks of the country held $111.0 billion in federal debt and the Fed held $131.0 billion. By the end of the third quarter of 1993 the commercial banks had increased their holdings to $719.7 billion and the Fed has increased its holdings to $321.6 billion.

While the Fed was creating $190.6 billion of essentially interest-free money for the government, commercial banks were being permitted to create $608.7 billion of interest-bearing money for the government. Now I believe it may be reasonably contended that if there was going to occur the creation of $799.3 billion ($190.6 + $608.7) for the purpose of finance the federal debt, then the Fed should have created more than a fourth and the commercial banks should have been constrained to create less than the three-fourths they created.

At times in the past (most recently in 1973) the Fed's holdings of federal debt constituted as much as 22.5% of the total. It is difficult to imagine any good reason why this percentage should have been permitted to dwindle to less than a 10% as of the third quarter of 1993. At times in the past (most recently in 1982) the holdings of federal debt by commercial banks have constituted as little as 13.3% of the total. It is difficult to imagine any good reason why this percentage should have been permitted to rise to 21.8% as of the third quarter of 1993.

The nearly $720 billion in federal debt now held by the commercial banks makes it necessary for the government to hand over to them between $30 and $35 billion annually in interest even at today's exceptionally low rates. At an average rate of 7%, the interest charges would soar to $50 billion per year.

William F. Hixson

Vol. 6, No. 4 — April 1994

Dark Secrets

In Canada even babes at birth, like newly appointed finance ministers, are said to swear by the independence of the central bank. Right-thinking folk are supposed to hear, speak and know no evil where high finance is involved. In the American financial press, however, the involvement of banks with risky derivatives trading has become the stuff of scare headlines.

Under the title 'Is your fund on steroids?' *Fortune* (29/11/93) wrote: "It used to be so simple. No more. In the 70s fund managers started messing around with puts and calls. The 80s brought a proliferation of futures and stock index options. Now some mutual funds, along with banks and corporations, are snapping up financial esoterica as fast as Wall St. can pump them out: swaps and structured notes; caps and floors: IOSs and POSs (interest and principal only strips). Horror stories abound of huge losses from these volatile and complex instruments.

"As interest rates started dropping last year home-owners refinanced their mortgages and owners of IOSs that give investors only the interest portion of a mortgage saw their investment plunge. Once the principal is repaid,the interest stream dries up. Auditors recently discovered that Ohio's counties, cities and schools had lost millions in IOSs. Now the state has banned that sort of instrument."

Originally some of these gimmicks were designed to protect producers from brusque price movements of raw materials they processed for resale. But speculators soon realized that these instruments could offer fantastic leverages for coups.

Derivatives are the Wild West of security trading, where the successful rustler, if he doesn't end up hanged, may become a living legend.The risks attached to highly leveraged derivatives are not only uncharted but unchartable.

The Wall Street Journal (17/3) tells part of the story: "Banks, security firms and other big traders rely heavily on portfolio insurance to contain potential losses when they buy and sell options. But since portfolio insurance backfired on investors in 1987, it goes by an alias these days — the sexier moniker of "delta hedging." Whatever you call it, the recent turmoil of European bond markets taught some practitioners the same painful lessons learned by earlier portfolio insurers. An option can gyrate wildly in value with even modest changes in the underlying security price; the relationship between the two is known as the option's 'delta." Thus dealers in these instruments need some way of hedging their delta to contain risk" The hedge itself requires hedging.

A basic difficulty in achieving that is that in every hedge there has to be a seller of options to accommodate each would-be buyer. But speculative trading has far outstripped the demand for hedging inventory risks in the real economy. As a result gambler is pitted against gambler in deals of the sort that in other arenas are enforced by breaking arms.

In theory, delta hedging takes place with computer-timed precision. "In a choppy market, dealers may suddenly not want to do the business because the risk management tools aren't in place."

The technicalities can become so tangled that only the odd specialist can claim to understand them, and he, too, could be bluffing.

Last September Juan Pablo Davila, a 34-year-old futures trader for Codelco, the

Chilean state-owned copper company, lost his employers the equivalent of 0.5% of Chile's annual gross national product or US $207 million. Metallgesellschaft, the huge German metal and energy concern, was brought to the brink of bankruptcy when it dropped a billion dollars in oil futures. Showa Shell, a Royal Dutch Shell affiliate declared a $1 B unrealized loss from a currency hedge.

Business Week (8/11/93 'Once Again Banks are Leaving Investors in the Dark') wrote: "Under today's accounting and disclosure rules it's almost impossible for outsiders to get anything but the sketchiest pictures of a given bank's derivative activities. Citibank's credit exposure (to derivatives) is now at least 86% of its equity, Morgan's is 141%, and Bankers Trust's is 213%."

The retiring Superintendent of Financial Institutions in Canada, Michael Mackenzie, has repeatedly expressed concern about our banks' involvement in derivatives.

William Krehm

Looking into the Mirror

The best way to learn what we really look like to others is to glance at a mirror. Similarly, to grasp how our Western economy works or fails to, there is no better way than to assess our efforts to help the former Communist countries to an enjoyment of the benefits of the market system.

The Wall Street Journal contributes to this in reportages by Barry Newman on Poland and by John Fialka on Russia. (23 & 24/2)

When Lech Walesa addressed the US Congress in November 1989, he expressed hope for a new Marshall Plan — Stalin had prevented Poland from taking part in the original one.

"By early 1993, the 24 richest nations of the West had made paper pledges of $70 billion to East European countries from Estonia to Albania. Poland alone got a chit for $25 billion. What happened to it? Fair question. Many aid dollars benefit donors more than donees.

"Poland ought to be aid's showcase. First to revolt, this country freed prices, checked inflation, beat recession. Yet the West, reluctant to give handouts or take big risks, has withheld large-scale aid to the small businesses that are fuelling Poland's transformation. Nor did the West channel aid to make life easier for millions more as unemployment shot up to 16%, welfare crumpled and living standards collapsed.

"The impact became clear last September. Three months before the Russians gave a shocking electoral victory to the far right, the Poles voted in the old left.

"Nobody knew that the whole system, from courts to banks, had to be scrubbed out before a torrent of private capital could wash away communism's slops. Nobody knew much of anything. Because they assumed that the market would do the work, the donor nations and aid institutions never set up a think-tank or command center to coordinate aid to the East. Their purpose was to put on an extravagant show, and buy a quick fix. Aid agencies were out to produce a laissez-faire economy at great speed.

"Under conditions attached by donors, more than half the country's potential credit must be spent on Western exports — from corn to economists — a practice called 'tied aid' long frowned on in the Third World.

"Paperwork holds up everything, due as much to rusty Communist laws as to Western fears of real or imagined fraud.

"The World Bank makes credits conditional on progress in reforms. When the Berlin

Wall came down, Steve Buckley had a Harvard MBS and a yuppie's salary with a San Francisco consulting firm. 'I'd have had a hard time finding Poland on the map,' he says. But he quit his job and flew to Warsaw, and without having seen the inside of a Polish factory before, he began giving advice to 20 Polish firms under an aid contract 'to stop the bleeding.'"

Reports were written that nobody read. Ignorance was no obstacle to consultants hired to rescue and sell state industries. An EU adviser can make $1,200 a day. Brussels awarded 546 contracts worth $286 million in 1991. Polish consultants got half a percent of that.

"Along with every other firm working in Poland, Buckley's firm expected to parlay the aid money into success fees for finding buyers for the firms they put into shape. In the case of 35 shoe companies and 28 machine-tool manufacturers, not a single bid arrived despite endless phone calls.

"Just as aid for Western advice mostly aided Western advisers, Western business has been the biggest gainer from the West's business loans. The money they are supposed to lend to inspire enterprise in the East often goes to Westerners, or it goes nowhere at all.

"Experts still fly in to improve Polish cherries, while Western duties kill Polish cherry exports. The Poles politely wonder if a tariff cut wouldn't lessen the absurdity."

The tale told by Fialka on Russia is no different. "The US has pledged $5.8 billion in aid to the former Soviet Union, most of it destined to Russia: there is dancing in the streets — though not in the streets of Russia. The chief celebrants? — hordes of US consultants who are gobbling up much of the US aid. Consider one example of how money is being spent. A camera closes in on a cluster of schoolchildren: 'My dad is a shareholder in a whole biscuit factory,' trumpets a young boy. 'So there!'

"Little of the money is targeted toward easing the economic strains of ordinary Russians. With cash-starved Russians trying to jump-start their fledgling businesses, we don't need 90% of technical-assistance money going to American experts,' says Aleksandre Jitnik, head of a Russian commission coordinating foreign aid. Marshall Goldman, professor at Wellesley College, recently told the Senate Banking Committee that Russian aid in the hands of US consultants and 'Beltway bandits' benefits Russians 'minimally if at all'

"James M. Silberman, an 80-year-old World Bank consultant and architect of the technical aid package of the Marshall Plan recalls that planners found it more effective and cheaper to bring 26,000 European business and social leaders to the US to learn rebuilding skills. The notion of big-spending, well-paid US consultants raking in aid 'was resented then and it is resented even more now.'"

Vol. 6, No. 5 — May 1994

Is God a Keynesian?

Apparently there is nothing like a catastrophe or "Act of God" to mobilize resources. According to *The New York Times* (1/28) Southern California is on the verge of an "earthquake boomlet." With damages estimated to run around $30 billion, one would expect a construction boom. But it is more than drywall contractors that are doing a land office business. Motorcycle sales are up, massage therapists are solidly booked.

At a recent press conference, Laura Tyson, Chair of the Council of Economic Advisers, predicted that the 4th quarter growth would be stimulated by what she called the "flood factor." The Midwest is now the most rapidly growing region thanks to the stimulus coming from FEMA (Federal Emergency Management Authority) payments connected with the 1993 floods. According to Mort Zuckerman of *US News and World Report*, two percentage points of the last quarter's growth resulted from the flood factor.

Earlier Peter Passell on the front page of *The New York Times* boasted that the effect of the World Trade Center bombing represented a net stimulus to the New York economy. All the replacement for bomb damage created jobs and the former surplus of office building space was reduced.

Still earlier, Florida benefitted from the "Hurricane factor." None of this would have surprised John Maynard Keynes who recognized that "Pyramid-building, earthquakes, even wars may serve to increase wealth, if the education of our statesmen or the principles of classical economics stand in the way of anything better."

President Clinton was rebuffed on his $16 billion stimulus package in early 1993. If Congress is reluctant to spend for reconstructing areas like Watts, perhaps the black community might resort to prayers. Luckily, there is some evidence that God is a Keynesian, perhaps the last one.

Lynn Turgeon

The Rubbing Out of J.M. Keynes

Last summer, as the 50th anniversary of the Bretton Woods Agreement approached, I decided to make a pilgrimage to the site of the conference that gave birth to the International Monetary Fund and the World Bank. At the Mount Washington Hotel, nestled at the foot of New Hampshire's White Mountains, the room in which the signing took place is suitably cordoned off, with pictures of the chief participants on the wall outside. The relatively obscure Russian delegate (M.S. Stepanov) is pictured, but, to my astonishment, there is no indication that John Maynard Keynes, the principal architect of the IMF and the World Bank, was present.

Lynn Turgeon

The Solidity of Our Fundamentals

As stock and bond markets tumble around us, we are reassured that "the fundamentals are sound," but no one bothers specifying what these fundamentals might be. However, the US House Banking Committee looking into derivative trading has offered glimpses into an alchemists' den complete with smoking alembics and shattered glass from unscheduled explosions.

A derivative is not a security — i.e. a share of stock or a bond — but a disembodied feature of a security. In his testimony before the Committee. George Soros, one of the most successful derivative traders remarked, "Some (of the derivatives) are so esoteric that the risk involved may not be properly understood even by the most sophisticated investor, and I'm surprised to be one."

Comptroller of the Currency Eugene Ludwig has remarked "his staff has come up with a list of more than 1,200 financial derivatives that are currently offered, with such names as 'harmful warrants,' 'worthless warrants,' 'death-backed bonds,' 'limbos' and 'heaven and hell bonds' — descriptions 'obviously designed to inspire confidence.'

Since October a lot of water has gone under the bridge — and there are several bridges missing." (*WSJ* 21/4)

"The largest funds have moved beyond stocks to roam the world looking for opportunities, moving from stocks to bonds, currencies to commodities. Typically, they borrow heavily, both from banks and brokerage firms. And their profits have verged on the spectacular, with many of the largest funds earning their investors more than 50% last year. Of course, some of their losses have been just as stunning, with many of the same funds losing half of last year's gain the past three months alone." (NY Times Service, *G&M* 14/4)

The potential for big profits has helped hedge funds attract ever more investors, both among the affluent individuals and institutions such as pension funds and charitable organizations. The Rockefeller Foundation, for example, last year allocated $130 million — 5% of its assets — among 10 hedge funds, in search of returns that are six to 10 percentage points higher than short-term government bonds.

"The trading strategies of the large funds have evolved in part because their funds have grown so big that it is difficult to make the returns they want simply from stocks."

Stanley Druckenmiller, chief trader for George Soros, in an interview in Jack Schwager's *The New Market Wizards* observed: "Soros has taught me that when you have tremendous conviction to a trade, you have to go for the jugular. It takes courage to be a pig."

Our banks are into this perilous game up to their eyeballs. *The Globe and Mail* (15/4) informs us, "Wood Gundy Inc. analyst Kathy Humber figures that the banks account for about 90% of the derivatives business. She estimates that the total face value of the banks' outstanding interest rate and foreign exchange swap contracts was just under $2.4 trillion as of last October 31. This was more than three times the $708.7 billion in contracts outstanding at the end of fiscal 1988." The Royal Bank with $743 billion was the biggest player. But a better indicator, she said, is the risk-weighted exposure."

There is in fact as great an asymmetry in many derivative contracts. The purchaser of a put has *the option* to sell his position. The seller of a put *must* buy at the option of the other side. Moreover, the "risk-weighting" of a bank's exposure is at best guesswork since it depends on the volatility of the derivative: that determines the chance of getting out with a profit before the skies cave in.

A series of mega-losses in derivatives by major corporations has enlivened the financial journals in recent weeks — General Electric's Kidder, Peabody Group Inc. dropped $350 million because of alleged "phantom trades and profits."

All this has a double bearing on the solidity of our "fundamentals.." First it makes at best heroic guesswork of "the money supply" by which our central banks still pretend to be steering the economy. Today our money is debt-money, and it does make a difference whether the debt is backed with real or imaginary assets.

There is, too, a moral dimension. The successful mega-trader in derivatives has become the king of the heap, raking in greater rewards by two or three digits than the most glamorous CEO of an industrial firm. Right until the moment when he may disappear into the bankruptcy courts or jail, he is preeminently our role-model.

wk

Vol. 6, No. 6 — June 1994

Awaiting a Translation from the Arabic

When an Arab conqueror set fire to the greatest library of antiquity at Alexandria, he uttered a line that calls to mind a monetarist central banker brushing off Keynes: "If what the Greeks wrote was true it must already be in the Koran, and if it is not in the Koran it is not true." And that took care of Aristotle for another five centuries.

However, in time some Arabs absorbed the cultural heritage of the conquered and carried it into Spain. From there Aristotle, retranslated from the Arabic, found his way back into Europe.

An incorrigible optimist may detect hints of similar retrieval of long buried economic wisdom in our newspapers — not in the editorial columns, but in its news pages. Good reporters get restive under too great demands on their credulity.

In *The Globe and Mail* (28/2) Bruce Little under the heading 'Amazing Facts' ponders "a nasty little trend" in the Finance Department's prediction of its revenues: it was out by 5% in 1991, by 8% in 1992, and by 10% in 1993." This then could be the equivalent of the grand moment when a Spanish-Jewish translator first set eye on a long-forgotten work of Aristotle in Arabic. Undoubtedly, as in Mr. Little's case, that bearded scholar found it easier to grasp the anecdotal than the underlying idea. In the *G&M* piece we read of possible reasons for surprises in the size of the deficit: disappointing rulings of the courts, a spurt of activity on the part of smugglers (because a good production of Carmen had come to town?), the failure to legislate in time for the remittance of the Goods and Services Tax on a six- rather than a four-month basis, an upsurge in tax-refunds, a 1992 slip in incomes below expectations. "Little wonder that Finance Minister Paul Martin has asked an outside consultant to study the way Finance predicts revenues."

To help such brave souls in their daunting chore, we offer a basic Keynesian teaching, once known to every economics freshman, but long since lost even to most outside consultants.

To deal with Mr. Martin's problem in the 1930s — revenues that insist on shrinking with every cut in government spending — Keynes took over the multiplier-accelerator concept developed by his student, Richard Kahn. Every increase in spending (government or private) through its ripple effects leads to an increase in consumer demand much larger than the initial spending. That is because the money spent will put people to work, and what they spend of their earnings will further increase consumer demand, and so forth. A converging series of spending increase will result. This "multiplier" effects in turn will trigger an "accelerator" effect: with a pronounced increase in the demand for consumer goods, investment in new productive plant will be stimulated. That will put further people to work. Their spending will add further to the multiplier effect. And the extended activity will broaden the tax-base at the same time that it takes people off the relief rolls. The process will thus feed on itself in a non-linear way (i.e. involving higher powers) until it outstrips the available supply of labour and productive capacity. At that point it can become inflationary and drive up prices *without* increasing real production. We are a long way indeed from such danger.

What our government is doing is running this powerful relationship in reverse gear. With the country wallowing in excess productive capacity and unemployed workers, it is slashing government spending. That reduces consumer purchasing power by several times the initial amount of the slashing of spending. A negative muliplier will trigger a negative accelerator. Mr. Martin has nagged off the ears of industrialists to make new investments, ("By God, if the business community doesn't start producing jobs in the next five years, there's going to be a fundamental shift in thinking." *G&M* 24/2) However, if there is insufficient consumer demand, it would be suicidal for them to do so.

What the economy is suffering from is a quarter of a century of an artfully planned unlearning process. We are in the position of medieval Europe awaiting those redeeming translations from the Arabic.

k

New Fare for Thrillers

The collapse of the Evil Empire has deprived mystery writers of plausible settings for secretive characters prone to abrupt disappearance. But the industry can take heart: the derivative-trading departments of some of our most venerable institutions are filling the gap.

In Chile, a 32-year old whiz-kid in charge of derivative trading suddenly wasn't there, but he left behind undeclared losses for his employer — a nationally-owned mining trust. These amounted to .5 % of the GNP. We have become accustomed to gauging our government debts as a proportion of the GNP, but doing so for speculative losses ushers in a new epoch.

In New York Joseph Jett, in charge of government-bond trading at Kidder, Peabody Group Inc, a General Electric Co. subsidiary, was suddenly fired when it turned out that he collected several million dollars in bonuses on his non-existing trading profits.

"Derivatives are side bets on things ranging from interest rates to currency values, stock market trends to the price of natural gas. Their names include options and swaps, caps, collars and floors, swaptions and captions, forward rate agreements and futures, straddles, strangles, butterflies and spreads."

In boardrooms an executive admitting that he did not understand the risks behind these seductive names would not only lose face, but possibly his bonus. As a result much of the discussion at such gatherings has come to resemble cocktail chatter in a Woody Allen film.

On Mathematical Illiteracy

We hear a great deal about the deterioration of mathematical education in our schools. To that is attributed much of the malaise of the North American economy.

But that is not our most threatening brush with that unforgiving subject. Even more costly has been the mathematical illiteracy of the central banking community. Where our elementary schools are striking out is teaching students to handle specific numbers. That — without condescension — might be termed "grocery arithmetic."

Our central bankers, however, turn their backs on a more fundamental type of mathematics — one that mathematicians refer to as "abstract structure." That is no way deals with specific numbers. Instead it is concerned with relationships and more basically the symmetry and asymmetry of those relationships. Matrix theory, for example, x-rays the structure of the equations that have to be satisfied simultaneously. Group theory enables mathematicians to detect common pattern of symmetry in operations in quite different fields and solve seemingly unrelated problems at a single crack.

Computers per se cannot replace the need for this sort of thinking — they themselves require the guidance of structural analysis. That is what software is about.

Our central bankers don't do much worrying about the software of economics. They have been staking the survival of our civilization on stabilising prices through higher interest rates. Let us apply a simplified version of symmetry analysis to check the odds in this gamble.

The notion of stability implies symmetry: any divergence from a centre of equilibrium must trigger countervailing forces that will bring the system back towards the equilibrium point. An example is the rocking of a cradle. When it moves off-centre in one direction, the pull of gravity tends to bring it back to where it came from. But even so you must take care not to rock the cradle too violently, otherwise its outward momentum will outstrip the ability of gravity to pull it back towards the equilibrium position.

If a movement off centre were to give rise to forces adding to the momentum in the same direction, the cradle would turn over and throw the baby onto the floor, or even out the window. That indeed is the way in which interest rates have stabilized our economy. Once the baby hits the pavement, it lies inert, even after the cradle has stopped rocking. It explains something that has our government baffled — why the economy is not recovering even with interest rates somewhat down.

An open mind would have warned us that the high interest rate policy to stabilize prices was bound to produce the wrong results. Our higher prices do not always indicate an overheated market with buyers, confronted with empty store shelves, bidding up prices. On the contrary we take great pride in the fact that unlike the case in Russia, our stores are well stocked — so well in fact that many shopkeepers have been going broke. These days higher prices are more likely to result from higher taxes to pay the usurious rates on the soaring debt.

Another case of misplaced assumption of symmetry: it simply cannot be taken for granted that equations can be read backward as well as forward, without further ado. If a pistol is fired against a man's head, he will drop dead. But if a man falls dead, it is by no means proven that a pistol has been fired.

But that sort of nonsense is fed into econometric forecasts by the equilibrium model that identifies any price increase with an excess of market demand. When you start with software so wide of the mark, you can feed the most accurate statistics into your computer, and it will come up with the wrong forecasts. But at that point, instead of reexamining the model for basic flaws of structure, right-thinking economists simply proclaim the misfired prophecy an enigma.

"Trade-offs," implying reversible one-to-one relationships, have become a staple of economic discourse. From the undeniable fact that, other things being equal, an increase of demand over supply will tend to push up prices, economists leap to the conclusion that every time prices go up, it is because of an excess of market demand.

Prices, however, can move up for any of many other reasons. For example, the very increase of interest rates. In 1983 47% of sewage disposal costs in the German city of Aachen could be traced to interest payments, and for the Federal Republic as a whole (1979) 77% of public housing costs went to interest payments. Yet the German central bank, in its monetarist fervour, pushed its interest rates up to more than double the US figure to "fight inflation."

That still does not tell the whole story. To make sure that they will have their loans repaid, banks and other lenders usually ask for security. When the central bank squeezes up interest rates, the value of such security drops. The borrower is therefore required to put up more collateral or his loan will be called in.

Nobody in business is unaware of these grim facts. Only our central banks shut their eyes to them. It is high time that we started a campaign against the mathematical illiteracy of central bankers.

William Krehm

Hixson's Corner — The Mobile and the Immobile of the World

Transnational corporations champion free trade because they want to be at liberty to make those product components most likely to result in pollution in the nation with the fewest environmental protection laws; to make the components that are most labour intensive under the sovereignty where there are the fewest occupational health and safety rules and labour is cheapest; make the sub-assemblies in another place and the final assemblies in yet another, and then juggle the accounting so that profits are shown to occur under the sovereignty where profits are least taxed. This assures the next best thing to the business ideal of total escape from any sovereignty whatever.

Transnational corporations are thus able to arrange things to their benefit because of what economists call the "mobility of capital." That is to say, corporations can shift their money, investments, or production from country to country with little impediment.

Unfortunately, for people who must make their living by working, there is no similar "mobility of labour" and hence workers enjoy no comparable opportunity to take advantage of differences between national sovereignties. Wouldn't it be wonderful for workers if they could, at one and the very same time, live in another country with the best environmental protection laws, live in another country with the best occupational health and safety laws, another country with the highest wages and longest annual vacations, another country having the best health care and old-age pension system, and another country where there were no payroll taxes, sales taxes, or income taxes on workers? Of course, such "mobility of labour "is *physically impossible.*

Since it is impossible to provide a mobility of labour comparable to the existing mobility of capital, fairness demands that the mobility of capital of multinational corporations be severely restricted.

The mobility of capital works in two very different ways. In the first case, it involves the abandonment of a factory in Country A where unions are strong, wages high, and fringe benefits large, and the erection of a factory in Country B where there are no unions, wages are low, and fringes nonexistent — this followed by the shipping of the factory's products to country A. This may be referred to as "flight of production capital" and results in a more or less direct confrontation between the agenda of labour and that of capital. The long-standing method of rendering in some measure ineffective the mobility of capital of this type is the raising of tariff barriers against products made in Country B. That is to say, the traditional method has involved the government of Country A placing limitations on free trade between itself and other countries.

The second class of mobility of capital involves the "flight of money capital" The confrontation in this case is less one between capital and labour than between capital and a government. Imagine that an administration enacts legislation protecting labour or the environment — legislation which capital for one reason or another finds repellent. Owing to the mobility of capital, holders of money are free to move it out of the country. Flight of capital in this case may result not in the erection of factories in foreign countries but in the purchase of "money market instruments" elsewhere in the world. This flight of money capital from a country depresses the international value of its currency and makes difficult or impossible the financing or refinancing of the country's debts. It is designed to so embarrass and to so pressure the government as to bring about the repeal of the legislation protecting labour or the environment not wanted by capital.

In earlier centuries labour and capital usually confronted each other directly in a given locality and the principal means of confrontation were essentially economic — the strike and the lock-out respectively. But strikes against factories that have been shut down and replaced by factories abroad are meaningless. Labour's traditional weapon has been rendered useless where the flight of production capital is involved. It is even more useless in cases of the flight of money capital. Confrontations between labour and capital now are essentially on the political rather than the economic plane.

The purpose of FTA and NAFTA was to validate the effectiveness of the flight of production capital by making possible the unimpeded flow of goods from countries that do not protect labour and the environment to countries that do. The multinational corporations have won this round, temporarily at least. But given that FTA and NAFTA could be reversed and a principal reason for the flight of production capital removed, there would still be no impediments to the flight of money capital. This potent weapon of capital against governments that behave contrary to the wishes of the holders of money capital would remain unobstructed.

I believe the best way to think about these matters is that a national government, a national sovereignty has become very nearly the only instrumentality by which the attempts of the owners of capital to destroy "safety nets" and to pollute the environment can be confronted. There is virtually no prospect of "international legislation" and certainly no international government that could enforce it.

William F. Hixson

Vol. 6, No. 7 — July 1994

Twin Comebacks

The signs are unmistakable. The rapacious right has overplayed its hand. Appetites for instantaneous megaprofits were presented as economic efficiency, and how could we have too much of a good thing? But the eighties have left behind a deepening chasm between the rich and the poor, and a hopelessly disjointed economy.

A year ago *The Economist* was accepting the monetarist dogma as gospel. But much has happened since. In Northern Europe, and in former Communist countries like Poland and Hungary electoral victories have gone to parties questioning the idolatry of the market imposed by the West. With little capital or private savings to acquire the privatised state industries, that evangel has left the ex-Communist lands awash in crime and scandals. The West itself is distraught with collapsing bond markets and a listing financial sector that it cannot begin to understand.

Reviewing some of these trends *The Economist* (11/6) devotes much of its issue to — of all things — 'A Future for Socialism.' "Socialism must continue to define itself less in terms of means (we will manage the economy and civilize the market) and more in terms of priorities (we will help society's losers)." But for at least a decade society itself has been a loser, mugged by speculative Finance gone berserk.

Statistics Canada has announced another comeback: the May Consumer Price Index — 0.2% *less* than a year ago — has brought back deflation for the first time in forty years. For many months now we had been warning that the country was already deep in deflation. Only the hopelessly flawed price statistics and government accountancy could obscure the point. Unrecognized public capital — whether bridges, education, mental health or the environment — has been consumed and not replaced.

Last February the US Fed instituted the first of four increases in the "fed rate" to "preempt" money traders' fears of a resurgence of inflation. And where the Fed had hoisted its rates by a single percentage point between February and May, the BoC responded with increases almost twice as great. It was like a crack addict losing both self-control and his moral sense.The bigger the dosage, the more powerful the addiction and the need for a larger fix. And the less his concern about whom he victimizes to get it.

Futures

It was only last March that Fed Governor Alan Greenspan told a congressional committee that money supply figures could not longer be taken as a reliable gauge of inflationary pressures, and that it was necessary for the Fed to take its cues from other statistics, including gold and commodity prices.

The present is a progress report on the results of this new dispensation.

The deregulation of our financial institutions begun over a quarter of a century ago was supposed to assure the public "one-stop" shopping for all financial services. The reality? The banks have turned their backs on loans to business. Before finding financing these days, longstanding clients of banks with impeccable credit records can easily wear out a pair of shoes.

In chartering a bank the state delegates to it a franchise to create money — i.e. to lend out more than its own capital plus borrowings. "Every dollar of the depositors' money is not in storage on the premisses. The art of banking is always to balance the risk of a run with the reward of a profit. The tantalizing factor in the equation is that riskier borrowers pay higher rates." (James Grant, *Money of the Mind*).

The deregulation of banking has not made it easier for banks to resist that temptation.

Step by step, as the restraints on their activities have been peeled away, the banks have plunged into riskier investments. And whenever they have got into difficulties, the state has waded in to save them not only with money, but with further deregulation proposed by the bankers themselves. The idea was to recoup their previous losses, but the effect was to get them into deeper grief — the classical syndrome of inveterate gamblers. There are times when it seems that banks are in to everything except their proper business.

The theoretical underpinning of monetarism is the belief that if you control the money supply you can keep prices flat. But by now few people — not even Chairman Greenspan of the Fed — believe that it is possible to quantify or even define what the money supply might be.

Scarcely had Greenspan declared commodities a key to stabilizing the economy than they joined the bond and currency markets as one of the biggest crap games in town.

"'Since Alan Greenspan's testimony, there has been a huge and building interest in commodities,' said William Byers, director of futures research for Bearn Stearns &

Co. 'Thus when grain markets are especially weather-sensitive, as they are now, bonds become directly sensitive to weather as well.'" (*WSJ* 30/5). "For all of 1993, investment in futures jumped 56% to more than $50 billion, and much of that increase came from pension funds. The influx can be read in two ways. First, smart investors are hedging their bets against a resurgence of inflation. The second lesson, pension funds' growing appetite for futures may have been pushing the commodities markets to unnaturally high levels."

"In recent months hedge funds and commodity funds have been pouring money into grains, copper, cocoa and other commodity pits as never before. And that's raising concerns that, at least on a short-term basis, the commodity futures markets no longer reflect the economic realities of supply and demand. Soybean future prices, for instance, rose the permissible daily limit May 23 on concerns about dry weather in the Midwest — and then plunged the next two days when rain fell throughout the Corn Belt. Silver, coffee, and cocoa futures, though unaffected in a fundamental way by rain or the lack of it, followed grain prices up and down," (*WSJ* 31/5). The article quotes a farmer: 'The presence of funds can make the markets a dangerous place for farmers using futures contracts to hedge their business risks.'"

To cap it all the *WSJ* (26/5) reported: growth in the mutual-fund industry has been driven by distribution far more than by investment performance. Unless a fund company has a large distribution mechanism, it should merge with a bigger company before it is too late. The only way for a fund company to maintain market share these days is to spend more money on advertising and customer service, and to pay more money to brokers and others who sell mutual funds.

And should you think we're kidding when we emphasize that the casino economy is elbowing the real economy off the map, there is the report in the *WSJ* (19/5) that the Kansas City Southern is trying to sell its flagship railroad unit to leave the company to focus on mutual-fund asset management.

Before long we will be left with an economy that is all flea and no dog.

Vol. 6, No. 10 — October 1994

The Perils of Amnesia

Loss of memory, one of the most tragic fates, is getting increasing attention from scientists. Strange then that the same affliction on a national scale should be actively cultivated by governments.

The Quebec election illustrates the point. The Parti Quebecois triumphed in seats winning 77 against 47 for the Liberals. But in the future referendum on separation, noses rather than legislative seats will provide the decisive count. Accordingly, the popular vote last month (PQ 44.7% as against 44.3% for the Liberals) offers hope that Canada may survive in one piece.

But that will call for a lively sense of history. It is always easier for the former oppressor than for the victims to forgive and forget. *Je me souviens* has been on Quebec motor license plates so long that by now even Anglo rednecks should be able to handle the translation. For two centuries after the conquest French-Canadians were hewers of wood and drawers of water. Quebec was the only place in the world where the

French language in many circles had a status not unlike that of Nahuatl or Quechua in Latin America. Since then a brilliant francophone intelligentsia and an affluent bourgeoisie have arisen Yet memory's sting lives on. That makes Quebec particularly sensitive to economic recessions contrived in Ottawa. Quebec is among the provinces hardest hit by the Bank of Canada's "zero inflation" antics.

Bloc Quebecois chieftain Lucien Bouchard, leader of Her Majesty's Opposition in Ottawa, has had a field day taking up the cudgels on behalf of distressed Canadians across the land from which he hopes to pull away.

The Parti Quebecois is declining to set a date for the referendum on separation. For good enough reason. With the software in place at the Bank of Canada, any recovery will at once trigger a judo chop of high interest rates. That will be the moment for the PQ Government to hold its referendum. There is then still a danger that Canadians will pay the ultimate price — the breakup of their country — for their folly in surrendering their central bank to the world's money traders.

Obituary — Lauchlin B. Currie

Lauchlin B. Currie was born in West Dublin, Nova Scotia in 1902 and died in Bogota, Colombia on 23/12/93. The information has come to us belatedly from Roger Sandilands of the National University of Singapore. Sandilands is the author of *The Life and Political Economy of Lauchlin Currie: New Dealer, Presidential and Development Economics* (Duke University Press, 1990). Currie's passing received no attention from our media. Canada is not given celebrating those of her heroes not turned out by cooky-cutter.

As much as any man, Currie was responsible for reshaping US monetary policy under Roosevelt. Possibly no other Canadian has had so great an impact on the world economy.

In graduate school at Harvard Currie came under the influence of Allyn Young. He stayed on at Harvard as assistant to Ralph Hawtrey and Joseph Schumpeter. The latter he considered a hopeless reactionary for his views on the "salutary" nature of the Depression. His articles on the monetary causes of the Depression and his support of deficit financing to get out of it ("Curried Keynesianism" that predated *The General Theory*) blocked his promotion at Harvard. But his work led Jacob Viner to pronounce him "too good for Harvard" and invite him to join the "freshman brain trust" at the US Treasury. He had become a US citizen shortly before.

Currie persuaded Marriner Eccles to present to Roosevelt his draft of what was to become the 1935 Federal Reserve Act making the Fed an effective central bank, as a condition for Eccles accepting the Fed chairmanship. He stayed on at the Fed as assistant director of research until 1939 when Roosevelt appointed him his personal adviser on economic affairs. He remained at the White House until FDR's death, developing his views on getting the country out of the Depression. Increasingly, however, he concerned himself with the financing of the defence build-up before Pearl Harbour. He was responsible for adding China to the lend-lease program, the civilian side of which he administered.

In 1943 after a mission to China he recommended the recall of General Jose Stilwell who had become unacceptable to Chiang Kai Shek because of his appreciation of the fighting qualities of the Chinese Communists. Despite this, his friendship with Harry Dexter White, who was accused of "leftism," earned Currie the enmity of Senator

Joseph McCarthy, and eventually created difficulties for the renewal of his American passport. At that point in 1958 President Alberto Lleras conferred Colombian citizenship on him.

Even under McCarthy, curbing bankers was apparently even more serious than anything having to do with Communism.

Since 1950 — apart from the period 1953-7 under a military dictatorship when he became a successful dairy farmer — Currie served as economic adviser to the Colombian government on the country's transition from a peasant economy to an increasingly urbanised one. Under the administration of President Michael Pastrana (1971-4) many of his views were incorporated in the official "Plan of the Four Strategies." This embodied Currie's "leading sectors" model of development, an early version of "endogenous growth theories based on ideas of Allyn Young. It stressed the role of non-inflationary "real" demand in generating self-sustaining "increasing returns" of an macroeconomic type. It "differs sharply from the internal economies of scale stressed by other endogenous growth models."

Currie spent his last four decades mostly in Colombia, taking a Colombian as his second wife.

Our "Inverse Floater" Economy

The US Federal Reserve's interest rate increases since February were meant to reassure money traders that the economy is stabilized and inflation is dead beyond resurrection. But what we are getting calls to mind the financial turbulence that brought down the pound, the lira and the Canadian dollar in 1992.

Remote from the carnivores of Wall St., Piper Jaffray of Minneapolis used to be described as "the little old lady of brokerage firms." Having existed for over a century, it was respected for its conservatism. But screeching headlines inform us that like a crooked Olympic weight lifter the little old lady was on steroids. Its shares plunged 20% on news that the $12 billions of mutual funds under its management had lost 23.5% of their market value in just six months. Its "sage, stable, and secure" investment funds had been souped up with a particularly deadly derivative ("inverse floaters"). That derivative can shed 20% to 40% of its value for every 1% increase in interest rates.

All sorts of good people and causes — The Minnesota Orchestra Association, local charities, municipalities, and trade union pension funds, government agencies — were caught in the $700 million loss. What could have launched so strait-laced a firm into such adventures?

The answer must be sought at greater depths than "inverse floater" derivatives. Indeed the Fed policy of battling inflation with high interest rates has transformed the economy itself into one vast "inverse floater." Whenever the real economy starts struggling out of the gutter, the Fed knocks it down again with higher interest rates. Mindful of that, the stock markets now sell off on the suggestion of a recovery, and rebound on news that the economy is running out of steam. The fictitious economy floats only when the real economy sinks.

The wealth assigned to speculators by this arrangement outstrips anything the real economy can support. As they devour more and more producers, the unsustainable interest rates eventually drop. Then passive investors suddenly miss the inflated returns to which they have become accustomed. The most conservative mutual funds come under pressure to produce returns higher than securities throw off in a depressed economy. This drives some fund managers to high-grade their portfolios with derivatives.

Last year's earnings are never enough. In mystic ascension the bottom line must ever soar. And as it does, gambling winnings are capitalised as though they were a solid stream of earnings, and are stripped in advance for a quick get-away.

Developments in the financial sector are reinforcing this trend. Staggering from crisis to crisis, the banking system is losing "market share" to mutual funds. Today mutual funds in the US control over $2 trillion of assets — equivalent to 85% of bank deposits, up from 10% in the early 1980s. The larger ones have even invaded the turf of the IMF and the World Bank and have begun directly laying down the law to Third World governments.

Within the mutual fund industry the shift has been from fixed-rate investments to equities. Recently US mutual fund portfolios contained about $670 billion of equities, $760 B of bonds and $580B of money-market assets.

In Canada mutual funds have made less headway — currently they amount to 6% of the American figure. But to encourage their growth the Ontario Securities Commission has just allowed portfolio managers to do business in the province without local offices or staff. Clearly the Rae government is anxious that we don't miss out on future Piper Jaffray bonanzas.

To nurse the banking system back to health, the Fed after 1991 brought in the lowest short-term interest rates in thirty years. That gave banks an abnormally profitable spread between what they pay depositors and the interest they earn on their portfolios of government bonds that now exceed their commercial loans in volume. Those low interest rates have provided a strategic opening for mutual funds.

The "securitisation" of mortgages, credit card and other debt — marketing securities supported by entire portfolios of such debt — has added grist to the mutual fund mill. Junk bonds and leveraged takeovers are flourishing again as though Mike Milken was never sent to the clink. Even Real Estate Investment Trusts (REITS) have resurfaced to offer seductively high yields and balance sheets that even their promoters are often unable to decipher.

As interest rates are screwed up to "preempt inflation," not only will people lose their jobs and businesses, but many affluent citizens will suddenly realize that with the collapse of their retirement funds they are far less wealthy than they used to be. That guarantees us in technicolour the meltdowns that the early nineties gave us in black-and-white.

wk

Vol. 6, No. 11 — November 1994

From time to time *ER* has chronicled with wonder the rising multi-storeyed structure of false diagnosis prescribing high interest rates as the cure. This is not to be confused with the caution of the chap who shores up his trousers with both suspenders and a belt. Rather it resembles the overkill of medieval executioners who hanged their victim, quartered him, committed the segments to the fire, and finally called in the priest to condemn his soul to hell for all eternity.

A key tool of those in control to make this possible has been the growing vocabulary of what George Orwell called *newspeak*. The latest achievement in this field reaches us from New Zealand where a neo-conservative leader has come up with "*retroactive consensus*." That covers squarely the case of our Liberals sweeping to electoral triumph with promises of full employment and then giving us more of the policy that led to the Progressive-Conservatives falling on their sword.

The Grim Reaper's Bottom Line

The bottom line has been the ultimate court of appeal of our policy-makers. All other considerations — health, education, the solidity of our bridges — are relegated to the "long run," long indeed for those run over. The Grim Reaper, however, does have his own bottom line.

The Globe and Mail (4/10) reports that in 1992 100,497 abortions were performed in Canada — 25.2 for every 100 live births. This was a 43% increase over the 70,000 number of abortions in 1987. "Observers on both sides of the [abortion] debate say that the increase is a cruel legacy of the recession."

Many of those never-to-be born children will be needed to support our rapidly aging population in the decades ahead. That is all the more so since we are restricting immigration.

For at least a quarter of a century it has been the simplifying premise of our policy-makers that wealth "trickles down" from the affluent to the lower orders. However, the wholesale impoverishment of the middle class that has been going on has not helped this bromide. At the same time the evidence is mounting that deadly diseases do trickle upwards. The recent suspension of Air Canada flights to India because of the plague in Gujurat sent shivers down the spines of first-class travellers. Abruptly we are reminded of a degree of symbiosis between the wretched of the Third World and the elect of the First.

Biologists are pondering questions with implications for economic policy. Isn't the killing of the host organism bad strategy for the virulent parasite? We are informed in a recent *Economist* that two mathematical biologists at Oxford did a cost-benefit analysis from the parasite's point of view. "A cold virus exits the crowded sinus via a runny nose; cholera clears a path through the gut; bubonic plague, roughly speaking, tries erupting through the skin of your groin. Harming the host in these ways can help the parasite prosper — up to a point. But beyond that point, the parasite risks killing the host before its offspring can enter the next one.

"In a recent book, *The Evolution of Infectious Diseases*, Paul Ewald puts this work into an ecological context. Parasites such as cold viruses that depend on a handshake or a close-range sneeze, cannot afford to be too virulent: a near-dead, bedridden host does less kissing and disease-spreading than a cold virus may wish. Other parasites, however, do not depend on direct transmission. Dr. Ewald concludes that the more frequently a type of bacterium uses water to reach its new hosts, the more virulent it is likely to be. There is evidence to suggest that less virulent bacteria displace more virulent ones when cities introduce water-purification systems, which block the waterborne transmission routes. Over time, natural selection will ensure that parasites with the optimum virulence enjoy the most reproductive success and supplant parasites that are either too vicious or too wimpish."

All this lends ghoulish overtones to the facts laid out in *The Wall Street Journal* (30/8, 'The Global Population Streams into Cities'). "By the year 2000 there will be 300 cities with more than a million inhabitants in the developing world, compared with 125 today, and eight of them will have populations of more than 15 million. The urban explosion brings another less-discussed problem: areas with population and the size of cities, but which lack a normal city's facilities. El Alto a new city about 9 miles from La Paz, Bolivia, is a case in point. Its population, now about 500,000 grows by about 9% annually. What's the lure? Bolivia has the worst rural poverty in the world with 97% of its peasants living below the poverty line. In El Alto most of the streets are just potholed dirt roads through which spills a mixture of raw sewage and garbage. Everything is missing here. Like running water."

That puts into proper perspective the amazing confrontation that took place at the annual meeting of the International Monetary Fund and the World Bank in Madrid early in October. The IMF has earned itself an unenviable reputation by imposing on Third World countries as conditions for loans: belt-tightening, high interest rates, and the slashing of government services. But now it has adjusted at least its rhetoric to the portents in the wind. Michel Camdessus, its managing director, demanded that the industrialized nations inject a further US $52 billion into the international monetary system to beef up the reserves of both the former East Bloc countries and developing nations elsewhere. This was countered by a group of G7 members who proposed IMF allocations be restricted to $23.4 billion in Special Drawing Rights of IMF currencies available only to ex-Communist countries.

India, Brazil and other developing countries refused to deal separately with the renewal of the present special lending facility to Eastern European countries that expires at the end of 1994. "We want a symmetrical world," India's Finance minister, M. Singh, told the press. It comes as a surprise that the G7 shows such insensitivity.'

Hans Tietmayer, president of the German Bundesbank, laid down the position — supported by the US — that 'inadequate stabilization and reform cannot and must not be compensated for by the artificial creation of liquidity.'

The long-term winners in this debate are likely to be the cholera and plague viruses.

The Booby-traps of Terminology

No well-led army rushes into battle without checking its ammunition. It would be a mistake for the critics of official economic policy to do less.

We refer to those who express their opposition to the policy of "licking inflation" with high interest rates in terms of "cost push." That expression is in vogue for price increases resulting from higher costs, whether such costs originate in the market or as a result of high taxation or mandated improvements in quality of goods and services. The trouble with that is that instead of clarifying it confuses the basic problem.

Though we have been living in a mixed economy for a half century, conventional price theory still tries explaining all price movements in terms of the balancing of market supply and demand. But the market makes up less than 60% of the Canadian economy; the rest is the public sector operating not by a market code but by political decision. The private sector is subject to costs fed into it from the government sector. If they are not to go broke, private firms must recover in their prices those costs that do not originate in the market.

If the central bank raises interest rates to make the price level stand still, producers will not only be unable to recoup these higher costs originating outside the market, but both they and their customers will come under the pressure of higher financing charges. And the government itself, having to pay more to service its debt, will be driven to jack up taxes still further.

That is why *ER* calls for the unbundling of the price index to show how much the upward price movement has been brought on by too much market demand, and how much may be due to an increase in public services or to higher mandated standards for the output of the private sector.

If laws impose less pollution of the environment, the cost of that must show up in a higher price level. But that is not more inflation, but less cancer. It is essential to use language that will express this difference. We have suggested "market inflation" for prices due to an excess of demand or a shortage of supply, and "structural price rise" for increases in the price index due to our getting more unpriced public services and higher quality in our purchases because that is mandated by the law.

Nor can we dismiss price increases that do not originate in the market as offering less value in return than those that are market-driven. For that would lead us to attribute greater value to the cigarettes we buy than for lung surgery partly paid for by the tax on tobacco.

Nobody likes paying more taxes. But whether they are good or bad depends on the use to which the revenue raised is put. Our quarrel with the term "cost push"" to cover all cost increases producers experience is that it fudges such enquiry. "Push" suggests something aggressive and pushy. But much of the "tax push" is in fact "pushed" — passive rather than active. It includes society's defence against "pollution push," "technological push," population push," "urbanization push," quite apart from "interest push."

The "cost push" terminology is the mother lode from which the present cutbacks of public services across the board derives. There is nothing necessarily pathological about the growing overhead costs of running our increasingly complex world. Unless our terminology reflects that, we are sunk before leaving port.

Adopting our adversaries' lingo is not popularization, but evading the problem at its root levels.

In the same spirit there are well-intentioned critics of BoC policy who argue that the Bank's estimate of the "natural rate of unemployment" is too high. The trouble is not how we calculate the "Non-Accelerating inflation rate of unemployment" (NAIRU) but the very concept of that "natural rate of unemployment." Accept it and it will lead you up the garden path. That is precisely why it was developed.

Some of our friends may consider the suggestion for unbundling the price index as "too theoretical" In fact it points out one of the most vulnerable chinks in our opponents' armour. Even the research department of the BoC has felt obliged to recognize the "inflationary bias" of the CPI, but of course they miss some of the really key components of this bias: the one-year write-offs of capital expenditures by the government which adds needlessly to taxation and price; and the effect on the CPI of the broadening layer of taxation to pay for necessary public services.

The crucial point is that the flawed CPI packs a devastating operational wallop. The moment it goes up, interest rates follow. Unbundle it to disclose the component of "overheated market" that might really exist and you destroy what is left of the theoretical justification for the BoC policy. Last February Governor Alan Greenspan of the US Fed acknowledged that the "money supply" is elusive and hence no good for predicting inflation. Shoot down their notion of "price stability" and they have nothing left to stand on.

The technique of unbundling the price index is simple enough. Essentially it consists of introducing new items such as environmental clean-up into the sample basket of goods and services on which the CPI is based. Each of such new items is priced at zero (since in fact it is neither marketed nor priced) and weighted by the total expenditures it entails in both the public and private sectors as a proportion of the Gross Domestic Product.

William Krehm

Line in the Sand

During the run-up to the Canada-US Free Trade Agreement (FTA), a group of progressive Canadian nationalists formed a political action group — The Council of Canadians. The COC's 30,000 active supporters represent a diverse group united in their commitment to the "protection and enhancement of Canadian political, economic, environmental and cultural sovereignty and to the promotion of democratic rights of Canadians and people around the world."

While ultimately unsuccessful in their efforts to stop the FTA and NAFTA, the COC has come away more determined than ever to fight for popular and national sovereignty in the face of "the corporate agenda." With the parliamentary opposition confined largely to Quebec separatists and the populist but right-wing Reform Party, many now consider the COC to be the main progressive opposition in English Canada.

It could well be that the COC's annual General Meeting held in Ottawa on October 14-16 marked a watershed in Canada's lamentable policy record of the past few years. A spirit of combative optimism pervaded the 350 people who had come from every part of the country. There was a feeling that a line had to be drawn in the sand in defence of Canada's social programs. As happened in New Zealand a decade ago, these are now being threatened due to the government's debt/deficit crisis.

Until recently the Council has been weak on economic issues. Its main economic prescription has been fairer taxation. Over the past year, however, there has been a great interest among COC members in the issues addressed by COMER, and there is a growing overlap in membership between the two organisations.

The COC invited COMER spokespersons John Hotson and William Krehm to address a working group on "Canadian Monetary Policy and Economic Sovereignty." The result was a resolution presented for consideration by the wrap-up plenary session. The motion, moved and seconded by Jordan Grant and George Crowell, who are members both of the COC and COMER, was overwhelmingly endorsed. It reads as follows:

"Whereas poor monetary and fiscal policy and loss of public control over the Canadian financial system have resulted in an explosion of debt,

"Whereas the current attack on social programmes is solely in response to the demands of the financial sector of the economy and bears no relation to the needs and capacities of the real economy,

"Whereas the cornerstone of any economic policy must be full employment and respect for the environment,

"And Whereas any attempt to regain control of the social and economic policy agenda is inextricably linked to reasserting control over the financial system,

"It is therefore resolved that the Council of Canadians make as an integral part of its campaign "Standing on Guard for Canada's Social Programmes" an education and lobbying programme on economic issues including the links between economic policy and social and environmental issues and the need to reassert control over our financial sector. Steps to be considered in the campaign shall include, amongst others, the following elements:

1. The use of capital budgeting at federal and provincial levels so that the public debt may be measured against the corresponding public assets;

2. Re-institution of the requirement for deposit-taking financial institutions to maintain reserves with the Bank of Canada;

3. The use of the Bank of Canada's existing authority to lend money to the provinces and municipalities at low interest rates for capital investment in such areas as human resources, public infrastructures, and environmental cleanup and in support of a full employment policy;

4. The restoration of a reasonable balance between Bank of Canada — created money and private bank-created money, and the discontinuation of the use of high interest rates and high unemployment to control inflation in favour of more targeted and humane measures of inflation control;

5. Financial re-regulation and tax measures to slow down the velocity of "hot" international money flowing into and out of the economy, ensure that money creation by the private banking system is directed to real investment and consumption rather than speculation and require that Canadian savings in tax-sheltered vehicles such as pension plans and RRSPs are used to create Canadian jobs rather than invested overseas;

6. Rethinking of our methods of measuring inflation and economic growth to take into account qualitative improvements such as the cleaning up of the environment and the value of unpaid work; and

7. Recognition that environment is not an infinite resource and must form the central part of any economic plan.

And be it further resolved that an economic policy working group be struck consisting of members of the Board of Directors and others to explore in detail the economic assumptions underlying the current policy agenda, and to identify and develop alternatives that are 'socially desirable, economically feasible, and politically credible' in conjunction with other like-minded groups."

Jordan Grant

Hixson's Corner — The "Natural" Rate of Unemployment vs. The Self-Regulating Market

The advocates of a so-called "command economy" have never been fewer than nowadays. But there is no basis for concluding from this that since government cannot provide an answer to all our problems it cannot be useful in providing a solution or partial solution to *some* of them.

As Karl Polanyi maintained in *The Great Transformation*, there are three areas in which "market forces" are particularly inept in confronting problems that inevitably arise. He refers to what he calls the "labour market," "the land market," and the "money market." According to the "theory of markets," supply, demand and price are so interrelated that there will always be a price at which supply and demand will come into equilibrium. There will then be a demand for all that is supplied and a supply for all that is demanded, The market will clear.

Applied to the "labour market," this theory says that there will always be a level of wages at which there will be no excesses of the supply of labour over the demand for it — there will be no unemployment. Paraphrasing Ricardo, "Should the number of working population exceed the demand nothing can prevent wages from falling even below the minimum necessary for existence, for there will no longer be any necessity for keeping them alive."

Near the point at which the "equilibrium wage" becomes a "starvation wage," the unemployed lose all interest in the theory of markets and demand that the government enter the picture and either provide "welfare payments" or become the "employer of the last resort" at a "minimum wage."

The staunchest defenders of a policy of leaving everything to market forces now talk of a so-called "natural rate of unemployment."But that amounts to saying that in present-day economies (unwilling to tolerate starvation wages) the demand for labour will not tend to rise to a level equal to the supply of labour. It amounts to saying that the theory of markets is inapplicable.

For things produced for the market, for true commodities (services included), "the market" works tolerably well. But labour (persons) is not produced for the market. People are produced for reasons entirely unrelated to markets. On the contrary, markets should be for serving people, not people for serving markets.

All theory aside, no advance in the welfare of labour, no improvement in the condition of people depending on wages or salaries may be attributed to "the market." In every case, amelioration has been in defiance of "market forces" and due either to labour organisations or to government.

No "market force" tended to reduce the length of the work-day from 16 to 8 hours or the work-week from 80 to 40 hours. Every improvement in the conditions of labour has, in fact, been due to something other than the "self-regulating market" — principally due to "government interference."

It is no longer credible that an economy can operate optimally or even with a minimally acceptable degree of compassion or humanity if only the government will restrict itself to providing defense against foreigners, prisons for the unruly destitute, and a proper mechanism for the foreclosure of mortgages and otherwise collecting debts.

William F. Hixson

Vol. 6, No. 12 — December 1994

Three Strikes and Out!

The most convincing thing that Clinton always had going for him was the enemies he made; but the election blew that up to the point of insult. He is left facing characters as antediluvian as Jesse Helms chairing key congressional committees. And Senator Alfonse d'Amato, of all people, may be wielding the gavel over an enquiry into a bad investment of a former governor of Arkansas long ago that lost mere pocket change compared to the misadventures in S&L land of the new Governor of Texas, name of Bush.

Most disturbing of all was the landslide approval in California of Proposition 187 denying education and social services to undocumented immigrant families. In that state illegals have long done underpaid work that went begging among native Americans. But then the Statue of Liberty, a continent away, has her back turned on California. Though Proposition 187 is likely to be quashed by the Supreme Court, the mood of the electorate opens the prospect of an underclass of pariahs, illiterate, hounded, and dehumanised.

At one level the elections signalled the syndrome of a lone superpower suddenly finding itself short of a superfoe. This has left the US with the task of redefining itself. For some the solution is internalizing the hatreds and physical menace for which the Soviet Union had offered an outlet. Significantly, a parallel phenomenon has cropped up in Russia in the neofascist spasms of Zhirinovsky.

It appears in antics of the gun lobby, unrelenting even after the shooting up of the White House, in the murder of doctors by crazed anti-abortionists, and in the passion for building penitentiaries seen not as "pork" but as the purest beef.

At the most basic level, the American people feel threatened by a faceless enemy sapping their manhood, their living standards, their country's preeminence abroad, their image of themselves. As a creeping socialist, Johnny Appleseed is out, but Western vigilantes, sheriffs who shoot from the hip and ask questions later are acquiring the sentimental appeal of Currier and Ives prints.

The Great American Dream has soured into nightmare. With the sharply regressive taxation of the past two decades, deteriorating public services, the espousal of bankruptcies and mass unemployment as the means of"stabilizing" the economy, the middle class has come to feel as threatened as those at the poverty line.

In his *Boiling Point, Democrats, Republicans and the Decline of the Middle-Class Prosperity* (1993) Kevin Phillips, an erstwhile Republican analyst, summed up the trend. Between 1977 and 1989 the effective tax rate paid by the lowest quintile of income was unchanged at 9.3%, but that of the top 1% dropped from 35.5% to 26.7%. "From 1979 to 1982, as the maximum tax rate on capital gains fell from 49% to 20%, the maximum income tax rate on unearned incomes dropped from 70% to 50% The effect on financial markets — once they were also reassured by disinflation — was to fuel a massive boom. The lower tax rates raised the after-tax return on and thus the value of financial assets like stocks and bonds. From 1978 to 1988 the number of persons with million-dollar annual incomes or more sky-rocketed from 2,041 to 65,303."

Under Roosevelt the Fed had been reinvented to prevent depressions. Today it singles out planned recession as the sole tool for "fighting inflation." The resulting lurching of interest rates has enabled speculative finance to pick the bones of the producing economy. And with a straight face all this is attributed to the market, and hence without appeal.

With information blocked, symbols acquire an overwhelming force. Remember the patriotic indignation when the Japanese were loading up with "American ikons" like Rockefeller Center at the peak of the real estate bubble? Something similar is afoot with the sinking US dollar defying the Fed's efforts to underpin it against the yen and the mark.

After World War II US dollars took over the role of international monetary standard held by gold in the twenties. But unlike gold the dollar is not a commodity: its value is bestowed by fiat. Having its currency accepted as an unofficial international standard is a bonanza for the issuing nation. It allows it to create at no cost much of the money base of the world.

But with that privilege goes responsibilities which the American authorities have hardly observed. When they churn interest rates to flatten a misleading price index, they are in fact disqualifying their currency to moonlight as international monetary base. That was also so when Washington deregulated American banking and encouraged wildly-leveraged gambles in derivatives. Every time speculators lose or win big, there is a deluge of dollars sploshing across national frontiers.

The outcome of all this has been the third major pratfall of American monetary policy in the last few years. The first was the collapse of the US Savings and Loan banks in a miasma of corruption. The second was the failure to foresee the incompatibility of the"zero inflation" via high interest rates with the Bank for International Settlements' Risk-based Capital Requirements that declared government bonds (of OECD countries) risk-free. As *ER* predicted two years ago, when the Fed pushed up interest rates again the banks sustained massive losses on their bond hoards.

In *The Globe and Mail* (14/11) Donald Coxe, president of Harris Investment Management Inc. of Chicago, connects the impact of that with the election: "Until Mr. Clinton, no president in our time made the care and feeding of bond investors a core component of his program. Mr. Clinton was led by such advisers as Wall St. whiz Robert Rubin to understand that if he delivered deficit reduction and a low-inflation, moderate-growth economy, interest rates would stay low to help fund his rather modest agenda of new social programs. But Clinton's defeat adds one more major source of strength to the big financial story of 1994: a the most formidable bond bear in history." Sinking bond prices due to rising interest rates have led to a massive flight of investors from American stocks. That has contributed in a major way to the fainting spells of the dollar.

Democrats and Republicans have joined to jail even petty criminals for life according to the good old baseball rule: "Three strike and out!" Surely the time has come to extend that principle to a monetary policy that, suppressing evidence and falsifying history, is driving the world over the cliff.

Bretton Woods Revisited

On October 15-17 the Institute for Agriculture and Trade Policy organised an intergenerational conference attended by many of the early leaders of the Bretton Woods system that produced the International Monetary Fund, the World Bank, and finally the World Trade Organisation which is scheduled to be voted on in Congress shortly.

Many of the original architects present were able to congratulate one another on the relatively successful development of international institutions in managing the global economy. Also invited were young economists and activists associated with the "Fifty Years is Enough" movement that is critical of existing international economic policy. The thrust of the young critics was directed at the contributions of the IMF to the increased pauperization of the Third World.

One of the purposes of my attendance was to discover the mechanism whereby Resolution 5 of the Bretton Woods Agreement was never carried out. Readers of *Economic Reform* may remember that this resolution called for the elimination of the Bank for International Settlements (BIS) because of its cooperation with Hitler.

The BIS was established in 1930 to service the loans — largely made under the Dawes and Young Plans — to Weimar Germany which allowed the Germans to go through the motions of paying reparations after World War I. Later, it was assumed that President Hoover's moratorium of 1931 rendered these bonds null and void. In fact the BIS annual report in 1980 recorded the final payment on the Dawes and Young Plans by the Federal Republic of Germany.

Resolution 5 was initiated by the Norwegian delegation. In the late thirties, when Hitler brought Bohemia under the Czech Protectorate and created an independent Slovakia under Father Tiso, the BIS seems to have allowed the Germans access to former Czechoslovak assets.

In July 1944 there was still considerable anti-fascist sentiment. The Norwegian delegation consisted of anti-fascist exiles, and very anti-fascist delegations represented other governments-in-exile.

By the time the IMF began operations in 1946, the mood had changed as the Cold War was beginning. In February 1946 the US Secretary of State Jimmy Byrnes was telling the Russians that if they wanted German reparations — promised by the Potsdam and Yalta Agreements — they should take them out of their "Soviet Zone."

The Russians attended the Bretton Woods Conference, and were represented by Stepanov, whose picture is on the wall in the permanent exhibit outside the Gold Room in the Mt. Washington Hotel where the Conference was held. Though there is no picture of Keynes in the permanent exhibit, they did have some pictures of him on an easel added for the Bretton Woods Revisited Conference.

Like everything else in the West, the IMF and the World Bank were converted into instruments of the Cold War, denying credits to East European members such as Czechoslovakia or Vietnam. The International Development Association was created as an answer to Khrushchev's foreign aid program to the Third World, lending to poor countries for forty years at one percent interest. The combination of the foreign aid and military competition eventually did the Soviet economy in.

Since the War had left Britain impoverished, the British received special treatment by the BIS. In gratitude the British representatives at the IMF proposed dropping Resolution 5 to Edward M. Bernstein, then the first Director of Research at the IMF. Bernstein, who had been the Chief Technical Adviser and Executive Secretary of the US Delegation to the Bretton Woods Conference in 1944, went along with the British position.

Lynn Turgeon
Professor Emeritus of Economics
Hofstra University

Vol. 7, No. 1 — January 1995

Behind Our Banks' Bonanza

It was enough to bring flushes to the cheeks of PR types not given to blushing. In lockstep with the US Fed the Bank of Canada had bumped up interest rates for the sixth time since February. Our chartered bank CEOs had taken turns predicting disaster if we don't gut our social programs. And then in the midst of this hand-wringing, the banks announced a super-bumper year. The Royal Bank, the largest of them all, chalked up well over a billion dollar profit. This was up 290% with a return on equity of 16.8% compared to 2.4% last year.

A brokerage spokesman (*Globe and Mail* 6/12) rushed in to claim that the banks' "collective return on equity of 12 to 13% for 1994 is 'dead in line' with the 25-year average." But Michael McCracken of Informetrica Ltd. put that straight: "What they're talking about is a nominal rate of return. Subtract inflation from returns in the 19-20% range in parts of the 1970s and 1980s and the 1994 tally is anything but average. They should be looking at the real rate of return."

The public is being warned not to incur the sin of envy. Hadn't the banks laboured, and increased their productivity? However, if we were able to identify the sources of our banks' prosperity in a setting of poverty and convince ourselves that there was no connection between the two, we could more readily take joy in their good fortune.

Even among economists there is a shocking lack of familiarity with the mechanics of banking. For a good twenty years we have had drummed into our heads that high interest rates are imposed by "the market" — as though that were a force of nature. We are told that humans can do little to bring those rates down, and are urged to pay them manfully and pull in our belts. But now in the awkward situation created by record bank profits, bits of truth are drooling out of brokers' mouths. "It's the Bank of Canada, not the commercial banks, that largely control rates, analysts note." (*G&M* 7/12).

We are asked to take pride that our banking system has come out of the difficult years in so much better shape than our trust and insurance companies. Unmentioned is the detail that our banks were allowed to pick up at bargain prices the segments of those distressed trust and insurance companies still worth the trouble — at times with government guarantees

The boom of the eighties left most of our banks with uncomfortable portions of their capital in defaulted real estate and other speculative loans. To bail them out the *Bank Act* was amended in 1991 to phase out the reserves the banks had to put up with the Bank of Canada to protect their depositors. These reserves had earned them no interest. The amendment to the *Bank Act* slipped through Parliament neither understood nor noticed by many MPs who voted for it.

Shortly before, the Bank for International Settlements had brought in new risk-based capital requirements to deal with banks' mounting liquidity problems. Government bonds were declared risk-free, calling for not a penny of the banks' own capital.

Together, these two measures have changed the face of banking in Canada. To recoup speculative losses the banks built up their holdings of government bonds which no longer required cash reserves at the central bank nor more capital of their own. Between December 1990 and August 1994 their portfolios of federal government bonds soared from $3.5 billion to $35.6B — i.e. by 900%. [The total federal debt held increased by 300% to $80 B.]

At the same time, the Bank of Canada cut its stock of government bonds from $10B in 1989 to $6.2B in September 1994 — i.e. by 38%.

When the BoC acquires federal bonds the interest paid on them comes back substantially to the central bank's sole shareholder, the government. When the banks hold similar bonds, that interest stays with them. Such indeed was the purpose of the exercise rushed through in the banks' hour of need. The banks are being paid simply for storing public debt in their strongboxes.

Assured of such effortless income, the banks have felt free to engage in high-leveraged gambles in currencies and derivatives. Legislation to prevent our banks from speculating and shorting our dollar is certainly overdue.

Under the polite term "fees," banks have begun demanding outrageous payments for routine services that bear no relationship to their costs.

The *G&M* (15/12) informed us that "Canada's largest banks coming off their most profitable year yet, are quietly claiming hundreds of millions of dollars in tax credits under a federal program designed to encourage leading-edge science. This is for computer projects that they would have introduced in any case. 'This may become the son of SRTC,' said a partner in one of the country's major accounting firms, referring to the Scientific Research Tax Credit, which was abruptly cancelled a decade ago after costing the government more than $1 billion in tax revenues and leading to a litany of fraud convictions."

Success, too lightly obtained, becomes addictive. And having had everything their own way, our banks are forever seeking fresh teats on that big, dumb cow, the government.

Regurgitation of a Whole Food Chain?

To promote its program for "restructuring" social services, the Minister of Human Resources had MPs across the land organize open townhall meetings. At these the proposed revisions to our social programs were presented as just an updating of legislation that no longer answered the needs of a changing world. There was no hint of any connection with the roaring deficit-reduction campaign. Yet only the brain-dead could overlook that the campaign for slashing the federal deficit centered on down-sizing social programs at a time of rapidly growing need.

Two of the meetings we attended offered revealing contrasts. The sociology of Toronto's ridings apes the jagged contours of its ravines. A highly affluent Rosedale district rubs elbows with near-slums. Despite this the Rosedale meeting managed to express its discontent in a basically orderly way.

The following evening a meeting organized at the Scarborough Centre by five MPs fell short of that. Scarborough is a blue-collar municipality with a fringe of opulence on the north. There blind indignation took over. Denunciations of immigrants, abusive recipients of unemployment insurance, and members of parliament consumed most of the available time.

A few days later in Montreal a mob of protesters broke into a consultation meeting on the proposed social reforms and, until the police arrived, trashed the furnishings.

From these meetings a momentous message to Ottawa emerged. Installing unbridled greed as automatic pilot for economic policy invites chaotic revolt.

But isn't salvation on its way from the sweeping free trade blocks that our government is so busily negotiating? Has our PM not returned from China with a

Kleeg-light tan and a trunkful of contract prospects? Precisely. Nothing better than China illustrates the abyss towards which our society is being stampeded. Shortly after Chrétien had walked down the Forbidden City aisle with nine provincial premiers as bridesmaids, *The Wall Street Journal* (2/12) headed a story: 'Honeymoon's Over on the West's Trade with Beijing.' Chinese banks have begun defaulting on their obligations to the West, contracts are being rewritten unilaterally by China.

In *Saturday Night* (12/94) John Fraser, former *Globe and Mail* correspondent in China, explores the subject. "When he recently visited China without official blessing, an old contact warned him of "the endemic personal and institutional corruption, the growing disaffection of the peasantry, and the rising brutality of the new cities. But surely, I reasoned, the new economic zones must work as safety valves, both by creating new industries and jobs, and as something to dream about." He was told that for every person who makes it to the new economic zones, five or ten are trying to get into them "There is something new in modern China — millions of people with no permanent home, no permanent work, nothing at all to lose. You are going to Guangzhou. Visit the railway station and you will meet them." Fraser found tens of thousands camping outside the station.

We have been locked into a single foodchain with those destitute Chinese millions. Streaming out of the overpopulated countryside, they enforce a world-wide "natural rate of unemployment" — to use the lingo of mainline economists. High at the top of that food chain are the financial makers and shakers who profit by the arrangement. But at the lower rungs and indeed most of the way up, lives are being "destructured." For "structure" in anybody's life implies a job, a home, security, and some continuity with the past. But that is what the millions camping around China's railway stations have been deprived of. And their pressure is felt not only in Canton, Shanghai and Hong Kong, but through cheap imports and the diversion of capital, in Europe and North America.

As the rich get richer and the poor poorer in China's swarming cities, we are likely to get not 1.2 billion customers for our exports, but a planet-wide contagion of social breakdown. It is not hard to foresee the default of loans guaranteed by our government to finance megaprojects such as the Three Gorges Dam that will strip more than a million people of their homes and land. Our government resists using the BoC to finance essential environmental projects in Canada that could put our jobless to work; but it is proceeding slap-happily to fund mammoth projects in China condemned both by environmentalists and economists not on the official bandwagon.

Stuck with its guarantees, our government will find fresh cause for hacking away at what may be left of our social programs.

wk

Don't worry about those trees. They're not in trouble after all. The 90% of the "pre-consumer" fibre in letters and envelopes mentioned does not come from "trees," but from "meadow waste." Officials of the Service at the Siskiyou National Forest recently planned to cut timber over a large area. This is usually called "logging," but the Forest Service calls it a "meadow restoration project." The Oregon Natural Resources Council calls the plan a ruse to produce almost two million board feet of timber. *Quarterly Review of Doublespeak* (10/94)

The Tinbergen X-Ray for Policy Fraud

Some decades ago the Dutch economist Jan Tinbergen, a Nobel laureate, tried bringing scientific method to economics. Having received his doctorate in physics rather than economics, he had a serious understanding of what science was about.

Control theory tells us that if n independent variables can be identified in a problem, no solution with less than n independent variables can work. Proposing a solution with a single independent variable to a problem with several such variables would be like putting a one-armed, one-legged wrestler in the ring against an intact opponent.

From this principle, Tinbergen deduced his "counting rule" for policy-making. If there are n independent goals to be pursued, no less than n independent policy instruments are needed for the job.

Tinbergen's proposal came when the central banks of the world were being taken over by the monetarists whose faith demands a bogus single-variable solution. Previously economic policy in the free world had set itself several goals — the greatest possible stability of employment, trade, prices and exchange rates. But in the seventies a well-organised campaign was launched to replace these multiple goals with a single one — price stability. And the one acceptable means for achieving that was higher interest rates. Tinbergen's counting rule would have debunked that Grand Design. It was ignored.

Let us improvise a notation to set up the Tinbergen test S(4) ~P(4) which will be defined to mean a Solution with 4 independent policy instruments has just enough degrees of freedom (independent variables) to achieve a Policy with 4 independent objectives.

Tests of this sort permit engineers to check the design of spaceships on the drafting board. They don't build their spaceship without such checks and send them into space only to find that they blow up or cannot be brought back.

Economists, however, adopt the contrary course. Even after their models have repeatedly crashed, they cover up their design effects.

In the fall of 1991 when the country had for a second time been brought into the deepest depression since the thirties, the BoC launched an all-out campaign to inscribe "zero inflation" into the Constitution and the *Bank of Canada Act*. This was to replace the provisions that require the Bank to use its monetary powers to moderate oscillations in trade, employment, prices, and exchange rates. In hundreds of speeches and editorials this was dismissed as a "mishmash" of goals that could not possibly work. What was kept from the readers was that it had worked well in the most lustrous decades of our economic history. Fortunately a parliamentary committee turned down the proposal.

What the Bank of Canada was proposing could be expressed in terms of our version of the Tinbergen model as follows: S(1) ~ P(1). The solution proposed was to shove up interest rates (by restricting the money supply) on the assumption that would give us non-inflationary prosperity — which by the Tinbergen control rule would have to have only a single independent variable.

A little examination, however, refutes the assumption of the one-dimensional nature of our "inflation" problem. Prices in a mixed economy can move up for very different reasons. The conventional model *defines* any price rise as a sign of too much market demand outstripping supply [i.e. the sole independent variable is the ratio of demand to supply]. However, if laws are passed to clean up the environment that will show up in increased costs and a higher price index. Rather than more inflation that is less cancer.

The "inflation" variable (statistic) lumps together a cluster of very different problems. It must be unbundled to reveal real causes, i.e. the independent variables. To get out of our present mess we must learn to distinguish "market inflation" due to an excess of demand over supply from "structural price rise" which reflects additional value delivered without purchase because of new regulatory laws, or additional taxation to finance essential public services.

When inflation was "licked" by defeating the economy, the deficit exploded, and replaced the one-dimensional official goal with another — "lick the deficit." However, it is impossible to balance a budget that writes off government acquisitions of land, buildings and equipment in a single year and enters their value on the books at a nominal one dollar. The slashing of government services and investment by assigning to money-lenders higher interest rates, merely causes society to come apart. But that is not recognised in single-variable trade-offs.

During WW II and the quarter of a century that followed, society's needs were addressed with a rich menu of policy instruments: forced savings of a portion of earnings to keep excess demand off the market, exchange controls, ceilings on interest rates, more equitable taxation, full employment, restraints on consumer credit, and when necessary price controls. High interest rates were ruled out because they would bleed the productive economy and the public treasury and leave us without resources for attacking society's real problems.

William Krehm

Vol. 7, No. 2 — February 1995

Year of Truth

1994 was NAFTA's year of instant truth. 85 million Mexicans had been presented to us as a beckoning market in an emergent democracy. For the purpose, democracy was redefined to mean the privatisation of public companies, letting bankers and security pushers set up shop with a minimum of regulation, and smothering inflation with high interest rates.

But with the fizz of a pricked tire, NAFTA suddenly gave up the hot air that shaped it.

On the very day it came into force, January 1, 1994, the peasant revolt broke out in Chiapas. Then the presidential candidate and a high official of the government party were assassinated. As marinated in corruption as Dutch herring in brine, the Institutional Revolutionary Party has been in power since the murder of a president-elect in 1928.

First had come the official protestation that Mexico would not devalue, then the local media were informed that the government was discontinuing its support of the peso. Only the following morning were the tidings shared with the outside world. During Xmas week the peso shed 40% of its market value.

However, some Mexicans had long since anticipated the "globalisation" of fleet-footed capital. From colonial times galleons loaded with treasure leaving for distant shores have been something of a national ikon; and not infrequently they were waylaid by blond buccaneers. Stanley Fisher, chief World Bank economist, estimated the flight of capital at the time of Mexico's default on its debt in the early eighties amounted to half the Mexican debt.

American investors had been hoodwinked into believing that Mexico was no longer Mexico because the president and finance minister had Ivy League diplomas on their office walls and swore to fight inflation with high interest rates.

What former President Carlos Salinas de Gotari's American enthusiasts were admiring was essentially what they saw in their mirrors. Only a week before, the Orange County bankruptcy in California as a result of the derivatives investments it had been led into had shaken American markets to their boots.

Orange County, in a sense, worked to Mexico's advantage. It left Washington in no mood for another financial earthquake. In no time flat $18 billion of credit lines were put together to help Mexico face its maturing debt. Of this the US is putting up $9 billion, and Canada C$1.5 billion.

The blame for the artificially high peso was pinned on the former government. Devaluation had been considered in 1993, but Salinas was anxious to ensure US congressional approval for NAFTA. So the peso was kept at lofty levels with high interest rates right until its collapse.

Logic instead would have dictated temporary exchange controls. But it is a central tenet of the monetarist faith that capital — even in its most carnivorous forms — must be accorded a diplomatic passport for moving unquestioned across frontiers.

NAFTA has destroyed whatever bargaining power Mexico had in dealing with its neighbour. The Zedillo government first announced the stepped-up privatisation of chemical plants, ports, airports, and highways. It stopped short only of the oil industry. But bankers merely had to give the screw another turn for Mexico to throw in the down-stream assets of the national oil company as collateral for its borrowings. This lets all the demons of Mexican-US history out of the closet again. The nationalization of their oil industry in 1938 was as much a reassertion of national self-respect as strictly economic policy.

The Bank for International Settlements Guidelines on Risk-based Capital Requirements for banks now declares the debt of all OECD countries "risk-free." A bank can buy the bonds of such a country without putting up a penny of legal tender or capital. The only restriction is that the borrowing country must not have restructured its debt during the five previous years. Mexico was accepted into the OECD last fall in recognition of its economic soundness. The last restructuring of its debt took place in March 1990. Had the present contretemps been delayed for another three months, it would thus have become possible for Canadian banks to load up to the gills with high-interest-bearing Mexican debt. At present the exposure of Canadian banks to the Mexican debacle is some $2.5 B. Our government is committing $1.5B to help bail them out.

The high-flying shenanigans of deregulated finance combining with the peculiar vulnerabilities of Mexico will haunt the world for years to come. Falling due in coming months are $18B of *tesobonos* (government bonds denominated in pesos but adjusted to the exchange rate with the dollar). As though that were not problem enough, these tesobonos form the basis for complex derivatives peddled by US investment houses. The resulting nightmares have induced the US government to supplement the initial $18 B standby fund with $40B of US guarantees. Both Democratic and Republican caucuses are supporting the bill.

The world's monetary authorities failed to foresee the fruits of their labours when they were already rotting under their noses. To cover up, their spin doctors are redoubling their efforts. There is, for example, the editorial in *The Wall Street Journal*

(12/1): "Mexico isn't the only US neighbour flirting with the financial abyss. Canada has now become an honorary member of the Third World."

Basic to Mexico's troubles is the lack since colonial days of the slightest trust between the various layers of society. In spirit Hernan Cortes still rides over the Indians.

Canada on the other hand has built up a high degree of mutual respect among its citizens. Nobody should be allowed to destroy that asset — not even the hot-panted financiers planning their next global scam.

Despite the efforts of the Mulroney government to remove them, the provisions are still in the *Bank of Canada Act* for handling our debt problem. We need only increase the BoC's holdings of government bonds to the 1975 level (20.8% as compared to the present 5.5%). We could repatriate at a discount any Canadian bonds (practically all of which are denominated in Canadian dollars) that foreign holders choose to dump.

On the other hand it takes foreign currency to support our dollar as we are foolishly doing, hamstringing our recovery en route. And the interest paid on government bonds held by the BoC does revert to its sole shareholder, the federal government. Bringing the BoC's proportion of the federal debt to the 1975 proportion would save $7.5B per year. That should ring a bell for our Finance Minister, Sisyphus Martin, in his budget-balancing labours.

The Virtues of Hindsight

Hindsight is an overly disparaged resource. It is actually the best protection against ideologies grown long in the tooth.

It took two world wars to jolt our monetarist bureaucrats out of their inherited beliefs. What is unusual in the present crisis is that the wisdom acquired with so much blood and treasure has been buried again. We are left with the financial sophistication that existed before 1914.

On the outbreak of the First World War, Britain raised its bank rate from 3% to 10% in a knee-jerk reaction to defend the pound. With the present monetarist dogma in place, that is precisely what our central bank does when confronted with any major emergency — whether flood or drought, earthquake of foreign war.

But a few days later on August 6th, 1914, came some realization that country's productive capacity rather than its gold reserves is the ultimate backing for its credit. The Currency and Bank Note Act underpinned the nation's entire debt. Against the Treasury's guarantee the Bank of England actually lent to acceptance houses up to 60% of any loan outstanding at the outbreak of the war. When the public was slow in absorbing the First War Loan the banks were called upon to pick up nearly one third of the issue amounting to £330M. To finance the banks' holdings of the war loans, the BoE lent them money at 1% below the bank rate.

It even began to dawn on the bureaucrats that the BoE could save the nation a great deal of money by holding more of the debt itself instead of financing the commercial banks to do so. Between 29/7/14 and 27/11/18 the Banking Department of the BoE's holdings of government securities rose from £10M to 62.6M — or from 13% to 33% of the central bank's assets.

In Canada something similar took place. We had no central bank at the time, but on the outbreak of WWI the Finance Ministry announced its readiness to advance Dominion notes to the banks against securities as collateral. This innovation, originally intended as a wartime measure, was put on a permanent basis by the 1923 Finance Act. But such increases in the money supply were left entirely to the initiative of the banks. The practice of allowing the banks to borrow from the government against commercial paper was carried forward in the *Bank of Canada Act* (1934) establishing provision for the banks to borrow from the BoC against "secondary reserves" — commercial paper discounted by them. Its purpose as in WWI was to temper periods of financial stringency. In recent years, however, financial stringency, rather than something to be relieved, has become the sole instrument in the fight for "zero inflation." Accordingly, that provision in the Act has lapsed into disuse. [It was actually repealed in 1980.]

In World War II Great Britain, the US and Canada adopted a deliberate policy of 'pegging' the interest structure at a low level, something that required the cooperation of their central banks. The Bank of Canada had opened its doors in 1935, and was completely nationalised three years later. The war taught our government how to make far greater use of its potential than had been done during the depression of the thirties.

In Great Britain the bank rate was reduced to 3% on 29/9/39 and to 2% a month later, and was held there throughout the war. With wartime conditions, it is unlikely that a high bank rate would have increased the supply of foreign exchange. High interest rates have since come to be viewed by our central bank as an unfailing way of making foreign exchange available. Nor do higher interest rates solve a country's foreign exchange problems even in peace. Were it so, the Canadian dollar would long since have carried away the gold at the Olympics.

In Britain the total central bank loans to the government amounted to only 8% of the increase in debt during WWII. The corresponding figure in the US was 9%.a During the first three years of the war this proportion in Canada actually amounted to 16% of the federal debt (compared with 19% held by the chartered banks). But when full employment put more money into private pockets, the central bank's holdings of government debt declined to 14%. The victory bonds were largely financed on the instalment plan: the victory bondholder borrowed 90% of the money paid for his bond from his bank, and to make that loan the bank put up only 10% as reserves with the Bank of Canada. The whole scheme was made possible because of the pegging of interest rates at a low level and rigorous price and exchange controls.

wk

Vol. 7, No. 3 — March 1995

In Quest of an Anorexic Economy

Under the Bourbons the nobility was exempt from taxation — i.e. from contributing to society's overhead costs. Our money-lenders are seeking a similar privilege. In our mixed economy ever more costly infrastructures are provided by the state. By their very nature many of these cannot be priced or marketed; instead they are paid for by taxation which filters into the price level. A flat price index in our society would excuse lenders from paying their share for public services.

In our society even consumption has become capital-intensive: the pacesetters of our economy are "big-ticket" items like homes, cars, appliances, post-secondary education. That makes borrowers acutely vulnerable to high interest rates used to flatten prices.

Repeatedly in recent years, interest rates have been pushed to the point of collapsing the economy. But once the economy is down for the count, interest rates plummet along with everything else, and retired people suddenly find themselves short of income. That sets the stage for the slaughter of the innocent as retirees scramble for more lucrative returns.

Central banks had promised an indefinite period of prosperity and low interest rates once we had "licked inflation." On the strength of that Wall St. synthesized derivatives combining the most bizarre notional features of securities. Pensions and mutual funds, municipalities gobbled these up in the hope of higher returns. But instead of the low rates promised, we have had seven increases by the Federal Reserve in a single year. That brought on the most devastating crisis in bond markets since 1929.

The Mexican economy, promoted as the great white hope, caved in under the sudden jump in the carrying charges of its historic debt.

Wall St. firms marketing highly speculative paper thrive on the churning of the economy with lurching interest rates. Whether they go long or short, in the confusion there is money to be made.

However, no worker has ever made a fortune shorting the labour market. Though rarely mentioned in the media, the "natural rate of unemployment" — the "Non-accelerating inflation rate of unemployment" (NAIRU) — has become the lodestar of right-thinking economists. No sooner does the economy show signs of picking itself off the floor than the Fed hits it on the head again with higher interest rates. That cannot possibly make sense for industrial firms.

"[The natural rate of unemployment] was developed in the late 1960s by Edmund Phelps and Milton Friedman. Phelps concluded that if unemployment stays one point below the natural rate for two years, it will cause a permanent one-point rise in the inflation rate — that only two years of unemployment one point above the natural rate will root out. Milton Friedman, the other father of natural-rate theory, has completely disavowed the forecasting use to which his creation has been turned. 'I don't know what the natural rate is, neither do you, and neither does anyone else.'"

But to have a duly anorexic economy, you must not only have enough people unemployed, but idle equipment and plant as well. And here again producers are pulling away from the "zero inflation" goal.

"Chrysler Corp.'s chief economist, W. Van Bussmann, [when] asked about the Fed's capacity utilization number of 90.7% for the auto industry, responds, 'It is misleading.' Not counted in the capacity data, he notes, is the potential to go to a third shift, to import vehicles from foreign plants or to eliminate traditional bottlenecks."

The time is ripe for forging broad alliances of all victims of a failed dogma that refuses to let go.

Meltdown!

Our readers will certainly have heard of *The Wall Street Journal* (12/1) editorial proclaiming Canada "an honorary member of the Third World." But they will search their newspapers in vain for a mention of a front-page *WSJ* column a couple of weeks later (30/1). We have had it drummed into our heads that the IMF will move in on us unless we slash our social programs to reduce our debt. There is, it is claimed, no other way out.

But shaken by the Mexican events, the *WSJ* revealed that there is after all another way:

"Unfettered private capital flows" made Mexico a financial basket case. In 1974, the year of the first oil shock, the OPEC countries syphoned off some 68 billion dollars more from the world economy than they spent on imports. And most of this money ended up on deposit with American banks. Partly because of its corrupt and compliant regimes, Latin America was chosen for the recycling ground for the oil money. The international financial organisations were perverted from their original purpose of balancing payment flows to extract every possible penny of interest on this recycled money. And all the while that debt was compounded at outlandish rates set by the US Fed "to lick inflation."

These payments outstripped by far the German reparation payments after World War I or the inverse reparations (victors to vanquished) of World War II under the Marshall Plan.

Bemused by fat fees and commissions, American banks in no time flat lent themselves into a state of undischarged bankruptcy. Their bad LA debts came to outweigh their capital by 150%. Repeatedly just enough "new money" was doled out to borrowers to enable them to make the minimum interest payments to keep their loans off the banks' books as "non-productive" debt. Today's peso meltdown is but the sequel to Mexico's 1982 default and the 1987 LA debt crisis. The essentials for the current blowup were in place when NAFTA was set up in a fury of mendacious hype.

Canadians must ask by what credentials our government goes on recycling Canada according to the tenets of a disastrously failed dogma. NAFTA and globalisation in general are basically a race to trawl the bottom of the world economy. But the lesson from Mexico is that there is no fixed bottom. The underdeveloped countries are far more vulnerable to high interest rates than the developed ones. Their debt load is greater, their social institutions more rickety. That means that when the Fed cranks up interest rates, living standards and society itself will collapse sooner in countries like Mexico than in Canada. But Canada will be under pressure to keep up with Mexico's fatal plunge.

k.

Sisyphus and His Rock

The scene might have been lifted from Greek mythology. Our Finance Minister, Mr. Sisyphus Martin, goes on eternally pushing his boulder up the mountain only to have it roll back on him. Friendly economists in brokerage houses inform him that with each rise in the US Fed's bank rate, the rock rolls back twice as fast as he has shoved it upward with so much groaning and self-congratulation. (*Globe and Mail* 18/1) They urge him to slash away at social programs still more zealously without wasting time on bogus consultations with the victims.

This has been going on for at least a decade.

Originally it was to "lick inflation." But early in January Alan Greenspan, chairman of the US Federal Reserve, complained to Congress that the Consumer Price Index could be overstating inflation by as much as 1.5%. From this Mr. Greenspan did not conclude that he ought to be more careful about shoving interest rates up further. What he was concerned with was adjusting federal benefits and tax brackets and exemptions downward to a more accurate price index. Similarly, Newt Gingrich, at a town meeting in Kenneshaw, Ga., threatened to cut off funding for the Bureau of Labor Statistics if it "can't get it right" within 30 days.

That would seem pizza-quick delivery to those of us who for years have been pressing for the unbundling of the grossly inaccurate CPI — for reasons that still escape Messers. Greenspan and Gingrich. When government proceeds to clean up our atmosphere, the costs will turn up in the CPI through the effects on prices of taxation and/or increased costs of producers. But the benefits, which are neither priced nor marketed, will elude the index [which after all deals only with price].

[On our side of the border] Statscan has not been encouraged to refine sensitive statistics. In August 1991 when Statscan concluded that the deficit was not due to increased spending but to a drop in government revenue and high interest rates, the Mulroney government made it eat crow on a reduced budget.

To dig ourselves out of our present mess, we must start by bringing our statistics and accountancy into line with reality.

The BoC has never asked how the interest rates it sets could fit into the real economy. It begins with the goal of making a highly flawed price index lie prone. But much of its movement merely reflects the rising costs of operating an increasingly urbanized, high-tech society. The difference in telephone rates in New York City and a town of 10,000 can hardly be considered inflation: it reflects the far more complex circuits connecting so many more phones. Linking people in a contemporary setting is even more costly.

Rethinking economics in terms of the interrelations of public and private sectors will disclose unsuspected options for managing upward price movement. The growth of essential public services within the economy has unsettled the traditional patterns of price. The conclusion to be drawn is not that essential public services must be cut, but that non-tax revenues must be found to lessen the government's dependence upon taxation.

Once we recognise the capital investments of government, we could seek out capital gains for the government. In the private sector, capital gains have become a holy cause, whereas in our government's finances, not even capital, let alone capital gains, are recognised.

To illustrate the point let's start with a bit of street smarts.

If unscrupulous operator A sells something to operator B and both are allergic to paying taxes, they can resort to a classic scam. A might invoice his sale to B at a lower price, and in return B lend money at a less than market rate. That would hardly please the tax authorities. But suppose the government became a partner in a legitimate version of such an arrangement. It could issue special tax-bonds offering certain tax-payers exemption (not just deferment) from taxation on both the principal and interest if they put the money into such long-term bonds at a fraction of the going rate of interest.

The government would recoup the taxation forgone not only in its interest savings, but through the likely erosion of the real value of the bond by the time it matured. It would be a 'swap' of taxes for lower interest rates — and both of these would help reduce the climb of the price level over time.

The plan would have a built-in hedge against inflation: if the tax-bonds were successful in moderating the price gradient [i.e. the secular price climb due to the changing structures of society] the state's capital gain at the end of the haul would be less; but the fight against price rise would have been won without wrecking the economy. If the structural price gradient continued steep, the capital gain would be greater and hence the state's dependence on taxation would be lessened.

Insurance features could be incorporated into the tax-bonds to help their placement. They could be redeemable at par in the event of the death of a bread-winner, disability, or protracted illness or involuntary unemployment. Since the coupon would be well below market, such redemption would in fact involve a bonus. With social programs being axed, this feature would be timely.

Our policy-makers must learn to start with a real social need and then seek a way of funding it that would move key parameters — taxes, prices, interest rates — downward, not upward. Tax-bonds are one of the many policies that could be designed around such neglected principles.

wk

Vol. 7, No. 4 — April 1995

Lessons out of Mexico

The lessons come pouring out from Mexico. *The Globe and Mail* (24/3) quotes Peter Godsoe, chairman of the Bank of Nova Scotia, "I must admit that the bank's $102 million investment in the fourth largest Mexican bank, obviously ain't what it used to be." Its value has fallen by two thirds in the few months since it was made.

Mr. Godsoe did a bit of whistling in the dark of the sort that bank managers are accustomed to hear from clients in trouble. "Scotiabank is taking a hard look at its equity stake in *Grupo Financiero Inverlat S.A.* [By next fall] the bank could write it down or become more active in acquiring a bigger equity interest."

The point is that the bank has not written down its admitted loss of $67 million. That is of importance to Canadians. Canada has replaced the reserves traditionally held at the BoC with capital requirements based on the risk of the different categories of investment.

But there is an immense difference between judging a bank's soundness by its reserves and by the amount of capital it has to support its debt. The first is held by the central bank in legal tender. The second can only be guessed at until accountants come around to evaluate the bank's portfolios.

If the accountants arrived at the Bank of Nova Scotia tomorrow they would find the *Inverlat* investment booked at $67 million more than Mr. Godsoe says it is worth.

Mr. Godsoe is "optimistic about Mexico's long-term prospects." But Mr. Godsoe was less than prescient at reading Mexico's future when the bank made that investment. Today Mexico is experiencing 90% interest rates. Inflation is rampant as the peso has lost 60% of its value. Government services are being slashed, and living standards which were already below those of 1980 have come down 30% since November. Unemployment is rising.

Has Mr. Godsoe given any thought of how Mexican society is going to stay in a single piece under such strains?

Detaxation Schemes

Historians are intrigued how it was possible for Britain — a country with one third the population of France — to defeat her so consistently in the wars of the 18th century. Most concur that much of the explanation lies in the funding of the British debt while France sank ever deeper into the clutches of her tax-farmers — the "privatisation" of tax-collecting. That permitted privileged individuals to intercept government revenues at their source. The result was the proliferation of corruption, the bankruptcy of the state, the bleeding of the productive classes, and eventually the French Revolution.

During the period when the modern state was seeking a way of organizing its tax collection, many interesting ideas surfaced. Some of them proved impractical because the conditions for their success were still not there, but they merit our critical attention. One such was the tontine lottery, named after an Italian clerk of Cardinal Mazarin of France, Lorenzo Tonti. A tontine is a fixed collective annuity paid to a group of investors and divided equally among the survivors until the last of them dies. One year before the Bank of England was founded in Britain in 1694, there was an attempt in Britain to raise one million pounds by a tontine lottery, but only 100,000 of this could be sold — the balance was raised by single-life annuities.

Not only does the tontine assure the investor income as long as he may live, but on a growing scale. That would provide against the effects of inflation, and still leave a premium for the survivors. Indeed, the premium could be so great that it would make sense to adjust downward the collective payment to the survivors after a reasonable period — say thirty years. In this way the state would not be burdened with the original payment to a few individuals who might live on beyond one hundred years.

Since the increasing average longevity of the population would be in part the result of government investment in health, environmental conservation and other public services, the government's gain from such an arrangement could rightfully be seen as a capital gain from public investment.

Combining features of a retirement fund, protection against inflation, self-liquidating government debt, and low interest rates based on the life insurance feature, the tontine compares advantageously with many of the instruments in the private sector. These, goosed with derivatives to produce greater yields, have led to tragic losses among retirees.

[The tontine also has immense social advantages over the current state promotion of casinos and electronic gambling machines. But no innovation that would contribute to funding public services without enriching the financial community seems to rate consideration.]

William Krehm

Boys Will Be Boys

Directly or indirectly, all derivatives are highly sensitive to changes in interest rates. And since for central banks today higher interest rates are the one therapy for all problems, that makes derivatives the financial equivalent of the atom bomb.

Not only are the gamblers at risk, but the very exchanges on which the trading is done. Listen to *The Wall Street Journal* (1/3): "For years, [Singapore] took great pride that its well-regulated markets had suffered none of the financial debacles that dogged Wall St, London's City and Tokyo in recent years. But the "it can't happen here" attitude ended this week. The disclosure that a 28-year-old trader at Barings in Singapore had caused losses of more than $1 billion, destroying his employer, is an embarrassment to Southeast Asia's main financial centre."

Repeatedly the central banks of the world have backed the financial firms in rejecting any suggestion of official derivative regulation. That was again apparent at the peak of the Barings drama when Fed chairman Alan Greenspan endorsed the repeal of the *Glass-Steagall Act* before the House Banking Committee. He attacked the "basic rationale for maintaining the Depression-era law — namely that the banks would be weakened if they expanded into other potentially risky, financial businesses. Noting that banks' net interest income has been declining, Mr. Greenspan warned that "unless there's a basic change, commercial banking will be in increasing difficulty" as investment and other financial concerns invade the banks' traditional customer base." (*WSJ* 1/3)

Significantly, Canada has long since enacted into law much of the deregulation that Mr. Greenspan is advocating. "Mr. Greenspan argued that the Barings debacle and others like it shouldn't impede moves to abolish what he called 'antiquated barriers.' Human nature is going to do what human nature has always done — bad things on occasion."

In short, "boys will be boys" Especially if they happen to be "our" boys.

Vol. 7, No. 5 — May 1995

Inflationary Hellfire?

In the monetarist evangel the German hyper-inflation of 1923 fills the role of hellfire in some primitive religions. Unless we nip inflation in the bud, we are told, it will inevitably become a runaway hyper-inflation. Supposedly this is what happened in 1923, when thirsty Germans had to push wheelbarrows of paper marks to the Bierkeller to buy a mug of beer.

In the early 19th century. Napoleon had a very simple way of financing his conquests — by exacting tribute from the conquered. That served as model for the Prussian Finance Minister in that country's later wars. After its victory of 1871, Germany extracted some five billion francs from France. It was an article of Prussian financial policy that the cost of wars were to be paid by the defeated enemy. Meanwhile those costs were amortized as a sure capital asset.

Karl Helfferich, the ultra-conservative Finance Minister throughout most of World War I, was "lulled by the conviction that borrowing was not inflationary if the ordinary budget were balanced, and resisted taxing profits and high incomes." (Charles P. Kindleberger, *A Financial History of Western Europe*, 1984, p. 293)

After WWI the French also stuck to the Napoleonic model. About $40 billion of reparations imposed by the Allies were "commercialised" — to use a more modern term— "recycled": Germany issued bonds to be sold to Americans and others against the eventual reparations payments.

[After its defeat in that war] nationalist passions in Germany flared high. Two German foreign ministers were assassinated for agreeing to the reparations. In January 1923 when German reparation deliveries of coal and telegraph poles to France were in arrears, French and Belgian troops occupied the Ruhr basin. The workers struck, with popular backing across the length and breadth of Germany. The German government printed more and more paper money. Yet it is significant that "in real terms the money supply shrank as printing presses failed to keep up with prices." "Money printing" was a cart stuck in the mud rather than a runaway horse.

The exploded mark had to be replaced with an entirely new currency. Under the Dawes Plan in April 1924 a loan of 800 million of the new Reichsmark was sold in various markets to provide Germany with some of the foreign currency to make its reparation payments. That, however, was intended only as "pump-priming." And it initiated Wall St. into the fatal game of foreign lending. The gush of American money for a while provided Germany with the foreign currency to pay its reparations, though to keep it coming the German government had to go on raising interest rates.

Little of all this money remained in Germany to meet the needs of the economy. And the high interest rates needed to fund reparations prepared the stage for Hitler. Matters came to a head when the N.Y. stock market boom of 1928-9 began competing with the Germans for the loans they needed.

After the Wall St. crash of 1929, the Young Plan revamped the reparations terms and the Bank for International Settlements (BIS) was set up in Basle to handle the purely notional transfers of foreign currency from Germany to her creditors. Within three years of the signing of the Young Plan the market value of the German reparation bonds accumulated by BIS was close to zero. The parallel with the recycled oil money debt of Mexico today is inescapable.

We are asked to believe that if interest rates had only been pushed high enough, there would have been no Napoleon, no Bismark, no German defeat, no reparations, no French occupation, no general strike. No history, just monetarist dogma.

wk

Haiku

With the dollar in free fall, Washington is putting the screws on Tokyo to brake the mystic ascent of the yen by lowering its interest rates. This would make it unnecessary for the Federal Reserve to ladle out further increases in its own rates — the one remedy to be found in its medicine cabinet. But the Japanese have already dropped their bank rate to 1% and have some major problems of their own. Not so long ago Washington contributed to these by leaning on Japan to *raise* its interest rates so that American banks could "enjoy a level playing field" in Japan. This inconsistency can be explained by Washington's unfailing belief in its own high morality and wisdom when dealing with other countries. The Japanese might be excused for considering it the MacArthur or the Commodore Perry syndrome.

The Wall Street Journal (17/4) reports that at the recent Pacific Rim Conference Japanese Finance Minister Masayoshi Takemura proposed to US Treasury Secretary Robert Rubin that the US issue yen-denominated bonds "as a kind of show of good faith in the dollar. With yen bonds, the US would be betting on the dollar. If the dollar rebounded the US would have to spend fewer dollars to pay off its yen debt. But if the dollar continued to fall, the debt under these bonds would increase." Some of our readers may recognise in the suggestion the spirit of the haiku — a form in which with a few subtle syllables a Japanese poet can evoke the essence of a sunrise or a goldfish — or if need be the flailings of an epileptic whale.

Through the international organisations the Americans themselves have imposed just such bonds denominated in dollars on the Mexicans (the *tesobonos* that contributed so much to the meltdown of the Mexican peso). A variant of the same idea prevents the Argentine central bank from issuing Argentinian money without 100% backing in dollars.

It was a study in contrasting national styles when Rubin turned down the suggestion: "US officials consider yen-bonds to be an admission of weakness — that the US can't finance its own debt. 'I said we had large, deep and effective capital markets.'" To which we can only add our Amen.

Rolling the New Governor on Our Tongue

The advent of a new Bank of Canada governor is always the occasion for edgy speculation — particularly because the pronouncements of the new dignitary *urbi et orbi* are couched in the Bank's own church Latin without translation into the vernaculars of this world. We thus depend in part on intuitive appraisal of the governor at his public appearances. As with vintage wines, we roll the performance on our tongues. Then, rather than swallow, we spit out, and consult our mouths for after-tastes.

Recently we caught up with the new BoC governor, Gordon Thiessen, at Glendon College. When Thiessen eludes a question, he takes the trouble to do so with charm and even self-deprecation. Canadian scholars might even ponder why one third of the BoC's governors to date have come from Saskatchewan — of all our provinces one of the most remote from high finance. But then Mr. Thiessen's predecessor was a Brit who for pomp and circumstances might have been presiding from elephant-back over the durbar of a long-vanished empire. To restore the balance it was almost mandatory that his successor be from Saskatchewan.

Openness was the keynote of the occasion, and the Governor did share with us the nitty-gritty of cheque clearance. On more crucial matters he was less forthcoming. The title of the talk was "Uncertainty and the transmission of monetary policy in Canada." Uncertainty, it emerged, was limited to doubts about the central bank's resolve to pursue its one goal of price stability; never for a moment was it allowed that the policy itself might be open to questioning. That eliminated all but high interest rates as a tool against inflation.

In 1983, when our central bank had already been in the clutch of monetarist dogma for at least a decade, its holdings of federal bonds amounted to 14.5% of the total outstanding. By 1994 this had fallen to 1.5%. It is still going down rapidly. When the BoC holds government bonds the interest from them reverts to its sole shareholder, the Government of Canada. When the chartered banks do so, that does not happen. As a consequence of the phasing out of reserve requirements since 1991 and the new Risk-Based Capital Requirements of the Bank for International Settlements in the late 1980s, the banks' hoard of government bonds has risen by over 900%. Not surprising since under these new rules banks can hold bonds without a penny of their own money. They are able to clip their coupons as a social security benefit.

That helped the banks out of their losses in high-flying real estate and leveraged buyout deals. It has also encouraged them into even riskier gambles. That makes it likely that they will be back at the government's door for further largesse. Since our banks take many of their cues from south of the border, it is of interest that *The Wall Street Journal* (10/4) should report the Controller of the Currency, Eugene Ludwig, finding "nearly universal slippage in credit standards. The standard minimum payment on credit cards is now 2% of the balance outstanding, down recently from 5%." And the largest home builder in booming Minneapolis reports that while 18 months ago is was unable to get a bank loan, "today it is being courted by bankers as far away as Boston and California. They are once again willing to finance the purchase of raw land."

Though the central bank cannot "set" long-term interest rates, holding even 14.5% of issued bonds as it did in 1983 would give it considerable influence on the longer-term market. In its rush to bail out the chartered banks it has thrown that away.

The high interest rates established by the BoC have provided the banks with probably the highest spread on deposits in Canadian history. Several major banks are paying depositors as low as 0.25% on their savings and relending it at double-digit rates. That has driven many retirees to put their savings into mutual funds for higher returns. To be able to pay such returns many of these funds have larded their portfolios with risky derivatives.

Money put out in mutual funds or abroad is beyond the control of the central bank. The banks' increasing reliance on fees rather than on interest charges for their income has a similar effect. The diversification of the banks' activities into such unrelated fields as insurance, stock brokerage, and foreign investments also places a growing part of banks' activities beyond the central banks' reach.

At the Glendon lecture, Mr. Thiessen repeated his opposition to any regulation of derivatives. He expressed a cheerful unconcern about the financial blowouts that have been increasing in frequency and depth throughout the world. The BoC could well be on a steady course of self-destruction. Unfortunately that could take our society over the cliff with it.

wk

Tax-farming and Privatisation

In a recent issue we noted that Britain's triumphs over France in the 19th century were in part due to her success in funding her debt rather than remaining dependent on the mercies of tax-farmers as was France. This fiscal revolution was made possible by the weakening of the grip of the aristocrats when Charles I lost his head. Charles P. Kindelberger comments on the process with tact: "Note that the necessity to alter a system of private business in the king's finances provides a possible counterexample to the thesis that progress in economic development is achieved only when property rights become clearly defined in private ownership."

Did the government bureaucracy lack the moral credentials for collecting its own revenues that private tax-farmers could show? On that there is room for doubt. Sir Thomas Gresham in the 16th century advocated farming out tax collection because "young merchants who had engaged in smuggling knew how to get goods ashore without payment of customs and hence would be more efficient as collectors than government officials if given the proper incentive." In France tax-farmers' accounts were audited, but with a delay of as much as ten years during which the tax-farmer might have passed on to other rewards.

Many tried reforming the French system — usually foreigners like the infamous John Law. Banks offered an alternative to tax-farmers for coming up with immediate financing when wars broke out. But the abuse of note issues by Law's banks to finance hare-brained land schemes in Louisiana had been so scandalous that for the next 150 years even the name "banque" was avoided in France (with a single exception under Napoleon). Euphemisms that replaced it included *caisse, comptoir, credit, societé*. Law, who arrived in France as a fugitive from British justice, may have contributed more to Britain's military victories than her generals in the field.

Despoiling the state treasury had long been regarded a birthright of the nobility. Only the guillotine during the Revolution and the *assignats* — paper money backed by the church estates — could finally uproot that tradition. Thirty-five tax-farmers were arrested in 1794 and 28 of them were guillotined — including the discoverer of oxygen. Antoine-Laurent Lavoisier's main occupation had been running the excise for his own account on goods entering Paris. His scientific work was relegated to early mornings and evenings plus one full day a week.

In England under James I tax-farm contracts granted to peers were resold to merchants at a profit of 27,500 pounds annually.

Taking their share off the top, tax-farmers had vast powers for dictating the distribution of the national income. Under the Bourbons the nobility were exempted from taxation in recognition of their duty to defend their country. Today the "zero inflation" goal of monetary policy seeks to exempt the bondholder from contributing to those components of price rise that have nothing to do with an overheated market — the cost of unmarketed public services and mandated standards. In one case as in the other the burden of taxation is shifted to consumption: the ending of regressive taxation such as the *dime* and the *gabelle* was an early fruit of the French Revolution. In recent years the thrust of taxation has been reversed.

Since the monetarist dogma took over central banks a quarter of a century ago, the money interest has acquired a more sweeping control of the public treasury than tax-farmers could ever pretend to. And it is exercised with a far lower profile. The central banks and the international financial organisations do much of their dirty work for our money-lenders. Higher interest rates have been established as the one accepted solution to any major problem — including those created by that very system.

William Krehm

Vol. 7, No. 6 — June 1995

Portrait of a "With-it" Banker

Since 1987, more than any other mortal, Charles S. Sanford Jr., chairman of Bankers Trust, has inspired the transformation of banking. And the thumb-nail sketch of him carried in *The Wall Street Journal* (4/74) shows that he makes no bones about what he has been up to.

"Mr. Sanford decided to move away from traditional banking by focussing on a business called "risk management." Henceforth banks would not only manage risk but help create it on a world scale. He preached the idea that everything in life involves risk, and that Bankers Trust could profit by creating products that would help companies recognize, quantify, mitigate and even capitalise on these risks. He claimed that derivatives could be used for everything from hedging risks and investing money to creating 'synthetic' mergers and acquisitions." The really smart folk simply place bets on what would happen as the less bright wasted their time growing wheat and manufacturing widgets."

"A former BT executive said, 'Charlie caused a mass hypnosis that led everybody to think not only that derivatives were a good business, but that we could depend on them as the new paradigm of the financial world.'"

In an address at the University of Georgia in 1989 Charlie proclaimed the philosophy of the new banking: 'The real risk in life turns out to be the refusal to take a risk.'"

Among the converts to the theses that Mr. Sanford nailed to his bank's doors were Canada's Royal Bank and the CIBC. In recent issues we reported their hiring wholesale the derivatives specialists of US financial firms come to grief by following Charlie walking on water.

In the words of *WSJ* the Bankers Trust "has stumbled badly and it now faces problems so serious that its future now may depend on Mr. Sanford's ability to reinvent it all over again. During the past year, after customers lost large sums of money from using BT derivatives, it became known that the aggressive pursuit of short-term profits led to the defrauding of at least one of the company's short-term customers. That, in turn, led to a sharp decrease in the demand for the company's most lucrative product, exotic derivatives."

Yet there was some logic in Canadian banks jumping into the derivative sea where BT was already sinking. Canada's banks have a more indulgent uncle than their US counterparts. To bail our banks out of their massive losses in the eighties, Ottawa relieved them of the need to hold non-interest-bearing reserves with the Bank of Canada to support their deposits — [apart from offshore tax-shelters like the Cayman Islands] Canada was only one of three countries to take such a step. That has enabled our banks to increase their holdings of government bonds by over 900% in the past five years, and tap the federal treasury of $3 billion without putting up a penny of their own. They are thus better positioned than the high priest of the new banking himself to convert his gospel into clinking coin.

However, Canada's Auditor-General, Denis Desautel, worries about the "capacity of the Office of the Superintendent of Financial Institutions to evaluate credit risks facing the banks from derivatives and securities activities." (*G&M* 5/12) Yet the BoC still opposes any regulation of derivatives.

As a result, as they respond to Charlie's call of the wild, they have lost interest in the humdrum business of [traditional] banking. And in the process they are creating far more risk than anybody can manage. When banks turn down loan applications from perfectly sound old customers, the next stop of the latter is likely to be a loan shark. And in that way the economy as a whole eventually becomes a bum risk.

Fortunately Charlie's fertile mind has come up with a cue for dealing with this: "I think we should get rid of our commercial bank licence" Ottawa then should pick up that bright thought to bring our banks back to banking. Those who insist on acting out Charlie's evangel should be asked to trade in their banking charters for casino licences more in keeping with the business of their choice.

William Krehm

Further Monetary Wizardry

The Wall Street Journal (27/4) updated us on the protean role of credit cards in our money supply: "In 1994 the gross charge volume on all cards was estimated at $437 B by Credit Card News. In an annual survey run by SMR Research, the amount outstanding on cards grew 24% last year."

Translating that into Canadian dollars we would get something in the $640 billion range. Estimating the Canadian equivalent as the usual 10% of the US figure, we arrive at something over $60 billion as the outstanding credit card charge volume for Canada — twice as large as the legal tender in existence. That figure, be it noted, does not give the total authorized limits of credit card borrowings — equivalent to bank lines of credit — but only the amount utilised.

The *WSJ* goes on to show how developments of credit card magic are further muddying the "money supply" waters. It quotes Stuart Feldstein, SMR's president: "The 'reward' programs have created a new American currency for consumers." Since its introduction, the GM card has signed on 12 million cardholders and more than 450,000 have actually used their 'reward' to help buy a car. Citibank is trying to set itself apart from the reward crowd with a "buyer-protection" program that provides buyers with cost-free replacement of purchases they might break. And so forth.

Which raises some philosophical questions. Logically the 'reward' — discounts on purchases — should be recognised by lowering the price index — and hence warranting less hysteria about inflation. But will it be? And shouldn't the 24% jump in credit card charges be incorporated in the "money supply." Were that done, it would throw the whole monetarist model further out of kilter that already appears. Less expensive forms of credit are being withheld to make room for the expansion of credit cards and other usurious forms of lending.

From an Open Letter to the Rt. Hon. Jean Chrétien

I read in *The Globe and Mail* (15/5) that you are much concerned about the loss of Canada's sovereignty — that it is unacceptable to you that the International Monetary Fund, Moody's and "25-year-old speculators in red suspenders" are now more powerful than our parliament in determining government policies. Further, I read that you hope to do something to dampen down speculation and work to reform the IMF and the World Bank to aid bankrupt countries at the G7 Summit in Halifax in June. Millions of Canadians share your concern and wish you every success in doing just that.

The papers are also full of the suggestion that while you personally are favourable to a "Tobin tax" on financial transactions — which could be used both to fund the UN and your own promise to repeal the GST — you have run into much opposition from "experts" who tell you that such a tax is "unworkable because certain countries would provide tax havens for currency traders."

Would Canada give up on speed limits because of speeders or repeal our laws against murder because certain countries provide havens for killers? When some country has the courage to enact a financial transaction tax it will be found to be easily collectable and, once a few stiff jail terms are handed out to scofflaws, highly enforceable.

Before seeking international innovations it is well to remember that sovereignty, like charity begins at home. Much of Canada's loss of sovereignty is a self-inflicted wound within your power to heal. Start with Mackenzie King's statement, "Without government creation of money, talk of Sovereignty and Democracy is futile.

John H. Hotson

Tactical Retreat — Reculer Pour Mieux Sauter

A tactical retreat is underway by the BoC to duck a hailstorm of misfired prophecy. The latest proof of this comes from David Laidler and William Robson, *Don't Break the Bank! The Role of Monetary Policy in Deficit Reduction* published by the C.D. Howe Institute. Though the tone suggests moderation, the document is a cover-up to preserve a militant dogma until it can resume its 20-year rampage.

That appears in the opening paragraph: "Concern over Canada's fiscal problems, coupled with reluctance to see federal spending cuts large enough to fix them, has led to suggestions that the Bank of Canada should run easier monetary policy to make the finance minister's job easier. Easier money's potential to produce higher inflation, however, makes such a strategy risky.

"Because the Bank appears to have become inadvertently tight during the second half of 1994, somewhat easier policy now would probably not put its 1 to 3% targets at risk." We love that "inadvertently." Whose inadvertence? Given the series of unsoft economic crashes brought on by the same high-rate policy over the past twenty years, it was no great sweat for COMER to predict a stubborn recession when the short-term rate was doubled in less than a year during 1994. The inadvertence was wholly that of the BoC and those academics and editors hoodwinked or suborned by a network run at public expense.

R&L warn that "Ottawa should look to its own spending, not to the BoC, for a solution to its fiscal woes."

But over one third of the government's spending is for interest imposed by the BoC. As late as 1980 the BoC held 19.5% of the federal government's funded debt, but by 1994 this had been reduced to 5.4%. When the central bank holds government debt, the interest on it reverts to the Bank's sole shareholder, the Government. When private banks hold it, it doesn't. If R&L really want to reduce government spending, they should begin by looking into the arrangements that made this possible — the phasing out of the reserve requirements that banks had to hold with the central bank and the new Risk-Based Capital Requirements for banks issued by the Bank for International Settlements that declared the debt of OECD countries risk-free requiring no capital of the banks that held it.

Instead R&L write: "Although very short-term interest rates are directly influenced by BoC policy, medium and long-term rates are subject to a variety of influences, among which expectations about future inflation are front and center." Presumably this is a shamefaced way of saying that the central bank has little influence on long-term rates. That is far from the case. In any market a considerable degree of influence must go with a 19.5% stake especially if the owners take to liquidating it in a highly public way. When our central bank, which is the financial agent of the government is seen unloading its government bonds, that can only push up long-term rates. For in effect it is an inside trader.

Their final conclusion is "that an analysis of likely market reactions to an overly easier policy suggests that the results might be higher, not lower, long-term results."

A quarter of Canadian government bonds are held by foreigners, and less than one percent is denominated in foreign currencies. The BoC can thus acquire with Canadian dollars of its own creation the money to purchase at a discount any Canadian bonds dumped by foreigners.

Most amazing, however, is that these gentlemen should have the brass to go on giving the government the worst possible advice: "A government that believed in the effectiveness of its inflation and deficit targets would issue more indexed and foreign currency debt." Were our government to issue debt in foreign currency it would need foreign currency not Canadian dollars to support its bonds under pressure. We would be completely in the power of foreign financial interests.

This is not the first time that R&L have pushed policy that would leave Canada at the mercy of foreign speculators. In the fall of 1991 commenting on a proposal for a lower Canadian dollar, David Laidler wrote: "It is hard to imagine US legislators failing to react if Canada were to attempt to gain competitive advantage through an active policy of devaluation and wage-and-price controls."

When the BoC hoisted our dollar by over 20% in relation to the US dollar with lofty interest rates, it was thus admittedly leading us into a trap easier to enter than to get out of. No protectionist US congressman could object to our shooting ourselves in the foot. If the Lord made us that stupid, it was simply to be considered the will of Heaven. But once we tried letting the dollar return to a realistic level, Prof. Laidler was there to warn us that our cousins to the south would hold us guilty of unfair trade practices.

A reading of this amazing document left us asking how much longer our Government and editors will go on taking Robson, Laidler and the Howe Institute as anything more than a bad joke too often told.

William Krehm

Vol. 7, No. 7 — July 1995

Keynes's Most Original Creation

It is becoming pretty obvious that the international monetary system is not working. So much so that the reform of the institutions that emerged from the Bretton Woods Conference of 1944 has become a popular media theme.

If there was a single purpose that animated the Bretton Woods deliberation it was: to prevent a replay of the depression of the thirties. No man had given more thought to the means of achieving this than John Maynard Keynes. The recent biography of Keynes by the editor of his opus, D. E. Moggridge, enables us to follow the evolution of his ideas. Eventually, in very watered-down form, they led to the IMF and the World Bank. After 1975 monetarism took over the international institutions and reduce them to grotesque caricatures of their founders' intent.

As early as 1941 Keynes had outlined the plans for a supra-national bank, the Clearing Union, that would prevent the polarization of debt and credit among have and have-not nations.

"Social changes affecting the position of the wealth-owning classes are likely to occur or be threatened in many countries. The whereabouts of "the better 'ole' will shift with the speed of the magic carpet. Loose funds may sweep around the world disorganising all steady business. Nothing is more certain than that movement of capital funds must be regulated."

From this he concluded that exchange controls would be needed. Foreign transactions would have to be channelled through central banks, and the central banks for their part would conduct their international transactions through the Clearing Union. Each country would denominate its currency in terms of the Clearing Union's unit of account, which in turn would be expressed in gold. But while gold could be converted to the Clearing Union's unit of account, they could not sell the international currency to buy gold. That established the clearing bank money as the reserve money of the international system.

Initially each country would receive a credit for drawing on the Clearing Union equal to one half the sum of its average exports and imports over the preceding five years.

Trade imbalances between two countries would appear on the Union's books as an overdraft for the debtor and a positive balance for the creditor. A deficit country could not overdraw its account by more than 25% of its quota in a year. As its overdraft grew, so would the rate of interest it paid to the Union. If its debt reached half of its quota, it could be required to hand over what gold reserves it had, and be allowed to export capital only with the permission of the international bank. Should it still not rein in its spending, it could be asked to leave the system.

These constraints on debtor countries were balanced by obligations of creditor nations. As their balances with the Union rose, the exchange rate of their currency would move up, and foreigners would be allowed to withdraw the balances of investments held in that country — measures that would tend to equalize the balance of payments. Surplus countries would receive no interest on their balances with the Union. Indeed, they would be required to *pay* interest on the excess of their balances with the union exceeding 25% of their quota. The interest collected would go to finance programs of the international community — international police forces, relief and reconstruction.

More than *The General Theory*, Keynes's work on the Clearing Union must be considered his most strikingly original creation. But rather than the exact details, the bold thrust of the plan is of interest today: an adjustable international payments system that would discourage irresponsible spending by debtors and force the creditors to put their credit balances back into the world economy.

Keynes's views received a sympathetic hearing even from the notoriously staid British Treasury. The reason was given by Keynes himself : "We in particular, in a distressed and ruined continent, will not [be] the most suitable candidate for the dole, however real our difficulties. The assistance for which we can hope must be *indirect* and a consequence of laying the foundations for a sounder political economy between all nations."

But there was the US Congress to reckon with. Keynes not only had to convince Harry Dexter White representing the US Treasury, but to handle White's preoccupations with Congress. The concern there was about the US collecting its debts, and about inflation if there were no mechanism for reducing the total credit available through the Union. When first confronted with White's plan, Keynes put his finger on the nub of the matter: "He has not seen how to get around the gold standard difficulties and has forgotten about the useful concept of bank money."

But in the final count the debate was not between Keynes and White, but between the respective clout of the US and war-sapped Britain. Realizing this, he ended up explaining to British critics that "the real risk is that there will be no plan at all and that Congress will run away from their own proposal."

With the enthronement of usury a quarter of a century later as the one stabilizer of the economy, the IMF and World Bank were perverted to quite the opposite of their original purpose. They were set to dictating the slashing of social programs, wage roll-backs, and devaluations that rigged the terms of trade against the debtor nations. They ended up as "enforcers" breaking arms and lives, collecting on IOUs held by the Grand Casino that the world economy had become.

wk

We Do Not Eat Our Unemployed

Statistics Canada (*The Globe and Mail* 6/6) reports goods-producing industries operating at 84.8% of capacity during the first quarter of the year, unchanged from the previous quarter. This represents a flattening of the surge in the statistic that had driven it up from 80.5% in the first quarter of 1994.

Bruce Little of the *G&M* comments, "With industrial production slowing and additional capacity available, the stage is set for utilisation rates to edge lower.." To offset this, we have the routine optimism of Finance Minister Paul Martin that "the slowdown is just the inevitable 'pause' he expected on the road to longer-term growth and prosperity, so that there is no need to adjust the government's policies." The Finance Minister — perhaps in the interest of economy — might be using the very releases of his Tory predecessors.

The fragmentary recovery experienced up to last fall was strictly in the market sector of the economy. But it was at the expense of the household sector — family units that do not sell their internal services. When manufacturing firms modernise their machinery to eliminate workers, it may seem to increase the productivity of the market sector. But it could do so at the expense of the household sector. For the good jobs lost to the "increased productivity" will reduce family income. It may be that the husband will have to accept less skilled work, and that to make up the drop in his earnings, the wife will have to find employment at the check-out counter of a supermarket. That may deprive her children of their mother's care for much of the day.

This does not mean that we are against improved technology; but we must check to see whether the seeming "prosperity" in the market sector is bleeding the household sector. And if it is, we must make good the damage.

If the economy is expanding, it can provide new jobs of like quality to replace the old ones. But our economy is being run according to what economists choose to call "the natural rate of unemployment" — enough unemployment to keep an admittedly flawed price index flat. Since Mother Nature has been brought into the picture, let us see how vastly what Mr. Martin is up to differs from Nature's way of achieving balances. Her predators kill enough prey for their needs, but sated lions will watch herds of antelopes move by without taking them out .The lions are not under any compulsion to establish their credentials for "leanness and meanness" or to "kick ass" for market share. Nor do we eat the workers that we cull. Instead they are left to moulder. Their families often become dysfunctional and prove a burden to society for generations. But to have curiosity about such matters you would have to abandon the "pure and perfect market" that by ignoring the other subsystems of our mixed economy is bound to produce increasingly impure and imperfect results. Society, the ecology, and the public sector must be brought into our accountancy.

Though manufacturing is becoming ever more capital- rather than labour-intensive, the contrary is the case with human care. There the investment is largely in training people, and in providing children with adequate services. To say that we cannot afford this merely indicates that our accountancy is so misleading that it assumes that the market can pilfer the resources of the household sector at no cost to society.

Nothing written above detracts from the importance of limiting the working hours of the employed. That would not only spread the work around, but allow workers to spend more time with their families.

William Krehm

Illegal Acts in Roosevelt's Bedroom?

In reviewing Robert McNamara's *In Retrospect*, reviewers have picked up the author's claim that Dean Acheson resigned as Under Secretary of the Treasury in 1933 because of differences with the New Deal over monetary policy. McNamara is not clear whether he himself was fired by Johnson or resigned on his own to become head of the World Bank. I suspect the same may have been the case with Acheson's "resignation" on November 16th, 1933. In *The Secret Diaries* of Harold L. Ickes, Vol. 1, p. 174, Roosevelt is quoted as follows:

"There is something that I want to say here in the family in case I die. After I *fired* Dean Acheson as Under Secretary of the Treasury (our emphasis), Lewis Douglas set out to make a written record. If things went wrong he wanted to be in a position to show that on such and such a date he advised the President not to do thus and so. Of course, he makes a very good watchdog of the Treasury, but I don't like it."

What were the disagreements between Roosevelt and his adversaries (such as Acheson) within the Administration?

At the time Dean Acheson, Lewis Douglas and James Warburg represented the "deflationist" position within the Roosevelt brain trust. Roosevelt, however, was more conscious of the sharp deflation in prices by about one third between 1929 and March 1933 when he took office. He was looking for some way to "reflate" the economy and was especially pressured by agricultural interests.

The economics establishment was dominated at the time by Irving Fisher, who had pronounced the achievement of permanent prosperity in early 1929. Earlier Fisher had introduced the so-called "Quantity Theory of Exchange" into our economic thinking. Later this was revitalised by Milton Friedman and the monetarists as part of their counter-revolution against Keynesianism. The orthodox prescription for the way out of the Great Depression was to further reduce wages.

In fact, the Bruening government in Germany actually succeeded in getting German workers to accept a roughly 10% cut in pay. Likewise, the British government devalued the pound in 1931, which in effect lowered wages for sales abroad — an attempt to cut prices back into world markets. To his credit Herbert Hoover saw wages as an important source of purchasing power, and refused to go along with the Germans or the British. Partly as a result of their misguided policy, the Germans managed to produce 40% unemployment compared to only 25% in the United States. That Hitler exploited in his initial electoral success in the polls.

At the time there were two rather obscure agricultural economists and statisticians at Cornell University — George Warren and Frank Pearson — who had studied the historical relationship between gold and the general price level. Their conclusion: raising the price of gold would be a means of reflating prices and getting the economy going again. (Warren had been dubbed "Rubber dollar Warren" by the deflationists). Roosevelt thus went against the conventional monetarist establishment when he ordered his Reconstruction Finance Corporation (RFC), headed by Jesse Jones, to buy gold at progressively higher prices starting at $26.67 per ounce and ending at $35.

Acheson claimed that there was no legal authority permitting Roosevelt to raise the price of gold. But each morning Henry Morgenthau, the new acting Secretary of the Treasury and a former student of Warren, along with Jesse Jones would come to FDR's bedroom to determine a small increase in gold prices until they reached their initial goal. These so-called "illegal acts" were denounced by the establishment. The new $35 per ounce price was confirmed by Congress in the Gold Reserve Act of January, 1934.

While the capitalist powers were largely unsuccessful in restoring the prewar international gold standard after World War I, the British tried pricing gold and the pound at their prewar equivalence. The result was catastrophic: Britain was the only major economy to suffer from double-digit unemployment in the 1920s. As early as

1923 Keynes had concluded that the gold standard was deflationary. Keynes no doubt thought of Warren and Pearson as money cranks, since he — like Hitler's economics Czar, Walther Funk — was more inclined to get away from the 'barbaric' metal completely.

The general price level did rise after the increase in gold prices, although by the beginning of World War II, the index had still not recovered to the level of 1929 (which itself was lower than the 1920 price index). All through the Great Depression the Federal Reserve acted as though there was primarily an inflation danger. After the 1935 reforms eliminated the influence of the Treasury on the Fed, the Fed (now chaired by Marriner Eccles) doubled the reserve requirements of the banks within a year and helped bring about the sharp drop in activity in 1937/8 that has been dubbed the Roosevelt Recession. In addition, they sterilized" (i.e. refused to count as part of the monetary base) large inflows of gold from Europe seeking a "safe haven" in the late 1930s. While some economists talked of "going off gold" the predominant thinking was still influenced by the gold standard.

Shortly after Pearl Harbour, FDR clamped down on the bankers to win the war. In early 1942 nominal interest rates were "pegged" around 2%, where they remained until the Treasury-Fed Accord of March, 1951. During the subsequent 45 years, the Fed has been chronically fighting inflation to the point where — as Alan Greenspan now admits — even the Fed's own index of inflation is running betweeen 1 and 2 percent per year. In Japan, where there has been virtually no real growth for four years, there is actual deflation according to official statistics. In the deflation of the early 1930s, the real interest rates hit 12 percent, a record high. In the 1980s and currently, real interest rates have averaged about 5%, considerably higher than the less-than-one percent real interest rate from 1945 to 1980. When looking for an explanation for the world-wide stagnation (outside of East Asia), these high interest rates should be considered a prime suspect.

Lynn Turgeon

Hixson's Corner — *Pax Vobiscum*

It is reasonable to suppose that everything the government does at every level, everything every private corporation does, everything every individual does, could be done more efficiently. Waste and corruption are pervasive and there is room for improvement everywhere. But all the furor in the US about "streamlining" government, particularly the federal government, is motivated less by an intention to increase efficiency than to slash social programs.

The Department of Defence may or may not be the most wasteful, corrupt and inefficient of all the branches of government, but it is certainly near the top of the list. And the dollar amount of DOD appropriations for which there is no significant "value received" undoubtedly dwarfs that of any other branch. Nevertheless, all the talk is about reducing expenditure for items like Medicare, Medicaid, Aid to Families with Dependent Children, and unemployment compensation — not about reducing expenditures for the DOD where they would be most appropriate.

In terms of 1994 constant dollars, US annual military spending for 1948 through 1989 averaged $250 billion. In the last year of Carter's administration, a year when USSR strength was at a peak, the figure was $235 billion. So what did Clinton propose in 1994 as an average for 1995 through 1999? An average of $260 billion each year and $1.3 trillion total. He has since decided that somewhat more will be needed and Republicans heartily agree. The Soviet Union has disintegrated, the Warsaw Pact is history, there is no power or foreseeable combination of powers threatening or likely to threaten the US. Yet its leaders propose more military spending than during the Cold War.

For 1993 US military spending amounted to $291 billion. The military spending of Japan, Germany, Russia, China, France, and the UK averaged $32 billion per country — about 11% the US amount. Are we crazy? Annual military spending per each US citizen in 1995 will be near $1100. Per capita annual military spending in Germany, Japan, Russia, and China amount respectively to $380, $320, $120, and $20. Are these figures signs of national paranoia or are they better explained as a pay-off for the huge campaign donations of defence contractors? They certainly bear no relationship to existing or likely threats to US security.

Present plans call for the retention of 8,300 nuclear weapons into the 21st century. They call for 14 Trident submarines carrying nuclear weapons and for 450-500 Minuteman III missiles. Whatever the excuse for such armaments in the past, the excuse has no present validity.

Finally, it must be noted that since 1990 the US has been the largest international seller of conventional arms — hardly the best way to promote a peaceful world. The latest year for which I can find statistics is 1992. In that year the US signed agreements to sell $13.6 billion in conventional arms to Third World countries. Russia agreed to sell $1.3 billion and all other countries, $9.0 billion. According to the Center for Defence Information in Washington, "The Clinton Administration is encouraging US arms makers to increase exports to maintain jobs and help the balance of payments problem."

Pax vobiscum.

William F. Hixson

Vol. 7, No. 8 — August 1995

A Trial Balloon to Shoot down

His sainted namesake notwithstanding, Tom d'Aquino has for a decade flapped his wings over the Canadian scene like a bird of ill omen. As executive director of the Business Council on National Issues, his job has been to present the greed of transnational corporations as our destiny.

The Toronto Star (31/5/95) quotes d'Aquino at a recent conference on US-Canadian trade sponsored by the University of Toronto's Centre for International Studies: "This was not an issue free-trade proponents had wanted to raise during the free-trade debate' [but] d'Aquino argued that there was not an adequate 'institutional infrastructure' to deal with the growing integration of the two countries." And George von Furstenberg, a visiting professor at the U of T from Indiana University, was on hand to spell out what that might mean: "Canada could negotiate a voice in a new North American central bank in exchange for giving up the Canadian dollar and the Bank of Canada."

"Gary Hufbauer, a prominent US trade expert from the Institute for International Economics in Washington, was even franker: 'We will see a substantial decline in the US as a provider of a social safety net in the years ahead,' he predicted, warning this could conflict with the Canadian agenda of providing health care and other social benefits. Companies in Canada could demand a cut in Canadian benefits to bring them closer to US levels, along with tax cuts, or threaten to move their investments south of the border.'"

The absorption of the BoC by the Federal Reserve System of the US would be a decisive step in destroying Canada as an independent country with a view of society that is increasingly diverging from that imposed by the US.

The same pattern turns up in the imminent privatisation of the CNR and the discontinuation of many railway lines across the country. At two critical stages of our history, transcontinental railways and the BoC in turn made possible our survival as a distinct nation. But now all that is being disposed of as a redundancy.

It is strange, too, that this should be happening when some of those promoting our switch to the US dollar should be rejecting with indignation the proposal of the Quebec secessionist movement that an independent Quebec could go on using the Canadian currency. In a recent article Mordecai Richler lamented professional satirists are finding it increasingly tougher matching the one-liners of reality. The latest escapade of the d'Aquino team underlines the point.

Mailbox

Walter Stewart, author of *Belly Up* and twenty other books, has written me as follows:

"A couple of days after our fortuitous meeting in Ottawa to talk to the Standing Committee on Industry, I phoned my good friend Mr. X[†] and asked him if he knew that the reserve requirement had been lifted on Canadian banks.

"He said, Huh?

"Then he said that he didn't believe it because, 1) it was economic nonsense, since it would leave the government with no lever save high interest rates to control inflation; and 2) he had never heard nor read about it, and such a change must have been accompanied by huge publicity.

"I replied that I gathered from you that the thing was slipped through in 1991, and deliberately downplayed.

"He was bemused, baffled, and enraged.

"I got in touch with the publisher of my original book on the banks, *Towers of Gold, Feet of Clay* and proposed a sequel to be produced in 1997, with the working title *The Towers are Still Gold, the Feet are Still Clay*.

"I now have a contract to write that book."

w.k.

[†] We do not have permission to use the actual name of Mr. X, a minister in previous Liberal administrations and an economist of note. [Subsequently that permission was forthcoming. It was Eric Kierans.]

F-word

The Toronto Star (25/6) reported that on May 6 our Finance Minister used the "f-word in talks with the banks." The bank representatives had protested against the government Export Development Corporation competing with the private sector. When asked whether the banks would assume all the risks of financing export by small and medium-sized business, they replied, "Oh, no. We have a responsibility to our shareholders."

A "senior official" is quoted: "Paul [Martin] feels that the banks, protected by the *Bank Act* and the taxpayer-underwritten Canada Deposit Insurance Corp. have failed to respond to the needs of small businesses."

Human Food Chain

Over the past forty-odd years Guatemala has provided more than its share of the world's blood-drenched news. It made horrible reading, but it was all so remote. Until recently few Canadians would have known where to seek Guatemala on their maps.

In 1944 one of the most sanguinary of Central American dictators, Jorge Ubico of Guatemala, fell victim to "friendly fire" out of Washington. The US propaganda beamed on Europe during the war had been translated by Central Americans into local terms. Up to then Guatemalan highland Indians had worked on the coffee plantations for 10 cents a day, and were at times delivered roped together to the lowland plantations by the army. Came the revolution and wages rose to $1 a day. Inevitably that pushed up prices as well. That raised a question that orthodox economists have neither asked nor answered: do price increases in such a context constitute inflation — i.e. something pathological — or the phasing out of a social system imposed by the Spanish conquerors in the 16th century?

With globalisation underway that unanswered question is echoing across the world in ever more troubling ways.

Guatemala's democratic experience was cut short in 1954 with the overthrow of the democratically elected government of Jacobo Arbenz engineered by the US. Washington has an engagingly simple model in Latin America: instead of allowing existing social structures to be disturbed, it claims to be concentrating on economic growth in the belief that democracy will automatically follow.

To see how that model is standing up we need only refer to *The Wall Street Journal* (3/7), a publication beyond suspicion of leftist influence. "Whenever it awards contracts to apparel makers [in Guatemala] J.C. Penney Co. has them sign a code of conduct forbidding any violation of local labour law. Virtually everybody applauds the intent of the codes, and the stated penalty for violations — immediate severance of the contract. But no one applauds the way the codes are enforced.

"Visits to factories supplying Penney turned up workers under the legal age of 14 paid less then the minimum wage of $2.80 a day and forced to put in unpaid overtime for work days as long as 15 hours.

"'It's common for these companies to close the doors and force the workers to stay all night working, says Guatemalan labour inspector Juan Castillo Rodriguez, sitting at his battered desk in a grimy office.'

"Says Ana Mendoza de Rivera, chief of the Labour Ministry's child-worker protection office: 'We don't have the people to investigate' what she estimates to be 300,000 illegally employed minors." Her office, with a staff of five, has no telephone.

According to human rights organisations in the last few years more than 40 unionists have been murdered or "disappeared."Owners say that the retailers pressure them relentlessly to pare costs to the bone. 'The ethics of the world market are very clear,' says Carlos Arias Macelli, owner of a maquila here that makes apparel for Penney. 'Retailers will move where it's cheapest.'"

And that makes the "natural state of unemployment" that drives Canada's destiny not the million and a half officially unemployed in Canada, but perhaps a billion of un- or under-employed in our globalised world.

At long last we have come to realise that life in the ocean from plankton to cod and salmon is all one food chain. Our fishery minister, Brian Tobin, has gone so far as to mobilise Canada's navy and TV cameras to impose some decorum on foreign fisherman too eagerly globalising the great waters. But globalisation has made those of us on land a single food chain with the Third World as well. Speculative capital sits on the top run of this ladder closest to heaven, while those beneath fight to determine who eats and who is eaten.

William Krehm

Vol. 7, No. 9 — September 1995

Scalars and Vectors as Tools in Economic Theory

Newton and Galileo before him had to sort out into scalars and vectors the concepts of mass, velocity, momentum, acceleration before they could start serious enquiry into the laws of the universe. Without a similar exercise economists can only go on spreading confusion about the workings of our mixed economy.

A *scalar* (from the Latin *scala* for step or ladder) is an absolute quantity with no sense of direction. A *vector* (from the Latin for "carrier") is a spatially directed quantity.

The mass of a potato, for example, is a scalar. But when I drop a potato its mass gets pulled towards the earth's centre of gravity. The scalar is multiplied by a vector, gravity. The product of a scalar and a vector is always a vector.

Now let me set up a diagram of our mixed economy with just three subsystems to keep it simple: the market economy, the public sector, and the ecology. We must keep track of the effects of whatever we do in the market sector on these other two subsystems. Unless we do, we risk depleting their resources with disastrous results. We must then deal in vectors that carry the effects of market events into the other subsystems. This is indicated by the arrow-headed vector lines in our diagrams running both ways between the three subsystems — market, public sector, and ecology.

VECTOR MODEL

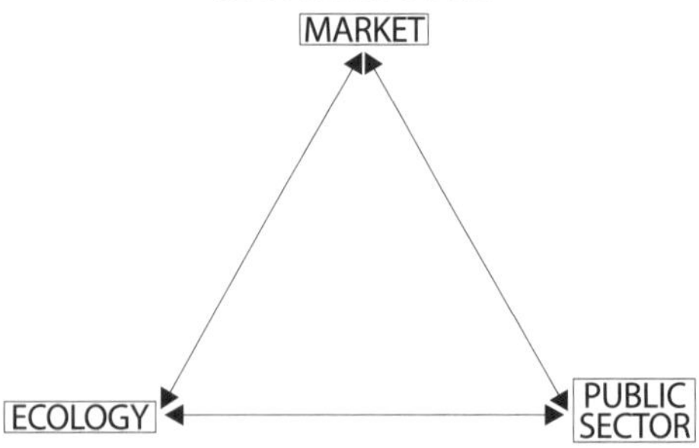

The effects of market policy in the other subsystems will echo back into the market. If we overfish the Grand Banks eventually the cod will disappear and leave thousands of Maritimers out of work, with traumatic effects on the budget-balancing fervours of our federal Finance Minister.

The official model deals essentially only with scalars. The market is assumed to be self-balancing, i.e. to oscillate around equilibrium points. Applying a scalar where a vector is appropriate can lead us to believe that a dropped potato will not fall to the earth and stay there, but behave like a yoyo, returning to where it came from. The price level, wages, employment, and all else according to the official model tend to behave in that way. And if they don't in practice, interest rates will be raised by a sufficient scalar to reduce employment by another scalar to squeeze the price level down by yet another scalar to the programmed equilibrium level.

There is little curiosity about the vector of consequences that may be crossing the boundary lines of the market into the other subsystems. The equilibrium points indeed become black holes gobbling up everything approaching them. Communication, on the other hand, takes place only by vectors. (To be delivered letters must be addressed). As a result there has been no serious communication between the subsystems of the economy. That, however, is a synonym for chaos.

In both physics and the economy scalars and vectors can combine into more complex *operators*. Thus waves combine amplitude (a scalar), frequency (a scalar), acceleration (vector) to deliver energy (scalar) to a given destination (vector). Remove the vector concept from this and what is left is a dead universe. Its parts do not communicate.

There can, of course, be bogus vectors as well as bogus scalars. The "domino" theory, which inspired American policy in Vietnam in the sixties and seventies and in Central America to the present day, was a bogus vector. It warned that if Ollie North didn't overthrow the government of Nicaragua, Communism would take over Texas and even Montana. The collapse of the Soviet Union proved that a false vector.

The domino effect in the North American Free Trade Agreement is real. It is pulling our economic and political standards in the direction of those enjoyed by Mexico, and pushing those of Mexico down towards those of Central America and Bangladesh. This can only lead to social breakdown. [In actual fact the domino model is linear dealing with upended dominoes aligned in an appropriate fashion. Globalisation is multidimensional with the effects radiating in every possible direction.]

Zero sum games (I win only what you lose) are scalar concepts. Positive and negative sum games ("win-win" or "lose-lose") have a clear vector dimension. That is crucial to meaningful policy design.

Recently somebody sent me a copy of a paper originating in or close to our government. It bore the title *Options for Eliminating Deficits and Reducing Debt.* In it occurs a statement that illustrates the above point: "The government could reduce the interest rates it pays on outstanding debt by making such interest tax-free. But what it gains in lower interest rates it would lose in lower tax revenues." The government in other words would cede a scalar and receive a scalar in return and the result would be a wash in a scalar "zero sum" game.

However, let us reformulate that example in vector terms, and at the same time step up the power of the arrangement. In our version the government would not only make the interest paid on certain of its bonds tax-free, but make the taxable income invested in such lower-coupon bonds *exempt* from taxation. The reduction in interest rates and the tax brackets to which such exemptions are applicable could be elaborated by actuaries to conform to desired standards of progressiveness.

For a quarter of a century, conquering inflation and deficits have been the very pivots of policy. Perceived inflation, however, was fuelled by a growing tax-burden that denatured our price signals. And high interest rates, imposed to suppress that inflation, have accounted for much of the government's deficits and debt. Interest rates and taxation have goosed each other on an upward course.

In contrast, the proposed *policy operator* would direct the key parameters of taxation and interest rates downward rather than upward. Surely, if you are concerned with inflation and deficits, downward rather than upward is the direction that these parameters should. go.

Lower interest rates and lower taxation will give us less inflation, higher employment. That in turn will make available the resources to deal with society's real problems.

William Krehm

On the Perils of Number-Crunching

We are drowning in an ocean of information and disinformation. In such a situation any figure, especially if accompanied by a chart, may promise terra firma under our feet. That, however, could prove a dangerous illusion.

In a neglected article Keynes criticised Jan Tinbergen's statistical testing of business cycle theories. In the 1/95 issue of *ER* (see p. 156) we carried a piece on his test for flaws in policy-design at the drafting board stage: at least the same number of independent variables are needed in any proposed policy solution as can be identified in the problem it is supposed to address. But the mere fact that so gifted a man, professionally trained as a physicist, came a cropper as one of the founding father of econometrics, should alert us to the treachery of the number-crunching sport.

"For Tinbergen," wrote Keynes, "the economist specified the theories and it was the job of the statistician to compute regression coefficients and thus determine the relative quantitative importance of variables postulated *a priori*. As subsequent observers have pointed out, judgment is allowed to play an important role in deciding whether an explanatory variable should be retained or discarded. Tinbergen makes the least possible preparation for the inductive transition to break the period under examination into a period of sub-periods, with a view to discovering whether the results of applying our method to the various sub-periods taken separately are reasonably 'uniform.' To econometricians this would be the equivalent of testing for structural stability. The notion of testing the quantitative influence of factors suggested by a theory as being important is very useful. The question to be answered, however, is whether the complicated method here employed does not result in a false precision beyond what either the method or the statistics actually available can support. It may be that a more rough-and-ready method which preserves the data in more recognisable form may be safer.

"My point against Tinbergen is this. In chemistry and physics and other natural sciences the object of experiment is to fill in the actual value of various quantities and factors appearing in an equation or formula; and the work is done once and for all. In economics this is not the case. In fact, by filling in figures, which one can be sure will not apply the next time, so far from increasing the value of his instrument, he has destroyed it. All statisticians tend that way.

"The pseudo-analogy with the physical sciences leads directly counter to the habit of mind which it is most important for an economist to acquire."

A few years later† a French economist, Jacques Austry, wrote: "In general econometrists dangerously impoverish the notion of structure by identifying it with coefficients of reaction and parameters determining the system. The definition of J. Tinbergen (*Econometrie*, 1953) is the following: "Structure consists of the characteristics that are not immediately observable involving the manner in which the economy reacts to certain changes. In econometric terms, they are coefficients" [i.e. multipliers attached to variables]. In this way we end up with a conception that defines as structural relations: the functions of offer, of production, of costs, etc.; and as coefficients of structure: the elasticity of demand to marginal costs, etc...Far from situating the phenomenon under observation in its total social context, such a notion of structure cuts up the latter by means of coefficients."

Indeed, the distortion of reality comes from two directions: from the coefficients which freeze an economic model into a system by choosing the coefficients that provide the best fit with the historical statistics to make the chosen model plausible; and from the statistics themselves that embody misconceptions of the same theoretical model. Thus our price index and our official figures for 'savings' will reflect the attempt to write off government investments in a single year. The figure for government debt ignores government capital assets. Our Gross Domestic Product ignores our despoliation of the environment and the household economy, etc. Not only is it "garbage in, garbage out," but there is a built-in gatekeeper that ensures that inputs reflecting reality [ignored by the model] will be shredded to useless waste.

There is something else that makes the whole "regression" procedure suspect. It boxes the past for burial. Long gone is the time when the past was a living present able to throw out a challenge to economists to predict where it was headed. Econometricians occupy themselves with that past when it has become defenceless against being laid out for the wake in garb of other people's choosing, and prettied up for the comfort of the survivors.

There are better tests for assessing competing models. For example, *Economic Reform* has eight years of publication behind it during which it predicted quite accurately where the goal of stability through high interest rates and pumped-up unemployment was leading. Enjoying command of the media, the other side has left behind a far more opulent paper trail. Comparing their respective forecasts would be a serious way of testing models. Those respective predictions are valuable, dearly-bought data. They must not go unused.

N.B. Keynes's criticism of Tinbergen's econometrics in no way invalidates his "counting rule" examined by us previously.

William Krehm

† *Méthodes mathématiques et sciences de l'homme, Revue économique*, 1959, p. 416

Carousel Logic

"The crowning achievement of marginalist theory was to have merged the concepts of valuation and distribution. Automatically by the mechanism of the pure and perfect market each factor of production was supposed to receive exactly what it contributed marginally to the creation of value. Valuation and distribution were but two aspects of the one event.

"This led to some remarkable circular reasoning. Thus in his classic book *The Sources of Economic Growth in the United States and the Alternatives before Us* (1961. p.31) Edward F. Denison employs this axiom of marginalist theory to establish the respective contributions of factors such as education, capital, etc. to the increase of productivity. 'Under competitive conditions, in equilibrium, each unit of any factor of production of uniform quality will receive the same income. According to the marginal productivity theory, the amount of this income per unit will equal the value of its marginal contribution to production. And both will equal the value of the marginal product of a unit of the factor. The basic assumption of my approach is that the economy of the US is not so different from this description as to invalidate the use of the average return per unit of each factor as a measure of its marginal value product.'

"So far so good. But how then can the same adherents of marginal theory take the increase of wages or of the costs of the other factors of production as the basis for apportioning responsibility for 'cost-push' inflation? What on one occasion is taken as the measure of the factor's increased productivity in on the other seen as the index of his guilt in bringing on inflation." William Krehm, *Price in a Mixed Economy — Our Record of Disaster* (1975), p. 25

This self-balancing marginalist model underlies the nonsense policies that have reached a terminal stage in tearing the world apart. It is a mistake for well-meaning academics to go on messing up the minds of students with such stuff either because they mistake it for high science on the strength of the mathematical symbols it is expressed in; or because, as 'just theory,' they convince themselves that it doesn't matter. Theory in fact is the genetic code of our thinking.

Vol. 7, No. 10 — October 1995

Wild Oats

Samuel Johnson described oats as a grain eaten by horses in England and by people in Scotland. I don't know how the Scots are faring these days, but Canadians are finding it harder and harder to locate plain rolled oats in their stores. That is because the dominant manufacturer in the field is aggressively moving into "higher value-added" variants. These have sugar additives, special flavours and fancy trade names and fetch several times the price of what the Lord created. At my supermarket the unadorned product of a competitor is still stocked, but for months no price has been posted on it. Clearly the reigning corporation in nailing down shelf-space has contrived to put all competition to its special brands *hors combat*.

These oatmeal wars bear a striking resemblance to our monetary policy. As with oatmeal, for some decades now our central bank and government have systematically swept off the shelves every possible alternative to high interest loans for dealing with the one goal they have set themselves — suppressing inflation. First the ceiling on interest rates was removed. Today the only limit that crimps money-lenders' style is in the criminal code — 60% per annum. Price and exchange controls that performed well in dealing with emergency situations during and after the Second World War are not even mentionable in polite bureaucratic society.

The federal government is the sole shareholder of the Bank of Canada. Yet it has espoused the evangel beamed out of Switzerland by the Bank for International Settlements asserting the independence of central banks from their governments. Properly billed — as theatre of the absurd — our monetary policy must be judged a great success.Just find another sole shareholder aching to amend the law to deprive shareholders of a say in their company's affairs!

It is a universally accepted principle that when a monopoly exists in the private sector (say, railways or utilities) its revenue must be regulated by a public authority.

But our government has not only removed all constraints on what the banks can or cannot do, but it has chosen higher interest rates as the one means of controlling the economy. And if the promised stable prosperity does not result from high interest rates, they are simply pushed higher.

There is a rub in all this. The boundary between absolute monetary virtue and criminal financial scams grows faint. In the 1920s Charles Ponzi of Boston earned himself a sort of immortality by borrowing money at high interest rates to pay the interest on what he had already borrowed. If initiated by the central bank, that today would pass not for the sort of financial strategy that put Ponzi in jail, but for "sound fundamentals."

Economists have simply lost the habit of relating the rewards of financial manipulation to the real economy. A few months ago a grandiose promotion in the US, not inaptly named "New Era," offered wealthy investors 50% each six months in interest with the story of the money being matched by anonymous philanthropists waiting in the wings. The tax-shelter allegedly resulting from the supposed philanthropic contribution would allow the investors to shield these 50% half-yearly interest payments from taxation. All of which was packaged with overtones of religiosity. The denouement should cause us to reflect on how far we have come: when the ploy collapsed, investors bearing surnames like Templeton, Rockefeller, and Buffett turned out to have been caught in its net.

Black Patch

At a time when more and more Canadians are worrying what they will be doing when their food bank shuts its doors, a World Bank study has found that the average Canadian is virtually a millionaire, topped only by the Australians. (*The Globe and Mail* 18/9)

Such is the nonsense that ensues when somebody slaps a dollar sign on natural resources that won't and shouldn't be exploited for generations to come, if ever, and lets the market code blind us to the constraints of all the other subsystems of our mixed economy: the public sector, the ecology, the household economy.

Marketing our natural resources for a fast buck could certainly increase the wealth of some citizens and thus help bring the national "wealth" average to dazzling heights. Society's well-being is another thing. It requires the functioning of all other subsystems. If it takes two parents to work to pay the mortgage and child care is slashed to balance the government budget, well-being goes down because the household sector has been robbed.

It is therefore important to decide whose "wealth" we are talking about and in what time-frame.

Even if we manage to integrate all known factors of the non-market subsystems into our reckonings, there will always be a residue of effects about which we will be in the dark. That should counsel humility towards nature and her mysteries — the ultimate wisdom of aboriginal peoples. Undermining the nuclear family in the advanced countries or the extended families of the Third World will compromise society's well-being unless public institutions are developed to fill the gap. The optical illusion of inevitable efficiency increase associated with the present craze for privatisations results from the black patches over the eyes of the privateers.

Dinosaur Dig

Those who aspire to success in financial reporting should begin by taking a course in paleontology. In their chosen specialty they will not be putting together dinosaurs from a few random bones buried millions of years ago; but, no less daunting, their task will be assembling a jigsaw puzzle from a few odd snatches of legislation that only a few months or years ago may have slipped through a dense wall of secrecy. Too often members of parliament vote on such items strictly on instructions from the caucus whip with little curiosity of what might be involved. The finance minister himself may have submitted the bill on the assurance of the central bank which had it on the authority of the Bank for International Settlements in Basel that this was the way to go.

And too often what is hidden from the public view does not add up to a viable beast.

In 1992 *Economic Reform* was the first publication to sound the alarm about such a misfit that was to cost Canadian taxpayers billions of dollars.

It was from the *Wall Street Journal* that I first became aware of the new risk-based capital guidelines of the Bank for International Settlements in Switzerland. These declared the government debt of advanced countries risk-free calling for no bank capital, while loans to business required 8% of the bank's own capital.

Then on a tip from a subscriber, I tracked down the 1991 bill that revised Canada's *Bank Act* to phase out the reserves that the banks had held with the Bank of Canada.

These two measures initiated from different sides of the great waters were responses to the one emergency. By the end of the eighties the portfolios of Canadian and international banks had been savaged by the speculative financial boom of the late eighties.

One of the purposes of the reserves that banks held interest-free with their central bank was to protect their depositors. Doing away with reserves at the very time that the banks got into hot water should have raised eyebrows. Then in a dusty box at the University of Toronto library I dug up a reference to Resolution 5 adopted at Bretton Woods in 1944 to have the Bank for International Settlements "liquidated at the very earliest possible moment." Amongst other things, this was because of the indecent haste with which it surrendered to Hitler the Czechoslovak gold in its care when the Nazis marched into Prague. That resolution had been expunged from public memory.

Today the BIS has more to say in the fate of the world than any country's elected representatives.When I chanced upon the phasing out of the Canadian banks' reserve requirements, I filled in a few missing bones with the assumption that reserves had been abolished for banks throughout the world. I reported that incorrectly in my 1993 book on the Bank of Canada. After all, the move in Canada had coincided closely in time with the Risk-Based Capital Requirements put out by the BIS for banks throughout the world, and right-thinking academics internationally were already disseminating the cover-up for the move: "Reserves should be abolished because they were an unjust "tax.""

The Toronto throwaway paper *Now*, while checking with the BoC data it had from us, that dug up the stark truth: ending reserves had been too strong a cup of tea even for the German Bundesbank and the US Fed. Only two other countries — the UK and Switzerland — did away with bank reserves.

[Later it emerged that this, too, was not quite the case. Offshore tax-shelters like the Cayman Islands had dispensed with them years before. A couple of years later *The Economist* reported that they still existed in several additional European countries, in some of which the central banks actually paid the banks interest on the reserves they held. Information on the subject was not readily available.]

Only when the archives of the secretive BIS are opened up, will we know the exact role it played in ending the reserve requirements in Canada. Together, the BIS guidelines and the end of reserves made for an explosive combination. For with no increase in capital needed for banks to acquire more government bonds declared risk-free, the banks' portfolio of government bonds swelled (900% over four years). The BoC for its part, made room for that by reducing its holdings of such bonds by 38%. It occurred to me that as soon as the central bank resumed licking inflation with higher interest rates the "risk-free" bond hoards of the banks and other financial institutions would shrink with disastrous results. That indeed happened in 1994 with the greatest deflation of bond values since 1929.

But that was still not the complete dinosaur. There was also the requirement of the Office of the Supervisor of Financial Institutions (OSFI) that the banks have 5% of their assets across the board in their own capital. But that only accentuated the flight of the banks from lending to business to government bonds.

Besides, legal tender reserves with the BoC are not to be compared — even remotely — with capital requirements. Whenever interest rates are pushed up, the bond assets of the banks lose value. If these assets are not sold at a loss, that loss does not appear on their balance sheets. It may be months before the overworked auditors turn up to sort out fact from fiction. Moreover the accepted bookkeeping for banks is to book securities they own at their historic value. That is [largely] what the current Japanese financial crisis is about, with major banks having lost 150% of their total capital. The difficulty of estimating what a bank's capital really is at any moment so far exceeds in magnitude the 5% OSFI capital requirements as to render them little more than window dressing.

With still a good many bones missing, the shadow cast by our monetary policy dinosaur is growing bigger and darker.

W. Krehm

Vol. 7, No. 11 — November 1995

A Nobel Prize for Snobelen?

At a meeting with departmental senior officials last July the education minister in Ontario's new budget-slashing government John Snobelen remarked with a chuckle: "We need to invent a crisis."

There was something symbolic about Premier Harris appointing Mr. Snobelen, a high-school drop-out, as his Education Minister. Possibly it was meant to signal that when the public budget for education is eventually balanced at zero, there will still be a future for the young — as ministers of education.

We are indeed considering nominating Mr. Snobelen for the next Nobel prize in economics. What brought that to our mind was the bestowal of that laurel on Robert Lucas, father of the doctrine of "Rational Expectations." While Snobelen laid bare the mechanics of high decision-making, Lucas was rewarded for having buried them under a glittering misuse of the word "rational." Boiled down to its essence, what Lucas tells us is that it is senseless believing politicians offering "jobs, jobs, jobs," because if they ever tried keeping their promise, the central bank would clobber the treasury with high interest rates. Snobelen was far truer to the Boy Scout oath.

When an official at that notable meeting asked him, "Do we bankrupt the ministry before positive change can occur?" Amidst laughter, Snobelen replied: "In my opinion, yes."

From the incident Phil Ryan of Carleton University's School of Public Administration (*The Globe and Mail* 10/10) concluded: "A certain type of politician, as Mr. Snobelen has revealed, specialises [not in finding solutions for problems] but problems for solutions. Two clever organisational theorists named James March and Johan Olsen, put their finger on this practice years ago. You begin with some pet project you wish to implement. You then wait for a problem to come along, or if you are as ambitious as Mr. Snobelen, you *make* a problem come along. You can then announce that you have found a solution to this problem, the solution being, of course, your pet project. "

The two "invented crises" today are inflation and the government deficit. But true to Snobelen's Law, they were created as panic buttons to serve a single solution chosen in advance: higher interest rates.

In either case the statistics deployed to establish the problems are hopelessly flawed. In recent years the research department of our central bank has recognised some of the lesser flaws in the price index that could be found in conventional textbooks decades ago. More serious distortions not in the textbooks are still ignored. For example, no unadjusted price index, precisely because it is a *price* index, can pick up the benefits of the unpriced and unmarketed output of the public sector. But through taxation its costs do show up in the price index. Yet nothing has been done to correct even the flaws that have been recognised. Why? Such recognition would *disinvent* the problem that implements the Final Solution.

wk

Penal Keynesianism

Gratitude is not a notable factor in policy-making. In the thirties when capitalism was teetering on the lip of the abyss, John Maynard Keynes rescued it by integrating it into society.

For that he has never been forgiven by the bankers whose necks he saved. Now that they are again in command, they have buried him with a stake driven through his heart to head off the possibility of his resurrection, come Judgment Day.

Yet Keynes's homespun truths go on reasserting themselves. With all the deregulation and slashing of public services and employment underway, we suddenly find Washington increasing its military budget even without a convincing enemy around. Why? Just to provide enough dog to keep the voracious fleas happy. Among the more irreverent economists that has come to be known as "military Keynesianism." A few months ago we found it necessary to coin the term for a parallel phenomenon with a big future: Penal Keynesianism.

As unemployment is pumped up as the means for "fighting inflation," society is becoming increasingly dysfunctional. Social services are being slashed with a cleaver. Crime is reported on the rise. Even Bill Clinton has espoused the "three strikes and you're out" principle, which in fact really means that "you're in — for life." With the present headwinds, politicians are prone to a strange alexia that puts the wrong word on their tongues.

The Wall Street Journal (28/9) informs us that the US prison population has tripled in the past fifteen years to 1.5 million. The Rand Corporation forecasts that in California, home to the toughest "three strike" laws, prison inmates will double in the next decade.

Richard Freeman of Harvard states that "prisons are capital-intensive, and money spent on anything else would create more employment." California, that in 1980 spent only 2% of its budget on prisons, is now spending 9%. Rand estimates that this will jump to 18% by 2002 at the present growth rate.

All this helps explain a statistical mystery on which our American cousins have been congratulating themselves: their relatively low rate of unemployment. Professor Freeman goes on to estimate that "the nation's official jobless rate, now at just below 6%, would reach 7.5% if the nation's male prisoners were counted as part of the labour force." He calculates that only one quarter of these would hold jobs if freed. And, of course, the armies of prison personnel take a further bite out of unemployment. All in all, we can foresee a time when the increase in the prison inmates will bring the US close to the "full employment" that the Fed considers so dangerous. That in turn will lead to more of the same — higher interest rates, greater unemployment, shrivelling social services and schooling, and more crime. So the country will be into a further chapter of prison building with the same results.

The "privatisation" of prisons is not only taking over in the US, but has begun spilling across our border. Some months ago, we reported the celebration in the business press of the doubly captive market that the booming prison population offers concessionaire suppliers.

Who said that Keynes had no future?

wk

Vol. 7, No. 12 — December 1995

Brawl over Tickets on the Titanic

Now that Canada has squeaked through the Quebec referendum, we are told that it is time for reassessment. But up to now the discussions have been restricted to constitutional matters with little attention to economic or monetary issues. The latter, however, are the unblinking eye of the storm.

Ottawa was shocked that only 40% of French-speaking Quebeckers voted against sovereignty in the recent referendum compared with fully 60% in 1980. It shouldn't have been. The 1980 and 1995 votes lie on opposite sides of a great divide. Around the time of the first referendum the international community of central banks announced that it would no longer concern itself with interest rates, but would concentrate on money supply targets. The only trouble was that with the latest deregulation of banking nobody could tell what the money supply might be. But then the real purpose of the move, as the sequel made clear, was to give central banks more leeway to push up interest rates in the shadows.

A massive shift of bank deposits had begun taking place from non-interest-bearing current accounts to the new interest-bearing chequing accounts not reckoned as money supply. Unable to understand what was happening, the Chairman of the US Fed, Paul Volcker, panicked and drove interest rates into the 20% range. The BoC followed suit.

That misunderstanding flattened the economy and kicked off the explosive growth of our federal debt.

In Canada this was topped off with John Crow's 7-year governorship of the Bank of Canada. Crow was determined to carve out a reputation as a super-Volcker, and for much of his tenure short-term interest rates in Canada were as much as five percentage points above the US figure. That hoisted the Canadian dollar up by 25% of its value, choked off exports and subsidised imports. And since Canada was preparing to enter the Free Trade Agreement with the US, it was a blue-chip program for disaster. High domestic rates led the provinces to do more of their borrowing outside the country in foreign currencies.

In 1991 when banks had lost heavily in mega-real estate and oil loans, the Government came to their rescue by ending their obligation to hold reserves against their deposits with the central bank. These reserves had earned them no interest. This legislation along with the Bank for International Settlements' new risk-based capital requirements, made it possible for the banks to load up with government debt without putting up any of their own cash.

Quebec was particularly affected by this. Unemployment figures for Quebec usually run about two percentage points higher than the national average. In 1980 when unemployment in Ontario was officially 6.8%, in Quebec it was 9.8%. By February 1994, these figures had risen to 10.7% and 12.5% respectively. A recent poll commissioned by *Time* showed that in Quebec 43% cited unemployment as the main problem facing Canadians and only 9% thought it was the danger of Quebec leaving Confederation.

The high costs of our monetary policy had boosted the federal debt from less than $83 billion in 1980 to around $500B today. That goes far to explain the massive shift of francophone votes to the separatist cause since 1980.

The BoC's policy not only fanned separatism in Quebec, but made provinces elsewhere in Canada less sensitive to Quebec's dissatisfactions.

For their part, the separatists played the social issue to the hilt. But until the last panicky days before the referendum, you would never have guessed from the English media that unemployment was a major issue. Serving up more constitutional cake in the months ahead will not help our Prime Minister save Canada.

A farcical side-show illustrated the innocence on monetary matters that is *de rigueur* among our politicians. Bouchard insisted on the right of an independent Quebec to go on using the Canadian dollar, while PM Chrétien argued that Quebec might be denied this. M. Bouchard could have made better use of his time in Paris as ambassador of Canada — a sort of travelling scholarship bestowed on a small-town lawyer by his then friend Brian Mulroney. There was no better place than Paris to learn how a country profits when another country accepts its currency as legal tender: it is equivalent to an interest-free loan to the issuing country. After all it was Gauliste France that blew the whistle on Washington's ploy in passing part of its war costs in Vietnam onto foreign countries using the dollar as their reserve currency. But M. Bouchard seems to have fumbled his homework both while in Canada and in France, And our anglophone politicians — with a few honourable exceptions — seem no wiser on this key matter.

Indeed, the Bouchard-Chrétien interchange on an independent Quebec and its right to use the Canadian dollar was like a brawl in a queue for tickets on the Titanic.

When Brokers Talk like Radicals...

When brokers start talking like radicals, it is a sure sign that something is rotten in Denmark.

The Globe and Mail (6/10) recounts the experience of Moss Lawson & Co. Ltd., when the Bank of Nova Scotia pulled its $1-million dollar standby loan. The firm, a brokerage customer of that bank for over 70 years, had never drawn down a cent of that credit-line in the 30 years it has been in place.

Brian Price, head of the firm, wrote the bank: "Since we are not owned by a bank, we wonder if bank policy is not to support any other dealer than the one you currently own. The answer appears to be yes. All but one of the country's Big Six banks have cut off non-bank-owned investment dealers' access to subordinated loans, a crucial source of regulatory capital, said several other investment industry executives. What concerns many industry players is that the banks are denying their competitors access to the type of capital they routinely provide to their own investment dealers."

After being turned down for a straight commercial loan by the large banks, Moss Lawson finally obtained a commercial loan against collateral with a small domestic bank — but the rate paid was prime as against 0.75% that it had paid for its standby credit.

The Scotia Bank spokesperson explained that the bank's dislike of subordinated lending in financial institutions is mainly because the risk-reward is not attractive. To which the investment industry executive replied "hogwash."

"The banks lost hundreds of dollars lending to Third World countries and the resource sector in the 1980s and commercial real estate in the early 1990s. The brokerage industry, by comparison, has been relatively free of casualties."

Our big banks have managed to parlay their repeated bailouts by the government into a monopolist "one-stop financial shopping" scam. For many Canadian businesses, small and not so small, that one stop threatens to be the cemetery.

k

Cutting an Issue: the Bank of Canada

In a documentary produced by the National Film Board of Canada in the late 1980s, the great Chicago-based community organiser, Saul Alinsky, made a comment that burned into my memory. He said: You can go into a community full of misery and social injustice. But you don't have an issue. You have to *cut* an issue."

Here in Canada politically active people concerned about human and environmental well-being are in confusion and disarray because we have not succeeded in cutting an issue. We have developed a richer understanding than ever of the dynamics of the social problems confronting us, and of their interactions with the vast network of problems that endanger the entire human community. But we have not been working effectively towards overcoming these problems because we have not successfully cut an issue. We have not zeroed in on some key factor at the heart of the many problems, nor have we devised a line of action that could mobilise many people with diverse, but related concerns into a common struggle focussed on a particular achievable goal.

Powerful, profit-oriented interests have taken control of the political agenda in Canada as elsewhere. They have reshaped our tax system and pushed through international trade agreements much to their advantage. They have reduced employment, are pushing down wages, and have the labour movement in retreat. They have accomplished these gains to the detriment of most of us and to the peril of the environment. Now they are on the verge of shredding our social safety net, claiming that our public sector debt makes such action, which they label "reform,"" inescapably necessary. They are intent on further reducing the ability of democratically elected governments to limit their power, and they seek to gain income from taking over portions of government activities where profit is possible.

If the three-year budget project Martin in February 1995 are implemented, the dismantling of Canada's social programs, the envy of many around the world, will become increasingly difficult to reverse. In Alberta the process is well under way. In Ontario Premier Mike Harris is imposing the most draconian cuts yet seen in Canada. Nevertheless, despite gradually increasing cuts over the past dozen to fifteen years, the damage is not yet irreversible. When the spending cuts announced by Martin will be passed down to the provinces and municipalities, the social programs that have made Canada a just and compassionate society will be devastated. Because, we are constantly told, we must reduce our public debt!

For most Canadians, it appears, the logic of this conclusion is beyond dispute. We all know from personal experience that there are only two ways of dealing with debt. One is to increase income and the other is to cut spending. We assume that the same logic applies to governments. They must either raise taxes or cut spending.

Operating within the confines of this logic, people concerned with maintaining our social programs have concluded that we must restore higher taxes on wealthy individuals and corporations. In her *Behind Closed Doors* Linda McQuaig has chronicled how such taxes were substantially reduced over the last two or three decades, while taxes on lower-income groups were raised. Increasing taxes on the rich makes sense. But voters are not convinced. The ability of the rich to resist tax increases by dominating public discussion through the media has won a sympathetic hearing from many ordinary people. They have found themselves working harder and longer, but nevertheless falling further behind. They have seen their taxes increase while social benefits have been eroded. Their hostility against taxes and their resentment against welfare recipients, however misguided, have played into the hands of the budget smashers.

Unable to raise taxes, are we at a loss to find ways of continuing to finance social progress? Not if we recognise the logic of federal government economics is different from that of family economics. The federal government has access to the additional tool of monetary policy. That tool is an extremely powerful one, but at present it is being perversely misused.

When, for example, the Bank of Canada pushes up interest rates to fight inflation, it drives the economy into recession, increases unemployment, reduces tax receipts and increases the public debt. Just as spending for social programs was not responsible for the burgeoning debt, so cutting social programs cannot bring the debt under control. The Martin budget calls for reductions over the next two years of $13.4 billion in spending, and projects that at the same time interest payments on the debt will rise by $16.2 billion!! Changes in monetary policy could enable us to bring under control the interest payments on the debt, without cutting social programs, and even without raising taxes!

Since its inception in 1988, *Economic Reform* has argued that the issue that we desperately need to cut here in Canada is the reform of monetary policy through the BoC. When we consider the potential beneficial impact of reshaping monetary policy, it becomes evident that we could hardly cut a more potent issue. Much more public understanding of this possibility is urgently needed.

At the October Convention of the Federal NDP COMER members succeeded in getting passed a strong statement on monetary policy as an amendment to the NDP Renewal Document. Others have been working with members of the federal Liberal caucus. The Alternative Federal Budget project in its second year now has a strong emphasis on monetary policy, thanks largely to COMER efforts. Let's keep pushing to cut this issue!

George Crowell

Vol. 8, No. 1 — January 1996

Genie out of the Bottle?

Metaphors are bridges for reasoning. Taking off from the familiar, they probe the unknown. But there is a catch. In the mouths of charlatans metaphors can be passed off as identities that block rather than open the mind.

Today the virtuous ideal of balancing budgets is putting knives to throats. Accordingly, gentle metaphors like "fine tuning" and "soft landings" are being replaced with others resounding with the finality of doomsday. Recently in Toronto Sylvia Ostry, the very model of a right-thinking economist, told her audience that it was too late to reverse what was happening. "The genie is out of the bottle and can't be put back." Unless we wanted to waste our time "like King Canute commanding the waves back."

Regal Canute, treated like just another giddy member of the House of Windsor, is warned against taking seriously such election-time fairy tales as "jobs, jobs, jobs."

When the North American Free Trade Agreement was being sold us, we were not told that we would be letting genies out of bottles. When, where, and by whom was that decision taken? Certainly not by Parliament.

In 1991-2 COMER was concentrating on defeating the government effort to put "zero inflation" in the Constitution and the *Bank of Canada Act*. But for all our prying, even we were not aware that a bill had already been slipped through a dozing parliament ending the reserves that banks had to put up with the Bank of Canada. During months of hearings of the Commons Subcommittee on Banking some months later, there was no mention of it. Only recently did we awaken to the crafty connection between the end of reserves and the attempt to consitutionalise "zero inflation."

When I mentioned it to John Hotson, he came up with the right metaphor — "a bull fighter distracting the bull with his cape."

In 1215 the barons at Runnymede laid the foundations for democracy by vesting the keys to the till in Parliament. Now central bankers have undone all that — and beyond all appeal!

The genie, having lied his way "out of the bottle," considers himself in control of things. But is he? In the past five years there have been several financial disasters of seismic scope. In the late 1980s and early 1990s there were the massive losses of banks in speculative mega-real estate projects. In the fall of 1992 came the shooting down of the British pound, the lira, the peseta and the Canadian dollar from the insane levels to which their central banks had hoisted them. In 1994 when the US Fed almost doubled its short-term rate within a year, there followed the greatest meltdown in the bond market since 1929. Then came the mega-scams in derivatives that bankrupted uncounted banks, municipalities, and trust funds. Finally topping all, Mexico, the white hope of NAFTA, collapsed in a cesspool of murder and corruption. All of these disasters were linked to the use of high interest rates as a stabiliser. Remarkably, however, not a single of these disasters was foreseen by the self-declared genie. They followed on the heels of his assurances that "fundamentals are sound."

There was no concern that the high interest rates imposed were beyond anything that could be extracted from the breathing body of the economy

In 1939 after a grinding decade of depression there were more holes than savings in Canadian pockets. Yet Canada was able to use the newly founded BoC to mobilise its resources for the war. As a by-product, the percentage of our federal debt held by non-residents was reduced from 30.4 in 1939 to 6.3 in 1946. And when peace came, we made good the devastation of fifteen years of joblessness and hostilities. A vast penniless immigration was housed, the baby boom generation educated to standards undreamt of before the war, a semi-rustic society transformed into an urbanised, literate one. An aridly provincial land experienced a cultural blossoming. How was this financed? Through reasonably full employment while inflation was held at bay with forced savings, price controls, and other methods that directly addressed our real problems.

A decade ago we were assured that such measures would be accepted only in times of crisis. It was too early then. Now we are told that it is too late. Anybody cheating at cards so clumsily would be thrown out of a gambling club.

wk

Let's Talk Bonds!

Bondholders have inherited the earth, so let's talk bonds.

R. Glenn Hubbard tells us that the "risk premium [on bonds] consists of two components." One is the "default risk" — the risk of the debtor defaulting. The second is the "variability risk" — the risk of the market value dropping.†

Both risk types are driven into the skies by the monetarist dogma that singles out "zero inflation" as the one goal of central banks. And to defeat inflation, only one policy is declared acceptable — higher interest rates. In that our central bank calls to mind the 18th president of the US, General Ulysses Grant, who claimed he could recognise only two tunes — *Yankee Doodle* and all the others. The policies that made it possible to finance our part in World War II — without inflation and while lightening our burden of foreign debt — are rejected out of hand.

Lurching interest rates do far more to destabilise the economy than the moderately mobile prices they were supposed to cure. That is best seen in the case of bonds.

The market value of a bond is determined by discounting its interest coupons by the foreseeable rate of interest over its term. A bond may be as solid as the rock of Gibraltar, but if interest rates go up, a shortfall arises between its coupon and the market rate. But there are two other factors in the implosion of bond prices. Even the coupons on old bonds are now discounted for present value (pv) at the higher rate of interest. And finally the principal payment when the bond matures is discounted at the new higher long-term rate. That rate is influenced by the spot short-term interest rate and central bank policy.

(With 10% rates, a dollar payable a year down the line is worth 90 cents today. One dollar due ten years away is worth 35 cents, Raise rates to 15% and a dollar due ten years away is worth only 20 cents.)

But these increased discounts are not confined to bonds. They affect the market value of every capital asset in the land in a *non-linear* way. Even the espousal of "zero inflation" by the central bank may push up the "variability premium" on all bonds, and, indeed, on all capital assets. For such a policy guarantees that there can be a substantial drop in the market value of the bond arising not from a defect in the bond itself but from central bank policy.‡

In the case of corporation bonds the effect of higher interest rates is still more crushing than in that of government debt. In the cast of government bonds of developed (OECD) countries the "default risk" is declared to be zero by the Risk-Based Capital

Requirements guidelines of the Bank for International Settlements. But that is not the case with corporation bonds. When interest rates shoot up, people lose their jobs, the demand for products and services shrinks, and firms have smaller net earnings out of which to pay the higher rates on their debt. Government debt grows as the tax-base shrivels. and civil servants are laid off at the very time that there is need for more emergency services. The soothing talk, of course, is of "soft landings," but the violent braking of the economy, with seat belts eliminated beforehand as an economy measure, guarantees that the recession will be traumatic.

With a stricken private economy, government bonds become more desirable, and, being in greater demand, their yield — which is the cost to the taxpayer on new issues — should go down. Hubbard (p. 48) writes: "From 1929 as expectation of downturn during the Depression, bondholders shifted from risky corporation bonds to government securities pushing yields close to zero. The spread between BAA-rated corporation bonds and long-term government bonds moved from 2% in 1929 to 6% in 1931."

Why hasn't this happened today? Largely because of the bad-mouthing of the government's credit by the government itself and its central bank. Since over 95% of our money supply (M3) is debt, and capital assets serve as collateral for much of it, high interest rates are a form of financial terrorism that undermines the entire economy.

Analysis along these lines is a key tool for understanding what is happening around us. It may require a little effort to grasp, but it offers more insight into our economic plight than a library of conventional textbooks.

William Krehm

† *Money, the Financial System and the Economy* (1994)

‡ The approximate formula for the drop in market value of a bond of n-year term, when long-term rates rise from i to I is the sum of two components:

a) The pv of the shortfall of the coupons of the old bond compared with the new higher interest rates. $[DI + (DI)^1 + ...(DI)^n]$ s where s = the shortfall of the coupons of the old rate i compared to the new rate I. DI = annual discount rate at I or 100-I/100.

b) Difference of the principal repayment on maturity P after year n calculated at the old and new rates: $[DI^n - Di^n]$ P

Note that as interest rates eventually drop with the imploded economy, the shortfall s moves from a positive to negative value, and the bond market shoots up as violently as it collapsed when interest rates jumped.

Financial Madam Butterfly?

Within the next year or two we are likely to witness a Japanese crash that will rock the world financial system to its Gucci shoes. That will not be without an element of justice. For Japan was pushed into its breath-taking casino economy by the militant ideologists who took over the show in Washington and the Bank for International Settlements.

Japanese banks lost massive amount of their capital in the collapse of the roaring US real estate market of the late 1980s. To bail them out, the Bank of Japan cut its discount rate to one-half percent. And to reflate the banks' capital, the government encouraged them to load up with US bonds. It assured the banks that it would keep the yen low in relation to the US dollar to shield them from exchange losses in such ventures.

That should sound familiar to Canadian ears, since up to a point it parallels the Bank of Canada's bailout of our own banks. The latter took the form of doing away with reserve requirements for the banks so that the banks could load up with another

$60 billion in Canadian government debt without putting up any cash of their own. Our government picked up the tab, since the central bank itself could have held that additional government debt and returned the interest as dividends to its one shareholder, the government. In Japan the BoJ made available funds to the banks at 1/2% to finance their acquisition of US debt that earned them 5.5 and 6%. [The Japanese arrangement was in a sense smarter than ours, since it was the US taxpayer rather than the Japanese that paid the shot. Moreover, it enlisted the support of the financial community for low interest rates, and a low currency that has permitted Japanese exports to earn the foreign currency for repairing some of the damage sustained in foreign speculations.]

However, there is nothing so imperfect as a perfect papering-over job. And when in 1994 the US Fed almost doubled its rates, the market value of existing bonds took the worse shellacking since 1929. As a result more of the Japanese banks' capital went down the drain.†

Between 1945 and 1970 the highly regulated Japanese financial system had provided cheap credit and strategic planning for industrial expansion. After 1970 pressure for much deregulation came not only at home, but more significantly from the us. Washington fingered those low interest rates and other regulation as "unfair" competitive advantage, while its geo-economic offensives contributed to cycles of credit boom and bust in the late 1980s and early 1990s.

Centralised planning in Japan goes back to the Meiji Restoration over a century ago when domestic funds were channelled into industrial modernisation. The banks and the government provided so large a proportion of investment funds that capital markets were hardly needed. Another important factor in the weakness of capital markets was the prominence of the holding companies, the *zaibatsu*, alliances of firms holding equity in one another's enterprises on a long-term basis. That kept much equity off the market.

US occupation authorities after WWII were torn between conflicting objectives. On the one hand to prevent a resurgence of militarism, they broke up the *zaibatsu* and decentralised their share capital. But before Washington's trust-busting nostalgia could take root under distant cherry blossoms, the Cold War gusted in. In its procurement the Pentagon found it simpler dealing with large rather than with small businesses. And Japanese fear of takeovers by predatory American firms inspired a "shareholding stabilisation strategy." Its stated goal was to keep savers and investors separate so that the intermediation of funds might enable the government to ensure cheap bank credit to industry. The BoJ and the Finance Ministry undertook to protect the banks should their industrial loans go sour.

These measures helped make possible an average annual growth of the Japanese GDP during the 22 years after 1951 of 9.2%. Cheap loans to strategic industries were at the heart of Japan's economic miracle.

Since the 1970s, under American pressure, deregulation has taken over. Industries are less dependent on banks for their financing and more on the money market. The end of the dollar's convertibility into gold in the early seventies flooded the world with depreciated dollars and improved American competitiveness on foreign markets. In response, Japan initiated an inflationary spiral of its own to reverse the rise of the yen against the dollar.

Washington, however, stopped at little to bully Tokyo into allowing interest rates to rise to international levels. Within two and a half years by 1988 the dollar value of the yen had shot up by 50%. That started an outflow of Japanese capital into US real estate investments. It also led to a four-fold increase between 1987-9 in the Japanese expatriation of their simpler, more labour-intensive manufacturing to South Eastern Asia. It was this rather than just "the free market" that put the tiger into that region's tank. Indeed, contrary to the version pumped out by the international financial bureaucracy, South Korea, Taiwan, Malaysia, Singapore, Indonesia and Thailand all tended to adhere closely to the Japanese model: powerful strategic planning, a close link among government, banks and manufacturing firms to provide plentiful and inexpensive credit where the national interest required. While adopting the rhetoric of deregulation, Asian countries have resisted opening up their economies.

Under constant diplomatic battering from the United States, the Japanese model has not fared so well in Japan itself. To compensate for the erosion of their export profits Japanese industries turned increasingly to financial gambling on world markets. Their disasters in derivatives, if less known, more than match those of Orange County, California. When in 1987 Washington's offensive suddenly switched from pressing for a higher yen to pushing for a lower one, financial speculation really shot into orbit. Between 1980 and 1990 the assets of Japan's twenty largest banks increased by 450%.

That is how Japan got where it finds itself — with a destabilised banking system, its social structures sapped, and its society increasingly polarised.

† *Money Power and Space*, edited by Stuart Corbridge, Ron Martin and Nigel Thrift, Basil Blackwell Ltd., 1994, especially the essays of M.T. Daly and Andrew Leyshon.

Vol. 8, No. 2 — February 1996

The LBO-ing of Government

With the exception of the Depression of the Thirties, the cycles of classical capitalism conformed to a basic pattern: after a period of recession, recovery would allow the economy to heal, paving the way for the next boom. Since the late seventies this is no longer so.

It all began with the progressive deregulation of what financial institutions could do with other people's money. The ceiling on interest rates came off in the sixties. In the seventies banks were allowed to wander far from their home turf to more exciting adventures. Deposit insurance made deposits ever available provided that the banks paid high enough interest. And the need to earn that sort of money drove borrowing institutions into ever more harebrained schemes.

In Canada, as ever, we danced in step with our southern cousins, and looked with pride at our Campeaus and Reichmanns who were doing leveraged buyouts (LBO-ing) on the world market with the best of them. With less fanfare our government was soon bailing out our banks from their massive losses from financing the sport.

Memories of the destructive potential of debt had died hard since the thirties, Executives of the 1960s and 1970s believed that their interest bills should not be larger than one sixth of operating profits. But by the late seventies a new generation of financiers had arisen. By 1968 the operating profits of firms taken over in LBOs could cover their interest burden only by an average proportion of 1:0.71.

The flagship of the new age was Kohlberg, Kravis and Roberts (KKR), a small partnership specialising in LBOs.

To bring in the new morality KKR relied on the persuasiveness of rich fees paid armies of lawyers, investment banks, and sundry advisers. They devised ways of shrinking the tax liabilities of the LBOed corporations, stepping up the depreciation writeoffs by goosing the book value of the corporation's assets. They propagated the mystique of LBOs being best for society by releasing "lazy capital."

Servicing that debt, KKR maintained, would spur management to new heights of efficiency. That took the form of mass firings, the selling off of attractive assets of the burdened firm, and the occasional suicide among managers entrusted with such agendas.

The "discipline of debt" became the new magic.

KKR made a point of keeping their distance from the management of the corporations they took over. Getting too close to the blood on the floor would interfere with their concentration on the abstract bottom line. They insisted on their managers owning not options but actual shares in their companies. In this way they stood to gain or lose immensely depending on their companies meeting the financial projections of KKR. Workers in the LBO-ed firms were spurred by the fear of being the next to go.

It was a landmark moment when KKR turned to Michael Milken of Drexel Burnham Lambert Inc. for financing. Milken was the next best thing to an automatic teller machine for huge instantaneous loans to finance LBOs. By the mid-1980s Milken was underwriting $20 billion of junk bonds a year — as much as the entire national debt of the US in 1940. What eventually brought him to disaster was that, while demanding equity as a discretional sweetener to bond-buyers to move the issue of junk bonds, it emerged that he kept much of it for his own firm. When one of Milken's major clients turned state witness, both the LBO and the junk-bond market unravelled.

Having bagged just about everything that moved in the private sector, the "financial engineers" moved on to do a LBO job on government itself. First, with the collusion of the Bank of Canada, our government was saddled with enough high-priced debt to undermine its social programs. For no good reason Canada's debt became the most generous junk bonds on the world market. In the light of that achievement Governor John Crow of the BoC must be seen as the equivalent of Milken in Canadian high finance.

The LBO-ing of our government is complete in every essential. To cope with this yoke of debt, federal and provincial governments are firing civil servants by the tens of thousands. Programs that had redefined Canada as a nation are being plowed under. A government deprived of its functions has ever less reason for surviving, and not surprisingly secessionist movements are cropping up throughout the country.

To ease this debt load, government investments — like units of a LBO-ed private firm — are being sold off. By the very dynamic of the LBO phenomenon, every privatisation can only spur the "financial engineers" into greater boldness. And for the opening barrage of this new chapter, even rusty, spiked cannon from ancient battles are being wheeled into line. John Crow sorties out of his well-earned retirement to fill pages of the press with letters denying that he had ever espoused "zero inflation."

The Toronto Star (20/1) gives us an inkling of still more daring coups in the offing. There the chief economist of the Royal Bank of Canada, John McCallum, broached "the possible case" for allowing mergers among the six major chartered banks left in Canada. "We are in the process of losing the competing advantage in banking we have enjoyed for a century" The "we" will be savoured by Canadians in modest business who have had their lines of credit called, because "our" banks have become "gung-ho" on world conquest. "The Royal Bank of Canada ranked 12th in the world. It has now slipped to 59th place." Mr. McCallum omitted to mention that the largest banks in the world are the Japanese who have lost much of their capital in mega-speculations. At this very moment they are being bailed out by their government on a scale carefully hidden from public view.

Mr. McCallum, a former critic of our banking system until he was hired by the Royal Bank, puts his reputation at risk with such nonsense.

Vol. 8, No. 4 — April 1996

Social Notes

The budget-cutting gospel is a simple one. Governments and businesses slash and slash their staffs and spendings, and the markets applaud and reward their effort with higher quotes for shares, and lower interest rates on bonds. Having appointed the market traders supreme judges, their approval is supposed to settle all things. But does it? Even after the chosen key statistics — inflation, deficit — have been knocked into shape, there is a tremendous disposal problem left. The millions thrown out of work do not disappear, but linger on spreading demoralization, self-hatred, to say nothing of disease. No right-thinking economist has yet devised a way of running a functioning economy in a broken-down society. Let us take a quick look at how things are shaping up in the world of reality.

Mexico

Neal Templin in *The Wall Street Journal* (4/3) tells of Enrique Mendez Mora, a Mexican civil engineer who had "earned more than enough building homes in Mexicali to support his family. After Mexico's worst economic crisis since the Great Depression put Mr. Mendez out of work, he crossed the border to harvest onions. When harvest ended, he landed a job in a US car wash.

"After investing years in education, hordes of Mexican professionals are performing menial work when they can find it. Throughout Mexico — a country with an underemployment rate of 26% — doctors, lawyers, engineers are waiting on tables or filling lowly clerical jobs.

"Even though Mexico still has only half as many physicians per capita as the US, there are doctors driving taxi cabs in Mexico City."

Mexico thought it had a free-trade agreement with the US to become the major low-wage supplier of the US market. It seems to have balked when confronted with the reality that US retailers intended to use NAFTA to open Mexico to goods produced by even lower paid Chinese workers. Mexico's bureaucrats are defending the home turf in the spirit of Pancho Villa. They are throwing up barricades of bureaucratic paper to obstruct the cheap Chinese imports favoured by US discounters, slowing down customs clearance, and slapping on tariffs up to 300%.

So much for our Prime Minister's travels throughout the Third World to win jobs for Canada. He could save a lot of carfare with similar results by visiting the hospices for the homeless in Toronto and Montreal in quest of markets.

Germany

The Wall Street Journal (6/3) gives us a sample of what is happening in the world's third largest economy.

"Ulrich Hartmann, the CEO of industrial giant Veba AG, is doing something unheard of in Germany: He's worrying about shareholder value. He has laid off thousands of workers, fired longtime managers and closed divisions that date back to Veba's beginnings — all in the name of investors. 'Our commitment,' he said, 'is to create value for you, our shareholders.'

"The developments at Veba, Germany's fourth largest company in revenue terms, underscore a trend catching hold in German boardrooms.

"But the German public — used to a fabled 'German model' of management described as 'capitalism with a human face' — remains deeply suspicious of the alternative way of doing business."

That model can be traced back to the discussions of the Socialist leader, Ferdinand Lassalle, with Bismark in the 1860s. For a century it was one of the cornerstones of Germany's economic successes. Since the Second World War the trade unions have had a part in the decision-making of large corporations.

During the thirties, the Weimar Republic, with unemployment at 20% and more, turned its back on that model, paving the way for the Nazi takeover. The German economic miracle after World War II was partly rooted in generous social services. When deflationary interest rates took over, the resulting unemployment was cushioned by the firing of millions of foreign workers, whose remittances to their homelands had been a major factor in keeping the economies of Yugoslavia, Turkey and other Balkan countries on an even keel. Had high interest-rate fanaticism not triumphed and the *Gastarbeiter* had been able to go on working in Germany, Yugoslavia might have survived in one piece.

But now the market efficiency model is eating at the vitals of Germany itself, as unemployment is pushing up towards 4,300,000, 11.1% of the labour force — a record figure for the past half century.

Meanwhile, it is leading to some strange alignments. Since the goal of maximising "shareholder value" leads directly to takeovers, it presents a challenge to the German banks that historically have controlled many German industrial firms. The *WSJ* quotes a management board member of Deutsche Bank saying that emphasis on shareholder value must be viewed critically. "She talks about corporate raiders who 'squeeze companies dry' and show no regard for workers. Minority shareholders, such as pension funds, are part of the problem, she says because they sell to the highest bidder."

After 12,000 workers were laid off at Veba's chemical division, Huels, Veba's profit rose by 40%. "'A year ago,' says Juergen Schrempp, manager of Daimler Benz, 'no one in the company knew what the stock price was.' Now the company keeps stockholders in mind with everything it does. 43% of Veba's shares are now in foreign hands. When their profit is high enough they sell and transfer to elsewhere in the world, leaving the social havoc created by the Hartmann policy behind them."

Book Review — *When Corporations Rule the World*

[Korten, David C. *When corporations rule the world.* West Hartford, CT : Kumarian Press, 1995. ISBN 1887208003]

David Korten fingers the tendency of too many economists to plant their conclusions in the assumptions of their arguments. Data may be fed into a preexistent computer model that incorporates premises not even declared. He cites the case of *The New York Times* using the theory of comparative advantage to bolster its support of NAFTA. The classical theory of comparative advantage, however, deals with natural resources, not with the relative wages paid in the trading countries. "Letters submitted by me and others to the editor pointing out the omission were not published."

The worrisome relationship between morality and "market efficiency" is handled with elegance. "The self-proclaimed 'value-free objectivity' of economic rationalism aligns easily with the elitist moral philosophy of market liberalism. Seldom has this been more starkly revealed than in a widely publicised staff memo by Lawrence Summers in his capacity as chief economist of the World Bank. Summers argued that it is economically more efficient for the rich countries to dispose of their toxic wastes in poor countries, because poor people have both shorter life spans and less earning potential than wealthy people."

He emphasises the parallel between the inflation of the prices of goods and services, the one concern of our central banks, and the inflation of financial assets promoted by deregulation. "In an economy awash with money and investors looking for quick returns, demand is substantially influenced by speculators' expectation that other speculators will continue to push up prices. Nicholas F. Brady, US Treasury Secretary under President Bush, observed: 'If the assets were gold or oil, this phenomenon would be called inflation. In stocks, it is called wealth creation.'"

When the speculative bubble finally burst on October 19, 1987, the Dow Jones Industrial Average fell by 22.6% in one day. "Investors lost over a trillion dollars on the NYSE in little over two months — an eighth of all homes, factories, office buildings, and other real estate, and roads. As Joel Kurtzman pointed out, this was enough to feed the entire world for two years, raise the Third World to middle class status, pay for one thousand nuclear aircraft carriers." But then Korten goes on to add: "In fact, this $1 trillion could not have fed the world for even five minutes for the simple reason that people can't eat money. There was no change in the productive capacity of any of those companies, or even in the cash available in their own bank accounts."

It is this contradiction that is pulling society apart. "The global financial system has become a parasitic predator that lives off the flesh of its host — the productive economy."

"Additional risks and economic distortions are created by a sophisticated class of financial instruments known as derivatives — bets on movements of stock prices, currency prices, interest rates, and even stock market indices. Future contracts on interest rates didn't exist until the late 1970s. Now such contracts total more than half the GNP of the us. In 1994 the total value of outstanding derivatives contracts was estimated at about $12 trillion — with growth projected to be about $18 trillion in 1994. *The Economist* has estimated the value of the world's total stock of productive fixed capital to be around $20 trillion.

"Derivatives are commonly purchased on margin. The largest players may not be required to put up any money at all. The more sophisticated derivatives are highly complex, and are often not well understood even by those who deal in them."

"The riskier and more destabilising forms of extractive investment have received a major boost from a new breed of mutual funds called 'hedge funds.' These specialise in short-term speculation and call for a minimum initial investment of $1 million. Many of the largest hedge funds produced a return of more than 50% in 1993, The downside risks are also substantial."

Korten quotes Felix Rohatyn, senior member of Lazard Freres & Co: "In many cases hedge funds and speculative activity in general may now be more responsible for foreign exchange and interest-rate movements than intervention by the central banks. Derivatives create a chain of risks linking financial institutions and corporations throughout the world; any weakness or break in that chain could create a serious problem for the international financial system."

So much for the wisdom of "the market" to which our governments and central banks have surrendered much of their power. Little wonder that when President Clinton proposed nominating Rohatyn to the Federal Reserve, Wall St. raised such protest that Rohatyn declined! As topmost storey of their casino, farthest from the real economy and closest to their god, central banks have embraced the derivatives trade, and rejected all proposals that it be subjected to government regulation.

Korten's summation: "To the global economy, people are not only increasingly unnecessary, but they and their demand for a living wages are a major source of economic inefficiency."

k.

Vol. 8, No. 5 — May 1996

In the Shade of a Tottering Tower?

Over a century ago the Americans solved the engineering problems of building skyscrapers. As more and more storeys were piled up, the foundations were strengthened to support their weight. How differently a similar problem is being handled in the economy!

We are told that we must put up with joblessness, fewer public services, and other inconveniences because the world economy is being 'restructured' – an expression that bristles with engineering know-how. However, if we summed up our global restructuring in a nutshell it would be: markets, especially financial markets, are to be freed from all constraints. When the prices of stocks and even derivatives go up, value, it is said, is being "created." But any upward blip in the prices of real goods must at once be repressed with higher interest rates. Those higher rates stimulate the appetites of those who juggle securities to add further storeys to the financial superstructure. But the same high rates eat away at the footings of the top-heavy structure. It should be obvious that such a construct must be increasingly exposed to the risk of collapsing or keeling over.

That is exactly what has begun to happen. The Bank for International Settlements (BIS), habitually as silent as the grave, has taken to issuing releases that smack of cover-up.

"In a report issued by BIS, central bankers from the world's 11 major industrial countries said many banks don't appreciate the size or complexity of settlement risk and that they lack formal mechanisms to measure and cope with their exposures. The amount at risk even to a single counterparty [another bank] could easily exceed a bank's capital. Some of the 80 major international banks studied acknowledge that their senior executives had never been fully briefed on the foreign exchange settlement process and the associated risks." (*Wall Street Journal* 28/03)

"The central banks threatened that in each country they might impose risk-management guidelines and verify compliance. The BIS also is willing to consider imposing similar limits on non-bank financial institutions active in currency trading."

Yet BIS and the central banks have consistently pressed for ever more deregulation of finance. Even when banks, mutual funds, local governments, and industrial corporations were losing astronomic amounts of money on complex derivative gambles, central banks recoiled in horror from any suggestion for imposing a modest tax on financial transactions. It would, they argued, lessen the "efficiencies" that result from giving speculative money a diplomatic passport. Worse still, it might reduce the very volume of money swishing across frontiers, that now — for good enough reason — suddenly alarms them.†

The emphasis of the BIS and central bankers remains on "self-regulation." What better guardian of the henhouse than the fox? After all, he has had so much experience.

Indeed, many of the risks BIS now deplores can be traced back to the Risk-Based Capital Requirements formulated by it in the late eighties. These allowed banks to load up with government debt with little or no capital of their own. That is why government debt of OECD countries were declared risk-free. But lurching interest rates make it impossible to say what the capital of a bank might be at a given moment. What BIS has wrought rules out any serious risk-management.

Before deregulation took over it was possible for industrialists to run their firms for the long-term rather than with an eye on making a quick killing on the stock market. The stock market has a logic of its own. Whenever a company shows an improved "bottom line," that is at once capitalised: i.e. the assumption is made that not only will the improved bottom line occur next year and for all time to come, but that the rate of improvement of that bottom line will repeat itself as well. Ditto the rate of improvement of the rate of improvement, and so forth to infinity. A management that neglects such an exercise will expose itself to a takeover.

Removing the ceilings on interest rates over three decades ago, and the ongoing deregulation of what banks can engage in, had made it possible for "financial engineers" to find bank financing for leveraged take-overs and speculative gambles. Providing such financing on highly lucrative terms has become a higher priority with our banks than serving "stick-in-the-mud businessmen" content to go on producing something that satisfies human needs. To escape the stigma of being "lazy," capital must fornicate and multiply all over the world 24 hours a day.

The net result was to run up storey after storey of fictitious finance at the same time that the supporting foundations in the real economy were being ground away. The world's financial skyscraper goes on pushing into the heavens by gobbling up its own foundations. That explains the unease that has suddenly overtaken BIS.

wk

† James Tobin developed the idea of such a tax applied by all countries, with its proceeds directed to financing the UN's peacekeeping and social initiatives. In Canada COMER members (Jack Biddell, Jordan Grant and others) developed a domestic version of such a tax that would be directed to replacing the regressive Goods and Services Tax. The Liberals, when in opposition promised to do away with the GST, but since elected has not given the proposal the time of day.

Fighting the Wrong Deficit

Most public discussion of the federal budget deficit accepts the premise that government spending cuts are necessary to reduce the deficit to pave the way for economic growth. There is a bipartisan consensus to balance the budget in seven years. The only genuine difference between the major political actors is over the scope of the spending cuts.

What is missing is any concern about the type of our deficits, whether they are active or passive deficits.

Active deficits are simply the result of the government spending more than it collects in taxes at full employment. Traditionally, wartime deficits provide the classic example of active deficits. Even a booming economy and steep federal income taxes during WWII could not cover the enormous cost of the nation's military spending.

Passive deficits, on the other hand, result from slow economic growth and the under-utilisation of capital and human resources. Unemployed resources do not pay taxes, but rather are an enormous drain on the fisc.

Today's deficits are largely passive in nature, resulting from anemic economic growth, high real interest rates, and high levels of unemployed human and physical resources. But deficit hawks assume, quite wrongly, that we are fighting active deficits.

The conventional remedy for large active deficits has been restrictive fiscal policies. Unfortunately, such policies only exacerbate the size of passive deficits. What little inflation we have comes from rising overhead costs per unit product associated with under-utilised capacity and high interest costs.

Timothy A. Canova and
Lynn Turgeon

BIS — a Hot Tip

We are indebted to a COMER member for a recent "junk-mail" edition of The Oxford Group stock market tip-sheet that declares BIS shares a hot buy.

"It owns over 6 million ounces in gold with 473,000 shares outstanding. At $395 per ounce, that alone puts the share value of BIS at $5,172.

"But it is also deep in cash reserves — about $1.8 billion worth. That adds a further $3,740 to each share value for a book value worth around $8,900.

"Like any good Swiss bank, it has hidden assets that don't show up on its official balance sheet. Among them, tracts of valuable land around Basel. These would bring the real value of the shares to about $18,000.

"Yet remarkably, this stock is selling for only $9,691 — roughly 50% below estimated value!

"BIS is one of the world's rare bargains.

"We think BS should get to its real value of $18,000 within the next five years. It's safe, private, has good profit potential, and a tidy 2.6% dividend paid in Swiss francs free of the 35% Swiss withholding tax. The stock has nowhere to go but up."

You may be surprised that BIS, which has a lot more to say about your economic future than your elected government should be so hot a tip on the stock market. The explanation can be found in William Krehm, *The Bank of Canada: a power unto itself* (Stoddart, 1993, p. 18):

"BIS's original shareholders were supposed to be central banks. But because of the isolationist stance of the US Federal Reserve, a syndicate of American commercial banks took up the shares reserved for the us.

"Today the BIS shareholders and members are still those central banks and what remains of the original US bank syndicate — not as is the case with the International Monetary Fund and most other international organisations, representatives of governments,

"Several central banks, including those of France, Belgium, and Denmark, along with the US syndicate, have sold substantial portions of their holdings to the public. But only the original subscribers can vote, with voting rights allotted in proportion to the shares originally held.

"Obviously BIS has done a thorough job of avoiding any contamination with democracy."

Vol. 8, No. 6 — June 1996

Planning the Next Bailout of Our Banks

It is high time that we draw up a rescue plan for our banks in their coming difficulties. Evidence that the occasion cannot be too distant is piling up at many levels. Most basic is the belief that to equip our banks to conquer the world further deregulation is necessary. That is like arguing for stripping the brakes of a high-powered car because they prevent it from "maximising" its momentum.

Bringing the banks back to attending to the needs of our economy must be one of the conditions for the next bailout of the banks. For this it will be necessary to restore the reserve requirements to the *Bank Act*. That done, the next step will be for the Bank of Canada to build up its holdings of federal debt to the levels that stood at in 1990, or roughly be adding to its inventories some 11% of the net funded federal debt — some $55 billion. This amount of debt taken off the market will have an effect in bringing down interest rates on all government debt, but particularly on medium- and long-term bonds.

It has been argued that adding $55 billion to the assets of the Bank of Canada will increase them by almost 200% from the present figure and by the time that reaches the chartered banks add perhaps $45 to $50 B to their legal tender holdings that serve as the basis for their money creation.

That is pure red herring. To understand the very different attitudes of our banks toward legal tender and credit money of their own creation, we can learn something from Gresham's Law. Thomas Gresham, a financier under Elizabeth I, is credited with being the first man to recognise that bad coin drives good coin out of circulation. If clipped coin is found on the market side by side with sound coin, the good coin is removed by private parties for hoarding and only the adulterated stays in circulation. Something similar is happening with our money supply today. It is far more profitable for banks to create their own money (i.e. credit) than to hold legal tender that they get from the central bank. In a bizarre extension of Gresham's Law, for them the good money i.e. the profitable money, is the credit they themselves create and the bad money that they leave circulating among the public is the legal tender or "billfold money." Legal tender is for them "bad money" because it earns no interest, it is money without gonads. The main purpose for which they used to hold legal tender was to put up the required reserves with the BoC, to meet the public's demands for legal tender (for example for stocking their ATMs), and to settle any balance in cheque clearance each day. [They will hold no more of the increased legal tender than what they cannot avoid. Since the ending of the statutory reserve requirements in 1994, their holdings of legal tender has gone down by almost 50%, and ways of economising on the cash they must hold for cheque clearances are constantly being perfected.]

Social Immune Deficiency?

Others have drawn on the analogy of a failed immunity system to explain the world's troubles. Diseases long believed expunged are cropping up again under the favourable conditions offered by our growing street population, unemployment, reduced social services and the use of antibiotics in livestock feed to promote growth. Microbe strains are developing resistance to our most trusted antibiotics; the slashing of research funds is not helpful in this deadly race. Entire hospitals in the United States are infected with new virulent mutations of microbes arriving from other continents. Where the Sermon on the Mount has been amended to read "Lean and Mean," the Sermon of the Microbes may compel greater attention.

In his *The Social Immune System and the Cancer Stage of Capitalism*[†] John McMurtry, however, transforms all this from a parable into masterful analysis. "When we think of a society's 'defence system,' we think of its armed forces. We have long been conditioned to this...Society's real system of self-defence, its public health process, is in this way deprived of its proper social resources and functions. Ever more invasive assaults on the protection and circulation of means of life within societies by environmental despoliation, redistribution of wealth from the poor and middle-income classes to the rich, and the radical dismantling of public forms of life-provision now attack society's life-defences."

"Public health regimes regulated by self-conscious scientific practices are a comparatively recent evolution, originating in Europe in the latter half of the 18th century. The intensive concentrations of propertyless humanity in rising production centres introduced new and deadly problems of runaway sewage, fouled water supplies, adulterated foods, contagious diseases, roaming street people, abandoned children, infirm aged without familial support — much as we see growing again in the unfettered "free market" cities of today. Surveying the increasing public-sector mediations of every aspect of our lives by protective regulation, one begins to recognise that this is a *social immune system.*

"In 14th-century Europe and Asia, up to three-quarters of humans suffered horrible deaths without the social immune defence we now take for granted. There have also been barbaric regressions in times of great social stress. Atavistic attacks on minority populations as 'unclean' or 'foreign' have been unleashed in murderous "defences" of a spurious social self. In these cases we see a disordered social immune system at work — a false recognition of a 'non-self' agent and response by extinctive attack or isolation. We have observed these social-immune disorders in various forms, from 'witch hunts' across Europe in the later 16th century to 'anti-subversive' exterminations in developing countries across the world in the Reagan period.

"One might argue that the idea of a 'social immune system' is only a metaphor, modelled on the intro-organic analyses of medical science. Considered more deeply though, the terms deployed by medical science in its descriptions of the immune system's operations are themselves *social categories.* The foundational concepts of the entire immune system lexicon began with the binary opposition of 'self' and 'non-self,' the primary distinction between individual persons and what they are not in the realm of human interrelations.

"A society that loses its former capacities to provide nutriment, protection against pathogens, or literacy education for its citizens is suffering from a disease of the social body. Whether this results from the seizure by a despotic oligarchy of the means of life and reproduction, or from more subtle mechanisms such as financial transactions that systematically enrich a section of the population at the expense of the rest, the attack on the health of the social body calls for a resistant response to the disease invasion. The sector that appropriates its life resources at the expense of the community also prevents an effective social reaction to the disease challenge by recasting *the response itself* as society's 'disorder.' It then attacks the bearers of society's immune response as 'enemies, terrorists, subversives,' etc. and seeks to destroy them."

In moving from this striking generalisation to specifics, McMurtry displays both insight and advantages of background. At the University of Guelph, he holds a chair not of economics, but of philosophy. That undoubtedly helped him develop a keen sense of structure in dealing with the economy and society itself — something that a doctorate in economics is almost guaranteed to blunt.

McMurtry's biographical note gives value theory as one of his specialties. Significantly, for over a century value theory has been banished from [the mainstream of] economic thinking. Yet there was a time when value — as distinguished from the latest market price — occupied a key position in economic literature. Variously defined, it covered the whole gamut of relationships that linked the economy to society. Some economists referred to it as 'intrinsic value'; John Stuart Mill compared value to the sea level constantly being ruffled by the turbulence of price. Adam Smith, canny Scot, operated with no less than three distinct value theories depending on the problem he was considering — much like the bifocal spectacles invented by his friend, Benjamin Franklin.

David Ricardo, a keen-minded broker, in his campaign against the Corn Laws had honed the labour theory of value to so sharp an edge, that from it Marx and other trouble-makers were able to draw highly subversive conclusions. After the Paris Commune had alarmed the propertied classes, a great need was felt for a theory that would fudge rather than emphasize social disparities. The mathematical model of a self-equilibrating 'pure and perfect market' developed by Leon Walras filled the bill to a T. All actors in the productive process were cast in the role of traders. Workers, too, were presented as weighing the relative advantages of working for the wages offered or savouring the joys of leisure in their parlours.

Value was superseded by the price of the last market transaction. Even Joan Robinson, a leftist Keynesian who dabbled in Marx, dismissed value theory as "metaphysics."

And now we are being forced to the realisation that what is not picked up by our value theory and passed on to our operational statistics and policy models, simply has no practical relevance. There is no way of restoring society to economics and economics to society without bringing back value theory.

McMurtry's sense of structure finds stimulating applications. "Karl Marx was the first to see what separated the capitalist organisation from all previous modes of social reproduction. It adopted as the initiating moment of its reproductive circuit *exchange value* rather than *use value*. Whereas previous exchanges by the medium of money had begun with a *use value* (e.g. shoes) that was then sold for the money to buy another *use value* (e.g. food), the capitalist mode of producing social use value was an inversion of this. It began with 'money' to be invested in *others'* production of *use values* that, once produced, were sold as commodities for more money." [M-C-M as opposed to the pre-capitalist C-M-C.]

"Again, in Marx's words: 'a definite part of the total capital dissociates itself from the rest and stands apart in the form of money-capital, *whose capitalist function consists exclusively in performing these operations for the entire class of industrial and commercial capitalists.*'"

"The mutation in this macro-circuit of money investment and profit occurs when money capital is no longer a phase within the circuit of the production and distribution of goods and services, but is exclusively committed at every stage of its growth to the direct multiplication of itself. This capital circuit mutation can take place when capital is no longer bounded by any national base, interest, or regulation, or by any other direct or indirect requirement to commit itself to a productive function beyond itself, but can receive more money for money without limit with no conversion into sustenance or services for any human, social, or environmental life organisation. These conditions satisfy our *carcinogenic formula* of $M\text{-}M^2\text{-}M^3\text{-}M^n$.

However, though Marx can provide us with important clues for diagnosing society's present syndrome, he can hardly help us out of the mess. That is because his absolutist view of the state as instrument of the dominant class hardly equips him to deal with the mixed economy that rose out of the Depression and the Second World War.[‡]

Nor is it just the distinct codes of the market and public sectors that must be grasped and reconciled. There in addition other essential subsystems, each with its own constraints — the ecology, the household economy, demography. The only manner of handling such a problem is by system theory that has long been routinely applied in other disciplines.

[†] *Social Justice*, Vol. 22, #4

[‡] In his *Histoire des doctrines economiques* (Paris, 1925, Vol 2, pp.57&58, Marx takes the French translator of Adam Smith, G. Garnier, to task for arguing for the productive nature of state services: "Of course, a Frenchman could not miss coming up with *Ponts et Chaussees* (roads and bridges). Arguing against Ganilh (p. 80) on the same point, he delivers himself of the following: "The tax on his wages that the worker pays the state and the Church is taken from him for services imposed on him. What he pays for education is blessedly little. As to his expenditures for the services of doctors, priests, lawyers, that is so much wasted money."

Mentioning the Unmentionable

On May 8th, Gordon Thiessen, Governor of the Bank of Canada, acted out the scenario of man biting dog and earned himself a front-page spread in *The Globe and Mail* (8/5). He announced his worry about "deflation developing within the next two years."

But within the week Mr. Thiessen, appearing before the Parliamentary Finance Committee, ate crow: "I probably will regret forever that I mentioned it." (*G&M* 16/5)

"It" referred to the D-word that has been unmentionable for at least two decades — deflation. Why should the head of the BoC "forever" regret mentioning his worry about deflation? That is what is what is on the minds of most Canadians. The Newfoundland Minister of Finance, Paul Dicks, forecasts a rise in official unemployment in that province from 18.3% to 19.4% as the budget-slashing proceeds. The BoC was founded in 1935 not to deal exclusively with inflation (none in fact existed) but to lift the country out of a deep deflationary ditch.

Even the research department of the BoC has long since recognised some of the lesser components of "inflationary bias" that flaws the Consumer Price Index. But nothing has ever been done to rectify these. On the contrary in his 1991 annual report the manager of the Bank for International Settlements (BIS), Alexandre Lamfalussy, dealt with the matter as follows:

"It has been argued that a quality-bias in price level calculations implies that inflation in the range of one to two per cent may be considered price stability for all practical purposes. Nonetheless, the move from an environment of low or moderate inflation to one of no inflation implies an important psychological shift."

You might imagine that that "important psychological shift" could be achieved by correcting the price index which would probably already show "zero inflation" or even some deflation present while the official meter still reads "two per cent inflation."

However, with an obvious reference to over-achieving central bank heads like our John Crow, Mr. Lamfalussy regretted that "it has proven difficult in recent decades to do better than merely low inflation and to move on to actual price stability, even in those countries with the best price performances."

Imagine nuclear physicists, perfectly aware that their figure for the critical mass of plutonium was inaccurate, going on building fission bombs without making the necessary correction!

Flying Feathers

"Interest rates are high because we have been living beyond our means and there is a lack of savings to be lent." This supposed truth has been drummed into our ears for a quarter of a century. Is it right or wrong? Just listen to *The Wall Street Journal* (15/3) in an article captioned 'To Make More Loans Banks Use Computers. Are they Going Out on a Limb?'

"At a time when many US consumers are beginning to creak under the weight of excessive debt, National City Corp. and many other large US banks are charging ahead, making more loans, regardless of rising delinquencies. They are turning to sophisticated computer credit analysis in a methodical effort to lend even more, [including] to marginally credit-worthy consumers formerly scorned.

"'In January personal debt, excluding mortgages, rose 12% to $1.05 trillion. Meanwhile, credit-card delinquencies have climbed to levels not seen since the end of the 1991 recession,' The American Bankers Association said yesterday.

"Is the banking industry going to make the same mistake of over-lending to consumers as it did in the 1980s with other kinds of debt, for leveraged buyouts, commercial real estate and developing nations? Bankers like David Daberko, CEO of National City Corp. don't believe so. For one thing, lenders are more adept at stemming potential losses sooner and charging risky borrowers higher rates, thus building in more margin for error.

"But the main reason is that they are using powerful computers to slice and dice large amounts of information about potential borrowers. Some bank regulators and observers warn that loan strategies built around 'predictive computer modeling' could backfire.

"'The ticking time-bomb is that more credit is being loaded on the shoulders of consumers who already are maxed out,' says Robert Heady, publisher of *Bank Rate Monitor*. More and more borrowers are going over the cliff into bankruptcy with no indication of the usual warning signs,' Fed Reserve Chairman Alan Greenspan recently told Congress.

"'I'd be more comfortable if I didn't hear bankers say they have sophisticated models to better handle risk,' says Lawrence Lindsey, pausing before he adds, 'because I simply don't believe it. I'm worried about the economy.' He recalls the banking industry's reluctance to do small-buinsess loans during the last recession. 'If a number of banks decide to pull the plug [on consumer loans] at the same time, it could shake the system.'"

Pushing consumer loans at a time when the stock markets allot massive rewards to corporations doing massive layoffs should be easy to recognise as nonsense without the aid of a computer.

The Mother of Lies Is Still Birthing

Even as its polls seem to be holding up by sheer levitation, the great Liberal Party has suddenly been stricken in the most vulnerable part of its anatomy — its credibility. Canada, it seems, may run out of political parties even sooner than out of money.

It all began with the Little Red Book (LRB), not Mao's but Chrétien's. Whatever questions were asked during the campaign, he parried them by waving the LRB "It's all here. Just read it."

That may yet prove a fatal error. At many of history's crucial junctures authors have been burned along with their books. Their purpose once served, some shrewd writers have themselves been known to burn their books rather than their bridges. This Chrétien has neglected to do. Enough people took to reading his LRB to cause trouble. Among much else they found the promise that the hated Goods and Services Tax (GST) would be abolished by the Liberals once elected.

It is not that anybody in government prefers lying, but politics has become a mug's game. For a quarter of a century monetary policy has been brilliantly organised to bypass democratic process and bring the world back to the good old days when bankers ran the show as heaven ordained. Matters have been so arranged that whenever Mother Hubbard comes to the cupboard, she finds it bare. This has been achieved with interest rates high enough to make a highly flawed price statistic say 'uncle.' By the time that price index was almost flattened, those interest rates had cleaned out the public treasury and another problem had taken over. Deficits had multiplied like holes in pockets during the Depression of the thirties. And now we are being told that we must get leaner and meaner to hold our own against Mexico and Bangladesh in the globalised market.

And in that way the Mother of Lies — that high interest rates would save the world from inflation — birthed the next Mega-Lie — "the deficit made us do it." And between them they have given rise to an endless progeny. The sincerity of the individual politician becomes irrelevant. The world's affairs have been arranged so that the revenues of government are preempted to money-lenders and speculators.

Vol. 8, No. 7 — July 1996

Thoughts for Fathers' Day

The Fathers of Confederation had a keener concern for the national interest in dealing with banks than our more recent ministers of finance. That emerges from a study by Trevor J.O. Dick and John Ford.[†]

Referring to the period immediately before and after Confederation, D&F write, "Relatively few large banks, each with multiple branches, were chartered and permitted to issue their own notes subject to a limitation based on the amount of their paid-up capital stock. Banks were not required to keep reserves. The government did not guarantee to redeem bank notes."

However, the restraints on the banks' money-creation were far stiffer in the post-Confederation period. "The security of bank note issue was assured by several arrangements. Bank stockholders were subject to double liability. [If a bank went broke, its shareholders not only lost their original investment, but had to come up with a similar amount to indemnify the holders of the bank's notes] All banks were required to redeem their own notes.

The banks' contribution to moving the wheat crop was efficient, but the needs of domestic industries less tied to the UK and the US were a lesser concern. As today, the banks were more preoccupied with attaining a high profile in New York and London. During the 1907 panic some Canadian banks became lenders of last resort in New York.

"After Confederation the Government introduced and expanded the use of Dominion notes, redeemable in gold, in an effort to recapture the seigniorage that the commercial banking system had preempted. In 1881 bank notes were restricted to denominations of 5 dollars and over [a large amount of money in those days] and 40% of the banks' primary reserves had to be held in Dominion of Canada notes. A Circulation Redemption Fund was established into which banks were required to deposit gold and/or Dominion notes to an amount of 5% of their average circulation.

"Altogether reserves constituted 30-40% of net bank liabilities before 1914."

The government's attempt to "increase the outstanding stock of Dominion notes relative to its gold backing in the early days of Confederation [did] economise on the cost of servicing the public debt. But though it undoubtedly reduced bank profits, it did not affect the money supply — the public could adjust its money holdings by buying and selling assets abroad, thereby forcing the banks to create whatever money supply it desired."

"This regime came to an end only when the government instituted a new means of money creation that enabled the banks to extend credit outside the discipline of the gold standard. Under the Finance Act, passed to help finance Canada's First World War contribution, banks could borrow reserves without limit from the government by pledging an equivalent amount of public debt. Redemption of Dominion notes in gold had been suspended."

Our Finance Minister, Paul Martin, could vastly improve his performance not only by consulting what was done by governments of which his own father was a distinguished member, but even by taking a cue from the Fathers of Confederation.

In earlier centuries when the monarch coined bullion, he took a markup known as "seigniorage." That might be 10%. Or if he clipped or adulterated the currency that, too, was seigniorage of an underhanded sort. Today the cost of issuing money supply in credit form is close to zero. Seigniorage thus approaches 100%.

The question is not, as our government claims, that money is "printed" when the central banks holds government debt, and not "printed" when the chartered banks hold it. In either case printing takes place only in a metaphoric sense. The real question is who gets the near 100% seigniorage on money-creation in its modern credit form.

† 'Canada and the Gold Standard, 1871-1914, a durable regime,' an essay published in *Monetary regimes in transition* edited by Michael D. Bordo and Forrest Capie, Cambridge Press, 1994.

Irrational Expectations

Economics has always been a cross between analysis and advocacy. The hybrid nature of the discipline, however, does not necessarily destroy its usefulness. We all of us had two parents who did not always get along. The trouble with economics today is that one parent has done the other in. From a struggling effort to understand reality, economics has become a shameless lobby.

A case in point is our Consumer Price Index, a powerful statistic whose merest wiggle prompts the central bank to push up interest rates and throw thousands into bankruptcy and unemployment. Yet it is some years since the Research Department of the Bank of Canada acknowledged that there was an "inflationary bias" in the CPI, i.e. that it reported more "inflation" than was actually there.

But instead of being abandoned, the misinformation generated by the flawed index is clearly prized — undoubtedly for its usefulness in pushing through an unavowed social agenda.

To catch this bird on the fly, we need only examine the current bond issues indexed to "inflation" in Canada and the US — RRBs for "Real Return Bonds."

These bonds are indexed to the CPI that ignores such unmarketed benefits as environmental clean-ups and interprets their costs as "inflation." The RRBs are based on the assumption that bondholders neither ingest nor defecate, and in no way benefit from adequate public infrastructures.

In this view bondholders must also be shielded against the price effects of natural disasters and wars. That, of course, means that the cost of such disasters will weigh all the more heavily on those who are not exempted, and will show up as still higher prices. This is clearly a powerful source of inflation.

We are now told that bondholders are intensely unhappy about these RRBs that protect them not only against inflation but against the cost of natural disasters that have nothing to do with market inflation. In *The Globe and Mail* (28/5) Greg Ip writes:

"Canada's federal government has issued real return bonds since 1991. But RRBs remain unpopular, labelled by one manager as 'Really Repulsive Bonds.' The RRB protects its owner against any unexpected rise in inflation that erodes the real value of fixed-income investments, by indexing both the principal and coupon to the CPI.

"RRBS have performed horribly. Daniel Kelly of CIBC Wood Gundy Securities Inc. calculated that in the past four years, the RRB has returned 19% compared with the conventional 10-year bond's 41%and the conventional 30-year bond's 49%.

"That's because [since] the first RRB was issued in 1991, expected inflation has fluctuated between 1 and 2%, so RRB holders have received a pittance in inflation compensation and conventional bond holders have been rewarded handsomely as their yield tumbled and prices rose."

When nominal interest rates drop because the economy is being deflated, existing bonds with higher than current coupons trade at a premium. While reproaching the rest of us for living too high off the hog, those who peddle and speculate in bonds, are not satisfied with having inherited the earth. They have staked a claim to heaven.

Happy Days Aren't Here Again

The Globe and Mail's Report on Business (6/96) carried a cover article by Anne Kingston, 'Inside Bank of Montreal's anxiety-driven ad campaign — Callous or Cool?' It tells us a lot about the moral canker at the heart of Canadian banking.

BoM Chairman Matthew Barrett (1994 pay package $1.9 million) "could teach Mother Teresa a few things about PR. Charming, smooth as a river-boat gambler, Barrett makes a point of eschewing the embalmed high-WASP Bay St. Banker stereotype. His brilliance is not credit analysis, but spin, image, optics." Entirely logical then that as soon as he became chairman in 1990 he chose for the bank's advertising agency a boutique, Vickers & Benson, that had helped craft the image of Pierre Trudeau and Jean Chrétien. His problem was that 'out there' the mood was getting ugly — understandably with the banks' successive record-breaking profits that coincided with soaring bank fees and a cavalier disregard of the needs of small business.

Barrett "approved a program of 'image' advertising that dwells on emotions rather than facts. It's Coca-Cola teaching the world to sing on a mountain. Suddenly an over-sweetened beverage equals brotherhood, harmony."

In 1993 the team produced a 60-second commercial titled *The Trial* that presented a typical Canadian being lowered in a cage before a mob of jurors who scoff at his determination to pay off his mortgage, give his kids a university education, and go south to escape our winters. The man insists that 'It's possible' The BoM logo is flashed across the screen, and without having committed itself to a thing, the bank has become associated in hundreds of thousands of brainpans with the little man's failing dreams. It won the bank the Bessie gold award for the best Canadian TV commercial in English.

"If we demonstrate the will to change, then may be, we thought, the people will give us as much credit as actually changing," philosophised Bruce Philip of the V&B agency. However, though the flocking of more customers to the BoM on the heels of these commercials supported that view, there was no lack of critics. *Frank Magazine* (evoking the thirties as did the bank advertisements) shot people in black and white holding homemade signs "Can banks change?" Another followed with the reply, "Hell, we don't even make change."

"Geoff D'Eon, producer at *This Hour Has 22 Minutes* on which the bank actually bought time, remarked on the campaign, 'Stylistically it's catchy. But its content is Orwellian. It's saying something manifestly untrue, but it's saying it with such a puffed-up sense of truth. It's scary.'"

Kingston quotes Barrett last October remarking on the creative efforts of the B&V people: "They're fine. I would have wished the public mood less dark, I'd rather be doing *Happy Days are Here Again*."

But the mood is likely to get even darker once the public learns the suppressed part of the story: Of the chartered banks' $5.2 billion in profits last year some $4 billion can be traced to a transfusion from the federal treasury to the banks. That is what has crumpled the Canadian economy and the lives of millions of Canadians.

Vol. 8, No. 8 — August 1996

From St. George to Couch Potato

Over the past two years Canada's 'inflation,' even as judged by an admittedly flawed price index, has averaged well under 1.5%. Were we to clean up the price index, it would undoubtedly show the economy to be *deflated*. Yet rather than the promised reward — the "long-term gain for the short-term pain" — we are experiencing another period of high unemployment and high *real* interest rates. The only difference is that the budgetary deficit has replaced inflation as the panic button that drives the show.

Like a versatile actor, the Governor of the BoC, Gordon Thiessen, has simply retired to the dressing room, changed costume and make-up, and reappeared under a different billing. The earlier scenario had cast him as St. George slaying the Dragon Inflation. Once killed, the monster was supposed to stay dead, and we, the damsel, were to be rescued once and for all.

It hasn't remotely worked that way. So St. George has transformed himself into a couch potato. Instead of confronting the fire-breathing monster with sword and buckler, he has hung up his armour and is content to watch the contest between the dragon and the market on TV. He has ditched adventurous knighthood for spectator sports — blaming the torrents of bad news on inevitable forces like globalisation; and having redefined the agenda he received on high as "rationality," on the failure of those other guys to "reform" briskly enough.

Even the pretense of serious analysis had been replaced by far-fetched metaphor. Prices in a complex urbanized society can move up for a variety of reasons having nothing to do with "too many dollars chasing too few goods."

The Bank of Canada was born out of the anguish of the Great Depression of the Thirties. Its purpose, still in the Act, was to get the economy moving again, not to plunge it into recession. The central banks of England, France, Germany, on the other hand, were set up to finance or to digest the booty of wars. The US Federal Reserve is a bureaucratic nightmare owned by private banks though almost all its earnings go to the federal government. The Bank of Canada, however, has a single shareholder — the Government of Canada. Its purpose rings out from the Act as clear as a church bell.

The change from hyperactive knight to couch potato has been so abrupt and unconvincing that you can't help wondering how St. George ever managed to get canonized. For example, if our central bank has less powers for influencing long-term interest rates as it claims, it is because it has deliberately surrendered those powers to the private banks. It has shifted its portfolio massively from long-term debt to short term government debt. It influences short-term rates by powerful interventions at the short-term end of the debt market, buying to drive down rates, and selling to drive them up. But on top of that it arranged to phase out the reserve requirements of the chartered banks.

You would have to go back to Joe Stalin's "most democratic constitution in the world" to find an instance where the reality and the letter of the law diverged so blatantly.

The High Cost of Waste

One of the most thought-provoking papers to reach us in many a moon was presented by Paul Hawken to an Ottawa gathering of the National Round Table over a year ago. As Mr. Hawken modestly emphasizes, the basic ideas in it had until recently eluded him as well.

"I read all the [environmental] material — a thousand articles and two hundred books, 25 million words. [But] how do we reconcile our living ecosystems and our commercial business system? But before I could begin [my book the *Ecology of Commerce*] I went into a real 'funk.' It was a meeting with William McDonough, Dean of Architecture at the University of Virginia, that brought me out of that. He had read my book *The Next Economy*, in which I said we don't have an economic, environmental or political problem, we have a design problem.

"McDonough pointed out that there are only three design principles that describe natural systems. First in nature, in living systems, waste equals food. There is no waste. Second, all living systems run off current solar income, they don't borrow from the carbonaceous period and burn it up to double glaze the planet in CO_2. Lastly, natural systems depend upon enormously diverse biological pathways for those efficient nutrient and energy flows."

"Probably the most interesting application of these principles today is through the work of Dr. Michael Braungart, a German chemist of the Environmental Protection Encouragement Agency (EPEA). In the eighties Braungart devised the "Intelligent Product Principles." They are a description of how existing industrial systems, which are linear take-make-waste systems, can make the transition to a cyclical, self-regulating take-make-take-make system which does not create waste All products are broken down into three categories: consumables, products of service and unsaleables. By consumables, he does not mean just that you can eat it. Biologically-speaking, the product has to be able to be placed outside on earth and broken down and consumed by organisms without persistent or biochemical effects. If it came from the earth it should be able to go back to the earth without killing anything along the way.

"A product or service is something much more complicated such as a television, VCR, automobile, refrigerator etc. Obviously you can't place these on the earth and have them consumed by organisms. So Braungart says that if you make something like a car, a TV, or other durable, you, as a manufacturer, own it in perpetuity. Instead of selling the actual product, a manufacturer sells a licence to use the service the product provides.

"The idea that we have a consumption problem in our society is actually upside down. We have a non-consumption problem because most of what we make cannot be consumed by anything at all. Therefore, it becomes waste. So I have this wonderful thing [a TV], that contains four thousand chemicals, most of which were invented since World War II. It has an explosive inner vacuum, a little bit of lead, some cadmium and, if it is made in South Korea, probably some mercury.

"If you incinerate it, nothing can eat the fly ash. What the Germans are saying is that products like this have to become food for Phillips or Sony. In other words, they are talking about industrial systems that begin to mimic natural systems in which waste equals food.

"So this thinking is producing a design revolution in Germany. BMW, Hewlett-Packard and others are now designing their products so that they have value when they come back, not just when they go out the factory door. You are beginning to see the invention of new polymers, new plastics, new materials because German manufacturers started to realize what was in their products — the free isosianates and the thermal plastic resin, the heavy metal stabilizers and forth. And they realized they don't want these back, so they went to their suppliers and said 'Make us something less toxic and more useable.'

"We have come to see the two ideas of environment and business as always requiring fine tuning, articulating a compromise. What engineers, designers, and industrial ecologists are saying is that in terms of the next industrial revolution, that's malarkey. The fact of the matter is, whether you approach this biologically, morally, economically or from the standpoint of competitiveness, all the arrows are pointing in the same direction. Let me give you a quick example.

"Let me tell you about the invention of what is called the hypercar. The idea behind it is to look at the car as a system instead of trying to work with incremental improvements and mileage efficiency. Only two percent of the energy in a car moves and stops you. The rest of the energy is used to move and stop the car itself. Paul McCreedy and Amory Lovins of the Rocky Mountain Institute and others have created a car made of carbon fibres that weighs about six hundred pounds. It is safer than existing cars because it is really hard to break carbon fibres They will mesh in but they'll go back to their original shape so they bounce much more than today's cars do. It's run with electric motors on each axle powered by hydrogen fuel cells and a small motor scooter engine. The engine provides the electricity at a constant RPM (revolutions per minute) and the hydrogen fuel cell provides energy for the four electric motors that are used with microelectronic chips to adjust their speed. These cars are on the road now in a prototype stage."

On engineering design Hawken is brilliant. However, when he comes to deal with the economics that must make the design revolution possible, he swallows handed-down bromides as credulously as any conventional automobile engineer. Thus: "neoclassical economics is just an ad hoc description of industrialism as it is right now." It is far worse than that. It is a shameless lobby for the continued ransacking of the economy by unlimited greed elevated to the official morality.

Just as there can be no waste in an ecologically sound product, there should be no human debris in a properly designed economy, for humans consigned to the role of waste become as toxic as any chemical.

Central Bank Watch

Central banks do have a problem. Their one goal is to keep credit choking-tight and interest rates hanging-high. But for that they must cultivate the image of engineers perfecting the magic shower-head of "trickle-down" to those beneath some of the golden spray enjoyed by speculators above. Moreover, to repay Bill Clinton for his second reappointment as US Fed chairman, Alan Greenspan must avoid piddling on the President's cakewalk to reelection. There are, too, memories of 1987 when the same Greenspan triggered the worst stock-market meltdown since 1929 by bull-headedly shoving up interest rates. Hence the increasing flow of gobbledegook churned out by the Fed.

The Fed's new buzzword is "opportunistic disinflation." (*Globe and Mail* 11/7/96) The new thinking is summed up in the passage: "When inflation is low but still above the long-run objective, the Fed should not take deliberate anti-inflation action but rather should wait for external circumstances — such as favourable supply shocks or unforeseen recessions — to deliver the desired reduction in inflation." That is quite a mouthful. To which are attached the usual reservations that go with trial balloons: "Officials at the Fed stressed that the document is only a staff study. The chairman hasn't taken any position."

Even so, this double-talk has elicited considerable indignation. "Some private economists argued that if this paper became official Fed policy it would raise concerns in financial markets about the central bank's inflation-fighting resolve." Sung Won Sohn, chief economist at Norwest Corp. in Minneapolis, said that the risk in waiting for a recession to reduce the level of inflation is that the central bank could slip back into the inflation spiral of the 1970s when the Fed failed to fight inflation vigorously enough. That forced Paul Volcker, then Fed chairman, to push interest rates up to levels not seen since the Civil War, triggering the 1981-82 recession."

There is more that is questionable about the "opportunistic dis inflation" than that. The essence of the conventional equilibrium model is the self-balancing market. If prices rise, they are supposed on their own to generate forces that pull them back to their equilibrium point. Lose faith in that and start fiddling around with interest rates to collapse prices by collapsing the economy, and you invalidate your model. [You are left riding a broomstick.]

The BoC's Latest Con Job

When last December Governor Thiessen of the Bank of Canada delivered himself of his remarkable denial that the multiplier exists, he rocked us with disbelief. However, we have since been able to piece together the tortuous path that led the Governor to place his head so temptingly on the chopping block. The evidence can be found in Peter Martin's *Inside the Bank of Canada's Weekly Financial Statistics: A Technical Guide*. Published by the Fraser Institute, Martin's book interprets the weekly financial statistics of BoC for 'street' folk. In putting it together he obviously worked closely with the BoC staff. The second edition that I quote appeared in 1989, fully two years before the bill for the phasing out of private bank reserves slipped through a dozing parliament. Yet the book treats the end of reserves as a virtual *fait accompli*. It reports that the questioning of the existence of the multiplier had already begun.

And on remarkable grounds. Chartered banks are ever under the temptation to keep their stocks of legal tender as low as possible. They consider legal tender sterile money, that unlike credit of their own creation earns them no interest; and they hold as little of it as possible.

That is why they took to viewing the week-end as a blessed hiatus. That had nothing to do with the Jewish and Christian Sabbaths, but because it exposed them to no cheque clearance surprises, while the interest meter on loans made Friday did tick on. During the first four days of the working week banks are always at risk of finding themselves short of legal tender to meet their clearance obligations. If their depositors write more cheques than expected in favour of depositors at other banks, the banks suffer an unforeseen leakage of legal tender. And if that leaves them short to meet their clearance calls, they have to borrow from other banks or the Bank of Canada at a penalty rate.

Because that cannot happen over the week-end, they learned to turn that to their profit by lending out as much short-term money as possible on Fridays. What resulted was a weekly bulge in the banks' short-term lending.

To deal with that abuse, "lagged reserve requirements" were brought in by the BoC in the latter eighties. Under this arrangement the average daily clearance needs during the *previous* month now serve as the basis for the banks' necessary in-till reserve. In the Martin book we find (p. 7) the following revealing passage: "Most textbooks discuss at length the so-called deposit multiplier and the impact on money supply that would result from the Bank supplying say an extra $10 million in reserves to the chartered banks. In fact, chapter 4 points out that the Bank does not believe that there is any direct quantifiable relationship between reserves supplied and M1 *in the short run*, because of the lagged reserve accounting. For this reason, the deposit multiplier concept, though theoretically correct, is not used by the Bank in its day-to-day implementation of monetary policy."

From this we can judge the validity of Thiessen's statement that "the multiplier the textbooks speak about does not exist." It is as though, having arranged with a creditor to change the interest payment dates on my loan, I cited that as proof that no such loan existed.

With the end of the reserves held by the banks at the central bank under the 1991 revision of the *Bank Act*, the only remaining reserve is the legal tender kept by the banks at their own discretion on their own premisses.

Peter Martin writes: "Excess cash [held by the banks to meet their clearance obligations] is the key to the BoC's whole control procedure. *Since the Bank has real control over excess cash* [by shifting cash out or into the different federal government accounts held in the chartered banks by the Draw-down/Repossess technique], *this variable becomes the true operating variable to implement monetary policy*." On the same page (130) Martin observes: "It is worth noting that excess cash reserves are, in fact, a very small part of the monetary base." In short while doing away with reserves that made it possible for the BoC to act directly on the entire money supply, the BoC has reduced its input to a marginal intervention on the very much smaller amount of cash needed for the daily cheque clearance. Such are the flimsy and quite irrelevant grounds for Thiessen's statement that the multiplier no longer exists.

Martin (p. 131) restates the position: "The BoC would maintain that the deposit multiplier concept, though theoretically nice, does not work in the short run and that using the money multiplier approach is bound to lead us astray *in the short run*." But that is only because the BoC has rejigged the rules to abdicate much of its influence on long-term rates by doing away with reserves, and by shifting drastically the distribution of holdings of federal debt from longer-term bonds to short-term Treasury Bills.

More recently the Bank has put an end to the weekly auctions of Treasury Bills that determined the short-term interest rate. Though the central bank was an active participant in buying and selling T-Bills, the auctions had been used for years to support the view that the market and not the central bank determine interest rates. Now the BoC openly sets the rate again.

At the height of the Cold War the Americans decided to keep part of their nuclear warheads in constant motion on trucks or submarines so that the Soviets could not pin-point them for a preemptive strike. The BoC's constant fidgeting with its administrative rules serves a similar purpose. It befogs the whole matter of money creation, and enables the good Governor to ladle out whatever misinformation might catch his fancy.

William Krehm

Vol. 8, No. 9 — September 1996

Our Banks' Blitz Strategy — Risk Transference

Time was when, the banker was amongst the most solemn citizens in the community. Like the undertaker, his daily experiences made him aware of the mortality of human hopes. And the banks' powers of money creation — formerly by their issue of notes and more recently by their ability to create credit far in excess of the cash in their tills — places them in a fiduciary role. On its mundane plane their position has its parallels with the priest who presides over an even greater miracle. But priests, frail human vessels entrusted with the sacrament, were never deregulated. On the contrary, they were bound by vows of chastity, poverty, humility, and love for their fellow man.

The essence of banking is risk management. But in recent years our banks have contrived to transfer the risks they incur increasingly to the public and to the state. There was a time when "Character, character, and character" was held up as the highest criterion of a banker making a loan. Lending was a labour-intensive process, for the bank ended up knowing almost as much about a client's business than the client himself. That has changed. Clients are left to the mercies of computers not programmed to deal with character, or for that matter to distinguish between a good and a bad credit risk. While slashing staff to the delight of the stock market, the banks have unloaded the costs of bad risks onto doting governments and their creditworthy clients.

For example, the banks take the initiative in soliciting credit card holders. Credit card lines are increased without the customer requesting it. But they are protected from the consequences of such financial blind dating by raising interest rates across the board. That a computer can handle with brio. Borrowers have become fungible — classified into a few broad categories that the computer can handle.

The same occurs on a more dramatic scale with many of our banks' ventures abroad, especially in the Third World. There interest rates tend to be higher than at home and thus more alluring. But the area of a businessman's expertise is in his own business and that expertise is based largely on mistakes already made. The farther a firm ventures from home the greater the risk. Lending hundreds of millions of dollars at a crack to a Mexican bank or acquiring a piece of the syndicated loan, may seem to bring great savings in staff costs and per unit lending, compared to monitoring the puny affairs of thousands of domestic borrowers. Here again the interest rates on glamorous mega-loans abroad would seem to assure the lending banks an adequate insurance premium. But to judge just what an adequate premium in problem-plagued countries like Mexico might be would require an intimate knowledge of that country and its ancestral gods and demons,

That not a small assignment. So instead, our banks have developed ways of risk transfer.

In the twenties, a surge of financial speculation led to the collapse of the banking system throughout the world. By the time Roosevelt assumed the presidency in 1933, 38% of American banks had shut their doors and one of Roosevelt's first acts was to proclaim a banking moratorium. Severe limits were placed on what interest rates banks could pay on deposits, what they could charge borrowers, what they could invest

The opening move in the risk transference saga came with the introduction of deposit insurance to prevent further runs on the American banks. Brought in over Roosevelt's misgivings, it was initially for paltry amounts, and given the severe restrictions on what banks could invest in, there was a limit to its capacity for mischief. But with progressive deregulation, the banks could pay or charge any interest rate not ruled out under criminal law, and could thus attract the money for their most hare-brained investments. Meanwhile, the amount of the deposit insurance per account has gradually risen to where it is $100,000 in the US and $60,000 in Canada. Depositors did not lose much sleep over what the bank might do with their deposits. It is enough for them to seek out the highest rate of interests offered, snug in the knowledge that if things went wrong, the government will pick up the tab.

In the S&L debacle of the eighties alone, Washington ended up stuck with a half trillion dollar bill, which is incidentally kept off-budget, i.e. not readily available to the public.

If the Americans left us behind in the idiocy of their deposit insurance practices, Canada has outstripped them in allowing our banks to pipe into the federal treasury as a virtual entitlement. Central banks' role as "lenders of the last resort" involves coming to the aid of financial institutions suffering from crises of liquidity, not of solvency. The first occurs when a bank is unable to convert enough of its net asset balance to meet its obligations; the second when such a positive asset balance does not exist. But that sage distinction is tempered by an unofficial directive that if a bank gets big enough becomes "too big to be allowed to fail."

Now it happens that banking in Canada is very much the affair of the Big Six, who by any criterion are big indeed. And so it came to pass in the latter eighties that these banks financed the mega-deals of real estate operators who had wandered far beyond their field of expertise. To help the banks out of their losses Canada became one of only three major countries to do away with the non-interest-bearing reserves that banks held with their central bank. At the same time the Bank for International Settlements, concerned with not dissimilar bank problems throughout the world, introduced its Risk-Based Capital Requirements that declared government debt of OECD countries risk-free, while loans to business call for 8% of the banks' own capital. Together the two measures have made it possible for Canada's chartered banks to increase their holdings of federal debt by some 60 billion dollars without putting up any cash of their own. Depending on where the central bank chooses to push interest rate this represents an ongoing entitlement of the chartered banks of between $4 and $5 billion a year. That approaches about 80 percent of the banks' record profits for the current year.

Vol. 8, No. 10 — October 1996

What Now Mr. Martin? The Unravelling of a Hoax

An unperceived revolution has taken place in US government statistics that makes nonsense of the central issue of the presidential campaign — the deficit.

Until last January Washington made no distinction between current and capital spending. Ottawa still does not. The budget they speak of is a cash-flow exercise that writes off all non-financial capital spending (buildings, equipment, land) in the year in which it is made. The same is the case with investment in human capital (education, health, welfare). The value of such investment is entered on the government's balance sheet at a token dollar. Such a budget can be balanced — if at all — only with wrenching effects on the economy.

Over the past two decades and more that bad accountancy has helped gut the economy.

First there is its inflationary effect on price. Picture what would happen if an oil company expensed its wells, pipelines, refineries in a single year. Even the attempt to balance such a budget would drive the price of petroleum products into the skies. By the same logic the absence of capital budgeting in government accounts was a major if unrecognized factor in the surge of prices that began in the latter sixties.

In the sixties the baby boomers were approaching university age, and to educate them to the new required standards, post-secondary campuses sprang up throughout the land. Then there were the public infrastructures needed for the exploding cities, and to serve countless new technologies. Such outlays, however, were not treated as investment. Because services they delivered were not priced, no unadjusted price index could pick up their benefits — for the same reason that you cannot read atmospheric pressure from a thermometer or temperature from a barometer. Yet the taxation to cover their costs did find its way into the prices of whatever was marketed. That effect on the price level was confused with an overheated market ("too many dollars chasing too few goods"). And the attempt was made to suppress it with ever higher interest.

Why has the correction been partially made in the US just now? Undoubtedly to help Mr. Clinton in the coming election. And why was it carried out in such stealth that even the financial analysts have overlooked it? We can only surmise the answer. In keeping with its passion for reassuring the financial community, the Clinton team has been content with the vastly improved deficit and debt statistics that have resulted. Politics dictated their not drawing undue attention to the king-sized can of worms they have opened.

In just three years (1992-4) recognizing the physical investment of the federal government resulted in a $618.5 billion lower debt figure. Carried forward to 1995 (and backwards to 1959), the change would far exceed a trillion dollars. And that, mind you, ignores the government's investment in human capital that certainly outstrips by far its physical capital assets. Once the Department of Commerce had revised the government savings figures the Federal Reserve Bulletin (table A-40) had no choice but to take over those figures, without mentioning what brought about the massive drop in the deficit.

So it has come to pass that all parties have been mum about the reason for this massive deficit reduction. Right-thinking economists have too much to answer for to blurt out that much of Clinton's deficit reduction was due simply to the introduction of elementary accountancy into the government's books — something they had resisted for decades.

COMER, however, feels that the cost to society of these rigged statistics has been too staggering to leave the job incomplete. As early as the latter sixties some of us were writing about the distortion introduced by the absence of capital budgeting introduced not only in the budget and deficit figures, but more important at the time, in the inflation figure. We understood that the sudden upward movement of the CPI in the latter sixties had less to do with "too many dollars chasing too few goods" than to the massive capital investments by the public sector that were being disregarded.

Had capital budgeting been brought into the accountancy of governments only enough taxation would have been raised to cover the depreciation of the public investment plus the interest on the undepreciated portion. But instead, excessive taxation was levied in the misguided attempt to pay off capital acquisitions by government in a single year. We identified that as a major factor in the perceived take-off of "inflation."†

We applaud the long overdue rectification of the US figures on public savings and investment. Obviously Canada must make the same rectification in its statistics. But we cannot leave matters there. By this accountancy dodge, hundreds of millions of dollars have been syphoned from the pockets of the producing population to rentiers and speculators; countless families have been broken, lives destroyed, and the unity of Canada itself compromised.

The time has come to put an end to all that and to make sure that it will never happen again. With the recognition of public savings and investment, we will have a meaningful balance sheet for our government. The price index must be unbundled to reveal how much of its upward movements really reflects an overheated economy, and how much merely the increased package of unpriced services. If there is in fact an overheated market with "too many dollars chasing too few goods" the remedy is not higher interest rates but higher reserves to rein in the banks' money creation. At present the nation's money creation, increasingly surrendered to our banks, is being used to finance their speculations and less and less to finance the producing economy.

The jig is up, Mr. Martin. The time is here to come clean.

William Krehm

† Some years ago I developed a simple method for unbundling the Consumer Price Index to reveal the extent to which the economy may really be "overheated," i.e. suffering from an excess of demand over supply. In essence it consists of adding to the sample basket of goods and services on which the CPI is based items for ecological clean up, non-marketed public services, mandated standard improvements, and other such unpriced benefits priced at zero (for they are unpriced) and weighted according to their total costs represents as a proportion of the GDP. In essence it dilutes the price index by the unpriced benefits. See: W. Krehm, *A Power Unto Itself — the Bank of Canada* (1993) p. 96.

Is the 1996 Presidential Race Based on a Statistical Error?

We are indebted to A. W. Caughey of Valencia, Pennsylvania for bringing to our attention a quiet revolution in the official US statistics that literally reduces to nonsense the central issue around which the presidential campaign is being run: the deficit.

Caughey writes: "Overnight the nation's savings data jumped by $135.2 billion for 1994 and even more for some prior years. This is due to the fact that the Bureau of Economic Analysis [under] the Secretary of Commerce now incorporates government investment along with private investment and net foreign investment in arriving at the total. Prior to January of this year, when businesses purchased assets with long lives, such as buildings or computer systems, the BEA (Bureau of Economic Analysis) treated the purchase as an investment to be written off yearly over the life of the asset. But when the government made similar purchases, there were treated as current expenditures, written off 100 percent in the year of purchase. The effect was to understate the nation's total saving and to overstate the government deficit.

"In January the BEA corrected this anomaly. By recognizing government investment, the national savings increased by $135.2 billion for 1994, $151.1 billion for 1993, $182.6 billion for 1992, and comparable amounts for prior years: 1995 data are available only on the new basis.

"The revised data now show gross government saving of $49.9 billion for 1994 instead of -$119.3 billion (deficit), and $79.1 billion for 1995. The 1995 data reflect a federal deficit of $88.7 billion offset by state and local government surpluses of $167.9 billion. The 1994 data show a federal deficit of $119.3 billion offset by state/local surpluses of $169.2 billion.

"But there are additional pieces of the puzzle to be considered. In 1994, the federal grants-in-aid to state and local governments totalled $195.9 B and in 1995 $206.1 B. This raises the question of which branch of government is really responsible for the federal deficit — the federal or the state/local?

"Also, the state and local governments repaid $43.4 B of prior borrowings (bonds, banks etc.) in 1994, and $51.5 B in 1995. Should not these repayments really be viewed as offsets to the federal deficit? After all, without the grants-in-aid, there would have been no state/local surpluses and no state/local repayments.

"All of which reveals the budget-balancing charade for what it is — an assault on public services expenditures. Budget balancing is valued not as a goal but as a process to undo the progressive legislation of the past sixty years.

"The foregoing data can be verified in the *Survey of Current Business* for Jan.-Feb., p. 13, *Economic Indicators*, p. 34, and the *Federal Reserve Bulletin* table A-40."

Fashioning the God of Clay

We hear a great deal about the omnipotence of the money market. Our central bank in particular professes its helplessness to do anything but consult, indeed anticipate its wishes. It is presented as being the embodiment of deeper natural laws that elude ordinary mortals.

It is surprising therefore that money market should in fact have been a creation of our central bank, and that it required a great deal of effort, artificial respiration and intravenous feeding to keep it alive before it was able to take over as the architects of our destinies. Listen to the testimony of George S. Watts who served in high capacities with the central bank for many years, and was indeed its first archivist. The introduction to his book was written by Gerald Bouey a former governor of the BoC. (*The Bank of Canada — Origins and Early History*, ed. Thomas K. Rymes, Carleton University Press, Ottawa, 1993.)

"During the war years and immediately after, the program of controls meant that there was less need for a market mechanism and that in practical terms any effective move towards an orderly introduction of a money market was out of the question. However, by the end of the 1940s it had become apparent, with the return to peacetime conditions, that not only was the need for innovative steps becoming pressing but that the strong postwar expansion of the economy was creating an environment in which efforts to foster a money market could be expected to have prospects for genuine success. For several years the Bank, in trading in treasury bills, had progressively widened the spread between its buying and selling levels in order to create an incentive for the charter-ed banks to look elsewhere for buyers.

These efforts had met with little success and in early 1953 a number of new steps were taken. The principal objective was to broaden the market for treasury bills and other short-term paper by encouraging some of the larger investment dealers to act as 'jobbers,' that is, to hold an inventory of short-term securities and other paper and to stand ready to buy or sell. With this end in view, the regular auction of treasury bills was changed from a fortnightly to a weekly basis, a nine-month issue was offered in addition to the three-month issue and the amount outstanding was gradually increased over the next few months from $450 million to $650 million. Concurrently, the Bank of Canada undertook to provide investment dealers who were prepared to take a jobbing position with an alternative means of financing inventories of short-term Government securities through the institution of Purchase and Resale Agreements (PRA). Under these arrangements, the Bank would, if required, provide participating dealers with short-term accommodation by purchasing treasury bills and/or short-term Government bonds under an agreement to resell the securities at a pre-determined cost to the dealer. Initially these facilities were made available to 'approved' dealers at a rate lower than that charged by the banks for call loans, but it was hoped that a true call loan market would develop and that the Bank would become a lender of the last resort.

"...It soon became apparent that the steps taken in early 1953 were proving more attractive than the call money arrangements with the chartered banks, and as a result the investment dealers that had been given PRA privileges were shifting their borrowing to the Bank of Canada. ....Despite the substantial increase in the amount of treasury bills outstanding, a non-bank market had not developed and the amount held by the general public was about the same as a year earlier. However the BoC's holdings of PRA had risen from nothing to between $15 and $25 million towards the end of 1953 and continued to rise to more than $70 million in June 1954.

"By June 1954 it was possible, with the co-operation of the banks, to take a further decisive step. The BoC had developed a group of approved dealers who were prepared to act as jobbers and the chartered banks agreed that they would provide day-to-day accommodation to these dealers, within the limits of their PRA arrangements with the BoC, on the pledge of the same type of securities that were eligible for PRA. At the same time, the chartered banks reduced their charges for over-certification. (The charge paid by a dealer for 'daylight overdraft' used to finance the purchase of securities sold later the same day. They were completely eliminated for certain money market transactions in 1957.)"

That is the way the BoC fashioned the clay god — the money market — before which it bows in reverence today.

Vol. 8, No. 11 — November 1996

Our Banks Go to Wall Street

We will all have been solicited on a parking lot by some seedy character: "Psst. Wanna buy an expensive watch dirt cheap?" Oddly enough these days our banks are engaged in a not dissimilar ploy on Wall Street.

To help them out of their staggering losses financing real estate and buyout deals in the late 80s, Canada's Parliament in 1991 passed a bill ending the requirement that the banks hold reserves with the Bank of Canada that earned them no interest and amounted to some 4% of their deposits. Depending on how high the central bank pushed interest rates, the banks' increase in their portfolio of government debt amounted to an undeclared government subsidy of between $4 and $5 billion a year — almost 80% of their record profits. When the central bank holds federal debt the interest on it goes back substantially to its one shareholder, the Government of Canada.

But our banks cannot go public with this dark secret.

Today our banks are getting listed on the Big Board in New York. They want to market their shares at prices reflecting this bonanza, but they don't dare go into the details — rather like the seedy chap offering us expensive watches at bargain prices through a corner of his mouth. Wall Street analysts complain that our banks' reports haven't been breaking down their information to show how much of their income comes from what sources. For good enough reason. To do so would risk alerting the Canadian public to the welfare the banks are enjoying at its expense.

So what the banks have been doing is buying back their stock to push up its market value. The Royal Bank has announced that it will be in the market for up to 10% of its outstanding shares. The CIBC has bought back 5%, and the TD Bank expects to repurchase no less than 17% of its stock. Since the banks are now creating over 97 percent of the Canadian money supply (M3) by making interest-bearing loans to the public, they prefer using such money of their own creation to finance their increasingly daring adventures — buying up interests in Mexican banks, taking over the derivative department of brokerage firms in difficulty in New York. On the other hand packaging their ongoing entitlement resulting from the end of reserves, after adding to it the further government handouts they are currently working on, is the standard way in which corporations go about maximising the proceeds of a coup — and assuring a quick getaway for the nimble-toed.

One reason Wall Street analysts have no understanding for the wondrous scam of reserve-free banking is that it does not exist south of the border. Even Canadians are unaware of the enormity our government's gift to our banks.

A masterfully orchestrated campaign of misinformation has been launched to allow our banks to merge. The reasons cited are enough to bring tears to the eyes of the thousands of employees they have laid off in these years of unprecedented bank prosperity. The Royal Bank moans that in 1970 was the 12th largest in the world while by 1994 it had fallen back to the 59th largest place. It omits to mention that the very largest banks in the world — Japanese banks — not too long ago were reported having lost far more than their total capital in mega-real estate and other gambles abroad. Nor do they bring up the detail that a few years ago they got themselves into serious trouble by financing the ventures abroad of the world's #1 largest leveraged buyout artist of US department store chains, name of Robert Campeau, and the world's largest developer of elegant office towers in several financial capitals of the world, name of Paul Reichmann. If you are not a banker, being very large does not necessarily save you from bankruptcy. Today our banks are abusing both their money-creation powers and their "too big to be allowed to fail" status to get into businesses that are wildly risky and have nothing to do with traditional banking.

We are being subjected to a tattoo of propaganda warning us "DON'T STUNT BANK GROWTH." The banks even have the arrogance to talk of "the current review of legislation is a chance for all Canadians to create a regulatory framework that puts the interests of the customer first by giving the Canadian banks the freedom to grow to innovate and to compete, so that they can give their customers world-class quality of service." (Matthew Barrett, chairman of the Bank of Montreal, *The Globe and Mail*, 2/10/96) That is supposed stir patriotic fervour in the breasts of the thousands of small clients who in recent years were simply informed that their lines of credit have been discontinued. Nothing personal, the banks were simply getting into bigger things like mega-deals down Mexico way.

But with so many releases on the need of our banks to merge, an important motive in this promotion is not even mentioned.

Though their statutory reserves with the BoC have been abolished, they still must hold enough legal tender for two other purposes: to meet their cheque clearances each day, and to satisfy the requests of the public for legal tender (wallet money). By far the greater of these two is their daily need for cheque clearance. Banks don't like holding legal tender — it earns them no interest — while the credit created by them does. But hold some legal tender they must so long as there are even six banks, because the credit they create can be lost to them by their borrowers writing cheques to accounts with other banks. When that happens, the original lending banks must remit the amount of the cheque to the bank of the recipient. Were there a single bank, that would not happen. Money created by a bank through loans would stay with it. Cheque-writing would become an internal affair. A single bank is still a big order. But five is better than six in cutting down such money leakage, and three is better than four. Besides once you allow a single merger, the combined principles of "too big to be allowed to fail" and the "level playing field" would prevent the government from turning down the next merger. The time has come for the public to insist that anybody in public office learn the basics of banking.

Book Review — *Bastard Keynesianism : the Evolution of Economic Thinking And Policymaking Since World War II*

[Turgeon, Lynn. *Bastard Keynesianism : the evolution of economic thinking and policymaking since World War II*. Westport, CT : Greenwood Press, 1996. ISBN 0313300240]

This engaging little book abounds in anecdotal material, lightly handled, yet bearing messages of significance.

There is much that I learned from it about Abba Lerner, one of the most productive of leftist Keynesians — this though I knew him in London in 1937, and caught up with him again in the latter sixties when he was a visitor at Waterloo University. By that time I was in close contact with John Hotson as we shared our realization that higher taxation, rather than a "weapon against inflation" as was then believed, actually contributes to higher prices. John told me that when he came up for tenure at Waterloo, Lerner had been helpful in overcoming the opposition of some influential monetarists.

Among much else Lerner originated the notion of "functional finance" (1943). This asserts that selling Treasury bonds to the Fed is a suitable alternative to federal taxation. The only logical reason for taxation, Lerner argued, is to keep consumption down — the case during the full employment of World War II. Keynes's initial reaction was that Lerner was an impractical dreamer. What I did not know was that "it required a personal confrontation between Keynes and Lerner, who considered himself a Keynesian and was shocked by his mentor's failure to recognize his offspring." Lerner, who came up from humble East-end London origins by the scholarship route, was not of the Cambridge set that played gadfly to Keynes on a more intimate basis. Without the swarm of close critics about him, Keynes would have been as incomplete as a beekeeper without a buzzing hive. Part of his genius was his ability to select from all that advice what could be integrated into timely policy.

When I met Lerner again in Waterloo in 1968-9, I was brimming with my newly developed ideas on the impossibility of understanding price behaviour in a mixed economy with a model that ignores the unpriced contributions of a growing public sector. I remember him as politely unresponsive. That came into better perspective when I read in the Turgeon book that in the seventies he actually coined the term "supply-side inflation." "The environmental movement, which, to some extent was initiated by Nixon on Earth Day, April 1970, began to attract the attention of legislators in the 70s and was responsible for increased amounts of what later came to be labelled "supply-side inflation" by Keynes's disciple Abba Lerner. Pollution was regarded as a good example of an external diseconomy with respect to the firm."

Lerner at no time challenged general equilibrium at its mathematical foundations as François Perroux in France and E. H. Chamberlin in the US had done. Indeed, very early he elaborated the ideas of the Pole Oskar Lange who from mathematical general equilibrium developed a model for a socialist economy. It is instructive that Lerner's "supply-side" terminology should have ended up as the marching song of the Reagan regime. To fit his terminology into the supply-demand framework of equilibrium theory, Lerner put the very different sources of "cost-push" into the one bag. He thus fudged the specific cause components of a given price movement. Thirty some years ago Federal Reserve Chairman William McChesney Martin remarked that, "the Fed had to take away the punch bowl just as the party begins." Similarly, the "Supply-side inflation" terminology cuts off the analysis just when it really starts getting interesting.

Further tidbits:

"The problem of servicing this huge [postwar, US] debt probably accounts for the extension of the pegged interest rates until the Treasury Accord of March 1951. Ironically, the pre-Hitler power of West German bankers was restored in a program to de-Nazify the German economy by John McCloy, the High Commissioner for Occupied Germany. In a further attempt to rid the Germans of Keynesian or Hitlerian influence, the tool of Keynesian deficit-financing was withheld by the postwar constitution until after the first major German recession of 1966-67."

"The chairman of the Fed has been treated as a 'sacred cow' far removed from criticism. In my view, bankers should be treated as the special interest group they are. Bankers as a group are not ordinarily affected by unemployment. But their self-centered policies should not be a burden to the rest of society."

"One wonders if some of the sluggishness in measured productivity might not itself be the result of the investment binge. There are three possible measures of productivity: labour productivity, capital productivity, and so-called factor or multi-factor productivity where both labour and capital are in the denominator. Typically we measure labor productivity with only the labor inputs in the denominator since the data are more reliable. But when we measure changes in labour productivity we are also measuring changes in capital productivity per worker. The artificial scrapping of perfectly useful machinery doesn't help improve labour productivity as conventionally measured. However, the artificial scrapping of capital — as a result of rapid depreciation and the investment tax credit — does bring down the cost of steel scrap, a major raw material in steel production. We are now exporting 8 percent of our steel output as a result of our comparative advantage in steel scrap, which emanates from the investment subsidies."

Turgeon exaggerates the net contribution of Sir Roy Harrod, close collaborator and early biographer of Keynes. He quotes Harrod's letter to *The Economist* (29/7/89), "A few weeks ago I had a conceptual break-through. A sharp distinction should be drawn between the effect on the general price level of a decline in aggregate demand, when initially it is running above the supply potential of the economy, and the effect of a decline of aggregate demand when it is below the supply potential." But anything so obvious would have needed no "conceptual breakthrough" had Sir Roy not had his head stuffed with general equilibrium theory. He was at least partly responsible for restraining Keynes from trashing that whole baggage to arrive at an understanding of the Great Depression. In his *General Theory* (p. vi) Keynes wrote of his "long struggle to escape from habitual modes of thought and expression...which ramify for those brought up as most of have been into every corner of our minds." Before Keynes could come to grips with the problem of Effective Demand, he had to develop a unit of value in which he could do his thinking on the broader problems of social accountancy — rather than start by assuming that the "pure and perfect market" is always self-balancing. He goes on to pen one of the most significant passages in all his work, and characteristically one that is practically never quoted by economists, "I sympathize, therefore, with the pre-classical doctrine that everything is produced by labour... It is preferable to regard labour, including, of course, the personal services of the entrepreneur and his assistants, as the sole factor of production, operating in a given environment of technique, natural resources, capital equipment and effective demand." (p. 213)

On reading the proofs of *The General Theory* Harrod wrote Keynes: "(Your) effectiveness is diminished if you try to eradicate every deep-rooted thought unnecessarily. I am not merely thinking of the aged and fossilized, but of the younger generation...It is doing a great violence to their fundamental groundwork of thought if you tell them that two independent demand and supply functions won't jointly determine price and quantity. Tell them that we don't know the supply function and that we can discover more important relationships governing price and quantity in this case which render the S and D [supply and demand] analysis nugatory. But don't impugn the analysis itself."

Such pressure from his peers led Keynes to do his most basic thinking in a very private manner, much as a gentleman performs his ablutions. In the words of G.L.S. Shackle: "Keynes spares his readers, even in the deliberately provocative *General Theory* the ultimate force of his conclusion uttered in speech, 'Equilibrium is blither.'"

From the individual economist's interests, many considerations counsel speaking half-truths in a language designed to cover the shameful parts of our society. But in pursuing respectability in this way the profession slips into a fallacy of composition — one that has made it an object of derision amongst thinking people.

Hopefully, when Turgeon's delightful little work reaches the second edition it deserves, he will find room for some of these missing quotations.

wk

Mystifying Money Creation

In *Economics* of Richard G. Lipsey, Paul N. Courant and the late Douglas Purvis (published 1994), the authors play down the role of the central bank in issuing the government debt that is our legal tender. Instead they dream up "the hypothetical Canadian Immigrants Bank of Commerce (CIBC). An immigrant arrives in the country and opens an account by depositing $100 with the CIBC. As a result of the immigrant's new deposit, cash assets has increased. The bank now has $80 in excess reserves, etc."

Ingenious? Tremendously so. For years right-thinking economists have argued that "money" cannot be created ("printed") by the economy itself "endogenously," but must be borrowed from the outside, or painfully "saved," i.e. taken out of consumption, before it can be invested. And there is an added bonus. As our wilting economy is inspiring our government to restrict immigration, there will be fewer immigrants to bring in those $100 deposits of foreign currency the authors seem to think that money creation of the country depends. That guarantees a further throttling of the economy.

By sheer coincidence I have an anecdote to go with this. In 1977 John Hotson somehow arranged for him and myself to take charge of the plenary session of the Canadian Economics Association at Fredericton (in those remote days such things were still possible). My paper summarized my book *Babel's Tower : the dynamics of economic break-down* that argued the impossibility of understanding what goes on in a mixed economy with a model that deals only with supply and demand on an idealised market, and ignores the output of the growing public sector that is neither marketed nor priced. My referee was none other than Richard Lipsey, head author of the book in question. Before hurrying away for a regrettable previous appointment, he delivered himself of a single remark:

"Give us another four years and if the present model hasn't worked by then, we will seriously consider abandoning it." And seventeen years later Mr. Lipsey gave us...the Canadian Immigrants Bank of Commerce (CIBC)!

wk

Hixson's Corner — Keeping the Argument and the Record Straight

Establishment economists say that any federal government expenditures not financed by tax revenues must be financed by borrowing. This sounds true to most people because personal experience teaches that spending not matched by earnings must be paid for by borrowed money. But the federal government has an option not available to individuals — it can create money. The federal government has, therefore, not two but three sources of funds to meet its expenditures: 1) tax revenues; 2) borrowing; and 3) money creation.

The Council of Economic Advisers (CEA) provides figures relative to federal government accounts for the decade of the 1980s (1981-1990 inclusive). Average annual amounts (all in billions of dollars and rounded) were: expenditures $950; tax revenues $780. The customary procedure is to subtract tax revenues from expenditures and call the difference ($950-$780=$170) "the deficit" and to say that this deficit must be financed by borrowing. On the contrary, it was, in fact, financed by borrowing only $156 and by money creation amounting to $14. It was, in fact financed 8 percent by the government creating money and 92 percent by borrowing.

The customary procedure is to call the $14 billion in newly created money, "money borrowed from the Fed" or "increase in the debt to the Fed," rather than properly to call it "money created by the government for itself via the Fed." The government's so-called "debt to the Fed" is as phony as a $3 bill — the government is not ever obligated to repay it and whatever annual interest the government pays on it is refunded annually. A debt, properly so-called, is an amount you are obligated sometime to repay and obligated meanwhile to pay interest on. I wish I was in debt for a zillion dollars that I never had to repay and, in effect, never had to pay interest on.

What seems to me the most important question raised by the above is this: why did the government rely so little on money creation in financing its expenditures? Instead of creating only $14 billion per year why did it not create at least twice that amount? The customary answer is, "But that would be inflationary." To which the answer is, "Not necessarily and even likely."

Again relying on the figures of the CEA, we find that on average for the decade of the 1980s the M3 money supply of the USA increased by $214 billion per year. $14 billion of this was money created by the government and $200 billion was money created by the private sector — mostly by "depository institutions," mostly by banks. That is to say, of all money created, the government created only about 6.5 percent (14/214) while letting banks create 93.5 percent.

I submit that there is not an economist alive who can prove that it would have been more inflationary if the government had created twice or four or eight times the percentage of the total (13, 26, 52 percent respectively) and if the percentage created by the banks had been reduced accordingly. When I say that the government should have created more money in the 1980s, I am not at all saying that the total amount of money creation should have been greater. I am saying only that more of the total amount of money created should have been created by the government. If anyone cares to argue that total money creation in the 1980s should have been less or more, well and good. But this is irrelevant to my contention that whatever the total, the percentage attributable to government should have been larger and the percentage attributable to banks should have been less.

Let us leave aside the matter of inflation, about which misconceptions so abound that the subject can hardly be discussed in less than 5000 words or even more. Inflation aside, I submit that there is not an economist anywhere who can prove that it would not have been more in the public interest had the government created twice or four or eight times the percentage of the total amount of money created in the 1980s and the percentage created by banks reduced accordingly. There is not an economist alive who could even make a plausible argument that this would not have been more in the public interest.

For what was done with the $2140 billion that banks created between year-end 1980 and 1990? $290 billion was loaned to the federal government. Think of it! The government could have created this $290 billion for itself and had it interest-free;

instead the government let banks create it, borrowed it from them, and, of course, paid them interest on it — is still paying them interest on it. Anyone care to make a plausible case that this was wise public policy?

Banks also made consumer loans amounting to $210 billion and business loans totalling $1640 billion. The wisdom of the loans of both types that were actually made is highly questionable. A good part of the consumer loan borrowing was spent on items the borrowers didn't need, couldn't afford, and would have been better off without. A good part of the consumer borrowing and spending was the result only of misleading advertising and uninhibited credit-card promotion by banks.

A good part of business borrowing was even more outrageously misspent.

A lot of it was spent helping companies in Wisconsin, Illinois, Michigan or whatever, turn their employees into the streets and relocate factories to Mexico, Taiwan, Singapore, or wherever.

A lot of it was spent promoting leveraged buyouts (LBOs) of one domestic company by another — LBOs that guaranteed to increase unemployment and to drive down the wages of those still holding jobs.

A lot of it went to loans to venal officials in rotten governments abroad who syphoned off large amounts for themselves and for kick-backs to the lenders; and who never intend to keep up the interest payments on what they borrowed, much less ever to repay the principal.

A lot of it went to broker-loans for speculation in stocks, bonds, silver, other commodities, and derivatives so complex that even their inventors do not fully understand them.

No one would argue that every cent the government spends is wisely spent, but isn't it obvious that there is far too much money creation by banks for very unwise spending and far too little money creation by government to, in the words to the Preamble to the Constitution, "promote the general welfare."

William F. Hixson

Vol. 8, No. 12 — December 1996

Correspondence — to William Krehm / from Finance Secretary of State Doug Peters

08/10/1996

Secretary of State, Finance

Ottawa

Dear Mr. Krehm:

Thank you for your facsimile of August 30, 1996 in which you propose the reinstatement of reserve requirements on the banks, to be administered by the Bank of Canada. I would like to provide you with an explanation of why the government eliminated reserve requirements on the banks.

Reserve requirements were initially put in place to facilitate the exercise of monetary policy by the Bank of Canada (the Bank). The idea was that the Bank could change the ratio of required reserves to bank deposits to affect the money supply. However, as financial markets developed and became more sophisticated, the Bank found manipulation of the reserve ratio to be an inefficient monetary policy tool. Indeed, the Bank never used its power to vary the primary reserve ratio, and its discretionary power to change the ratio was removed in 1967. The Bank has since developed more fine-tuned methods of influencing monetary and credit conditions, including open market operations, managing the government's cash balances at the banks and intervening in the overnight money market. For this reason, reserve requirements were phased out.

I would also like to respond to the proposal that reserves be used in conjunction with a policy of increased holdings of government debt by the Bank of Canada to help fund the national debt. Under this proposal, as the argument goes, the Bank would buy a larger portion of government bonds. To pay for them, and to counteract the inflationary effect, the Bank would raise reserve requirements, forcing the banks to increase their deposits at the Bank. However, the impact on the Canadian economy would be severe. To meet the increased reserve requirements, the banks would likely respond by raising interest rates and restricting their lending to individuals and businesses. In other words, reserve requirements would divert lending from the private sector to the government. This would run counter to the policy objectives of increasing bank lending to small businesses and of lowering interest rates. In fact, the monetary policy effects of even a small change in the reserve requirements — that is, high interest rates — could well swamp any interest savings to the government by having the Bank of Canada hold more of its debt.

The government is currently reviewing the financial institutions statutes. We have recently released a consultation paper outlining our legislative proposals. While a return to statutory reserve requirements is not part of these proposals, I appreciate your taking the time to make your case. I hope that my comments have been helpful to you.

Thank you again for writing.

Yours sincerely,

The Honourable Doug Peters, PC, MP

4/11/1996

Re: Your letter of 8/10/96

Dear Sir:

I wish to thank you for the trouble you have taken to explain to me why the Mulroney government eliminated the reserve requirements for our banks.

You begin with a statement that happily we can both agree upon: "Reserve requirements were initially put in place to facilitate the exercise of monetary policy by the Bank of Canada. The idea was that the Bank could change the ratio of required reserves to bank deposits to affect the money supply." However, you go on to justify the end of the reserve requirements with arguments that are seriously flawed. For example, "However, the Bank found manipulation of the reserve ratio to be an inefficient monetary policy tool. Indeed, the Bank never used its power to vary the primary reserve ratio, and its discretionary power to change the ratio was removed in 1967." Surely, if the Bank never used its power to vary the primary reserve ration, how could it have found it to be "an inefficient monetary tool?"

Nor is it strictly correct to say that the ratio of reserves was "never used." Though the law in force fixed primary reserves at 5% of deposits at the time, the first Governor of the Bank during his testimony before the Subcommittee on Banking and Commerce in 1939 was repeatedly asked why the Bank was insisting on 10% reserves. That was a deviation from the literal law in the direction of tightening money to fight inflation in a still depressed economy.

Moreover, the second major development in this late war period was the relatively permanent increase in the chartered banks' cash ratios which began in January 1944. In his evidence before a Commons Committee on June 27, 1944 Governor Graham Towers declared: "If the banks in general were aiming at a ratio of 15 percent we would know that. We therefore would not consider that we were taking an expansionary action unless we had put the ratio above 15 percent." The important thing to note is that it was this capping the banks powers of money creation to contain inflationary pressures rather than by raising interest rates that allowed the Bank to reduce the Bank rate from 2 ½ % to 1 1/2% on February 8, 1944 and continue low interest rates into the postwar period. It was this that helped prevent a postwar depression and reduce the federal debt from 140% of the Gross National Product at which it stood in 1946 to under 21% by 1975.

Two other important factors are missing in your argument. By eliminating the Bank's powers to vary the reserve requirement Parliament in 1967 took an important step in making high interest rates the sole major tool for combatting inflation. Moreover, you make no allusion to the detail that interest rates are the revenue of a privileged portion of the population. They add substantially to costs and hence to inflation until they have risen to the point of collapsing the economy, and then they too collapse. The constant churning of interest rates that results creates an environment of uncertainty in which few productive industries can prosper. But it does serve to inflate the speculative financial sector that thrives on the constant lurching of capital asset prices. That explains the amazing performance of stock markets when our real economy is inert. In the longer run, however, if persevered in, it must bring down on our heads a replay of the 1929 scenario or worse.

You go on to warn that "to meet the increased reserve requirements, the banks would likely respond by raising interest rates." If that were true, it would have played in reverse, and interest rates would have fallen when the reserve requirement was phased out. Nevertheless, that was far from the case. Moreover, you make no mention of the fact that Canada has been only one of three countries in the world — along with the UK and Switzerland — that put an end to reserves. And the timing and the conspiratorial way in which the 1991 bill was slipped through Parliament suggest that the motive was to bail our banks out of their massive losses of capital in financing such irresponsible ventures as Robert Campeau's shopping for US department store chains and the Reichmanns' adventures in New York, Toronto and London (UK). The reserves that banks held with the central bank were not only a policy tool but collateral to protect the banks' depositors. When their customers get into trouble, our banks do not release their collateral, but demand more. There is no good reason for our government adopting the contrary course at the expense of the taxpayer.

Surely enforcing the so-called "natural rate of unemployment" by means of high interest rates leaves our society at the mercy of the legendary "young men in the red suspenders" that gamble on the financial markets of the world 24 hours a day. Bring in the reserves again and some of these superachievers will be encouraged to seek careers in more socially useful endeavours.

Yours truly,
William Krehm
Chairman of the Board,
Committee on Monetary and Economic Reform

Mexico's Excess of History

Everybody," said the late Andy Warhol, "has his fifteen minutes of fame." Mexico's problem, however, is that it simply cannot stay out of the headlines. Having been "rescued" by Washington often enough, and its "sound fundamentals" vouched for, one might expect that it would finally be allowed to enjoy the blessings of obscurity.

Mexicans have themselves fingered part of their problem — "Poor Mexico. So far from God and so close to the United States!" It has never forgotten that it lost half its territory to its Great Good Neighbour, and is accordingly morbidly sensitive to slights from there. It has vast untapped oil reserves, something that the United States is running out of. Besides it has a tradition of corruption that opened the gates wide to Northern freebooters long before NAFTA. A continuity of globalisation stretches unbroken from the day Hernan Cortes set foot on Mexican soil; at no time did he lack traitors to warm his bed or cheer his board. Mexican history is the amazing record of how one ruling group, domestic or foreign, merely changing the rhetoric of the moment, has been able to slip into the cozy arrangements of its predecessor. The mestizo Liberal caudillos took over from the aristocratic traditionalists they had routed, the trade union bosses from the agrarian caudillos — all have taken turns in running the country like their private haciendas. And today in the age of NAFTA corporate America has fitted into this procession, missing scarcely a step.

Language has already developed a boneless flexibility for the purpose. The words democracy, elections, justice, people's choice, call to mind ladies of the night long accustomed to serving the most varied clientele without blinking. When it comes to mendacious cosmetics not even American television could teach Mexico a thing. In the hothouse atmosphere of globalisation evils already rooted in Mexico's past have proliferated. The only trouble is that once you add high technology to so rich a mix you run up against bounds set by biology.

The Wall Street Journal (29/10) under the headlines 'Mexico City Crime Alarms Multinationals. Foreign Investment could Prove to be the Next Victim.' "Crime is strangling Mexico City. While petty crime and corrupt cops have been standards for decades in this smoggy capital of 16 million people, the increasing rate of organised armed robbery, murder, rape and car-jacking in 1996 has shocked international risk analysts and foreign businessmen, not to mention Mexicans themselves. US Ambassador James Jones, has been quoted as warning that foreign investment may be affected if the situation doesn't improve.... 'Multinationals are no longer immune,' says Morton Palmer, head of a security consultant firm. 'In the past year I personally know of seven chief executives that have looked at the wrong end of a weapon in Mexico.'

"The country's steep recession has certainly played a role in the crime wave, but analysts warn that Mexico's weak judicial system and unsophisticated police force mean that incidents will continue to escalate if the economy improves." A US official also warns that 'American tourists are being targeted' by sophisticated criminal gangs operating around hotels and the US embassy in Mexico. Complaints filed with the embassy include eight murders, 68 armed assaults, and six rapes, and despite frequent contact with Mexican authorities, not one incident has resulted in a conviction."

However, let it not be said that all American corporations are so lacking in entrepreneurship as to fail to profit by this ultimate of deregulations.

Thus the same *WSJ* (01/11) comes up with another hardly less sensational set of captions: 'Private Banker Wooed and Then Sought to Drop Mexico's Raul Salinas.

Special Way to Move Money.' "For three years, Citibank private banker Amy Elliott strove to accommodate Raul Salinas de Gortari, brother of Carlos Salinas, Mexico's president from 1988 to 1994. [Citibank is the second largest US bank with a notorious record during the oil boom of the 1970s in providing a variety of services to wealthy Mexicans for stashing away bribe-money in secret accounts abroad.] Aware of his penchant for secrecy, Ms. Elliott set up an unorthodox system to help Mr. Salinas move millions of dollars out of Mexico in strictest confidence. But by early last year, her star client had lost his lustre: Charged with involvement in the murder of his former brother-in-law, Raul Salinas was held in a high-security Mexican prison. Ms. Elliott's bosses agreed she should travel to Mexico City to persuade his wife to take back the money he had placed with the Citibank, by then totalling at least $80 million. Her trip was unsuccessful, and today the money still sits in a series of accounts at Citibank, drawing scrutiny from law enforcement authorities in at least five countries. They are trying to determine how Mr. Salinas, whose maximum salary as a government employee was $190,000 a year, was able to stow more than $120 million abroad in Citibank and other banks.

"During two days of questioning in New York, Ms. Elliott provided Swiss, Mexican and US investigators with rich new details of Raul Salinas's relationship with Citibank:

• Indicated that she and her superiors didn't follow several procedures widely used by other banks to reduce the risk of money laundering;

• Said immediate superiors at Citibank involved themselves in important decisions relating to the relationship.

• Cast doubt on Mr. Salinas's assertion that his money came from friends who wanted him to manage an investment fund — his primary defence in Mexico's corruption case against him.

"Mrs. Elliott, who has worked at Citibank for nearly 30 years, remains an employee in good standing. Citibank is paying her attorney's fees.

"She said she didn't consider [Mr. Salinas's] wish to keep money outside Mexico unusual. Carlos Salinas was doing so many good things for Mexico and was restoring a confidence level to a country that hadn't had that for a while.

"Raul Salinas, besides being a brother of Mexico's president at the time, was himself a Mexican official. After five years at Conasupo, the state-owned food distributor, he was a consultant between 1990 and mid-1992 at the anti-poverty agency, known as Sedesol.

"Ms. Elliott waived Citibank's standard policy of requiring new customers to present two references. Ms. Elliott told investigators. 'Do I believe the Rockefellers have money? Yes I do.'

"Michael Zeldin, who used to head the money-laundering section of the US Justice Department, says the Salinas family didn't have great wealth prior to Carlos Salinas's presidency."

"At this time [before the fall of the peso in December 1994] many of Ms. Elliott's clients were moving their money abroad. But she didn't go to the same lengths to disguise their activities as she did with Mr. Salinas. Sympathetic to his concern about effects on the peso if it became known that a presidential brother was taking his money outside of Mexico, she devised a special system. 'It didn't seem strange to me that he wanted to do it this way because he was a Salinas,' Ms. Elliott told investigators.

"After Raul Salinas was jailed in Mexico, Ms. Elliott told investigators ex-president Carlos Salinas called to say he needed to be able to prove Raul was in New York the last week of August and the first week of September 1994 — a time when Mexican authorities claimed he was plotting the murder of Mr. Ruiz Massieu. She found a request form for the purchase of theatre and US Open Tennis tournament tickets. But when the former president arrived to pick them up, she told him, 'I would rather not be seen with him.' Instead, she watched from her office window as a colleague met Carlos Salinas and his father, who sat parked outside Citicorp Centre. When it finally dawned on her that the Swiss had frozen Raul's funds, she refused to come up with a scenario for moving those funds when Raul's wife requested her to. Mrs. Salinas was arrested in Switzerland when she and her brother attempted to see her safe-deposit box. Mrs. Salinas was later released and not charged.

Little has changed since the early eighties except that with the deregulation of banking and NAFTA Citicorp has some additional degrees of freedom to work in. After all it could argue that it is merely availing itself of a level playing field with the offshore money-laundering havens.

Vol. 9, No. 1 — January 1997

Reduced to Absurdity

Having over the years engineered the near-complete deregulation of the banks it was set up to supervise, the Bank of Canada finds itself in a quandary. For decades it had proclaimed high interest rates the one tool for fighting the inflation it saw under every bed. Those rates were the spiked cudgel with which it beat the economy out of shape. All this was done on the promise that once inflation was battered out of existence we would be rewarded with seamless prosperity for decades to come. It has not worked out that way, nor was it even intended to. High interest rates can bring down prices only by felling the economy with mass unemployment. And when that happens, interest rates too come down with a thud. That is the stage that we have reached today. Meanwhile the lurching of interest rates — summoning asset values out of the void and destroying them just as readily — has created the greatest orgy of stock market speculation on record. And our banks, having become financial conglomerates spanning every facet of financial markets from credit cards to derivatives, are driving this madness.

Most recently, for example, the Royal Bank of Canada has announced its entry into merchant banking. There are still limits in criminal law on interest rates in Canada — 60% per annum. But when the Royal Bank cancels the line of credit to a struggling but promising young firm, the latter can no longer go, as it once could, to a trust company and obtain a loan at a rate higher by a percentage point or two than what it paid the bank. With few exceptions the trust companies have long since disappeared down the maw of the banks. Our former client of the Royal Bank is therefore likely to end up as a suppliant at the door of Royal Bank's new merchant banking arm. Merchant banks make their loans not only for a fixed rate of interest but on top of that may muscle in for a participation which after a contractual number of years may have to be bought back by the borrower at its appraised value. That not only may bypass the 60% ceiling in our criminal law, but places the burden of redemption of the lender's capital gain on the borrower. And since as its former banker, the Royal is privy to our applicant's vulnerabilities, its merchant banking arm holds all the cards in the pack. This is what passes in official parlance as a "level playing field," also known as "single-stop banking for the convenience of the public."

It used to be the ultimate wisdom of central bankers, formulated by a former chairman of the US Federal Reserve, to "take away the punch bowl just when the party is becoming interesting." What the banks are drinking these days is stronger than punch. That is why raising interest rates at this juncture could bring on a market crash of 1929 proportions. That is the real reason why central banks are reluctant to raise interest rates to curb the inflation of assets on the stock market: would put a pin to the bubble in which our banks are more directly involved than ever because of their countless new brokerage, underwriting, and other financial tentacles. Banks, indeed, have come to share the interests and "culture" of the non-banking institutions that they have acquired.

And central banks, having transformed themselves from regulators into a lobby for the regulated, reflect this interest shift.

As a result we are witnessing a breath-taking miracle: central bankers who had dedicated the producing population to a life of austerity, have been reducing rather than increasing nominal interest rates to keep alive the unprecedented saturnalia of the stock market.

To fully grasp the enormity of this paradox, let us look elsewhere for guidance.

By nature mathematicians are lazy folk. Unlike economists they loathe number-crunching, and are always seeking simpler ways of testing propositions. One of their most elegant procedures for the purpose is what they call *reductio ad absurdum*. With nothing more than a pencil and paper, they assume the validity of the hypothesis in question, and then carefully, step by step, examine where it leads them. If it brings them to the opposite of the proposition assumed, they have a fool-proof demonstration that the hypothesis is false.

Although it modestly shuts its eyes on its feat, our central bank with its present nominal low-interest rate policy has convincingly debunked its central dogma that high interest rates will stabilize the economy. Unlike mathematicians they have achieved their stunning proof not with twenty-five cents worth of pencil and paper, but at a cost of millions of ruined lives and innumerable trillions of dollars of wealth.

That is not the only instance of our central bank reducing one of their cherished dogmas to absurdity. The central proposition of monetarism is that the price level is determined by the money supply as a proportion of the volume of transactions. That view, advanced by Milton Friedman, used to be considered on the lunatic fringe of economic theory. But in the late seventies, the central banks adopted this monetarist lemma to cover up what they were doing. They had driven interest rates up and up in their fight against inflation. Monetarism offered them a supreme advantage: it allowed them to duck their responsibility for the climb of interest rates. It allowed them to argue that their one concern was seeing that the money supply was not increased beyond what was needed to stabilize prices, and that they were ready to let the interest rate chips fall where they may.

But these same central banks had a parallel agenda of deregulating banks, and that soon made it impossible to know what the money supply might be. The late seventies saw the removal of the strict division that had separated interest-bearing accounts on which no cheques could be written from non-interest-bearing bank accounts on which cheques could be drawn. With deregulation hybrid chequing accounts that did earn interest were brought in. But the money supply had been defined as currency (i.e. folding money and coin) plus non-interest-bearing chequing bank accounts. No thought was given to the contradiction between the two agendas central banks were pursuing. So one fine day in the early eighties the chairman of the US Fed, Paul Volcker, noticed that deposits in the brand-new interest-bearing chequing accounts had jumped spectacularly. And he panicked. Now when a central banker panics, the first thing he does is raise interest rates. It is his equivalent of locking all doors.

Volcker drove up short-term rates into the 21% range. By the marvels of compounding interest, that contributed more to the government debts in Canada and the US than the growth of all social programs many times over. All sort of new definitions of money supply followed (M2, M3, M2A, etc.), each intended to prove that the price level indeed obeyed changes in the money supply as prescribed by the monetarist model. We even heard the argument from true believers: "We may not be able to quantify the money supply or even say just what it is, but we do know that it exists and that is enough to justify our policy." But knowing that the money supply exists hardly underpins the constant claims of our central bank to be "fine tuning." A few months ago Fed chairman Alan Greenspan threw in the sponge on the matter and declared that he no longer attributes importance to the money supply, but instead concentrates on other statistics such as unemployment, delivery times of orders, and much else. In essence our central bankers are flying by the seat of their soiled trousers.

Book Review — *War Finance and Reconstruction : the Role of Canada's Department of Finance 1939-1946*

[Slater, David W. *War finance and reconstruction — the role of Canada's Department of Finance 1939-1946*, with two chapters by R.B. Bryce, David W. Slater, 199 Crocus Ave., Ottawa, K1H 6E7]

We came by this interesting volume in a bizarre way. After months of negotiation the Executive of the Ontario Federation of Agriculture arranged a debate between Jack Biddell and myself for COMER and two champions of Bank of Canada policy. To defend its policy the Bank of Canada chose William Robson, who has made a career of that sort of thing, and David W. Slater, a prominent Keynesian. Even knowing the current scarcity of career opportunities for Keynesians of distinction, I was intrigued by the choice of Slater to defend the very people who managed to do away with the Economic Council of Canada that he had once headed.

We were informed that he was a last-minute substitute for David Laidler. Slater opened the debate by reading a document that seemed to betray the fine Italian fist of that other David, Laidler not Slater. I referred to the BoC's citing the German hyper inflation of 1923 to warn us what we would be in for if we neglected even a small amount of inflation. Connecting the two situations implied some miraculous retroactive effects: had Germany only pushed up interest rates high enough, it apparently would not have lost the First World War, the Allies would not have exacted crushing reparations, the French would not have occupied Germany's industrial heartland, the Ruhr, there would have been no general strike financed by Berlin overworking the printing presses, and there would not have been virtual civil war in the Ruhr and indeed throughout Germany. Whereupon Slater remarked, "Of course. I taught monetary policy for many years, and always emphasised that there was no connection between what happened in Germany in 1923 and our problem in Canada."

There were other patches of common ground in our interchanges with Slater throughout the discussion and in private. And shortly after, Slater sent us his book that sheds light on the brightest period of Canadian economic policy.

Who could sum matters better than Slater in the first chapter of the book: "In terms of economics, the war, despite all its sacrifice, was the road from depression to prosperity. The potential productivity and income of the Canadian economy turned out to be much greater during the war than they had appeared at the beginning. The potentialities after the war were even larger than those of wartime, despite the reduction in peacetime of several advantages of scale and specialization. Underestimates of potential early in the war curbed the war effort. But after the fall of France, Canada made all-out commitments and gradually achieved and sustained them.

"The war showed what could be achieved by a fully employed economy, compared with the output during the unemployment and underemployment of the 1930s." That is hardly the song that the Bank of Canada has been singing, and that the author joined the colours to defend.

The Slater book recounts the efforts of the Finance Department to whittle down the aid requested by the besieged UK to what it felt we could prudently afford. "Despite the primitive, uncertain and incomplete state of national income accounts, the government used them as the basis for determining what the country could afford to contribute to the [Commonwealth Air Training] plan. The method was to forecast national income for 1940 and subsequent years and determine the proportion that could be devoted to all government purposes, including the military effort. The calculation was based on a 10-per-cent increase in national income. Finance and the Bank's macroeconomic argument did take account of a number of factors that made the air training plan a good fit for Canada's war capacities: large uncluttered spaces for air training; plenty of lumber and building materials; experienced road buildings and underemployed construction firms; a large supply of rough carpenters off the farms; romantic interest in the air inherited from the Canadian aces of the First World War and the epoch of the bush pilots in opening up the north." And the men involved in such errors of judgement included the first Governor of the Bank of Canada, Graham Towers, and Clifford Clark, the guiding spirit in recruiting the young mandarins who were to run the Bank of Canada and the Ministry of Finance during its most brilliant period. Eventually "it became the watchword of war finance that anything that could be produced or devoted to the war effort could be financed."

Slater provides thumb sketches of the group responsible for rethinking the musty certainties of the banking community. A few like R.B. Bryce and A.F.W. Plumptre had studied under Keynes at Cambridge, others at Oxford and the London School of Economics. Clark set rigorous tests on monetary topics for applicants both at Finance and the BoC. Graham Towers, the first Governor of the BoC "was one of the few people in the banking community with a university degree and a good grounding in economics. He understood credit creation not only in the practical way of bankers, but in the broader economic and social sense of monetary economists."

"The seekers of more effective economic policies in Canada were also convinced of the need for constitutional change. They regarded the relief programs that were the main response by governments to unemployment and destitution as inadequate, inefficient, and unfair. Tax and expenditures policies and public work programs to improve income and employment were inhibited by the political structure as well as by worries over Canadian debts. Though the successful launching of the BoC had equipped the country with an improved financial structure and policies, the BoC was deeply concerned with the debt problems of Canadian provinces and municipalities."

"Taken together, all the wartime tax changes amounted to a virtual revolution in taxation policies. Canada moved from a regressive to a progressive system, from one in which only the minority paid income taxes to one in which the majority paid them, and from one in which the provinces and local governments collected the majority of tax revenue to one in which the federal government collected the most. Though tax levels would go down as the war gave way to peace, these key elements of the revolution would last into the postwar era." It needs only be added that this wartime revolution made possible a more just and caring society that is being undermined today.

"The ratio of gross national debt to GNP, as we now know it, peaked at 170 per cent, much higher than the 70 per cent that became so worrisome in the early 1990s after years of large government deficits."

"The price controls imposed in November 1941 were the most severe that any country used during the war. They froze every individual retail price at its level two months earlier. When the war began, wholesale prices were about 26 per cent below pre-depression values. The cost of living was about 17 per cent below the pre-depression level. Canada's real GNP increased by more than 65 per cent between 1939 and 1944."

Maintaining low interest rates was the kingpin of the government's strategy against inflation. "The government was committed to maintaining low interest rates into the postwar period, as Towers stated in the Bank's 1944 annual report. This implied government willingness through the Bank of Canada to support the price of government bonds if the public started to sell them heavily. The government was also committed to maintaining the consumer price ceiling at the autumn 1941 level into the transition period, and to gradual and orderly price and wage decontrol thereafter. The government believed in the fundamental interdependence of these policies. If inflation mounted, a spending spree could start, fuelled by the public's use of its liquid asset accumulations and the liquidation of the wartime savings. If the interest rate was to be held in such circumstances, the BoC would have to acquiesce in a further inflationary expansion of money and credit. But if the interest rates were not held, the market value of the public's holdings of government bonds would fall, perhaps triggering a sell-off. "The resulting success of Canada's restraint of inflation contrasted with the hasty deregulation of price controls in the us"

Slater's book has the immense merit of disinterring a crucial cut of our history.

wk

Cockeyed Price Index

One of the gross inaccuracies in the US Consumer Price Index fingered by the Commission headed by Michael Boskin in its report to the Senate is the disparity of the bases used in comparing upward and downward price movements. If chicken prices move from $1 to $1.50 per pound that shows up as a 50% increase. If the following year it falls back to $1 that — on a base of $1.50 — is seen as only a 33.3% drop. Over the two-year period then there will be a fictitious net inflation of chicken prices of 16.3%. The solution is simple enough, and has indeed already been adopted by Statistics Canada: using the geometric rather than the arithmetic mean for comparing upward and down price movements.

Other even greater inaccuracies of the CPI have not been dealt with by the Boskin report. And it remains to be seen whether those that have will be corrected. They are, after all, too useful for the implementation of Wall Street's agenda.

Vol. 9, No. 2 — February 1997

Reserves

For five years COMER has been talking about the ending of the reserves that Canadian banks had held with the Bank of Canada. Slipped through a comatose Parliament in 1991, the bill that achieved this had rated neither a debate in Parliament nor a mention in the media. It took COMER the better part of a year to dig up the facts and grasp their full significance. That done, it was clear to us that this would alter the very identity of our banks. Yet apart from a few brave souls who did listen, we might have been about talking of town planning on Mars.

But now considerable information has started appearing on that proscribed subject. That information offered hardly leaves the public much better informed about what is really at issue

The Economist (23/11) reported sharp disagreements amongst European central bankers on "minimum cash balances that commercial banks must leave with their central banks, supposedly to assist monetary policy. Bankers have long argued that they should not be forced to place these considerable sums into accounts which often pay no interest." This "is emerging as yet another obstacle on Europe's road to economic and monetary union.... Europe's commercial banks are watching nervously: the outcome of the tussle will go straight to their bottom lines."

But it is not just that "no interest is often paid" on the reserves. More important, those reserves are almost half of the denominator of the ratio determining the private banks' multiplier, i.e. their ability to create credit out of the void. The numerator of that fraction consists of interest-bearing near-monies (short term loans) that have come to make up the bulk of our money supply.

We are informed that "[Banks] must put aside anything from 1% to 17% of their deposits, depending on the country. Italy and the Netherlands pay some interest on this money; Germany, France and Spain pay none." Taking the worse scenario where the central bank pays no interest on the banks' reserves, this factor would cost the banks about 1% of their interest revenue in the case where reserve requirement was 1% and 17% in the extreme instance where the 17% requirement is in force.

Let us note the effect of reducing the denominator of the multiplier proportion given above. The phasing out of reserves in Canada reduced by 44% the banks' holdings of legal tender that earns them no interest — whether in their own tills or at the BoC. Shrink the denominator of the multiplier by 44% and you get an increase of the multiplier by about 79%. That will give you an indication of the real stake in abolishing the statutory reserves.

But the story does not end there. Parallelling the campaign to abolish reserves, there has been an ongoing deregulation of banks. This has made it possible for them to rush into the riskiest schemes for earning a big fast buck: underwriting stock and bond issues, brokerage, insurance, derivatives, real estate and currency mega-deals. Indeed it has been the banking deregulation agenda that has driven the demand for doing away with reserves, to make good the banks' periodic losses at the gambling tables. Quaintly enough, the banks were allowed to prescribe the therapy. It was as though Alcoholics Anonymous — perhaps as a cost-effective measure — were to fire its professional staff and allow the alcoholics themselves to run the show.

And that brings us to a still more revealing proportion: that between the total banks' assets to their legal tender. In 1975 that ratio was well under 40:1. Today it is almost 300:1. And we must keep in mind that 20 years ago there were strict limitations on what banks could invest in.

The Economist goes on to say "Germany's Bundesbank claims that it needs reserve requirements. The Bank of England counters that the minimum reserves are an ineffective monetary tool that sucks money into non-productive use. In any case, it argues, commercial banks keep reserves of their own to ensure they are not caught short of cash."

Here there is a willful misunderstanding. The statutory reserves fill several purposes. Historically, they were a consideration paid to the state for the assignment of part of its lucrative privilege of seigniorage. Originally seigniorage consisted of minting of coin, then the issue of notes (i.e. folding money), and finally the creation of credit money. Another role filled by the reserves was as collateral for the deposits the banks had accepted from the public. The reserves had to do with both the solvency of the banks, i.e. their positive net worth, and their liquidity — the ability to meet claims on them when due. Finally, reserves provided an alternative to raising interest rates when the economy was overheated. By simply increasing the percentage of reserves to deposits, part of the banks' lending powers were sterilized.

"The banks' own reserves to ensure that they are not caught short of cash," cited by the Bank of England addresses mostly daily cheque clearance. This has little to do with solvency which is essentially a bank's relationship with the entire economy rather than the leakage of bank-created credit from bank to bank. The latter occurs when a depositor in Bank A writes a cheque in favour of a client in Bank B. Quantitatively it is a phenomenon involving fewer digits than problems of solvency can acquire.

The article informs us that, understandably enough, "commercial banks across Europe — including the German banks which must park 2% of deposits with the Bundesbank — are united in opposition to any reserve requirements. If a harsh European reserve requirement arrives with a single [European] currency, they fear, they will lose business to rivals in America and Asia." Information on what reserve requirements exist in what countries is hoarded to such an extent that European bankers — and *The Economist* itself — seem to be unaware that reserves are still in force in the United States and in many larger Asian countries — at 3% currently or 50% higher than the Bundesbank reserves being discussed!

But there are still other considerations at work in the reserves debate. The projected Eurocurrency will embrace not only highly developed countries like Germany, France and possibly the UK, but countries that conform more closely to Third World living standards. That threatens the Bundesbank's tight rein on "inflation" — the official concept of which lumps together an overheated economy with the price effects of any expansion of public services which would allow, say, more Portuguese to see the inside of a secondary school.

"On November 18th, the Bank for International Settlements, the central bankers' central bank, suggested that higher reserve requirements could offset national central banks' falling revenues once the European Central Bank takes over the job of selling notes and coins."

Book Review — *Economic Fundamentalism*

[Kelsey, Jane. *Economic fundamentalism*. East Haven, Conn. : Pluto Press, 1995. ISBN 0745310443]

For the great neo-liberal experiment visited upon the world three countries were chosen as guinea pigs: New Zealand, Canada, and Sweden. What they had in common — modest-sized populations and advanced social systems — made it easier to push them onto paths where angels would fear to tread. The high technology of disinformation took care of the rest. Of the three New Zealand had the frailest economy to support its social programs. Its background as a lesser dominion made its politicians readier than their Canadian or Australian counterparts to swallow whole the doctrines in vogue in Britain and the United States.

Jane Kelsey has done a masterful job of analysing the New Zealand experience.

As in astronomy, it all began with a Big Bang, as of some monstrous celestial chamberpot crashing down to clear the way for the Creation. By the early nineteen-eighties the US Federal Reserve had adopted monetarism as its creed — the belief that reining in the money supply was the only way of "licking inflation." The money supply and not interest rates is what it claimed to have its eye on, and interest rates were supposedly just the way the cookie crumbled.

But at the same time the Federal Reserve was pursuing an agenda of financial deregulation that made it impossible to say what the money supply might be.

When the tidal waves of Big Bang washed over New Zealand, it brought on a political upheaval. Oddly enough, the Conservatives in power under Robert Muldoon were the party of greater state intervention, while the current generation of Labour Party leaders "were more modernisers than socialists, and had a sceptical and even hostile attitude to the state." The anti-statist winds gusting in from abroad thus helped the Labour Party to a landslide victory in 1984. Prime Minister Muldoon's refusal to hand over power at once, prevented the new Labour Government from devaluing the currency. As money poured out of the country in anticipation of devaluation, an exchange crisis provided the mother of opportunities for the "economic fundamentalists" in the Treasury. Had exchange controls not been ruled out by the new ideology, that crisis could have been handily managed in proven ways.

All had been well prepared for the occasion. Kelsey quotes the convenor of the Washington-based Institute for International Economics, John Williamson, who in 1993 retrospectively reviewed "the political factors that made the implementation of structural adjustment possible. When a major crisis occurs within the existing system, it creates new opportunities for actors who until then have been prevented from taking the initiative. Where a crisis does not occur 'naturally,' it might make sense to provoke one to induce reform. The most effective time to act is the honeymoon stage immediately after taking power, when the need for, and costs of, reform can be blamed on previous governments. The problem of sustaining the changes might be overcome by deliberately creating a group of beneficiaries likely to fight to protect the reforms."

Williamson's wisdom — refined in hundreds of coordinated think-tanks across the world — was applied to the letter in NZ. Kelsey quotes B. Easton: "'In each case the lightning strike involved a goal radically attained following a surprise announcement and a very rapid implementation.' Opponents were always on the defensive and left debating last week's reforms.'"

"During the government's first three-year term many of Labour's activists focussed on non-economic issues — anti-nuclear and disarmament — and the disaffected kept their criticism largely in-house." An increasing distancing took place between the Prime Minister, David Lange, and his Finance Minister Roger Douglas. When Labour was re-elected in 1987, Douglas hastened to bring in his economic program — "Rogereconomics" — to head off any reaction to the stock market crash of October 1987. This included a flat income tax and deep cuts in social supports. Lange tried resisting much of this, and forced Douglas's resignation from cabinet at the end of 1988. But eventually Lange himself was pushed out.

By 1990 the sharp deterioration in NZ's position had become evident. Unemployment shot up to an official 11.1% by 1991 compared to 3.8% five years earlier. Crime, family break-ups, youthful suicides followed the same pattern. "The dismantling of domestic protections was driven up by the image of an internationally competitive NZ economy footing it with, and sometimes leading, the major trading nations of the world. Expositions of free trade theory took on an air of scientific truth." Many of the cards NZ held in its bargaining with Australia and the US were thrown away in advance for ideological reasons.

The Reserve Bank was privatised, and the requirement that the private banks hold reserves with the central bank discontinued. Price stability was proclaimed its sole objective. When economists argued against this policy the Treasury retorted, "Given the broader international support received, we suggest that this lack of local academic support says more about the state of NZ academic economics than about the correctness of the Reserve Bank's policy." "When other countries were asking how best to supervise banks, Governor Don Brash [of the NZ central bank] was asking why they needed supervision at all."

All this has seriously prejudiced the position of the Maoris who make up more than 13% of the population. Their *Treaty of Waitangi of 1840* with the British Crown promised them the means of pursuing development according to their tribal values. But under the neo-liberal governments lands and resources on which Maori claims are still pending have been sold off to foreigners. This bodes ill for civil peace.

The Value Crisis of the Global Market

In global market competition, "value adding to the inputs of capital investment" is the final goal of societies. Life has become the means to enable the capital expansion of investors, rather than capital the means to enable life's survival and development.

When, for example, a number of years ago the Club of Rome introduced its concept of "the limits of growth," it was not LIFE'S growth that it was concerned to limit, but "economic growth;" or to be more precise "the increase of money-measured market growth." Growth of LIFE in a comprehensive sense, its movement and mental reach, is a value which we claim is ultimate. Except for strange minds like Schopenhauer, growth and development of life in this sense is the good of all goods.

When we think of "development" now, we do not think of the unfolding and expression of LIFE'S capacities for articulation, diversification, and increased vital powers. Rather we are taught to think of an opposite process — the levelling of life-habitats and natural environments for the building of profit-producing infrastructures. "Development" means how much Money-Value has been added to an economy by marketable activities. For market increases of value-adding development continuously result in life-depleting outcomes. More and more the air cannot be safely breathed, the earth's aquifers are more fouled, the fresh and sea waters lifeless, and larger numbers of citizens and their children are malnourished.

In a leaked memorandum, the Chief Economist of the World Bank in 1991 recommended that less developed countries (LDC's) achieve "welfare enhancement" by accepting increased migration of "dirty industries" and "toxic wastes." His reasoning consisted of three arguments. First, the liabilities resulting from the destruction of people's health was far less in these countries because "the forgone earnings from increased mortality" were far less than elsewhere. Secondly, the already existing pollution in non-industrialized countries, such as those of Africa, was "vastly, inefficiently low" compared to other countries. Thirdly, the "demand for a clean environment" has "very high income elasticity," meaning that money-demand for it varies with the money income of people. The World Bank's Chief Economist concluded that the "economic logic" of dumping poisonous wastes in the Third World is "impeccable."

In short, we have come to a point where the life of people, societies and the planet itself have been so subjugated to the rule of the money code that the most life-invasive and morally grotesque consequences of its reasoning appear "rational" and "impeccable." One may recoil from such brutal implications once they are spelled out, but the value program keeps these implications out of view. It is locked into a sequence of destroying life to gain more market value. This sequence is then confirmed as good by increased GDP's, which are society's measure of progress and growth. From a code of value based on life-enhancement, we can readily recognize the lethal disorder in this value-program. Only what fits the market's value metric is computed by it, or deemed "economic."

Karl Marx, to put it mildly, held no brief for the capitalist system. Yet even he could not envisage anything quite so efficiently anti-human as what is taking over today. He was the first to see that the law of capital's process inverted all previously existing systems of social metabolism and exchange. Previous exchanges through the medium of money had begun with a Use Value (e.g. shoes) that was then sold to others for the money to buy another Use Value (e.g. good). But the capitalist mode of producing social Use Value was an inversion of this. It began with 'money' to be invested in other's production of use values, that once produced were sold as commodities for more money: Money>Commodity>More Money or M-C-M' as opposed to the pre-capitalist C-M-C.

The current mutation of this macro-circuit of money investment and profit occurs when money is no longer a phase within the circuit of the production or distribution of goods and services, but is exclusively committed at every stage to the direct multiplication of itself. What results is the carcinogenic formula M-M-M....M.

This market sequence of choices and exclusions is straightforwardly pathogenic. Its mutation of investment contradicts even the theoretical ground of its founder. Adam Smith began from the value premise that the market and the pursuit of money gain should be a means for society's well-being, and not the other way around. But not one of his assumptions in this respect has survived in the global competition for money demand which rules the world today. Smith, in fact, conceived of money itself as bearing value only in "circulating consumable goods, provisions, materials and finished work," i.e., as a means of serving human needs and wants.

The life code of value can be formulated in the sequence:

Life –> means of life –> More Life (L –> M of Life –> L)

In this formula Life means organic movement, feeling, and thought. Means of Life, in turn refers to whatever enables life to be preserved or to extend its vital range. Clean air, food, water, shelter, affective interaction, environmental space, learning contexts, and participation in the decisions governing one's life are all such means of life.

The money code of value, in contrast, follows the sequence: ($ –> M of L –> $)

In this money sequence of value, the means of life are what money uses as a middle term to become more money. Money is any quantity of addable exchange units which things of life-forms are worth in the market, or which money can buy or demand.

More money, not more life, is the regulating objective of thought and action. Life is resequenced as money. The more money that results in the hands of the investor of money, whatever may happen to life, the better the sequence is for this value-system. It does not calculate into its value judgement whether life has gained or lost — even the vital life range of the principal who ends up with more money. This too is an externality. This value program cannot factor into its calculus losses of life of any kind because they have no place in its debits. Since this sequence of value begins from the assumption that more money can produce and buy more goods or utilities, it therefore follows from its value system that more money sums is always better. This cognitive slippage at the very base of the money value program is not recognized. It ends in the failure to distinguish between wealth and the money demand on wealth. This can lead, if its logic is not seen through, to the stripping of the life-world by money demand until the life fabric can no longer hold.

John McMurtry
Professor of Philosophy
University of Guelph

Vol. 9, No. 3 — March 1997

An Open Letter to Our PM

The Right Honourable Jean Chrétien
Prime Minister of Canada
Ottawa ON K1A 0A6

Dear Mr. Prime Minister:

The Globe and Mail (02/14) quotes your statement before a business luncheon "We will not budge in our fiscal discipline. We can't give up now. Not when so many have sacrificed. Not after so many years of failure by our predecessors. Not when we are so close."

The $64 question is "Close to what?" Reducing the official deficit to zero, and then wiping out the debt are questionable goals on several counts.

To begin with, the public accounts makes no distinction between current spending of the federal government and capital investment. The *Canada Year Book* (page 22-6, 1988 edition) informs us that "fixed capital assets, such as government buildings and public works, are charged to budgetary expenditures at the time of acquisition or construction and are shown on the statement of assets and liabilities at a nominal value of $1.00." I would be lacking in the respect due your office, if I thought for a moment that you were unaware that a deficit arrived at by such bizarre accountancy cannot and should not be wiped out. Instead, the investment of the government in physical and human capital should be recognized as such and amortized over the period of its likely usefulness.

It was Liberals who nationalized the Bank of Canada and made it so efficient an institution for ending depressions. The interest paid on federal debt held by the Bank of Canada comes back to the government, the Bank's sole shareholder, as dividends. At the close of the war the proportion of federal debt to the GDP stood at just about twice the present figure — at 143%. However, reasonably full employment, vast investments by government, made it possible to catch up with fifteen years of neglect of our infrastructures, and the assimilation of a vast, mostly penniless immigration. Yet by 1975, because of low interest rates and an expanding economy, the proportion of federal debt to GDP had been reduced to less than 22%.

For its part, the American government in recent months has started moving in the general direction of recognizing government investments. In January, 1996 the Bureau of Economic Analysis of the Department of Commerce, corrected the write-off of federal investment in a single year.† As a result the revised data show gross government saving of $49.9 billion for 1994 instead of a deficit of $119.3 billion. Over the past decade the revised figures brought down the debt by over one trillion dollars, thus contributing not only to President Clinton's re-election but to the relative strength of the US economy. Those figures of reduced deficit and debt suggest, Mr. Prime Minister, that you should follow Mr. Clinton's example. That would make it possible for you to satisfy your Finance Minister's mania for balancing the budget without ruining both the country and the great Liberal Party. Should Mr. Martin prove difficult, we are confident that your celebrated street smarts will prompt you to ask why he has not written off the cost of the ships in his shipping line in a single year.

As things stand, much of the "fiscal discipline" of which you seem so proud consists of slashing grants to the provinces who in turn pass on to the provinces the dirty work of victimizing the most vulnerable sectors of our society. Meanwhile the country is becoming pocked with pot-holes in every area, physical and moral. We are headed back to the thirties, when the cry of "budget-balancing" resounded throughout the land. The most spendthrift of all policies, however, is to count on the supposed "natural rate of unemployment" to stabilize the economy.[‡] Unemployment per se is in fact "unnatural," and the "jobs, jobs, jobs" promise in your Little Red Book was doomed even when made, by the very doctrine that guides your Finance Ministry and our central bank today.

It is certainly not enough that Mr. Martin, like the good Lord, giveth and taketh. What he "gives" is for the benefit of the TV cameras and is by far outweighed what he will continue to take to implement the hidden "natural rate of unemployment" program.

You refer to the "sacrifices that so many have made" that makes it impossible for you "to give up." The fact, however, is that our banks and other financial interests, have profited inordinately at the expense of those on whom the sacrifices have been inflicted. As a result of the progressive deregulation of banking, by 1990 our banks had lost much of their capital by financing such hare-brained schemes as Robert Campeau's ambition to buy up every department store chain in the US. To bail them out of their plight, the Mulroney government in 1991 slipped a bill through Parliament ending the need for the banks to hold reserves with the Bank of Canada as a portion of their deposits. By virtue of this legislation our banks have been able to increase their holdings of government debt without putting up any legal tender. They have accordingly increased their holdings of government debt since then by $60 billion. That (along with the legal tender made available to them from the ending of the reserve obligation) has amounted to a subsidy of over $5 billion dollars annually to our banks. That has enabled our banks to turn around on a dime — and the dime was not even their own. From suppliants carrying begging bowls they have developed an arrogant grasp without precedence in this country.

Nor can you blame it all onto Mr. Mulroney. The decline in the bond holdings of the Bank of Canada has fallen in relative terms more rapidly since your government took over than during any like stretch under Mulroney — by over 24% between January 1994 and June 1996. Since 1975 the Bank of Canada's inventory of federal debt has dropped from 22% of the outstanding debt to just over 5%.

All this has plunged our banks into an identity crisis. It has contributed to create the greatest inflation of financial assets on record. You take great credit for our low nominal interest rates. The truth is that neither the US Federal Reserve nor the Bank of Canada dare raise interest rates — which they formerly have been quick enough to do when the unemployment rate went down ever so little. That is because it would prick the hot-air balloon that the stock market has become. Were reserves still in place, the financial inflation could be cooled by raising the reserve requirement without raising interest rates.

If your government has a back-up plan for when our current financial spree goes the same way that financial speculative booms have already gone in Japan, Mexico, South Korea and Thailand, we have yet to hear of it.

William Krehm
Publisher of *Economic Reform*

[†] Source: *Survey of Current Business for Jan.-Feb.* p.13; *Economic Indicators*, p. 34; and the *Federal Reserve Bulletin*, Table A-40.

‡ "In an interview with Southam News last month, Deputy Finance Minister David Dodge — Martin's right-hand man — pooh-poohed the idea that Canada's rate could be reduced much below what it already is. The so-called natural rate of unemployment, Dodge said then, is about 8 percent. Any attempt to push the unemployment rate below that level, he went on, would lead to inflation." Thomas Walkom in *The Toronto Star* 19/2.

Vol. 9, No. 4 — April 1997

Do We Really Need an Economy When Our Casinos Are Doing So Well?

Globalisation was advanced as a win-win ticket, but for most citizens of all three NAFTA countries the results have been lose-lose. Jobs have disappeared, and living standards have declined.

Helene Cooper in the *Wall Street Journal* (21/2) tells a cautionary tale out of Nogales, Arizona. After years of watching service jobs emigrate across the street to Nogales, Mexico, the Arizonians had high hopes when new employers began coming in. At a recent meeting in the high school, civic leaders boasted of the 5.6% growth in local manufacturing jobs, compared with a 0.5% drop nationally. But someone lamented the town's overall unemployment rate: 22.6% and rising. Ross Perrot, it seems, was half-right. NAFTA does produce a giant sucking sound as jobs head south — but mainly to the US border states of Texas, Arizona and California. Seeking to supply nearby Mexican plants, the maquiladoras, American auto-parts suppliers, plastics companies and others are opening factories on US soil to make the complex components that the assembly parts need but that low-skilled Mexican workers can't produce.

However, the new US factories can't make them, either, unless the companies go north to hire managers, technicians and skilled workers. Nogales had neglected vocational, science and even English-language training for its residents.

Like other border towns, Nogales has long relied on providing shops and services for Mexican visitors. With its Spanish-speaking populace, it was the perfect place for Mexicans to pick up US goods quickly. And residents didn't need much schooling to get decent jobs in the stores. Now those jobs are mostly gone, done in by NAFTA and the 1995 devaluation of the peso. The devaluation boosted retail business in Nogales, Mexico, where Americans shop, but obliterated it in downtown Nogales, AZ, where goods suddenly cost 35% more in pesos. In the US town, the main street has one shuttered store after another.

In the words of Lori Wallach, director of Public Citizens' Global Trade Watch (*Globe and Mail* 25/2): "NAFTA has become the trade agreement from hell. The United States has gotten clobbered and that has a lot of members of Congress nervous." Instead of reexamining the assumptions on which NAFTA was based, the Clinton administration has just pushed its expansion to yet other countries. But (*WSJ* 31/3) "Clinton will likely postpone an April trip to Mexico and a May trip to five Latin nations. The official reason: Clinton's lack of mobility. But US plans to expand free trade to Latin America also are going nowhere."

Rather than starry-eyed globalisation, Washington is being driven by the risk "of losing ground to European and Asiatic competitors moving into the us's economic backyard." The prospects — as in the thirties — are for sharpening trade wars amongst the mega-powers.

In all three NAFTA countries, the very traumas suffered by the mass of the population have produced bonanzas for a small elite. For speculative finance it has been decidedly win-win all the way.

The case of Mexico illustrates the point. During the Second World War and in the first postwar decades, the terms of trade between the two countries were shamelessly manipulated in the us's favour — first by freezing the prices of strategic materials that the American war machine needed but refusing Mexico the goods it wanted to import in return for those exports because of wartime scarcities. With a lot of money around resulting from the wartime exports and little to spend it on, inflation flared in Mexico. Then in the immediate postwar Mexico was pressured into keeping its export prices low "to fight inflation." With the oil crunch of the 1970s, much of the billions of US money pouring into Mexico stuck to politicians' fingers. And with that gigantic debt in place, the US Federal Reserve pushed interest rates into the 20% range in the early 80s "to lick inflation."

Mexico earned applause throughout Latin America by defaulting on its $100 billion foreign debt in August 1982. Alarmed, Washington rushed in to restructure Mexican and other Third World debt as "Brady bonds," denominated in US currency and partly guaranteed by the American Treasury. Their option of using Brady bonds to buy local equities gave Americans a bargain-basement way of picking up pieces of the Mexican economy. Temporarily, that removed the harsh edge of the relationship between the two countries, and prepared the way for what has probably been the greatest two-way con job in the history of world finance — the North American Free Trade Agreement.

The corrupt Mexican political establishment benefited by the glowing PR that poured out of the White House. By grace of their pin-striped suits and the Ivy League diplomas on their office walls, Mexico's political elite was sold abroad as democratic statesmen. Money flowed into Mexico in torrents. And a year after NAFTA was signed the scam blew sky-high. The peso devalued by 13% in December 1994, and was down fully 45% less than four months later. But by then many properly plugged-in Mexicans had long ago sent their winnings out of the country. The scale of the collapse put the international financial system at risk, and the Clinton government desperately patched together a rescue package of $50 billion, with Mexico's oil revenues serving as collateral.

But even this monumental bust was to turn out a win-win game for the nimble-footed with deep pockets. Listen to *The Economist* (24/2/96): "A year ago, prices collapsed after Mexico's financial crisis. But between April, 1995 and the end of the year, an index of "Brady bonds" compiled by Salomon Brothers climbed by 43%. On February 20th [however,] the Brady bonds index fell by 3%. The reason is that Brady bonds trade like American Treasury bonds on amphetamines. When the American market rallies, Brady bonds soar; when Treasuries falter, Bradys fall. In part this is because Brady bonds are partially backed by American Treasury bonds. More important, when bond markets rise, yields tend to drop. That makes riskier assets such as Bradys, more attractive. Yields on 30-year Treasury bonds now stand at 6.4%; when stripped of their collateral value, benchmark Mexican bonds yield 15.2%. In Brady bonds the US Treasury had put together as tricky a derivative as ever came out of Wall Street.

Their Mexican post-bailout bonanza is opening new vistas for financial buccaneers. It has brought them a liberating idea: who needs a functioning economy if the casinos are able to do so well without one? The bigger the financial crash, the more money is to be made as the market recovers. The end result is like fishing with dynamite. Of course, it is hardly the level playing field we hear so much about — the guy with the sticks of dynamite does have an advantage over those who surface belly-up.

Between March 1995 and January 1996 Bulgarian bonds, described by *The Economist* article as "some of the dodgiest paper in the market," surged an extraordinary 60%. The *WSJ* (6/3/97) informs us that "fixed-income analysts in London and New York fret over the exchange rates of hryvnias (Ukraine), liuns (Moldava) and tenges (Kazakstan) and sweat over decisions whether to liquidate Russian T-bills and take positions in municipal bonds issued by the Siberian city of Novosibirsk. Last year, the performance of this young market blew the top off any other [debt] market in the world. Most Western investors in Russian T-bills [pulled in] returns of about 50% in dollar terms. What does it matter that even Moscow doesn't publish budgets?"

The Answers Lie Beyond Number-Crunching

Ninety-five percent of what currently passes as economic research consists of number-crunching. Let us take the example of Pierre Fortin, one of the most charming and well-intentioned of our academic economists. Among critics of the Bank of Canada's disastrous "zero inflation" policy, Fortin has probably received the most media coverage.

His talent and dedication are blunted, however, by his confining himself to number-crunching within the framework of the official model. When the Finance Ministry experts argue that the "natural rate of unemployment" is 8% (or 9 or 10), Fortin is out there defending the good cause — stating that the "natural rate of unemployment" is lower, say 5, or 6. In doing this he apparently overlooks that he is legitimising the "natural rate of unemployment." There is no use trying to track down the correct value of a relationship that is in itself cooked up to serve a perverse cause. Unemployment of those who can and wish to work is in itself "unnatural." It cannot be left on Mother Nature's doorstep. It has no correct value since the very concept is incorrect.

Vol. 9, No. 5 — May 1997

A Bond Rating Service Appraises Our Banks

The Dominion Bond Rating Service (DBRS) is not unfamiliar to Canadians. For years it has served our government as the bogeyman to intimidate the public into accepting its slashing of social programs. The DBRS's constituency, bondholders, flourishes on bond interest. Accordingly the DBRS sees its duty as keeping an eye on the risk involved in holding a particular bond. They are particularly concerned with the ratio of borrower's income to expenditure.

But though no great friends of social programs, they do favour a functioning economy. Speculators, on the other hand, can thrive on the bankruptcy of creditors and debtors alike. On such occasions debt and assets can be bought up cheap, and eventual recovery may deliver stellar capital gains to those with depth of pocket and cunning.

The late French economist François Perroux emphasized that each particular revenue has its own "life-style" (*comportement*). Speculative profits are rarely reinvested in annuities or stuffed in mattresses. Nor do they often go into founding new industrial firms. They are more likely to seek out still more daring speculations. And from the salaries, options, and perks that CEOs help themselves to these days, it is clear that corporation executive, too, are not above such foibles.

Naively confident that where interest rates are high and wages low enough, fundamentals are sound, our banks are plunging headlong into Latin America where deepening poverty strains society's seams.

In such ventures the ratio of the banks' holdings of legal tender to their total assets rose from 97:1 at the end of 1989 to a current 295.4:1 The government and its intervention in the economy" has created a monstrous degree of "moral hazard." That arises when investors are given incentive to assume inordinate risks by the knowledge that others will absorb their losses. In this instance the "other party" is the government that under the unwritten "too big to be allowed to fail" principle, underwrites our banks' wildest gambles.

Along with other key players, our banks have recently discovered that speculative gains can be made from major financial calamities. Indeed, the revelation seems to be dawning that a functioning economy is strictly not necessary for success in their new role. Spastic heavings of exchange and interest rates can offer them their greatest opportunities.

Because of this, an important change has taken place in the banks' position in society. To help us understand this, we must again refer to François Perroux — this time to his concept of "the dominant revenue."" In every historical epoch the welfare of society as a whole comes to be officially identified with the quantity of a privileged revenue. Under feudalism, it was the income of the landowning nobility. Under industrial capitalism it was the flow of industrial profits. In a mixed economy, [as in the sixties when Perroux wrote this] the rate of profit was the result of a complex combination of public and private, of market and extra-market actions." Then with the increasing deregulation of interest rates and banking, control passed to bondholders. But globalisation, and deregulation have created a universe of churning interest rates, exchange rates, and of just about everything else. Speculative capital gains have come to replace interest on money-lending as the dominant revenue.

"DBRS also has doubts about claims by some banks that because of advanced new lending methodologies, they will never again experience losses of similar magnitude to those they sustained in the last recession. Historically, the banks have shown a talent for finding new ways to blow their brains out from time to time."

William Krehm

Saskatchewan Secrets

There is a type of novel that enjoyed particular popularity some decades ago. In it the same events are told and retold by two or more of the characters from their particular angles of vision. The effect can be bizarre with heroes and villains changing place as in a square dance.

That came to mind on reading of Saskatchewan's close brush with bankruptcy in 1993. (*The Globe and Mail*, 22/03) In a self-congratulatory mood NDP Premier Roy Romanow announced a $370 million surplus for 1996-7. This has permitted his government to cut its sales tax by two percent. Higher wheat and potash prices have of course had much to do with this. "Mr. Romanow discovered when he took office in 1991 that his government had inherited a financial straight jacket after a decade of deficit spending by the Tory government of Grant Devine. Saskatchewan Finance Minister, Janice MacKinnon, met secretly in Ottawa with her federal counterpart, Donald Mazankowski to explain how close the province was to defaulting on its debt payments of more than $15 billion.

"Mr. Romanow did not reveal the terms of the federal bailout, but in March 1993, the *Globe* disclosed that federal officials were quietly canvassing the country's financial community to draw up contingency plans in the event some provinces were no longer able to raise money in foreign bond markets. A plan was discussed whereby the Bank of Canada would arrange emergency borrowings for unnamed hard-pressed provinces which might be shut off international capital markets. Both Mr. Romanow and federal officials denied the reports at the time.

"This was at a time when the International Monetary Fund had issued sharp warnings to Ottawa and the provinces about the level of public indebtedness."

Today Premier Romanow is generous to a flaw in giving credit to his perceived benefactors: "I must pay a little tribute to Mr. Mulroney here, because he was able through his minister of finance to grease some payment from the federal government to Saskatchewan."

No country and no province has an oversupply of heroes, and praise in recent years has rarely crossed provincial boundaries. Accordingly *ER* is loath to discourage such kind remarks between heads of governments. However, why was there need of so many secret meetings, so many generous heroes in Ottawa, and cloak-and-dagger stuff when right in the *Bank of Canada Act* in item (j) of its Section 18, there has been since its adoption in 1934 a provision for the central bank to "make loans to the Government of Canada or the government of any province, but such loans shall not at any one time, in the case of the provincial government, exceed one-fourth of the government's estimated revenue for its fiscal year." The wobbly state of provincial finances was a constant concern throughout the thirties and was the reason section 18 was put in the Act.

Section 14 of the same Act establishes the ultimate responsibility of the federal Government for the general policy of the central bank.

Besides, before really earning the "little tribute" that Premier Romanow so generously bestowed on him, Mr. Mulroney had a certain moral debt to discharge in the matter. It was his all-out support of Bank of Canada Governor John Crow's high-interest-rate mania that accounted largely for the state of the finances not only of Saskatchewan but of the other provinces. In his most measured, persuasive tones Premier Romanow could have explained to Mr. Mulroney and his own electorate the real source of the province's crisis, and the ways of dealing with it already enshrined in the *Bank of Canada Act*, rather than putting the burden on the most vulnerable portion of the population.

Had the Bank of Canada been used as the Act prescribes, the IMF could have been sent packing. The big, bad wolf was of Ottawa's own making: its determination to carry out the directives of the Bank for International Settlements in Switzerland. The BIS has no mandate from the Canadian electorate.

In the negotiations with Quebec, Premier Romanow has proved himself a constitutionalist of note. He should apply those talents in appraising the extent to which the Bank of Canada respects its charter.

Vol. 9, No. 6 — June 1997

Book Review — *It's Your Money*

[Hixson, William F. *It's your money*, with an appendix by William Krehm, *The Bank of Canada — a misused tool*. Toronto : COMER Publications, 1997. ISBN 0968068111]

Stuff Banks Hope We Don't Know

William F. Hixson looks like an Old Testament prophet in a good mood. Elijah, perhaps, on one of the days when he spotted the ravens, and realized they were going to feed him.

Hixson is a prophet, of sorts, hurling his thunderbolts not at Jezebel, but at her modern counterparts, the commercial banks.

Hixson has written a book, *It's Your Money,* which joyfully smites the tribe of bankers hip and thigh.

The author is a retired professional engineer and successful businessman from Kentucky, who has written two other books, and a bevy of articles for economic journals, about banks.

He doesn't like them much. He thinks they are grasping, greedy and out of control. Well, nothing new there. But the theme of this book, and the reason why it is of interest to Canadian as well as US readers, is that it deals, in some detail, with the way banks all over the world make up money, rent it out many times over — and collect interest every time.

He writes: "Suppose a person owned a farm and tried to rent it to five, 10, 20 or 30 different tenants at the same time, and collect rent simultaneously from all of them. He would never get by with it, of course. The scam is too obvious...

"But suppose a person owned a dollar and tried to loan it out to five, 10, 20, or 40 different borrowers at the same time and collect rent simultaneously from all of them.

If he were a banker, he would get by with it easily, although, when one thinks about it, the scam is only a little less obvious."

This is a fair sample of Hixson's writing: clarity itself.

The book is important because we're going through a patch of historical revision. Our banks, which have never previously denied that they made money up on the premises, have suddenly decided that this isn't what they do at all.

They borrow from depositors and lend to depositors, that's all. They are "financial intermediaries." The reason for this new line, which has been adopted by the governor of the Bank of Canada, Gordon Thiessen, is that our banks have managed to get rid of most of the reserve requirements that formerly kept a curb on how much money they could create.

In Canada, as William Krehm points out in a shrewd Afterword to Hixson's book, they managed to wipe out primary reserves entirely, with almost nary a word spoken, beginning in 1991.

This means that, instead of being able to make up eight or 10 dollars for every dollar of real wealth they hold, the banks can now create more than 40:1 in the US, and as much as 100:1 in Canada.

It seems rather risky, so the banks have put forward the tale that they don't create this money, they just borrow it.

Hixson, hitching up his pants, and snapping his suspenders, replies, "Oh, Yeah?," and takes the argument apart.

The nub of his thesis is that, if the money banks lend was money they borrowed, there would be a rough parity between increases in bank deposits and bank loans over a period of time. Instead, bank loans have increased, and continue to increase, at about 10 times the rate of deposits.

In other words, "What banks loan is, for the most part, money they create."

With high reserves (in Canada, not long ago, banks had to have up to $18 on hand for every $100 loaned) there was a strict limit to the money-creation process, but, as the reserves came off, the banks became more expansive, more profitable, and, Hixson argues, more open to abuse and even to financial disaster.

The ultimate irony is that banks, both in Canada and the US create money and then turn around and lend it to the government at steep interest rates.

Hixson contends that governments ought to do much more of the creation, and collect much more of the profits of creation.

Walter Stewart

Stewart, author and humorist, appears in The Toronto Sun *Mondays. The above review was published on 28/4.*

A Link Between the Bank for International Settlements and the Nazis' "Dental Gold?"

Early in May the US government released a report summing up its review of 11 million pages of documents on the role of Swiss banks in dealing with the flow into Switzerland of gold plundered by the Nazis. Some of it had been extracted from the teeth of its death-camp victims.

It was no secret at the beginning of the war that the Germans were running out of gold and foreign exchange. The stream of gold that began flowing into Swiss banks could thus have been recognized as loot. For the first time this report provides hard evidence that the booty picked up in central banks was blended with the jewellery and teeth fillings of its extermination camp victims. In this doubly gruesome money-laundering the Swiss banks collaborated profitably. The heirs of Nazi victims encountered stubborn resistance when they applied for the release of the deposits made with the banks by their relatives. Some of this money had been earmarked by the Nazis for financing a revival of their movement after their defeat. Without the cooperation of Switzerland and its banks the Nazis could hardly have sustained so long a war.

The record of the neutral nations with respect to the Nazis' victims leaves much to be desired, but even so Switzerland stands out for its abject self-seeking. After the war, the Swiss finally agreed to hand over to the Allies some $58 million — a third to a quarter of the Allies' estimate of its own gold shipped by the German Central Bank to Switzerland. But the Swiss also undertook to send $120 million of German-looted gold to other countries. That obligation was never fulfilled. Meanwhile the value of gold has more than decupled.

The Americans had cracked the code used by the Swiss in communicating with their Washington Embassy; and were thus privy to the negotiating tactics of the Swiss. Nevertheless, the Truman administration struck a poor agreement and then lost interest in enforcing it. They threw away their bargaining leverage by unfreezing Swiss assets in the US. Part of the explanation was the increasing absorption of the State Department with the Cold War: right-wing Germans were coming to be seen as future allies. They achieved prominence at the new Bundesbank and in the new international banking bureaucracy that was being created.

It is not surprising then that a key aspect of the Nazi gold loot problem would appear to have been sidestepped by the Undersecretary of Commerce Stuart Eisenstat, who directed the historical study. That was the possible involvement of the Bank for International Settlements (BIS) in this episode. Unlike the League of Nations organizations and those of the present United Nations, BIS is strictly an organization of central bankers. Government officials are not even allowed to attend its sessions. From the beginning this provided an ideal channel for bankers to circumvent elected governments.

At the Bretton Woods Conference of 1944 at which the financial arrangements of the postwar world were planned, on the initiative of governments-in-exile, Resolution Five was adopted that called for the liquidation of BIS at the earliest possible moment. That was because it had earned itself a reputation for accommodating Nazi Germany.

By the fifties, however, BIS came to be seen as an ideal bunker from which the campaign of the world banks could be conducted for the reconquest of the positions they had lost in the thirties. In 1951 the US Government announced that it would not insist in carrying out Resolution Five of Bretton Woods.

And since then it is from BIS that just about every important step in deregulating the banks of the world emerged: "zero inflation" as the one tool for "stabilizing" the economy; the doing away with reserves held by banks with their central bank; the "independence" of central banks from their government.

Now, in the light of the US Government report, the role of BIS during the war must be revisited.

Vol. 9, No. 7 — July 1997

Our Vanishing Money Supply

We have just come through an election campaign in which the main issue — the deficit — was based on misinformation. Not inaptly, an irreverent Quebec journalist compared the performance to a small boys' peeing match: party leaders took turns in promising to wipe out the deficit a year or two sooner than their rivals. Some even offered to cut taxes while at the head of the budget-slashing pack.

What went unmentioned was that the federal debt is the legal tender of the land, performing the function gold did in bygone periods. The annual deficit is the increase in our money supply that makes possible increased economic activity and more jobs. Eliminate the deficit and you throttle the economy with a shrinking money supply. It is highly unlikely that our Finance Minister is unaware of this elementary fact. But it has been carefully hidden from a gullible electorate.

But we are entering an intriguing period when truth bursts forth from the mouths of prevaricators. After years of warnings about government deficits ruining the land, financial circles are suddenly disturbed by the shrinking supplies of new government debt issues. Listen to the *Wall Street Journal* (27/5):

"Hey buddy, can you spare a bond?

"As the [US] federal budget deficit drops and new corporate debt shrinks, a dwindling supply of new bonds is aiding the bond market, and could keep interest rates lower in the years ahead. Thanks to a growing economy and slowing government spending, the budget deficit is now just $69 billion, or less than 1% of gross domestic product, a 24-year low. The figure is down from a 4.1% average in the '80s. As a result, the government finds itself turning to the debt markets for help less frequently.

"Indeed, the balanced-budget scenario is based on dubious assumptions, such as that the economy won't meet a serious setback. During the next economic slowdown, the government may feel the need to boost its expenditures. Those who subscribe to the new paradigm, posit that low-risk, long-term bonds could be the favoured asset of the next decade, as they become more scarce."

However, if the modest recovery now underway should give way to a deepening recession, the whole vision of a deficit-less future will be blown to kingdom come. By the current logic we will be faced with the need to go on downsizing government services at an even jollier clip. Or admit that the policy made no sense in the first place.

There is a polarized relationship between government debt and the stocks, bonds and other paper assets of the private sector. The former is legal tender that by law *must* be accepted in discharge of any debt. Accepting cheques on banks for the purpose is optional. But banks do not like holding more legal tender than they can get away with under the existing regulations. For them cash is sterile money — holding it earns them no interest. Good money in their eyes must breed like rabbits, and bring forth ever more bumper litters. Ideally, it is credit of their own creation based on as thin a sliver of legal tender as possible.

Ever since the fifties the governments of the West have moved consistently to accommodate the banks in this respect. Step by step they have reduced the cash (legal tender) that the banks had to hold with the central bank to back the deposits they hold. At the same time they have removed the restrictions on the investments that the banks are allowed to make with the credit they create. Throughout history the powers delegated to banks to create credit out of the void ("money creation") have gotten them into trouble. That climaxed in 1929 in the stock market crash that helped bring on the Great Depression of the thirties.

The Bank of Canada was set up to put the commercial banks on a strict diet and to help the country out of the Depression. But by the fifties the banks had recovered and had begun intriguing to be allowed to return to their old bad habits. Four decades of deregulation ensued. Whenever the banks got themselves into difficulty they were allowed to prescribe the form of the government's bailout — undoubtedly the most monumental case of homoeopathy on record. At the beginning of the nineties the banks were in deep, hot water from financing gigantic real estate and financial gambles. To rescue them, the primary reserves that the banks had to hold with the Bank of Canada were abolished entirely. That was the equivalent of the Security Commission allowing gamblers on the stock exchange who had lost their capital by speculating on margin, to require no cash at all for further purchases. So radical was the operation, that it was carried out with a stealth that calls to mind bank-robbers pulling off a job under cover of darkness.

As a result our banks today are all over the map. They have taken over most of the trust companies, the brokerage houses, merchant banking, underwriting of bond and stock issues. They are lobbying like mad to swallow up the insurance industry. They are buying up pieces of banks in increasingly unstable countries of Latin America and Asia. All the while the probable deflation of the real economy is transparently masked by a stock market that refuses to go down. In part that is because the central banks have hesitated to raise interest rates fearing the resulting damage to an inflated financial system.

In the United States currently a bill has passed a congressional committee that would allow banks to own gasoline pumps and grocery stores. In fact with deregulation bankers have become brokers and stock salesmen in drag. They have undergone an identity change more drastic than a sex-change operation — with the added feature that the surgery is conveniently performed on innocent third parties.

Accordingly, every device has been employed to keep the stock market in ascension. Globalisation, privatisation, mutual funds, derivatives, have all played their part in this. But though it has enriched many in a few years beyond all expectations, the situation has a fatal weakness: it devours its shrinking base. Becoming top-heavy, it must inevitably keel over. The supply of legal tender into which the speculative assets can be converted has dwindled. For years now our financial institutions presented the public debt as "#1 enemy" — including the not insignificant portion of it our government incurred to bail them out. But in doing this the financial sector was shutting their own escape hatch for getting their winnings to a safe haven. To grasp the bizarreness of this situation, we must refer to a classic law in economic literature — Gresham's law.

Thomas Gresham was a financier under good Queen Bess 400 years ago. And the law attributed to him says that when good and bad money ("clipped" or adulterated coin in the period) circulate side by side, the bad coin will drive out the good — i.e. those in the know will fish out the good coin for hoarding. We have already noted that for banks "good money" is normally not legal tender but credit of their own creation. Because the federal government is the sole shareholder of the BoC the interest on government debt held by it reverts to the government in the form of dividends. The result is a virtually interest-free loan for the government, i.e. "bad money" in the banks' books.

But the banks' "good money" has been increasing so wildly, that the feeling is spreading on Bay Street that the time has come for "locking in" their winnings, that is, converting them into legal tender that will not be exposed when the stock market's joyride "hits the wall." That is tantamount to declaring yesterday's "bad money" today's "good money," and unloading speculative stocks and bonds onto the proverbial "bigger fools."

A Matter for Serious Investigation

Canada's recent election was spun largely around the government deficit and how rapidly it should be done away with. There was no questioning how reliable the deficit figure might be. And yet for many years the answer, unchanged from year to year, was readily available in the *Canada Year Book*. Thus In the 1988 edition you will find it on page 22-6. In the 1967 edition — the earliest I could readily get my hands on — it appears on page 117. In either case the passage, word for word, is identical: "The statement of assets and liabilities is designed to disclose the net debt, which is determined by offsetting against the gross liabilities, only those assets regarded as readily realizable or interest- or revenue-producing. Fixed capital assets, such as government buildings and public works, are charged to budgetary expenditures at the time of acquisition or construction and are shown on the statement of assets and liabilities at a nominal value of $1.00."

Such a budget cannot and should not be balanced, since it ignores investment in physical and human infrastructures. Even the attempt to balance such non-accountancy could only add to the perceived "inflation" — consider what would happen to the price of gasoline if Imperial Oil wrote of the cost of its oil fields, pipelines, and refineries in a single year. This hipshot accountancy underlay the two panic buttons that have driven our political and economic life for the past three decades: inflation and the deficit.

I first analysed this relationship in 1970.† At that time this bizarre flaw in the accountancy received no attention whatsoever in the international literature. Some years later Robert Eisner did magnificent work on the subject — concentrating on the connection between it and the perceived deficit. When *Economic Reform* began publishing in 1988 it threw its modest resources into spreading information on the matter. Most copies of *ER* were sent to members of legislatures across the country and in the fullness of time some of them even came to be read.

Recently I noticed that the above-quoted explanation of how our deficit is calculated no longer appeared in the 1997 *Canada Year Book.*

Democracy is inconceivable without a minimum of unmanipulated information. And to probe the state of that valuable resource in our land, I set out to find when the above-quoted passage on capital expenditures had been suppressed. It was unchanged in the CYB from the earliest edition that I could readily get my hands on (1967) to 1990 (page 22-5) But by 1994 it was no longer there. Its suppression was not too long after *ER* had begun making a noise on the subject.

Was the elision due perhaps to a lack of space? Hardly. In the 1997 issue you will find a page of rhetoric on Inflation and Interest Rates that might have been lifted from the Finance Minister's political speeches. Since the bogus statistic served as centrepiece of the electoral campaign, it skewed the results as much as a mass stuffing of ballot-boxes could have. The matter demands serious investigation. It would be a good question to ask from the floor of the House of Commons.

wk

† *Price in a Mixed Economy*, Toronto, 1975

Vol. 9, No. 8 — August 1997

Have the Banks Taken Over Our Government?

Whatever illusions about the state of Canada's democracy survived the recent elections are taking a brutal pounding. The elections were spun almost wholly around the deficit. The major parties did not so much as mention allowing our banks to merge. Yet even before the brief campaign was half-way through, *The Globe and Mail* (14/05) reported a task force on financial legislation being "pledged" to let the free market operate with as little government intervention as possible. "Pledged" by whom, to whom, and with a hand on what bible?

The background of the Task Force's original chairman suggests the answers. Mr. James Baillie comes to us neither from banking nor from supervising banks. A lawyer, he served as head of the Ontario Securities Commission whose job is to keep the Toronto Stock Exchange pure. From abundant evidence before and since his departure from that post in 1990 — his success at that task left something wanting. In the midst of the election campaign the greatest scandal in the history of mining, Bre-X, shook the world. An Indonesian promotion headed by a recent bankrupt that did its mining in investors' pockets rather than in the ground was not only listed on the TSE but included in the basket of stocks on which its index is based.

The response from those with a background in bank regulation has not been slow in coming. On June 25th Michael A. Mackenzie, former head of the Office of the Superintendent of Financial Institutions (OSFI), addressed the Conference Board of Canada on "Ownership Rules and the Future of Banking in Canada." His central point was the increasing vulnerability of banks as they race to become bigger. "There is no responsible government in the developed world that does not take a strong interest in the prudential supervision of major banks and will [not] go to great lengths to ensure that they do not fail. The failure of a clearing bank would have enormously disruptive effects. It is interesting that nowhere has this 'too big to fail' doctrine been put into writing....Learned academics, journalists and stockbrokers in love with open markets are claiming that banks are no different from other sectors and ownership restrictions have no place in the global economy."

Let us eke out the meaning of Mr. Mackenzie's remarks — for 'the too big to fail' principle of banking is not the only crucial detail about banking that is rarely mentioned in polite society these days. Remove the 10% ceiling on shareholdings in banks and our mega-banks from six would soon be down to five, four, etc. to a single one. En route the urgency of not allowing them to fail would become greater. And why should a government that has been so diligent in slashing social and other services embark on such a path? What could be behind this lemming dash to elevate having the world's largest banks to a national objective?

In 1991, when our banks were up to their nostrils in bad loans from financing leveraged buyouts, speculative real estate empires, a bill was slipped through a dozing Parliament phasing out the statutory reserves that banks had to put up with the Bank of Canada as a proportion of their deposits. Those reserves earned them no interest. For years before and after Second World War such reserves had amounted to 10%, but by 1991 they had already been whittled down to less than 4%. With their abolition, the ratio of the total credit banks could create to their legal tender had been increased from about 24:1 in the general direction of infinity.

Banks don't like holding cash (legal tender). Since it earns no interest, they consider it sterile money. And with the end of primary reserves the only cash they still hold is what they need to meet their net cheque clearances each day with other "clearing banks" [and to stock their ATMs]. Were our six banks reduced to five, such "leakage" would be lessened. Moreover, allow one merger and you are committed to allowing all. You will end up having a single private bank and all cheque clearance would become an internal affair tying up no legal tender at all. And then the one leak-proof bank could gamble its head off, secure in the knowledge that it had become supremely "too big to fail." The government would be ever there, like a doting uncle, to pick up its gambling tab.

Even before the bill phasing out of reserves, the Bank for International Settlements had published its Risk-Based Capital Requirements that declared the debt of OECD countries to be "risk-free" requiring no capital of the bank's own. It became possible for Canada's banks to load up with another $60 billion of federal debt without putting up any cash of their own. At the same time they were relieved of keeping over $2 billion in cash as reserves with the Bank of Canada. For our banks the two measures added up to an ongoing entitlement of at least $6 billion annually. With the $2 billion released from reserve duty, it was possible for them to create new credit under the new deregulation to just about any amount they set their hearts on. From such investments their earnings could be phenomenal. As could their losses.

The banks in fact have moved away from banking. In 1946 the ratio of our banks' assets/liabilities to the legal tender they held had stood at 11:1. By 1990 it had risen to 102:1. And then by 1996, with the end of reserves, it had soared to 292:1.2 Not only was the leverage wild, but an increasing amount of the investments consisted of pieces or entire banks throughout Latin America, brokerage houses, a heavy involvement in derivatives on their own and for clients' accounts, insurance, overstretched credit cards, and much else.

Mackenzie has yet other concerns. Expressing agreement with a statement of a former President of the Federal Reserve Bank of New York, E. Gerald Corrigan that "banks are special," Mackenzie enlarges, "I concur with this view, because I believe that the banks in every country in the developed world are at the centre of financial and economic activity. I am, as he was, talking about the major clearing banks as distinct from other financial intermediaries. It is these that provide most of the credit indispensable to business, governments and the public. They effectively operate the payments system."

A few years ago, Mr. Mackenzie would have referred to the "fractional reserve" system and to "money creation" that permitted banks to make loans many times greater than the cash they kept in their vaults. These powers of "money creation" were expressed as a "multiplier" that was explained in all the elementary textbooks (including one by the Canadian Bankers Association). But as the multiplier moved in the direction of infinity, the very notion of "fractional reserves" or "money creation" was banished from polite discourse.

In November 1995, the Governor of the Bank of Canada, Gordon Thiessen, told a parliamentary subcommittee that the "multiplier" that had been taught in our textbooks no longer existed. In fact it had exploded to such size that the banks' spin doctors deemed it prudent to deny its very existence.

Mr. Mackenzie avoids scarlet words, but goes far towards spelling out the reality: "In all but name, [our banks] have become universal banks. Each is now a financial conglomerate doing business on its own books or through affiliates: domestic commercial and retail banking; international corporate banking; mortgage banking; securities underwriting and stockbroking; mutual funds; transacting derivatives and foreign exchange products, property and casualty insurance; life insurance; merchants banking and venture capital. In varying degrees, they have substantial overseas interests, including participations in foreign banks. They also hold substantial government debt as assets." What is straining to break through in these lines is that the banks' tremendous leverage backed by the implicit guarantee of the government, gives them an immense advantage over the established actors in any area they choose to invade. They create their own credit, where the others must raise theirs by borrowing at interest from the same banking system, or through stock or bond issues. While the talk is all of "level playing fields," the playing field is in fact practically upended to the banks' advantage.

But these advantages are not without their risks — especially to the taxpayers and society that are on the hook for the banks' overweening ambitions.

Mackenzie examines the objectionable features of a "closely-held" financial institution. "The business objectives of the major shareholder drives the capital and business strategies of the bank. More often than not, the controlling shareholder wants to tap the deposit base of the bank to further other objectives. There should be a separation of banking and commercial and industrial interests. Close connections will likely distort credit allocation and link the fortunes of the bank to those of related commercial enterprises."

The High Explosive at the Heart of Our Government's "Stabilization" Policy

The combination of the ending reserves and deregulating what banks can invest in, is lethal . It will guarantee us deficits from the resulting bank bailouts, credit-crunches, and recessions for decades to come.

If you think that we are exaggerating, just note how events have changed their speed and course since the election and Mr. Baillie's initial release. To quote The *Globe and Mail* (28/6), "Until this week James Baillie thought he had another 14 months to ponder the future of Canada's financial services sector. On Tuesday, the day that talks were confirmed between Royal Bank and Trilon Financial Corp. [for the merger of the Bank with London Insurance], Mr. Baillie was asked to come up with criteria the government can use in approving mergers and acquisitions by July 11. Mr. Baillie said in an interview that it is 'regrettable' there will no longer be enough time for broad public consultation on the issue of mergers because it is difficult for the legislative process to keep pace with market events."

And then *The Globe and Mail* (4/07) reported chairman Baillie as "involved in one of the deals that caused Ottawa to seek his Task Force's advice on what rules should govern mergers": the takeover of National Trust by the Bank of Nova Scotia. Mr. Baillie it appears was a director of Midland Walwyn Inc., a brokerage house, and Manufacturers Life Insurance Co. when he was appointed to chair the Task Force.

Postscript

On 5(07) *The Globe and Mail* reported the resignation of Mr. Baillie. *The G&M* went on to add, "Bankers are urging the Task Force to stick to its schedule despite the sudden departure of its chairman." Mr. Scott Mullin, vice-president of the Canadian Bankers Association, "noted that a discussion paper published by the Task Force June 13 has laid out all the major issues it expects to deal with during its deliberations." That list, however, had omitted every question that must be asked in defence of the national interests. Amongst these are the following:

- How many of the world's very largest banks have been in intensive care and since when because of the capital losses sustained in their speculative acquisitions?
- Since the Canadian public is on the hook under the "too big to fail" principle, surely it has a right to know what further risks are being downloaded on it. Accordingly, the Task Force consider and make public the effects of deregulation on the banking systems of such countries as Thailand, Malaysia, Indonesia, South Korea, the Philippines, Japan, Czechoslovakia, etc. and the degree of risk increase that our banks are taking on as a result of deregulation.
- The details of the last bailout of our banks, including the phasing out of the primary reserves, the effects of that deregulation on the government debt that they held and used to hold, and the cash that they had to put up to increase their government debt holdings.
- How does the Task Force envisage the next bailout by our government of our those of our banks that are too big to fail now that there are no reserves kept with the Bank of Canada?

The Great Canadian Bond Shortage

The millennium would seem to have arrived by registered mail. Just a few years ago we were told that we the people had been living so high off the hog that the country was drowning in debt. Now all that is in the past. By "staying the course," a veritable Ulysses lashed to the mast, Finance Minister Martin has delivered the goods. The *Globe and Mail* (11/07) informs us that Ottawa has stopped new borrowing "for the first time in 25 years, issuing no new bonds a year earlier than expected." Surely, this should be an occasion for fireworks. So why the groans from the high-priced seats?

Well, it now seems that banks, mutual funds, pension funds, and the entire financial community have need of government debt for safe investments yielding a steady flow of income. But weren't we assured that the government's credit was in the gutter, and that to refurbish it we had to slash social services, while keeping interest rates high enough that a million and a half Canadians might serve the Fatherland by rotting in foodbank lines?

What was kept from the public was that government debt is the legal tender that underpins our money supply. Until World War I the basis for all debt formation had been gold or silver. By law they were the stuff that creditors had to accept in payment of what was owed them. But since the twenties — impelled by necessity, and only dimly aware of what they were doing — governments began replacing gold with just plain government credit. This trend had started with paper money supposedly convertible into precious metals, but in the fullness of time even the pretence of an equivalence with a given weight of gold was dropped.

When gold or silver were legal tender, it earned their holders no interest. Likewise, the new legal tender held at its point of origin — the government and its agencies — costs it only a nominal rate of interest. That is because modern central banks return the bulk of their net profits to the government.

Private bankers in recent years have improved on that formula — they invented they expanded the category of government debt that did earn the banks interest. For the federal government it translated into an equivalent growth of its deficit and debt. Meanwhile the Bank of Canada kept real interest rates at heights that savaged the tax-base and contributed further to the explosion of the federal debt.

Though Finance Minister Martin is taking full credit for the wilting of the deficit, other factors contributed to that result. The slashing of federal grants and services is giving rise to other deficits. On the very same day that the bond scarcity was announced, *The Globe and Mail* reported that the federal Health Department is disbanding "its in-house drug-research laboratories and will rely instead on scientific research from universities, foreign regulatory agencies and the pharmaceutical companies that apply to have their drugs approved." Since the government elevated the revenue of money-lenders — interest rates — into the one tool for keeping a hopelessly distorted price statistic flat, our government seems to have lost all sense that conflicts of interest can arise. Assigning the approval of new drugs to the folks who make them is no way of keeping the reputation of Caesar's wife lily-white.

Vol. 9, No. 9 — September 1997

Ottawa Confesses to Privatisation Scam

On page 33 of the *Bank of Canada Review* of Summer 1997, under the heading "The direct impact of privatisation on the federal government's fiscal position" reproduces a brief item from the *Public Accounts of Canada 1995-96*. First it deals with the case of public assets organized as Crown corporations: "If the federal government expects an asset to generate revenues sufficient to cover operating and capital costs, it generally records its investment at cost, reporting it as the gross book value. It revalues its investment periodically to reflect changes . . . in market value, and these allowances for valuation are charged to budgetary expenditures in the year in which they occur. Because the federal government may have charged substantial allowances for valuation to previous years' deficits, privatisation can result in an accounting profit, which reduces the deficit, even though the government may have invested more in a Crown corporation than it receives when the corporation is privatised."

The writer goes on to cite the case of the privatisation of Petro-Canada which reduced the federal deficit by $154 million and the CN privatisation that brought it down by $171 M, even though the government made the sales at substantially less than their cost to it.

But the real interest of the piece deals with government assets not organized as Crown Corporations: "In contrast to commercial Crown corporations, full-cost recovery for many federal assets, including bridges, ports, and telecommunications systems, was never considered either feasible (because the asset is a public good) or desirable (for public-policy reasons). The federal government financed the cost of acquiring and maintaining such assets through budgetary appropriations, recording their book value as a nominal $1 even though the government invested huge sums of money in them and may have incurred significant debt to finance them. Consequently, if these assets are privatised, all of the sale proceeds can be applied against the deficit, as the $1.5 billion received from the sale of the air navigation system was in the 1996/97 fiscal year. *The federal government is gradually moving towards full-accrual accounting, whereby the cost of acquiring physical assets is spread over the asset's useful life through annual depreciation charges, and thus the true cost of such assets will be more accurately recorded in the future.*" (our emphasis) The most astounding word in this clump of bureaucratic prose is the "gradually" in the passage "The federal government is gradually moving to full-accrual accounting. . ."

Very little else in economic policy is done "gradually" these days. Certainly not privatisation. Note the case of the sale of Toronto's airport, rammed through by a government immediately before an election, an election that practically wiped out the party in question.

Since the above item in the BoC Review admits belatedly that we do not even know what the costs or value of the assets privatised might be or what the net deficit and debt are, that the privatisation is supposed to make more manageable, such non-accountancy amounts to a standing invitation to scams. One would think that the full-accrual accountancy is what should be rushed through, and until it is, privatisations are what should be pursued "gradually."

Market Monotheism?

With "the market" assigned the place earlier societies reserved for their gods, there is need for a caveat. For it is an arbitrary assumption that the new creed is the monotheism it claims to be. On this new Olympus there are many competing deities, and not only do they engage in playful adulteries, but devour one another. And since that brings into question their immortality, some reflection is in order.

Decades ago when economists were less cynical, some of them did not just assume that "the market" was self-equilibrating. Now and again one actually looked for the mechanisms that corrected imbalances wherever they might appear.

A good example was *Money, Interest and Prices* (N.Y., 1965) of Don Patinkin. Patinkin's proof of the balancing magic of markets was that as prices moved up, the cash holdings of entrepreneurs lost real value, and that put businessmen in a more sober mood. Patinkin even struck a lyrical note: "the wonders of the 'invisible hand' never cease." This would certainly be the case if active investors made a habit of holding large cash balances. However, entrepreneurs usually operate with borrowed funds. That reverses Patinkin's "real-wealth" effect. Price stability gets the back of the "invisible hand" as inflation shrinks the real indebtedness of entrepreneurs. That spurs them on to further boldness.

By the mid-sixties, however, there was more serious thinking being done. In the English-speaking world John Kenneth Galbraith concluded that there was need to countervail the powers of oligopoly with intervention by government, trade unions and citizens groups. But Galbraith's preference for social insight over the preening of mathematical feathers, doomed him to be forever an outsider among economists.

In France critics of the self-balancing market found a more receptive hearing because of the strong national tradition in that sense. The outstanding figure amongst the French economists, François Perroux, showed that, far from being self-balancing, the markets of the real world were rather theatres of power.

Both Galbraith and Perroux stopped short of recognising the impossibility of understanding a mixed economy by the code of a single of its components — the market. For clearly that could not recognize the contribution of the public sector, the household economy, and the ecology, whose benefits are neither priced nor marketed. You might as well try reading the time of day on a barometer. But as the power structures within the market grew in girth and muscle, little encouragement was given to questioning the self-balancing market.

The whole purpose of camouflage, after all, is to pretend you are what you aren't. Increasingly economic theory became a cover-up for massive corporate aggression on two fronts: 1) against nonmarket sectors; 2) against less powerful actors within the market — labour, smaller and medium-sized businesses.

Let us mention some aspects of this.

• Ignoring the positive contribution of the public and other non-market sectors. This required burying the work of Keynes and others who had made possible financing the Second World War, and the postwar Reconstruction.

• The use of a single statistic as a panic button for imposing a targeted policy. The strategy became throwing the opponent off balance. In turn the function of the panic button was assigned to the price index (as measure of "inflation") and the government deficit. Nor were the notorious inaccuracies of these statistics allowed to stand in the way of the good cause. Even where some of the "inflationary bias" of the Consumer

Price Index had been recognized, not only in the standard textbooks but by the research department of the Bank of Canada itself, no correction was made. And the government deficit is arrived at by writing off investment in the public sector in a single year — something that would not be tolerated in the business world.

• High interest rates were declared the one answer to the panic created by either of these buttons. All rival solutions were denied to exist.

The panacea promoted was an uncapped increase in the revenue of an already powerful class. The obvious conflict of interest involved has never been addressed.

• Of all available tools, manipulating interest rates is the most profoundly destabilizing. To see this you need only consider how the value of a capital asset is reckoned. Any increase in current earnings is extrapolated into the future, and then its present value is arrived at by discounting these future revenues by the current rate of interest. If the rate of interest doubles, the value of a bond with the old coupon, if it has long enough to run, can fall by a third or more. Contrariwise, if the rate of interest drops, bonds paying the previous rate can become worth much more than par. And since bonds, plant and real estate serve as collateral for loans, shifts in interest rates can convert sound debts into bad debts.

• In the new globalised world higher interest rates will have contrary effects on different markets. Thus a steep rise in the interest rates in country A over that of country B will tend to depress the stock market of A by increasing the cost of portfolio investment. This will create losses for investors of country B who have invested on the stock market of A. On the other hand the same higher interest rates by attracting more short-term money from B to A will strengthen the exchange rate of Currency A

in terms of Currency B. Instead of just "the market" what we have are two distinct markets with opposite responses to the one "blunt" tool to which central banks have reduced their policy kit.

But that is not the end of the tale. The higher interest rates, strengthening the exchange value of A's currency will put A's producers at a disadvantage in meeting competition both on foreign and domestic markets. And to plug the resulting hole in its trade balance, A will become still more dependent on sucking in foreign short-term money with higher interest rates. Meanwhile an economy depressed by the high interest rates will yield less taxation to the government. And the government's pyramiding debt will be at a higher rate.

In short in the dealings between two countries, A and B, there is not just a single market ("*the* market") but a Babel of markets outshouting one other in different tongues. And as economies move towards chaos, fortunes are made in the resulting mega-gambles. Rather than confined to A and B, the pattern is reproduced amongst more countries than there are letters in the alphabet for labels.

And as this happens, the main beneficiaries shift from the rentier group to bigger-than-life speculators. In the early 1980s rentiers had become the favoured economic group as nominal prime rates were pushed into the twenty percent range.

But the collapse of the Mexican peso and economy in December 1994 led to a great revelation. Mexico, the world's greatest debtor, had just been accepted into NAFTA and the OECD. It was praised to the skies for its "sound fundamentals" by the Deputy Secretary of the US Treasury, and as a bonus for conformity its democratic credentials were declared impeccable. The when all this collapsed in bankruptcy, blood and corruption, it first looked as though the financial system of the US might be compromised. That is why Washington hastily patched together a $50 billion rescue line-of-credit.

But subsequent events led to some second thoughts. The crisis opened up Mexico like an oyster on the half shell. Its oil production — long an untouchable national ikon — was put up as collateral for its new loans. With the drop of the peso, wages and living standards were cut by almost half. The terms of trade shifted drastically in favour of the United States, and through the maquiladoras and NAFTA automatically strengthened Mexico's position as purveyor of cheap labour to the world. Mexican Brady bonds partly guaranteed by the US treasury rose by almost half within the year after the meltdown. In a flash it dawned on Wall Street that it was not strictly necessary to have a functioning economy for "the market" to prosper. Big enough crises in successive countries could prove more profitable. It was the nearest possible thing to fishing with dynamite.

The bizarre effects of all this can be found in the investment advice ladled out in just about any financial publication. Thus in the "Report on Business" of *The Globe and Mail* (9/08) you can read under the heading "Swaying to the Latin Beat" the opening paragraph: "Investment quiz. Where are the world's hottest stock markets? North America? Europe? Asia? Nope — Latin America, a region that historically has been better known for ballooning debts, revolutionary turmoil and wrenching instability than for runaway stock markets. Boy, have things changed. Morgan Stanley Capital International's Emergent Markets Free Latin American index gained 42.9 percent over the first half of the year, well ahead of the 32.8% for the Group of Seven Markets."

But can all this be sustainable? With its rich experience in bending language to its needs, Wall St. was not going to be stopped by a detail like that. That, in fact, is what the Multilateral Agreement on Investment (MAI) is about. If the world is opened up so that no country can defend itself by impeding the comings and goings of speculative capital, or inhibit what it does once it comes to a country, the best of all worlds will be assured. As the currency of one country drops, that of others automatically rises. If one stock market collapses, footloose money flocks to those in ascent. In that way the great gamble can go on day and night with an unbroken succession of crises knocking down living standards to create ever fresh opportunities.

But what if society itself collapses in the process? Would that not put a dent in "sustainability?" For all practical purposes in the circles that count society has been declared a redundancy. And there are countless off shore havens like the Cayman Islands where every serious operator has long since set up *pieds a terre* to keep his winnings sustainable.

After all if we can land a man on the moon and a exploration craft on Mars why should a stock market headed for outer space be impossible? Whether the stock market goes up or down is determined by whether demand for stocks exceeds their supply or vice versa. And to keep the market climbing the rest of the economy is being plucked to provide the necessary stock market demand. First there are the privatisations of government assets achieved at ridiculous low prices in keeping with their being carried on government books at a nominal $1.00. Once privatised, and the proper schedule of user fees slapped on, the return can easily be made high enough to justify a capitalisation far beyond the cost of their privatisation. And then as pension funds are allowed to carry more stocks on ever-rising stock market. And the number of mutual funds and funds of funds bid well to exceed the number of listed stocks. The latter for years have been depleted by mergers and takeovers.

In this new environment the new pattern is superblock trades. So scarce are shares — just about any shares — that according to the *Wall Street Journal* (11/8), "Gone are the road shows and lengthy meetings with prospective investors. Instead, the underwriter buys the entire block of stock from the seller at a fixed price, then spends the next 24 hours putting together a group of buyers. As most money managers struggle to cope with large amounts of new cash, after years in which stocks have soared and holding cash has hurt performance, superblocks have been a godsend, some say." Then the *WSJ* goes on to quote chief investment officer at American Express: "The biggest risk for us is that we don't get enough time to do our due diligence."

The stock market in fact is being force-fed with as much professional cunning as the old fashioned "boiler rooms" and "bucket shops" that whipped up phony demand by trading each other's stocks. And both the US Federal Reserve and the Bank of Canada, sensitive to the banks having become mere wagging tails of the brokerage firms acquired by them, do not dare brake the greatest asset inflation spree on record. Such is the strange climax to a holy war to "lick inflation."

But is the stock market's asset inflation really related to the simple "inflation" that we were told was to be wrestled down to "zero." There is a very simple test for that. Has a Jaguar salesman been known to refuse to sell his latest model just because the buyer was paying for it from his latest stock market winnings?

It used to be that the central bank would raise interest rates when average wages went up a half a percent, but the stock market would not be allowed to shoot up a thousand points without being unchallenged. But that is no longer so. That is because our bankers and the Bank of Canada have become concerned about pricking the stock market bubble with any increase in interest rates. In the process of serving the banks that it was supposed to supervise in the national interest, the Bank of Canada has dismantled all the alternatives to raising interest rates that used to serve for controlling inflation — including the statutory reserves that banks used to hold with the BoC. These could be raised to cool an overheated economy *without raising interest rates.* Today it is in the position of the aeronautical engineer who designed a high-flying plane without landing gear.

To reach a ball-park figure of what the present market boom adds to the money-supply (and hence to inflation) let us take the following figures from the *Toronto Stock Exchange Review* of July 19, 1997. The total equity trading on the TSE for the half year prior to June 1997 was $200 billion compared with $301 billion for all of 1996. Assuming that stock on average traded once a year and taking the TSE figures for the total stock trading across Canada (it was actually about 2/3rds), we have the amount of equity in the Canadian stock markets equal to about $400 billion. The average increase in market prices in the last year was 20% hence the profits made amounted to some $80 billion. That amounts to the almost twice the total capital of our chartered banks. Even if retained, shares can be borrowed against. What we have had on our stock markets these recent years approaches hyper inflation, but the sort of hyper inflation that the central bank smiles upon, because it lines the pockets of the proper people.

wk

Neglected Aspects of the Health Care Debate

Let us begin by reproducing an article from *Economic Reform* (9/1991) long before the crisis in health reform had overtaken us.

Ice Floes in Our Future?

Not only is science prolonging life, but it is revolutionising its quality for the aged. Yet such things do come with price tags.

In the past 35 years our birth rate has fallen from almost four births per woman to an all-time low in the 1.7 range. By the year 2010 the post-war baby-boom generation will be entering retirement age. That could mean that by 2020 the retired population, which stood at 3% in 1976, could reach as much as 10%.

The logical thing would be to put our infrastructures in tip-top shape against the day when there will be far fewer active people around to do so. Instead Ottawa has concentrated on driving up the army of unemployed to a level where it would give our central bank the "zero inflation" it has set its heart on. The present engineered recession has already cost us at least $100 billion in lost Gross Domestic Product and it is far from over. After that extravagance, we are told that we can afford nothing else — least of all foresight.

The politicians in the advanced countries are increasingly preoccupied with the ethics of euthanasia, i.e. whether to allow medical assistance to the terminally ill wishing a dignified exit. But the strain on our ethics will be infinitely greater if we ever have to decide whether to permit old folks in excessively good health to go on living. The Inuit used to put their old folks on ice-floes and send them into the ocean. But such customs were imposed by poverty. If we bring such solutions on ourselves, there will be no tradition to bestow its absolution.

To make matters worse, those arrangements have placed a portion of the seniors of the advanced countries — through no fault of their own — in the position of profiteers. Central banks have persisted in trying to lick "inflation" with interest rates as steep as might be needed to do the job. They have shut their minds to the evidence of a quarter of a century: interest rates that devour the greater part of society's net operating income can achieve "zero inflation" only by moving in the direction of a zero economy. All this effects a massive transfer of wealth from the working population to the holders of debt. Most of that debt is held by pension funds and retired folk.

Many seniors were thus able to profit by money rates kept artificially high when younger people were losing their jobs and their homes to these same rates.

Our senior citizens have a valuable contribution to make as a bridge with a past that is being buried and denied. And the physically fit among the aging could help cover the costs of this increasing longevity. By remaining productive on a part-time basis, they would avoid confinement in an age ghetto. But that is hardly possible when more and more middle-aged citizens are being pressured to take voluntary retirement, with little prospect ever again of finding suitable work.

It is true, of course, that Canada will never run out of ice-floes. That is the one case where our monetary policy is laying the basis for an expanding domestic market. And since the same monetary folly is being cloned throughout the world, perhaps even for a bustling export industry.

Since that piece was written, that troubling vision is well on its way to becoming a reality. And if we actually reach the point of sending our old people out on ice-floes, there will be no lack of spin doctors to present the solution as a triumph of multiculturalism and a salute to the Inuit. Medical science goes on producing every more dazzling miracles — replacement tissues, recoding genetic systems, but all these have their costs. Meanwhile the politics of health care are increasingly driven by "the bottom line."

The Wall Street Journal (14/7) reports new drugs to prevent the toxic effects of chemotherapy that allow patients to bear up under longer treatment to get at the cancer. The rub, however, is that these drugs do not come cheap, and are often not even mentioned by the doctors unless the patient broaches the subject. $100 for an intravenous infusion, or $50 for a couple of pills is not unusual. And cost-cutting through bribes and menace is promoted in the corporations that have taken over US health care. Some of these corporations are handling mastectomy cases as outpatients, and bundling them out of the door a few hours after surgery.

The "voice of the market" which prescribes these arrangements drowns out other voices from higher moral terrain. And yet beneath all the fanfare what scores are being kept are far from flattering to the "free market" wisdom banging at our doors. Thus *The Globe and Mail* (1/8) informs us that "Universal medicare is probably the reason poor people in Toronto do substantially better than their Detroit counterparts when they have cancer, say the authors of a five-year study published in the *American Journal of Public Health*. Its authors conclude that earlier detection, faster treatment and better health care, available to all Canadians through Medicare, are probably key to notably better survival rates after the initial diagnosis. Previous comparisons of US and Canadian cancer rates have not taken socioeconomic status into consideration and they found almost no difference in cancer-survival rates. But this study seems to be yet another indication of the failure of the US health-care system to look after some of its neediest citizens most of whom have little or no health insurance.

"Compared to their Detroit counterparts, poor women in Toronto have a survival rate for breast cancer that is 30% higher, for ovarian cancer 38% higher and for cervical cancer 48% higher. Low-income men in Canada's largest city have a survival rate for prostate cancer that is 21% higher, and twice as many men in Toronto were alive after a lung-cancer diagnosis than in Detroit. The data were adjusted to the fact that a higher proportion of poor people in the US are black, in case the propensity for cancer varies with race."

In the last analysis we are confronted with something broader and deeper than just medical ethics — the inescapable question of what society itself is about.

And on that point there has been in recent weeks an avalanche of evidence that has received little attention in the Canadian press. And yet this could not fail interesting Canadians since the debates of health care systems both here and in the US pit the supposed efficiency of the American privatised system vs. Canada's universal health care.

Four different US government agencies, after an investigation involving no less than 700 agents, swooped down on hospitals of the Columbia/HCA Healthcare Corp., the largest company in the field. Three middle-level employees were charged with conspiring to defraud the government. If convicted on all counts, each of these could draw 25 years in prison and a fine of over $1 million. But that is only the first phase of the investigation. *WSJ* (31/7) remarks, "law enforcement officials familiar with the case noted that the first indictments typically target lower-level employees [to] try to persuade [them] to cooperate to implicate higher-ups."

This opens an unscheduled chapter of one of the great sagas of take-over and privatisation in the US economy. Columbia/HCA Healthcare is by far the largest player in its field. Indeed, the American business press is busy making comparative tabulations of the methods and habits of the hero of the present drama, Richard Scott, and Michael Milken, the junk-bond king of the of the eighties. There are their 4:30 a.m. breakfasts and 6 a.m. strategy sessions; Milken's warrants permitting his group part ownership in junk-bond companies(that eventually put him in jail) and Scott's limited partnerships by which doctors had an equity interest in the hospitals they worked in; their sensitive use of the mother tongue: "High-yield bonds," never "junk-bonds" (Milken), and "Tax-paying hospitals," never "for-profit" hospitals (Scott), and so forth. It is hard overlooking a certain reverence shown them in the business press even after their downfall. In another era one could picture traders picking up futures for a tibia or a finger of the fallen hero to serve unborn generations as an inspiring relic.

And yet the beginnings of the epic were humble enough. Thomas Frist Jr., a young Tennessee flight surgeon fresh out of the army had a vision. Why couldn't hospitals be run like Holiday Inn hotels? Holiday Inns changed the way people travel, bringing economies of scale, better quality and product. Instead of operating as charitable institutions, he saw them making profits by mobilising their buying power and management smarts.

At the end of the rainbow, however, was the massive spending of the federal government and private insurers just waiting for 'a financial engineer' of bold imagination. Between 1968 and 1981, Dr. Frist's HCA acquired 171 hospitals, and then he started adding related businesses — ambulance companies, laboratories, laundries. However, by the late 1980s when managed-care moneys were drastically slimmed down, HCA began finding the going tough.

Enter Richard Scott, a 34-year-old lawyer. If Dr. Frist was essentially an insider looking out, Scott was an outsider looking in. In 1987 he had begun by acquiring two small Texas hospitals, and when shortly afterwards he tried negotiating a take-over of HCA, he was laughed out of court. But by 1993 he had successfully pioneered networks of outpatient surgery centres and healthcare clinics that sought to capture as much as possible of the managed care revenue around. He introduced a new vocabulary into the business. Patients became "customers" and diseases "product lines." From a $100 million budget for TV and billboard advertising to Columbia-brand hats, shirts, license tags and even a theme-song, he applied just about every marketing trick available, and cracked the whip over the staff to achieve 15% to 20% growth rates. Stressed-out managers who could not stand the pace quit.

He had no use for the traditional arm's length relationship that existed between doctors and large urban hospitals. The purpose had been to prevent doctors as shareholders from profiting by any treatment not strictly necessary they might be tempted to prescribe. Columbia's "bottom line" seemed to become his major concern as he pressured his subordinates to reduce support staff and purchasing.

The strategy paid off. By 1993 Dr. Frist, discouraged by the new environment, sold out to Columbia. Frist, whose family retained control of 25 million shares retired to a passive role as vice chairman. Between 1994 and 1996, Columbia's revenues grew by 37%, and profits, over 60%. After languishing at around $20*s* a share it recently touched $32. According to regulators and former employees some of this was squeezed out of patients. In the corporations' hospitals the emphasis was on "revenue centres." For example, their blood banks received their blood from the Red Cross under a contract that ruled out its being sold to patients at a profit. In 1983, nevertheless, the IRS determined that at least one Columbia Hospital booked a tidy profit at its blood bank.

In March federal agents raided Columbia/HCA establishments in El Paso. In July they hauled away documents from 35 of its facilities. The publicity sent its stock into a dive. On July 25 Scott resigned. Dr. Frist took over again, vowing to straighten matters out with the federal regulators. However, Dr. Frist himself still has matters to clear up with the IRS going back to the eighties. *WSJ* (1/8) reports Dr. Frist remarking that over the next 100 days, Columbia "will evaluate all of Columbia's options — including a leveraged buyout, a recapitalization, selling out or buying another company."

"One option Columbia has studied for putting the current controversy behind it is merging with Tenet Healthcare Corp. of Los Angeles (formerly known as National Medical Enterprises). Earlier this week, Tenet agreed to pay $100 million to settle claims filed by former NM patients and their families who charged the predecessor company admitted people into its psychiatric institutions who didn't need to be hospitalized. Three years ago, NM paid $380 million to settle federal fraud charges.

Vol. 9, No. 10 — October 1997

Economic Trireme

Alan Greenspan, chairman of the US Federal Reserve, has smashed the legendary champagne bottle on the bow of the trireme that our economy has become. In the hold, shackled to their benches the slaves work the oars. There, in the real economy inflation has not only been licked, but deflation has set in. But on the top deck the passengers wallow in every luxury while speeding to an uncertain destination. There is even a vomitorium where they can disgorge so that the joyous feast and the dice may roll on. Ask no longer whether we have "inflation" or "deflation." In this best of all worlds we have both, properly ordered. One in fact feeds on the other, and nobody on the bridge is sober enough to discern the rocks ahead.

"In a speech at Stanford University, Mr. Greenspan noted the 'extraordinary rise' in the stock market, but avoided anything resembling a warning about 'irrational exuberance' such as he issued in December. The Fed [the chairman said] focusses primarily on the prices of products not on assets such as stocks and real estate." (*Wall Street Journal*, 8/9) Yet ever the wily survivor, he did slip in a bit of hedging with the remark that in the late 1980s Japan demonstrated that 'soaring asset prices' can undermine an economy even if prices for goods and services are stable.

Last December when he delivered his "irrational exuberance" remark (*WSJ*, 5/12) he was told by Wall Street types to butt out and concern himself wholly with product inflation. Mr. Greenspan is cunning enough to recognize that the banks, combining their powers of money creation with deregulation, have taken over brokerage houses and much else to become the preeminent makers and shakers in the world of mega-deals. Today they move and quack like brokerage firms rather than banks. And, the central bank, founded to keep the banks in line, has been reduced by its own doing to taking their orders.

So it has come to pass that the Fed hesitates to raise rates that would prick the hot air balloon. Since the winnings from stock trading can be spent like currency, they are in fact an inflationary expansion of the money supply. Yet this is merely taken as a just reward for our having "stayed the course" and "wrestled inflation to the ground." To justify the arrangement, the mass of our population has been cast as "consumers" thriving on the cheap goods flooding in on us through the open gates of "globalisation." What is glibly passed over is that people come on stage as "consumers" only when they have first found roles as producers. But "globalisation" adds the wretched of the earth to the dead weight of the planned domestic unemployment to keep our commodity prices flat.

The message from on high is that when the workers have learned to lower their expectations and cultivate the humility befitting their station, they will be rewarded with at least a degree of stability in their fortunes. But the very design of the globalised world, assuring the unimpeded flow of investment, has shattered that promise. To a degree this was achieved by the North American Free Trade Agreement; but the Multilateral Agreement on Investment being prepared in the demi-shadows will tighten the commitment. It proclaims investment a super-citizen armed with a diplomatic passport to come and go at its pleasure.

To attract investment with its greater "efficiencies," it is enough for the currency of an underdeveloped country to be knocked down by speculators. But like the tides, the ebb and flow of this arrangement is unceasing. This keeps the rowers in the hold of our trireme doubled over their oars. On the upper deck the constant churning of the world economy creates opportunities for mega gambles — if the exchange of one currency falls in one country it automatically rises in another like the opposite pan of a scale. And since the stock market winnings are capital gains, if not completely sheltered then taxable at very low rates, the mood on the upper deck is unclouded by the slightest twinge of conscience. The absolving code word is that these privileges of the favoured "create jobs." The financial profits of the financial sector have been sanitized under the label of "value added," but a more fitting designation would be "value extracted." For ultimately it is unpaid labour that is the prize of these mega gambles.

A great deal of human ingenuity over the centuries went into devising this near-perfect arrangement. Whenever capitalism overreached itself in inhumanity, the "dismal science" stepped in to serve as a fig-leaf for its shameful parts. Essentially it saw profits not extracted from value already produced but as "value-added," i.e. created in the course of trading including stock market high-jinks.

Entrusted with part of the creation and distribution of credit, banks have the duty of keeping a keen eye on the uses to which the credit they create is put. It must be closely enough related to real production to ensure that it will come back crowned with interest. There was a whole "real bill" theory of banking in vogue a century ago based on this — it assumed that if the banks just limited themselves to discounting the real bills resulting from the orders of producers everything would work out fine. Of course, it didn't because it ran up against the problem of inadequate effective demand that Keynes addressed in the mid-thirties. But in recent years the monetarist dogma that has taken over the banking system has effectively hidden all dependence of the financial system on real production. The bills discounted and borrowed against can be famously unreal. If enough demand is fed into the stock markets to exceed supply, the market goes on climbing like a hot air balloon.

And the banks, increasingly deregulated, are grabbing commanding positions as brokers, underwriters, insurers, vulture capitalists, mutual funds owners, derivative pimps, and whatever. Increasingly they are turning their backs on the dull business of banking proper. That leaves much of the real economy exploited rather than served. Just about everything that moves or it is hoped can be made to move is being absorbed into public companies so that underwriting fees may be earned, brokerage commissions raked in. The stock-market is being stuffed with contrived demand much like a Strasbourg goose fattened for the killing.

The flaw in the situation is that in order not to back up the price of stock must be kept rising at least at the rate already attained. For the acceleration of their climb has been worked into their price. As a result their lofty levels and momentum become as oppressive as an equivalent burden of debt.

On the Privatising Front

You may have read in *ER* that the accountancy in place in Ottawa and Washington makes it possible for our governments to sell off the White House or the Parliament Buildings for $1,000 and book a $999 capital gain — because its value was entered on our government's books at a token $1. And on doing so, you perhaps muttered, "those fellows have got to be exaggerating ." The truth is that we just don't have the imagination to top reality with anything we could dream up.

If we are guilty of anything it is understatement. The $1.00 entry for capital assets that the government enters on its books is for items it bought and paid for. If you are talking about natural resources, since they weren't bought, government accountancy treats them as though they have no value at all, not even $1. To find a parallel you have to go back to the Pilgrim Fathers acquiring land from the Indians with a few glass beads and a dose of small-pox.

Take the front page story in the *Wall Street Journal* (3/06). Last April the policymakers in Washington were so gung ho on balancing the budget that they skipped all the usual preliminaries in putting out to auction licences for airwave bands. There were no reserve bids. "Potential bidders were not given the time to develop business plans and line up financing. Telecommunications-equipment makers weren't sure what to build or what to spend. The government was strictly offering a pig in the poke. As a result Clark McLeod's firm, McLeod USA, paid $1 each for four licences that gave him the right to provide wireless communications to 15 million people in Iowa, Wisconsin, Minnesota and Nebraska. The licenses will play their part in Mr. McLeod's big plan to sell bundled local and long-distance, cellular, paging and Internet services across the upper Midwest. Bryce Nemitz, a company vice-president deadpans: 'Our CFO guaranteed we could double our money.'"

In our reports of what is possible we cited $1 as the figure the asset appeared on the government books. Here the same amount is the actual *price* in a privatisation *sale*.

"Thirteen prior FCC auctions of rights to use the electromagnetic spectrum had in the past brought in $23 billion for 4,249 licenses — or about $5.4 million a licence. But the latest auction looks more like a fire sale, with bidders offering a measly average of $106,000 a piece. BellSouth and the Atlanta-based Baby Bell, snagged licenses for Kentucky, Tennessee and the Carolinas for just $1,002 each. And like McLeod USA, two other companies paid $1 each for Missouri, Minnesota and Wisconsin licenses."

Mr. McLeod sold his first company to MCI Communications Corp. for $1.25 billion. He obviously had a better grasp of what he was up to than the government.

The Figaro of Our Newly Baked Mega-tycoons

In other cultures hairdressers have filled functions just beginning to be taken over by Web sites today. Contributing to this is probably the circumstance that most of their clients are female, who on subjects that really matter are the more communicative of the sexes. Not surprising then that hairdressers should alongside other creative artists give tongue to the spirit of our age. Figaro, Beaumarchais's barber hero who achieved his second immortality in the Mozart opera, voiced the resistance of the ordinary citizen to a licentious nobility. In our times the dominant message clamouring for utterance is from those suddenly enriched so far beyond their dreams that they have not had time to develop a style to frame their good luck.

It is quite in order then that in an article on the Figaro of Toronto's nouveaux ultra-rich, *Toronto Life* ("Mister Glitter" by Sarah Hampson, September, 1997) we should be regaled with insights into the life problems of our new upper crust in these new austere times. At $200 per cut for the first sitting and $105 thereafter, the stunning second wives of newly minted financial magnates are adoring clients of Robert Gage. Gage himself is a primary school drop-out who casually claims descent from a Norman knight who fought beside William the Conqueror in 1066. His more immediate family in England were in fact hairdressers. His wisdom is larded with nippy references to his own bisexual adventures — almost invariably with aristocrats. In the same building is an equally fashionable cosmetic surgery clinic to which he occasionally refers his distinguished clients.

Among Mr. Gage's clients is Ann-Marie Sten, 42. "She has been known as Khashoggi's Mistress since her claim to fame is her love affair years ago with the Saudi arms dealer. Now she's referred to as the Professional Girlfriend. It was at a party of Peter Munk, the Barrick Gold CEO, that she was paired with the chairman and CEO of the Bank of Montreal Matthew Barrett by Mrs. Munk, who used to romp down the same modelling runways as Ms. Sten. Five weeks later it was announced that they would be married."

The Globe and Mail (29/8) reports on the wedding. In a charming speech, the new

Mrs. Barrett "joked that she wants her husband to alter the bank's name to Bank of Monaco." She lived in Monaco until her marriage. The *G&M* comments: "We know depositors would love the subtle allusion to gambling with their money."

"It was a great week for Matthew Barrett — he also got to announce his bank's record third-quarter profit of $372 million. For a wedding gift, Bank of Montreal's board might consider paying the entire sum as a special dividend to the chairman and his new wife. It could be in the form of place settings in their favourite china, Dynasty by Minton. At $1,500 each the quarter's profit would buy 248,000 settings."

At this point *ER* must confess belittled by being reduced to quoting others on what we were coming to consider our turf. In the September issue of the "Report on Business Magazine," a veteran money manager writing under the name "Loose Lips" tells of having attended the Barrett wedding in the company of a colleague of his firm, designated as George.

George exploded: "'For Christ's sake I don't care what the analysts say, I don't want to own BMO any more, not the way Barrett's behaving. A broker or software exec is one thing, but this guy is chairman of 'Canada's first bank.' What's this guy going to do next, buy a casino?'"

"I moved to the next question: 'What'll we replace BMO with? At 6% of our portfolio we need about $80 million of another stock.'"

"'Wait a minute,' George sputters. 'Compare last year's annuals to the 1987's. These banks aren't showing asset growth in domestic loans any more; if you back out loan-loss recoveries from the real estate blowout, they are flat. They are not growing their traditional businesses in Canada.'

"I'm now pointing my finger. 'Buying US brokers, acquiring Canadian trust companies, life insurance companies, proprietary trading — that means playing the market, buying Mexican and South American banks, New York derivative groups; this percentage growth has nothing to do with Canadian banking.'

"'Exactly right!' George is now indignant. 'These bastards are taking 200 years of slow and steady franchise growth, by some of the toughest and most disciplined businessmen this country has ever produced, and spraying their stock around in the financial supermarkets of the world.'

"'Plus they have the gall to preach to Ottawa that all of their ownership constraints be lifted, so they can make the big takeover score,' I add.

"Then to me [George] adds: 'The end is beginning. Look at the way these bankers are overpaying for London Life, and National Trust, and Oppenheimer. And we have to own the one run by the biggest pirate, the guy who wants to get rich and will realize the stock prices are all bullshit so he can't wait too long!'

"I couldn't resist, 'The kind of guy with an expensive second wife.'

"'Okay, okay, so let's take our BMO weighting up another 2%,' George says."

We couldn't possibly had said it better.

Excerpts from Comments on the Discussion Paper of the Task Force on the Future of The Canadian Financial Services Sector

While inviting discussion on the issues raised, the paper of the Task Force slips in answers that preclude even the mention of alternative policies. And amongst those shut out are some that served us well during the most vibrant period of our history.

The Bank of Canada was founded in 1934-5 by a Conservative government — precisely because the private sector had proved itself famously non-vibrant. Under a Liberal government the central bank was nationalised. Because of that the interest paid on any federal debt held by it reverts to its sole shareholder, the government, in the form of dividends.

When chartered banks hold the same debt, however, that interest stays with them Any serious discussion of our financial institutions must start out from this fact. Shifting the holdings of government debt from the BoC to the chartered banks may serve as a hidden means of subsidizing them to bail them out from the consequences of their speculative excesses.

Of course, the central bank cannot load up with government debt without limit. Until recently when the legal tender created by it to acquire the bonds reached the chartered banks as deposits, it provided the money base for loans many times its amount.

But a whole menu of devices existed for preventing this. Not the least of these were the cash statutory reserves the banks had to leave with the BoC as a proportion of their deposits. These earned the banks no interest. Until 1967 they served as a means of cooling an overheated economy *without raising interest rates*. All that was necessary was to raise the ratio of the statutory reserves to bank deposits. But in 1967 an amendment to the *Bank Act* ended the powers of the BoC to vary the reserve requirement. Interest rates became the one means of controlling inflation. This seriously upset the balance between lenders and borrowers. It has been the main factor in the run-up of government debt.

At the end of the Second World War (1945) the ratio of the federal debt to the GDP amounted to 144.9% — approximately twice the peak reached in recent years. 10.5% of that enormous debt was held by the BoC at a virtual zero interest rate. Along with the low ceiling on interest rates banks could charge, that made it possible to catch up with the backlog of maintenance, expansion and modernisation of our infrastructures after a decade of depression and five years of war. From a semi-rural country the country developed into an urbanized industrialized one. A vast and mostly penniless immigration was housed and assimilated. Yet while all this was done by 1975 the ratio of federal debt to GDP had been reduced from 144.9% to 21.3% in 1976.

This was made possible by a close collaboration between Parliament and the private sector. More often than not the initiative was Ottawa's. That should alert your Task Force to the perils of ideological mantras like "Parliament cannot legislate vibrancy." (p. 5)

In the 1980s the ambitions of our banks to expand into new fields had left them in serious straits. Much of their capital had gone to finance leveraged take-overs and mega-real estate deals, Latin American loans, and much else. In banking circles then as now mega-loans were assumed to result in efficiencies of scale. Perhaps the names of Dome Petroleum, Robert Campeau and the Reichmanns will ring a bell in the minds of the Task Force.

It was to help our banks recoup their losses that an amendment was slipped through Parliament in 1991 phasing out the reserves that our banks held with the central bank. Such reserves are still a requirement in the United States.

Shortly before, the Bank for International Settlements (BIS), a sort of central bankers' bank the shares of which you can buy at your brokers, introduced the Risk-Based Capital Requirements that declared the debt of OECD countries risk-free. Business loans, on the other hand, called for 8% of a bank's own capital.

However, with progressive deregulation cum globalisation in a world of lurching interest and exchange rates, it is not possible to say what the capital of banks may be at any moment. Legal tender put up as reserves with the central bank, on the other hand, was for real. That is a distinction that should be central to your deliberations.

Right in its opening paragraph the *Bank of Canada Act* sets forth the goal of the Bank to "mitigate fluctuations in the general level of production, trade prices and employment, as far as may be possible within the scope of monetary action." In 1991 a richly orchestrated campaign was launched to do away with this "mishmash" of goals in the Act and replace it with a single one, "zero inflation." After months of hearings before the Bank subcommittee of the Standing Finance Committee of the Commons all caucuses joined in rejecting the proposal. This most unusual event was not reported by our media.

Even after the rejection of the move to put "zero inflation" into the *Bank of Canada Act*, the central bank essentially behaved as though the deed had been done. High interest rates and the resulting over-priced Canadian dollar continued to bring on mounting unemployment, until speculators outgunned the Bank of Canada and shot down our dollar by some 30% in October 1992. The BoC has since taken credit for the modest revival of our exports since then, yet only after our central bank had run out of foreign currency defending the dollar had it been allowed to drop to more realistic levels. The cost to the Government of that ill-starred defence has never been disclosed.

Along with the Risk-Based Capital Guidelines of the BIS, the end of the statutory reserves had made it possible for the chartered banks to load up with government debt while putting up little or no additional capital of their own. The *Bank of Canada Review* gives the relevant figures. In December, 1990, these added up to $23.6 billion. By September 1996 they touched $80.7 billion. To that must be added the reduction of the legal tender owned by the banks made possible by the ending of the statutory reserves. Banks avoid holding more legal tender than is necessary because it earns them no interest. Between the foregoing two dates this had dropped from $5,808 M to $3,642 M — a difference of $2,166 M. But even before reserves were abolished the release of that amount of legal tender would have allowed the banks to create 24 times as much credit — or over $48 billion.

But as we shall see, the end of reserves rapidly moved the multiplier for the banks' credit creation on a given money base in the direction of infinity (i.e. the denominator of the multiplier approached zero). For most of 1995 government bond yields — depending upon their term — varied from 7% to well over 8%. The end of reserves thus meant a hidden annual subsidy to the banks by the government of well over $4 billion. If you add the increased credit-creation made possible by the release of $2.1 billion of legal tender formerly put up as reserves, you almost double the value to the banks of the abolition of the reserve requirement.

To provide elbow-room for the banks to increase their holdings of government debt, the Bank of Canada curtailed its own inventory of federal bonds from $9,751 M in 1990 to a low of $5,053 M in June, 1996.

When COMER finally put together the details of this hushed-up government bailout, the banks and the government retorted that it was only right to have ended the reserve requirement, because it was an unfair tax on the banks. It was in fact, not only collateral for the deposits accepted, but a token consideration for the surrender of most of the government's historic rights of *seigniorage*. These derive from the traditional monopoly of the monarch to mint coin, passed through the issuance of paper notes, to the creation of legal tender in the form of government debt managed by the central bank. They are also a modest payment for the government's deposit insurance, to say nothing of the implicit guarantee for banks become too great to be allowed to fail.

By dint of repeating that the money they created was their "own money," bankers have come to believe it. That plunged them into an identity crisis. They proceeded to act not as responsible bankers but as speculative financiers. And having put itself in the position of accomplice of the banks by the semi-conspiratorial way in which reserves were abolished, our government has apparently ended up considerably in their power. In November, 1995, the Governor of the Bank of Canada, told a Commons committee that the multiplier that determined what credit a bank could create for a given unit of reserves, no longer exists. In fact by mid-1997 the ratio of chartered bank assets to the legal tender in their possession has risen from 11.1 in 1946 to 317:1.

Moreover, this leverage has been run up through loans and investments in high-risk areas. The money-creation franchise assigned to the banks by the government implies a fiduciary role. A certain quantum of money (mostly credit in our times) is necessary to meet the needs of the economy. It serves as infrastructure. If more than what is needed is created, the effect is inflationary; if less it is deflationary. We even hear proposals to pay off the federal debt. What then would be used for legal tender? Bank credit that simply disappears when good debts become bad debts during a recession?

Once the view has been imposed that credit created by the banks is just "their own money" the constant improvement of the bank's bottom line tends to become the banks' sole concern. Today our banks, having acquired brokerage houses, insurance firms, credit cards, merchant banking and mutual funds, are active on the stock and option markets on an increasing scale. The necessarily conservative bank culture is rapidly being replaced with the culture of the stock market. You can judge that not only from the feverish growth of their earnings in a frail economy. And it is only a few years ago they had lost or immobilised much of their capital. And in the midst of such ever mounting affluence, there is certainly no need for continuing the $5 billion plus entitlement introduced by the ending of reserves.

Having sketched out some of this crucial background, let us proceed to specific passages in the Discussion Paper:

• p. iii "The underlying philosophy is that competition and disclosure should be the principal motivators of financial institutions to operate in the public interest."

Before assigning the task as "principal motivators of financial institutions" to competition and disclosure, it would be well to consider whether these mystic principles might be just buzzwords.

An article by Barrie McKenna entitled "When trade deals mock trade ideals" in *The Globe and Mail* (2/9/97) concludes that "The tendency to cave in to US demands to limit exports — in return for stable access to the US market — is leading some to question whether the North American free-trade agreement is a misnomer.

"Perhaps the real name, some observers say, should be the North American Managed Trade Agreement, or NAMTA . . .

"The US pattern is to threaten the use of anti-dumping laws and other retaliatory measures. The foreign country then settles out of court as it were, by agreeing to such euphemisms as 'voluntary export restraints' or 'voluntary import expansion remedies.'"

This, of course, is no new discovery. John Kenneth Galbraith in the sixties, and the French economist, François Perroux developed their views of the markets of reality as theatres of power struggles rather than the ideological fiction of "free and perfect markets."

The Discussion Paper shows concern lest our financial institutions be prevented from ranking amongst the world's largest financial institutions by a refusal to allow them to merge. Let us recall then that the self-balancing "free and perfect market" model that is supposed to guarantee "level playing fields" simply assumes that all players are of such infinitesimal size as to make anything they do or fail to do individually without effect on the market. There is thus an internal contradiction in what the Task Force advocates.

• p. iv "The discussion paper notes the expansion in the size of pooled funds (mutual funds, pension and segregated funds of life insurance policies) . . . . Has their growth created risk for the Canadian system, and are they contributing to the extent that might reasonably be expected to the development of entrepreneurial and knowledge-based businesses in Canada?"

For the past quarter of a century and more monetary policy in Canada has been reduced to "fighting price inflation" with higher interest rates. Since much of our price rise had less to do with an overheated market than with the unavoidable provision of public services essential for a rapidly urbanizing, high-tech society, the only way of keeping prices flat was to create enough unemployment to bring on a chronic recession. Though rarely advanced by the government during elections, this has under the moniker of "Non-accelerating Inflationary Rate of Unemployment" (NAIRU) has been the benchmark of central bank policy. The goal "zero inflation" (which would call for still more unemployment than just non-accelerating inflation) deflated the real economy, and resulted in a mass transfer of wealth to lenders.

However, with deregulation banks have become financial conglomerates, with an ever-increasing involvement in the stock market. One consequence of this has been a marked change in central bank policy. While keeping a keen watch to detect the slightest increase in the Consumer Price Level, central banks have done nothing to dampen the unprecedented asset inflation on the stock market. They don't dare precipitate a market sell-off by raising interest rates; nor are they encouraged by the financial community to do so. Instead to keep the stock market in continuous ascent, it is being force-fed with every sort of demand. Privatisations of every conceivable public service — health care, highways, prisons, schools — are being promoted as a means of reducing the budgetary deficit. But the stark fact is that we are without a clue as to what the budgetary deficit might be, or in fact what it is about.

Some of us in COMER have been saying this for decades, but in its last issue the *Bank of Canada Review* (page 33) quotes a most remarkable passage from the *Public Accounts of Canada 1995-96*: "The federal government financed the cost of acquiring and maintaining such assets through budgetary appropriations, recording their book value as a nominal $1 even though the government invested large capital sums of money in them and may have incurred significant amounts of debt to finance them. Consequently, if these assets are privatised, all of the sale proceeds can be applied against the deficit, as the $1.5 billion received from the sale of the air navigation system was in the 1996/97 fiscal year. The federal government is gradually moving towards full-accrual accounting, whereby the cost of acquiring physical assets is spread over the asset's expected useful life through annual depreciation charges, and thus the true cost of such assets will be more accurately recorded in the future."

What this says is, in effect, that if the Parliament buildings were privatised at a price of $1,000 it would show the deficit and debt reduced by $999. Clearly with such accountancy there is no way of judging whether the privatisation of any asset makes sense. It discloses that the deficit may have served essentially as a panic button to justify slashing social programs. The obvious thing would be to put further privatisations on hold, and speed up the introduction of full-accrual accountancy in our governments affairs. Then we could all judge whether specific privatisations make sense or are folly — or worse.

But the opposite course is being pursued. Not only is "full-accrual accountancy" being introduced "gradually," but no mention of the subject has even appeared in the media.

And once the notion of government capital is brought in, it cannot be restricted to the "bridges, ports and telecommunications systems" mentioned in the *Public Accounts* quoted by the *Bank of Canada Review*. Equally important is the money invested by all levels of government in human capital — health. education, welfare. For the past half century economists have recognized — partly on the basis of the surprisingly rapid recovery of Germany and Japan from the physical devastation of World War II — that investment in human health and skills is the most productive of all investments. But the expenditure our government on such "most productive of all investments" is being slashed blindly to feed the speculative boom on the stock market.

• p. iv "A special initiative, taken primarily by the banks, to deal with concerns has been the creation of ombudsmen. Do these concerns with institutional responsiveness sufficient merit to require some initiative by government?

Indeed they do. It is absurd to even suggest that an ombudsman appointed and paid for by the banks rather than by the government could possible provide a serious defence of the interest of the small borrower.

• p. iv "Access to financial services by low-income and other potentially disadvantaged customers..."

The Task Force must consider whether it is not in place to restore a ceiling on interest rates that chartered banks and other financial institutions can charge. At present the only ceiling on interest rates that exists is in the criminal code — 60% per annum.

This situation in a supposed "level playing field" should be reviewed and addressed. Even a ceiling of say 15% of real interest — i.e. adjusted for any inflation — would be a vast improvement and provide the banks with generous elbow-room for legitimate banking.

The Task Force must recommend obligatory public courses at the high school level in the elements of compound interest, with special reference to credit cards of retail firms as well as banks. Literacy in the field is as vital as elementary health education — for once a person falls into the clutches of usury at compounding rates, to say nothing of advance payments and other sordid tricks of the trade — he will have neither means nor morale to look after the well-being of his family.

• p. iv "it may be difficult to support the application of regulations dealing with various issues to regulated institutions while not applying corresponding regulations to unregulated institutions." Severe limitations on interest rates and other regulations should be applied across the board to all financial institutions.

• pp. v and vi the lifting of the 10% ceiling of any class of shares of the particular institution. This is an obstacle to mergers and take-overs of one financial institution by another. This is seen "as having important implications for competition..."

It is impossible to discuss this and related issues without clearly disclosing certain fundamental facts about our banks which are not even referred to in the Discussion Paper:

1. Deposit-taking banks differ from other industries in one important respect. They have powers of money-creation — i.e. powers of lending out or investing many times the cash in hand. That puts them at a murderous advantage at competing with other

industries. It has been a great factor in our banks making an almost clean sweep of our domestic brokerage houses.

2. Why is there no mention that the world's very largest bankers most of which are Japanese have lost much of their capital and are surviving at cost to the taxpayer?

Why is there no reference to the massive crises that in recent months have swept the financial systems of just about every S.E. Asian country plus South Korea and Hong Kong, and is showing up in Taiwan and China itself? Why is deregulation taken as a given not open to discussion? In practically each of these countries currently sinking into financial crisis, severe foreign exchange controls have been introduced. That is the great No-No of the deregulation gospel.

3. Our banks are moving into unknown industries and unknown countries with a quite irresponsible leverage. And behind them is the unwritten rule — amazingly not even mentioned in the Discussion Paper — of being too large to be allowed to fail. That means that the average Canadian is at risk if they fail in their grand adventures, while of course, should they succeed, they will simply accelerate their profits and rewards to their top executives.

Conclusion

Without disclosure of these basic issues, your task force will be doomed to become just another of the mock-consultations that have been the bane of our public life this past decade. Moreover, it is late in the day, and unless your Task Force looks into the premisses of the policies you seem to support, it runs a great risk of being left with egg on its face. For it is unlikely that the greatest asset inflation on record, feeding on a deflated real economy, can continue indefinitely in its ascent.

William Krehm
Editor, *Economic Reform*

Vol. 9, No. 11 — November 1997

Hats off to Our Accountants!

A most unsettling blow has come to Ottawa's economic dogmas from the Canadian Institute of Chartered Accountants (CICA) Public Sector and Auditing Board (PSAAB). This body was set up in 1981 to provide better information, decision-making and accountability in government. Recently it issued its report. It comes out squarely in favour of introducing the distinction between investment and consumption in the public sector — i.e. to depreciate and amortize public physical investments instead of writing them off in a single year.

The two major pretexts to push through the downsizing of social programs — inflation and the deficit — emerge as fraudulent. There are those of us in COMER who made the point when the process was at its merest beginnings. Now CICA is speaking out on the matter. That stands in glorious contrast to the behaviour of other professional groups — beginning with economists and the media.

That report, indeed, comes when the Bank of Canada, with the open support of our Finance Minister, is once again increasing interest rates in a "preemptive" strike against inflation — this at a time when the unprecedented asset inflation on the stock market does not even rate "postemptive" restraint. And our chartered banks — deep in their gambles — have responded to the Bank of Canada's move by raising their rates twice as much as the Bank of Canada's increase. The banks, it would seem, really need the extra money to support their wild and wilting gambles in Thailand, Latin America and the New York derivative casino.

Critics of this ruinous policy must catch up with years of neglected homework to make full use of the CICA (www.cica.ca) report.

Not All Money Is Created Equal

Money arose to free mankind from the saddle sores of barter, but early in its career it took over other functions. It is a medium of exchange, a store of wealth, and unit of accountancy. In all these capacities it must be reasonably immune to the tooth of man and time. And above all it must be fungible. Fungible, from the Latin *fungor* — "I serve as" — has acquired a special meaning. A substance is fungible if any part of it is indistinguishable from any other. It thus provides a universal standard. This quality of fungibility is a requirement for money in all its functions (a word that harks back to the same Latin root). It is only because of its fungibility that money can serve as the common denominator of the items traded.

Historically, money is anything that society will accept as such. In primitive societies sea shells did the job. In the early American colonies, where gold and silver were scarce, beaver skins or (in the case of French Canada) pieces of playing cards were pressed into service. But these were far from satisfactory. Precious metals filled the bill far better. Yet dependence on geological cataclysms of billions of years ago and the hazards of exploration was painfully confining to the evolving commerce of the late middle ages. Banking arose to fill the gap. Merchants leaving on lengthy trips had good reason for taking as little coin with them as possible. They entrusted their fungible gold with a goldsmith in return for a non-fungible draft on his correspondent in the city of their destination. Before long the goldsmith realised that he was called upon to surrender the gold in his trust only months later. Meanwhile he could get away with lending out the deposits left him at interest several times over. This discovery immediately promoted him from goldsmith to banker. And — with the occasional mishap — he has hardly stopped moving on to grander things ever since.

Wars have ever been the mother of invention. Whereas money breeds conservatism, and bankers have always been inclined to invest their wares with mythical powers, under the stress of war the most daring makeshifts are resorted to. When precious metals ran out, credit took over. And a quarter of a century ago even the pretense of currency being redeemable in gold was abandoned. Today central banks are selling their gold stocks because they no longer serve a purpose.

As a result the problem of fungibility is resurfacing in quite novel aspects.

Credit comes in two vastly different form. The debt of governments is fungible because the undivided power and resources of society stand behind it. It is legal tender that *must* be accepted in payment of any domestic debt. Private debts, on the other hand, lack that attribute. However, most people choose to leave their cash on deposit with banks. They use cheques and credit cards for paying their bills.

But such private debt is not fungible. First of all, its credibility will be determined by the creditworthiness of the debtor. In the case of deposit-taking institutions this is strengthened considerably by state-backed deposit insurance. Moreover, there is an unwritten law, founded on rich precedent, that when a bank is too big to be allowed to fail a government does not let it fail. And Canada's banks have long been very, very big. To honour this unofficial law our central banks serve as "lenders of the last resort." That, however, is an understatement: repeatedly it has proved itself "bailer-out of the first resort."

There is another non-fungible characteristic of private debt: the amount of interest it earns. The interest paid by the government on debt held by the central bank is effectively zero. The same is the case with "folding" money held by the public. In the case of government funded debt held by the Bank of Canada the interest collected by the central bank finds its way back to the government, which is the sole shareholder of the central bank, as dividends. Even where the central bank is privately owned — for example, the US Federal Reserve — all its earnings beyond a modest figure are passed on to the federal treasury. That makes such debt perfectly fungible — every unit of it is worth exactly as much as the next.

However since the bailout of the North American commercial banks in the early nineties, the trend has been for the central banks to hold less government debt while the private banks held more. That in fact was largely the form that the rescue of the banks took. But the ugly facts of that fateful event have been covered up with an outpouring of ideological argument. The shift of government debt held by the central bank from 20.8% of the outstanding debt in the latter 1970s to a mere 4.2% currently has been justified on the most improbable ground: it was argued that the government which had just completed the greatest stroke of philanthropy in history was untrustworthy to create money through its central bank.

On the other hand the chartered banks who so recently had been the beneficiaries of that charity are presented as the only fit financiers of the government. Nonetheless the new Risk-Based Guidelines of the Bank for International Settlements declared government debt "risk free" requiring no capital for the banks to acquire. At the same time the deregulation of banking had been pushed to the point where in June 1997, the Canadian chartered banks' assets amount to 317 times the legal tender they held, as compared to the ratio of 11:1 in 1946. These are indeed swinging trustees appointed over our government's financing, and their hands are deep in the pockets of their ward.

When the non-interest-bearing reserves that the banks had held with the Bank of Canada were phased out in 1991, they were replaced with risk-based capital requirements under the new Bank for International Settlements' guidelines. But trading legal tender reserves held with the Bank of Canada for capital requirements was replacing perfectly fungible collateral with non-fungible assets difficult if not impossible to check in good time. But so deeply mired were economists in piety that they failed to notice the destruction of the fungibility in the criteria for the supervision of our high-flying banks. Tax-payers are likely to pay dearly for that oversight.

Decreasing the interest-free money creation of the central bank for the government, and increasing vastly the money-bearing government debt created by the private banks has done away with the essential fungibility of most of our money supply. Not only will one government bond issue be different from another in market value because of its different coupons, but the market value of each individual sample of government debt will change as the central bank raises or lowers the bank rate. And fiddling with the bank rate has long since become the one tool left to the government to satisfy its obsession with making a highly flawed price index lie flat. Whenever bond rates move up, preexistent bonds with a lower coupon fall below par, and vice versa. This contributes vastly to the churning of the economy which is as natural an environment for speculators as water is for fish.

W. Krehm

Out-Mulroneying Mulroney

We have been sold a bill of goods on the levelling of all barriers that might impede the free flow of speculative monies across frontiers. Its advocates presented it as both the ultimate solution of all human problems, and something impossible to resist — a rare case in theology of the inevitability of heaven. Behind closed doors more sweeping plans are under way for making this agenda more absolute and binding. But as these proceed, all over the globe evidence has been erupting that the vision is neither heaven nor inevitable. First there was the meltdown of the Mexican financial system in December 1994, and now there is the deepening trouble of the banking system of East Asia — from Japan, South Korea, Thailand, Malaysia, Indonesia, which threatens to spread to Hong Kong, Taiwan and China itself.

With every new collapse of deregulated finance, we have been offered a stock argument by the Neocon spin-doctors: the countries suffering the trauma had not proceeded quickly or thoroughly enough with "restructuring" — the code word for deregulation. But an interview with Roberto Zahler, in the *Wall Street Journal* (18/9) leaves that in shreds. An alumnus of the University of Chicago, the Vatican of free-marketry, Zahler was president of Chile's central bank between 1991 and 1996. It was during his tenure that Chile imposed restrictions on the inflow of short-term money into the country described by the *WSJ* as "among the most successful experiments of their kind." We quote passages:

WSJ: Why worry more about short-term and portfolio investment than foreign direct investment in factories and natural resources?

Zahler: I am very concerned about inflows of short-term and portfolio investment because they generally generate bubbles in asset prices and in the financial sector. And bubbles generate a transitory apparent wealth, stimulating spending and distorting the value of bank collateral. You should favour what I call risk capital as compared to financial capital. Long-term risk capital is more in the nature of long-term sustainable capital coming into the country.

With short-term capital inflows, when things are bad in the country, which is precisely when you need them, the investors go out. They usually come in when things are very good and you really don't need them.

In Chile, in the first years of the '90s, we had a very reasonable macroeconomic framework, and because of that we had huge amounts of capital, foreign direct investment and all sorts of capital coming. Then we said, "This is precisely the moment when we should try to screen this capital, because if not, we will have too much of a good thing."

WSJ: What benefits do the merging-market countries get from big hedge funds speculating in their currencies and flooding their banks with short-term money?

Zahler: To be very honest, from short-term, financial capital inflows they get very few benefits.

First, investors usually don't have enough information about the emerging markets in which they invest. For a huge American or Japanese or Swiss investment fund investing 1% of their assets, it is not worthwhile to have lots of resources invested in researching characteristics of some small countries. They probably will not discriminate between countries. This may create huge changes in exchange rates and prices of stocks and bonds that don't reflect changes in fundamentals. These investors can make huge amounts of money, not only in terms of weeks or months, but even in terms of days or hours.

But in the process of making that, they can generate such instability in foreign exchange and capital markets in an emerging country that they complicate an implementation of independent monetary policy, but the overall strategy of development of a country. I think if you can discourage them, that is something that is very reasonable for an emerging market to do."

Despite our notorious national modesty, Canadians can hardly describe themselves as an "emerging country." It is many times as large and as industrialized as Chile. Yet if it was not an "emerging land," under Mulroney it chose to become a submerging one — opening wide the gates to hot money of every sort, and indeed surrendering its national policy to its whims. Why then in the midst of the gathering disaster of deregulation, does everything seem set — with MAI in the wings and much else — for pushing on further from where Mulroney left off?

Vol. 9, No. 12 — December 1997

"De-leveraging" — the Saxon Tongue Is Enriched with a New Word

Not so long ago that Gordon Thiessen, Governor of the Bank of Canada, told a parliamentary committee that the multiplier — the proportion of credit created by our banking system to the legal tender it holds — no longer existed, though, he admitted, that had been taught to generations of students. The fact was that not only does it exist but since the ending of the cash reserves that banks had been required to hold with the Bank of Canada, it has shot skyward. Reducing the denominator of any ratio to zero is in fact the quickest way of getting to heaven.

We have been publishing an updated summary of that critical proportion from time to time to document the phenomenon. We know of nobody else who has — though it is the statistic that would have forewarned us of the traumatic asset inflation that is overtaking the world. (p. 372)

If Governor Thiessen had not been so busy suppressing all record of the thirties, he would have known that an economy is deflated by tight money, the money supply — which today consists wholly of debt — implodes and disappears. Debt, once defaulted, ceases to be money.

Instead, little more than a year ago he told a parliamentary committee that he will never forgive himself for having mentioned the word "deflation."

And when an economy is seriously deflated, you can no more ignore it than you can an earthquake. But, of course, having suppressed the old word, you are put to the trouble of coining a new one for the phenomenon.

The new word a leading *Wall Street Journal* article has come up with is "de-leveraging." It adds nothing to the elegance of the language but it does get some important folk off the hook. The caption of the piece, "As Risk Becomes a Four-Letter Word, Markets Shudder," would suggest that Nobel awards notwithstanding, risk has not become quite manageable. The authors Michael R. Sesit and Laura Jereski don't underestimate the extent of the problem: "October's global turmoil is forcing traders, investors and market analysts to grapple with a new problem: why do the flutterings of Asian markets create tidal waves that swamp a restaurant owner in Brazil?"

"The answer, in a word, is "de-leveraging." "So far, the de-leveraging has been getting little notice. But not so the volatility it causes — evident not only in the 554.26-point drop in the Dow Jones Industrial Average on October 27, but in the continued global aftershocks that rocked investors from Hong Kong to Brazil last week.

"At the same time, borrowing costs are rising sharply for developing-country bankers who themselves bet on high-octane, emerging market debt or stocks. Feeling the pinch, they are getting stingier with their own clientele at home: the restaurateur and other business borrowers. As the enormous borrowing shrinks, mercurial markets have become more prone to volatility. That's because 'investors are [selling] in one market] to cover losses in others. You lose a certain amount of your equity, then you lose the ability to leverage.' A few institutions, confident about their knowledge of smaller markets, see the current volatility as an opportunity to increase their exposure to emerging markets. Several days ago J. P. Morgan gave another $1 billion for emerging-markets investments to the bank's proprietary traders.

"Just how much leverage there has been in global markets is a mystery. But here's one clue to how much it has grown: the surge in emerging market debt trading in the wake of the 1995 Mexican bailout. Through June 30th trading in emerging-market debt instruments, more than twice as high as the 1995 volume, had attained an annual rate of $6 trillion. Korean banks snapped up Brazilian banks, and the redoubtable George Soros led the rush into the former Soviet empire.

So it is to be expected that the 317:1 leverage of Canadian banks will come down — but the statistic will lag the reality. That is because our banks will take their good time writing off their unrealized losses, because they have been losing not only leverage but with it their capital. Declaring that would bring them afoul of the BIS risk-based capital requirements. Better, as in the late 1980s, to wait until the next government bailout had been arranged, and then charge their capital losses against the philanthropy received. And having negotiated that, there will be such revival of animal spirits, that the bank CEOs will resume their public strictures on the profligacy of the public sector.

And Now Come Further Fee Increases

Whenever the banking systems as a whole gets itself in real hot water, the government has a problem on its hands. It can hardly write cheques to get the banks out of their difficulties. Instead ways must be found to effect a covert transfusion of wealth. This calls for some ingenious cover up, and the banks are brought in for their not entirely disinterested expertise. There are several paths to strike out on. The first is to increase the spread between the banks' cost of funds and their revenue — the rate spread. By doing away with the statutory reserves in 1991-94 at the same time that the Bank for International Settlements risk-based capital requirements declared government debt risk-free requiring no additional capital to hold, lowering the bank's cost of funds was achieved on a really grand scale. You simply cannot improve on zero. The banks were able to increase their holdings of federal debt by $60 billion. And then, while deploring the shortage of savings in the land, the banks lowered the interest it paid on its savings account to ½% — in the case of the CIBC actually ¼% per annum. While the banks lowered the rates they paid depositors the central bank improved the spread at the other end by pushing up interest rates. Following the banks' advice, the government also introduced further deregulation so that the banks could go out and triumph in those far-off fields that always look so green. Or failing that they could at least chalk up some losses there that would shelter the government largesse already received. And finally, it was declared they would depend more on fees.

With the troubles into which the world financial system is again sinking it was therefore predictable that there would be a new wave of banking fee increases. And indeed, the *Wall Street Journal* (11/11) under the heading "New Charges Make Banking More Confusing" reports most poetically, "A decade-long flowering of bank fees keeps sprouting new thorns." Citibank will triple the minimum balance required for unlimited free checking to $600 and raise the fee for falling below that level from $7.50 to $9.50. Some banks will tag on automated-teller-machine charges, and/or charge for mailing cancelled checks back to you. Others charge $2 extra for using a teller instead of an ATM."

Dominoes

Years ago when the Cold War was going strong, the domino model held sway. If Ollie North didn't overthrow the Sandinista government in Nicaragua, why the Reds down there would be tipping over the lily-white democratic regimes of Honduras, Guatemala, and taking Texas in no time flat. It was by grace of that theory that the Americans got into Vietnam faster than they eventually managed to get out.

But applied to the world's stock market misadventures in late October, the domino model — moving as it does in a single line — would understate things. A ripple model — like the concentric shock waves of an earthquake — would give a better idea of what is happening. Currency and stock market crises are moving out from their Thai epicentre towards all points on the compass. They triggered multilateral[†] sell-offs all over the globe — in North and South America, Australia, Europe, and even in Russia.

Yet nobody on high even so much as mentioned the word "domino." Instead we were assured that fundamentals were, are, and will be sound. This covered up the fact that the model they have peddled for a quarter of a century had become dysfunctional.

The mechanics involved are simple. With all barriers, legal and moral down, speculative money, riotously multiplied by banks become stockbrokers, surges over oceans and frontiers night and day. Nothing remains of the old moral code other than the command: "Go forth and multiply."

But there is a catch. Between low wages and high bottom lines there are tensions and incompatibilities that can attain explosive force. To keep hot short-term money in place once it has been borrowed, interest rates must be raised. And that is poison to the stock market and to the local economies as a whole.

In his *World Power and World Money* (Harvester Wheatsheaf, 1993) Andrew Walter makes the point that the international monetary system in the decades 1870-1914 was less a gold standard than a gold exchange standard with very little conversion of currencies into gold actually taking place. What kept the economies in their international dealings relatively stable was the very minor role played by the manipulation of international short-term rates. The gold reserves of the Bank of England were far too limited to allow it to function as world lender of the last resort. The much larger hoard of the Bank of France made it relatively unresponsive to gold drains from an unfavourable balance of trade.[‡] Most capital movements — from London to the Empire and North and South America, from France and Germany into Russia, assumed the form of long-term investment in infrastructures — notably canals and railways. The limited movement of short-term funds was partly responsible for the stability of the system. Insolvency of borrowers left the real investments financed in place and functioning. Often the borrower came out ahead at the lenders' expense —US railways were a notable case. Today, technology and the deregulation of our financial institutions according to the monetarist evangel have assigned an increasing importance to speculative short-term funds.

The Multilateral Agreement on Investment (MAI), if adopted, will open the door to replays of the Asiatic financial meltdown on an ever-escalating scale. Emerging countries are learning the hard way to make the distinction between hot short-term money and investment in productive facilities. They are also becoming increasingly vocal on the subject. We in Canada, however, have been slow to pick up the point. For two decades and more whenever the Bank of Canada screwed up interest rates another notch, the CBC read us the boiler-plate — "It was to attract investment." It was in fact "To choke off real investment."

After two months of spreading financial disaster, an official line is emerging to explain the extent of the Thai debacle: native corruption. Every land has its particular background and Thailand's has not been particularly blessed. During the Vietnam War it served as a glorified brothel for the American troops on furlough. Amongst the many virtues for which it was lauded in the Western financial press was its low public spending. This was made possible not only by Bangkok's rudimentary sewer system, but by the wide-spread child prostitution that largely makes do for social security.

Though it reproduces entire pages from the *Wall Street Journal*, the Toronto *Globe and Mail*, significantly, used none of the *WSJ*'s excellent coverage out of Thailand for many weeks after the crisis had struck there. With everything in place to slip in the MAI, why complicate so noble a purpose with facts? But by November 1st when Thailand had already helped bring down the Toronto Stock Exchange, our "National Newspaper" caught up with Thailand. John Stackhouse on the spot reported the Thai Prime Minister's winged words: "there was no reason for investors to leave his country when they could get three caddies on any golf course, one to carry your clubs, one to hold your umbrella and one to massage your back." He added: "Middle class Thais were able to borrow more than a year's salary to buy shares on the soaring stock exchange. Thailand's currency fell to a new low again yesterday, 40% below where it stood three months ago. Thailand and Indonesia failed to invest in secondary schooling and higher education. They found they could not compete for many higher-value industries such as electronics. Many of their basic manufactures — in areas such as toys, clothing and footwear — moved to China."

Thailand's popularity with Western mutual funds and transnational corporations flooded the country with short-term debt. Much of this was denominated in American currency, and with the national currency itself linked to a basket of dollars, yen and the money of other trading partners, the scene was set for disaster. To defend the currency against the raids of speculators, interest rates were raised — to as much as 300%. This immediately triggered a stock market meltdown. Small investors who had no difficulty borrowing against the stock, suddenly found their life's savings wiped at the same time that they lost their jobs as businesses close their doors. Financial turmoil has passed into political instability.

And all this against the chorus from Washington that "fundamentals remain sound, but reform and disclosure must be sped up." The greatest lack of disclosure is, in fact, on the part of Washington that continues presenting the combination of deregulation and high interest rates not only as *a* means of stabilising the world economy *but the only means of doing so*.

Above all mum is the word on the obvious connection between the East Asian meltdown and the dogma underlying the proposed Multilateral Agreement on Investment.

High interest rates have proven themselves once again a sure way of transmitting exchange difficulties to the world's stock markets. They chalk up massive bad loans, hopeless unemployment, and annihilate the tax base.

† Multilaterally as in MAI, the Multilateral Agreement on Investment. What we are experiencing in fact is a timely demonstration of the effects of the OECD's proposed MAI which is being prepared in the semi-shadows to be thrust on the world as a *fait accompli*.

‡ From Marcello de Cecco, *Money and Empire: The International Gold Standard 1890 — 1914,* (1974) Walters quotes the percentages of gold reserves held in 1910 by: Britain (4%), France (15%), Germany (4%), Austro-Hungary (6%), and the US (33%).

Vol. 10, No. 1 — January 1998

Like the Pox after Carnival Time

Like the pox after Carnival time — with a clear preference for the most alluringly masked — the Eastern Asian meltdown has spread from Thailand, to Malaysia to Indonesia, the Philippines, to South Korea, to Japan itself.

The quacks have had a field day. As the plague turned up in each new country, they began by proclaiming "fundamentals" to be "sound" and went on to prescribe more of the same: there had been too much restraint, too much puritanism in the celebrations. The Lord of The Free Market, they ruled, had been offended.

Japan and Taiwan, rich in foreign currency and deeply involved with the stricken countries, moved to come to their aid. But Washington held up a forbidding palm. The cure must be ladled out by the International Monetary Fund (IMF) so that the patients would undergo the necessary pain of restructuring along lines dear to Washington. Prescribed by the IMF for at least a quarter of a century, its therapy consists of slashing social services, raising interest rates, removing all impediments to the free movement of money into and out of the country. The services of this stern enforcer had been until recently required only in Third World countries, or the battered ex-Soviet states.

But now the IMF's clientele have moved up the social ladder. At the head of the list are the "Asian tigers" whose rates of growth, high morality, and emphasis on family values rather than on social welfare, had drawn the thunderous applause of the free market gurus. Why then is the demand for the IMF's dread services, rather than dwindling, attaining undreamt of proportions?

In the words of the *Wall Street Journal* (10/12): "The IMF has been at the centre of several multibillion-dollar bailouts since the 1994-95 Mexican peso crisis, *which for the first time put the global financial policeman in the position of having to deal with a huge, sudden exodus of private capital from a vulnerable developing nation — instead of the chronic current-account deficits the IMF had usually addressed.*" [Our emphasis.]

"New problems require new approaches," says US Deputy Treasury Secretary Lawrence Summers. But wouldn't restraints on the free movement of foreign speculative money across frontiers do the job — as it used to for the UK and Canada in the postwar period?

Washington began by whistling in the dark in descending minor scale. First only the impact on US foreign trade was considered, then the capital of its mutual funds, banks, and other financial institutions alluded to. Now the danger is admitted to be one of systemic failure. The defaulted Asian debts are so many black holes down which the equity of sound banks and corporations on other continents can disappear.

Day after day the Korean currency, the won, was losing the maximum permitted daily 10% of its value in terms of the dollar — by December 12th it had parted with more than 40% in a single week. The largest IMF bailout packet ever assembled — $57 billion, put in place earlier in the month — had already proved inadequate.

"Clumps of ominous-looking black-clad riot police, clutching clubs and huge plastic shields stood guard outside several merchant banks, keeping worried investors from rushing inside to demand their money." In an attempt to save the snowballing disaster the government is offering to guarantee short-term loans to securities firms.

The deficit and debt, exaggerated by faulty accountancy, served as the panic buttons to trigger the wholesale slashing of social programs..

The pattern had been endlessly improved since the 1920s. This happened partly by serendipity as financial adventurers followed their ravishing appetites. Initially the beneficiaries were money-lenders, great and small. But as deregulation proceeded, and the variety of deposit accounts and financial instruments multiplied, the central banks simply lost control of the financial system.

The result was an ever more violent lurching of interest and exchange rates. Advantage and ultimate control shifted from the passive rentier to the mega-speculators who could win fortunes by targeting unsustainably overpriced exchange rates or stock markets.

In the 1920s and 1930s public infrastructures and social services had been simple and few. But with the postwar urbanization and technological revolutions an extensive public sector had arisen. An embracing propaganda campaign presented public investments and services as invariably wasteful and private ones as ever efficient. Privatisation at bargain-basement rates was defined as always good.

This became one of the devices for fuelling the largest, wildest, and most sustained stock market booms on record. Public services had their budgets cut to the point where their standards could not be maintained, and then they were sold — in whole or in part — to private entrepreneurs. Where the public services continued it was in a deteriorated form, while those who can pay the shot availed themselves of upper tier private services.

Once privatised, infrastructures are listed on the stock market. There the bonanza of their take-over terms is capitalised and becomes negotiable into ready cash. The alchemy of such capitalisation draws on many areas. Thus in the United States between 1979 and 1982, the maximum tax rate on capital gains was reduced from 49% to 20%, and powerful lobbying is under way to remove it altogether. That acted on the stock market like a magic carpet. For it is the after-tax return on an investment that is the name of the game. Capitalised, it underpins the price of a stock.

But the sleight of hand of capitalisation is applied to the stock market itself and its indexes. If it has risen, the assumption is made that the *rate* of its increase will continue into the indefinite future, and that, too, is built into its prices.

But the resources available to support this game are soon exhausted. Taxes on capital gains and income cannot be decreased indefinitely — and public assets that can be privatised below value are in dwindling supply. Hence the untiring prowl for new means of keeping the market aloft and rising. Currently moves are under way to achieve the privatisation of retirement funds, allowing increasing portions of such funds to be invested in distant lands, where the borderline between ignorance and optimism is necessarily hazy. And above all there are the ever vaster gambles in derivatives — disembodied features of stocks, bonds, interest rates, currencies, stock market indexes in every conceivable combination.

The deregulation of the banks has permitted them to take over almost the entire brokerage industry, plus insurance, mutual funds, while the cash reserves they had to hold with the Bank of Canada to back their deposits have been phased out. This has enabled them to enlarge their leverage immensely. From 11:1 where it stood in 1946, it has now attained a record 317:1 — and an increasing amount of this is invested in central and Eastern Asia, Latin America. Banking in fact has itself become a super-derivative.

Along with the United Kingdom and Switzerland, Canada has been one of the few countries to do so — if one excepts the offshore havens like the Cayman Islands, the Bahamas, that are little more than financial bordellos.

Hot, short-term money flocked into emerging economies, and then, as interest rates were pushed up "to fight inflation," they brought down the domestic economies, usually beginning with the stock market.

And when the US Fed almost doubled short-term rates in the course of 1994, it delivered a judo chop to debt-ridden Mexico on a scale that threatened to shatter the US banking system. Fear rather than philanthropy prompted Clinton to patch together a $50 billion rescue program for Mexico.

But a few months later Wall Street was thrillingly surprised. As conditions for the bailout, Mexico was made to slash its slender social programs, raise its interest rates, open its economy wide to foreign investment. The IMF stepped in to dictate belt-tightening to people who had lost their trousers.

This not only turned the terms of trade even more in favour of foreign investors, cheapened their imports of Mexican products and the Mexican labour employed in their maquiladoras, but all this was transmuted into quite fantastic profits on Mexican securities acquired at the depth of the meltdown — 50% and better. Such interest-induced disasters were suddenly recognized as the financial equivalent of fishing with dynamite.

The Mexican experience had revealed to international high finance the high profits to be had from churning the monetary systems of the world. Even better than military conquest a financial meltdown made it possible to dictate the terms of surrender. That experience echoes through the MAI drafts.

But there is a catch — even from the victors' point of view. To understand this, we must revisit the phenomenon of capitalisation. Mathematicians long ago foretold its essence when they formulated the exponential function. This has a very special feature: its rate of growth and the rate of growth of its rate of growth (respectively known as its first and second "derivatives") and indeed all its derivatives right to infinity — equal the value already achieved by the function itself.

It is in fact the mathematics of the atomic bomb. It underlies the behaviour pattern of investment funds. Indeed, the banks themselves have become living embodiments of the exponential function.

So on one hand you have the financial world restructured as an uncompromising exponential function. On the other side is the food chain that must fuel this prodigy. Expanding production is not enough for the job. Except in the case of great technological innovations in their early years, increases in real production tend to be linear — i.e. having to do with simple momentum rather than acceleration. Moreover, by the monetarist model in force, the real economy is kept in a chronic condition of under-performance with high interest rates and unemployment. What we have then is a financial sector constantly overstimulated being supported by a real economy constrained to underperform.

To get over this discrepancy, it becomes necessary periodically to smash the weaker economies so that their capital assets can be "liberated" at distress prices, and put together again by "financial engineers" so that they may ride the capital gain up-draught.

William Krehm

A Footnote on the Exponential Function

The malignant potential of the exponential function is not to be confused with great but far lesser powers of compound interest, though some economists have been known to do just that.

A popular illustration of the ravages of compound interest involves the infant Jesus. Had the Virgin Mother on His birth invested in His name a silver shekel at a modest rate of compound interest — and on the assumption that the mature Jesus had not driven the money-lenders from the Temple — the investment would by now have exceeded in silver the mass of the globe. But note well that was at a fixed rate of interest.

Compound interest does not mess around with the dimension of time. To pocket this dazzling result even on parchment, our tiny Investor would have to wait almost two millennia. Dealing with abstract mathematical structure, the exponential function telescopes time. It was constructed by mathematicians to the specification that the rate of growth and the rate of growth of the rate of growth and so forth to infinity would equal the value already reached by the function itself (in mathematical lingo these are the first second, third, and higher derivatives).

The formula was readily structured with a bit of differential calculus, developed by Isaac Newton from the binomial theory that he also formulated. You may have encountered both of these in your final year of high school, or your freshman year at university.

The exponential function underlies the design of the nuclear bomb, of environmental and demographic disaster. Rather than something to be learned by rote it is a subject for endless meditation.

But do our speculators perform these complex calculations? They don't have to. The exponential function is implicit in the concept of capitalisation, of projecting "past performance" of a stock into the future, the whole driven by unlimited greed elevated to the supreme virtue in our society. The exponential function with its infinity of equal derivatives shapes the graphs that market analysts study. Occasionally — as in Bre-X — where there was no past performance to be extrapolated into the future, the market will even overshoot the exponential curve itself.

There is in all humans an unhappiness with the tooth of time. Some will address the problem by attempting to create something that may outlive them: family, selfless deeds, creative works. Others may settle for face-lifts. But capitalisation in this age of MAI seeks to capture the future by the tail and confine it in numbered accounts in sheltered tax havens. That threatens civilization with annihilation in many dimensions.

It Is An Ill Typhoon That Blows Up No Profits

There is an old adage that "it is an ill wind that blows no good," and in our globalised world there is no good reason for not stretching that to include typhoons in the China seas.

The Wall Street Journal (15/12) tells the story. "Just when it seemed that 50-years of free-trade momentum had ground to a halt, the economic shambles in Asia got things moving again. In a landmark pact reached at the World Trade Organisation [WTO] in Geneva early Saturday, 102 countries agreed to open their banks, insurance companies and other financial institutions to foreigners. The pact covers about 95% of financial services trade and means big banks and insurers in the US and Europe will get freer access to developing-world markets. Until now these have resisted making meaningful concessions fearing an onslaught of foreign competition would endanger their home-grown industries.

"'This is the biggest trade deal the US will ever do because there's no sector in the

US economy that will ever come close to approaching the financial-services sector,' US Trade Rep. Charlene Barshevsky said. 'The commitments made cover $17.8 trillion in global securities, $38 billion in bank lending and $2.2 trillion in insurance premiums.'

"But most trade officials conceded that it was the global financial and currency turmoil, not the torturous negotiations at the WTO, that forced big emerging economies in Asia, Latin America and the Mideast to improve their offers to the levels sought by the US."

Indeed, before the financial typhoon blew up over the China seas, the prospect of achieving their goal through the WTO had seem so unpromising, that the big business strategists had devised another course.

Paul Hellyer in his fine little book, *The Evil Empire* (1997) tells the story. "It began with the US Council for International Business which recruited the US government as its stalking horse. Along the way it has gained the support of international banks and multinational corporations, including some in Canada. The Canadian government has been aggressively promoting a treaty called the Multilateral Agreement on Investment (MAI) which has been negotiated in great secrecy by the 29-nation Organization for Economic Cooperation and Development in Paris. Originally slated for signature in the spring of 1997, the current deadline for approval is sometime in the spring of 1998.

"The treaty would make it impossible for Canadian legislators to alter or improve environmental standards for fear of being sued by multinational corporations whether operating in Canada or not. [It] would encourage multinationals to reverse a century of social progress by moving production to countries that allow sweatshops and child labour in the knowledge that there would be nothing we could do to prevent those products from entering Canada. What we are talking about is a virtual world without borders ruled by a virtual dictatorship of the world's most powerful central banks, commercial banks and multinational companies."

Now the disaster of the very free market dogma has brought its sponsors a completely unforeseen windfall. . Their victims have been delivered to them belly-up like dynamited fish.

We are thus witnessing the penultimate chapter of a tale that began towards the end of World War II when the defeat of Hitler had been achieved with the offer of new hope for the world's underprivileged rather than a resumption of the thirties.

The IMF was first planned over 50 years ago. If you wished to have a relatively stable, functioning world producing enough to raise living standards across the world, it was necessary to structure the flow of goods services and purchasing power over a relatively "level earning field."

But a deregulated market in which the player with the sharpest fangs triumphs was hardly the way of achieving that. (See 'Keynes's Most Original Creation,' page 174.)

The Civil Commons — Selling Out The Academy

One of the more poignant reminders of our condition comes from the University of Toronto, a place currently selling its academic stock to business bidders under the leadership of President Robert Prichard is one of the new breed of university presidents who spend ever more of their time ingratiating themselves to the rich to solicit funds, while euphemising the business-led stripping of public educational funding as "New Challenges" for corporate-style restructuring.

Collaboration in high places is a well-known phenomenon of occupied societies. A while ago, a business donor demanded the right to prescribe curriculum for the University of Toronto's Faculty of Management in exchange for his money gift. No problem. The business school quickly crouched to agree, and its senior professoriate publicly expressed confidence that the faculty could meet the new standards prescribed by their business patron.

Not to be outdone by the subjugation of its Faculty of Management, the U of T subsequently solicited a $6.5 million-dollar handout from the notorious financial manipulator, Peter Munk, who the year before had bribed a daughter of Indonesia's military dictator to obtain the rights to the Bre-X gold find, itself a swindle. Munk had further distinguished himself the year before that by publicly proclaiming that the mass-murderer General Augusto Pinochet of Chile was owed a debt a gratitude by us all for saving North America from the ravages of socialism. Here was obviously a man to be courted. Munk came through with the $6.5 million just prior to U. of T.'s conferral of an honorary university doctorate on Munk's business colleague and friend, George Bush, who had earned his own special recognition by such de facto crimes against humanity as destroying civilian infrastructures to protect US corporate oil interests in the Middle East in 1991. That an estimated 400,000 children died from the damage was not an issue to detain the mutually profitable exchange of academic awards for business favours.

Still, the award of an honorary doctorate to such a recipient with no hint of moral or academic standard guiding the affair incensed many still alive U of T faculty. Their most courageous members walked out of the ceremony in full academic regalia, and suffered the predictable censure of *The Globe and Mail* the next day. The new breed of academic administrators have firm corporate support for their resolve not to let educational or moral scruples get in the way of business patronage, or future directorates for academic administrators. This is the deepening university-market linkage celebrated by the new order as "the way ahead."

The collapse of the academic backbone now reaches deep into Canada's national research infrastructure. Consider a recent letter from the President of the National Science and Engineering Council to Canadian universities. The NSERC president, Dr. Tom Brztustowski, is expansive in his praise of his Council's research grants which are unashamedly in service to the imperative of private corporate profit and sales. Brztustowski celebrates such stirring advances in research for the benefit of Canadians as "the magic threshold of 250 sales that makes it [a private corporate jet] a money maker."

The Quebec multinational, Bombardier Inc., is the miracle-working corporation in question. Minister of Finance Paul Martin earlier justified such research and other subsidies to big business in times of savage cutbacks to social infrastructures as the only way to "play in this game." But to have NSERC research money going to develop private corporate jets when university students are being simultaneously converted into debt-slaves to banks to pay off ever higher education costs — well, what in Marie Antoinette's France was more in contempt of the public interest?

The sad truth is that the public funds for the university and higher research in general are being rapidly converted into a slavish function of technological development for private corporate profit, and the heads of our research institutions are only too anxious to serve the new order as their god.

The NSERC president's rise to leadership of Canada's higher research sector is a revealing one, preceded by years of outspoken advocacy for the corporate agenda. He earned his spurs as a standard-bearer in the public educational sector when he presided over it as Ontario's Deputy Minister of Education in the late 1980s, a leader of the very system which other business programmers now proclaim has been misled and must be restructured. Never mind. The truth is what you can get people to believe at the moment. But being a man of more enduring principle, Dr. Brztustowski proclaimed the overriding purpose of all public education as follows (emphasis added):

"I contend that *the one global object of education* must be for a greater capability of the people of Ontario to create wealth... [to] export products in which our knowledge and skills provide the value added... to develop new services which we can offer in trade in the world market."[†]

The enthusiasm of public bureaucrats to join in the corporate crusade for more borderless wealth for private corporations is a servility which quickly takes root in the academy's careerist culture. But an innocent question insists. Where does all this fit in with the University's historical and constitutional mission of "advancing and disseminating knowledge and learning" with "no deference to established interests"? The tragedy is that the continuous underfunding of the universities has led to a situation where senior administrators are increasingly appointed on the grounds of their willingness to turn any deal for business funds, including selling out education itself for a small fraction of the budget. This is the market's vaunted leveraging technique, taking control of enterprises with little input of cash. But beneath the magic of the money leverages, the mind-set of education bureaucrats has come to be indistinguishable from their masters. Education is accepted as a function of the global market, which itself is a process ruled by a single imperative — turning money into more money for money investors.

He declared in late November that all of the humanities as well as sociology and geography were no longer of use in the new world order. "The graduates," he opined, "have very little hope of contributing to society in any meaningful way." People of intelligence were understandably alarmed at the swing of the Harris axe at their heads. But they may not have realized the full significance of the event. Harris was announcing the moral epistemology of the total corporate culture. The meaning of life is to serve profit-making needs. The truth is what sells.

John McMurtry

[†] Cited by William Graham, "From the President," Ontario Confederation of Faculty Associations Bulletin, 6:15 (1989), 2-3.

Vol. 10, No. 2 — February 1998

MAI Shot down over the China Seas

Wave upon wave of woe washes out of the former Asian Tigerlands. Insolvent banks trigger the collapse of currencies and stock markets, disturbing balancing acts thousands of miles away. "'In Indonesia alone, the ranks of the unemployed are expected to swell by as much as 50% this year to at least 6.5 million job-seekers,' says Labour Minister Abdul Latief. Add to that 800,000 to 1.5 million of Indonesians forced to leave Malaysia, and the social and political fallout worsens for the world's fourth most populous state." (*Wall Street Journal*, 9/01)

The *WSJ* cites the case of an Indonesian bricklayer drawn to Malaysia by wages of $6.73 a day — double the going rate in Indonesia. Today he fears for his job when he still needs another year to repay the $400 dollar fee owing the labour agent who brought him to Malaysia. With the corrupt Indonesian regime already tottering as it resists the IMF's pressures to close down insolvent corporations of the ruling Suharto family, it isn't hard foreseeing the chaos as the millions of unemployed are herded from one country to another.

The Strolling Players

Unless, of course, you happen to be the US Deputy Secretary of the Treasury or the head of the International Monetary Fund, two gentlemen who flew all the way from Washington to the China Seas to put the arm on recalcitrant near-bankrupt governments. The latter, even with their reserves of foreign currency running out and short-term loans coming due, have actually started talking back!

It reads like a Gilbert & Sullivan scenario. You will have heard all about the President of Indonesia, the 76-year-old Suharto, whose fatherly love is such that he is unable to deny his children anything they set their hearts on. Only a few months ago he was reassigning the non-existent Bre-X gold from the enterprising Canadian promoters to other corporations backed by rival junior Suhartos. Concessions and government subsidies for automobile companies, shopping malls, skyscrapers, hydroelectric dams, and the clove monopoly, were handed out by the affectionate father as from a year-round Christmas Tree.

Little more than six months ago (*Wall Street Journal* 30/12) the IMF handed top marks to Indonesia "for its prudent macroeconomic policies, high investment, and savings rates, and reforms to liberalize markets." But now it is punishing the same Indonesia so severely, that Joseph Stiglitz, chief economist of its sister organization, the World Bank (*Wall Street Journal* 8/01) protests "You don't want to push these countries into severe recession. One ought to focus on things that caused the crisis."

If the IMF focussed on the things that had "caused the crisis" it would have to put itself in the dock. For at the top of that list would be the one medicine that the IMF ladles out — high interest rates. Those rates drove the East Asian industrialists and bankers to do their borrowing abroad in US dollars so that they might pay 9% rather than 18%.

Deregulation encouraged banks to invest in every sort of speculative gamble from office skyscrapers to derivatives. And when the new industries could no longer find easy markets, the house of cards crumbled. The situation could have been saved by imposing exchange controls and restricting non-essential investment in good time. But that was ruled out by what the IMF calls — most quaintly in view of the interest debtors are forced to pay on them — "free markets."

Jeffrey Sachs of Harvard told John Stackhouse of *The Globe and Mail* (13/01), "I believe that the IMF has got it so badly wrong that they're going to change direction. They are in a process now of squeezing these economies so inappropriately that they're pushing [them] deeper into crisis. The currency adjustments have virtually destroyed their banks. South Korea's auto producers are cutting back on their production sharply even though their export profitability has soared. The parts suppliers are going bankrupt because they can't get the working capital. Rather than simply paying off the foreign creditors, a lot of this IMF money should be channelled to provide working capital for exports."

To the question, "Should Indonesia declare a moratorium on debt?" Sachs replied: "It makes sense to avoid a debt moratorium if possible, but I've always believed that there are worse things than debt moratoria."

Indeed. When Roosevelt was inaugurated early in 1933, the mighty United States of America was in a crisis hardly better that of Indonesia today. 38% of the banks had shut their doors and one of the first things the new President did was to declare a banking moratorium. From that arose the drastic reform of the banking system with ceilings on interest that banks could pay or charge, and restrictions on what they could invest in.

Enter The Carpet-baggers

Not everybody is wringing his hands over the misfortunes of the Tigers so suddenly deprived of their stripes. Dow Jones Service (*G&M* 31/12/97) reports Chase Manhattan Corp., General Electric, General Motors Corp., and J.P. Morgan & Co. Inc amongst the vultures attracted by carrion aroma. With the compounding of stock market and currency collapses, "everybody and his brother are over there looking for acquisition targets," says Cay von Rumohr, Cowen & Co.'s director of equity research.

"Companies with the best chance of succeeding with acquisitions are those that have explored purchasing before the current economic crisis emerged."

This is the equivalent of stalking one's prey — a tactic of both lions and jackals. It also imparts some logic to the International Monetary Fund's prescription of high interest rates as a condition for its assistance. That, too, is a familiar hunting tactic — the use of a "beater" to drive the quarry, crazed with fear, out of the bushes.

A Powder Train of Vulnerability

In the early days of the crisis-solving the IMF and US hugged the moral high ground and bemoaned the lack of transparency of Asian banks. However, it should be noted that as the Deputy Secretary of the Treasury, Mr. Summers responded to every stage in the unfolding of the East Asian crisis as previously to the Mexican meltdown, with the assurance that "fundamentals are sound." Since that was grossly misleading for millions of small investors puzzled where to place their retirement money, Mr. Summers and his government are in a poor position to raise the question of transparency.

The lack of transparency of the Malaysians, Thais, South Koreans, and Indonesians could only be matched by the minimal curiosity of the bankers about whom they were lending to. And now it seems the wily Indonesian President Suharto is not adverse to a little blackmail before surrendering the financial empires of his family members and his cronies.

What makes the situation particularly ticklish for Washington is that "according to figures from the Bank for International Settlements, Japanese banks had lent $23.1 billion to Indonesia, rivalling the $24 billion owed Japanese banks by South Korea. No one knows just how much money Korean banks lent to Indonesia and how many Indonesian corporate bonds they bought in their global search for higher returns. 'The Koreans were up to their eyeballs in Indonesia.'"

The lines of vulnerability then lead from Indonesia to Korea, to the Japanese banks, and given their huge US bond hoard, to the US. The currency market, on which the players are big, realizes this. That is why the rupiah continued its downward course, by 6.5% after the IMF deal was signed. However the Western press headlines fatuously emphasized the 6.9% rise of the stock market rather than the currency drop.

The stock market at present has so little going on that even small transactions show up big. But what happens to the currency embraces everybody and everything. When the rupiah goes down Indonesia's $65 billion debt, contracted in US dollars, becomes ever more oppressive and drives more firms into bankruptcy.

The IMF has laid down its usual punitive conditions for temporary financing: these include a budgetary surplus equal to 1% of the GDP; increased excise taxes, scrap infrastructural projects, cut subsidies on fuel and most foods, restructure the financial sector and phase out most marketing and import monopolies. Suharto has his reasons for opposing these — some very good, some very bad.

Indonesia is reputed to hold $20 billion of foreign exchange reserves — enough to play a hand or two of poker. Beyond that he is resisting the foreign bankers' demand that the government accept responsibility for the private as well as the public debt. To counter that the government has thought out loud about declaring a debt moratorium which would have drastic repercussions throughout the region.

Mexico's debt default in the early eighties made anti-American waves throughout Latin America that must still be fresh in Washington's memory. At a deeper level popular resistance to the corrupt Suharto regime is growing by the day.

Because of the 72% plunge of the rupiah to date, living expenses are soaring as many of hundreds of thousands of workers are losing their jobs. The industrial towns of Java are seething with despair. Security forces are controlling the streets after mobs here and there have already attacked food stores.

Singapore and Hong Kong are being drawn into the eye of the storm. During the first ten days of the new year the Hong Kong market fell by 22% — more than its decline during the previous ten months. And here again, there is little information about the involvement of the Singapore banks in Indonesia. The latter do not report on their non-performing loans or on the distribution of their loans by country. Some analysts estimate the percentage of Singapore Bank loans that are nonperforming at 5% or 6% — about the rate in the US during the Savings and Loan crisis of a decade ago, compared to 1% or 2% figure usual in healthy banking systems.

The effect on Hong Kong is more readily documented. Hong Kong banks long served as intermediaries investing money from Thailand in South Korean junk-bonds that served to finance much of its former growth. Now disaster has struck at both ends of this chain. Peregrine Investment Holdings Ltd., not so long ago "Asia's most powerful home-grown investment banking firm, has overnight appeared on intensive care because a $265 million bridge loan to an Indonesian company was not repaid. That led to the cancellation of a $200 million capital injection by the giant Swiss insurance Zurich Group, and affected the prospects of its own creditors including First Chicago Corp..."

The *WSJ* (12/01) emphasizes the long reach of Peregrine's troubles: "Also worrisome is the so-called counter-party risk of banks and other financial institutions that have engaged in currency swaps with Peregrine. Peregrine helped many Indonesian and Thai companies issue large amounts of debt securities denominated in rupiah or baht. When many potential bond purchasers were reluctant to assume foreign-exchange risk themselves, Peregrine would itself take on that risk. Often Peregrine paid a bank with a high credit rating to act as guarantor and pay the client in US dollars." Now with Peregrine practically *hors combat* these banks are left on the hook. One of Peregrine's close associates has been Li Ka-shi, well-known in Canada for his real estate and other investments. The repercussions may thus be felt in Canada's real estate and other markets. East Asian students are already dropping out of Canadian universities where the high fees they paid have helped our universities get by on shrinking government grants. No man is an island, and in any case all islands are volcanic in this globalised world.

The Next Bailout of The Banks Is Already Planned

To better follow what is going on in East Asia, one must sort out three distinct classes of problems. These do, however, overlap. There are jurisdictions like Japan, Taiwan, Hong Kong, and China that have large foreign currency reserves, but whose banks have either lost much of their capital or find it frozen in non-performing loans. A key motivation in South Korea's bailout has been Washington's concern that the spill-over of Korea's troubles could trigger the collapse of the shaky Japanese banking system. That in turn would certainly bring on massive liquidation of the Japanese banks' hoard of US government bonds. That bond hoard has its own peculiar history.

To bailout the Japanese banks from their losses in the late 1980s, they were encouraged by their government to accumulate US federal debt. Accordingly they borrowed money from their central bank at 0.5% to finance their holdings of US bonds yielding 6% and more. The low yen and the booming exports that resulted provided the dollars for the purpose and secured the banks against exchange losses. The sudden liquidation of these holdings could lead to a collapse of the US bond market, and drive up interest rates with murderous effect on the US stock markets.

"That is why ideology has been laid aside and there is such undoctrinary enthusiasm for having private Korean debt to the Japanese banks changed into obligations guaranteed by the Korean government.

To appreciate why, we must hark back to an equally schizophrenic arrangement sponsored by the Bank for International Settlements, the central bank of central banks and keeper of the purest deregulated monetary faith. This was the BIS Risk-Based Capital Requirements to help banks around the world over their speculative losses. These requirements declared the debt of OECD countries to be "risk free"; banks could purchase it without putting up any capital of their own. In the light of that, private debt guaranteed, no matter how feebly, by the South Korean government could help the Japanese banks meet these BIS standards.

The monetarist dogma has unravelled in the Far East. Declaring high interest rates the one lever for managing the economy had a great deal to commend it to those who live on interest. But as a tool of monetary management it makes no sense. It provokes head-on collisions between the interests of the stock market, balance of payments and the support of the local currency. Along with deregulation, it enhances the prepotence of those with access to both savings pools and powers of money creation — in particular Wall St. whose currency is the reserve currency of most of the world.

The New Buzzword out of the Murk — "Transparency"

With the east Asian banking crisis spreading world-wide, we no longer hear the assurances from the US Treasury that "fundamentals" in the stricken countries are "sound." Instead "a new buzzword" has come to the fore — "transparency." The IMF reproaches the afflicted banks with a lack of "transparency," while the Bank for International Settlements, where deregulation, the substitution of "capital requirements" for reserves in legal tender were hatched, complains that "international banks ignored warning signs from East Asia in the first half of 1997 and continued to lend fresh money to South Korea."

BIS does not cite its own timely warnings on the subject which, if they existed, would certainly strengthen its case.

Lending by global commercial banks to South Korea rose during the first half of

1997 by $4.9 billion to $103.4 billion by mid-1997. Short-term loans made up 67.9% of the total amount, due to be repaid within a year or sooner. European banks were the most aggressive in fighting for loan business in South Korea and Asia as a whole, their share rising from 30.5% to 35.1 during the previous year. Japan's troubled banks, though still the largest individual group of creditors, saw their share drop from 24.3% to 22.9%.

No matter how unforthcoming the international financial institutions have been in seeking ways of addressing the unholy mess, some key information is coming to light. Dearly purchased, this should not go wasted.

Bankers are firm believers in the free market and in governments keeping their snouts out of banking affairs. Right? It would appear not quite. Thus the *Wall Street Journal* (2/1) writes: "US bankers remain deeply concerned that they don't know the true scope of lending problems in Japan because of poor disclosure. The Ministry of Finance last week estimated that problem loans totalled $223 billion, but many bankers believe the figure is much higher. 'Do we really know exactly what the loss ratio is at all of the banks?' asks one US banker close to the discussions. 'A lot of people don't think the Japanese government does. The way some banks in Japan ran was that a district manager would be perfectly happy to hide a loss for a long time in his own little office. When do these finally percolate back to corporate headquarters, and was that ever counted before?' Still, the failures this fall of Hokkaido Takushoku Bank and brokerage house Yamaichi showed US bankers that Japan could absorb large blows. Bankers also are pleased with Japan's recently approved plan to use public money on the banking crisis, though the money isn't being disbursed as quickly as some Americans would like. Unlike other Asian countries, Japan has huge stores of cash reserves on hand."

So much for leaving matters to the all-wise free market. But the really amazing paragraph in the article comes next. "As discussions among US bankers continue over a long-term solution for Korea, the Japanese are letting it be known that they are likely to support any plan that turns private South Korean debt into obligations guaranteed by the Korean government, whether debt is repackaged as bonds or as straight syndicated refinancing of some kind. The reason: Even a government guarantee from an industrialized nation like Korea, no matter how feeble the guarantee is, would help Japan's banks meet global standards of soundness and stay active in international markets."

Japan's loans to Korea and elsewhere are mostly denominated in US currency. Accordingly they grow in value whenever the dollars edges higher against the yen. That calls for more capital denominated in yen.

Transparency and non-transparency accordingly are largely in the preacher's eye.

Denouement

In well-constructed plays and less well-planned crimes, the final act brings surprising disclosures. The present financial crisis in East Asia is no exception. At times it even seems that the doctor might be exploiting the helplessness of his patients for purposes that old Hippocrates would not have approved...

The *Wall Street Journal* (15/12) has been led to some un-Christmas-like reflections on the subject. "Around the region, bankers and traders are fretting that governments will refuse to take the medicine prescribed by the International Monetary Fund, or, worse, that the IMF got the prescription wrong. The new and worrying outlook for Asian currencies, particularly the Indonesian rupiah and Korean won, is that they have fallen victim not to speculators or government driven devaluations, but to panic demand from companies about to go bust. Many companies in Asia have borrowed heavily in dollars; now that the dollar has soared in value against local currencies, these loans are suddenly worth much more in terms of rupiah and won. In South Korea, where the won has fallen further against the dollar than any other Asian currency, there is hardly any company that is solvent.†

Korea's economy — having ridden the opportunities put in its way by the Cold War — became the 11th largest world economy. Its investments in many part of the world remind one of Japan during its most dynamic successes. "For years its conglomerates (*chaebols*) operated with debt loads that were several times as large as their equity capital." They brought together the most diverse industries and were but the ultimate instance of the Merger and Acquisitions craze that has kept Wall Street above the clouds during the past few years. Favouritism in the distribution of credit, now suddenly deplored, was presented on occasion as a superior family ethos.

Rather than the level playing field it is celebrated to be, the deregulated market of the West often just removes barriers to the ambitions of those with access to the largest capital pools. That empowers the plugged-in to take advantage of tight money to devour the less well-connected. The moment of truth comes when the lenders demand the repayment of their loans all at the same time. At the bottom the East Asian crisis is simply the Western system come to flower.

And because of its spectacular success in playing that game, Korea was evolving as a serious competitor of US interests. "Many of the planned Korean investments (now put on hold or worse), were symbolically important, heralding South Korea's debut last year as a full-fledged industrial country and its conglomerates as big-name multinationals. [Its] Daewoo Corp., leading the parade of Korean businesses abroad, just this year broke into the United Nations' list of the world's 100 largest corporations. Distant Uzbekistan, in Central Asia, earned the nickname Daewoostan because of Daewoo's investments there. Foreign investment in much of Eastern Europe was similarly dominated by the chaebols. They had plans for increased invasion of the US market itself. "Next year the six biggest Korean conglomerates tegether planned to invest $80 billion abroad by the year 2000, very much in the Japanese pattern but concentrating on markets where the Japanese had not made their presence felt."

To make all this possible the very language was rejigged to confuse and misinform. Take the word "reform" that has become the categorical imperative which sets the price of the IMF's life-lines cast to the drowning. All embracing, it is never really defined. At times it includes corrections so desirable that one could recommend them for the US itself — for example, discouraging corruption and favouritism in granting credit and trade concessions.

But what are we to say about the demand for the immediate liquidation of firms made insolvent by dollar-denominated debt? Here the position of the US and the IMF surely smacks of the lemma, "Do as I preach, not as I practice." When the S & L scandals overtook the US in the eighties, there was no insistence that the insolvent institutions be sold off overnight. That would have endangered the entire financial system of the US. Instead they were gathered into the broad bosom of the state and sold off in a more or less orderly way over the greater part of a decade. Nor has it ever been documented that political favouritism was entirely absent in the process.

Why then the insistence on an overnight liquidation of the insolvent firms as a condition for assisting the stricken countries to meet next week's dollar obligations?

And why the utter exclusion of the most proven first-aid by which debtor countries used to meet their foreign exchange commitments without having the flesh picked off their bones? For example, temporary exchange controls?

† In the light of the shattering currency crises in East Asia, Canadians must review the advice peddled by David Laidler and William Robson in their *Don't Break the Bank! The Role of Monetary Policy in Deficit Reduction* published by C. D. Howe Institute in 1995: "A government that believed in the effectiveness of its inflation and deficit targets would issue more indexed and foreign currency debt."

Vol. 10, No. 3 — March 1998

From the East Comes Light

If with considerable delay, light has begun streaming in from the Far East on two of the most dramatic issues facing Canadians — the proposed merger of two of our largest banks and the proposed Multilateral Agreement on Investment (MAI). Our Prime Minister has even scoffed at the Royal Bank's argument for that merger on the grounds it has fallen from its previous position as 12th largest in the world to the 57th. We were delighted to see somebody in the government finally picking up what we had been saying for many months: the Japanese banks that are the world's very largest banks have been surviving on alms from the taxpayers for some years. Canadians have no more interest in helping our banks win the banking Olympics, than they had in helping Robert Campeau become the world's largest collector of department store chains.

The Indicator (p. 372) that *Economic Reform* publishes from time to time tracks the crucial ratio of our banks' assets to their legal tender. In 1946 it was 11:1. In 1990, on the eve of the phasing out of reserves it had — with extensive deregulation of banking — already attained a value of 102:1. By the second quarter of 1997 it had already reached 348:1 and was rapidly soaring.† Moreover, the rise in the leverage of the banks' investments was parallelled by the increase in their riskiness. For such a banking system to reproach the East Asian banks for their lack of transparency, is a clear case of the kettle calling the pot black.

These are the statistics that our Prime Minister must ponder in taking a stand on the merger of the Royal Bank and the Bank of Montreal. To discuss it only in terms of the merged banks' staff reduction is to trivialize the issue. Adequate banking services are a life-and-death need for any economy. To depend for that on the competition of international banks won't do. The large international banks are more interested in competing with our banks in profitable underwritings, derivatives, and the big-dice gambles that have come to define international banking.

Our government must make available a new class of banking charters that will limit their holders to small and medium-scale banking for consumers and business concerns. Such charters would be valuable assets and would not go begging. Nor would there be a lack of personnel with rich experience in traditional banking to staff and train this new category of banks. Our banks' downsizing of their staff engaged in retail banking guarantees that.

In addition the reserve requirement must be brought back for all deposit-taking financial institutions. A backup plan must be drawn up to for the bailout of our banks the next time they get themselves into trouble. The above figures on the banks' exploding asset leverage underline the urgency of such a step. We cannot risk finding out once more that the bailout has taken place behind the backs of the public. *Transparency is a bright and shiny word, but like charity it begins at home.*

The Multilateral Agreement on Investment is also on trial in Eastern Asia, and the verdict is coming in loud and clear. Outlawing exchange controls at the very time that finances are being globalised makes as much sense as would the banning of sand bags and dykes in areas threatened with flooding. The deregulation of banking has allowed international lending institutions to prove themselves as responsible for the East Asian mess as the local borrowers. Unlike the IMF, the World Bank has expressed that conclusion. For our government to lock the country into commitments that have already failed so resoundingly in East Asia, would be the height of irresponsibility.

† [It is understating the point to include the scant legal tender held by the banks today in the denominator of this crucial ratio. For it fills the operational needs of the banks, and is not available as collateral for the money created by the banks.] This alarming trend resulted both from both deregulation and the systematic whittling down of the reserve requirement leading to the completion of its phasing out in 1994. The figures Mr. Chrétien can find in the *Bank if Canada Review*, Fall 1997 p. S25 (C6) total liabilities of the chartered banks for the second quarter of 1997 $1,203,149,000 and legal tender held by the banks on page S14 the sum of columns B403 (BoC notes and coin) and B404 (deposits at the Bank of Canada).

The Common Sense Revolution Rides the Subway in Toronto

Toronto has long prided itself on being a well-run city of clean streets and minimal violence. However, if you come to Toronto and ride on our gleaming subway these days you may note that the passengers on the platform are lined up with their backs against the wall. Why? Thereby hangs a tale.

Part of the so-called Common Sense Revolution of the Harris provincial government was to balance its budget, and even before doing so, to cut taxes. And to make that possible social services have been slashed across the board. Among much else the beds in psychiatric institutions have been reduced. That is why Torontonians have been startled to encounter clearly deranged fellow citizens on the street shouting obscenities at nobody in particular.

More recently the fruits of the "Common Sense Revolution" in this area have assumed still more alarming forms. In late September, a 23-year old law clerk was pushed to her death from the platform of a downtown station by a deranged unknown, and died after at least two cars had passed over her. Since then the copy-cat pattern seems to have asserted itself. Attempts to push people onto the tracks of Toronto's subway have averaged about one a month. Paul Copeland, the lawyer defending the accused in a recent incident of this sort, sums it up: "There's a lot of disturbed people out on the streets, there are a lot of people falling through the cracks, and it's frightening." (*The Globe and Mail*, 7/02)

"A Canada Post letter carrier, John de Marco, who has been riding the rails on his delivery rounds for 30 years, offers yet another perspective. 'Commuter behaviour has deteriorated sharply. People are quicker to let themselves go into a rage. You're in a vulnerable position.' One suggestion is for plexiglass barriers at platform's edge, which would open only when an incoming train comes to a full stop. Another is that a subway employee be posted on each platform to watch for suspicious types. The Toronto Transportation Commission security chief would rather see the money spent on mental-health care programs. Public-spending trends, however, are heading in just the opposite direction ...cutbacks consistently seem to penalize the neediest.

"'Where do people go to express their rages?,' asked Lilleth Finkler of Parkdale Community Legal Services. 'People lost their housing because the funding is gone. They lose their social assistance. Their doctors leave to go to the US Their social workers get laid off. So where do they go?'

"'If I want to scream in my house, I don't disturb anyone. But if someone lives in a very small room, with very little soundproofing, someone's going to call the cops to complain.'

"'And the same may hold true on a bus or a train. A lot of people are a little crazy around this town as of late.'"

Did the Emperor Ever Wear Any Clothes?

What follows is an exchange between William Krehm, and John Crow, former Governor of the Bank of Canada.

Round One — "Banks Go Begging"

Letters to 'Report on Business,' *The Globe and Mail*, Monday, January 26, 1998.

Re Terence Corcoran's column "Bankers get out begging bowls" (Jan. 14).

By the time the CIBC made its pilgrimage to Ottawa on behalf of its insolvent client, the Reichmanns, the bailout of the banks themselves from these and other losses had already taken place. It took the form of the phasing out of the reserves in legal tender that they had to hold against their deposits, which was slipped through Parliament in 1991.

This, combined with the Bank for International Settlements' risk-based capital requirements that had been drawn up in the late 1980s, enabled our banks to load up with government bonds without putting up a penny of their own legal tender. The BIS guidelines declared the debt of OECD countries (the OECD includes South Korea) risk-free, requiring no supporting capital for banks to acquire.

In fact, of course, nobody's bonds can be completely risk-free, as claimed by the BIS. It is enough for central banks to raise interest rates for all existing bonds to drop in value.

The bailout of our banks by the Bank of Canada enabled them to increase their holdings of federal debt by about $60 billion. That has allowed them to tap into the federal treasury for about $5 billion annually, mostly in interest payments. If those bonds were held by the Bank of Canada itself, the interest paid on that federal debt would have substantially reverted to the government in the form of dividends.

The continued deregulation of what the banks can invest in has made it possible for them to engage in dare-devilish gambles, not excluding the purchase of banking interests and derivatives in East Asia. This, in turn, guarantees that they will be travelling to Ottawa with their begging bowls once again in the not-too-distant future.

William Krehm
Toronto

Round Two — "Banking Rules"

Letters to 'Report on Business,' *The Globe and Mail*, Monday, February 2, 1998.

Re the letter from William Krehm (Banks go begging — Jan. 26).

Mr. Krehm suggests that the phasing out of chartered banks' required cash reserves against deposits was inappropriate and that it was "slipped through" Parliament. I beg to differ. Admittedly, the removal of bank reserve requirements was not a Bank of Canada initiative — the bank has no jurisdiction in this area. However, the bank was consulted by the Department of Finance and indicated it was in favour of the action on grounds of competitive equity. Non-bank deposit-taking institutions bore no such reserve requirement, though they were increasingly getting into commercial banking. Accordingly, the reserve requirement constituted a discriminatory tax on the banks. The Bank of Canada also assured the minister that the elimination of these reserve requirements would not diminish its capacity to implement monetary policy.

Regarding the introduction of Bank for International Settlements' risk-based capital requirements, one must distinguish between credit risk and other kinds of risk. The initial risk-based capital requirements focussed largely on credit risk. It is in that context that the Group of 10 countries agreed to put a zero weighting on credit risk for the central government debt of Organization for Economic Cooperation and Development countries. Choosing the countries for whose debt this weighting would apply was difficult, and the criterion of OECD membership was seen as a fair compromise. But at no point was it declared that such debt was entirely risk-free or that interest rate risk did not matter.

The BIS agreement has since been refined to incorporate into the capital calculations other kinds of risk beside credit risk. Also, both in Canada and elsewhere, national regulators have insisted all through the BIS exercise on banks holding a basic minimum amount of capital regardless of the particular mix of their assets.

To see all this, as Mr. Krehm does, as a "bailout of our banks by the Bank of Canada" is simply perverse.

Finally, I totally disagree with Mr. Krehm's wish that the Bank of Canada should somehow have bought the $60 billion of federal debt he estimates was acquired by the chartered banks. The banks financed this acquisition by raising deposits from the public. What Mr. Krehm appears to be proposing is that the overall rate of Canadian money creation be determined by the pace at which the supply of government debt expands. He may wish to suggest that the way out of his box is to impose a massive cash reserve requirement on chartered bank deposits. But this brings us back to where we started — a discriminatory tax on banking that, furthermore, varies with the size of government debt.

John W. Crow

Toronto

Knock-out

Tuesday, February 3, 1998

Re Banking rules from John Crow (2 February) commenting on my letter of 26 January.

Mr. Crow's letter abounds in quasi-facts that do not stand up under inspection.

A few samples:

The Bank of Canada when consulted by the Department of Finance on the removal of the legal tender reserves that banks had held with the Bank of Canada and earned them no interest, "indicated it was in favour ...on grounds of competitive equity. Non-bank deposit-taking institutions bore no such reserve requirements."

Canada then could have followed the American example of extending reserve requirements to non-banking deposit-takers. Instead, by phasing out the reserve requirement it put Canadian producers at a competitive disadvantage with their US counterparts since it allowed our banks to load up with another $60 billion of federal debt without putting up a cent of capital of their own.

This contributed to the federal debt which prompted Governor Crow to push up short-term rates five percentage points above the American figure. (The interest on government debt held by the BoC reverts substantially to its one shareholder, the Government of Canada.)

"Accordingly, the reserve requirement constituted a discriminatory tax on the banks."

It was in fact a token payment for the government assigning seigniorage to the banks — the right to create money that today is almost wholly debt. In addition the government backstops deposit insurance, and bails out banks "too big to fail."

Even the Bundesbank and the US Fed have retained the reserve requirement. But perhaps the greatest cost of the reserve phase-out, is the identity crisis of our banks brought about by the government and the central bank repeating that reserves were "their own money being unjustly taxed." Without that the present display of arrogance by two of our largest banks in a mating mood would have been unthinkable.

"BoC also assured the minister that the elimination of these reserve requirements would not diminish its capacity to implement monetary policy."

In fact the end of reserves was only the latest of a series of measures that have completely undermined the capacity of the central bank to control monetary policy. As late as 1970 reserves had consisted of 10% of deposits plus secondary reserves (interest-bearing paper) of 8%. By 1990 they had been whittled down to about 4%. Until 1967 it had been possible for the BoC to cool an overheated economy by raising reserves. Today raising interest remains as the lone "blunt tool" of the BoC to control inflation or defend our currency.

"Regarding the introduction of Bank for International Settlements' risk-based capital requirements, one must distinguish between credit risk and other kinds of risk."

We always have, but the only relevant fact is that the BIS requirements permitted our banks to load up with some $60 billion of debt as though there was no risk involved. And that is why the international banks, contrary to their deregulation dogma, are bargaining for South Korean government guarantees of defaulted private debt. In that way, it would appear on their books as risk-free.

"The banks financed this acquisition [of the $60 billion increase in government debt] by raising deposits from the public."

Not so. When a bank takes in $1 as a deposit it appears as an asset in its till and as a debt on the other side of the ledger. It in no way changes its capital position. Mr. Crow can confirm this by consulting the nearest accountant.

"What Mr. Krehm appears to be proposing is that the overall rate of Canadian money creation be determined by the pace at which the supply of government debt expands."

It is odd that Mr. Crow should think so when he is defending money creation by the banks by a ratio (assets over legal tender in their possession) whose denominator is approaching zero. Phasing in reserves would in fact discourage the banks from holding their present mountain of government bonds. In 1946 that ratio was 11:1; by 1990 it was around 102:1. In the first quarter of 1997 it had attained 317:1, three months later it was 347:1.

Moreover, the Office of the Superintendent of Financial Institutions has confirmed to me that "in the vast majority of cases the derivatives held by banks are off their balance sheets." Derivatives are highly leveraged bets on futures that led to the bankruptcy of Barings and other banks famous and infamous.

With financial deregulation, no one can say what a bank's capital might be at any moment. A 10% reversal of the stock market, on top of the E. Asian disasters ricocheting across the globe, can wipe out the greater part of our chartered banks' capital. That is why Mr. Thiessen was so hesitant to raise interest rates to defend the dollar or cool the most extravagant asset inflation in our history.

Now that he has finally done so, we are put to every sort of risk. Repeatedly during the War and after, Canada effectively defended our dollar with temporary exchange controls. And banks of course, were obliged to stick to banking, rather than engaging in overseas adventures. Their enhanced demand for foreign currency for these heady games cannot but contribute to the present weakness of our dollar.

William Krehm
Toronto

Get Thee to a Monastery, Mr. Thiessen

Pity poor Governor Thiessen of the Bank of Canada. He inherited the top post in a world so magically simplified that to run it all you had to do was lean on a single button.

But the formula no longer works. The Bank of Canada, set up in 1935, had originally put the chartered banks on a tighter rein to pull the country out of the Great Depression. The banks were severely limited as to the interest they could charge, and the investments they could make. But by the early 1950s, with the Depression behind them, the banks began lobbying for deregulation. Step by step they were allowed to slap on what fees and interest rates they wished. A revision of the *Bank Act* was slipped through Parliament in 1991 to end the reserves they held with the Bank of Canada. Long since whittled down from 10% to around 4%, these reserves had served as collateral for the deposits made with them. By raising the reserve requirement, the central bank had been able to brake the banks' lending *without* raising interest rates.

Then something began happening that is not unusual in the relations of regulating authorities and the industries in their charge. The dog on the leash took over and dragged its master where it wanted to go. In time the banks were digging up every flower bed and had a hind leg cocked at every tree in the neighbourhood. They took over 80% and more of the brokerage houses, they acquired derivative departments, gambled for their own account on the stock, commodity, and currency markets across the world. They lost interest in providing the dull banking services the country needed..

Until several months ago, it was apparent that Governor Thiessen was too frightened to lean on his one magic button — high interest rates — to rein in the asset inflation that had taken over the financial sector. The Canadian dollar was under pressure that redoubled as the East Asian crisis progressed. But raising interest rates to protect our dollar would bring the stock market crashing.

Eventually Mr. Thiessen did raise interest rates not once but twice. And he is likely to go on repeating that move as the international financial system unravels. What else can he do, with his ingrained belief that he has only that "single blunt instrument"? That defines the "main enemy" for him — "inflation." To maintain that creed its opposite — "deflation" — can't even be admitted as a possibility.

On (8/05/97) *The Globe and Mail* reported Mr. Thiessen worrying about "deflation." But only a week later (*G&M* 16/05), Mr. Thiessen had assured the Commons Finance Committee "that he will probably regret forever having mentioned 'it.'" One must ask why?

Especially since it is increasingly clear that today deflation is spreading across the globe. Unemployment in Germany has risen to the highest since World War II — 12.6% and has resulted in cuts in jobless benefits, and nation-wide demonstrations. The Commodity Research Bureau index (heavily weighted with agricultural products so important in North American exports) fell to a 3.5 year low last month (*WSJ* 5/02/98). Industrial commodities were down nearly 10% in late September "after sliding for more than two years — the largest decline in a half-century." Crude oil prices have dropped 25% since the fall. The East Asian collapse for the time being has up to now been felt in the US more through a shrivelling of its exports than by a flood of cheap imports. The short-term credits that would allow a jump in ultra-cheap East Asian exports are still not available to East Asian producers. When they are, they will further depress world prices.

Against this background, Parliament must cross-examine Mr. Thiessen on his vow never again to pronounce the word "deflation." Just who exacted that view from him and why? Failing a satisfactory answer, Mr. Thiessen must be released so that he can get himself to an appropriate monastery where vows of silence are more appropriately made and kept.

William Krehm

The Fly in the Soup — Deflation

Redefining Deflation

The similarities between now and 1929 are overwhelming. Then, too, there was no commodity inflation, though that is what the bankers and economists were looking under every bed for. The stock market kept on soaring. Economists put that down to the dawning of "the New Era." Right to the day of the crash. Something very similar is occurring today.

The performance could hardly be complete without William Robson of the C.D. Howe Institute. "[Robson] said he wouldn't use deflation even to describe several years in which the overall price level fell by half a per cent annually. 'That's pretty close to price stability.'" We have yet to hear him say that he would not even describe several years in which the overall price level rose by half a percent annually as inflation. Then *G&M* goes on, "He would reserve the word for a period when 'prices are falling so fast that the best investment you make is money in your mattress.'" If that should occur you may be sure that Robson would be defining deflation as when you no longer *had* a mattress to put your money in.

Vol. 10, No. 4 — April 1998

The Civil Commons — Coup d'état by Silencing : What The Corporate Media Do Not Let Us Know

The meltdown of the 'miracle economies' of Asia has given rise to some perplexity. How could all of these economies which had 'the fundamentals right' suddenly collapse together overnight?

Since the unregulated international financial system which caused these failures cannot be wrong, the fault must be the simultaneous and sudden sin of the economies involved. But people are beginning to disbelieve this fairy tale. They know something else is afoot.

For just as the Multilateral Agreement on Investment (MAI) is being negotiated to open all the economies of the OECD still further to these deluges of unregulated money flows, the miracle economies themselves lie bleeding on the floor.

So what does the International Monetary Fund do to rescue the failing system as it careens across continents leaving ever more broken societies in its wake? It leads a publicly-funded rescue package to lend ever more billions to keep the hot money going — over US$100 billion at last count.

But make no mistake. It is not Indonesia or South Korea or Malaysia or any other country which is being "bailed out" by this bottomless pit of emergency loans. It is this ruinously deregulated financial system itself and, more directly, the loan capital of international banks which stand to lose big from unpaid interest and debts if the money is not kept churning to them by the injection of countless billions into drained national accounts.

It is the foreign banks and creditors who lent the money who are, in fact, being bailed out. All that is being received by these mortally wounded societies is massive new debt to keep paying their external creditors back, along with a large dose of more financial deregulation to colonize them further.

At some point, the world's public who are paying for this stripping of their societies to enrich the high-volume and velocity flood of deregulated money around the globe will awake from the nightmare imposed upon them by this mindless model of 'market freedom.' My bet is that we are beginning to already.

John McMurtry

Vol. 10, No. 5 — May 1998

Springtime of Megamatings

The delirium of mergers has reached proportions where any multibillion dollar bank that does not find a partner yesterday considers itself doomed to the long-toothed solitude of a Victorian spinster.

American banks in their thousands, cast a shadow on anything that can happen in Canada which entered the exercise with only five really large banks. After only two betrothals, the sole remaining biggie, Scotia, is reduced to seeking a spouse south of the border.

In the Canadian press all this is generally taken to confirm the inevitability of the process, due, as it were, to the flood of banking hormones devised by some super-broker above the clouds to ensure that life itself will go on. The perception in the US is less unanimous.

Thus on the front page of *The Wall Street Journal* (16/4) Greg Ip writes: "It's a good thing individuals are willing to pay such high prices for stocks, because Corporate America isn't."

Significantly, in both the US and Canada the bank mergers are being done without money changing hands. Instead shares are swapped, and the next day the market celebrates the event with an explosion of the value of the banks' shares. That means that instead of putting their money where their mouth is, insiders are cashing in on their generous options and leaving their shares to outside hopefuls. That is an unfailing sign that Moby Dick is blowing off.

And then there is the detail of the unwritten "too big to fail" law. This has been in force since Paul Volcker in 1984 bailed out the Continental Illinois Bank from its Eurodollar adventures. There is hardly a bank involved in the present pairings that has not already had such regal bailout treatment in earlier bank crises. The current merger merely adds a belt to their red suspenders for ensuring that their trousers do not droop to half-mast in the trials ahead.

The whole spectacle confirms an important fact that few economists have awakened to: as a result of deregulation our banks have undergone a mutation and switched their food chain. They have become stock-market-driven, and would be amongst the first to go up in smoke if central banks pushed up interest rates to restrain the stock market orgy.

Having triggered the biggest stock market crash since 1929 in 1987 by doing just that, Federal Reserve Chairman Alan Greenspan is bright enough to pay less heed to elusive "money supply" statistics, the touchstone of monetarist dogma. Instead he talks about myriad other statistics like railway car loadings. He has even expressed concern about asset inflation against a background of economic deflation.

Through their deregulation of banks, central banks have left only one "blunt tool" in their kit — high interest rates — to control any form of inflation. But since that will implode the stock market, they have no alternative but to keep aloft that magic flying machine that finds itself without landing gear.

Towards that end much of the capital accumulated in the public and private sectors over a half century is being ransacked. The slashing of capital gains taxes itself has added billions to the real capital worth of stocks. The demand of mutual funds and funds of funds is outstripping the shrinking supply of shares that supports the crazy structure. The latest move in this direction is the conversion of mutual insurance companies into public companies and the proposal to have 30% of Canadian deferred taxation pension funds to be invested in the stock market. The churning of exchange and interest rates has been fashioned by the IMF into a wrecking technique to reduce emerging economies to debris for stoking this play.

Nationsbank had its start in the rich pickings from the S&L banking mess of the 80s, and today is the lead partner in the second biggest merger to date. Its partner, Bancamerica, featured in at least two costly bailouts in previous decades. Citicorp which is going to the altar with Travelers Group was similarly bailed out in the early eighties and again in the early nineties. . What is inevitable is less the merger process than the precipitous end it must come to. And then the rest of society will by further downsized in aid of the mega-upsizers.

But what about the increased efficiencies? *WSJ* (14/04) quotes a Federal Reserve Board report that concluded that "'average fees charged by multi-state banks are significantly higher than those charged by single-state organisations,' and the very biggest banks have been among the most aggressive deployers of surcharges." *WSJ* goes on to tell of an elderly woman who paid a bill with a cheque on Citibank for $20 that never arrived. Phoning her bank to stop payment, she was told there would be a $25 charge for stopping payment on the cheque. Recently National City Corp, has begun charging customers $20 an hour, and a minimum of $10 for 'research' which includes such tasks as helping customers balance their checkbooks."

What efficiencies may emerge from the computer technology are hijacked to support bloated market evaluations based on inflated multipliers of projected profits. The fact is that our banks have simply changed their line of business. That was determined in the Bank for International Settlements Risk-Based Capital Requirements that requires 8% of their own capital for business loans while government bonds require none, and derivative gambles can be kept off the bank's balance sheets.

Nor is allowing more foreign banks to open shop likely to be of great help. These banks have served as role models for our banks in their present insanity. Unless we get down to the root causes of our banks' identity crisis, we will be trivializing the mega-crisis that lies ahead.

Pre-nuptial Suggestions

• Reserves should be brought back beginning modestly to the 3% range that US requires of its banks. That would put our banks at no competitive disadvantage since US and German banks must still put up such reserves with their central banks. It should be made law that at all future bailouts of our banks the reserve requirements be raised — say by 2%. The need for a further bailout of our banks would be a clear indication that they have not used responsibly the leverage granted them by previous deregulations.

• A ceiling on interest rates should be brought back. At present the only ceiling that exists is under the criminal law — 60%. A real interest ceiling (nominal interest rate less the flawed official rate of inflation) of 25% in civil not criminal law would be an improvement.

• A new category of bank charter should be made available that would limit bank loans to a maximum of $2 million to a single customer, and require the new bank to open at least one branch in a community of less than 20,000 that has been left without bank services. Despite such limitations such charters would be highly valuable assets and will not go begging. And the personnel for staffing them will be available from our megabank downsizings. The appearance of such banks would result in a mass transfer of modest accounts from our megabanks.

'If Finance Minister Paul Martin turned down the merger proposals it could wipe out millions of dollars of value off the TSE in a single day and cause a crash,' one banker speculated."

No previous stock market operators had enough power to permit themselves the overtones of blackmail that the *Globe* story radiates. What the banks are proposing is that government — which they have long argued should be kept out of the economy — must not only bailout the banks, but guarantee the stock market at whatever level the banks choose to drive it up to.

A Spreadsheet for Our Mixed Economy

Each subsystem of our economy, by its very definition, has its specific constraints that must be respected if society is to go on functioning. It is only in terms of these constraints that the subsystems can be monitored. The crucial point, missed by economists, is that the balance sheet of such non-monetary subsystems as the ecology, the household economy, the demographic subsystem cannot at their most meaningful level be drawn up in money terms.

If this is not kept in mind, we end up with bizarre laws like the one in the US that allows firms to sell their unused pollution quotas to others who may wish to pollute beyond the allowed limit. That in effect capitalises the right to pollute even of industries that may be abandoning their operations. As a limiting case, this might be compared with endowing all citizens with a modest murder quota — say the right to expunge 1/1,000,000th of a human life for each person who would be free to sell that right to someone who wished to take up murdering on a grander scale.

Expressed in graph form, this basic principle for the management of a mixed economy can be formulated as follows: The subsystems of a mixed economy are divided in two distinct categories at two levels. In the first division on one side we have the marketed and priced subsystem — the market — which always speaks in terms of price. On the other side of this first division we have the unpriced systems — the public sector that *is* "monetised" (i.e. expressed in money terms — derived from government *costs*) but *not priced since its benefits in general are not sold by the government*. In the second division we have those subsystems that are neither "monetised" nor priced: the household economy, the ecological and demographic subsystems.[†]

At the most basic level the unpriced and unmonetised subsystems must be formulated in terms of their specific constraints. For example, the Carbon Dioxide subsystem of the second order within the Ecology will show the maximum level of CO_2 pollution that may be safely permitted (*the level of tolerance*), and beneath it a graph to show the trend of pollution reached currently and for some years back. In this brief treatment we are using the CO_2 subdivision of the ecology as a proxy for all other ecological subdivisions, for example, the ozone layer, mercury poisoning of our waterways, nuclear pollution, etc. And we are using the ecological subsystem in turn as a proxy for all the non-monetary subsystems — e.g. the household economy, the demographic.

Only in a *secondary chart* of a non-monetised subsystem can the specific problem of each of these be translated into money terms. Such translation will be based on the estimated cost of repairing the damage currently being done to the particular subsystem — *whether the damage is being made good or not*. If the damage is not being made good, the cost of doing that must be deducted from the Gross Net Product of the economy. If damage inflicted on the subsystem in the past is being repaired, that must be shown as a capital investment.

There is no common dimension for aggregating the subdivisions of the ecology — i.e. adding up the damage of mercury poisoning of our waters with the carbon dioxide polluting of our atmosphere. Only when these primary graphs have been translated into monetary terms can such aggregation be carried out.

The priorities of the cleanup for the various types of pollution in our budgeting will depend on how closely they have approached their respective limits of tolerance, rather than their relative costs.

The primary graphs of the subsystems and the "monetised" versions of those graphs may be ranged vertically over the chart for the national GDP to align the time frame, the only dimension common to all graphs in the one column will be that of time. Time shown as common ordinates of the various graphs will help identify causal relationships. At a first glance any marked movement of the graph within a sub-system will alert us to any significant move towards the limit of tolerance.

Once the data from the non-monetised subsystems have been translated into monetary terms and incorporated into the GDP series (and graphs) the great task remains of devising programs that will provide the necessary growth of the GDP which the market subsystem requires to continue functioning *without* undermining the functioning of the other subsystems.[‡]

† "Monetised" is put in quotes because it does not refer to using gold, silver, or debt or whatever as "money." The costs of the public or any other unpriced sector are expressed in money terms in a purely notionalised way. We might coin the word "monify" to express this.

‡ All this can be summed up as the *eigenvalue* of a matrix of the economy. The technique is familiar to all mathematical economists, but is rarely applied to anything but the modern version of that great problem of medieval theology, how many angels can dance on a pinhead?: calculating equilibrium points of the economy *assumed* to exist. For the matrix of the three subsystems we have chosen the private sector, the public sector, and the Carbon Dioxide subdivision of the ecology as proxy for all non-monetised subsystems, in their monetised form explained above. This matrix is manipulated by standard procedures into its *eigenvalue* form: the matrix consists entirely of zeros with the exception of the diagonal elements:

1 0 0
0 1 0
0 0 1

where successive lines represent

x+0+0
0+y+0
0+0+z

each letter representing the condition of a subsystem. The *eigenvalue* xyz is arrived at by multiplying the terms of the diagonal together. If all three subsystems are functioning the *eigenvalue* is 1. If a single one has been knocked out (i.e. reduced to three zeros) one factor of the diagonal will be a zero and the *eigenvalue* will be zero. This simple and very familiar technique sums up the reality of our problem — that all subsystems of the economy must be functioning for the economy *and* society to survive. *N.B. The graphs are purely notional to illustrate a method. No attempt has been made to obtain data relevant to the unnamed jurisdiction referred to.*

[To be able to manipulate the system matrix into eigenvalue form, the matrix must be symmetrical i.e. self-balancing. That a purely market matrix is definitely not. But a market matrix plus enlightened policy would ideally add up to a self-balancing system for which an eigenvalue would be available.]

Comments on The Submission of The Competition Bureau to The Task Force on The Future of The Canadian Financial Services Sector

On perusing this submission, you wonder whether it was written on the same planet on which the East Asian crisis was unfolding. The Discussion Paper of the Task Force argued "vibrancy cannot be legislated." In its way the Discussion Paper had already been a *tour de force* of reality-denial. But "applauding" it five months later, the Competition Bureau tops that record.

The advice to limit "governmental intervention [to] what is reasonably necessary" rings strange when in South Korea the IMF was twisting the arm of the government to guarantee debt of the private sector.

"Effective competition among the participants in market, drives [the banks] to perform in the interest of their customers." In recent decades our banks have undergone an identity crisis that has completely changed the business they deem themselves to be in. They have gone far towards turning their backs on their traditional customers and left many of them out in the cold.

Along with these powers of money-creation entrusted to the commercial banks went severe restrictions on what they could engage in.

Let me quote from an article by Donald Coxe entitled 'The Made-In-Japan Credit Crunch' in *Canadian Business* (October 1991). Mr. Coxe, whose column appears regularly in *The Globe and Mail*, is an investment banker based in Chicago.

"Once upon a time international bankers were stuffy, prudent men who thought the business of banking was lending money only to those deemed to have an excellent chance of paying it back. Owners of shares in the big banks were happy with low growth and reliable dividends. Into this Eden came twin temptations — easy money and fast growth.

"The serpent was born during the Kennedy and Johnson eras when the US began running huge balance of payment deficits. At first, those extra dollars moved into the coffers of central banks abroad. But when those central banks became overstuffed with dollars, they declined to take more. The outflow of dollars began silting up in banks abroad.

"Thus was born the Eurodollar, the first money without a country since the days of the gold standard. As such it was free of the controls, the deposit requirements of central banks and the exchange controls imposed on all other currencies by their home countries' central banks.

"Then came the Arab oil shock and a leap in the US balance of payments deficit. The Arabs were suddenly awash in dollars. Those new dollars poured into the Eurodollar pool at a rate that overwhelmed the banks' ability to re-lend the funds. Rejecting prudence, banks competed furiously to lend money to every strong man in the Southern Hemisphere. By 1982 industrial world bankers had lent $1 trillion to the Third World.

"Punishment came in the form of expulsion of most big US and British banks from the high credit ratings of Eden. And as the financial strength of the top US banks succumbed to Third World debts and energy loans, the leadership in global banking moved to Tokyo. In 1972 most of the biggest global banks were American. Ten years later, only two were among the top 15. Today not one of the 15 biggest global banks is based in North America. Eight, including the five biggest, are Japanese.

"All these changes have stretched the abilities of the central bankers of the industrial nations. Under the leadership of Paul Volcker, they had agreed in 1982 to a "too big to fail" approach to banks in the Eurodollar market. That means that if one of these 40 or so biggest banks in the world went down, its home country central bank would pay off its Eurodollar depositors in full. That's why Volcker was forced to violate US law in May, 1984, when Continental Illinois, the seventh-largest US bank went down. Although Eurodollar deposits were totally uninsured, he used Federal Deposit Insurance funds to pay off holders in full.

"Why should the fall of just one bank have such catastrophic consequences? Because more than US $400 billion a day courses through the international system. [These figures relate to 1991 when the article appeared; they are several times higher today.] Beyond that mind-boggling amount of cash is the *trillions* of dollars worth of derivatives, such as futures, swaps and other exotica that jump from computer screen to computer screens in banks and brokerage houses throughout the world.

"So the central banks decided to write a global banking rule book. In July 1988, they reached agreement [under the Risk-Based Capital Requirements of the Bank of International Settlements] at Basle. The essence of the BIS rules is that each bank must have 8% of capital against loans to businesses or individuals, but needs no capital for investments in debt of Organization for Economic Cooperation and Development governments. Of particular importance was a concession to the Japanese banks: [in counting their capital] they can use up to 45% of the unrealized gains on their stock holdings. [Hence] a sharp fall in that unruliest of markets, Tokyo, will trigger credit contractions around the world.

"Although few Americans realized it, their long economic boom in the 1980s was fuelled by the spectacular growth in Japanese banking operations in the US. By 1989 US agencies of Japanese banks accounted for 50.5% of the total growth of those loans in the federal reserve system — a share far greater than the Japanese share of the new automobile market.

"Where did they get the money? The Japanese simply took over the Eurodollar market globally after the US banks had blown their wads on Third World loans. The Japanese then used these low-cost funds to make loans to top-rate US borrowers.

"Unable to compete in day-to-day loans to blue-chip companies, US banks turned to [financing] the boom in commercial real estate and leveraged buyouts to rebuild their balance sheets. They didn't even display the intelligence of lemmings, which wait four years before they plunge together over the abyss.

"That the Japanese banks were able to grow at such incredible rates was due to the Tokyo stock market, which soared by nearly 500% between 1982 and 1989. Then the governor of the Bank of Japan slashed Japanese money supply growth to the lowest level in history — from 13.5% to 3.5%. That burst the bubble. The Nikkei index of the stock market plummeted from 39,000 to 24,000. [Currently it is below 14,000.]

"Don't worry that the Japanese banks will go bust. All they need to do to meet the BIS rules is scale back their business loans. And if that weren't worrisome enough for the US economy, most of the big US banks are having to retrench to meet the BIS tests, because writedowns on their real estate and leveraged buyout loans are taking their regulatory capital below the 8% range.

"Banks in some major European countries are also feeling the BIS pinch."

Almost at the same time as that article was being written, a revision of the *Bank Act* was slipped through Canada's Parliament, phasing out the non-interest bearing reserves that banks had to hold in legal tender with the central bank, approximately 4% of the deposits they had accepted. That proportion had over the previous decades been whittled down from 10%.

But the experience of the Japanese Central Bank in attempting to "cool" a wild asset boom by slashing the money supply has left its mark on the world's central bankers. Where the solvency of the banking system had come to depend on the level of the stock market, using that "one blunt tool" had become a lethal menace to the banking system. In Japan this situation had arisen because the banks could count 45% of their unrealized stock market profits as capital. Higher interest rates nationally or internationally would mean a capital loss on their immense holding of US bonds — as much as 17% of the outstanding total.

In Canada the vulnerability of the banking system to higher interest rates arose in a different way. The end of reserves along with the BIS Risk-Based Capital Requirements had made it possible for our banks to increase their holdings of federal government debt by some $60 billion dollars without putting up a penny of legal tender of their own. This amounted not to a one-time bailout but an ongoing entitlement to the banks of at least $5 billion a year.

That and the progressive deregulation of what banks could invest in, made it possible for our banks to acquire over 80% of Canada's brokerage businesses, along with strong positions in all other financial areas. That has made them hardly less sensitive to what goes on in the stock markets than the Japanese banks.

This has been a major factor in the lower interest rates of recent years. Our central bank — like the Fed and the Bank of Japan — simply does not dare to push up interest rates since it would prick the stock market bubble and bring the entire financial system crashing.

The quality of the banks' assets have deteriorated under the influence of the "leave it all to the free market" expounded in the Competition Bureau's submission. Since loans to business require 8% of capital, while government debt calls for none at all, loans to businesses and individuals are the first to feel the credit pinch when a bank has suffered capital losses.

Ironically, the more sophisticated the strategies for reducing risk to individual bankers and investors, the greater the risk to the total financial system if one link in the electronic chain is broken. Moreover, the most dangerous exposures of our banks — derivatives — rarely even appear on their balance sheets.

In the accompanying Appendix we quote from a paper 'Derivatives and Global Capital Flows: Application to Asia,' presented at the recent Eastern Economic Association conference by J.A. Kregel of the University of Bologna and the Jerome Levy Institute. It discusses a couple of examples of the type of so-called "hedging" against foreign currency risk in emerging countries that is widely practised. The globalisation of our banks signifies their getting deeper into such situations, and when they turn out very different from their billing the most certain effect is the withdrawal from perfectly creditworthy Canadian firms back home.

The pattern of the globalisation-deregulation of our banks over the past quarter of a century has been a simple one. Encouraged to lay aside the responsibilities that went with the powers of money-creation assigned to them, our banks lost no time in gambling themselves into further insolvency. Approval of the proposed merger, will guarantee that the banks will be back with their begging bowls for the next bailout.

Appendix — Excerpt from 'Derivatives and Global Capital Flows: Applications to Asia'

Presented by Jan Kregel at the New York meeting of the Eastern Economic Association (28/2/98).

"Most people are now familiar with standard derivative contracts used in risk hedging such as forwards, futures and options. While foreign currency forwards remain the province of bank foreign exchange dealers, standardised futures and options are now traded in organised markets. Banks operate primarily in what is termed the over-the-counter market. ."The majority of OTC activity involves tailored combinations of standard financial instruments packaged together with derivative contracts. These contracts involve little direct lending by banks to clients and thus generate little net interest income; however, they have the advantage, after the introduction of the Basle capital requirements, of requiring little or no capital, or of being classified as off-balance sheet. In addition, they generate large fee and commission income. Rather than committing their own capital, the banks serve as intermediaries.

"The role of the active global bank is thus no longer to maximise its profits by seeking the lowest cost funds and lending them for the highest risk-adjusted return, but rather in maximising the amount of funds intermediated to maximise fees and commissions. ...It is precisely the role of most derivative packages to mask the actual risk involved in investment and to increase the difficulty of assessing the final return on funds provided. By extension, this should also create difficulties for regulators and supervisors.

"These particular aspects can be most clearly seen by reference to structured derivative contracts that expanded dramatically during the 1990s. Standard limitations restrict investments to assets with a minimum of risk given by an investment grade credit rating. This meant that a large proportion of institutionally managed investment funds cannot be invested in emerging markets. Structured derivative packages, created by global investment banks, have often provided the means by which these restrictions could be overcome.

"As an example, consider a one-year dollar-denominated note paying a guaranteed above-market interest rate, but with the amount of repayment of principal linked to the index of a foreign asset, say the Thai baht/dollar exchange rate. Since the asset is denominated in US dollars and the interest is guaranteed and paid in US dollars the notes carry a AAA credit rating and are carried on the balance sheets of investors as the equivalent of a US Treasury bill. Yet, the above-market interest rate on the note is generated by the fact that the buyer of the note has implicitly sold a put option on the Thai baht at a strike price just above the current market rate. This is equivalent to having purchased Thai currency. If the baht depreciates below the current market rate, then the buyer of the note as the writer of the option incurs a loss which is covered by a reduction in the amount of principal returned at maturity.

"Alternatively, the contract could have been constructed by lending the principal (less the discounted value of the guaranteed dollar interest payment which is invested in a one-year Treasury bill) directly to a Thai bank by buying a bank acceptance. The implicit assumption is that the $/baht exchange rate would remain constant so that the baht interest and principal repayment can be converted at maturity to a value in dollars equal to the original principal. If the baht devalues relative to the dollar, then the amount available to repay the principal will be lower. The buyer thus has the entire principal at risk, only the interest is guaranteed. ...There is no way for the US investor to evaluate the use of funds made by the Thai bank, and there is little incentive for the US bank to do so, since once the issue is sold, the entire foreign credit and foreign exchange risk is borne by the US investor."

One way or another the package is set up to convert water into wine of the highest vintage, bearing the imprimatur of the international financial authorities who have "transparency" ever on their lips.

On the Shrivelling Statutory Reserves of the Banks in the US Federal Reserve System

From these figures it is clear that what was accomplished in Canada — phasing out bank reserve requirements completely within less than three years — is being accomplished gradually but determinedly in the US. As the increase in monetary base-money created by the government through the central bank has consistently gone down, the banks were given ever greater leverage for the creation of interest-bearing money by reducing the reserves of legal tender they had to leave with the Fed as non-interest-bearing collateral.

US Federal Statutory Reserves

	Dec 93	Dec 94	Dec 95	Dec 96	Jul 97
Total Reserves	60.55	59.4	56.89	50.06	46.89
Required Reserves	59.48	58.24	55.11	48.64	45.68
% change from previous year Req Reserves		-2.85	-5.36	-11.74	-6.09
Monetary Base	386.88	418.48	434.52	452.67	464.25
% Change		8.17	3.83	4.18	2.55

Adjusted for Changes in Reserve Requirements, in $ billions. Source: Federal Reserve Bulletin, *October 1997*

The Current State of the Japanese Banks

An updating of Coxe's 'The Made-In-Japan Credit Crunch' (p. 318) will give us important clues to the current enigma — how the US stock markets go on flying into the sun without the wax holding their wings coming unstuck. All the necessary information is handily packaged for us in *The Wall Street Journal* (31/03): "The Tokyo stock market plunged nearly 3% Monday, dropping the once-swaggering market into a once unthinkable: third place, behind not only the US but London.

"According to Goldman Sachs & Co, at the close of trading Monday, Japan's total stock-market capitalization stood at $1.881 trillion. The comparable number for Britain's domestic market was $1.942 trillion. Total stock-market value in the US towered above both at more than $12 trillion. The descent of Japan to No.3 is particularly poignant because Japan's markets so triumphantly reached the #1 spot in the 1980s, *when the seeds of Japan's current troubles were being sown* [emphasis ours]. In 1989 Japan was at the pinnacle of its financial power, and the combined value of all the companies listed on its exchanges was 10% greater than even the value of US stocks."

One reason for this shift in ratings is that London has risen 15% to date this year, compared to 11.1% for the US while Tokyo has inched up a mere 6.6%. Fuelling the new highs on stock markets throughout Europe is an epidemic of privatisations to meet the entrance requirement of prospective EMU members down to 60% of GDP, mergers, and the withdrawal of investment from the Asia.

As they pushed their way to the position of the world's largest, Japan's banks lost much and even more than their total capital. To help them cope with that ticklish detail, they were allowed to count their inventories of shares as capital reserves. As a result every stock market blip shows up on the fever chart of Japan's ailing banks; it therefore determines what lending to businesses they can do. This has made the Japanese economy in a very real sense an appendage of the stock market.

That is why the central bank has kept interest rates abysmally low, in defiance of Washington's jaw-boning. In an attempt to lift stock-market prices, the government is proposing to pour ¥971 billion from the state-run postal savings and insurance system into the stock market.

"'Basically, the stock value lost by Japan has been picked up by the US,' says Christopher Eoyang of Goldman and Sachs in Tokyo." The mass withdrawal of American and other portfolio investment from the Far East on the heels of the recent meltdown has added new momentum to the ascension of the American, Canadian and European markets. This was predicted to us some months ago by J.W. Smith of The Institute for Economic Democracy of San Luis Obispo, California.

The upshot of all this recalls the withdrawal of the Romans towards the citadel from the uttermost limits of their crumbling empire. The repatriation of capital from troubled Asia is likely to be followed by similar developments in Latin America, a region vulnerable to the deflation of oil and metal prices, quite apart from some epic belt-tightenings imposed by the IMF. Late in March Ecuador devalued the *sucre*. A new round of economic implosion may be in the works.

What is remarkable about the Japanese situation is that the world's second largest economy, has a more than ample reserve of foreign exchange, but suffers from many of the symptoms afflicting the emerging countries of the region. Bankruptcies and unemployment are at all-time highs. Inventories of automobiles and other products are piling up. And at this very time, when a third of the country's banks are immobilised with bad debt, the Big Bang of financial markets is being initiated.

Large foreign banks from the Americans through the Europeans right to the Canadian are poised to make major inroads because their Japanese counterparts are in no position to defend even their home turf, let alone compete for foreign business. Indeed a new wriggle has been introduced into the BIS Risk-Based Capital Requirements for banks. Reported in *The Wall Street Journal* (1/04), because of new capital-adequacy rules, based on a formula mandated by the BIS, banks operating internationally are required to maintain capital equal to 8% of their loans.

As a result 35 of 80 Japanese banks have been downgraded from the "international" to the "domestic" category, and have closed their overseas offices. On the other hand "domestically operating banks," required to maintain only 4% of their loans outstanding, have risen from 67 to 102. It should be explained that "loans" requiring such "capital backing" do not include debt of OECD countries which are declared "risk-free" or even "mortgages" which require only half the amount.

Nonetheless when interest rates do go up the market value of the "risk-free" OECD debt will plummet. Indeed, the very concept of "capital" constantly becomes very iffy, unless the auditors of the state go through the entire portfolio of each bank with a fine comb. An international enquiry on BIS, its role and its record, is overdue.

But isn't financial reform just what Japan's economy needs? That is what it says in the official hymn book, but some of the slated reforms are precisely more of the sort of thing that contributed to the downfall of Japan's proud banking system. Thus the full deregulation of securities derivatives — hitherto banned as illegal gambling — comes into effect at once. The ban on securities houses handling unlisted or unregistered stocks is being lifted. Foreign exchange transactions and capital flows abroad are being deregulated.

However, 60% per cent of Japanese private financial holdings, estimated at $10 trillion that has been left as deposits yielding as little 0.1% will now be free to leave the country for investment in foreign mutual funds. Initially that could provide an upward blast for Western stock markets unequalled by anything seen up to now. But with the real economy of the world increasingly stressed on one continent after another, the ultimate result is hardly reassuring.

Cleanup Costs

In the months after the Mexican peso meltdown in December 1994, a lot of money was made by speculators who bought Mexican assets at bargain basement levels. Is that not proof the casino that international finance is leading to a more efficient world economy? A dispatch of Bloomberg News (*Globe and Mail* 9/04/98) provides the answer. "The acquisition of new troubled loans along with a more realistic estimate of all the loans, boosted the cost of rescuing Mexico's banking system to US $64.7 billion. The size of the bailout program is now equal to about 14.4% of GDP, up from an earlier forecast of 11.9%. This will be paid over 30 years." Interestingly enough a report by the Indonesia Bank Restructuring Agency (*Globe and Mail* 10/04) places the tentatively estimated cost of restructuring Indonesia's banking system at 15% of the GDP. Uncannily the estimates at this stage of either country hover around 15% of GDP. That might give you an idea of what the ultimate cost to Canadians of the proposed Canadian bank mergers might be.

The Civil Commons — The Truth of Global Competitiveness

"Global competitiveness" is to the contemporary corporate market what "doing God's work" was to the medieval Church — the omnibus self-justification for what would otherwise be recognized as criminally pathological behaviour. Across the world, corporations deprive families of their livelihoods, pollute and loot the environment, and demand that all governments divest themselves of their regulatory powers to protect life. As the juggernaut runs wild, few people stop to question the meaning of this "global competitiveness" itself.

Competition can be healthy or unhealthy in nature, whatever form it takes. Competition is *healthy* when the overcoming of limiting conditions confronting the competitors *enables a wider and deeper range of life by their competing*. It is *unhealthy* when the opposite happens, and the competitors are reduced to ever narrower ranges of vital life by their competition.

Athletes, for example, compete healthily when both they and their oppositions get better at what they compete at — running, jumping, throwing, lifting, and so on. At best, all achieve what they couldn't achieve before, and the margin of "*better*" is an *extension of the scope of life's capabilities*. Athletic competition is the paradigm of all competition because the margins of increase are clear, time-limited and embodied. One knows what is better by a better time, a higher bar, a longer distance, a heavier weight. A similar transparency of value gain, or decline, is available to us in the wider realm of social life. Societies too can get better, or worse, in their health or morbidity, literacy or illiteracy, civil decency or ignorant brutality. In the current competition of the global market we are clearly not becoming more competitive at these *goods of life*. We are becoming rapidly worse. What global market competition is, in fact, contending against is *life's vital capacities themselves*: invading, reducing and stripping every condition of life to turn the world into ever more money for money investors. Humanity's primeval urge to overcome limits has in this way been harnessed to a program that is consuming life itself. Because it is a closed program, its stripping of the living bodies of societies and their environments do not pose a problem to it. Its goal is only to turn everything into more money demand for corporate stockholders.

The way in which we can tell the losses of life underneath the pretences of gains is by the deficits of life's reproduction under this global market's rule. Everywhere we look, life deficits are evident: the rapid decline of species and biodiversity, of the air we breathe, of water and water resources, of solar and atmospheric quality, of forests and fish stocks, of the health of society's members, of levels of literacy and education, of the rights of all to public communication, and so on. There are many basic indicators of life-gain or life-loss which tell us how well or badly we are doing in the ultimate game, and these are the measure of how truly competitive or non-competitive a social order is.

The game of life, like life itself, is many-sided. Humanity's life gains or losses play out on many levels — child nutrition, accessible housing, disease ratios, air quality, water purity, literacy rates, biodiversity, forest cover, soil quality, physical fitness, noise levels, public and green spaces, social and artistic communication venues, higher education graduates, wildlife habitats, and so on. These are the true measures of a society's competitiveness. These gains or losses of life are all identifiable by *margins* of change up or down. Together they register a changing score-sheet of a society's true competitiveness at knowing how to live as societies. This is real life competition, not money-game competition. If we are winning, the lives of members of society and its environmental host are becoming more comprehensive in their vital capacities. If we are losing, and losing badly, these life capacities are increasingly reduced, degraded and extinguished. We are now losing badly.

The money-count method of success is a *lapsed paradigm* of competing at the life game. Its metric is blind to life's gains or losses; it counts only gains and debits of money. This is why a car crash that destroys people and property counts as a *gain* in corporate market scores like the GDP. It is consistent with the money-count method of competing that societies achieve ever higher levels of profits, stock-exchange rises and global trade aggregates, while civil and environmental life are cumulatively eroded, wasted and destroyed. This is, in fact, what is happening to our societies now. As in a carcinogenic invasion, the money sequence keeps multiplying itself by eating the life body which is its host.

Competition first becomes *pathological competition* when it does not raise life to higher or more enabling levels of thought, feeling and action, but *reduces it* to ever lower levels. On the micro-plane, we can see the pathological pattern of competition in a sport like hockey in Canada — ever fewer people gaining in life capacity by playing it, and ever more people becoming merely spectators at violence-entertainment sites. Nuclear war is an ultimate example of pathological competition. Once entered it must destroy tens of millions of lives on both sides of its obliterative contest, and perhaps the planet itself. Nuclear war is still believed in by minds locked into its program, just as the Business Council on National Issues still believes in destroying societies to make corporations more profitable. But such pathological sequences of destroying life to be "more competitive" are no more necessary or inevitable than a disease is. They are to be recognized and fought in the same way.

Corporate market competition has become the globe's primary disorder. It does not enable more comprehensive, vital life for humanity or the planet — not the world's species and environmental habitats, not the increasing hundreds of millions of malnourished, unemployed, homeless, insecure and money-subjugated people, and not the world's societies which have all been variously stripped of their social infrastructures. *Life's* sequences of growth and development on every plane are on a downward slide. But a grass-roots war is being waged against this race to the bottom to reduce corporate costs, and this grass-roots fight is beginning to win. The MAI Treaty, for example, was set for passage this month. It would have dismantled every social defence against total transnational ownership of societies' economies across the world. But it was chased back into the pathogenic den of the corporate mind-set from which it hatched — until it creeps back out again in a new guise.

Healthy life resists what attacks it, and counter-attacks until it prevails. We are seeing now the return of the immune response of the civil commons to what is invading societies across the planet. The battle will be long and hard. But the overcoming of a disease invasion is how life adapts and grows on the social as well as cellular level of life-organization. By overcoming threats to its vital organs and capacities, a society like an organism develops more competent ranges of life capability. Disease is evolution's provocation, and social disease conquered is history's moving spring.

John McMurtry

Vol. 10, No. 6 — June 1998

Atmospherics: an International "Tiff for Credit for a Lot of Nothing"

G7 time is back again, and it was undoubtedly in anticipation of its massive photo opportunities that Kodak shares recovered a bit on the stock market. If you closed one eye, whirled around to the music of the *Nutcracker Suite* for a half hour and then stood on your head, you could possibly detect some of the progress on which the members congratulated themselves.

The meeting, for example, was scheduled to be followed by one of the Group of Eight that includes Russia. That, in a sense, said it all. The fall of communism, rather than the expected victory of a sorely tried people, turned out merely to have replaced the dogmatism of the almighty state with the rapacity of the almighty market. The benefits to the financial mafia are in greater evidence than the improvement of the lot of the ordinary citizen.

The European Union, for its part, is founded four-square on the independence of the EU's central bank. France may have its atomic bomb but the master in the new European house was made clear by the appointment of the German candidate as first head of its central bank. That deprives the constituent countries and the EU itself of all power to address their real problems. Deficits cannot be run up even during a depression. That ties the hands of governments to do anything about unemployment which from over 12% in France, climbs to as much as 25% in parts of eastern Germany.

The real lesson of what is happening in Indonesia has clearly eluded the G7. If you concentrate your concern on a single addled price statistic and pile sacrifices and degradation on the bulk of the population, society will start coming apart — eventually into bloody chaos. And en route there will be growing crime, cynicism, and moral rot.

A month before the meeting our Finance Minister Paul Martin was blowing his little horn: "Minister Martin would try selling the rest of the G7 on the idea of a global banking watchdog to prevent the recurrence of the Asian financial crisis. The proposed international banking regulator would be loosely modelled on the federal Office of the Superintendent of Financial Institutions (OSFI) in Canada and particularly initially would be voluntary. The new regulator could, however, raise concerns about banking problems within countries and recommend changes. And even though the participation in the system would be optional, Mr. Martin envisages a worldwide reach for the regulator. It's an idea that has been working over in his mind for a couple of months, a Finance Department official said. At the G7 [meeting] in Halifax in 1995 the summit moved to set up a signal to prevent a recurrence of the Mexican crisis."

Surely Barrie McKenna, the author of the article, had his tongue in his cheek in writing of the G7 move to set up a signal prevent a recurrence of the Mexican crisis at a time when just about everything structured and promoted in East Asia was crumbling in anguish and gore around the G7's ears.

As for OSFI, proposed by Mr. Martin as the model for his world regulator, it has a record of becoming aware of bank troubles only when they have burst into full crises. Its criterion for the health of a bank is that it have capital equal to 5% of its assets across the board. That capital, however, though originally raised in cash, is increasingly invested in assets which do not exclude Korean bonds, or in derivatives that do not even appear on the bank's balance sheet. Moreover, its limited budget necessarily restricts OSFI for its information on the banks' condition to their published statements. Since our banks are engaged in "kick-ass" ventures across the globe that could hardly get OSFI or the international monitor very far.

In Mr. Martin's initiative there is little more than PR atmospherics — atmospherics plus a pinch of infantilism. Thus French President Jacques Chirac, "heralded the move as 'important progress' but claimed ownership of the idea for the French — the reinforcement of the international monetary system has been a priority since the Lyon meeting of the leaders two years ago in France."

What is involved is a tiff for credit for a lot of nothing. The Bank for International Settlements (BIS) has been working on a code of regulation of derivative trading ever since the British pound, the Canadian dollar and a fistful of other currencies were shot down from their artificial heights by speculators who outgunned the central banks in 1992. Nothing has come out of the BIS studies. Derivatives have been an important factor in the present East Asian crisis.

More than fatuous press releases, what is needed is a rethinking of the entire deregulation process that has built up towards terminal disaster over a quarter of a century. If he really wants to prevent the recurrence of financial meltdowns — at home and abroad — Mr. Martin must begin by coming clean. Charity, as ever, begins at home.

On the Joys and Grief of Delphic Utterance

In our last issue under the heading 'Time for Thiessen to Go' we quoted *The Globe and Mail* (24/04): "Governor Gordon Thiessen of the Bank of Canada says Canadian stocks aren't overvalued and have more to appreciate as the economy expands. ...Rising US stock prices have raised concern among analysts that investors may have pushed values to levels that are unsustainable and that could lead to a market crash. ...While Canada's stock market would be affected by a US stock collapse, Mr. Thiessen said there is a lower probability of a similar crash in Canada."

We noted that since our banks had attained a leverage of liabilities to legal tender on hand of 347 to one, "the notion of a 'lesser probability of a crash in Canada when one takes place in the US' is so bizarre that one must ask what this noted inflation-fighter is smoking."

We received from the Bruce Yemen, Chief, Communications, Bank of Canada a denial that the statement attributed to him in the *G&M* had been made by the Governor. We requested and received from Mr. Yemen the complete transcript of the Governor's April 23rd remarks before the Senate Committee on Banking, Trade, and Commerce. We also contacted Bloomberg News which was the source of the *G&M* quote, as well as another wire agency whose version substantially coincided with that of Bloomberg. Working our way through the 40-odd page transcript, we were left to ponder, once again, the advantages and drawbacks of the Delphic utterance that goes with godly powers. Let us sample the transcript.

Senator Austin: "I would like to ask whether the Bank of Canada at this moment is watching the potential asset price inflation circumstance, whether the pricing of equities and the high P/E ratios are of any concern; and whether the excess liquidity in the equity market, particularly in the mutual funds, is driving an irrational economic picture?"

Mr. Thiessen: "The role of monetary policy is traditionally to focus on what we call the real economy — the production of goods and services and the prices at which these goods and services are sold. Virtually every central bank in the world sees that the best contribution it can make to maximise the production of those goods and services over time is to keep the inflation rate very low and that should be the focus of monetary policy. You will note I have not said a word about the price of assets: it is the price of goods and services."

That is a most amazing mouthful. The cardinal tenet of monetarism — the doctrine that has controlled the world's central banks for the last twenty years — is that "inflation is always a monetary phenomenon." That means that when prices rise, the reason is that there is too much money around; and that by restricting credit and raising interest rates that will be remedied. In the short run, monetarists admit, it will result in unemployment and bankruptcies, but in the "long run," by squeezing inflation out of the economy, it will work out to everybody's advantage. Yet the high interest rates, the resulting bankruptcies and unemployment are very real, but the alleged long-term neutral benefits to all are strictly a matter of faith. Mr. Thiessen, however, flits over the real short-term agony of the productive sector, and treats the credo as hard fact. He calls the wild speculative gambles of the financial sector — the mega-mergers, the stock market puffery and all that — "the real economy," and expects us to accept the unemployment, bankruptcies and suicides that planned recessions bring on as the illusion.

Thiessen goes on to add. "You will note I have not said a word about the price of assets; it is the price of goods and services." But the Senator's question was precisely about equities and assets. In short the Governor did not even attempt to answer the question.

But even so he could not let the subject go, and continued: "That having been said, we are all well aware of what happened in Japan where the prices of assets particularly real estate and equity prices, went up very high. There was a speculative bubble, and when that bubble broke, it had all sorts of consequences for the real economy. I have doubts about the issue whether monetary growth is driving that. The degree of change that has gone on in the financial sector in virtually every country in recent years has been so enormous that judging exactly what you can make out of those aggregates, especially those that are broadly defined, is very difficult.

"In Canada, we are in the process of redefining our aggregates. We had something called M-2; then something called M-2 plus, and now to something called M-2 plus plus because the world keeps changing. Therefore, I would be very hesitant to attribute too much to what is happening to M-3."

But all these M's were introduced by the monetarists because they could not get the money supply — originally M-1 — non-interest bearing deposits and legal tender — to support their central dogma that "inflation is always a monetary phenomenon." They had no choice but to go on redefining the money supply. All the while they insisted on pushing through their deregulation program, because that was really where the interests of their constituency, the financial institutions, lie.

That is why Gordon Thiessen's statement on money calls to mind a Danny Kaye patter, or the elaborate dance of an exotic bird trying to lead a predator away from the hidden nest where its eggs are to be found.

There is no reference, for example, to the key statistics on the explosion of our chartered banks liabilities/assets to the legal tender still kept by our banks.

In 1946 the ratio of the first to the latter were 11.1: 1. Today it has risen to 347:1. Mr. Thiessen will find the figures in the *Bank of Canada Review*, page C6, Series B5400 for the liabilities and for the legal tender page C1, series B403 (bills and coin) plus Bank of Canada deposits (series 404). That in itself sounds a tocsin. But on top of that the quality of the assets for which the banks have run up those liabilities has deteriorated greatly. And even then the reality is still worse than the figures, because the bulk of the derivative plays in which they are involved is kept off their balance sheets. If the gambles in which our banks are engaged drop 15% across the board in the next market crash, our banks will be out their entire capital. And to bail them out, Canadians will be told that we have been living beyond our means, and that a new, even greater pogrom against our social services must be undertaken.

But back to Thiessen's prose: "I would be far more inclined to suggest that major changes going on in the world are being reflected in the stock market. One might say it is very likely there is an exaggeration of those changes. Interest rates are much lower than they were."

[That is hardly the case if we consult *real* interest rates and consider not only the highly distorted Consumer Price Index, but the deflation on the commodity markets.-*Ed.*] "Productivity growth, because of technological change, particularly in the US, is rising." Productivity measurements are even more confused than the CPI — and to a large extent refer to the profits earned through financial manipulations."I am much more inclined to that explanation for profits than I am to one that relates to monetary aggregates."

Here we have a repudiation of the central dogma of monetarism. Why doesn't the good man come clean and explain what if anything is left of that dogma? And why society must be condemned to continue wearing it like a smelly albatross around its neck? "However, there is no question that everyone worries that if those markets become too speculative and then crash, they will have some implications for the rest of the economy. We are monitoring them very closely, but more than that I find it difficult to say."

However, Tim E. Noel, Deputy Governor of the BoC, was there to qualify even these weasel words of his superior: "The wealth effect of stock market prices is far from sure. If you go back to 1987, the last time we had a stock market crash, there was very little impact on the economies of the western world as a result of the break in stock prices."

The "wealth effect" occurs when consumers, without having bought or sold anything, find that the capital assets that they own — houses, cars, paintings, or even stocks — have gained substantially in market value. But the crucial effects of a stock market crash consist less of such "wealth effects" than the selling out of margin accounts, bankruptcies and unemployment. These effects may take two or three years to fully surface. That was the case after the 1929 crash when the US banking system closed its doors in 1933. The consequences of the 1987 crash were far more serious than Mr. Noel would have us believe. They were the reason for the institution of the Risk-Based Capital Requirements of the Bank for International Settlement that provided a bailout plan for distressed banks across the world. These proclaimed the bonds of OECD countries risk-free requiring no capital for banks to acquire. Canada went the BIS one further by doing away with the 4% of the cost of such bond acquisitions that had to be put up at the Bank of Canada against the bonds they purchased.

Amidst the verbal fog, pity the poor financial reporter who must send his editor a lucid statement of the Great Man's remarks. We note that at the date of this writing the *G&M* has still not published the Bank of Canada's correction.

Two Pillars of Globalisation

The present push towards globalisation rests on two pillars of faith: technology and the "kick-ass" campaign for market shares.† Big is beautiful, and big is so efficient as to be inevitable, and nothing no matter how big is quite large enough to satisfy corporative mega-greed. Suddenly, however, both of these are visibly crumbling.

We have many case histories to choose from, but we will stay with Boeing, since its achievements rests heavily on both these pillars.

In *The Wall Street Journal* (24/04) we read: "On a floodlit runway corner, a spanking new Boeing 777 is rolled out for the visiting pooh-bahs of Air France. Lasers zap an image of the Eiffel Tower onto the 150-ton airliner. Boeing Co. officials chortle. They have tucked it to arch rival Airbus Industrie, based in Toulouse, France, by selling Boeing's most technologically advanced model — to a French airline.

"But off in the shadows a slew of unfinished 737s are mute evidence of long months of assembly-line foul-ups. The giant aerospace company has become a giant paradox: reeling in disarray at the very time, amid a world-wide aviation surge, it should have been rolling in dough. Boeing has a windfall of orders it can't fill, a competitor it can't shake and a pile of troubles that would dwarf a 747. It suffered its first loss in 50 years in 1997 and reported a 91% drop in first-quarter 1998 profit.

"Boeing was so obsessed with protecting its 60% market share that it was drawn into brutal pricing wars with Airbus."

While unwilling to deliver a single civilian order to its rival, Boeing was focussed on gobbling up the international military aerospace business as well. It acquired McDonnell Douglas Corp. and the defence and aerospace units of Rockwell International Corp. [With all that underway] it had no time even to follow the growing mess in its commercial department. A badly prepared assembly line was improvised, and now the company is not only bleeding hundreds of millions of dollars, but witnessing a defection of unhappy customers to its rival.

Deregulation, supposedly the fount of all virtues, turns up at various stages of this ongoing drama. "The commercial jet business has long been prone to booms and busts, but today's circumstances contrived to produce an odd mixture of the two. New markets opening up in Asia and Latin America and spreading deregulation have spurred record spending on aircraft orders."

With only two serious suppliers in the field, the result should have been a sellers' market. But the contrary has occurred. Boeing and Airbus are competing viciously, making every bid a battleground. Each order ties the buyer to the seller for as much as 20 years. So cuts of as much as 20% off list are a common occurrence. Governments should be studying this phenomenon of two raging giants stricken with mad-cow disease. There is no indication that they have even awakened to the problem.

"Boeing was poorly positioned to meet the surge of orders. It sharply cut its work force during the last slump, in the early 1990s in a drive to slash parts inventories — the so-called "lean manufacturing." That netted the company an immediate accolade in the form of an upward spurt of its shares. "Boeing evolved 400 separate computer systems which aren't linked. The company offers customers a wealth of design choices. The combination of green workers and great haste [resulted in] lots of mistakes and production bottlenecks. One veteran 747 production crew member recalls spending a weekend chasing parts stockpiles around greater Seattle, trying to find rubber seals for jetliner doors. Parts were rushed in by taxicab. Rookie workers muddled by on the line, while managers were pulled off to be trained in new technology. The clear beneficiary of the chaos is Airbus. It is supplying airlines that can't get deliveries from Boeing. United Airlines recently shut Boeing out of an order for small jets."

Similar dramas are being played out to one degree or another throughout the economy. And it knocks into a cocked hat the stock market's evaluation of companies by the lemma that big means efficient. Sooner or later that too must eventually have its effect on the indexes.

† We owe this elegant expression to the CEO of the Royal Bank of Canada, the senior partner in our largest proposed bank mating. When you can get something from a bank these days without paying a fee, the occasion is not to be passed up.

The Myth of Our Technology-Driven Society Comes Apart

Remember our local scholars reading from the prepared kits sent them by the rightist think tanks? They assured us that there was no use trying to stop the globalisation and megamerger trend. It was, they said, technology-driven and inevitable. Trying to stop it would be like King Canute commanding the waves. Even the bad metaphors came prepackaged.

Well evidence to the contrary is now pouring in from several directions.

In *The Wall Street Journal* (30/04 'Some Firms, Let Down By Costly Computers Opt to De-Engineer. Memories of the Robot Craze') Bernard Wysocki Jr. writes: "The dark side of the corporate information revolution is coming into view. Companies across the country are seeing their cutting-edge computer systems fail to live up to expectations — or fail altogether.

"In 1996, Pacific Gas & Electric Co. began spending tens of millions of dollars on a system developed by IBM that would handle customer billing and many other tasks. But deregulation hit the California utility industry much faster than PG&E had expected. Suddenly it had the vastly more complicated responsibility of keeping track of fast-changing prices and multiple suppliers of electricity. 'We were heading towards disaster,' says Damien P. Brooks, a senior project manager with the giant utility. And so PG&E scrapped the fancy IBM system. Today there is a new four-year project under way, but this time PG&E has kept its 30-year-old first-generation computer system, which it is upgrading and replacing only gradually."

Such mega-system failures are turning up "at a dizzying rate," brought on by the interactions of high-pressured changes in the business world, the ever greater complexity of software, and "technology boosters' can-do mentality, even when they can't."

The Massachusetts research company Standish Group International Inc., studying the experience of 360 firms, found that 42% of the firms' information technology projects were scrapped before being completed. "But the backlash is [just] beginning." A new generation of executives has come to understand that behind the most sensational successes in the computer field there may lurk the old well-known supersalesman bred to a degree of cheek, greed and overstatement hardly less staggering than the technology itself. Microsoft's present discussions with the anti-trust department in Washington is filling in the picture with some amazing details.

"What's emerging is a search for a better balance between manpower and computer power, often resulting in some 'de-automatisation' of an organisation's information systems." Obviously, this is going to clash with many stock-market evaluations that by now are built into our indexes: those sensational rises of the market appraisals of stocks based on how many thousands of employees they have laid off. Nor is the problem likely to respect the mega-bank mergings recently announced.

"When companies mismanage technology, or the machines themselves fall short, the losses are huge. Struggling Oxford Health Plans Inc. has blamed many of its financial problems on gigantic computer snafues. In extreme cases a failed system has helped sink a company as executives of Fox-Meyer Drug Co. discovered in 1996 when the company's brand-new $65 million computer project failed."

"More senior executives are rebelling against constant upgrades of software, ever more complex and prone to breakdown. 'If our products failed as often as Windows 95, we would have been out of business long ago,' says Howard Selland, president of Aeroquip Corp, of Maumee, Ohio, an automotive supplier."

Wysocki closes his article on a cheerful note: "The current turmoil brings back memories of the robot craze that swept parts of industrial America in the 1980s. The most infamous example was at General Motors which in 1985 opened a highly automated factory in Detroit. Multimillion-dollar robots erroneously put Buick fenders on Cadillac cars. Spray-painting robots began spraying each other. Only when the robot population was reduced did productivity improve."

Letter to the Editor:

A Note on 'A Spreadsheet For Our Mixed Economy' (*ER* 5/98)

A reader has sent us the following comment: "Another great issue of *ER* — dealing also with issues of ecology. However, your taxonomy needs to reflect that the economy markets are actually SUBSETS of ecosystem and human societies (NOT the other way round, as you imply)! That's why the effort to price everything will always fail. Non-monetarised sectors can never be accurately monetised."

There is a misunderstanding here. The Spreadsheet does not imply that the ecosystem is a subset of the human economy. That you could see by consulting the "limit of tolerance" of each subdivision of the ecology (e.g. the CO_2). When that limit is crossed the whole system is undermined. Of course society itself is in a sense a parasite on the ecology. In other contexts we, like anybody concerned about the assault on the environment, have repeated that *ad nauseam*.

As you are aware, set and subset have precise meanings in mathematics. A subset must be entirely contained within the set. There must be no overlap. That is hardly the case with the ecology and the mixed economy. The reality of the mixed economy contains many forces that are alien and even threatening to the ecology. That is why such a spreadsheet is essential. The same can be said of any species — otherwise it would not take predators to enforce a workable balance within the ecology.

As the title 'A Spreadsheet for our Mixed Economy' makes clear, our point of departure is the Mixed Economy — that is what we are speaking about. Shakespeare may be a greater playwright than Moliere, but when we are writing about Moliere, we devote more attention to him.

All this falls into place if we think in terms of system and subsystems rather than sets and subsets. Let us take the automobile as the example of a system. For it to function, all its subsystems — the electromagnetic, the fuel (chemical), the mechanical, the electronic — must each and every one function. Averaging out their conditions will not suffice. If a single one becomes non-functional the car cannot move. Nor is it relevant to recite the hierarchy that exists between electromagnetism and chemistry, for example. They are neither subsets of the car nor is the car a subset of any of them. There is a lot about each science involved that is irrelevant to (i.e overlaps) automobile design and maintenance. Ed.

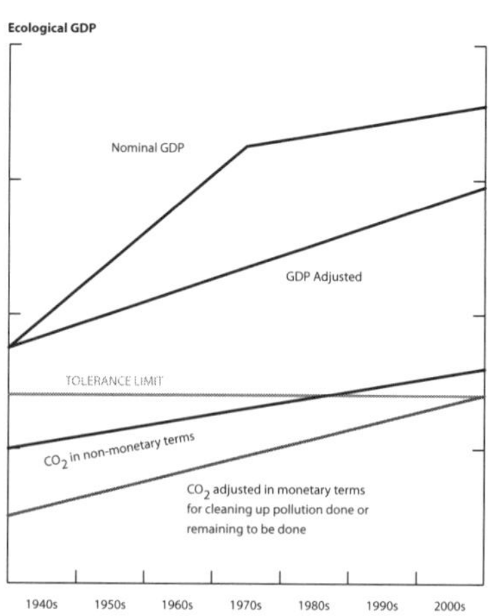

The $64,000,000,000,000 Question

The $64 trillion question in the current quiz program is just what, if any, are the limits to the upward swoosh of the world's stock markets? Let us then begin with a few hard facts.

The monetarism that has shaped our destinies for a quarter of a century is, on the surface, a simple enough faith. It holds that the price level should by the workings of the market always lie flat. Any upward movement of the price index is taken as a certain sign that there is too much money around. The central bank must therefore intervene to restrict credit and drive up interest rates. That done, in the long run (the length never actually specified), everything will fall into place to the advantage of everyone. For money, we are assured, is perfectly neutral.

There is, of course, no lack of evidence both from those who have a lot of it, and from those who have very little, that money, far from being neutral, is weapon with a murderous cutting edge. The lack of it can break up families and drive people to suicide and war. Its abundance can deliver governments, bound hand, foot and tongue, to private individuals. Though the basic monetarist faith was touchingly simple, it came with an undisclosed agenda attached: the utter deregulation of the economy including its financial sector. There has never been a suggestion of postponing such deregulation until some of the promised "neutral" blessings began rolling in. Rather there would seem to be an urgency for those in control to strike while the iron is hot, and get things done while opportunity was still there. That smacks of a sense of raw, unneutral power rather than a belief in what they were preaching.

The present magic flight of our stock markets is not driven by the basic monetarist dogma: that high interest rates are the unfailing cure for just about every ailment known to man. High interest rates are in fact deadly poison to stock markets. Let us draw up a brief list of the devices that have served to keep them rising and in the process shifting trillions of dollars from the most vulnerable sectors of the population to entrenched financial groups.

1. Our banks have undergone a mutation, during which they have changed their very food chain. Time there was when barring the local undertaker, the banker was the most solemn citizen in town. Not surprisingly, for he had been entrusted with the administration of a miracle — money creation. That enjoined a severe discipline. Though in a figurative sense they may have distributed wine and wafers, it was inconceivable that these priest-like characters should end up taking over wineries and bakeries in a battle for market share. That, however, is what has come to pass.

The miracle of money-creation is more easily understood if we track its history. Originally drafts on banks were redeemable in precious metals. When there was clearly not enough gold to go around, banks turned to issuing their own notes. But backing those notes, they had to leave a percentage of legal tender — government debt — in Canada, first with the Ministry of Finance, and with the Bank of Canada after it opened its doors in 1935.

In the early 1970s even theoretical equivalence between gold and the currency disappeared. Money became government debt and nothing else. That reduced it to an abstraction — a medium in which miracles are more readily brought to pass.

Repeatedly when bankers got themselves into difficulty by disregarding their vows, banks were allowed to write the scenario for their bailout by the government. By mid-1994 the cash reserves the banks held with Bank of Canada had been done away with.

Along with the Bank for International Settlements Risk-Based Capital Requirements, this allowed them to increase their holdings of federal debt by some $60 billion to a total around $80 billion without putting up any cash of their own. This has been the equivalent of an annual subsidy — an entitlement — of at least $5 billion. With the removal of restrictions on what banks can invest in, this subsidy has been parlayed into the acquisition of brokerages, insurance companies, derivative boutiques, to the point where the ratio of bank assets to the legal tender in their possession has soared from 11.1:1 in 1946 to 347:1 currently.

2. The monetarist dogma was that "inflation is always a monetary phenomenon," i.e. it depends on money and little else. But these days money is entirely credit — either that of the government which is legal tender that *must* be accepted for the discharge of a debt, or of a bank and other private credit which is accepted on the basis of trust. But in the process of deregulating banking to permit them to perform their miracle on an ever more massive scale, the banks and the central bank fudged the evidence by which their doctrine could even be tested. As financial deregulation proceeded, the variety of interest-bearing near-moneys multiplied, and soon central banks went on dreaming up new categories of "money supply" etc. to cover each new "near-money" that appeared: M-2, M-2 plus, M-2 plus plus, M3, and so forth. "Near money" is interest-bearing credit accepted as money in contrast to cash or "legal tender" that does not bear interest. For example, credit cards — which make up the largest asset of some major banks — are not included in our money supply. Nor are stock market winnings arriving in such bumper year-round harvests. And yet no Jaguar salesman has been known to turn down an order from somebody because he was paying for a matching pair of Jaguars ("His and Hers") with stock market booty. We have then the paradox of our central banks that see inflation under every bed and respond to it with higher interest rates but are today stone-blind to the greatest asset inflation that is readily monetised into bank credit.

3. There is a deeper explanation for this. With their acquisition of brokerage and underwriting houses, the banks, from depending upon interest as their main revenue, have become stock-market driven. That explains the reluctance of the Federal Reserve in the US and the Bank of Canada to apply the "one blunt tool" to which they have reduced their kit — interest rates — to douse the greatest asset inflation in history.

Over the years central banks whose duty it was to monitor the private banks, have come to do their bidding. In the words of a former chairman of the US Fed, the duty of a central bank is "to take away the punch bowl just as the party gets going." What the banks are drinking these days is much stronger than punch. But raising interest rates would prick the hot air balloon that the stock market has become, and devastate the banks as well as the rest of the financial community.

4. The increase in the private bank holdings of government debt has done more than allow private banks to pipe into the government treasury on an ongoing basis. It is changing the nature of money. Even where the central bank — as in the case of the US Fed — is entirely owned by private banks, some 99% of its earnings are remitted to the government treasury. In Canada since 1938 the government has been the sole shareholder of the Bank of Canada, and that makes the process of money creation still more transparent — the remittance of the central bank's earnings is made as dividends. But the important point is that when private banks have so vastly increased their holdings of government debt, more of our money becomes interest-bearing and less of it (M1) is interest-free as were gold, and bank notes.

During the Great Depression, an Argentinian-German economist, Silvio Gesell, had a bright idea or bringing idle money back into the real economy. Every month a tax stamp of small amount had to be affixed to the money-bill to keep it valid. A penalty was thus imposed for hoarding what was a resource in critically short supply — credit. What has happened in recent years is the exact opposite — less and less non-interest-bearing money is being created (legal tender or cash). It has been replaced with interest-bearing credit — "near monies." That massive increase in interest in one way or another finds its way into the bond and stock market.

Gesell's idea caught Keynes's fancy and he incorporated it into his draft proposal for the post-war world financial institutions — wealthy nations that build up large international payments balances had to reinvest them in the debtor countries under penalty of gradually forfeiting their balances to the international community.

5. The mutation undergone by our banks has deprived the central bank of the means and will to contain the greatest asset boom on record. For the moment our governments and the market players whose interests they have come to serve are distracted from the dilemma by the record profits that continue rolling in. By the rules of capitalisation the rate of return and the rate of increase of the rate of return and so forth to infinity must be matched year after year. (All these derivative rates are embodied in the graph of past performance that is a feature of stock analyses.) Otherwise, Pegasus's wings become unstuck. To postpone Judgment Day there is only a single recourse: transforming society's capital accumulations into forms where they can serve to keep the glorious potlatch going. At Bretton Woods Keynes lost out to the American bankers.

6. The privatisation of public investment has been a powerful way of fuelling the unending stock market ascent. The lack of serious bookkeeping in the public sector of Canada, the US and the UK imparts great depth to this resource. Capital investments of the government are written off in a single year, and are entered on the government's balance sheet at a token $1. Despite the urgings of the Auditor General for some years, and some vague talk of introducing capital budgeting, nothing has been done.

The only possible explanation of this is the usefulness of such non-accountancy for the Hidden Agenda of the monetarists. Firstly, to exaggerate the degree of real inflation and justify the high interest rates. Were Imperial Oil to write off its wells, pipelines and refineries in a single year, the price of gasoline would hit the skies. There is no reason to believe that the effect is any different when books are kept this way by government. Secondly, when the government deficit and the debt became the panic buttons, citing the debt without the capital non-financial assets that offset it, provided the edge of hysteria needed to push through the wholesale slashing of social programs. With the value of the Parliament Buildings, entered on the government books at a symbolic dollar they could be sold, say for $1,000 and the resulting $999 would result as a capital gain that could be applied patriotically against the national debt.

Meanwhile such basement-bargain privatisations, can be floated on the stock market with great profit to the promoters. This hardly improves the much-lamented morality of our public life.

7. The reduction of the tax on capital gains has enhanced stock values across the board. For it is the after-tax profits that tend to be capitalised ("the name of the game") and compared with what is available in the real economy.

8. The move is on to increase still further the availability of tax-deferred pension funds for investment on the stock market. This is one of the many ways of adding to the flow of money bidding for listed shares that with the epidemic of mergers are coming into ever shorter supply.

9. The demutualisation of mutual insurance companies would not only put vast new pools of capital in the hands of the public but add to the available stock.

10. Since the Mexican meltdown of 1994 the International Monetary Fund has refined its technique of serving as a wreckers' ball to break up distressed economies in the Third World and the Emerging countries. This makes it possible for vulture capitalists to pick up valuable pieces at bargain-basement prices, and position themselves strategically within those economies

11. The influx of cheap commodities and industrial products from the emerging economies restructured by the IMF contributes to the deflation of the real economy in the developed countries, and thus enlarges the elbowroom for the financial economy to inflate its take. Any increase in the profit margins of a producing firm is at once capitalised into capital gains for shareholders. Insiders with options to cash in benefit as well from a third multiplier — they have been able to carry large inventories of call on company shares without putting up any money.

12. Corporations listed on the stock market have been pursuing a policy of reducing their dividend payments, and using the liquidity conserved to buy back their own shares. This helps keep their prices climbing. Such undistributed cash may make possible further acquisitions, which tend to lift stock prices still higher. There is also a tax advantage in receiving less as dividends and more as capital gains on the sale of shares.

13. Rewarding executives with options to a greater extent than with salaries allows an enhancement of a company's balance sheet and hence its stock market performance. Salaries turn up as a current expense; options do not. Until exercised, under current accounting rules, companies do not have to count the cost of stock options against their net earnings.

14. Significantly more of the mega-mergers — particularly those done by the banks — are consummated without money changing hands. But it is not unusual for the market value of the engaged corporations to soar by many billions. That, of course, allows insiders to cash in their profits. This is a classic sign that the market boom has entered its final stage when insiders stage their timely getaway.

15. Much of the derivative trading consists of an underlying security with the derivatives that are supposed to shelter the investor from the exchange risks. Such instruments seek to combine some of the interest premium of emerging country securities with derivative hedging against the risk that is the reason for the premium. Since philanthropy is not so widespread on this planet for third parties to take over such risk knowingly, there is a fatal flaw in the arrangement. Banks may sell the package and leave the passive investor with the problem. This is known as "credit enhancement" which to well-attuned ears is itself a warning. Most of these packages, in fact, leave either the principal of the underlying security or the interest flow incompletely hedged since there are not enough proceeds from the sale of derivatives to cover both the principal and the revenue flow against currency risk. If the local currency falls drastically enough the package is in trouble. By that time the financial institution that put the package together and sold it is in the clear. It does not, however, make life easier for the purchaser, or for the authorities that exercise surveillance over such markets. Such derivatives have contributed to the stock market's levitation.

16. There was a time when "stock market analysts toiled in relative obscurity, writing reports on companies, making earning forecasts and recommending which stocks investors should buy or sell. All that changed in the 1990s. The boom on Wall Street has transformed many analysts' roles. Instead of simply assessing stocks they

increasingly promote them. If analysts aggressively tout a company's stock, their firm stands a greater chance at snaring an advisory role and the fat fees that follow. Now analysts can be stars, receiving bonuses of several hundred thousand dollars for big underwriting deals. Bash a stock, and your firm could be shut down." (*Wall Street Journal* 18/05) The *WSJ* names names of lone heroes who call the shot honestly, even though it can cut their earnings to a million a year instead of seven times that figure for more accommodating colleagues.

The takeover of brokerage firms by the banks has led to a revision of the very language. *Sell* is simply unutterable unless the company is just about in the bankruptcy courts or subject to a criminal investigation. *Hold* now means *sell*, and so forth.

We are back in fact to the fixed quiz programs in the early days of TV where the phrase "the $64,000 question" arose. The sponsors of the program took it upon themselves to arrange the winners beforehand to obtain a victor who would be a suitable image for Revlon's products. That led to a congressional inquiry. But there is no sign of that happening with the promotion of stocks by analysts.

This is by no means a complete list of the devices that are keeping stock markets soaring. Since they are draining the resources of the real economy and society itself, accumulated over a half century, there is no possibility of the phenomenon continuing indefinitely. To believe that there is, is to espouse perpetual motion.

William Krehm

The Civil Commons — Why the Global Free Market Is Neither

The master term of the global market's representation of itself is, as we know, "*the market*." "The market" is always in control, always infallible, and always to be obeyed. It requires, demands, punishes and restructures societies' production, distribution and survival across the planet. With transnational corporate oligopolies as its moving parts, it is the immutable law-giver of humanity's material condition. Or so it is believed.

In this Old Testament conception of "the market," an invisible and unerring hand of stern judgement produces economic miracles one day, and economic meltdowns the next, usually of the same societies. It pushes stock markets to new highs, attacks government social spending, transforms social orders overnight, and generally comports itself in ways that are understood as once God was comprehended by the godfearing. It is always right, no more resistible than the laws of physics, and deviation from its rule must inevitably end in disaster.

Yet we find that whenever we go to any *real market*, we move within an entirely different world. We may be in central London or Paris, an Indian or African village, an older town of Canada or Germany on the weekend, a Latin American plaza or a Far Eastern backstreet on any morning — everywhere there is a real market, a living community gathering together to exchange what each needs to enable their and their families' lives.

This free market is not remotely like the oligopolist corporate system which now calls itself "the market." It is not an hypostasised aggregate of borderless money investors focussed solely on having more money demand, nor controlled by transnational corporations and financial syndicates entering and exiting societies in nanoseconds to increase profit margins as the single ruling objective of their being. There is not a single aspect of life in common between this real free market we enjoy in the flesh, and what re-engineers societies across the world as the "global market."

How could such opposites be everywhere called by the same name? How could the real free market be swallowed and pushed to the margins everywhere by what calls itself "*the* market," and no one wonder why this mega-machine is designated as what it destroys?

The free market we experience in real life needs to be remembered to recover from the amnesia of the global system program. It is made up of ordinary people meeting in a publicly owned space. The goods are all foodstuffs, mostly fresh, often live, grown typically by their sellers. No one force-plays with a sudden invasion or desertion of money demand. All are friendly and jovial as on a festival day. The buyers and sellers talk with one another of the health of their families, their shared community, and local affairs. Not a place in the real free market can be privately owned, and the quality of goods is not hidden under wraps or chemically engineered for false appearances. Everything is sold without packaging or in recycled paper. The articles for sale always serve a need, and never a demand-created want. Creation of desire beyond need by operant conditioning does not exist. There is no monopolist or oligopolist distortion of supply or demand. Every good sold, unless the market is being undermined, expresses the local region's culture. Prices of different vendors are immediately comparable, directly negotiable with the owner, and no hard sell can entrap anyone in the open venue. Relations of community mediate everywhere in the real market with no closed doors or distant manipulators controlling the transactions.

No non-contributing stock-owner can make a profit out of the real free market. Bank and credit cards do not structure the transactions, nor appropriate a hidden margin from either vendor or buyer. Paper debts and interest charges cannot enter the producer-and-buyer-controlled process. No waste or pollution is generated by the direct transactions of individuals exchanging for what they need, and nothing is sold to harm people's lives. Because no one from outside the market can get rich from producing nothing for it, it is democratic. Most profoundly, the sequence of exchange is serves the growth of life on both sides, not the growth of money as an end-in itself.

The real free market was a great advance of the community's control of its own life when it was no longer subjugated to kings, lords or municipal monopolies for the privilege of its existence. It was an opening of liberty when ordinary individuals could freely exchange with each other in a public space to acquire the foods or crafts they chose to produce or buy. Money here was not a weapon to reduce others to instruments. Money in the real market is a universal medium of exchange that enables individuals to transact across differences of jobs and goods without incommensurables of worth standing in the way.

We might conclude that the real free market *is* truly "individual," "free" and "democratic" as a social form of life. While all of these properties are also claimed by the global corporate "market," all of its justifications draw on properties of its opposite, the real free market, to sustain the profound confusion between them. Not even the medium of exchange they depend on is the same, any more than pocket money is the same as interest-and-financial-charge-bearing instruments without cash reserves — the drive-wheel of the global system. The question, then, arises again. How could these opposed forms of life be collapsed into identity without the notice of economists and logicians? How could they be so pervasively confused that no terms in the technical literatures of the social sciences distinguish between them? How could such an equation of contraries so control world culture that public policy decisions continue everywhere on the basis of what is, in effect, a systematic lie?

Yet the difference between the real and the unreal is not only repressed in the mass media. It is also repressed in school texts, economic courses, and professional economic models themselves. Indeed, one finds that just about everyone justifies the global corporate market *in terms of* its opposite, the real free market, even though the consequences of doing so are like steering world life while asleep.

John McMurtry

Vol. 10, No. 7 — July 1998

A Fallback Plan for the Mega-bailout of Our Merged Banks?

The Honourable Paul Martin, PC, MP

Minister of Finance

Dear Mr. Martin:

Cheers for your resistence to the pressures for hastening the approval of the proposed bank mergers. Certainly enough is happening in the world to warrant delaying such approval until the government has assessed the full implications of the East Asian meltdown. This, you will remember, was completely unforeseen by the Discussion Paper of the Task Force on the Future of the Canadian Financial Services Sector, nor even recognised when it was already taking place.

Before our government can in good conscience take a position on the mergers, it will have to do a great deal of catch-up in public discussion on the previous bailout of these same banks from the consequences of their speculative excesses in the latter 1980s. At that time all information on the bailout was carefully withheld both from Parliament and the media.

Central to that covert operation was the 1991 revision of the *Bank Act* phasing out the reserves banks held with the Bank of Canada. As late as the mid-seventies such primary reserves, which earned the banks no interest, had amounted to 10% of a bank's deposits plus secondary reserves of interest-bearing government paper of 9%. By 1991 the primary reserves had already been whittled down from 10% to 3%, and secondary reserves abolished altogether. Likewise the BIS Risk-Based Capital Requirements introduced in 1988 had declared the debt of OECD countries risk-free that banks could acquire without putting up capital of their own. Together, these two bailout measures made it possible for Canada's chartered banks to stock up with $60 billion of additional federal debt to a total of about $80 billion without putting up any legal tender of their own.

When the central bank holds federal debt, practically all the interest paid on it finds its way back to the Bank's sole shareholder, the Government. On the other hand, when banks hold such debt, such interest stays with them. In this way an ongoing entitlement was given to our banks of over $5 billion dollars annually.[1] When this ingenious arrangement of the bailout was eventually uncovered by COMER, the government joined the banks in protesting that it was "their own money." The government thus helped plunge our banks into an identity crisis, representing the surrender of almost the entire franchise of money-creation to the banks as the removal of an unjust tax. Without that our banks would never have achieved the arrogance to which you were treated, Mr. Minister, when they surprised you with their public announcement of their merger plans.

US banks, be it noted, are still required to hold statutory reserves with the Federal Reserve amounting to 3% of their deposits. The reserve requirement continues to exist in Germany and other European countries. Restoring them in Canada therefore would not put our banks at a disadvantage vis a vis their main competitors. Discontinuing them, on the other hand, placed us in the category of the Cayman Islands and Luxembourg, and other "tax shelter havens" that are in fact financial bordellos where anything goes.

The end of reserves and the BIS Risk-Based Requirements have, along with other deregulation, made it possible for our banks to attain a ratio of assets to legal tender in their possession of 347:1 (compared to 11.1:1 in 1946).[2] Such outlandish leverage makes our banking system immensely vulnerable to the growing turbulence of the world's stock markets. It is time, Mr. Minister, that your department awakened to this fact. Your present failure to do so threatens the great Liberal Party with the fate of the Progressive Conservatives.

Deregulation, takeovers and mergers have altered our banks' food chain. Today they are far more dependent upon the stock market than on traditional banking income. That explains the reluctance of the Bank of Canada to address the present unprecedented asset inflation. Given that and the inordinate leverage cited, it may well be that before the present deadline for your government's decision on the proposed banks mergers — the end of 1998 — our banks will have lost much of their capital in stock market and currency implosions.

It is therefore urgent, Mr. Minister, that you give thought to how the next bailout of our banks could be structured. Since statutory reserves no longer exist, their further reduction to that end is not available. The government could, of course, privatise the Parliament Buildings and the St. Lawrence Seaway which are on its balance sheet at a nominal $1. If a couple of billion dollars were obtained in such an operation, a capital gain of $1,999,999,999 could be booked and used to reduce the debt. That, however, would not begin to cover the banks' possible losses on over $1.3 trillion of assets spread adventurously all over the globe.[3]

There is not a single neo-conservative dogma that has been left standing by the financial meltdown sweeping over the world from the Far East. Governments are supposed to keep out of financial matters? Then why has the IMF with the backing of Washington twisted the arm of the South Korean and other governments to guarantee the debt of private foreign banks so that they could still manage to pass the BIS capital requirements?

Against this background it is grotesque that the Governor of the Bank of Canada should still not have repudiated his vow never to mention the word "deflation" again.[4] Canada is cutting an absurd figure as it slips into the deepest deflation since the thirties with its central bank head plighted never again to utter the "D-Word." Section 14 of the *Bank of Canada Act* bestows on you the power, and its Preamble the duty[5] to reinstate that excessively timely word into the BoC's vocabulary. Do you really want to go down in history as the Finance Minister who led the country into a replay of the thirties gagged and blind-folded?

Basic to a fall-back plan for the next bailout of our banks, would be the reintroduction of reserve requirements as they stood in 1991 and still exist in the US today. This would reduce the banks' ability to hoard government debt without outlay of legal tender. The slack would be taken up by the Bank of Canada rebuilding its holdings of federal debt. In the mid-seventies this amounted to over 22% of the outstanding debt;

today it is below four percent. Of course, the amount of that debt has risen vastly in absolute terms, but that was largely because more of it has been held by the chartered banks — for long periods at interest rates wildly hoisted by the central bank to the point of crumpling the tax-base. Reversing that trend — cautiously, step by step — will make available interest-free finances which the Government can apply in part to bailing out the distressed financial system as that need arises. But this time the bailout must not be on terms prescribed by the banks, but rather designed to bring the banks back to serving the producing economy.

Banks that get themselves into greater difficulty than the average of the industry must be required, once rehabilitated, to leave with the central bank more than the standard 3% reserves for a specified period. When banks consent to restructure clients' defaulted debt, they usually demand more collateral, not less. In any future bailout of our banks the government must follow that example.

Once restored, the reserves can be used instead of higher interest rates to cool the economy when it really is overheated. By raising the necessary reserve ratio temporarily, the volume of lending banks can do will be curtailed.

Exchange controls, rather than high interest rates, must become once again the preferred temporary instrument for defending a currency under pressure. By now it should be clear that churning the economy and the currencies with high interest rates benefits only the mega-speculators.

The sloshing of hot short-term funds across funds must be impeded. The Chilean model of requiring a 30% one-year deposit of the total amount of a foreign loan to be made with its central bank could be followed. This in no way affects real foreign investments, but rules out purely speculative money inflows — absolutely in the case of short-term money and with a maximum tax in the range of 2% in the case of one-year funds.

The maintenance of employment in the event of bank mergers is certainly important, but cannot become the main consideration in approving the proposed mergers. Far more important is what use the banks make of their hugely expanded powers of money creation. Nor is increased presence of foreign banks the solution, since the large international banks have served our banks as role models in their merger-mania. To reduce the issue to such terms is to trivialise it. The powers of money creation concern the very life-blood of the productive economy, and significantly enough the very subject has been expunged from public discussion.

To really deal with the problem, two routes must be followed. The present laws governing credit unions must be studied to determine whether their access to cheque-clearance and other banking infrastructures can be extended to make them more effective competitors of our chartered banks in serving small and medium-sized businesses.

A new class of banking charter should be made available that would limit the loan to each client to, say, $2 million. With each charter granted, would go the obligation to open a branch in a small population centre left without a banking branch. Despite such limitations and obligations accompanying this new type of charter, it would still represent a valuable asset, and would not go begging. Since our large banks have turned their backs on small and medium-sized business loans for headier adventures, we can predict a massive movement of clients from the current mega-banks to those operating under the new charters.

We trust you will give these proposals careful consideration and act to prevent an unnecessary public subsidization, once again, of the private banking system.

William Krehm
Publisher-Editor
Economic Reform

c. Harold Mackay, Chairman, Task Force on the Future of the Canadian Financial Services Sector, finservtaskforce@fin.gc.ca

[1] This understated amount is a very sizeable proportion of the current earnings of Canada's chartered banks. But it should be noted that the declared earnings of our banks not only are net of considerable speculative losses abroad, but of writeoffs incurred in connection with recent takeovers, technological improvements, restructurings, and the preparative work on the proposed mergers.
[2] The figures for December 1997 given in the *Bank of Canada Review*, show this ratio having dropped to 317.7:1. This probably reflects the first losses from the East Asian implosion.
[3] The exact figure of our chartered banks' liabilities can be found on page C6 of the *Bank of Canada Review*. This does not include the risks involved in Over the Counter derivatives such as "interest swaps" which are not carried on our banks' balance sheets.
It should be noted that the Financial Accounting Standards Board [www.fasb.org] in the US has recently ruled that such derivatives be reported in US banks balance sheets at their current market values beginning in 1999 (*Wall Street Journal*, 2/06/98). It is to be hoped that Canada will lose no time in introducing this same change in our banks' accountancy in the interest of the transparency recommended by the IMF to East Asian countries.
[4] "Mr. Thiessen assured the Commons Finance Committee 'that he will probably regret forever having mentioned it.'" (*G&M* 16/05/1997)
[5] "to mitigate by its influence fluctuations in the general level of production, trade, prices and employment, so far as may be possible within the scope of monetary action."

A Change in Derivative Accountancy in the Works?

Tucked away in an inner page of *The Wall Street Journal* (2/06) is an item 'FASB Approves Controversial Derivatives Rule' that might cause greater turmoil than getting the famous computer software on corporation computers for the good year 2000.

"After 10 years of heated debate, US accounting rule makers have approved sweeping changes in how companies account for derivatives. The new rule for the first time requires corporations to report the fair-market value of derivatives on their balance sheets so that investors can better grasp their effect on profits. The rule takes effect for fiscal years beginning after June 15, 1999.

"Derivatives are financial contracts whose values are derived from those of underlying assets such as bonds, stocks or commodities. Some $65 trillion of derivative contracts exist today according to industry estimates. 'Derivatives can, in a heartbeat, turn into a $10 million or a $100 million liability for a company. But investors never get to see them,' said Edmund L. Jenkins, chairman of the Financial Accounting Standards Board. 'Now they will, thanks to the new standard.'

"This marks a victory for FASB and closes out one of the most controversial chapters in the rule makers' history. Many banks had lobbied Congress to block the rule, arguing that it would introduce enormous earnings volatility, and last year Federal Reserve Chairman Alan Greenspan asked FASB to drop it.

"Some congressmen, meanwhile, have backed legislation that would effectively knock the FASB out of its standards-setting role and instead shift that responsibility to the SEC; [such] legislation so far has picked up very little support. (It was Congress that pushed the FASB in the first place to issue a derivatives standard, after Orange County, Calif., suffered huge losses from its derivatives investments in 1994.)"

By sheer coincidence, the county's leading investment banker at the time, Merrill

Lynch & Co., has just settled for $437.1 million the county's lawsuit against it for the derivatives loss incurred as a result of the firm's advice. Other investment firms are likely to negotiate similar settlements, but the bond-rating firm, Standard & Poor's, is prepared to defend itself in the courts for having given the county top-rating shortly before it declared bankruptcy due to its derivatives losses.

This is another example of an effect that will increasingly downgrade stock market performance, and might be called "adjustment of overshooting capitalisations" In the present case derivative losses do not appear on the balance sheet resulting in an exaggerated bottom line. That performance along with any improvement over last year, and any improvement of the rate of improvement are extrapolated into the indefinite future in placing a price on the stock. Then comes an adjustment in accountancy that lowers these performance rates. Clearly, the adjustment in share value that will have to take place is a non-linear affair reaching into the remote future. The same effect occurs, when the foreseen efficiencies resulting from a merger or a downsizing of staff fail to occur. The essence of the matter is that market promoters by the capitalisation process tend to overvalue shares in a non-linear way. Reality, once it asserts itself, will have to bring on similarly non-lineal rectifications.

Derivatives

Below we quote an excellent paper by Adam Tickell, Professor of Geography at the University of Southampton, 'Dangerous derivatives: controlling and creating risks in international money,' which sheds light on the importance of the new rule proposed by the FASB:

The development of modern derivatives stems back to 1848. [In that year] the Chicago Board of Trade [CBOT] laid the foundations for much of the late twentieth century financial system. At the centre of a vast agricultural hinterland [the city] saw the development of "to arrive" contracts which allowed grain traders to sell their grain at an agreed price and deliver it later. In 1865 the CBOT adopted the first formal rules governing these futures contracts. Even in these early days, however, contracts were traded speculatively and 'men who don't own something are selling that something to men who don't really want it.'

In 1972 the Chicago Mercantile Exchange created the International Monetary Market which permitted trading in currency futures: the first derivatives contracts not based on physical products. [This] laid the basis for the development of more esoteric and abstract contracts later on.

The most basic form of derivative is a variant of the form that developed in Chicago in the 1860s: the future. A buyer of a future agrees to pay a given price on an agreed date for an asset (ranging from agricultural commodities to foreign currency), while the seller of a future agrees to sell on the same terms. Futures enable a buyer to lock into a given price and provide certainty. To ensure that buyers of futures can afford to meet their commitments, they are required to deposit an initial margin payment before they are allowed to trade on an exchange. [The payment] varies according to the volatility of the market and the type of asset being traded. For example, trading government securities futures requires smaller margin payments than trading futures based on equities.

A swap is an agreement to exchange cashflows between two parties and is effectively made up of a series of futures contracts. Interest rate swaps dominate the market and typically involve the 'counterparties' to the trade agreeing to exchange their interest rate liabilities. For example, if Firm A is borrowing money at variable interest rates it may wish to protect itself against rising interest rates. It can then agree to pay fixed interest rates by 'swapping' its borrowing for fixed interest rates with Bank B.

The third common derivative tool is the 'option.' In exchange for a premium, options give buyers the right either to buy (in the case of a 'call option') or sell (in the case of a 'put option') an asset at a predetermined price. Buyers will exercise that right if — and only if — interest rates move in their favour. ...Sellers, on the other hand, expose themselves to theoretically unlimited risks in exchange for a premium (and will therefore hedge their exposure themselves). Sellers of options receive premium income for potentially limitless losses and for this reason most sophisticated options traders both assume that they need to trade sufficient options for premium income to be able to cover inevitable losses (in the same way as household insurance companies pay for claims by pooling the risk).

Banks and brokers have developed these three basic forms of derivative instruments into more complex variants, largely by combining features of each. Swaptions, for example, are options to buy swaps and allow purchasers flexibility effectively to terminate another swap contract. For example, if a firm has a ten year swap A which it believes it might wish to end after five years, it could buy the option to buy a swap (a swaption) which had the opposite characteristics of its original swap A and would therefore cancel the costs of A. However, if circumstances mean that it wishes to continue with its original swap, then it will not exercise its swaption. Other, more complex, derivatives include exotically named instruments such as 'butterflies,' 'differential swaps,' 'strangles,' 'condors' and 'straddles.'[1]

Derivatives provide institutional investors, corporate treasury departments, and bank risk management departments with a number of significant benefits over trading the underlying asset. Their principal advantage is that they allow investors to hedge risk, in effect acting as insurance against adverse market movements. Second, some derivatives provide signals to the wider financial markets which, advocates claim, reduces uncertainty. In the case of commodities, rising futures prices may be a stimulus for increased production. Third, derivatives significantly reduce the costs of diversifying portfolios, because investment managers can expose themselves to derivatives based on baskets of stocks rather than on a smaller number of more volatile stocks. Fourth, derivatives are relatively cheap because they effectively operate on leverage. US Treasury futures, for example, require an initial margin payment of only 1.5% of the value of the Treasury Bonds.

However, despite their risk management function, derivatives have managed to achieve something of a bogey status since they first entered the public conscious-ness during the early 1990s. This is because they not only allow institutions to offset risk, but have also been implicated in a series of high profile losses which have undermined the financial viability of companies, banks and government entities.

In conditions of a perfect market derivatives are unable to effect the price of underlying assets (such as exchange or interest rates) and all they can do is to allocate risk between different players in the market and as they spread that risk more widely they should provide a wider systemic stability.

Yet perfect markets do not, of course, exist. Derivatives are traded in real markets where some players have some specialist knowledge, for example, that others do not have, while the very complexity of some instruments may lead to 'market risk.' Despite the increasing sophistication of models, there continue to be inaccuracies in the measurement of risks inherent in specific instruments.[2] Derivatives are more prone than other financial products to liquidity and credit risks. Credit risk is more common and occurs when the counterparty to a trade is unable to meet its obligations. The opacity of some derivatives, the potential for high gearing and the non-linear risk structure implicit in many means that credit risk is a particular problem of derivatives.

As an IMF study put it, derivatives reinforce the on-going process of global financial integration.[3]

A systemic crisis could be triggered by one of three things: default by a major player; a sudden shift in the prices of derivatives in the financial markets sufficient to undermine the viability of a major player; or the inability to net out obligations and receipts. Derivatives are traded in two ways: on organised and regulated exchanges, and 'over-the-counter' (OTC). Exchange traded derivatives are less flexible than OTC products, have standard structures, require that money is placed with the exchange as a guarantee and that extra margin payments have to be made against adverse market moves. Furthermore, the organised exchanges cooperate closely with clearing houses and so, in effect, the exchanges become counterparties to the trades.

Over-the-counter derivatives are tailored products which have no protection from the exchanges and are held off balance sheet. As a result, they are cheaper and more flexible, but their risk profile is higher and the products can be less easily sold to third parties. To liberal commentators, critics of OTC markets miss the point:

"the nimble nature of the OTC markets readily permits — indeed actively encourages — the introduction of new products. Any attempt to stifle the innovative thinking of the many highly intelligent figures involved ... is an utterly moronic piece of reactionary thought worthy of the worst moments of twentieth century socialism. If a company wishes to risk its capital by creating a new product, then let it."[4]

However, concern about the absolute and relative growth of the OTC markets is not confined to left wing commentators, but include senior regulators and participants on organised exchanges. This is because the OTC markets are less liquid than exchanges and during periods of turbulence they have enhanced the potential for a widespread collapse of market liquidity and backwash throughout the whole financial system.

Furthermore, during the 1990s it has become clear that other factors have exacerbated the levels of systemic risk in the international financial system.

First, there has been the emergence of large, integrated financial conglomerates with highly complex financial and corporate structures. One of the contributory factors in the collapse of Barings, for example, was the lack of clarity in the reporting lines engendered by the complex nature of the bank's corporate structure. Second, an increasing share of international financial transactions is dominated by a small number of institutions from a small number of countries which have the geographical networks, specialist knowledge and technological expertise to command market power and manage internal risk. In foreign exchange, for example, the top ten dealers have increased their market share from 31% in 1990 to 43% in 1997 and by the end of the century over 75% of the market is expected to be controlled by the top 15 firms. Such concentration contributes to instability because if one of the dominant institutions were to get into difficulty the contagion effect would be more serious.

"These institutions tend not just to be each other's largest counterparties, but also to have extensive dealings with many of the same customers around the world and to be members of the same clearing houses and exchanges. Risk exposures can build up undetected by existing monitoring systems."[5]

Although the globalising tendencies in finance have undermined some of the authority and power of national regulators, this is only a partial process and supervisors remain active in attempting to prevent crises in the financial markets. However, it is also important to remember that national-states actively encouraged the internationalisation of finance in general, and the development of derivative markets in particular, which is contributing to increased levels of systemic risk.

The collapse of the post-war financial order, when money was largely national in character and currencies were little traded and largely at fixed exchange rates, undermined the basis of the international regulatory environment. From the development of the Eurodollar markets, in which banks could evade US regulatory jurisdiction of their dollar holdings, in London in the 1960s, international banking began to cease being solely an ancillary to trade and investment and began to develop its own dynamic. In the United States these pressures, as well as intensified competition from non-bank financial institutions that had been stimulated by the deregulation of the New York Stock Exchange in 1975, encouraged banks to lobby Congress to relax the regulatory 'burden,' in the face of opposition from the Federal Reserve Board. The lobbying was hugely successful, leading to the *Depository Institutions Deregulation and Monetary Control Act* (1980) and the *Garn-St. Germain Depository Institutions Act* (1982), both of which dismantled bank regulations, and the establishment of the international banking facilities (IBFs) in 1981 as a direct challenge to the Euromarkets.

As Eric Helleiner has emphasised, the failure of the Federal Reserve to dictate the US regulatory environment was a seminal moment in history of international finance for three reasons. First, it demonstrated that financial institutions could [now] arbitrage between national regulatory systems and choose the one most conducive to their business aims. If one state attempted to impose a more burdensome regime than was to be found [elsewhere], it could either be undermined by a 'racc to the bottom' or it could find its business progressively seeping to other states. Second, the establishment of IBFs, free from tax and domestic US regulatory restrictions, led directly to competitive deregulation in countries which wished to compete with the US and UK as a hosts for financial institutions. Third, the failure of a conservative approach to bank regulation and macro-economic management heralded the development of neo-liberal financial regulation. Therefore, by the early 1980s the three pillars of the emergent 'pro market' regulatory order were born: regulatory arbitrage; regulatory competition; and regulatory neo-liberalism. The Basel Accord on capital standards [issued] in 1987 [by the Bank for International Settlements] became the 'cornerstone of a new regulatory order.'

As Helleiner (1996) points out, "the regime's strength should not be overstated. It was focussed only on the narrow task of preserving global stability through lender-of-last-result, regulatory and supervisory activities..."

Indeed, as derivatives were the fastest growth component of the financial sector, supervisory authorities positively encouraged product innovation in the exchanges within their jurisdiction at the same time as promoting exchanges internationally.[6]

The collapse of Barings Bank in 1995, when a single trader managed to evade both internal controls and external supervision in order to effect a series of disastrous derivatives trades, proved to be a seminal moment in international approaches to derivatives regulation. Although the British authorities initially attempted to isolate the impact of the event by claiming both that it was unique to Barings and that the involvement of derivatives was incidental, less publicly supervisors began to take the potential threat from derivatives far more seriously. Within three months of the Barings incident, regulators of the major financial centres issued the 'Windsor declaration' which signalled their willingness to force greater disclosure of information about derivatives exposure, to ensure that derivatives exchanges shared information, and to develop co-operative structures so that regulators could successfully intervene during emergencies.

[Yet] it is important to recognise that pro-market regulation is inscribed with a series of ideological understandings about the role of the state. The development of a transnational policy community in finance centred on the BIS, which is largely technocratic and free from democratic accountability, serves not only to set the tone for the international co-operation, it also sets the parameters of thinking. In the case of derivatives trading, the policy discourse still largely adheres to liberal understandings of market rationality (exemplified by the emphasis on disclosure as a means of overcoming the market imperfections). Technocrats have internalised a liberal logic. [In] response to Congressional moves to increase the supervision of over the counter derivatives, Alan Greenspan, chairman of the Federal Reserve Board, argued that

"there appears to be no reason for government regulation of off-exchange derivative transactions between institutional counterparties."

Credit rating agencies have increasingly assumed a governance role in international finance. Yet it is a form of governance which may be fragile, is unaccountable, and excludes alternative ways of seeing the world. It is, of course, entirely in keeping with a regulatory order which understands markets as being essentially rational. Shortly before the bankruptcy of Orange County in 1995, both Moody's and Standard and Poor's issued very strong grades for the municipality; while high grades were also issued on the sovereign, financial institution and corporate debt of East and South East Asian countries prior to the crisis of 1997.

Adam Tickell

[1] A. Tickell (1996) 'Making a melodrama out of a crisis: reinterpreting the collapse of Barings Bank,' *Environment and Planning D: Society and Space*, 14, 1, 5-33

[2] Indeed, bad price theory and bad stabilisation models will create risk as happened in September and October 1992 when speculators operating with leverages as high as 1000:1 shot down a series of currencies including the British pound and the Canadian dollar with immense profit. (*ER*)

[3] Group of Thirty (1993) *Derivatives: practices and principles*, Washington

[4] Black S and Young P (1997) 'Exchanges vs OTC trading' *Applied Derivatives Trading* 20 (November)

[5] Group of Thirty, 1997, p. 8

[6] Indeed, it seems at times as though the derivatives business has itself become, like our large banks, "too big to be allowed to fail." Tickell cites the case "when in 1991 the House of Lords ruled that debts incurred by British local authorities in the swaps market had been illegally incurred, the governor of the Bank of England lobbied ministers to introduce retrospective legislation to preserve the integrity of the markets."

[Adam Tickell is a Professor at University of Southampton in England. A longer version of the above paper is available from Prof. Adam Tickell, Department of Geography, University of Southampton, Southampton SO17 1BJ, or email a.tickell@soton.ac.uk. 'Dangerous Derivatives' forms part of a book Rogues, regulation and the culture of finance *to be published by Guilford, NY.]*

Vol. 10, No. 8 — August 1998

The Rising Cost of Spin-Doctoring for Our Banks

Pity that there are no indexes compiled for the cost to our banks of their spin doctoring. For such a statistic would shed much light on a region of shadows.

Time was when critics like COMER simply were simply treated as unmentionable. Now, however, that seems to be changing. In the May-June issue of *The Canadian Banker* Harvey Schachter's article 'The Great Debate' refers to the submissions of COMER to the Task Force on the Future of the Canadian Financial Services Sector in his very first paragraph. But the purpose was hardly to inform the reader of content. Instead by juxtaposing our submission with the Saskatchewan Federation of Labour's use of the venue "to sing some old anti-bank songs by the Wobblies (Industrial Workers' of the World)," there was an artful attempt to present us as unfriendly to banking in a far-out way. Our submission, however, could better be described as an effort to lure the banks back to banking.

I was represented as "Expounding on the waning fungibility of money and [my] other economic theories." In actual fact there is nothing esoteric about "fungibility" — it is the quality of a substance by which any unit is identical with any other unit. Thus gold or cash issued by the government is fungible. Bonds which do earn a specified rate of interest, on the other hand, are not fungible — their market value will depend not only on the soundness of the issuer, but on the current level of interest rates. A bond with a fixed rate of interest will drop in market value if the central bank raises the bank rate.

Fungibility acquired particular importance when the Discussion Paper of the Task Force was published. That was because the junk bonds of Thailand, Malaysia, Indonesia, South Korea carried high interest rates often in US currency, and the ability of the issuing government to honour its obligations was called into question.

None of this was so much as mentioned in the Task Force's Discussion Paper issued when the Thai crisis had already struck. However, that made the concept of "fungibility" more rather than less important and certainly no private preoccupation of mine. It does make a difference whether our banks keep reserves in Canadian tender — as they had to until 1994 — or in fancy Indonesian bonds.

But the importance of the fungibility concept does not end there. It is becoming widely recognised that our key growth statistic — the Gross Domestic Product (GDP) — measures the well-being of the economy by lumping together the additional spending to cope with disasters such as oil spills, earthquakes, the raping of the environment, divorces, crime, epidemics and activities that contribute to society's well-being. Indeed, proposals for replacing the GDP with a statistic put together from more fungible components in this respect are becoming ever more frequent. Remarkable that this should not yet have reached the ears of the CBA's scholars.

The same goes for "[my] other economic theories." Though flattered at the suggestion that the notion of money creation is an invention of mine, I must decline the compliment. Most of COMER's submissions to the Task Force concerned the money creation which, with the phasing out of the reserve requirement in 1991-94, has become a nigh-monopoly of the banks and other financial institutions. Though the banks and the Governor of the Bank of Canada deny that money creation even exists, we can cite an impeccable witness to the contrary.

In 1945 the Canadian Bankers' Association — the proprietor of *The Canadian Banker* — published *A Background of Banking Theory* by W.T.G. Hackett, economist of the Bank of Montreal, that stated: "When the government borrows by selling securities to the central bank there is made possible *an expansion of chartered bank deposits* equivalent to about *ten times* the value of the bonds thus sold, which would bring about *an approximately tenfold addition to the money supply*." (p. 54) The ending of the requirement that the banks put up non-interest-bearing reserves with the BoC in 1991 pushed that multiplier up from 10 to around 70. Currently the ratio of our banks' assets:liabilities to the legal tender they hold is 317:1. With deregulation the quality of those assets has declined greatly to include bonds of Indonesia and South Korea, and fancy derivatives.

But returning to the concept of "fungibility." It embraces not only bonds and other debt, but street-walkers, journalists and economists. As the demand for certain services soars, the fungibility of these professions tends to decline. We can only assume that *The Canadian Banker* is not ungenerous with writers and scholars prepared to impart an amiable twist to certain crucial facts.

William Krehm

Vol. 10, No. 9 — September 1998

First Aid for Our Swooning Dollar?

Our swooning looney has interrupted our Finance Minister's self-congratulations, and reduced him to a an unconvincing stutter about "sound fundamentals." However, since the weakness of the looney is to an extent just the flip side of the inordinate strength of the US dollar, should we not be looking there for some of the roots of that phenomenon?

Certainly, Canada's dependence on resource exports, and the scramble of refugee money away from the financial killing fields of Asia, have played their part in the problem. But dominating the scene and contributing to the imbalances that are tearing the world apart is Clinton's sudden success in doing away with his deficit. That has acted as a powerful magnet drawing money to the US. It made possible the fantastic stock market boom that only now seems to be coming to a steep untidy end.

And crucial to Washington's taming of its deficit was a quiet change in the way it kept its books. Before January 1996, when the federal government purchased capital assets such as buildings or computer systems, the Bureau of Economic Analysis (BEA) treated the transactions as current spending and wrote off the investment in a single year. The value of the acquisition was put on the government's balance sheet at a token $1. In contrast the practice in the business world is to depreciate and write off such capital goods over their useful life.

At the beginning of 1996, BEA quietly corrected this anomaly, which had exaggerated the real deficit. This increased the national savings statistic by $135.2 billion for 1994, $151.1 B for 1993, and comparable amounts for prior years. 1995 data are available only on the new basis. Carried forward to 1995 and backwards to 1959, the change exceeded a trillion dollars. And that, mind you, still ignores the government's investment in human capital. The above figures can be can found in the Survey of Current Business for Jan. — Feb. p 13, Economic Indicators, p. 354, and the Federal Reserve Bulletin table A-40.

Robert Rubin, the Secretary of the Treasury has applied to US foreign policy the arbitrage skills that earned him the chairmanship of Goldman, Sachs on Wall St. The problem of the Clinton Government was short-term and in revising the statistic on government savings and the deficit Mr. Rubin's arbitrage technique worked like a charm. Instead of raising the issue of capital budgeting as a theoretical issue and applying it across the board, he quietly concentrated on a single statistic. That gave him the deficit figure that he needed, that bond traders go by in setting yields. Artfully he avoided stirring up the sleeping ideological dogs of the right.

Our Finance Minister should come out of his lethargy to do the same as the logical first step in rescuing the looney. The ground has been thoroughly prepared for him. On page 33 of the *Bank of Canada Review* (Summer, 1997) he can read a quotation from the *Public Accounts of Canada 1995-6:* Full-cost recovery for many federal assets, including bridges, ports, and telecommunications systems, was never considered either feasible (because the asset was a public good) or desirable (for public-policy reasons). The federal government financing the cost of acquiring and maintaining such assets through budgetary appropriations, recording their book value at a nominal $1. Consequently, if these assets are privatised, all of the sale proceeds can be applied against the deficit, as the $1.5 billion received from the sale of the air navigation system was in the 1996/7 fiscal year. The federal government is gradually moving towards full-accrual accounting, whereby the cost of acquiring physical assets is spread over the asset's useful life."

Doing at least what the Americans accomplished two and a half years ago is the logical first step in the rescue of the looney. The second is for Mr. Martin to order our banks to stop speculative betting against the Canadian dollar. Shorting it should be allowed only when that is a means of hedging a real trade transaction.

William Krehm

Retrospect — a Half Century Later

The Colombian subsidiary of the Spanish publishing house Planeta has just published a new Spanish translation of William Krehm's *Democracy and Tyranny of the Caribbean.* Described as "a classic," it appears in its Black List collection of "cursed and prohibited books, censored and persecuted or simply condemned to oblivion because of what they recounted. Some were confiscated in the printshops before they were even bound. Others were picked up in bookstores and burned. Many of their authors had to choose between jail, exile or the cemetery." The collection includes names as distinguished as German Arciniegas, the celebrated Colombian historian. We shall be publishing excerpts from Krehm's introduction and to his coverage of the first round of Central American revolutions for *Time,* inspired in large part by the hopes aroused by Allied propaganda during the Second World War, but brutally repressed by Washington. David Halberstam in his book on the Fifties sees in the overthrow of the democratically elected Arbenz government of Guatemala in 1954 Washington's first application of a policy of military interventions in LA that through follow-ups in the Dominican Republic, Brazil and Chile eventually led the US into the Vietnam disaster.

A half century has passed since I wrote this book. The first Spanish version appeared in Mexico in 1949. The English original, however, saw the light of day in an edition by Lawrence Hill only in 1985. It had been blocked under the US State Department's "voluntary censorship," introduced during the hot war and carried forward with improvements into the cold. Since that takes us back some years before Senator McCarthy's day, I was in fact dealt a foretaste of its amenities.

Beyond the high adventure this brought me, it disclosed how deeply US statesmen, in shaping the destinies of their southern neighbours, had become infected with Latin America's "magic realism." Under its spell the past becomes the future and the future the past; the dead never quite loosen their grip on the living; and language ceases to mean what it says. Little gets buried; most things of consequence are left to rot. I do not have to remind the countrymen of Gabriel Garcia Marquez that from this compost the greatest contemporary literature was about to sprout. But as in 19th century Russia, all this has not come cheap.

Cost-accounting on that score had scarcely begun when begun when I became engrossed with Central America. American war propaganda had uncorked so bright a vision of the future that even sceptics were swept along. The demeaning thirties and the horrors of the conflict had left humanity tipsy with hope. When I returned to Canada in 1948, people had difficulty grasping that the tale I told could actually happen in so Brave and New a World. At the time little to challenge the State Department's version of matters in the isthmus saw print. Today, however, good books on Central America abound. They bear witness that my worst forebodings about American policy in Latin America were understated.

Years later when the Cold War was already bringing in its bitter harvest, George Kennan came to be rated a moderate. In March 1950, however, as the State Department's Soviet expert, he fitted Latin America into the global scheme as follows:

"If Europe turned anti-US, LA would be all we had to fall back on. We should not hesitate before police repression by the local government since the Communists are essentially traitors. Better to have a strong regime in power than a liberal government if it is indulgent and relaxed and penetrated by Communists."

I reported how the Communists had discredited themselves in several Caribbean countries by complicity with Washington's favourite tyrants. If their fortunes improved later, the State Department had only its own folly to thank.

This political agenda was paired with a no less remarkable economic program.

"In 1950 Assistant Secretary of State for Inter-American Affairs, Edward Miller, admitted that LA had unfairly suffered because during the war the US unilaterally administered price controls that kept raw material prices down, and then after the war allowed the price of US goods to shoot up. In other words, Washington fixed the market in its favour not once, but twice."

Later on such rigging of the terms of trade was to be institutionalised through the International Monetary Fund.

Yet Miller went on to warn of the perils connected with his country's postwar prosperity. Inflation had raised its ugly head. Cocoa beans were up 40% and cotton 30% and the Cold War loomed costly. Latin America must do its bit in the defence of democracy by keeping the lid on the prices of its exports even if that meant price controls. Latin America, having been there before, was less than enthusiastic. Disillusionment could be cut with a knife at the Bogota Panamerican Conference of 1948 and the assassination of the popular leader Jorge Eliecer Gaitain triggered a violent regurgitation of mendacious propaganda. The *Bogotazo* (public anti-American demonstrations) turned out a watershed in US-Latin American relations. From there on they deteriorated at an alarming pace.

Washington had a simple explanation for all its problems south of the Rio Grande:

the Communists were burrowing in its backyard. It responded by putting dependable military allies in charge. Despite the opposition of Chile, Uruguay and Mexico, the Military Defence Assistance Act was passed by Congress in 1951, establishing closer links with LA armed forces. The armies were to be trained at the Panama Canal Zone's School of the Americas. A disproportionate share of the program fell to Central America — among the officers graduating between 1949 and 1964, 1,639 were from Costa Rica, 2,969 from Nicaragua, 810 from Honduras, 358 from Salvador, and 958 from Guatemala, while only 178 were Mexican, 165 Brazilian, and 259 Argentinian.

Under the plan US forces would look after LA's regional and global defence, while "country missions" — counterinsurgency at home — were to be the affair of the local armies.

And it was all to be done on the cheap. With the advent of the Cold War, Europe and Asia had first call on Washington's purse. By 1948 the US had earmarked almost $13 billion of its foreign aid for the reconstruction of Western Europe, while LA was allotted only 2.34% of the total aid. Eisenhower and Foster Dulles felt that development moneys should come from private investors and Export-Import Bank loans, topped off with government financing of the military budgets.

For a while the "payback" from such an investment seemed great. By the end of 1954 military dictators were in the saddle in 13 of the 20 LA countries — a 20th century record. And the centrepiece of the achievement was the overthrow of the Arbenz government in Guatemala in 1954.

That had been brought on by Guatemala's agrarian Reform Law that expropriated 234,000 uncultivated acres of land from the United Fruit Company. The compensation offered was based on its assessment for taxation — $1 million. UFCO asked 16 million. Of the company's 3 million acres only 139,000 were actually under bananas. The rest was kept fallow — the company said for protection against disease, but possibly, too, against competitors.

In democratic countries such matters would be settled in the courts. UFCO's holdings — an estimated 40% of the country's arable lands — had been bestowed on the company for a song by compliant dictators. It had virtually written the tax and custom laws under which it operated. And it had already rejected the proposal of the previous Arevalo government for the renegotiation of its contracts.

Arbenz was planning roads and railways that would threaten UFCO's transportation monopoly based on its railway from the capital to either ocean. Sanctimoniously as on a harp UFCO played on its many strings in Washington. Dulles (once a UFCO lawyer) refused to consider the matter just in terms of bananas: "If they gave me a gold piece for every banana, the problem would remain communist infiltration."

As a matter of course Guatemala had supported major American initiatives at the UN. What condemned Arbenz in Washington was his daring to tamper with a venerable social system that reached back to the Spanish Conquest.

The CIA began training a few hundred Guatemalan exiles under Col. Carlos Castillo Armas on an UFCO plantation in Honduras. In November 1953 John E. Peurifoy arrived in Guatemala as US ambassador. While his Spanish was rudimentary, he did bring a rich experience in suppressing left-wing insurgence in Greece. When Foreign Minister Guillermo Toriello explained that the army used to deliver highland labourers roped together to coastal planters, Peurifoy retorted: "Agrarian reform had been instituted in China, and today China is Communist."

With such omens in the heavens, Arbenz sought arms where he could — from

Czechoslovakia. Had they been available from the US, he surely would have given it the business. On June 18th, 1954 Castillo Armas crossed the frontier with 150 men but got nowhere in skirmishes with Guatemalan troops. Then the CIA blanketed the country with radio reports that Castillo's forces were bearing down on the capital. When two of Castillo's three planes were shot down, replacements were rushed in from Nicaragua and elsewhere to frighten the population by dropping sticks of dynamite on the capital.

Then came Arbenz's fatal error — he tried arming a worker-peasant militia. The officer corps refused to cooperate. Arbenz handed over the presidency to an army colonel of liberal tendency. Ambassador Peurifoy, a pistol in his shoulder holster, at once called on the new president and got him to sign over his office to Castillo. All that remained was for Foster Dulles to go on TV to congratulate "the people of Guatemala" for having remedied the situation "themselves." At the same time Peurifoy was boasting that he had carried out his assignment just 45 minutes off schedule. And Castillo Armas had already begun the execution of several hundred Guatemalans.

I remember Arbenz, who had been my neighbour in Guatemala City, as someone who for dedication, talent and urbanity would have graced the public life of any First World country. His ultimate epitaph came from an American official years later, when the death squads armed by the US had gotten completely out of hand and the unmarked graves in its Guatemalan backyard ran into many thousands: 'What we'd give to have an Arbenz now!'"

The Self-debunking of Economic Dogma

The carnage on the world's stock market is a passing picnic alongside the self-debunking of what has passed for economic science.

Donald Coxe, chair of Harris Investment Management Inc. who moonlights as a superb columnist of *The Globe and Mail,* pinpoints the farce. "Wall St.'s best and brightest bulls have been reassuring frightened customers that a bear market is out of the question because Asia's crises prevent the US Federal Reserve from raising rates.

"The essence of this argument is that the Asian Plague is not just killing Asian economies any more: economies and stock markets as far away as Russia, Brazil and Mexico are infected with the virus. Therefore, the Fed dare not tighten, even though the US economy is strong, wage rates are rising because of labour shortages, and consumers are so confident they are spending 99.4% of their disposable incomes.

"According to this, a stock market with the highest price-earnings ratio in history is secure because conditions range from the grim to the catastrophic in countries with 40% of global gross domestic product. Melvin Coznowski, *Mad* magazine's famed optimist ("What, me worry?") is alive and well and setting strategy on Wall St. The Asian Plague is now the key reason for *buying* stocks, not *selling* them. All plagues are global, all profits are local."

That new logic becomes entrenched with a bit of exercise. Thus on 18/08 the day after Russia, on the heels of Yeltsin's solemn assurance that it would never happen, allowed the ruble to drop by as much as 34%, and proclaimed a moratorium on certain of its bonds, the Dow Jones shot up well over a hundred points to celebrate the prospective withdrawal of dollars from Russia and Eastern Europe.

Wall St. defines a correction as a 10% drop in the leading indexes. A bear is a 20% drop in those indexes. There is nothing more "scientific" about these definitions than about the Street's other pronouncements. Be it, however, noted that the key indexes are based on baskets of high-capital blue chips that mutual funds concentrate on because they alone can provide an outlet for the enormous amounts of the cash awaiting investment. As a result the bear market of smaller cap stocks that has been going on for months does not even show up in the Dow Jones Index.

Deeply rooted in official economic theory is the dogma that just as there is no other god but Jehovah or Allah, there is no other value other than price; and price is the point at which supply and demand meet to clear the market. Consider then the situation where all dykes, all road bumps, just about everything that impedes the flow of greed-crazed money from any point on the earth to any other has been removed, and ask what the inevitable effect of that must be on the market prices of stocks. All cannon — especially the big ones — must be loose on vessels navigating the turbulent seas.

A few months ago President Clinton himself was putting through telephone calls to the government chiefs whose banks, currencies and stock markets had imploded, urging that they deregulate their economies as the IMF required. Clearly Mr. Clinton might have employed his time less harmfully with whatever he was up to with Ms. Lewinsky than peddling such poisonous stuff. Thousands of editorials appear throughout the world with each rising sun urging bigger and more radical "reforms" — a term that has been high-jacked to designate the removal of all constraints from speculative capital and its movement. This helped drive stock quotations to levels that bear no relationship with the earnings of companies. And those levels contribute to money supply, to bogus collateral which stores up further and larger troubles ahead.

These days more and more writers are scampering for an explanation of what has overtaken the world economy. But because of the utter devastation of economic thought over the past decades, the efforts for the most part are picturesquely clueless.

In *The New York Times* (Oped, 2/08) David E. Sanger — inevitably — brings in the Domino Theory. "For a year now the domino theory has been making a comeback, this time paired with the newest buzzword in foreign policy: Contagion. The general idea is the same — if one country's economy is permitted to implode, it could start an uncontrollable set of events around the world — even if it has less to do with guns and Communists than with currency reserves and the psychology of panicked investors. 'The financial domino theory has actually proven more accurate than the national security domino theory,' Lawrence Summers, Deputy Secretary of the Treasury, mused last week.'Vietnam fell and other countries didn't. But you saw what happened after Thailand.'

However, the comparison is lame. The "domino theory" refers to the toppling over of a series of dominoes *appropriately aligned on end.* That has nothing to do with the current East Asian "contagion." Asset inflation through financial and trade deregulation came to the emerging world from Wall St., not vice versa. It was enforced with arm-breaking fervour by the IMF, and it moves neither in a single direction nor in a straight line, but every which way.

Its patterns are determined by marauders, ready to duplicate any speculative operation that has proved lucrative in any other part of the world where the circumstances seem favourable. In the nineties we have witnessed two quite novel speculative coups that proved lucrative at once adopted into the repertory of the mega-speculators and carried to other parts of the world. The first was the shooting down of the overpriced British pound, Canadian dollars, a hutch of other European currencies and the Canadian dollar. Today our banks are using derivatives not only to profit by the monetary disarray in Asia, but to topple the Canadian dollar.

The second instance was the quick transformation of Mexico within a matter of months in 1945 from a disaster-hole for foreign investors, to a land of gargantuan profits. That was because the Mexican economy offered sensational bargains for those who bought up the pieces at bargain prices. That pattern too is being repeated not only in Asia, but in Canada.

Even greater discrepancies are surfacing between the process of policy-making and the reality it seeks to shape. In *The Wall Street Journal* Judy Shelton, professor of international finance at Duxx Graduate School of Business Leadership in Monterrey, Mexico, writes: "Welcome to today's world of international monetary relations: global currency stability by political extortion. We have reached the untenable point where the performance of global financial markets depends not on how efficiently they channel private capital into productive investment, but rather on implicit threats to monetary stability made by calculating politicians. In the absence of a structured international monetary system, jawboning currencies has been raised to an art. Remember that the stability of the renminbi [the Chinese currency] depends solely on the continued willingness of Chinese officials to keep shelling out accumulated reserves of hard currency and gold to buy up renminbi on world markets — a practice that could get very expensive. For the Chinese government expects both economic and political compensation. For Mr. Clinton to express his personal gratitude for a stable renminbi is inappropriate. Shelton — herself a true believer — goes on to some damaging details:

"By linking monetary stability and foreign policy, the Clinton administration undermines any pretence of intellectual consistency in judging the exchange-rate policies of other nations. In November, 1994 the US Treasury turned down the $6 billion in loan guarantees it had offered Mexico the previous year 'on ground that Mexico was not ready to follow its recommendation that it devalue its currency. On the Asian front, Mr. Rubin [Secretary of the US Treasury]and his deputy, Lawrence Summers, have from the outset supported the devaluation advice of the IMF . The region's crisis was triggered a year ago when Thailand devalued its currency."

"If it was so foolish for Thailand and Mexico to attempt to stabilise their currencies against the dollar, how can it be so laudable when China opts to do so?"

That is quite a question. The answer is sketched in an article of *The New York Times Magazine* (17/07), 'The Calculator' by Jacob Weisberg. It describes how Rubin applies to US policy the arbitrage skills that earned him the chair of Goldman, Sachs on Wall St. It dwells on his prowess in remaining cucumber-cool in 1979 while betting a good portion of the partners' retirement funds that inflation and oil prices would continue high. Rubin himself is quoted: "We had one month in which we lost more money than the firm made in the prior year." He remained so cool because — to his own satisfaction — he had "calculated" (guesstimated would be a more prudent expression) the odds that the market would move in either direction. Transferred to US financial policy-making vis-a-vis the rest of the world, the notion of using Wall St. arbitrage skills is bizarre.

For on Wall St. you are successful when you cash in your chips with a profit. And even if you lose big, the world spins on. But if Mr. Rubin succeeds in pressuring Thailand and Indonesia to devalue their currencies and raising interest rates and the IMF bails out the foreign banks from their imprudent loans, though that might seem the end of a successful gamble, it is not necessarily so. Mr. Rubin's "model" does not even recognise the existence of "society" other than the money market, let alone the possibility of society coming apart if the slashing of employment and the local currency price are pushed far enough.

Meanwhile, though the pickings are rich for bold, deep-pocketed buccaneers, the moral cost to society is considerable. Jacob Schlesinger, writing in *The Wall Street Journal* (17/08) sums this well: "Russia, has in one form or another, been in the sick ward for seven years and just last month received a bailout package of nearly $23 billion. That raises the question — still unresolved in Asia — of whether the official solutions only make problems worse." Then he quotes Richard Medley of Medley Global Advisors: "This disputes the notion that we're in a smooth transition into the end of history, as was assumed."

Washington's Questionable Advice to Others

No matter how questionable the advice that the US has given Japan over the years, never was it short on sanctimony. As often as not its counsel ran counter to what it imposed earlier or what it itself practised at home. An article in *Economic Reform* (*ER*) of July 1991 provides some background.

The Myth of Japan The Saver

We nurture myths about other cultures, often to underpin myths concerning our own. A case in point is Japan the Saver that owes its prosperity to a compulsive habit of stuffing its socks with yen.

There was always an evident flaw in that version. For as the bombs fell on Hiroshima and Nagasaki, Japanese saving could only have been modest. Yet from the moment of peace Japanese recovery took off like a rocket to make fools of Western economists and their savings theories.

The truth is that Japan owes much of its economic miracle to focussing on the needs of the real economy. The most promising industries were identified, and financing directed to them at modest rates. But this preferential allotment of credit in recent years came under sharp fire from the central banks of the West on both doctrinal grounds and to lessen the competitive advantage that lower rates gave Japanese exports. *The Wall Street Journal* (8/2/90) quoted Bundesbank President Karl Otto Poehl: "We thought the yen would move in parallel with the European currencies, but it didn't happen. The main reason was that Japan wouldn't raise its interest rates." When that pressure grew, Japan acceded, but devised far riskier ways of providing its key industries with inexpensive financing.

The International Herald Tribune (27/6/91) carries an article by Carl Gewirtz showing Japan to have been the largest borrower on international markets over the previous decade. Japanese bond issuers now have some $317.7 billion of bonds outstanding — nearly double the paper issued by US firms.

But significantly, almost a third of the bonds issued by Japanese firms on international markets — the equivalent of some $133 billion — had warrants for their conversion into common stock.

The idea was to have the bonds redeemed before maturity with equity shares. Since the Nikkei index of Tokyo stocks had soared almost 300 percent between 1983 and the end of 1989, that seemed a reasonable prospect. But the higher interest rates imposed on Japan by pressure from the West nipped the plan in the bud. Between 1989 and March 1991 the Nikkei index dropped from 38,915 to 26,292 — low enough to make it unlikely that the warrants of some 80% of the convertible bonds will be exercised. [The Nikkei is currently in the 13,000s.]

That means that over the coming three years bond issues with unbelievably low coupons (because of the once promising warrants) will have to be replaced with new bond issues at far higher rates — in foreign currencies.

By imposing higher interest rates on Japan Washington undermined a policy of low interest rates that fed a stock market boom not unlike the one on which the US prides itself today. And for years that kept Japanese exports brisk and unemployment low. But international deregulation and the problems of the US banks in the eighties left the field of speculative Eurodollar and US real estate financing to the Japanese banks. They lost no time wading into it up to their eyebrows. Policies imposed by the West in this way contributed as much to the Japanese banking catastrophe as anything hatched on Japanese soil.

You would never suspect so checkered a background to the Japanese crisis if you listened to US Treasury Secretary Robert Rubin hammering away with the advice of "reform, reform." But "reform" has multiple meanings, many of them contradictory — for example the deregulation of banking and the banning of exchange controls to brake the movement of short term funds. Nor has this ardour for "reforming" other folks stood in the way of the US and Western governments bailing out those of their own financial institutions that were "too big to fail."

Spreading The Financial Bailouts

Partly for cultural reasons, and partly to prevent the collapse of its financial system the Japanese have traditionally taken another approach. Listen to *The Wall Street Journal* (7/7) "Debt and recession are hammering Takao Suzuki's machine shop, but his bankers won't let him fail. And in that regard, he isn't unique: his is only one among thousands of businesses, big and small, that Japan insists on keeping afloat — at great expense. Mr. Suzuki and his company, Suzuko Kogyo K.K., owe five banks a total of nearly $2 million, more than 10 times the revenue he expects this year. Yet his banks keep rolling over his debt and lowering his interest rates even though he is having trouble paying back his old debts. In Tokyo's Ohta Ward, six thousand or so family-run machine shops bang out goods from stamped metal to high-tech components for Hitachi and Mitsubishi. Dozens of these businesses fail each year.

"What is surprising, at least to the non-Japanese eye, is how *few* are failing — especially as Japan confronts its worst recession since WWII and tries to cope with banks that are so bad off they need public funds to survive. By restructuring the loans of deadbeats, banks are able to keep loans out of their bad-debt column. Mr. Suzuki's biggest lender is backed by a claim on a building on which three other banks also have claims. But the property's value has plummeted so foreclosure would mean losses that the bank can ill afford."

Mr. Suzuki, by the *WSJ*'s own telling is really not a deadbeat, insofar as he has never defaulted on a loan. He "secures his loans with whatever he can: his home, his rental property, his land." The trouble is that through no fault of his the market value of all that security has shrunk drastically. But Washington had more to do with that than Mr. Suzuki.

By the American bail out system, not only were banks too big to fail saved from the consequences of their irresponsible gambles, but the liquidation of smaller businesses provided brilliant opportunities for vulture capitalists to pick up flea-market bargains. For all that is wrong with the Japanese approach, it does spread the public largesse a bit more fairly. It is true that until the insolvent banks are put right with government money — what other recourse is there within the system? — the banks cannot begin repeating the same speculative climb to disaster. But should they be allowed to?

Perhaps the banking system should really be "reformed" bringing in regulations to restrict it to banking for the real economy rather than allow it to engage in every sort of gamble.

Vol. 10, No. 10 — October 1998

Book Review — *The Bankers : The Next Generation*

[Mayer, Martin. *The bankers : the next generation.* New York: Truman Talley Books, 1997. ISBN 0452272645 (1998 Penguin pbk.)]

Martin Mayer is an old hand at reporting just about every aspect of banking. He has served on official committees in the field. His most recent work is particularly timely since it is tremendously useful for an overview of the financial and monetary crisis that is so clearly in the offing today.

It is generally held that the banks started their comeback from the working-over they were subjected to under Roosevelt only in 1951 when the Treasury Fed Accord began unpegging interest rates. That, however, is a simplification of the facts. As early as 1938 when the tightening of credit by the US Fed brought on the so-called 'Roosevelt Depression' "federal banking regulators reacted with a 'Uniform Agreement' to establish a historical cost (book) valuation standard. Orders went out to examiners to reduce the placing of improper emphasis on maturity if ultimate payment seems reasonably assured."

Professors Donald Simonson and George Hemplel noted that 'by focussing on loans' ultimate collectibility, this provision ignores the fundamental economic tenet of the time value of money. The historical cost accounting framework concealed the true value of the institutions' net worth.' A quarter of a century later, the Financial Accounting Standards Board validated this neglect of the time value of money by approving FAS 15, a rule permitting financial institutions to carry restructured loans at par on their balance sheets so long as all prospective payments on the loan, principal and interest together, would *total more than its face value* (our emphasis). It was under this rule that banks were permitted to continue to carry their obviously impaired loans to less developed countries at full book value, though these loans were being traded for less than half that value on the international market."

Obviously this created a shortfall of the "transparency" that the developed countries have been so strongly recommending — retroactively — to the devastated countries of East Asia

The succession of bank bailouts by their governments over the past quarter of a century has reduced or completely abolished the legal tender reserves that banks held with their central bank. This has assigned to them more of the money creation of the economy, with the central bank obligingly reducing its own role in the field. To cover this up, central banks have denied that banks create any money at all. They claim that their business is essentially "intermediation" — taking in deposits on which they pay interest and relending it to others at a mark-up. There is a very simple test for this statement.

Through much of the eighties when the bank-rate was in double-digits much of the time, Canada's banks were paying their deposits as little as one-quarter of one percent. The obscene spread between such rates and what they were charging their borrowers caused swarms of depositors to shift their business to other financial institutions. In the words of Mayer: "Insured customer deposits, the essential link between the bank and its community, now fund only 17% of the assets in the American banking system. Thus the great bulk of the money a bank now has to lend is not the transaction balances of its customers but investment funds, which the individual or corporate customer has placed with the banks — a role he could just as easily assign to his broker or mutual fund or insurance company [that do not create the money that makes up their deposits]. The cant line of the late 1970s and early 1980s was that the banks were being 'disintermediated' — that people who wanted to make money on their money were abandoning their bank accounts to put their money where the grass was not only greener but grew faster."

Fleshing Out The Classic Bank Scandal — The US S&Ls

Much has been written about the US S&L scandal, but Martin Mayer draws the most complete picture that we have chanced upon.

"The 1980s were by no means the first time that the viability of the S&Ls had been called into question. They were originally voluntary associations in which people pooled their money to make it possible for members to get mortgages on their houses without falling into the hands of loan-sharks. (Banks, which had short-term deposits were not supposed to make mortgage loans; national chartered banks were forbidden to lend on the security of real estate until the Federal Reserve Act of 1913. If any number of members needed their money back, the mortgage-lending association was not very likely to have it, because it couldn't call in its loans.)

"Thus S&Ls were cooperatives in which members bought non-negotiable shares, not "banks," which took deposits. Thousands of these state-chartered associations went bankrupt in the Great Depression, when the general deflation meant that houses were worth less than the mortgages on them."

To keep the S&Ls liquid, Roosevelt founded a Home Owners' Corporation that bought up mortgages from the S&Ls, and a Federal Housing Administration to insure home mortgages to make them suitable for investment by insurance companies. But the basis of the S&Ls continued to be shares, not deposits as in the case of banks. That means that they could not promise a given return, since dividends can only be paid from profits. People could take cash out of their S&L shares but couldn't write cheques on their shares to third parties.

As early as 1966 when the Vietnam War had started driving up interest rates it was clear that the S&Ls were headed for trouble. Money could be withdrawn from their shares on demand, but they lent on 30-year mortgages. And as interest rates soared, the market value of long-term mortgages at fixed rates fell steeply. S&Ls, particularly those in California started getting money where they could, promising future "dividends" far higher than banks could offer under the Fed restrictions on interest rates. They had to keep up with the rates available from the new money funds.

Most of the future trouble was hatched in California. "Most S&L operators were builders, and most of them were cowboys who wanted all the perks of big-time corporate life for themselves and their buddies. With California's tremendous clout in national politics the attempt was repeatedly made to prohibit the enforcement on "due-on-sale" clauses in American home mortgages that required the buyer of a home to pay off the existing mortgage and negotiate a new one at prevailing rates. There were clashes of interest between S&Ls with state-charters and those operating under federal charters. To paper over these differences, both legislative houses in California made the fatal decision that the "way to the level playing-field was to give state-charter S&Ls enormously expanded asset powers — the right to develop property themselves, make commercial loans, buy junk bonds, make direct investments in non-financial businesses and so forth. The Nolan Act permitted S&L operators to own stock in and lend money to any business. Charles Knapp told analysts that his American Savings and Loan was going to use insured deposits to acquire Merrill Lynch and at one point it did become the largest shareholder of American Express. Charles Keating acquired Lincoln Savings and Loan with the help of Mike Milken of Drexel Burnham, and promptly became a prime customer for his junk bonds. This expansion of asset powers meant that the taxpayer through deposit insurance was to be a co-venturer with an incredible crew of speculators, incompetents, and thieves. It set up the Federal Savings and Loan Insurance Corporation for unimaginable losses in the succeeding years. One of its great innocent advocates was Alan Greenspan who accepted a $40,000 fee for writing a letter to the Federal Home Loan Bank Board praising the business acumen of Keating and the theory that said it was fine for Keating to use insured deposits to fund Milken's paper mill."

What inspired this incredible chapter was that between 1978 and 1982 interest rates were shooting up and many S&Ls were stuck with long-term mortgage portfolios that on the average yielded less than their cost of funds. And in this setting the maximum insurance for a single account was raised from $40,000 to $100,000.

And then comes a passage in the Mayer book that should be carefully pondered by our legislators today on either side of the international border: "Behind all this turmoil lay the unpleasant truth that the S&Ls were losing their social and economic function. Part of the original New Deal legislation had been authorization for a Federal National Mortgage Association which would sell bonds and buy mortgages. Private enterprise had not responded to the invitation so the government itself started Fannie May as a customer for the mortgages the Federal Housing Administration would ensure. In 1970 the Home Loan Bank Board formed Federal National Mortgage Corporation ("Freddie Mac") bonds that "passed through" to their holders every month what the homeowners paid on their mortgages — so that the S&Ls securities could improve their liquidity by "securitising" and selling some of their mortgages. [Because] Fannie and Freddie securities did not have to be registered with the SEC these 'government-sponsored' enterprises were by 1980 becoming by far the largest mortgage holders in the country.

"On the other side of the cage, S&Ls were losing their grip on consumers. Banks were offering savings accounts, and mutual funds were offering a range of high-yielding uninsured alternatives for the people who used to put their money into S&Ls." Then comes the clinker that puts our coming bank mega crisis in proper light: "The question of who *needed* S&Ls was there to be asked. Nobody asked it." It is a question that should be asked of our banks today.

But the fun really started when the S&Ls were already hopelessly insolvent. "Even by the highly permissive accounting standards of federal regulators by 1981, the S&Ls were supporting $650 billion of assets on a net worth of $32 billion — and would lose more than $4.5 B of that in Reagan's first year. If the assets were marked to market, the industry had a net worth of *negative* $80 billion. So the Home Loan Bank Board [took] a gamble doing what it could to keep the S&Ls going until interest rates turned around and their mortgage hoard became profitable again. Capital requirements were lowered to 3% of assets; deposits bought from brokers had been permitted only to a total of 5% of all deposits; now the fraction of deposits which came through paid brokers would become unlimited. Keating of Lincoln S&L paid Prudential-Bache 4.68% commission to bring him money.

Procedures for rescuing insolvent S&Ls were changed so that an institution that acquired an insolvent S&L could capitalise the difference between the net worth of the institution acquired and the price paid as "goodwill" that could be written off over as many as forty years. "The logic of goodwill" is that businessmen are rational, so when one company pays another more than its net asset value, that business must have "tangible assets" — a franchise, a location, a brand name, a customer list — that will generate future income. Depreciating this goodwill over forty years legitimated fraud, since the average duration of a mortgage was twelve years. As the low-rate mortgages were paid off, instead of writing off the goodwill acquired by purchasing them at a price below their face value, the S&L could take a profit and pay dividends to its owners — forgetting about its obligation to write off the surviving 70% of the goodwill on its books."

Then there was "Memorandum R-49" approved in September 1981, which encouraged loss deferral." Under it S&Ls could sell loans on which they showed a loss and amortize the loss over the life of the loan. There would, of course, be an immediate loss — and that loss the S&Ls could show in the books they kept for the Internal Revenue Service. The 1981 tax, passed the month before, had set up a "crazy harbour" system by which companies could carry back to the five previous years losses taken after 1980, and get a refund on past taxes."

But all this was topped off by the subsequent discovery of the little S&L world of unbounded opportunity by Wall St. "The debilitation of the industry is in large part the result of its contact with a more predatory form of life. A real estate developer in Dallas describes the scene: 'When the salesmen from Wall St. worked over the S&Ls here, it was like rocket scientists selling to drivers of Conestoga wagons. And all around the encampment were the regulators scratching their heads.' For once they had this paper Wall St. had sold them, the S&Ls could trade it, following the wonderful guaranteed models of 'risk-controlled arbitrage' that these brilliant people had designed just for them. Just like the derivatives the corporate customers were sold in the 1990s, after the S&L market dried up."

But this is not just dead history. The analogy with what happened with our banks in their past bailouts and what is likely to happen in the next one is disturbing. Our banks have turned their backs on their traditional function that did serve a social purpose. Instead they have gathered the franchises bestowed on them and used them to concentrate on wildly leveraged gambles throughout the world in areas where their own experience is marginal. Before our government takes a position on the proposed bank mergers, it must look beyond the fashionable buzzwords, to the record of the US S&Ls, and the catastrophe of Japan's megabanks, and explain to the public how our banks are to be rescued when the extent of their imprudence has fully surfaced. If Ottawa hurries through its approval of the merger plans without such preliminary analysis, it will be assuming an awesome responsibility. This time we can assure our political leaders that it will not pass unnoticed. That is what *ER* is about.

Editorial Note on Evaluation of Canadian Bank Portfolios

Since it is clear that historical evaluations are used in the United States in auditing the portfolios of US banks, we contacted the Canadian Office of the Superintendent of Financial Institutions to verify the situation in Canada in this respect. The reply received by telephone (10/09/98) is the following:

The portfolio of the bank is divided into two categories — the trading consisting mostly of short-term securities for the bank's own account. The evaluation here is at market. The investment portfolio up to a 20% participating share of the total security issued is valued at its historic cost. For holdings in excess of that is at market. The bulk of the portfolio is thus valued at its historic cost.

Derivatives are not carried on the balance sheet.

More Mexico Leads the Way

Our times could well end up known as the age of Mexico.

The current round of currency meltdowns began there when the steep devaluation of the peso interrupted Washington's snow job presenting Mexico as a thriving democracy worthy of NAFTA membership. High-level murders in a setting of corruption betrayed the reality as the Mexican economy went belly up. Clinton rushed in to patch together a $50 billion rescue program to prevent the mighty American financial system, already staggering from its own derivatives scandals, from following Mexico into the precipice.

But within a few months Mexico, ever the country of miracles paid for with human sacrifice, proved a bonanza for foreign speculators. Securities bought at distress discounts, produced 50% returns to nimble foreign speculators. This introduced the world to the "Mexican effect," the financial equivalent of fishing with dynamite. On the strength of that Mexico regained its position in Washington's rhetoric as a showpiece of deregulation, a model for other emerging lands. But like a Hollywood starlet on the make, Mexico simply won't stay out of the headlines.

The Wall Street Journal (28/8/98) informs us that the threat of inflation is back with a new 19% drop in the dollar value of the peso. What modest recouping of real wages has taken place since the traumatic collapse of 1994 are being lost once more.

To remedy all that the Banco de Mexico (B de M) has announced a complicated reserve scheme that suggests an experiment in designing the bailout of the world banking system from the next crisis that is already upon it. That presents some problems, since the statutory reserves that banks have to put up on an interest-free basis have already been whittled down to 3% of deposits in the US and completely abolished in a few countries like Canada and Mexico. Months ago *ER* has wondered out loud what form the coming bailout will take, and the latest news out of Mexico suggests that the same problem is preoccupying our international monetary institutions.

The *WSJ* reports that as of September 2nd commercial banks in Mexico will be required to deposit at the central bank 1.25 billion pesos each trading day until the amount of 25 billion pesos (US$2.56 billion) is reached. *The novel feature is that "on these reserves the cental bank will pay the banks the prevailing 28-day inter-bank rate. And the money so obtained will be used by the central bank to replace all the liquidity drained from the system in short-term open-market operations."* [our emphasis]

The B de M claims its "aim is to reduce long-term interest rates, which officials say have shot up too high as a result of the unexpectedly rapid depreciation of the peso." Shortly before the central bank set a 27% minimum on one-day government paper, and the net result of these moves has been to send all interest rates of all maturities soaring. This has put downward pressure on Mexican bank stocks. Analysts predict the measures could backfire given the jitters crippling markets there. By taking deposits from the banks and putting them right back into the money market, the risk is that the money will be switched to dollars 'and go right out the door.'"

We perceive another purpose that could be served by the confusing measure. With the statutory reserves abolished in Mexico, it is no longer possible to come to the help of the banks by reducing them. The logical extension then is for the central bank to pay the commercial banks the going rate of interest on new reserves they will deposit with the Banco de Mexico. A few months ago we noted that payment of market rates on banks statutory reserves was being proposed in several European countries when the European Union comes into effect. This would, of course, violate the very essence of legal tender that is not supposed to vary according to the movement of interest rates.

The Mexican move is but another sign that even the sponsors of deregulated globalisation are realising that the model is not working and cannot possibly work. The same message comes out of Hong Kong (*WSJ* (7/9). "The city's economy is faltering, its stock market is floundering. The key to a turnaround, economists say, is how the government deals with the HK dollar that has become much stronger against most currencies in the region thanks to its fixed exchange rate with the US dollar. The government has three choices, none of them ideal."

• Maintaining the HK's dollar peg to the US $ at the rate of $7.80 HK will continue [through high interest rates] the downward pressure on stock and property prices.

• Breaking the peg or re-pegging it at a lower rate are both big gambles [that] might spark a confidence crisis that would make things worse.

• Dollarising the HK currency or retiring the local currency and using US dollars instead.

Of course, there are other alternatives that are never mentioned, because they imply the surrender of the power position of international finance in the present set up. The fallacy underlying the policy menu offered is that the floating currency rather than a complete program is just a powerful tool. The crucial factor never mentioned is: who will manage the floating currency and in whose interests? And what other provisions will go with the arrangement to determine in whose interest will be served?

By now it should be clear that the present arrangement of floating currencies is based on a grotesque conflict of interest that simply cannot be sustained.

The news out of a growing part of the world bids well to outstrip anything in the thirties. Globalisation has dismantled great parts of the subsistence economies that assured at least wretched survival to most of the world's population. Emerging and Third World countries have become dependent on the money economy that has now failed them. In the statistics on "growth" the destruction of the subsistence economies was never considered.

In the same issue of the *G&M*, John Stackhouse reports from Jakarta that Indonesia's economy will be shrinking by 20% in the coming year. Every day 15,000 people lose their jobs according to an ILO study. By the end of the year it is expected that "100 million people — half the population of this most populous country in the world, will live in poverty. As a result a growing number of respected Indonesians are pushing for more aggressive government intervention, to the point of taking over faltering companies rather than selling them at fire-sale prices to foreign investors.

"Once held up as a model for developing countries, Indonesia's economy is what an aid official called 'freeze-dried.' A well-educated work force and solid economic infrastructure remain, long with one of the world's richest troves of oil, minerals, and timber.

"[But] for companies that survived the rupiah crash, there is no trade financing or working capital to speak of. Fifty-five of Indonesia's banks are under government supervision, and most of the rest are unable to give new loans. After flooding the banking system with money last winter to keep it afloat, the central bank is now trying to soak up as much liquidity as it can. The bank offered interest rates last week of 70% on deposits."

What we are witnessing is a breakdown of the dogma of deified greed that brought on the catastrophe.

A good first step would be to take up the search for solutions with Keynes's vision of the postwar world that placed an equal burden on debtors and creditors in maintaining a monetary balance. See 'Keynes's Most Original Creation,' p. 174.

Vol. 10, No. 11 — November 1998

Re-equipping the World to Meet the Trials Ahead

In mid-October COMER was invited to appear before two sessions of the Standing Committee on Finance of the Commons held in the Toronto area. The first was a pre-budgetary review, and we were included in the 2-hour round table with a delegation on child poverty. The next day we appeared at the session devoted to the report of the Task Force on the Future of the Financial Services Sector that has just been issued. In both instances COMER's contribution filled an essential missing link — explaining why the bottom had fallen out of the public treasury so that there seemed to be no resources to address critical social needs. Quite literally the food has been snatched from the mouths of impoverished families to provide the bailout for our high-flying banks. The present over-extension of our large banks even before their proposed mergers makes it all the more urgent to extend the powers of the credit unions and the few surviving trust companies, and to issue a new class of bank charter specially directed to the needs of small business.

COMER's part in the hearings was a far cry from the first gala consultation that Finance Minister Paul Martin organized in a luxury downtown hotel with a full panoply of fifes and drums shortly after the Chrétien Government came to power. On that occasion John Hotson, Jack Biddell, who had served as head of the Ontario Section of the Anti-Inflation Board under Trudeau, and I were left cooling our heels outside the conference chamber while scores of invited experts were given three minutes each to recite the official mantra about jobs, jobs, jobs becoming abundant once high interest rates had killed inflation, inflation, inflation stone-dead.

The contrast was heartening. However, a tremendous amount of damage has been done in the interim. The history of the Bank of Canada and its role in financing Canada's part in the War and the immediate post war decades has been buried deeper than the regulatory six feet. The COMER brief:

The present crisis involves more than an implosion of stock markets. Even more traumatic, it has undermined the most cherished dogmas of a quarter of a century.

Thus the world's stock market greeted the Japanese government's plans for a third of a trillion dollar bailout of their troubled banks with a wild rally. But wasn't the main article of faith of neo-liberalism that the government must keep its snout out of the economy? And government after government along with the IMF and the World Bank have declared for temporary exchange controls — until now the ultimate no-no of the new dispensation.

For many years elections have been fought around the deficit. Concern for it throttled our social programs. And yet the stark fact is that we have no idea what the real federal deficit might be. You will find the problem summed up in the *Canada Year Book* — in the 1988 edition on page 22-6: "Fixed capital assets, such as government buildings and public works, are charged to budgetary expenditures at the time of acquisition and are shown on the statement of assets and liabilities at a nominal value of $1."

Even the attempt to balance such a budget can only add to perceived "inflation." Consider what would happen to the price of gasoline if Imperial Oil wrote off its oil fields, pipelines and refineries in a single year. This hipshot accountancy provided the panic buttons that have driven our politics for the past two or three decades: first 'inflation,' and then the deficit that was largely the result of the high interest rates imposed by the Bank of Canada to flatten a misleading price index.

Recently I noticed that the above explanation of how our deficit is calculated was no longer in the *Canada Year Book*, 1997 edition. Democracy is inconceivable without a minimum of unmanipulated information. To probe the state of that resource, I set out to find when the above passage on capital expenditures had been suppressed. I was able to trace its presence unchanged in the *Year Book* from 1967 to 1990. But by 1994 it had already been ploughed under. That was not too long after COMER had started making noise on the subject. Some months ago I contacted Statistics Canada and asked the following questions: "When was the above passage in the *Year Book* first published? When was it removed? Why?" I am still waiting for an answer.

I suggest that your committee take up that query from there. What we are sliding into is not a cyclical depression, but something far worse. Bit by bit over at least three decades the world has been rejigged and deregulated for the convenience of speculative finance. Even the language has been twisted towards that end. The real economy has been ransacked to keep the grand speculative potlatch going. In our monthly newsletter, *Economic Reform*, we have been publishing what we call The Indicator. This is the ratio of the chartered banks' assets to the cash in their possession. It is based on statistics published in the *Bank of Canada Review*. In 1946 it had been 11.1:1. A few months ago it had attained a value of 358:1 — an increase of 3300%.

Moreover, with the deregulation of what banks can invest it, the quality of those assets has deteriorated dramatically. The Office of the Superintendent of Financial Institutions will inform you, as it did me, that basically those assets are reported by the banks at their historic costs rather than at their current market value. Those assets currently exceed $1,300,000,000,000 and the total capital of our chartered banks amounts to about $50 billion. Their capital then represents less than 4% of their assets and North American stock markets in recent months have fallen almost 20% while some of those in East Asia as much as 80%. Months ago we warned that our banks would be back for their next bailout by the government even before the deadline for their merger had arrived.

In the months ahead the world economic meltdown can swallow not only our banks' capital, but Mr. Martin's cherished budgetary surplus many times over. Before light can be restored to the end of the tube, there will have to be a review not only of banking, but of the entire corpus of economic theory. It falls to your committee to take the first step to make that possible by putting the government's accountancy in order. Without that economists lack even the basic statistics to start digging ourselves out of the present mess.

And for that the path has already been cleared for you. On page 33 of the *Bank of Canada Review*, Summer, 1997, you will find an item from the *Public Accounts of Canada 1995-6*. In part it reads, "In contrast to commercial Crown Corporations, full cost-recovery for many federal assets, including bridges, ports, and telecommunications systems, was never considered either feasible (because the asset is a public good) or desirable (for public-policy reasons). The federal government financed the cost of acquiring and maintaining such assets through budgetary appropriations, recording their book value as a nominal $1 even though the government invested huge sums of money in them and may have incurred significant debt to finance them. Consequently, if these assets are privatised, all of the sale proceeds can be applied against the deficit, as the $1.5 billion received from the sale of the air navigation system was in the 1996/7 fiscal year. The federal government is gradually moving towards full-accrual accounting, whereby the cost of acquiring physical assets is spread over the asset's useful life through annual depreciation charges, and thus the true cost of such assets will be more accurately recorded."

The astounding word in that passage is "gradually." Putting the governments' books in line with accountancy principles would have revealed that the "inflation" statistics used as a panic button to justify a regime of high interest rates and high unemployment were misleading. And those mistaken debt and deficit figures are what currency traders go by in setting a value on our dollar. A more realistic balance sheet of the Government's affairs would have provided a more effective defence of our currency against speculative attacks than piddling away billions of foreign currency for that purpose as the Bank of Canada has done.

With its current accountancy our government could sell the Parliament Buildings for $1,000 and book a capital gain of $999 which could be patriotically applied against the debt. Or the St. Lawrence Seaway which is not a Crown Corporation for $5,000. There is in fact talk of privatising the Seaway. But so long as it is on the books at $1, the government is clueless about what a fair price for it would be. *It is privatisation that should be done gradually in cases where it makes sense, and the introduction of serious accountancy into the Government's bookkeeping is what should be put on the fast track.*

Other urgent steps towards equipping society to overcome the crisis: High interest rates have over the past decades been elevated to the only means of stabilising the economy. The meltdown that is upon us is in fact the ultimate proof that a more destabilising measure could not have been devised. High interest rates, moreover, are the revenue of not the most altruistic group in society — money-lenders and speculators. There is thus a gross conflict of interest in such a choice that should have been addressed long ago.

High interest rates feed directly into all costs, and can bring down prices only by collapsing the economy. And when that takes place interest rates fall along with everything else. Reserves held with the central bank as a proportion of the banks' deposits should be brought back. But above all the public should once more be made conscious of the fact that the creation of money — which is wholly credit in our day

— is a privilege of the state (seigniorage) that has been assigned to the private banks under the terms of their charters. Once that is made clear there is a whole menu of measures that the government can resort to *other than high interest rates* — to defend our dollar. It could instruct the banks to cease shorting of our currency or financing such shorting of the currency by their clients under risk of losing their charters. Then the CEOs of the banks will be brought into line by their concerned shareholders. Legitimate hedging against currency risk by producers will, of course, not only be unaffected by such a measure but will be helped. At present legitimate non-speculative future trading connected with production and trade makes up about 5% of the entire option trade. Often it is swamped by the gambling of mega-speculators.

There are essential steps to be taken to reestablish the orderly functioning of the international financial system that could not be included in our submission. The role of the Bank for International Settlements must be examined publicly. The BIS is the den in which most of the policies that have led to the present world meltdown were planned. To introduce into the world financial system the transparency that our governments have recommended so strongly to the East Asian countries the BIS, whose stock you can buy through your broker, must be reduced to the status of a purely commercial bank with no special connections with central banks other than that of its own country — Switzerland.

William Krehm
Chairman, COMER

Vol. 10, No. 12 — December 1998

Locked in Deregulation's Vicious Circle

The granddaddy of deregulation was that of the banks. Its furtive beginnings can be traced to the first years after WWII, even before the Treasury-Fed Accord of 1951 had weakened the ceiling on interest rates. That was long before the Western world had even begun regulating disease, unemployment, and hunger. Today you cannot pick up your newspaper without being hit in the eye with headlines on the latest disaster of financial deregulation. Across the world mega-bankruptcies vie with mega-scams and riots for front-page space. But response of the G-7 powers to this is always the same: the dosage must be increased. It has been deeply embedded in the rhetoric and even in the language.

Deregulation has been made synonymous with freedom when it in fact it is the dead opposite of a democratic system, since those who have imposed it have been released of all responsibility for the results of their policies. By definition they are an act of God. The extent of the scam has begun being recognised in the very financial press.

Holman W. Jenkins Jr. in *The Wall Street Journal* (11/11) reports on the turmoil in the largest US match concluded some six months between Citicorp and Travelers Group. So violent have the domestic altercations been between the two that James Dimon, the president of the resulting Citi-group "came flying out last week like a watermelon seed under high pressure. He had been charged with getting Citibank's commercial bankers and the investment bankers at Travelers working together, but it seems his last useful act was to stop them throwing punches at a management retreat the week before.

"As will be recalled, folding Citibank into the Travelers insurance-and-everything empire was supposed to teach the planet a new way of banking. Rather than a financial super-market, we favour the analogy of a private welfare state. All around the world, government-run pension and insurance systems are getting creakier by the hour, and millions of people in the developing world have no systems at all. There's big opportunity here. We hope Citigroup will one day issue its own banknotes to compete with jittering national currencies."

"But even the supermarket metaphor could be applied more consistently. In the web age, anybody will be able to click his way to the cheapest investment and insurance products from competing suppliers. The only reasons to prefer the one-stop shopping of the unwieldly, bureaucratic Citigroup are trust, trust, and trust.

"Before my customer throws all his money at them, he'll want to be assured of a few things. He doesn't want to open his paper and read that his bankers just blew his $350 million on obscure bond derivatives as the guys at Solomon [of Citigroup] just did.

"He doesn't want to be peddled worthless Russian bonds because his bankers are sucking up to Boris Yeltsin—the fate recently of Goldman Sachs customers. He doesn't want to worry about his fund accounts being stuffed with stocks and bonds because Citigroup's corporate underwriters couldn't dump them on anyone else.

"Under the present archaic structure, Wall St. is riddled with such conflicts of interest between the 'buy' and 'sell' sides.

"For all the rocket science and clanging rhetoric about how everybody else's business should become more focused, there is something ineffably retrograde about Wall St."

In short, the American granddaddy of all our financial deregulations is in deep trouble. The deregulated financial system both begat and conceived the subsequent deregulations and privatisations in the real economy. It nurtured and toilet-trained them, brought them to the altar, and when it felt the need, buried them. An unceasing flow of privatisations and mergers has become a necessity for the merged financial institutions' own survival. Having gobbled up brokerage houses, merchant banks, underwriting firms, they depend on the continued magic ascent of the stock market.

Basically there are two possible factors that drive stocks—company earnings and interest rates. Earning growth is hardly a factor today. The two analyst firms that track corporate earnings—First Call Corp, and IBES—concur in their appraisal of the recent quarter for American corporations since 1991. First Call found a drop in 3rd quarter earnings of 3.3%, and IBES, with somewhat different accountancy, places the fall at 4.1%. No material there for a stretch-out of the bull market.

Interest rates are another matter. The US Fed cut its target for the fed-funds rate (at which banks borrow overnight from one another) at the end of August, again in mid-September, and most recently in mid-November—in every instance by a measly one quarter of a percent. Meanwhile small businesses were reduced to using their credit-cards because banks are the grand absentees when it comes to financing small businesses. The *WSJ* (19/11) carries the shocking report: "'A few years ago, credit cards were considered bad or dangerous for businesses, but now they are clearly acceptable,' said Nancy Pechloff, managing director of Arthur Andersen's enterprise group. A record of 47% of entrepreneurs use credit cards as a financing source, double the number from just two years ago, according to an annual survey of consulting firm Arthur Andersen and the National Small Business United. 'Needless to say, it's not a cheap way to finance a business, but I didn't have a lot of choices,' said Bill Lindsay of Benefit Management Design Inc. of Denver. He's paying 18% a year interest which is almost usurious, but you can't beat the ease and speed of credit cards.'"

Moreover, in most cases it is the same banks who postpone indefinitely approving a business loan, that are behind the credit cards that provide it to him instantly and sight unseen, at twice the same interest rates. This being the case, Alan Greenspan's paper-thin slicing of the fed rate has a limited relevance to most modest businesses. They are already providing the blood transfusion to help our banks recoup their losses from their latest adventures under deregulation.

Even more amazing is the extent to which the patchy revival of the bull market has depended on outright disaster of financial institutions throughout much of the world. That has made the US a safe haven to which money is flocking because the American-imposed deregulation model is in deep crisis on all continents. The "Stocks also got a big fillip from, of all things, bonds. Frightened professional investors had driven stocks down during the August turmoil and one of their main havens was US government bonds," driving up their prices and hence depressing their yield. Then as Russia virtually defaulted on some of its bonds, investors poured more money into US Treasuries. The yield on the 30-year Treasury bond fell from 6.9% in April to 4.71% on October 5th, the lowest in 31 years. With the return on bonds so low, many funds shifted from bonds to US stocks." Everything seemed to conspire to stuff more demand into the stock market. The prospects of the stocks bought seemed almost a secondary consideration. Finally the unworldly academic model of the "pure and perfect market" where price is determined only by the proportion of supply to demand seemed to have been realised. The link between the financial markets and the real economy has been sundered.

Meanwhile the earnings prospects of producing companies are not helped by the incipient flooding of North American markets with goods from Asia and Russia at liquidation prices. Under the impact of this Washington is mixing its deregulation sermons to the heathen with ugly protectivist noises about keeping dirt-cheap Russian steel and Korean cars out of its market. Again we are being brought back to the stark landscape of the Thirties.

The US stock market cannot go on feeding indefinitely on the collapse of the economies elsewhere in the world. Even if the Dow Jones were to touch 100,000, the damage already done to the prospects of human kind would prove beyond repair. And much of that destruction is carried out precisely to prolong the stock market's ascension.

* Please Note: Due to circumstances, the article that is indicated in the Article Titles to be in this place, 'Undistributed Earnings,' has been replaced by 'Locked in Deregulation's Vicious Circle.' No Index entries are available. We apologise for any inconvenience.

Indicator

Leverage of Chartered Banks in Canada			
Year	Total Assets (Millions)	Legal Tender (Millions)	Leverage
1939	$3,396	$269	12.60
1943	4,602	371	12.40
1946	7,233	653	11.10
1971	40,286	2,489	16.20
1980	252,933	6,568	38.50
1990	588,895	8,767	102.10
1996	992,544	3,356	291.90
1997	1,336,085	3,728	358.00
1998 (06)	1,365,766	3,762	363.50
Sources: *Bank of Canada Statistical Summary for Early Years* and *Bank of Canada Review*			

It is important to note that legal tender still held by the banks is not available as security for their liabilities but is the bare essential needed for their operations.

These fall into two categories—the currency needed to stock their ATMs and that needed to meet their net cheque clearances with other banks.

Should the proposed mergers of four of our large banks go through, obviously some of the present leakage will become clearances within the banks. Hence the amount of legal tender held for this purpose will drop, resulting in a substantial increase in the above crucial ratio.

That indeed is one of the purposes of the proposed mergers.

Postscript

Finance Minister Martin Nixes the Bank Mergers

The front-page headlines of *The Globe & Mail* (14/12) screamed : 'Martin slams door on banks' mergers to set back process by at least two years.' Then followed the reasons: the Report of the Competition Bureau expressing concerns about the drop of competition arising from the proposed mergers; and the Office of the Superintendent of Financial Institutions, which "reviewed the impact of the deals on the safety and soundness of the financial sector." Inevitably there was mention in the article of the role in the drama of Mr. Martin's ambitions to become our Prime Minister. Having cast himself in the public mind as Butch Martin, darling of Bay St. for balancing the budget by throwing our society dangerously off balance, he has now withdrawn to his dressing room to fix his face for winning the Liberal leadership as a humane and caring Martin — the man who stood up to our mammoth banks in their rutting season.

We do not wish to be killjoys. Martin's refusal to approve the proposed bank mergers has certainly brought him to a wrenching parting from his close friends in circles that count. In the *G&M* several days later (18/12) Peter Cook from his European listening post lost no time serving up a sample of what Martin has exposed himself to. "The Liberal government [claims to be] committed to introducing measures that will ensure a strong, competitive Canadian-controlled financial industry. Apparently no thought was given to the underlying contradiction in this. With the market capitalisation of the largest Canadian bank coming in at one-fifth that of the largest Swiss bank and one-third of the largest Dutch bank, who is kidding whom? How competitive will a Canadian-controlled financial services industry be?" As the winner of the COMER Business Journalist Award bestowed some years ago for the most thorough turnabout on the country's monetary policy, Mr. Cook must know better. After all it is a year since even our PM picked up the detail that the worlds' very largest banks — all Japanese — had gambled themselves to near bankruptcy and for years have been wet-nursed by the state.[†]

Let us applaud Mr. Martin for his stand — if only with the tips of our fingers, sparing the palms of our hands for when he really catches up with his homework. Of the reports of the Competition Bureau and the Office of the Superintendent of Financial Institutions (OSFI) it is the former that is highlighted in government circles. But the latter is by far the more important. It alludes, albeit it in hushed tones, to the risk to which taxpayers have already been put by our banks' speculative moves away from traditional banking.

As important as their constraint of competition and their impact on employment may be, these are not the most important threats of the proposed bank mergers. Far greater is their menace to Canada's survival in one piece as a functioning society.

Over the past quarter of a century, the traditional controls over our banks have been systematically lifted. These had been put on the creation and distribution of money for valid reasons that reach back towards the beginnings of society. With the privilege of money-creation goes a fiduciary responsibility that only in recent decades has come to be seen as a restraint of trade to be done away with. The label commonly applied to the unlovely result has been the conversion of the economy into a Grand Casino. But that is an understatement, for it is hardly the practice of the owners who run the gaming establishments to take the leading part in the gambling. That, however, has been the case with our deregulated financial sector. It has become a flying machine without landing gear, its unending ascension fuelled by the consumption of the real economy.

A Background Information release of OSFI itself explains why that institution is reduced to merely hinting about what should be shouted from the rooftops: "OSFI did not identify [in its Report to the Minister of Finance] issues which would be likely to have a material adverse impact on the financial viability of either merged bank."

For at least two years *Economic Reform* has tried coming to the aid of our Finance Minister by publishing an index of this terrifying problem. We call it the Indicator — the ratio of our chartered banks' assets to the legal tender in their possession. Since 1946 to mid 1998, with the whittling down of the statutory reserves of legal tender that the banks had to hold with the Bank of Canada and their finally phasing out in 1994, that ratio has risen from 11.1 to 363.5 and it is still rising. At the same time the deregulation of what the banks are able to do with other people's money and the credit they create, the quality of those assets has fallen drastically. Moreover, for the most part by a whimsy of official accountancy those assets are reported at their original cost rather than at their market value. It would be enough for the banks' assets to shrink less than 5 percent across the board for their capital to be wholly wiped out. But our Indicator, based on figures published by the Bank of Canada, has received zero acknowledgement by the government and the media.

That is why it must have come as a shock to most Canadians to read the headline on the front page of the *G&M*'s *Report on Business* (19/12) informing us that Standard and Poor's Corp. has raised red flags about the operations of Canada's big banks, citing concerns ranging from high-risk lending to capital markets exposure. It put the Bank of Nova Scotia and National Bank of Canada on credit watch and revised the outlook to negative from stable on Canadian Imperial Bank of Commerce and Bank of Montreal.

This announcement issued just days before this book went to press thus completes the cycle from our first issue over 10 years ago when we foretold where "zero inflation" would lead. With the S&P downgrading we get a whiff of reality behind the incredible puffery that our government has permitted our banks.

This leaves Mr. Martin with a lot of homework before he can redeem himself as Minister of Finance, let alone pass on to becoming Prime Minister.

† Yet we haven't despaired. Mr. Cook is too canny a practitioner not to hold up a moist finger from time to time to see what winds are blowing. One of these days, should we revive our COMER Prize for Business Journalists, we are confident that Mr. Cook will not be out of the running for that prestigious award a second time — for his courageous rethinking of official pieties.

Bibliography

Bordo, Michael D., Forrest Capie, eds. *Monetary regimes in transition.* Cambridge [England] ; New York, NY : Cambridge University Press, 1993, c1994. ISBN 0521419069

Budhoo, Davison L. *Enough is enough! Dear Mr. Camdessus: an open letter of resignation to the Managing Director of the International Monetary Fund.* New York : New Horizons Press, 1990

Canada Year Book, Statistics Canada

Chossudovsky, Michel. *The globalisation of poverty : impacts of IMF and World Bank reforms.* Penang, Malaysia: Third World Network, 1997. ISBN 9839747231

Corbriddge, Stuart, Nigel Thrift and Ron Martin, eds. *Money, power, and space.* Oxford, England; Cambridge, MA : Blackwell, 1994. ISBN 0631181997

De Cecco, Marcello. *Money and empire : the international gold standard,* 1890-1914. Oxford : B. Blackwell, c1974. ISBN 0631157506

Denison, Edward Fulton. *The sources of economic growth in the United States and the alternatives before us.* [New York] : Committee for Economic Development, [1962]

Eisenstein, Louis. *The ideologies of taxation.* New York, Ronald Press Co., 1961

Ewald, Paul W. *Evolution of infectious disease.* Oxford : Oxford University Press, 1994. ISBN 019506058X

Grant, James. *Money of the mind : borrowing and lending in America from the Civil War to Michael Milken.* New York, [N.Y.] : Farrar Straus Giroux, c1992. ISBN 0374169799

Greider, William. *Secrets of the temple : how the Federal Reserve runs the country.* New York; Toronto : Simon and Schuster, c1987. ISBN 067147989X

Hawken, Paul. *The next economy.* New York : Holt, Rinehart, and Winston, c1983. ISBN 0030626315

Hawken, Paul. *The ecology of commerce : a declaration of sustainability.* New York, NY : HarperCollins Publishers, c1993. ISBN 0887306551

Heilbroner, Robert L. *21st century capitalism.* New York : Norton, 1993. ISBN 0393035166

Hellyer, Paul. *The evil empire.* Toronto : Chimo Media, 1996. ISBN 0969439458

Henderson, Hazel. *Building a win-win world : life beyond global economic warfare.* San Francisco, CA : Berrett-Koehler, 1996. ISBN 1881052907

Hixson, William F. *It's your money*, with an appendix by William Krehm, *The Bank of Canada — a misused tool.* Toronto : COMER Publications, 1997. ISBN 0968068111

Homer, Sidney. *A history of interest rates.* 3e. New Brunswick : Rutgers University Press, c1991. ISBN 0813516285

Hubbard, R. Glenn. *Money, the financial system, and the economy*. Reading, MA : Addison-Wesley Pub. Co., c1994. ISBN 0201547082

Ickes, Harold L. *The secret diary of Harold L. Ickes*. New York : Da Capo Press, 1974. ISBN 0306706261

Kelsey, Jane. *Economic fundamentalism*. East Haven, Conn. : Pluto Press, 1995. ISBN 0745310443

Keynes, John Maynard. *The general theory of employment, interest and money*. London : Macmillan, 1936

Kindleberger, Charles Poor. *A financial history of western Europe*. 2e. New York : Oxford University Press, 1993. ISBN 0195077377

Korten, David C. *When corporations rule the world*. West Hartford, CT : Kumarian Press, 1995. ISBN 1887208003

Krehm, William. *A power unto itself : the Bank of Canada : the threat to our nation's economy*. Toronto : Stoddart, 1993. ISBN 0773756213

Krehm, William. *Democracies and tyrannies of the Caribbean*. Westport, CT : Lawrence Hill & Company, 1984. ISBN 0882081691

Krehm, William. *Babel's tower : the dynamics of economic breakdown*. Toronto : Thornwood Publications, c1977. ISBN 0889630011

Krehm, William. *Price in a mixed economy : our record of disaster*. Toronto : Thornwood Publications, 1975. ISBN 0889630003

Laidler, David and William Robson, *Don't break the bank! The role of monetary policy in deficit reduction*. C.D. Howe Institute

Lipsey, Richard G., Paul N. Courant and Douglas D. Purvis. *Microeconomics*. New York : HarperCollins College Publishers, c1994. ISBN 0673469816

Martin, Peter James. *Inside the Bank of Canada's Weekly Financial Statistics : a technical guide*. Vancouver : Fraser Institute, c1989. ISBN 088975117X

Mayer, Martin. *The bankers : the next generation*. New York: Truman Talley Books, 1997. ISBN 0452272645 (1998 Penguin pbk.)

McConnell, Campbell R., Stanley L. Brue and William Henry Pope. *Economics : principles, problems, and policies*, 5e. Toronto : McGraw-Hill Ryerson, c1990. ISBN 0075498006

McMurtry, John. *Unequal freedoms : the global market as an ethical system*. Toronto : Garamond Press, 1998. ISBN 1551930056

McNamara, Robert S. *In retrospect : the tragedy and lessons of Vietnam*. New York : Times Books, c1995. ISBN 0812925238

McQuaig, Linda. *Behind closed doors : how the rich won control of Canada's tax system—and ended up richer*. Markham, ON : Viking, 1987. ISBN 0670816787

Moggridge, D. E. *Keynes*. London : Macmillan Press, 1976. ISBN 0333197992

Orwell, George. *Nineteen eighty-four : a novel*. New York : Harcourt, Brace & World, c1949

Patinkin, Don. *Money, interest, and prices : an integration of monetary and value theory*. 2e. New York : Harper & Row, 1965

Phillips, Kevin P. *Boiling point : Republicans, Democrats, and the decline of middle-class prosperity*. New York : Random House, c1993. ISBN 0679404619

Plumptre, A. F. W. *Mobilizing Canada's resources for war*. Toronto, The Macmillan Company of Canada Limited, 1941

Polanyi, Karl. *The great transformation*. New York, Toronto : Farrar & Rinehart, Inc., 1944

Rymes, Thomas K., ed. *The Bank of Canada — origins and early history*. Carleton University Press, Ottawa, 1993

Sandilands, Roger J. *The life and political economy of Lauchlin Currie : New Dealer, presidential adviser, and development economist*. Durham : Duke University Press, 1990. ISBN 0822310309

Schloss, Henry Hans. *The Bank for International Settlements; an experiment in central bank cooperation*. Amsterdam : North-Holland Pub. Co., 1958

Schwager, Jack. *The new market wizards : conversations with America's top traders*. John Wiley & Sons, 1995. ISBN: 0471132365

Slater, David W. *War finance and reconstruction — the role of Canada's Department of Finance 1939-1946*, with two chapters by R.B. Bryce, David W. Slater, 199 Crocus Ave., Ottawa, K1H 6E7

Stewart, Walter. *Belly up : the spoils of bankruptcy*. Toronto : McClelland & Stewart, c1995. ISBN 0771083041

Stewart, Walter. *Towers of gold, feet of clay : the Canadian banks*. Toronto : Collins, 1982. ISBN 0002170248

Tickell, Adam. *Rogues, regulation and the culture of finance*

Turgeon, Lynn. *Bastard Keynesianism : the evolution of economic thinking and policymaking since World War II*. Westport, CT : Greenwood Press, 1996. ISBN 0313300240

Volcker, Paul A. *Changing fortunes : the world's money and the threat to American leadership*. New York : Times Books, c1992. ISBN 081292018X

Webography

Selected list of World Wide Web (Internet) sources.

Bank for International Settlements
www.bis.org

Canada — Bank of Canada
www.bank-banque-canada.ca

Canada — Canadian Bankers Association
www.cba.ca

Canada — Competition Bureau
strategis.ic.gc.ca/SSG/ct01250e.html

Canada — Office of the Superintendent of Financial Institutions
www.osfi-bsif.gc.ca

Canada — Statistics Canada
www.statcan.ca

Canada — Task Force on the Future of the Canadian Financial Services Sector
finservtaskforce.fin.gc.ca

Committee on Monetary and Economic Reform
www.comer.org

Hazel Henderson
www.hazelhenderson.com

International Monetary Fund
www.imf.org

Japan — Bank of Japan
www.boj.or.jp

John Maynard Keynes
www.wam.umd.edu/~mglondon/London/Keynes/keynes.htm

Organisation for Economic Co-operation and Development
www.oecd.org

The Globe and Mail
www.globeandmail.ca

The Wall Street Journal
www.wsj.com

UK — Bank of England
www.bankofengland.co.uk

US — Bureau of Labor Statistics
stats.bls.gov

US — Bureau of Economic Analysis
www.bea.doc.gov

US — Federal Reserve
www.federalreserve.gov

World Trade Organization
www.wto.org

World Bank
www.worldbank.org

Index

D

E

F

G

H

I